Y0-BRR-919

WOMAN: DEPENDENT OR INDEPENDENT VARIABLE ?

WOMAN:

Dependent Or Independent Variable?

EDITED AND AUTHORED BY:

RHODA KESLER UNGER
MONTCLAIR STATE COLLEGE

FLORENCE L. DENMARK
GRADUATE SCHOOL AND UNIVERSITY CENTER
CITY UNIVERSITY OF NEW YORK

PSYCHOLOGICAL DIMENSIONS, INC.
NEW YORK, NEW YORK

WOMAN: DEPENDENT OR INDEPENDENT VARIABLE?

DEDICATION

To my parents for a non-sexist upbringing; Burt, for making it all possible; and Laurel and Rachel, so they won't have to go through it all themselves.

DEDICATION

To my husband, Robert W. Wesner, our children:

Valerie, Pamela and Richard Denmark

and

Kathleen, Michael and Wendy Wesner.

To my mother, the memory of my father,

my sister Shirley, and to my extended family:

Uncles Sam and Herb

ACKNOWLEDGEMENTS

We would like especially to thank Sandra Tangri, U. S. Commission on Civil Rights, and Jacqueline P. Wiseman, San Francisco State College, for their help in the formative stages of this volume. They were both gracious and effective in suggesting alterations and additions to the manuscript before it reached its final form.

We would also like to thank our colleagues at our respective institutions for their suggestions in the rewriting of the textual materials contained in the book. In particular, we would like to single out for thanks Margarita Garcia, Moira LeMay and George Rotter of Montclair State College and several former doctoral candidates taking the Psychology of Women seminar at the Graduate School and University Center of City University of New York.

A number of graduate and undergraduate students were also of great assistance in the preparation of the book. We would like to thank Audrey Bricker, Sheila Marshall, Susan McCandless, and Nora Rubinstein for their assistance with the glossary, and JoAnn Linburn, Roseanne McConville, Anne Mulvey, Salvatore Randazzo, Doris Takooshian, and Jeanne Viviani for assistance in the preparation of the manuscript.

We would like to extend our warmest appreciation to Joseph Matarazzo, University of Oregon, Medical School, who was encouraging during a period when books on women's studies were not a "hot" property and whose comments on an earlier draft of this book greatly assisted in its improvement.

Last, but not least, we would especially like to thank our publisher, Robert W. Wesner, who helped organize the book and provided invaluable critical comments.

PREFACE

This book was written and put together in order to aid in the definition of a new field of study—the psychology of women. Until recently, most of psychology was male defined and male oriented. Now, however, the concept of being female is being viewed from a fresh perspective. New studies are being done and older ones are being reexamined. Since we feel that it would be premature to promote an *a priori* definition of the psychology of women, we have tried to define it denotatively, by pointing out those studies and issues which are critical. We have juxtaposed various points of view in order to focus on the relevant issues. These points of view revolve about the "nature-nurture" axis and most sections of the book have been constructed to move from the most biological position appropriate to an area to the most environmental-social position in that area. In general, we hold that an interactional viewpoint is most appropriate to all areas covered by this book. The question is *not* whether biological *or* social factors produce sex-characteristic behaviors, but how much of such behaviors is affected by *each* variable?

In addition to providing material for the growing number of courses in the psychology of women, an another purpose of this book is to make evident the existence of this field as an area of expertise for individuals of both sexes. One is not qualified to teach the psychology of women just because one is a woman just as one does not teach child psychology because one has been a child. Part of the reason for the large size of the book is to encompass in a single volume the extreme range and depth of materials appropriate to the area.

The book was made possible by the cooperation of many—only a few of whom could be thanked by name. More importantly, the climate for the book and others of its kind was made possible by the hard work of many others. The formation of the new APA Division 35 which aims to study the psychology of women is only one indicant of this new climate. It is very exciting to be present during a period when a new subject of study is being opened up. And we hope that our book will assist in its development.

Contents

Introduction   3

Section I. Sex-Role Sterotypes   9

  1. Introduction   11
  2. The Stereotype of Femininity   19
    Viola Klein
  3. Evaluation of the Performance of Women as
    a Function of Their Sex, Achievement, and
    Personal History   31
    Gail I. Phetersen, Sara B. Kiesler, and
    Philip A. Goldberg
  4. Female Roles in Women's Magazine Fiction,
    1940-1970   41
    Helen H. Franzwa
  5. Male and Female in Children's Books   55
    Mary Ritchie Key
  6. Male-Female Perception of the Female Sex
    Role in the United States   71
    Anne Steinmann and David J. Fox
  7. Women as a Minority Group   85
    Women as a Minority Group: Some Twenty
    Years Later   103
    Helen Mayer Hacker

Section II. How the Therapist Looks at Woman   117

  8. Introduction   119
  9. Some Psychological Consequences of the
    Anatomic Distinction Between the Sexes   127
    Sigmund Freud
 10. Women as Psychiatric and Psychothe-
    rapeutic Patients   137
    Phyllis Chesler
 11. Sex-Role Stereotypes and Clinical Judg-
    ments of Mental Health   163
    Inge K. Broverman, Donald M. Broverman,
    Frank E. Clarkson, Paul S. Rosenkrantz,
    and Susan R. Vogel
 12. Between Men and Women   177
    Benjamin B. Wolman

13. Women in Rage: A Psychological Look at the Helpless Heroine   195
   Jean Mundy

Section III. The Development of Sex Differences and Sex Roles   217

14. Introduction   219
15. A Note on Sex Differences in the Development of Masculine and Feminine Identification   231
   David B. Lynn
16. Parents' Differential Reactions to Sons and Daughters   247
   Mary K. Rothbart and Eleanor E. Maccoby
17. A Developmental Study of the Effects of Sex of the Dominant Parent on Sex-Role Preference, Identification, and Imitation in Children   263
   E. Mavis Hetherington
18. Woman's Role in Cross-Cultural Perspective   275
   Corinne J. Weithorn

Section IV. Sex Differences in Cognitive Functions   297

19. Introduction   299
20. Roles of Activation and Inhibition in Sex Differences in Cognitive Abilities   311
   Donald M. Broverman, Edward L. Klaiber, Yutaka Kobayashi, and William Vogel
21. Comments on "Roles of Activation and Inhibition in Sex Differences in Cognitive Abilities"   355
   Mary B. Parlee
22. Parental Education, Sex Differences, and Performance on Cognitive Tasks Among Two-Year-Old Children   367
   N. Dickon Reppucci
23. Problem of Sex Differences in Space Perception and Aspects of Intellectual Functioning   379
   Julia A. Sherman
24. Pattern Copying Under Three Conditions of an Expanded Spatial Field   395
   Barbara K. Keogh

25. Effects of Sex of Examiner and Subject on
    Children's Quantitative Test Performance   409
      Darhl M. Pedersen, Martin M. Shinedling,
      and Dee L. Johnson
26. Social Factors Influencing Problem Solving
    in Women   417
      L. Richard Hoffman and Norman R. F. Maier

Section V. Is There Psychosexual Neutrality at Birth?   435

27. Introduction   437
28. Early Hormonal Influences on the Develop-
    ment of Sexual and Sex-Related Behaviors   447
      Robert W. Goy
29. Sexual Dimorphic Behavior, Normal and
    Abnormal   473
      John Money
30. Attachment Differences in Male and Female
    Infant Monkeys   487
      Gary D. Mitchell

Section VI. The Unique Female Condition: Menstrua-
    tion and Pregnancy   501

31. Introduction   503
32. Hormonal Interaction, Menstruation, and the
    Oral Contraceptives   509
      Margarita Garcia
33. The Influences of Mother's Menstruation on
    Her Child   529
      Katharina Dalton
34. Patterns of Affective Fluctuation in the
    Menstrual Cycle   537
      Melville E. Ivey and Judith M. Bardwick
35. Effects of Oral Contraceptives on Affective
    Fluctuations Associated with the Menstrual
    Cycle   553
      Karen E. Paige
36. A Psychoendocrine Study of Pregnancy and
    Puerperium   591
      C. Richard Treadway, Francis J. Kane, Jr.,
      Ali Jarrahi-Zadeh, and Morris A. Lipton
37. Postpartum Psychiatric Syndromes   605
      Frederick T. Melges
38. The Case for Human Cycles   627
      Rhoda Kesler Unger

Section VII. Female Achievement: Internal vs. External Barriers   633

39. Introduction   635
40. Sex Differences in Expectancy of Intellectual
    and Academic Reinforcement   649
    Virginia C. Crandall
41. Experimental Arousal of Achievement
    Motivation in Adolescent Girls   687
    Gerald S. Lesser, Rhoda N. Krawitz, and
    Rita Packard
42. Toward an Understanding of Achievement-
    Related Conflicts in Women   703
    Matina S. Horner
43. Early Childhood Experiences and Woman's
    Achievemnt Motives   723
    Lois Wladis Hoffman
44. Encountering the Male Establishment: Sex
    Status Limits on Woman's Careers in the
    Professions   751
    Cynthia F. Epstein
45. Empirical Verification of Sex Discrimination
    in Hiring Practices in Psychology   773
    Linda S. Fidell

Overview: Some Aspects of Female Sexual Behavior   787
    Florence L. Denmark
Additional Readings   796
Glossary   799
Index   823

Introduction

Can sex be regarded as an independent variable built into the organism by chromosomes, genes, hormones, and so on, or is sex a dependent variable largely determined (except for physical structure) by the postnatal experiences of each individual as defined by a particular culture's definition of sexual gender? Is sex a variable that determines most of an organism's psychological characteristics, or do the manipulations to which an organism is subjected during its development determine sex? We do not expect to resolve this controversy, but we hope this book may help to clarify the issues involved. Whether one regards the variable as independent or dependent depends upon how narrowly one defines sex. However, whether one defines sex only in terms of physiology or only in terms of psychology is itself a controversial issue.

We are taught in many areas of science that a dichotomy is often the result of too simplistic an approach to a problem. Nevertheless, arguments on the hereditary versus the environmental nature of the causal factors of sex differences pervade the study of the psychology of women. The old nature-nurture controversy that most social scientists have dismissed continues to recur here. Why? A partial answer is probably because we cannot perform the definitive experiment. We can never acquire a group of opposite-sexed twins and raise them in different environments. And no environment, acts in the same way on organisms of different sexes.

A paper by Hebb[1] may serve to illustrate the interactional approach we believe to be most fruitful for understanding the etiology of sex differences. If one raised a group of animals that were genetically identical in different environments, their subsequent behavior would be different. We would then attribute 100 percent of these differences to environmental influence. If one raised a group of animals that were genetically mixed in identical environment, their subsequent behavior would be different. We could attribute 100 percent of these differences to hereditary factors. If the same behaviors are involved, how can differences be

---

1. D.O. Hebb, Heredity and environment in mammalian behavior. *British Journal of Animal Behavior,* 1953, 1, 43-47.

due entirely to genetic factors and also be due entirely to environmental influences? Hebb points out that what one is really studying is the variance of behavior. When one source of variance is constant, all variation must be due to the other source. This kind of manipulation does not make environment less important than heredity for a certain behavior. It only means that the relevant environmental influences are much the same throughout the group. It does not preclude finding another group with similar heredity and less similar experiences so that the level of the behavior in question varies with environment rather than heredity. All behavior must be the result of some level of hereditary factors interacting with some level of environmental factors.

One reason that so many sex differences seem to be attributable to build-in factors may be that cultural forces tend to impress a particular environment and role upon a female. No matter what her intellectual endowment, a female is expected to function mainly as a wife and mother. Her rearing is geared to this end. If there is little variance in environmental influences upon females as compared to males, naturally most of female behavioral differences will be attributable to biological influences.

There are also semantic problems inherent in the nature-nurture controversy. All unlearned influences are not genetic in origin. Developmental changes in the organism may occur in response to both genetic blueprints and environment. The organism always brings his or her environment along. Should we classify hormonal influences as genetic or environmental factors?

It is also necessary to make a distinction between distal and proximal causes of behavior. The factors ultimately responsible for the origin of a behavior may not be the same factors that modify it once it has originated. Moreover, behavior may be altered by still other factors that had no part in either the etiology or the further development of that behavior. Arguments on the relative contribution of genetic and environmental factors to the male-female differences in personality characteristics and some forms of intellectual competence have an interesting parallel in the recent controversies over racial differences in intelligence. In both cases proponents of some form of biological determinism tend to make broad inferences from the subhuman to the human condition. Sexism is not yet as well established a source of bias as is racism. Nevertheless, individual potential is still a far better predictor of human behavior than membership in any racial or sexual group.

While we have not attempted to inculcate any particular viewpoint, we have found that working on this book has made us more aware of the actual and potential sources of bias in studies on women. There are far more similarities between the sexes than differences between them. However, journals rarely publish negative results. Thus, only the data on sex differences wend their way into the literature, unnecessarily magnifying the differences between men and women rather than the more important similarities.

Women social scientists are faced with a dilema. If we accept and make use of previous research, as is expected of good scientists, we may perpetuate scientific mythology that has little basis in fact. To ignore previous research, however, leaves a completely unstructured field. Although we believe that much of the research on sex differences has been biased in various ways, we do not feel that data that contradict a "woman's lib" viewpoint should be ignored. Despite an anti-Freudian bias, for example, we have found ourselves, including what may appear to be more than a fair share of Freudian-influenced theory and research. Whether or not one agrees with Freudian theories on the nature of the sexes and the psychological differences between them, research on women has been greatly influenced by these theories. While one may lament that many studies represent a reaction rather than a positive conceptualization, the fact remains that little original work has been done. As Phyllis Chesler[2] and others have pointed out, we need new myths about women.

In fact, in preparing this volume we had to wonder why so little research has been done on the subject of women. One factor responsible for this relative dearth is that most researchers are male. No matter how they rationalize it, people tend to investigate matters that interest them. Hence we find a great deal more research on sex differences in analytic thinking than on sex differences in language development. Although we did not consciously attempt to do so, we have found that over half of the papers chosen for this book were written by women. This percentage is much higher than the percentage of female investigators in the scholarly fields from which the articles were drawn. Even if we assume that part of the scarcity of articles is due to the low percentage of female researchers, the number of articles on women's studies is still far lower than one would expect.

Until recently, it was not considered respectable for competent (meaning accepted by male colleagues and male-oriented institutions) women scientists to investigate women's issues. Females have tended to accept the view of male teachers, researchers, and co-workers that such research was not generally valuable to science. Several years ago one of the authors, with a

2. Phyllis Chesler, *Women and madness.* Garden City, N.Y.: Doubleday, 1972.

5

degree in experimental psychology, found herself apologizing for her involvement in this field. One purpose of this book is to help redefine psychology to include the study of women rather than sex differences — the back door through which much past research has become acceptable.

We feel that it is important for women psychologists, sociologists, anthropologists, doctors, lawyers, and all women professionals to remain part of their own fields. They must not end up talking only to each other. Although the female identity can be defined independently of the male identity, women scholars must not become experts only in women's issues. These issues are relevant only in the context of larger areas of knowledge. If women's studies are not integrated into the various disciplines, it will be very easy to dismiss such studies as particularist, unimportant offshoots of major fields of study. After all, it is a major tenet of women scholars that male behavior is meaningless when female behavior is not taken into account.

An important purpose of this volume is to delineate the major issues in the psychology of women. We have not chosen to attempt an encyclopedic compilation of all relevant areas of research. Instead, we have chosen a number of controversial or unsettled areas and included papers that represent various positions in each of these areas. We do not believe that all of the papers we have included represent the best works in their particular field. In fact, we have noted a number of methodological and logical flaws in some of the papers. Our justification for inclusion of some relatively weak studies is that they represent theoretical positions of importance. The juxtaposition of various theoretical positions can be very useful in a field where a great deal of further research is required. By foregoing one particular focus, the book will be more objective and can be used by instructors with different theoretical points of view. Students, moreover, can perceive that no one particular viewpoint is generally accepted as the "correct" one. Since it is the contradictions between differing theories and differing interpretations of the same data among scientists that generate research, we hope to convey to the student a sense of enthusiasm of the "things happening."

The articles were selected with a bias for empirical research. Although a number of review papers have been provided, we believe that most of the issues in the area must be resolved by insightful research, and every effort was made to include this kind of material. Unfortunately, a very limited amount of empirical data was available for the section on women and therapy. Nevertheless, the salience of this issue resulted in its inclusion with primarily position papers.

Seven sections have been selected to present some of the major issues prevalent in the field.

Each section contains a general introduction or overview of the area, which is followed by its own references. Each reading included after the introduction retains the original references of the author. An extensive list of additonal references is provided at the end of each section, along with topics for student papers and projects. At the end of the book, the reader will find an overview of some aspects of female sexuality, as well as a selection of general references, and there is a comprehensive glossary.

We have begun the book by presenting materials on sex-role stereotypes which appear to underline dramatically the different ways men and women are treated in our society. This area should serve as an excellent introduction to the subject for those who have not yet been sensitized to it, and should provide material for discussion for readers who are already somewhat aware of the issues. Although this material is no less scientific than the materials on physiological processes, it is much more motivating to the student.

Next we cover materials on how the therapist deals with women. This chapter becomes a logical extension of that on sex-role stereotypes. Third and fourth, we cover materials on the development of sex roles and sex differences in a number of behavioral and cognitive areas. Such data should enable students to evaluate the degree of truth in some of the stereotypes previously examined.

Fifth and sixth, we deal with some of the internal variables relevant to sex comparisons—the degree of prenatal influence upon sex-typed behaviors and the physiological phenomena unique to women. The question of how much these factors contribute to a unique female psychology may be discussed here.

In the last section we deal with female achievement. Here we are concerned with the behavioral results of the phenomena discussed previously.

There is no reason why the order cannot be rearranged at the discretion of any particular instructor. For example, the material may be presented in an age-development context—the first section dealing with birth and prenatal influences upon behavior, the second with development of sex roles, the later sections concerned first with the adult woman and later with a focus on society and the way it affects women. An instructor could also decide to eliminate one or more of the sections, when it is not relevant to a particular course, without losing continuity.

The book does not claim to exhaust the problems or issues relevant to the field. For example, the reader may wonder why such an important topic as female sexuality is not covered in a section of its own. However, it became clear to us that female sexuality is a very detailed subject. Since various instructors may wish to cover this topic in depth, while others wish to cover it not at all, we felt that by providing an overview with additional references, we would allow instructors flexibility in teaching this subject. Certain other areas have not yet been clearly identified and conceptualized. Cross-cultural and cross-ethnic materials were limited when they were not central to a particular issue. Not everything can be included in one book. We chose to eliminate some important areas such as marriage and the problems of the aging woman in order to delve more deeply into those areas that we have covered. Such omissions do not mean this material is unimportant; it only points out the need for still greater dissemination of research concerned with women.

We hope that this book will help continue the legitimization of studies on women. It is impossible for any reader to agree with all the theoretical viewpoints expressed by the various authors. It is also impossible for any reader not to feel that some paper she/he considers particularly relevant has been ignored. We hope you will let us know what these are. Information retrieval is particularly difficult in this area, where not one scholarly journal has been published as late as 1974. Material had to be searched out from a number of diverse sources and even came from studies in which sex was incidental to the major issue. Although we tried to be impartial, we believe that reading these materials will probably feminize many readers. We know that it did feminize the editors.

Section I

Sex-Role Stereotypes

1 Introduction

Despite some cultural variation, long-standing distinctions in sex roles have emerged. In fact, long before psychology or sociology was concerned with sex roles, religious authorities had perpetuated quite rigid sex-specific patterns of behavior.

Judaic-Christian tradition directed the female to be a faithful servant to her husband. Indeed, the wedding ceremony refers not to man and woman, or husband and wife, but to man and *his* wife. Rabbis and priests have been exclusively male, and God is always presented in masculine terms.

The social sciences have joined religion as authorities in this area of male/female roles, and have continued this old tradition. Beginning with Freud, theories of sex distinction complete with scientific halo have evolved into clear-cut sex stereotypes.

Females are characterized as emotional, passive, soft, and generally weak. Males are depicted as inquisitive, objective, strong, and aggressive. The majority of women are housewives and mothers, whereas men define themselves in terms of occupational goals outside the home. The high-status professions are dominated by men.

Social learning and cultural conditioning encourage females to conform to one criterion and to think of themselves in so-called feminine terms. Males conform to a different criterion.[1]

An excellent description of the female stereotype is presented by Viola Klein (1950). Klein notes that our society searches for the "Essential Woman," and our ideology perpetuates a stereotype of woman. This stereotype provides an oversimplified, "short-cut

---

1. It should be pointed out that many anthropologists have stressed consideration of a variety of cultural patterns and that any linking of psychological traits with sex is coincidental.

explanation of all sorts of peculiarities in individual women's behavior'', and a model that educates generations of women to conform to certain attitudes and values. Woman has always been seen as an appendage of man, whether she be the ''good'' mother type or the ''bad'' courtesan type. Thanks to its strong emotional tone, this traditional stereotype of woman has persisted even when the underlying social structure has been vastly broadened for women by modern developments. As a result, both men and women feel uncertain and anxious about their sex roles.

Klein feels that the very terms ''masculine'' and ''feminine'' are too vague to be useful. They vary from one society to another and even change within a given society as social conditions alter. The alleged dichotomy between them only serves to inhibit individuals and retard society's progress.

Klein calls for an end to the age-old struggle between the sexes in the name of a new philosophy stressing the common human ideals of both men and women, while valuing the widest range of individual differences, regardless of sex.

In contrast to Klein, many social scientists believe that stereotypes are useful in providing orientation and enabling individuals to cope immediately with their environment before making finer distinctions. Waite et al. (1967) note that clear differentiation of sex roles is an important stage in the six-year-old's development. The danger is that stereotypes become fixed and do not allow for variation unless such variation is considered an exception.

A long-established tradition, whether positive or negative, is hard to change, and rigid sex stereotypes may not be conducive to individual growth and maximum use of human potential. A study by Phetersen, Kiesler, and Goldberg (1971) illustrates this point. One hundred and twenty first- and second-year college women were asked to evaluate eight paintings on the basis of the artist's technical competence, his creativity, overall quality and content of the painting, emotion expressed, and estimation of the artist's future success. One half of Ss were given female artists' names and one half were given male artists' names. One half of the paintings were designated ''entries'' in an exhibit, the other half were designated ''winners.''

This study confirmed that females rate the technical competence and future success of male artists higher than female artists when their works were thought to be merely entries, but that they rated them about equally once the women were recognized as winners. In so doing, they seemed to be simply expressing their own previously held attitudes and those of society at large that women are less well motivated, less technically competent, and less likely to succeed in careers, *unless* there was concrete evidence to the contrary.

These findings suggest that female career advancement is inhibited by women's tendency to devalue other women's performance in competition, as well as by similar male tendencies. "Even work that is equivalent to the work of a man will be judged inferior until it receives special distinction, and that distinction is difficult to achieve when judgment is biased against the work in competition" (p. 117).

Women, like minority groups, tend to accept the attitudes of the dominant majority—in this case, white Anglo-Saxon males. Their misjudgment of themselves "should contribute to an actual lack of achievement . . . they should be less willing to try to achieve and less supportive of their fellow women's efforts" (p. 114).

This study illustrates the observation that variations in status attach to different stereotypes and that cultural values ascribe status differentially to the two sex roles. The male role is preferred, and both males and females take this view. It is also considered less deviant and less unusual for the female to take on characteristics of the male stereotype than for the male to adopt female stereotypic characteristics. This is understandable since in the female's case it would reflect an increase in status, whereas for the male it would be a step down.

Our language encourages this image of a man's world. "He" is the general pronoun; we refer to "mankind," not to womankind or humankind. Men retain their own names at marriage, in contrast to women, who take on their husband's name and are usually categorized according to their marital status as "Miss" or "Mrs."

The mass media also perpetuates these sex-role stereotypes. Through advertising, women are told that they will be unhappy and valueless until they model themselves after the lovely young models in the ads. They are also told that they will find security via the clean washes produced by the housewife in a different kind of ad.

Helen Franzwa provides the results of a thematic content analysis that was undertaken to discover how females are portrayed in the fiction of several woman's magazines from 1940 to 1970. The young single woman is portrayed as interested in finding a husband. Stories involving married women portray the wife as dependent on the husband and defined through her husband and children. The widow-divorcee is independent and able to cope without a man, but in comparison to the men who appear in their lives they are incompetent. They end up remarried before the end of the story. The spinster in fiction is lonely and useless because of her failure in love. These stereotypes are found in the great majority of stories, with little change from 1940 to 1970.

With few exceptions (Waite et al., 1967), studies of children's books report that these books provide a rich source of sexual stereotypes (Feminists on Children's Media, 1972; Bailyn, 1959; Child et al., 1946; Key, 1971; Weitzman et al., 1972; Stefflre, 1969). An example of the type of distortion pervasive in these readers is found in the brief but interesting report of Stefflre (1969). He has examined the current status of the woman worker in elementary readers and basic texts for grades one through six sold by six major publishers. The books distorted contemporary reality by transmitting the following messages: practically all men work but few women work; women are *either* married *or* working; practically no mothers work; and two-thirds of women workers are employed at the professional level. According to recent statistics, however, nearly half of all adult women work; 60 percent of the women who work are married; a sizable minority of mothers work; and "more women work at clerical and sales occupations, at factory manual occupations, than at professional occupations which account for only one-sixth of employed women" (p. 101). The readers further distort reality by showing 33 percent of women in "masculine" jobs.

Stefflre concludes that such discrepancies require "supplementary actions by the counselor and teacher to give a more accurate picture of the place of work in the life of the modern woman" (p. 102). He suggests, for example, exposing students to women in occupations other than teaching as role models.

One of the best summaries of existing literature in this area, as well as an additional analysis of children's books, is presented by Key (1971). Key notes that the prejudices about sex roles held by the majority of members of our society are perpetuated in children's reading material. Males are the central characters in the great majority of the stories; the absence or near absence of females is also typical.

It is difficult to determine whether children's textbooks and literature reflect the structure of society in terms of sex roles, or whether they influence children's views of sex-role differences. However, children do have clear expectations about adult activities divided in terms of sex. Hartley (1961) examined children's perspectives on sex roles. She interviewed at length 134 New York City boys and girls, about equally divided between ages eight and eleven, upper-middle and lower-middle class, and those with working and nonworking mothers. She found that the children had clear-cut expectations about the tasks assigned to women (primarily homemaking, serving, and making small decisions) and to men (mostly outside the home and very wide-ranging).

Disagreement on 20 percent of the items, however, suggests considerable cultural heterogeneity or individuality of sex-role patterns. The feelings children perceived as associated with these activities seemed to suggest considerable female contentment with socially assigned roles and little desire for the traditionally masculine.

Children of working mothers scored highest on egalitarian experience and variety of views on sex-role assignments. Lower-middle-class girls scored much higher than upper-middle-class girls on *both* female role acceptance and male role striving, suggesting that the home-career conflict is primarily an upper-class problem.

Rosenkrantz et al. (1968) questioned college men and women and found that they agreed on male and female stereotypes. They defined their self-concepts along sex lines and generally agreed that the masculine stereotype was more favorable. To view sex sterotypes as ascribing not only roles but also status adds another dimension to the dichotomy. It moves the two stereotypes even further apart and adds pressure toward conformity to the sex stereotype. Such conformity would typically result in the incorporation of a feeling of inferiority into a woman's self-concept, while the male would just as easily incorporate superiority into his self-image.

Steinmann & Fox (1966a) conducted a study on male-female perceptions of the female role in the United States. They took data on responses to thirty-four statements in the Inventory of Feminine Values from sixteen cluster samples totaling 1260 American men and women from New York City. The important finding here was the fact that females, although they repudiated the stereotyped female sex role in their personal ratings, believed that males desired the stereotyped traits. Their view of the "ideal" woman was less self-actualizing than their own self-evaluation. Male Ss' perceptions of the female role were also less stereotypic than the woman Ss' perceptions of their ideal role.

Ironically, the ideal woman men delineated is not significantly different from the women's own perception of themselves. The discrepancy between the woman which women believed men desire and the ideal woman that men said they desire is so broad as to suggest a real lack of communication between men and women in regard to each one's desires about what role women should assume.

The ambivalence of women as a group was reflected in bimodal responses on such questions as whether a woman has a duty to be active or create something important. The men also showed a conceptual ambivalence in their responses. While the men agree on a more liberal point of view than women attribute to them (as far as accepting women's avenues of fulfillment outside the home is concerned), they took a relatively traditional position on specific items. For example, they reject self-realization as the most important aspect of a woman's life, particularly if children are involved. Thus men are apparently giving contradictory cues to women, and women therefore often do not have any clear perception of what men want in a woman.

Steinmann and Fox postulated that this might result in contradictory behavior on the males' part, with a resultant sex-role uncertainty on the part of the female. A study by McKee and Sherriffs (1959) yielded similar results.

There are numerous studies concerned with cross-cultural perceptions of sex-roles (Havighurst et al., 1965; Rabbie, 1965; Seward and Larson, 1968; Steinmann, 1971; and Steinmann and Fox, 1966b). Despite certain cross-national differences in concept of adult sex roles, all groups (including both male and female Ss of different ages) displayed the familiar traditional sex-role stereotyping for men and women. Steinmann (1971) also reported cross-cultural findings that were in agreement with her earlier study (1966a), although women did reveal a more active self-concept as well as a more active "ideal woman."

In contrast to the traditional male-female role dichotomy, Hacker (1951 and 1972) draws an analogy between the stereotypes of women and of blacks. Hacker (1951) was well in advance of other women who later arrived at the same conclusion, that women have minority-group status. In her report in this volume Hacker notes that women still occupy a low status position, but that they are no longer acquiesent. Women have been set in motion. Many radical women see separatism from males as the only solution to changing existing inequities.

Most women's groups would rather see a modification of existing roles than a breaking off of male-female relationships. Hacker also notes that vested interests in the status quo must be overcome and that an appropriate social milieu that encourages equality must be created.

If sex stereotypes are constructions of reality rather than reflections of it, then they are subject to change. If Jane must be mother and wife, although she would be far happier as a physician, and if Bill is made to compete in the world of business and forego his artistic ability, then we have limited both Jane's and Bill's sense of self.

REFERENCES

Bailyn, L. Mass media and children. *Psychological Monographs,* 1959, *23,* 1-37.

Child, I.L.; Potter, E. H.; and Levine, E. M. Children's textbooks and personality development: An exploration in the social psychology of education. *Psychological Monographs,* 1946, *60,* 1-54.

Feminists on children's media, sexism in children's literature. *United Teacher's Magazine,* February 1972, M1-M4.

Hacker, H. M. Women as a minority group. *Social Forces,* 1951, *30,* 60-69.

Hartley, R. E. Current patterns in sex roles: Children's perspectives. *Journal of the National Association of Women's Deans and Counselors,* 1961, *25,* 3-13.

Havighurst, R. J.; Dubois, M.E.; Csikszentimihalyi, M.; and Doll, R. *A cross-national study of Buenos Aires and Chicago adolescents.* New York, Karger, 1965.

Key, M. R. The role of male and female in children's books—dispelling all doubts. *Wilson Library Bulletin,* October 1971, 167-76.

Klein, V. The stereotype of feminity. *Journal of Social Issues,* 1950, *6,* 3-12.

McKee, J. P., and Sherriffs, A. C. Men's and women's beliefs, ideals and self-concepts. *American Journal of Sociology,* 1959, *64,* 356-63.

Pheterson, G. I.; Kiesler, S. B.; and Goldberg, P. A. Evaluation of the performance of women as a function of their sex, achievement, and personal history. *Journal of Personality and Social Psychology,* 1971, *19,* 114-18.

Rabbie, J. M. A cross-cultural comparison of parent-child relationships in the United States and West Germany. *British Journal of Social and Clinical Psychology,* 1965, *4,* 298-310.

Rosenkrantz, P.; Vogel, S. R.; Bee, R.; Broverman, I. K.; and Broverman, D. M. Sex-role stereotypes and self-concepts in college students. *Journal of Consulting and Clinical Psychology,* 1968, *32,* 267-95.

Seward, G. H., and Larson, W. R. Adolescent concepts of social sex roles in the United States and the two Germanies. *Human Development,* 1968, *11,* 217-48.

Stefflre, B. Run, mama, run: Women workers in elementary readers. *Vocational Guidance Quarterly,* 1969, *17,* 99-102.

Steinmann, A. Cross-cultural perceptions of women's role in men and women as of 1970. *International Mental Health Research Newsletter,* 1971, *14,* 12-16.

WOMAN: DEPENDENT OR INDEPENDENT VARIABLE?

Steinmann, A., and Fox, D. J. Male-female perceptions of the female sex role in the United States. *Journal of Psychology*, 1966, *64*, 265-76(a).

——— and ———. Male-female perceptions of the female role in England, France, Greece, Japan, Turkey, and the United States: A cross-cultural study. Paper presented at the 19th Annual Meeting of the World Federation for Mental Health, Prague, 1966 (b).

Waite, R. R.; Blom, G. E.; Zimet, S. F.; and Edge, S. First-grade reading textbooks. *The Elementary School Journal,* 1967, 366-74.

Weitzman, L. J.; Eifler, D.; Hokada, E.; and Ross, C. Sex-role socialization in picture books for preschool children. *American Journal of Sociology,* 1972, *77,* 1125-49.

2

Klein presents an excellent general article that provides a basic fundamental definition of the feminine stereotype. She points out that while no one would assume that the great variety of differing temperaments, characters, abilities, and interests of males could be summarized under one psychological type, our society searches for and perpetuates a stereotype of women.

This article is well written and well argued, and presents some significant insights into this area of sex stereotyping. Thus Klein notes that certain psychologists have tended to show that women as a group have distinctive mental or temperamental traits, largely because of their biological functions. These usually include passivity, sensitivity, attention to details, devotion to individuals rather than abstract ideas. Sociologists and anthropologists, on the other hand, have stressed the variety of culture patterns and the coincidental alignment of psychological traits with sex.

According to Klein, we had best recognize that there exists in our society, especially in the media, a stereotype of women as chiefly interested in domestic affairs, fond of children, longing for romance and eternal youth, and measuring their success and failure in terms of marriage and popularity with men, rather than a career. In addition, we artificially dichotomize masculine and feminine character traits. Once this artificial opposition is realized, the first step toward greater solidarity of the sexes will be taken.

One further point noted by Klein is that the history of woman's emancipation fostered a spirit of rivalry between the sexes in one of two directions: either toward equality with men in careers, or else toward specialization in those careers where, by virtue of women's alleged special qualities, they were said to have distinctive contributions to make. In key areas such as social justice and international peace, for example, these latter hopes were not borne out in practice.

The Stereotype of Femininity*

Viola Klein

"Why is there no recount of the personality of woman that you could hand over to undergraduates to read?" I was recently asked by a lecturer in gynaecology who, conscious of the intimate relationship between mind and body, feels he would not do justice to his subject unless he included in his course at least five lectures each year on the Psychology of Woman.

Underlying this question, as, indeed, most thinking on the subject of feminine psychology, is the assumption that Woman represents a psychological type in the same way as "introvert—extrovert," "cyclothyme—schizothyme," "phlegmatic," "sanguinic," etc. are distinct psychological types.

Innumerable attempts have been made to define this type, to describe the mental traits supposed to be characteristic of the human female. They are not matched by equal endeavors to establish a "Psychology of the Human Male." Indeed, the mere suggestion of such a possibility would, rightly, be considered absurd. The Male is not one psychological type: the great variety of differing temperaments, characters, abilities and interests cannot be summarized under one heading if any purpose is to be served by classification at all.

Why, then, should there be this consistent search for a common denominator among the variety of feminine characters, this search for the Essential Woman, the "Eternal Feminine"?

It is because, although there is no uniform feminine "type," society carries, as part of its ideological baggage, a stereotype of Woman, a sort of rough model purporting to contain the *essential* characteristics, while all the *existential* features are but variations on a basic theme. Stereotypes—defined by Kimball Young as false classificatory concepts to which, as a rule, some strong emotional-feeling tone of like or dislike, approval or disapproval, is attached — are popular means to simplify, indeed to oversimplify, a complex social reality. They are a device to sum up a strange and thus bewildering situation in one simplified symbol, a kind of logogram which reduces a situation to the minimum necessary to be understood by common consent. One has only to think of the roars of laughter evoked on a music hall stage by the mere mentioning of

---

* From *Journal of Social Issues*, 1950, 6, 3-12.

the word "mother-in-law" to be reminded of this shorthand function of stereotypes.

It is in the nature of stereotypes as parts of prejudice that they should be applied not to ourselves but to others. While we see ourselves and the members of our own set as individuals, we are apt to generalize about members of the out-group and to label them in sweeping terms. Thus it is not surprising that in our chiefly man-made civilization a situation should have arisen in which woman is thought of as a psychological type while man is not.

The stereotype of woman has two distinct functions: on the one hand it gives a short-cut explanation of all sorts of peculiarities in individual women's behaviour; whether she is strong-willed or meek, single-minded or hesitant, gentle or quarrelsome—she is supposed to possess a particular version of whatever trait she manifests and her stubbornness or submissiveness, her capriciousness or lack of humor will all be found "typically feminine." On the other hand the stereotype holds up to woman a sort of mirror which has previously been treated so as to show her reflection in a peculiar light or at a particular angle. To see yourself as others see you—what Cooley calls "the looking-glass self"—is a very important part of the educational process concerned with the transmission of attitudes and values. Thus a model is set up for others to imitate. Conformity is at a premium, whereas deviation from the norm is fraught with a variety of penalties, from feelings of frustration and inferiority to social ostracism and outright condemnation.

To be sure, the traditional typology recognized not one but two feminine types, the "good" and the "bad" woman—Eve and Lilith, the Mother and the Courtesan, as Weininger defined them: the woman to whom sex is chiefly a means to produce children, and the woman who seeks it for the sake of the pleasure it affords her by itself. In either case her relationship to the opposite sex is the focal point from which her personality is viewed and both types are characterized exclusively with reference to their attitude to men, not in regard of any mental or temperamental traits. Thus woman is seen as an appendage to man—on whom, in fact, she was socially and economically, as well as emotionally, dependent—not as a personality in her own right.

This traditional picture of woman had the appeal of simplicity and was the "ideological superstructure" of a social system in which woman's role was equally narrowly circumscribed. Thanks to its strong emotional tone it has outlived its material basis and has lingered on long after the underlying social structure has been transformed. Today women have assumed a great variety of social functions and responsibilities apart from, and in addition to, their relations to the other sex and claim to be judged on their individual merits rather than by the degree of their conformity to an out-of-date stereotype.

Difficulties, however, arise on a number of levels. For one, the traditional linkage of psychological characteristics with sex and its contrast to the practical realities of everyday life have caused in many women a feeling of uncertainty of their sex role. If women are as active and aggressive as life in a competitive society requires, have they, on that account, become less feminine? Can a woman who is interested in mathematics or mechanics or logic still claim to be a "complete" woman, and is she so regarded by others? Or, she will ask herself, is there anything fundamentally wrong or odd about her? This uncertainty is all the more harassing as in our rapidly changing society the desire to "belong," to be reassured, to conform to an accepted norm, is increasingly gaining weight. The many questionnaires published in all kinds of periodicals, and particularly, it seems, in women's journals, in which the reader is given a chance to rate himself, serve this very purpose: to reassure the individual that he, or she, fits into a set pattern. The tendency for quantitative measurements of personality traits, prevalent in contemporary psychology, also goes to meet this demand for norms and provides the standards of comparison.

A second difficulty arises from the historical circumstances of women's emancipation. It was carried by an *avant garde* whose aim it was to widen the sphere of economic and political activities open to women and to force a breach into a solidly masculine world of affairs. Thus they had to maintain, and to prove, that women, as a class, were in every respect "just as good" as men. In the competitive struggle for jobs "equality" was the catchword.

But in the sphere of ideologies, it was maintained that women had a distinctive contribution to make; that they were possessed of qualities which were not sufficiently represented in public life; that they would add a new facet to it and thereby make it not only more complete, but all the richer and happier.

Many pinned their hopes for greater social justice, national sanity and international peace on the increasing contribution of women, in the same way as many people expected these aims to be achieved by greater participation of the working classes. Both these groups were untried forces, unspoiled by power, and those who were anxious to create a better world looked to either, or to both, for salvation. "As long as man is oppressed and down-trodden, as long as the compulsion of social injustice keeps him in subjection, we are at liberty to hope much from what has not yet had opportunity to burgeon, from all the latent fertility in the fallow classes. Just as we hope much from children who may eventually grow up into quite commonplace people, in the same way we often have the illusion that the masses are composed of a finer clay than the rest of disappointing humanity."[1] Thus writes the disillusioned Andre Gide after his return from the USSR: "I think they are merely less corrupt and less decadent than the others, that is all."[2] Come to power they show the same faults and vices as the classes which have ruled hitherto—naturally, for they are made of the same fallible human stuff.

The belief, not in the common humanity of all, but in the intrinsic merits of some particular section of mankind which, so far, has not had an opportunity to prove its mettle has led to disappointment in the case of women as well as that of the "common man." Faith, to be preserved, has to be in something abstract or supernatural. It does not, as a rule, bear confrontation with its object.

Thus, many a keen feminist was disillusioned when woman suffrage did not produce peace, abolish militarism, or in any other way make a marked change for the better in world affairs. The disappointment was, in most cases, not with one's own judgment but with women for not being up to expectation.

In another respect, too, the originators of women's emancipation overshot their mark. Being Victorians in their mental make-up, they tended to underrate the force of the sexual instinct. Concerned as they were to create new jobs for women, to prove their equality and to open up roads to independence, they concentrated on careers, and on careers only. "Marriage mortality" was the term applied to those who fell by the wayside in this struggle. They were a dead loss to the "Cause," which demanded whole-hearted and single-minded devotion. Having to choose between marriage and career, being subjected to the rival pulls of love and ambition, imposed a strain on women that was too great for most to withstand.

Among the generation that inherited the spoils of feminism without having to fight for them, there were many who asked themselves whether, in the competitive game, it was not better to "specialize." Were they to put the emphasis—as their mothers had done—on doing the same things equally well with men, or rather to concentrate on the things which they, as women, could do better? But if so, what were the activities for which they were particularly suited? Thus, while preserving the spirit of rivalry between the sexes, many women tried to shirk the issue of "equality" by

1. Andre Gide, In *The God That Failed.* Crossman, Richard (editor). New York, Harper and Brothers, 1949. Page 194.

2. *Ibid.*

moving the competition on to another level.

In this way, the conflict of specialization versus universalism, one of the big dilemmas of our time, has also affected the woman's problem. It has led to the peculiar result that, at a moment in our historical development when the range of activities in which sheer physical strength is a decisive factor has been reduced to such an extent as to make egalitarianism a practical possibility, many women began to doubt its wisdom.

At present, therefore, egalitarianism has arrived at a crossroad and the time is ripe for stocktaking and for a reassessment of the values involved. At this critical point it behooves us to survey, once more, both our potentialities and aims; to ask whether women have achieved what they set out to do and, if so, whether their purpose, and the purpose of humanity, is best served by continuing along the same road.

The problem of women's careers is, of course, closely linked with that of feminine psychology. It hinges on the question whether women, as a group, show distinctive mental or temperamental traits that fit them better for one type of work than for another. *As a group,* they have, of old, been excluded from remunerative work; *as a group,* they tried to enter the economic field. Do they, also *as a group,* show psychological characteristics that collectively mark them off from the rest of humanity? Even if this question be answered in the affirmative, it still remains to be decided whether these traits are, like class or national characteristics, the result of upbringing, social and economic conditions and historical background, and therefore bound to change with the alteration of any of these factors, or whether they are linked with the physique and biological function of women.

To this question both practical experience and the various sciences concerned tend to give divergent answers. While the social changes of recent years in our own society and comparison with other patterns of culture weigh heavily on the side of social conditioning, biologists and, on a different plane, psychoanalysts stress the important bearing of the sexual function on mental development.

An interesting example of this conflict of opinions is afforded by Margaret Mead, who, by her book *Sex and Temperament,* [3] has done more than anybody else to underline the relativity of the terms "masculine" and "feminine" when applied to psychological characteristics. She has shown in this and other publications the great malleability of human nature and given examples of

---

3. Margaret Mead, *Sex and Temperament in Three Primitive Societies.* New York, W. Morrow, 1935.

variations in behavior patterns of men and women which in some societies go as far as the direct reversal of our accepted standards. Recently, in *Male and Female*,[4] however, Margaret Mead has come out in favor of a theory which explains feminine psychology in terms of women's biological function. Though she still maintains, as before, that to assign certain psychological traits and certain social roles to one sex rather than another means forcing Nature into a straight-jacket and causing frustration and neuroses to great numbers of individuals who won't fit into the mold, she nevertheless asserts that from birth on—which itself, in her view, is a different experience for the two sexes—the life and the mental outlook of a girl are shaped by her potential maternity. A boy has to be active and to prove himself through achievement; he has to *"become"* in order to be reassured; a girl simply *is.*

"The life of the female starts and ends with sureness, first with the simple identification with her mother, last with the sureness that that identification is true, and that she has made another human being."[5] This assumption implies a fundamental difference in character structure between men and women which would necessarily cut across variations in culture patterns and in individual temperaments and abilities. It is in direct contradiction to the views expressed by the same author in many places, even in the same book, e.g.: "Every known society creates and maintains artificial occupational divisions and personality expectations for each sex that limit the humanity of the other sex. One form that these distinctions make is to deny the range of difference among the members of one sex . . . our failure to recognize the very great variety of human beings who are now mingled and mated in one great melange that includes temperamental contrasts as great as if the rabbit mated with the lion and sheep with leopards. Characteristic after characteristic in which the differences within a sex are so great that there is enormous overlapping are artifically assigned as masculine or feminine. . . . We may go up the scale from simple physical differences through complementary definitions that overstress the role of sex difference and extend it inappropriately to other aspects of life, to stereotypes of such complex activities as those involved in the formal use of the intellect, in the arts, in government and in religion. In all these complex achievements of civilization, those activities which are mankind's glory, and upon which depends our hope of survival in this world that we have built, there has been this tendency to make artificial distinctions that limit an activity to one sex, and by denying the actual

---

4. Margaret Mead, *Male and Female, A Study of the Sexes in a Changing World.* New York, W. Morrow, 1949.

5. *Ibid.,* p. 158.

potentialities of human beings limit not only both men and women, but also equally the development of the activity itself."[6] Thus, as a social anthropologist Margaret Mead stresses the variety of culture patterns and the purely conventional coincidence of psychological traits with sex; under the influence of psychoanalytic theory she links the two. The split between the two disciplines manifests itself even within the same mind; it is more outspoken where the conflicting schools of thought are expressed by different representatives.

At this juncture, when the question of psychological sex characteristics and their origin is so undecided, it is probably best to leave the issue in abeyance and to confine ourselves to the statement of two facts: First, that there is, in our society, a stereotype of Woman which has a practical reality. Retail traders — who, after all, know their business — cater for it; advertisers appeal to it; film producers and editors of women's journals direct their activities with this ideal consumer in mind. It represents the lower common denominator of contemporary womankind as established by mass observation and market research. According to it the majority of women, or rather the abstract Woman, is the homemaker, interested chiefly in domestic affairs: she is fond of babies and devoted to her children's success; she is attracted by "glamor" and longing for "romance"; she is vitally interested in her appearance and pays attention to minute details; her success or failure is measured in terms of marriage and appeal to the other sex, generally, not of a career. To preserve the semblance of youth is therefore her main concern. This is the popular and much publicized stereotype, the Woman to whom radio programs, posters and sales catalogues are addressed, whose instincts are appealed to and whose vanity is flattered by skillful salesmanship. It is the model set up to aspiring young girls by pressure of public opinion and to which they will be eager to conform.

The second fact worth noting is this: There are in our culture notions of feminity and masculinity as two contrasting sets of personality traits and, though these terms are by no means clearly defined, the dichotomy as such is well established. It is customary to refer to some qualities of character and behavior as "feminine" and to others as "masculine," though these terms do *not* mean, as the dictionary states: "of female sex, of woman" and "of male sex," respectively. Rather, they are meant to express a kind of tone quality, a subtle nuance superimposed on each personality trait. Every person, it is generally agreed, possesses both masculine and feminine traits, is, in fact, a mixture of the two. L. M. Terman and

---

6. *Ibid.*, pp. 372-374. Many more passages in a similar vein could be quoted. . . .

C. C. Miles, in their *Sex and Personality: Studies in Masculinity and Feminity,*[7] tried to establish a scale by which personalities can be measured in terms of their relative masculinity and feminity and they applied their score—carefully worked out on the basis of questionnaires and tests of attitudes, opinions, interests, emotional response, and so on—to different social groups, classified by occupation, age, education, and other factors. Their very interesting findings show, among others, that high scholarship students score more highly feminine than low scholarship students, or that policemen, as a group, have a higher feminity score than mechanics.

As will readily be seen from these examples, feminity is a quality divorced from sex and possessed in varying degrees by individuals of either. It is impossible to nail down what the term, so widely used and so generally accepted, really means.

At the time of writing, for instance, there is in London an exhibition of paintings by the Impressionist Berthe Morisot. Not one critic failed to mention the feminine charm of her pictures, the "exquisite feminity" of her art, etc. although both in style and in subject matter her paintings are entirely in line with the impressionist school and do not differ in any essential from the works of Renoir, Manet or Corot whose influences are clearly visible. Why, then, are her landscapes, portraits and still-lives "feminine" whereas Renoir's are not—except for the fact that they are known to be created by a woman? Sensitivity and loving attention to detail—which in this connection are possibly meant to be the feminine characteristics—are typical of all the impressionists, though Berthe Morisot was the only woman among them.

Compassion and devotion to individuals rather than causes have, also, often been called feminine traits, though chiefly when possessed by women. Men who are outstanding in these virtues are on that account not usually labelled feminine.

Absence of aggressiveness has sometimes been characterized as a feminine virtue and much has been made of this notion by those who advocate greater participation of women in public affairs on the ground that this would strengthen the pacifist element in politics. Here again, not only were the chief exponents of "non-violence" men, but the women who have entered politics did, on the whole, not differ from the average male politician. If they did, they would not have been elected by the men and women voters of their constituencies.

Thinking in concrete images rather than abstract ideas has been

7. Lewis Madison Terman and Catharine Cox Miles, *Sex and Personality: Studies in Masculininity and Femininity.* New York and London, McGraw-Hill, 1936.

described by some others as a feminine characteristic. On the basis of this assumption, the vast majority of mankind would fall into the category of feminine minds.

Ultimately, feminity has been said—and said with the authority of psychoanalysis—to consist in passivity, or, to use Freud's terms, in a "preference for passive aims." The passivity which, in Freud's view, is typical of woman's role in the sexual act pervades all her personality. Margaret Mead's assertion that at the very start of life, effort, an attempt at greater self-differentiation, is suggested to the boy, while a relaxed acceptance of herself is suggested to the girl, is another version, a different interpretation of the same assumption that feminity fundamentally is passivity.

The degree of passivity or initiative, in the sexual act as elsewhere, differs in individuals of either sex; and among the many varying influences on the development of personality, identification with one or the other parent is only one of many cross-currents. Longing for surrender and for a passive drifting-along is a tendency present in many men and women and is, in our competitive society, increasingly difficult to realize for either.

Women today show initiative in matters of sex as well as business. To call them "masculinized" because they have, on the whole, adjusted themselves to modern living conditions—or, on the other hand, to call "feminine" men who prefer the pen to the sword, or domestic felicity to the "struggle for existence"—means stretching the terms masculine and feminine to the limits of their meaning. What is termed "masculine" or "feminine" differs from one society to another, according to the way in which a culture defines the respective roles of men and women. If these roles change as a result of altered social conditions, new psychological adjustments of both sexes follow. To refer these changes to a supposedly absolute scale is to minimize the importance of cultural factors in the formation of a personality. Not to mention that, as standards of measurements, the conventional terms masculine-feminine are much too vague and undefined to be useful.

If, admittedly, men and women represent composites of masculine and feminine characteristics in infinite variations, it seems pertinent to ask what purpose is to be served by classifying personality traits according to sex altogether. The dichotomy which, as has been generally agreed, does not correspond to any real temperamental division along sex lines only tends to create uncertainty about the degree of their maleness and femaleness in the innumerable intermediate personality types. It causes doubts, and sometimes anxieties, about their adequacy as members of their own sex in people who differ in some irrelevant characteristics from an, in fact, purely fictitious norm. To unfold freely the potentialities of their personalities both men and women have to think of themselves as human beings first, as males and females afterwards. Their maleness and femaleness will develop all the more fully the less it is hampered by fear lest a deviant taste or interest may mark some fundamental deficiency.

The question, then, whether in the competition for jobs women ought to specialize in fields which suit their feminine abilities and inclinations best cannot be answered in the affirmative, for women differ in their interests and temperaments as much as men do. To label some occupations masculine, others feminine, means to bar people of either sex from activities for which they may well be temperamentally suited and which they might accomplish with success. This exclusion is done not only at the expense of in-dividual happiness but also to the detriment of human advance.

To free women from the social and economic disqualifications from which they had suffered for centuries was the feminist aim. This liberation was important for them not qua women but qua human beings—just as the liberation of slaves happened for the sake of their humanity.

Today, when so much has been achieved—when so many roads to freedom have been opened and the dividing line between the temperamental characteristics of the two sexes have been blurred by so much overlapping—the time has come to lay aside the battle-axe and to stop the competitive struggle between the sexes. What matters, at this point, is to re-emphasize the value of the individual personality and to call back to mind the common humanity of men and women. The ideals worth striving for, such as truth, justice, freedom, goodness, sympathy, fair play, are unrelated to sex and can be achieved—or aimed at—by both. Peace is an ethical postulate and a necessity for the survival of mankind; there is no point in making it a competitive issue between the sexes by maintaining that pacifism is a feminine virtue. This would only make peace all the more difficult to attain by enhancing the aggressive tendencies in men who would feel they had thereby to assert their masculinity. And the same which is true of peace applies to any other human value.

It will not be easy to give up the age-old struggle between the sexes, to overcome the in-group solidarity of each and its an-tagonism against the out-group. It may be too deeply rooted, too much ingrained in the relationship between men and women.

But to realize the artificiality of a juxtaposition of masculine and feminine character traits is a first step towards a greater feeling of human solidarity between the sexes. Moreover, the ideology of equality is today sufficiently well established to be, at least, generally paid lip-service. Finally, the free mingling of boys and

girls at school, of men and women in work and sport, has substituted a number of new solidarities—"school tie," club,
profession—which may contribute to a lessening of in-group
feelings among the members of each sex.

This is a useful preparation of the ground for a philosophy which
is not egalitarian, in terms of one sex as against another, but in-
dividualist and which stresses common human ideals while
allowing the widest range to individual differences.

3

Does being a woman place one in a disadvantageous position when ratings of competence are made by other women? This study was an attempt to reconcile the findings of Goldbert [1968] that educated women rated identical papers higher when they were attributed to male authors, and of Pheterson [1969] that uneducated women rated papers by mena dn women equally. The latter result was apparently due to the fact that these uneducated women considered any published article as prima facie evidence of success.

In this experiment, women were asked to rate paintings rather than written papers. When the paintings were designated "winners," the competence and success of male and female artists were rated equal. However, when they were "entrees," the competence and future success of the male artist was much higher than that of the female. The authors hypothesize that women might overvalue a woman who has succeeded, thinking that she has overcome greater odds than successful men.

The significant study suggests that female career advancement is inhibited by women's tendency [as well as by similar male tendencies] to devalue other women's performance. Thus, one effect of sex stereotyping is to inhibit career advancement for women and serve as a barrier to achievement. It is somewhat surprising that women serve not only as the object but also the source of prejudice. Women no less than men are influenced by their culture to internalize sex stereotypes and apply them.

Evaluation of the Performance of Women as a Function of Their Sex, Achievement, and Personal History*

Gail I. Pheterson, Sara B. Kiesler, and Philip A. Goldberg

A study was designed to investigate the conditions under

---

* From *Journal of Personality and Social Psychology*, 1971, *19* (1), 114-18.

which women are prejudiced against women. Paintings were shown to 120 college women for evaluation. Half of the subjects thought that the artist was female, half thought that the artist was male; half thought that the painting was an entry in a contest, half thought that it was a winner. Some questionnaire data showed that women judged the entry paintings by men to be significantly better than the identical paintings by women. Winning paintings were not evaluated differently depending on sex. Obstacles faced by winners or entrants had no effect. It was concluded that women who are attempting to accomplish are judged less favorably than men, but that women who have successfully accomplished work are evaluated as favorably as are men.

One explanation for the apparent failure of women to achieve as much success as men is prejudicial evaluations of their work by men (cf Klein, 1950; Scheinfeld, 1944). If men undervalue the accomplishments of women, women also may do so. Women's misjudgment of themselves should contribute to an actual lack of achievement. If women devalue their own and each other's work, they should be less willing to try to achieve and less supportive of their fellow women's efforts. The present study investigates the conditions under which women devalue female performance.

Goldberg (1968) designed a study to investigate prejudice among women toward women in the areas of intellectual and professional competence. College women were asked to evaluate supposedly published journal articles on linguistics, law, art history, dietetics, education, and city planning; for each article, half of the subjects saw a male author's name and half saw a female author's name. The results confirmed the hypothesis that college women value the professional work of men more highly than the identical work of women. Women devalued female work for no other reason than the female name associated with the article. Sensitivity to the sex of the author served to distort judgment and thereby prejudice women against the work of other women.

Using the identical procedure, Pheterson (1969) explored prejudice against women among middle-aged, uneducated women. The professional articles were on marriage, child discipline, and special education. The results did not support the findings of Goldberg. Women judged female work to be equal to male work; in fact, evaluations were almost significantly more favorable for female work than for male work.

The differing results of Goldberg and Pheterson were perhaps due to the different subjects used, to the different articles, or to some combination of the two. One plausible explanation might be that the printed articles had different significance for the two sets of subjects. College women see the printed word frequently, are taught to be critical, and may take the publication of a paper relatively lightly. They might have viewed the articles simply as vehicles for presenting ideas or proposals. Uneducated women, on the other hand, might regard the publication or even writing of an article as a big accomplishment in itself, regardless of the specific ideas presented. Perhaps all women judge women less favorably than men when evaluating their proposals or unfinished work because men are more likely to succeed. That is, given a piece of work which has uncertain status, the man's, rather than the woman's, is more likely in our society to eventually be successful. On the other hand, women may judge the recognized accomplishments or already successful work of women to be equal to or even better than the same work of men. Success is less common for women. A contrast effect may cause people to overvalue achievement when they expect none. Also, women may overvalue female accomplishment because they assume that women face greater obstacles to success and therefore must exert more energy, display more competence, or make more sacrifices than men.

The present study was designed to investigate the divergent results of Goldberg (1968) and Pheterson (1969) and, further, to test the previously presented arguments. Women were aksed to judge paintings created by men and women. Some paintings represented attempts to accomplish, that is, were entries in art competitions. Other paintings represented actual accomplishments—they had already won prizes. The first hypothesis was that women will evaluate male attempts to accomplish more highly than female attempts. The second hypothesis was that women will evaluate female accomplishments as equal to or better than male accomplishments.

The above hypotheses suggest that people judge successful persons more highly when they have more odds against them (as women presumably do). Thus, a woman's accomplishment might be praised more than a man's accomplishment because women face greater obstacles. Our culture shows great admiration for the achievements of the handicapped or underprivileged (Allport, 1958). A third hypothesis was formulated to explore this admiration and its influence on female judgments. It stated that women will evaluate the accomplishments of people with personal odds against them more favorably than the accomplishments of people without such odds.

WOMAN: DEPENDENT OR INDEPENDENT VARIABLE?

METHOD

Subjects

The subjects were 120 freshmen and sophomore women students at Connecticut College. College women were used to permit a replication of the Goldberg (1968) study within the experimental design. They volunteered in student dormitories for immediate participation in the fifteen-minute task.

Experimental Design

There were three experimental manipulations constituting a 2 X 2 X 2 design. Eight paintings were presented to small groups of subjects for evaluation. The sex of the artist, the status of the painting, and the personal odds faced by the artist were manipulated, such that for each painting half of the subjects thought that it had been created by a male artist, and half thought that it had been created by a female artist; half thought it was a prize-winning painting, and half thought it was just an entry in a show; half thought the artist had faced unusually severe obstacles, and half thought the artist had faced no unusual obstacles. Each subject participated in each experimental condition, evaluating all eight paintings sequentially. The identity of each painting was counterbalanced among subjects, so that all conditions were represented for each painting.

Procedure

Subjects were seated in a room equipped with a slide projector and screen. Each subject was given a booklet and was told to read the directions:

Slides of eight paintings will be shown in conjunction with brief biographical sketches of the artists. After viewing the slide, turn the page and answer five evaluative questions about the painting. No personal information about your identity, talents, or tastes is required. This is a study of the artistic judgments of college students.

The subjects were then instructed to read the first artist sketch, inspect the project painting, turn the page and answer the appropriate questions, and then proceed in the same manner for each of the eight slides.

Gail I. Pheterson, Sara B. Kiesler, and Philip A. Goldberg

Eight slides of unfamiliar modern art paintings were used. To accompany them, fictitious artist profiles were composed to include the eight experimental conditions. These profiles appeared in the booklets in different orders for the different subjects. Half of the profiles described a female artist, and half described a male. Their age, residence, and occupations were briefly described (identical for male or female). For example, "Bob (Barbara) Soulman, born in 1941 in Cleveland, Ohio, teaches English in a progressive program of adult education. Painting is his (her) hobby and most creative pastime." Cross-cutting the sex manipulation, half of the profiles described the painting as a contest entry (e.g., "She has entered

TABLE 1

MEAN COMPETENCE RATINGS OF MALE AND FEMALE
ARTISTS WITH WINNING OR ENTRY PAINTINGS

Status of painting	Sex of artist	
	Male	Female
Winner	3.483	3.483
Entry	3.562	3.354

this painting in a museum-sponsored young artists' contest"), and half described it as a recognized winner (e.g., "This painting is the winner of the Annual Cleveland Color Competition"). In a third manipulation, half of the profiles described the painter as having had obstacles to success (e.g., "An arm amputee since 1967, he has been amazingly productive as an artist").

After each slide, the subjects turned a booklet page. Five questions asked the subjects to evaluate the paintings on a scale of 1-5, with higher ratings representing more favorable evaluations. After every slide, the following questions were posed: (a) Judging from this painting, how technically competent would you judge Mr. (or Miss) ——————— to be? (b) How creative would you judge Mr. (Miss) ——————— to be? (c) What rating would you give to Mr. (or Miss) ——————— for the overall quality and content of his (her) painting? (d) What emotional impact has Mr. (or Miss) ——————— instilled in his painting? (e) Judging from this painting, what prediction would you make for the artistic future of Mr. (or Miss) ———————.

After all eight slides were shown, the study was explained, and the subjects were asked not to discuss it.

Results

The questionnaire data were analyzed using four-way analyses of variance, with three experimental conditions and subjects as the fourth factor. Three questions asked the subjects to evaluate the artists; these were assumed to be directly relevant to the hypotheses.

The first question technical competence, revealed an overall rating of the male artists as significantly superior to the female artists ($F = 3.99$, $df = 1/119, p < 05$). There was a significant Sex X Painting Status interaction ($F = 5.42$, $df = 1/119, p < 05$). Inspection of the mean ratings of males and females under winner and entry conditions indicates that the main effect of male superiority was attributable to the entry condition and showed no differences in the winner condition. Means in the entry condition differed significantly in favor of men ($t = 1.99$, $p < 05$); means in the winner condition were identical (see Table 1). All other main effects and interactions were not significant.

TABLE 2

MEAN RATINGS OF ARTISTIC FUTURE OF MALE AND
FEMALE ARTISTS WITH WINNING AND
ENTRY PAINTINGS

Status of painting	Sex of artist	
	Male	Female
Winner	2.970	2.987
Entry	3.062	2.812

The question concerning the artistic future of the artist produced results paralleling the competence data (see Table 2). There were significant Sex X Painting Status interaction ($F = 4.52$, $df = 1/119, p < 05$). Males evaluated significantly more favorably than females for their entry paintings ($t = 1.92$, $p < 06$). Evaluations did not differ significantly for the winning paintings, although evaluations tended to favor the female winners.

A third question, asking about the artist's creativity, yielded no significant differences. (Intuitively, these data are not surprising, given the ambiguity of the term "creative." Also, "creativity" has some feminine connotations which judges may not wish to attribute to men, even when they believe the men are better artists.) In addition, the subjects evaluated the paintings themselves, equally among conditions (their quality and their emotional impact). Bias apparently was directed toward the performer, rather than toward his or her work.

The data presented above support our first and second hypothesis. Women value male work more highly than female work when it is only an attempt or entry; however, this bias dissipates when the work advances from entry to winner. The third hypothesis concerning the odds condition was not confirmed; there were no significant differences among the odds conditions.

DISCUSSION

Some professional women have claimed that their work is evaluated by men less well than it would be if they were men (e.g., Klein, 1950). The recent data of Goldberg (1968) and Pheterson (1969) have added a new dimension to the attitudinal factors inhibiting female success. Under certain conditions, even women are prejudiced against the performance of other women. The present study investigated one aspect of this prejudice. Women evaluated female entries in a contest less favorably than identical male entries, but female winners equally to identical male winners.

The implications of this finding are far-reaching. The work of women in competition is devalued by other women. Even work that is equivalent to the work of a man will be judged inferior until it receives special distinction, and that distinction is difficult to achieve when judgment is biased against the work in competition. According to the present data and those of Goldberg, women cannot expect unbiased evaluations until they prove themselves by award, trophy, or other obvious success. Obvious success is perceived differently by some groups than by others. The present research was based on the speculation that uneducated, middle-aged women perceived published articles as signs of obvious success, whereas college women perceived such work simply as a presentation of ideas. Women were prejudiced against female ideas but not against female success. The manipulation of entry and winner in this study permitted controlled examination and confirmation of that speculation.

A question might be raised regarding the strength of the present findings. Of five questionnaire items, only two supported our hypothesis. These were the first question (technical competence of the artist) and the fifth (the artist's future). However, a priori reasoning would suggest that these were the very questions where one would expect bias against women to occur. As mentioned earlier, creativity is ambiguous and may have feminine connotations. The paintings themselves were abstract, unknown, and also difficult to judge on the dimensions covered (quality and emotional impact). If people are expecting men to perform better than women, they should have the strongest expectations about tasks on which society has already labeled men as superior. In everyday life, many professional men are regarded as technically competent and are successful; we see fewer women in these positions (girls are not raised to be engineers or business executives). Thus, the subjects might simply be described as reflecting attitudes in society at large. They assumed the men to be more competent and predicted a more successful future for men *unless* there was evidence to the contrary, that is, that the women had, in fact, succeeded. The subjects probably did not have very strong convictions about whether men are more creative than women (husbands usually leave such creative tasks as home decorating and sewing to their wives). The quality and emotional impact of an abstract painting is also unlikely to have aroused strong attitudes favoring men. We argue, then, that our questionnaire data reflected the differing expectations which women (or men) have about men and women. That is, a woman will probably be less competent and her accomplishments fewer than a man, although she may be as creative (but probably not in science or business) and certainly as "emotional." Such an analysis implies that the subjects were not really judging the artists or paintings at all, but were simply expressing attitudes they held prior to the study. This, of course, was our purpose.

The third hypothesis, which predicted evaluations of paintings by people with odds against them to be more favorable in the winner condition than evaluations of identical paintings by people without odds, was not supported by the data. It is possible that the odds manipulation was too obvious. Perhaps some subjects were immediately aware of their special admiration for achievers with odds and therefore controlled their responses or underrated them, thus masking any positive bias the odds may have instilled. Informal subjects' feedback after the task supports this explanation. No subject suspected the importance of artist sex differences; however, many subjects reported the suspicion that they were expected to overvalue paintings of the handicapped or underprivileged. This suspicion may have caused a reaction which obscured prejudicial responses. Remaining to be demonstrated, then, is the hypothesis that obstacles make successes seem greater.

Why do women devalue each others' performance? If one accepts women as a group which has important similarities to

Gail I Pheterson, Sara B. Kiesler, and Philip A. Goldberg

minority groups in our society, the answer is obvious. The members of minority groups, and women, have less power and fewer opportunities than do the dominant group, white Anglo-Saxon males. Self-defeating as it is, groups feeling themselves to be the target of prejudice nevertheless tend to accept the attitudes of the dominant majority. This process has also been called identification with the aggressor (Allport, 1958). Women, then, when confronted with another woman who is trying to succeed in some endeavor, will assume that she is less motivated, less expert, or simply less favored by others than a man would (all these assumptions may be perfectly true).

Our data suggest that women do not devalue another woman when she has attained success. Without evidence, we think men do not either. In fact, a woman who has succeeded may be overevaluated. The present study apparently did not afford a proper test of this hypothesis. Perhaps if the artists had been identified as famous and really superior, women would have been rated more highly than men.

REFERENCES

Allport, G. W. *The nature of prejudice.* New York: Addison-Wesley, 1958.

Goldberg, P. A. Are women prejudiced against women? *Transaction,* April 1968, 28-30.

Klein, V. The sterotype of femininity. *Journal of Social Issues,* 1950, *6,* 3-12.

Pheterson, G. I. Female prejudice against men. Unpublished manuscript, Connecticut College, 1969.

Scheinfeld, A. *Women and men.* New York: Harcourt, Brace, 1944.

4

Helen Franzwa, a member of the Communications Department at Hunter College, CUNY, is interested in the way the roles of women are communicated to readers of fiction in three women's magazines, Ladies' Home Journal, McCall's, and Good Housekeeping. Stories from two issues per year of each magazine sampled at five-year intervals from 1940 to 1970 provide the basis of the most informative and well-illustrated content analysis. A total of 122 stories were analyzed in terms of the roles portrayed by the female characters. As depicted in these stories, the only proper role for women was housewife and mother. The never married women and the childless wife are considered deviant. The single woman tried to catch a husband; the married woman was dependent on her husband, had children, and felt that being a housewife was the best career of all. Divorced women and widows tried to cope without a husband, but really needed a man in order to be successful and complete. The spinster is depicted as being useful and having failed in life.

As was true with children's fiction, there is also bias in the presentation of women's roles in women's magazine fiction. Females are not absent from women's magazines, as was frequently true in children's stories, but they still fit the stereotype of passive and dependent. Their sphere of activity is basically limited to the home. The central characters of these stories may be women, but their lives revolve around men. Surprisingly, there was little change in type and percentage of such themes over the years from 1940 to 1970. If a woman worked, it was only because she had to or to catch a husband. Women were portrayed as shouldering more responsibility during the years of the Second World War, but only because it was their patriotic duty until the men returned from the service.

It would be interesting to see whether changes in life style as well as efforts by women's groups to see women portrayed in a more realistic manner will have a pay-off in both adult and children's reading material.

Female Roles in Women's Magazine Fiction, 1940-1970

Helen H. Franzwa

What is the proper role for women in the middle of the twentieth century? If one were to use short stories in women's magazines as a guide, there would be only one answer—housewife and mother. Such a conclusion should come as no surprise to anyone who has followed the women's liberation movement. Betty Friedan has already made the point in *The Feminine Mystique.* In a chapter entitled "The Happy Housewife Heroine" she notes in regard to the content of women's magazines: "Fulfillment as a woman had *only one definition for America women after 1949* —the housewife-mother."[1] Neither should it come as a surprise to those who read women's magazines. Their very reason for existence has traditionally been to provide information on home arts and child care. One would expect that their stories would follow a similar editorial line.

What is the nature of this line? What do the magazine stories say about the housewife-mother role? Do they suggest other roles for women? How are these roles depicted? Is there any perceivable bias in the presentation of roles for women?

The purpose of this paper is to report the results of thematic content analysis which was undertaken to discover how females are portrayed in the fiction of women's magazines. One hundred twenty-two stories appearing in *Ladies' Home Journal, McCall's,* and *Good Housekeeping* were analyzed[2] for themes[3] expressing

---

1. Betty Friedan, *The Feminine Mystique* (New York: Norton, 1963), p. 38.

2. These three magazines were chosen because they are the only publications that have been continuously directed toward the female market from the turn of the century to the present time. (T. Peterson, *Magazines in the Twentieth Century,* 2nd ed. Urbana: University of Illinois Press, 1964), p. 165. The sample consisted of stories drawn from two issues per year selected at five-year intervals. The particular issues within a given year were selected with the use of a table of random numbers and remained constant across all three periodicals.

3. Themes were formulated from the plots and expressed attitudes of the stories. For example, if the major female character of a story is childless and if she or other characters express the attitude that she

values associated with female roles.Upon completion of the sampling, it was obvious that the formulated themes suggested four major roles for women, each defined by her relationship (or lack of a relationship) with a man: young, single (premarital); wife-mother (marital); widowed-divorced (postmarital); spinster (nonmarital). The themes associated with these roles are presented below.

The young single woman. Two major themes are associated with the young single woman: (1) "Marriage is inevitable for every normal female" and, for those who want to bring about the inevitable more quickly,(2)"To catch a man you must be less competent than he, passive, and virtuous."

"Being a woman her real career was to fall in love"[4] is a label that could be applied to many fictional females who were portrayed as being in a temporary premarital state, despite the fact that seventeen stories had plots revolving around women who were *not* acutely interested in getting married. This theme might be alternatively titled, "Marriage will come, even when you least expect it." One or two of the plots will illustrate the theme: A young secretary with no place to go at Christmas is invited to her boss's home. She meets his mother, is proposed to, and accepts despite the fact that she and her boss had heretofore been on a last name basis, had never spoken outside of a work situation, nor had she been even vaguely interested in him. Another marriage results when a man bumps into a young woman in the train station. Immediately smitten, he acquires her address and promises to write. They correspond, and upon his return a few months later, they marry.

Although in many stories marriage is portrayed as inevitable for young females, there are more plots that explore the nature of the hunt for a husband. Twenty-nine such plots appeared in the sample. Typical of these stories is the giving of advice on how best to accomplish this goal. The advice, briefly stated, is that to catch her man, she should be less competent than he, she should be passive, and she should be virtuous.

Be less competent. Twelve stories explore the theme of the incompetent female and the success incompetence brings her in

---

has thereby wasted her life, the formulated theme for the story would be "The childless woman has wasted her life." More than one theme per story was recorded, if apparent. The number of stories with similar themes was tabulated; the number of reported themes does not, therefore, equal the number of stories sampled.

4. Margaret Cousins, "Love Is a Complicated Thing," *Good Housekeeping,* March 1955, pp. 55 ff.

catching a man. Briefly explained, the theme has as its basis the assumption that the male must always be superior to the female. The stories reward those females who are less competent than the male by having him propose; they punish the more competent female by having her lose her man. This is a prevalent theme and deserves extended illustration.

The most recent such story in the sample appeared in 1965. Here, a totally incompetent female who can barely manage day-to-day existence because of her bumbling awkwardness is given a secretarial job by the husband of a former college roommate. *Despite* her total incompetence the husband's boss fails to notice—and then, *because* of her total incompetence, he falls head over heels in love. The husband is rewarded for his cupidity by being made his boss's partner.

The author apparently likes the theme of the successful incompetent female, for in 1960 he has another story that is almost identical in formula. Here he focuses on a woman who "manages her own immensely profitable surgical supply house." She has won the state tennis championship four years straight, she looks like a "Greek goddess," but, alas, "her world is coming to an end because she can't find a husband." Why is such a capable woman such a duffer in the husband-hunting department? We could infer that it is because she is so generally capable, but nothing is left to inference. The husband of this woman's sister exclaims in utter frustration:

> [Camilla] had never learned Rule Number One. This is the maxim every girl memorizes with her high school algebra, and it reads: "Never let him know that you're smarter (or stronger or wittier or a better piccolo player) than he is." I had no idea why she had missed this lesson. All I knew was that if she hadn't learned it by now, she never would, and I could round up every unattached male in town and still be wasting my time.[5]

In the end, however, Camilla is successful. She meets an artist and, fortunately for her, in art she is a total incompetent. In stunned disbelief the next morning she tells her sister and brother-in-law, "Why should he love me? I mean I'm an absolute cretin about art. I mean, I couldn't think of an intelligent thing to say all evening!" She marries the artist, they fly off to Venice, apparently tossing aside her "immensely profitable surgical supply house,"

---

5. Robert Knowlton, "Never Let Them Know," *Good Housekeeping,* September 1960, pp. 80 ff.

and the brother-in-law gets a raise.

Brief quotations from other stories containing the incompetent female theme will serve to indicate its widespread diffusion:

> She's a darn nice gal. She might even be a knockout gal, but she argues too much. She knows too much. She knows more than I do. . .[6]

> I'm the man. The man knows everything. He knows everything and he tells the woman; that's the way nature planned the formula.[7]

> He looked at her full of her silly woman errors, sweet and helpless. The tide of love swept over him.[8]

Be passive. A second theme in the "how to catch a husband" stories suggests that the woman must be patient and passive in her pursuit. Ten stories explore this theme in which aggressive behavior in seeking a mate is seen as a strictly male endeavor. The female may place herself in a likely place in which to find a husband—usually in an office—or she may just happen to be discovered by a likely prospect, but she never goes prospecting herself. If she loses a man, thereby, it is just too bad.[9]

The plight of the female frustrated by the passive role in which the culture has apparently cast her is explored in "Midnight of a Bridesmaid." The bridesmaid is in love with the groom and is crying over her loss. She discovers that a close male friend is in love with the bride. During a commiseration session she thinks to herself,

> He at least had been in a better position than she. He was a man. He could have fought for Barbi, swept her off her feet or done a dozen other things that were a man's right. Women were laughed at when they stormed the castle and

---

6. Elizabeth Dunn, "Men Are Better than Women," *Ladies' Home Journal,* March 1950, pp. 58 ff.

7. Nel Heimer, "The End of the World—But Not Quite," *McCall's,* September 1960, pp. 85ff.

8. Margaret Cousins, "Love Is a Complicated Thing."

9. In this section only those stories that *directly* deal with passivity are discussed. In many (if not most) stories in the entire sample women are portrayed as passive individuals, but this characteristic is not the focal point of the story. Here the issue is: Should she *actively* pursue the man or wait for him to pursue her? Generally, she waits.

were repulsed. Nobody laughed at a man who plainly showed his devotion. Even if he failed in his endeavor, nobody laughed.[10]

Three stories featured girls who would like to telephone the man and in each case they refrain; instead, they remain passively beside the unringing telephone. In one story the girl tells her sister that she would like to telephone her boyfriend to patch things up but she would become an "old maid" before doing so.[11]

Be virtuous. Display of a number of virtues as a means of attracting and holding a man is a third theme in these stories. Women who remain true, confident in themselves and in their men, who are thoughtful, gracious, selfless, and eternally understanding, are very much appreciated by the men in seven stories. These stories follow a highly similar formula. A couple is engaged or approaching engagement. The virtue of the female is tested, she passes the test, and the man happily and confidently marries her. In one story the girl did not pass the test, was rejected by her fiance, and remained unmarried through the rest of the story.

For the young single woman two themes illustrate the temporary premarital state she is in. Either she finds herself in love and about to be married or she is actively looking for a husband. If she is to be successful she must appear to be less competent than he, she must not be aggressive, and she must be virtuous. Once the woman has got her man, she then moves into the next stage of her life—the marital.

The married woman. The nature of being a wife is one that the stories portray as involving total dependence on and devotion to one's husband. The first two themes that illustrate these facets of the wife's role are (1) "Married women don't work" and (2) "To keep your man you must . . . " In addition to these two themes there are numerous stories that validate the role of housewife-mother, supporting the theme (3) "Being a housewife-mother is the best career of all." Minor themes supporting the housewife-mother role are (*a*)"To solve your problems have another child," and (*b*) "The childless woman has wasted her life."

Married women don't work. Fourteen stories feature the theme that married women don't work. In seven of them marriage is postponed, rejected outright, worried over, or rocky because the

---

10. Vina Delmar, "Midnight of a Bridesmaid," *Ladies' Home Journal,* March 1955, pp. 63ff.

11. Florence Soman, "Sisters Are Like That," *Ladies' Home Journal,* March 1950, pp. 56ff.

husband can't support the wife. In every case of unmarrieds it is a male decision that the marriage can't go on because his income is insufficient. In three cases, the fiancee offers to work, but he rejects her offer. Typical of these stories is one that appeared as recently as 1965. The young man is a Ph.D. candidate. The female has a good job in a publishing house, but he rejects marriage because "I can't afford it. . . . "[12] Similarly in 1965 an intern says, "It will be many years before I can start supporting a wife, and no wife of mine is going to work while I'm learning my trade."[13] In 1940 a young couple realize that they can't live on his salary. She offers to work; he replies: "I don't think that's so good. I know some fellows whose wives work and they might just as well not be married."[14]

Throughout, the underlying assumption of this theme appears to be that a wife who works is a threat to the male ego: "If a man can't support a wife, what good is he?"[15] In one case this worry is clothed with concern for his wife's health: "She'd be worn to a shred and a tatter"[16] if she worked.

There were two stories (one in 1945 the other in 1950) in which the wives worked and were successful in their careers; both lost their husbands. One wife's husband came back to her, however, but not until he had learned that she had been (inexplicably) fired. He demanded that she join him and "rest her feet and her brains and just take care of her husband. I guess that's what I've always wanted all this time, a dear dumb little wife to work for."[17] Their son (who had severe identity problems because of his mother's success and his father's lack of it) is happy because "suddenly the world made sense to me and I knew what it was all about. People working and taking care of one another, women in one way and men in another."

To keep your husband you must . . . Along with dependence on husband is devotion to husband. Numerous stories had plots that

12. Ruth Lyons, "The Lost Days," *McCall's,* May 1965, pp. 102ff.

13. Josephine Bentham, "With Love and Cold Water Soap," *McCall's,* August 1965, pp. 90ff.

14. Margaret Culkins Banning, "Enough to Live On," *McCall's,* February 1940, pp. 11ff.

15. Decla Dunning, "A Place to Be Born," *Good Housekeeping,* March 1950, pp. 38ff.

16. Josephine Bentham, "With Love and Cold Water Soap."

17. Margaret Lee Runbeck, "A Man with Woman," *Good Housekeeping,* January 1950, pp. 36ff.

centered on how to keep your husband happy: build up his ego, don't threaten him, be virtuous. The behaviors attendant to keeping your husband are virtually identical to those involved in catching him, so I am presenting them under the same headings.

Be less competent. One would hope that upon marriage female pretense of incompetence could be relaxed and wives could feel free to be themselves without worrying about comparisons or competition, but two stories stressed the point that to keep your husband you must continue to make it clear that he is the smarter and more able of the two. Women who displayed abilities surpassing those of their husbands had serious problems with their husbands as a result. Five other stories made the point that the wife was clearly the less capable of the two and *for that reason* she was desirable.

In the two cases of female competence, the women were superhousewives who excelled in every facet of the job. In one case the wife continually found herself alone and one evening reviewed her marriage. She concluded that she "had tried to be perfect in every way."[18] After a long heart-to-heart talk with her husband she discovered that she had been too perfect; he didn't believe that he could be as perfect in his work as she was in hers and was withdrawing from the relationship because he couldn't meet such high standards.

Five stories portray the stupid wife keeping her husband in much the same way the stupid female captured him in the first place. In the best example of this plot a beautiful, talented divorcee tries to take an ugly, untalented woman's husband away from her. She loses and even the wife can't figure out why. Her husband tells her: "I love you because you aren't beautiful. I love you because you think it's the ice cubes that make the refrigerator cold. I love you because you aren't witty . . . "[19]

Be passive. Passivity within marriage is not a popular theme. It is not that wives are portrayed as aggressors or even as independent; indeed, most wives are not portrayed as aggressors or even as independent; indeed, most wives are not portrayed as wanting any kind of independence at all. Because passivity is assumed, there is no conflict upon which to base a story exploring the consequences of aggressiveness or independence. The husbands are generally presented as the decision-makers, with the wives passively ac-

18. Chariotte Edwards, "Life Begins on Friday," *McCall's,* March 1950, pp. 50ff.

19. George S. Albee, "The Ugliest Woman in Town," *Ladies' Home Journal,* April 1955, pp. 62ff.

cepting the decisions.[20] The only story I discovered which explored female independence did so on an exceedingly trivial level. A graying mother decides that she would like to dye her hair. She sends up trial baloons and soon discovers that her children oppose it—mothers are supposed to have gray hair. Her husband and father oppose it—it's cheap and beneath her dignity. She is just about to succumb to their wishes when she realizes that she is a person in her own right and *she* wants to have it dyed.

Be virtuous. The same virtues that got a man in the first place are presented as useful in keeping him. The devoted, loving, selfless wife is much appreciated. Four stories focus on such a woman, the most important of which appeared in 1970. A young wife finds that her husband's promotion has resulted in long periods of loneliness. She believes that "women are incomplete without men"[21] and feels lonely, empty, and afraid. She soon discovers that her neighbors have the same problem and handle it by heavy drinking and carousing. She decides that she *will* be happy because in being so she can be more helpful to her husband. She rejects her friends, signs up for a sewing course at the YWCA, and, apparently, the marriage is saved.

Being a housewife-mother is the best career of all. Throughout the 1960's and in 1970 the role of housewife-mother is validated extensively. She discovers that she is the soul of the family and that being a housewife-mother is more rewarding and fulfilling than any other occupation. This theme did not appear in the sampled stories prior to 1960, apparently because the role was not so much under attack then. As late as 1970 there were three stories that featured this theme, but the most obvious defense of the role appeared in 1960 when a mother of five visits a childless friend now fabulously wealthy. The visit is a disaster except that she validates herself as a housewife-mother. She is racked by guilt in taking the first trip of her married life. She takes pictures of her children along to give her "courage and identity." On the plane she thinks about her family: "I miss you all atrociously already. I wish I'd slit my throat before I ever told Leslie I'd come. . . . I could have slip-covered the entire living room for what the plane ticket cost." She ends the visit abruptly, answering her protesting friend: "There's nothing left of me to see. I don't exist without my family. That's why I've got to go. I miss them all too much to live. I'm a wife and

---

20. One major exception to this generalization appears to be in deciding to have another child. Women are sometimes portrayed as making this decision alone. See "To solve your problems have another child."

21. Virginia Gillette, "A Love to Share," *Good Housekeeping*, November 1970, pp. 96ff.

mother. For better or for worse. That's all I want to be."[22]

In all of this validation of the housewife-mother role, one wonders if there just might be too much protest that the role is really that worthwhile. This wonder is further extended by the stories that acknowledge her feelings of boredom, uselessness, and loneliness. These stories do not get at the reasons for such feelings; instead they suggest having another baby.

To solve your problems have another baby. Four stories took notice of the uselessness many housewife-mothers feel when their children are growing up. In each case the wife is described as feeling lonely and bored. A new baby is the obvious solution to her problem. The following story illustrates the theme. A thirty-six-year-old housewife-mother of two (seventeen and twelve) spends a "long, lonely day" daydreaming about how babies had made her marriage "Fresh and young," but alas, it hadn't lasted. She feels lonely and unneeded by everyone. She decides privately to become pregnant and then announces to her family that she is pregnant and why she wanted another baby. Although they accept the idea of a new baby readily, they are astounded that she should feel useless. Her husband validates her role:

> Don't you know the home is built around you? Don't you know it's you we come back to, always? What would we do if you weren't here when we come back? . . . The house would be empty and cold, just four walls and a roof, all its warmth and spirit gone . . . a house without a soul.

She concludes, "They were a unit bound together by love. If it was her love that held them, then they would be together always."[23]

The childless woman has wasted her life. Twelve stories discuss the feelings of the childless woman. In some she is featured; in others the heroine derives personal satisfaction from favorable comparison to childless women. They are frequently described as having wasted their lives. They are lonely, bored, guilty, unfulfilled, and unhappy. Despite the fact that four have professional careers and two are exceedingly rich and travel extensively, they appear to derive little personal satisfaction from life and apparently have no worthwhile outlets other than the unfulfilled one of motherhood.

Typical of these women is the wife of a college professor. A schoolteacher prior to marriage, she quit her job despite an agreement that they would remain childless. After three years she

---

22. Nancy Ferard, "The Holiday," *McCall's,* September 1960, pp. 86ff.

23. R. W. Alexander, "So Dear to My Heart," *Good Housekeeping,* May 1965, pp. 88ff.

is bored being a housewife and says to her husband, "A good marriage has children in it. . . . It didn't seem to matter at first, but I feel useless. As if I'd cheated life."[24] Her husband finally agrees to have children. A return to teaching is not considered as a possible solution to her boredom and feeling of uselessness.

Similarly, a spinster, speaking of herself and her two maiden sisters, says, "Alice and Mae have had such empty lives. They never married, they've never had children. . . . "[25] In order to avoid wasting her life and being "a drain" on her parents, a woman marries a man she doesn't love: "She wanted a home; she wanted children."[26] A childless woman is accused of turning "her husband into the baby she can't have."[27] Another is described by a mother of five as being "a pauper in this highest bracket of wealth."[28]

The widow-divorcee. In contrast to the married woman and the husband-hunting single woman, the widow-divorcee is portrayed as a woman who, despite the fact that she is without a man, wants to remain independent. She is proud of herself and of her ability to cope with child-rearing and breadwinning without a husband. We as readers soon discover, however, that these women are deluding themselves. Far from being competent, they can hardly cope at all. As readers we worry about the development of "proper" sex roles; we worry about the sanity of one little girl; we even worry for the very life of one child left in the hands of these women. There is a major thread of similarity between these women and their single counterparts, and this is that no matter how competent and independent they may *think* they are, in comparison to the men who crop up in their lives they are incompetent. And before the end of the story they find themselves married to knights in shining armor who are eager not only to marry an incompetent are also eager to take on her family.

Typical of the incompetent divorcee-widow stories is that of a young beautiful widow who declines a proposal from a very eligible bachelor who is forever pointing out how her children need a father. She changes her mind when the bachelor saves her son from drowning after he had strayed into deep water (she couldn't

---

24. Nelia Garner White, "According to My Wife," *McCall's,* April 1955, pp. 35ff.

25. Jerome Weidman, "Something to Remember," *Good Housekeeping,* January 1950, pp. 46ff.

27. Virginia Gillette, "A Love to Share."

28. Nancy Ferard, "The Holiday."

swim that far). "It was a strange feeling after two years of trying to *be* everything and *do* everything, and she liked it. What a fool she had been to have thought she could do it all alone — earn the money, keep the house, mother them and be a father at the same time."[29] A second intrepid lover reaches the widow through her son. Being raised by mother, grandmother, and cook, the boy has no male models. The suitor spends most of his time with the boy and thereby wins his mother.

The spinster. The last category of women in these stories never had a man. There were twelve spinsters in the sample, all labeled as such within the context of the story. Some of these women have already been described under the theme "The childless has wasted her life," so there is no need to repeat that aspect of their description here. There were other stories that focused on husbandlessness, and it is to these that we will turn our attention. Similar to the childless woman in general, the spinsters are depicted as lonely, useless creatures who are unhappy because of their failures in love. Despite the fact that they have relatively high-status jobs (college professor, director of a girls' school, director of a museum), they don't appear to derive much personal satisfaction from their careers. Instead, they are depicted as lonely and morose; one even goes mad.

Two possible exceptions to this rule occur in which the spinsters talk of their being needed in their jobs, but they do not speak with conviction. For example, a reform school teacher describes herself in the following manner: "[I am] a spinster forever. I teach short-hand in a girls' state reform school and tell myself that this is where I am needed. What I really mean is that I need to be here."[30]

It seems to be impossible for the spinster to have a normal relationship with her work — in comparison to having a man, her work is dull, meaningless, and unimportant. Again, the existence or nonexistence of a man in the life of the woman is portrayed as being of utmost significance to her.

I have argued throughout that the stories sampled in the women's magazines portray females as half persons who are completed and fulfilled only by a man. First, the stories are easily divided into categories that focus on the female's marital state; second, the major interest of most female characters is to catch or keep a husband; third, single and married female characters learn that to catch and keep a husband they must show him that he is

29. Brooks Baldwin and B. F. Gorham, "Just Before Dawn," *Good Housekeeping,* February 1945, pp. 34ff.

30. Susan Morrow, "The Promise," *Good Housekeeping,* May 1965, pp. 94ff.

the single most important part of their lives; fourth, divorced-widowed female characters can't raise children without a man and expect them to grow up physically and emotionally healthy; fifth, spinsters cannot expect to lead a fulfilling life through a career.

Children in a woman's life are portrayed as being of lesser importance than is the man, but they are nevertheless presented as vital to her emotional well-being. First, mothers who are lonely and bored because their children have grown can solve this problem by having another child. Second, women who have never had children are invariably characterized as lonely, bored, unfulfilled, and wasteful of their time.

In none of these stories do we see whole, emotionally healthy women (married or single) who are complete in and of themselves. In almost none of these stories do we see married women who have any interests of their own that have nothing to do with their husbands or their children.

At the outset of this paper I wondered if there were a perceivable bias in the presentation of roles for women in women's magazine fiction. I believe that the answer to that question has been made obvious.

5

Mary Ritchie Key teaches linguistics at the University of California at Irvine. She chaired a group of honor-society women who researched the material on sexual stereotypes dealt with in this paper.

The article combines a summary of existing studies concerned with sex discrimination in children's books as well as an additional analysis of books to document these findings further. While not a high-powered study, this article was selected as most representative of those in this area because of its breadth as well as its recentness.

Key points out that children's literature perpetuates the antifemale myths and prejudices of society, and most other studies independently support this conclusion even without awareness of other research. Key includes some evaluation of the relatively small number of other studies that indicate opposite conclusions, i.e., a tendency to downgrade the male. She cites criticisms of several of these studies which indicate their highly biased assumptions.

One of the major points made by Key, both from her own research and that of others, is the relative absence of females in children's stories. This is true of Old and Middle English literature as well as current material. In textbooks at least 75 percent of the main characters are male. In group situations the males are preeminent. Females are frequently presented in relation to males. They don't do the things people do in real life. Girls and women are passive or unpleasant, one-dimensional or castrating. They are not very likable.

The article does end on a positive note and mentions some remedies that are being processed.

The Role of Male and Female in Children's Books — Dispelling All Doubt

Mary Ritchie Key[1]

. . . Bill said, "I will sit in front and steer the sled, Joan, You sit in the back so that you can hold on to me."[2]

Textbooks and children's literature are under scrutiny these days by persons interested in the full potential of both male and female. It is being discovered that the above quote appears to be typical of the general atmosphere in children's literature today: *Boys do; girls are.*

In general, children's books show that boys: climb, dig, build, fight, fall down, get dirty, ride bikes, and have many adventures, while girls sit quietly and watch. Boys are taught to express themselves; girls to please. According to an infamous little book called *I'm glad I'm a boy! I'm glad I'm a girl* (Windmill, 1970), "Boys invent things," and "Girls use what boys invent." Illustrations showing a little boy inventing a reading lamp and a little girl in an easy chair reading under his lamp are captioned by these phrases.

The theoretical basis behind this is, of course, Freud's hackneyed "biology is destiny," without regard for a balanced consideration that psychology can also be destiny."

At this point it is difficult to judge how much influence children's books have in shaping the child's life. One cannot be certain whether the structure of society is simply reflected in the books, or whether the books are further determining the structure of society. Leah Heyn, for one, speaks of the role in child growth that

---

1. The Research Committee of the Gamma Epsilon Chapter of Delta Kappa Gamma took the topic expressed in the title as a study project. Members of the committee collected materials and made analyses of several series of books. As chairman of the committee, I compiled the reports and worked them into this larger study. References to these analyses will be made by name only, since none of this was previously published. The contributions were from the following members: Marguerite Pinson, coordinator of bilingual education; Marguerite Sharpe; Marjorie Taylor, coordinator of library services; and Laura Wright.
2. Glenn McCracken and Charles E. Walcutt. *Basic Reading* (Lippincott, 1963), California State Department of Education, 1969, p. 41.

children's books have and feels that books do, indeed, have an influence in terms of the development of the senses, idea reinforcement, knowledge expansion, and the liberation from the child's born-into environment.

In any case, it is clear that the prejudices and myths held by the majority of the members of society are perpetuated in children's literature. For example, John P. Shepard's study[3] in 1962 showed that the characters "strongly tend to be clean, white, healthy, handsome, Protestant Christian, middle-class people. Villains much more often turn out to be ugly, physically undesirable persons of non-Caucasian races, often either very poor or of the wealthy classes." In this study however, the categories investigated did not include the sex variable which is under investigation today.

One of the earliest statements in the recent acknowledgement of sex prejudice in children's books was made by the well-known anthropologist John Honigmann, in *Personality in Culture* (1967):

> Reflecting a poorly concealed bias in American society, central characters in the stories are male more than twice as often as they are female. Surely this confirms the reader's belief that one sex is more important than the other, even if that isn't the only way he finds it out. Stories frequently differentiate male and female roles, just as our culture does. They generally leave female characters to display affiliation and nurturance and to flee danger; rarely do girls display traits of activity, aggression, achievement, or construction; seldom do they win recognition. In other words, girls are pictured as kind, timid, inactive, unambitious, and uncreative. Furthermore, characters in the story who are nurtured by a central character are mostly female, suggesting that females are likely to be in a helpless position. . . . The school readers portray males as bearers of knowledge and wisdom, and also as the persons through whom knowledge reaches a child [pp. 203-204].

This statement was, in part, based on a 1946 study by Irwin Child and others.[4]

The idea that sex prejudice is the only prejudice now considered socially acceptable seems remarkably applicable to the books

3. John P. Shepard, "The treatment of characters in popular children's fiction," *Elementary English* 39 (November 1962), pp. 672-676.
4. Irvin L. Child, Elmer H. Potter, and Estelle M. Levine, "Children's textbooks and personality development," *Psychological Monographs* 60.3 (1946) pp. 1-7, 45-53.

found in the field of education, one of our most respected institutions. One writer, Marjorie U'Ren, notes that textbooks written for co-education early in this century present a much more favorable picture of women and girls than do textbooks written from 1930 on. The atmosphere has changed since then. In 1946 Child did a content analysis and concluded that "The most striking single fact of all . . . about the differences between the sexes is that the female characters do simply tend to be neglected."

STUDYING THE STUDIES

During the last two years over a dozen different studies have been made on children's books: picture books, early childhood books, teen-age books, general library books, a series for minority groups, and California textbooks, which *every* child in California is exposed to. The remarkable thing about these studies is that, although they often make statements which are identical or similar and they reinforce the conclusions of one another, there appears to be no awareness between them of the other studies. They seem to have sprung up spontaneously across the nation, from student, mother, writer, professor, administrator, teacher, and librarian. The studies overwhelmingly document discrimination and prejudice against females in children's books.

Before proceeding further to the focus of our statement, let us stop here to evaluate other recent studies which seem to indicate opposite conclusions, namely the studies of first-grade reading books by Blom *et al.*; Waite *et al.*; Wiberg and Trost;[5] and others which these articles quote. For example, the Wiberg and Trost article concludes that children's books have "a tendency to denigrate the masculine role." Blom, Waite, and Zimet show that "A large number of stories were in the boy-girl activity category (46 percent) as compared to boy activity (26 percent), and girl activity (28 percent) . . ." "Active Play, Outings, Pranks, and Work Projects were related to boy activity. Quiet Activities, School, Folk Tales, and Real Life with Positive Emotions were related to girl activity." Such statements are somewhat misleading and must be

---

5. Gaston E. Blom, Richard R. Waite, and Sara Zimet, "Content of first grade reading books." *The Reading Teacher* 21.4 (January 1968), pp. 317-323; Richard R. Waite, Gaston E. Blom, Sara F. Zimet, and Stella Edge, "First-grade reading textbooks," *The Elementary School Journal* 67 (April 1967), pp. 366-374; John L. Wiberg and Marion Trost, "A comparison between the content of first grade primers and the free choice library selections made by first grade students," *Elementary English* (October 1970), pp. 792-798.

tempered with other facts and other perspectives. In addition, the terminology of studies such as these obfuscates. What is meant by "ambiguity in sex role, sex role appropriateness, oedipal conflict, sex of activity, sex preference?"

Other facts to be considered, for example, are how many boys and how many girls figure as the central character of those so-called "boy-girl activities" comprising 46 percent of the studies mentioned above. Worley counterbalances with other facts:

In most of the stories examined, the central character was a boy and the plot development reflected male circumstances . . . there were twice as many stories reflecting male story situations as there were stories reflecting female story situations.

He suggests that:

A larger proportion of basal reader stories should involve a female as the central character. The heavy emphasis given male figures creates a distorted and perhaps harmful sex role image for all readers (p. 148).

Other perspectives to be considered concern the judgments made about what, indeed, is a girl-activity and what is a boy-activity. It is highly possible that *all* activities that six-year-olds participate in could be either boy or girl activities, if the youngsters weren't socialized to what adults *think* they should do. There don't seem to be great differences in muscular ability, and this age is still a long way from child-bearing functions — two activities which are, indeed, not culturally learned. It would appear from the evidence presented in the studies I am summarizing that a significant number of scholars, persons in education, and lay people disagree with the stereotyped roles assigned to boys and girls in the foregoing studies. Apparently females also like to climb trees, explore caves, go fishing; feel invigorated with accepting responsibility; and can accept leadership with equanimity.

WE NEEDN'T HAVE FEARED?

This present paper is a result of a two-fold apparoach: a survey of studies already made, and an analysis of some actual books to confirm statements made. In our committee discussions while formulating plans for the project, we were concerned about how one would come to conclusions as to whether or not the text or pictures showed discrimination. How would one avoid subjective, biased statements? We needn't have feared! In many cases, there was no analysis to do because of the absence or the paucity of females either as protagonists or supporting characters. It would appear that modern children's literature follows true to the tradition of early English literature. George K. Anderson commented on the place of women in Old and Middle English literature:

> Indeed, the relative insignificance of women in the social scene marks the Old English period as different even from the Middle English. Women had a hard enough time of it at best in the Middle Ages, partly because they had no opportunity to do much of anything except in the domestic sphere and partly because Christian tradition traced the fall of man to a woman. . . . If we were to judge by Old English literature alone, we would conclude that only queens, princesses, abbesses, a few wives, and a scattering of mistresses comprised the female population of England at that time.[6]

In the *Be a Better Reader* series for the seventh grade, story after story unfolds without any female in existence. It is the exception when a female is a real part of any scene, such as in a farm story in which the mother and daughter are depicted as more thoughtful and intelligent than the boy and husband.

The absence or almost absence of females is also typical of *The Roberts English Series: A Linguistics Program* (Books 3 to 8), especially the later books. In Book 6, out of thirty main sections, only two focus on the female. One section discusses a poem of comparison between the jaded and weary hill-country wife (not woman, but *wife*) and the prairie wife who owns "one last year's dress" and whose life is a series of long, dull, lonely hours (pp. 132-133). The other section treats a humorous (?) poem about a remarkable (neurotic?) little girl "who didn't let things bother her very much." The "Things" she deals with are an enormous bear, a wicked old witch, a hideous giant, and a troublesome doctor (Ogden Nash, in Book 6, pp. 262-264). Book 8 has three sections out of thirty in which females dominate the scene. One is "The Solitary Reaper," another is a story about a crotchety old aunt. The book, and the series, end with the third and final piece about a

---

6. George K. Anderson, *Old and Middle English Literature from the Beginnings to 1485,* Vol. I of *A History of English Literature.* New York: Collier Books, 1962.

female, "The Hag," a witch who rides off with the Devil to do their mischief.

Some of the other recent textbooks adopted or recommended for second through sixth grade in California were analyzed by U'Ren, Gail Ann Vincent, and our committee. In these books at least 75 percent of the main characters are male. The stories about females are not as lengthy. Often the stories about males include no mention of a female, although the stories about females include males with whom the females interact. The mother figure is typically presented as a pleasant, hardworking, but basically uninteresting person:

> . . . she has no effect upon the world beyond her family, and even within the family her contribution is limited to that of housekeeper and cook. . . . She enters a scene only to place a cake on the table and then disappears. Or she plays foil to her husband by setting him up for his line. It is mother who asks, "What shall we do?" and by doing so invites a speech from father (U'Ren, p. 7).

Librarian Marjorie Taylor confirms this: "Daddy is the predominant character. His are the ideas, the main portions of the conversations, "where the action is."

Vincent's study concentrates on the socialization of the female in the California textbook series. References are made to previous studies on sex-role concepts. Lawrence Kohlberg's[7] study, for example, is said to show that children age five to eight "award greater value or prestige to the male role." "He also finds that identification with the father and other male figures increases dramatically for boys during these years, whereas preferential orientation to the mother in girls declines." Females are not seen interacting together as are males. In the one instance where girls are grouping together and excluding boys ("I *never* play with boys"), they are ridiculed by the boys. Vincent observes that the reverse, i.e., girls ridiculing boys for similar behavior, never occurs. Taylor also documented stories where high value is put on all male activity. In *All Through the Year* by Mabel O'Donnell (Harper & Row, 1969), when the children are going to play detective, Mark shouts, "Boy, this is going to be fun. . . . No girls can be in on this. Just boys. . . . "

With regard to physical tasks, Vincent observes that boys are more competent than girls in the California textbooks: the boy fixes

---

7. Lawrence Kohlberg, "A cognitive-developmental analysis of children's sex-role concepts and attitudes," in Eleanor Maccoby, ed., *The development of sex differences,* Stanford University Press, 1966.

his bike and rides it while the kneeling girl admires him; the boy shoots a basket, while the girl tries and misses.

In creative activities the males also excel: a boy is the best painter; a boy is the best storyteller; father is the best at riddles; a boy wins a contest in snow-sculpting.

In children's books, females do not have the freedom to inquire, explore, and achieve. Margaret Mead is quoted as saying, "Man is unsexed by failure, women by success." This indoctrination starts early. Vincent analyzes the repeated theme of a female not suc-ceeding and notes that when a girl does initiate a tree-climbing episodie, punishment is the result (a broken leg for one boy), and a grandmotherly character scolds her for shameful behavior: "What's wrong with you?"

With regard to pictures and illustrations, U'Ren found that many California textbooks included females in only about 15 percent of the illustrations. In group scenes, invariably the males dominate. In *The Roberts English Series: A Linguistic Program,* which includes a great deal of poetry, many of the poems are written with pronoun referent unspecified as to sex, e.g., "I, me, we, they." The pic-tures accompanying the poems, however, with the exception of Book 3, are almost all male-dominated. In Book 4, eleven poems are illustrated thus, with none illustrated by a female or female-dominated picture. The prose story of Daphne (p. 65) is illustrated by three pictures in which Apollo and Cupid hold the scenes. Daphne is shown only as the transformed laurel tree. In the text, which is presented in three sections, Daphne doesn't enter the story until the second section. Thus, even when a story is sup-posed to be about a female, the actual pictorial and textual presentation may diminish the female.

THE AWARD WINNERS

Alleen Nilsen analyzed the winners and runners-up of the Caldecott Award during the last twenty years. Presented annually by the Children's Service Committee of the American Library Association for the most distinguished picture book of the year, this exclusive award makes for wide distribution of these books across the country. Of the eighty books analyzed, Nilsen found that the titles included names of males over three times as often as names of females. One-fourth of the books had only token females. In the last twenty years, the presence of females in the Caldecott books is steadily decreasing. This statistic parallels other statistics which are commonplace today, such as the percentage of women in administrative positions in education and the percentage of women professors, which is less now than it was in the 1930s. Among the forty-nine Newbery Award winners of 1969, books about boys outnumbered books about girls some three to one.

Elizabeth Fisher studied books for young children found in bookstores and libraries. There were five times as many males in the titles as there were females. The fantasy worlds of Maurice Sendak and Dr. Seuss are almost all male.

In children's books, there is a significant reversal of the usual use of "she/her" for animals and inanimate objects. I have discussed pronoun referents in another study of the linguistic behavior of male and female.[8] Grammar rules and usage indicate, among other things, that large animals are "he," small animals are "she," and other inanimate objects are usually "she." Admittedly there is a great deal of confusion and inconsistency in rules and usage, which I point out in the paper. Storybook animals in our children's books, however, are almost all male, and female animals tend to carry names of derogation or are objects of derision: Petunia the Goose, Frances the Badger, and the sow who entered the Fat Pigs contest (Wodehouse, in The Roberts English Series 8). Personifications of the inanimate are invariably male; for example, in The Roberts English Series. While no sailor worth his salt in real life would refer to a ship as "he," our children's books have boats, machines, trains, and automobiles which carry only male names and gender. This contradicts T. Hilding Svartengren's study[9] where he showed that these items were referred to in literature by the referents "she/her."

THE BUTT OF THE JOKE

The treatment of females in comedy is another area of concern in children's books. Too often the butt of the joke in poems and stories is a female. The Roberts English Series:A Linguistics Program in chock full of such "funny" poetry by writers such as Belloc, Nash, and Thurber.

As far as role identity is concerned, when women are mentioned or pictured, they are usually shown in relation to men or as accouterments to men. Virginia Woolf pointed out that in literature as a whole this is the situation. In one of the Newbery Award winners,

8. Mary Ritchie Key, "Linguistic behavior of male and female," to be published in Linguistics: An International Review.
9. T. Hilding Svartengren, "The use of the personal gender for inanimate things," Dialect Notes 6 (1925), 1928-1939, pp. 7-56.

our next generation was advised, "Accept the fact that this is a man's world and learn how to play the game gracefully."

Books written for teen-age boys often tell them that females do not exist; life moves on without girls or women. The worlds of Mark Twain (*The Roberts English Series 7*) and Robert Louis Stevenson (*The Roberts English Series 8*), without a single mention of a female, are being reiterated in contemporary literature. The *Field Educational Checkered Flag Series,* written for boys, is such an example (Henry A. Bamman and Robert Whitehead, California State Text, 1969). When females do occur in books written for young people approaching adulthood, the girls and women are not like the people whom young men will meet in real life.

What Do Big Girls Do?

The following list, compiled from one of *The Roberts English Series,* written for junior high students, gives a comprehensive covering of what females do in Book 8:

- Count votes for males who were nominated;
- Accompany men to the hunt;
- Find their beauty is short-lived;
- Sit with their fans in their hands and gold combs in their hair.
- Put cream on their faces and "lie in bed staring at the ceiling and wishing [they] had some decent jewelry to wear at the . . . Ball";
- Poison their husbands;
- Die because they "never knew those simple little rules . . .";
- Get eaten up by alligators;
- Cut and gather grain and sing to no one;
- Listen to men give speeches;
- Rear children;
- Do silly, ridiculous things (James Thurber);
- Ride with the Devil.

Diane Stavn analyzed for attitudes about girls and women novels which are known to be popular with boys. She made two observations: ". . . the sweeping, sometimes contradictory" incidental comments about the female sex, and "the fact that the girlfriends and mothers are almost always unrealized or unpleasant characters—one-dimensional, idealized, insipid, bitchy, or castrating—while sexually neutral characters, such as little sisters and old ladies, are most often well conceived and likable." For example, the girl friend of jazz freak Tom Curtis turns out to be "merely a mouthpiece to relate information about other characters in the book and a sounding board for their ideas and problems." In general, the girls accompanying these teenage boys are inadequately fleshed out, tinny, paper thin, made of the stuff of angels, gentle, feminine, fairly quiet, doomed to be unreal. Good old Mom, on the other hand, often is depicted as "an insipid lady who flutters around chronically worrying and inanely commenting."

Stavn does discuss a few books where boys can come away with pretty good feelings about girls and women. The following quotes, however, seem to outweigh the good attitudes:

Women in the States . . . have forgotten how to be women; but they haven't yet learned how to be men. They've turned into hippies, and their men into zombies. God, it's pitiful!

Remember—she's a female, and full of tricks.

Men . . . liked to talk about women as though they had some sort of special malignant power, a witch-like ability to control men.

Polly . . . says "I'm a witch . . . I *was* being nasty . . . Girls just do those things, I guess. . . ."

Even old girls like my mother. If she hadn't torpedoed my father's idea to buy a garage, he might not have taken off.

[Polly] . . . began to think she should run the show. That's where I had to straighten her out. And after I got her straightened out she seemed happier.

Boys and young men are reading quotes such as these at the time of their lives when their thoughts of female relationships are predominant, and they are formulating ideas about the kind of woman they want as a partner—or are developing patterns of rejection altogether.

After reviewing the current lists of girls' books, one anonymous observer noted that a preponderance of stories about love, dating, and romance occurred among the themes identified. According to her literature, a female has no alternate life styles, but lives in a limited world with no control over her future. Nilsen calls this the "cult of the apron" and notes that this conditioning starts early. Of fifty-eight picture books which happened to be on a display cart of children's literature at Eastern Michigan University last year, twenty-one had pictures of women wearing aprons. Even the animals wore aprons! — the mother alligator, mother rabbit, mother donkey, and mother cat.

It is well known nowadays that 40 percent of all mothers work, and yet many studies indicate that there is not one mention of a working mother in the particular group of books reviewed. A notable exception is Eve Merriam's *Mommies at Work* (Knopf, 1961). And a notable discrepancy is the *Bank Street Readers,* a series designed for the inner-city child. In the three books, only one mother is shown as a working mother, a woman who serves in a cafeteria.

Social Studies Texts

In Jamie Frisof's analysis of social studies textbooks, men are shown in or described in over one hundred different jobs and women in less than thirty, and in these thirty jobs, women serve peoplr or help men to do more important work. Men's work requires more training; men direct people and plan things; men go places and make decisions; at meetings men are always the speakers; men make the money and are the most important members of families. The pictures in these social studies books show men or boys more than seven times as often as women or girls. Rarely are men and women working together or seen in equally competent roles. In short, these socializing books "do their part in preparing girls to accept unquestioningly their future as unimportant, nonproductive, nonadventurous, and unintelligent beings."

Regarding professional persons depicted in children's books, Heyn points out that among the several books in the field of health and medicine, without exception the doctor is portrayed as a white male — nurses and receptionists as female.

U'Ren and Vincent report that one of the California textbooks gave an account of Madame Curie, where she appears to be little more than a helpmate for her husband's projects (Eldonna L. Evertts and Byron H. Van Roekel, *Crossroads,* Harper and Row Basic Reading Program, Sacramento: California State Department of Education, 1969). "The illustration which accompanies this section reinforces that view of her. It portrays Madame Curie peering mildly from around her husband's shoulder while he and another distinguished gentleman loom in the foreground engaged in serious dialogue."

DIALOGUE

It might be well at this point to examine other examples of dialogue which occur in children's literature. Linguistic behavior is culturally taught, as are other expressions of behavior. In surveying the dialogues which occur in these books, one notes a pathetic lack of conversation with bright, adventurous females of any age. Rarely is there a give-and-take dialogue in which a female is shown to be capable of making a decision or where the input of the female is intelligent and useful information. The things which girls and women say in these books too often reflect the stereotypes of society: "Women are emotional."

In *The Story of Mulberry Bend* (William Wise, Scott Foresman, 1965), we read, "One little girl thought they were so beautiful she began to cry."

During a scene about fishing and baiting the hook, the girl says, "I can't . . . I don't want to touch those things." "Of course you don't, here I'll do it for you." And then she would have lost the pole but Johnny grabbed it in time (Nila Banton Smith, "Cowboys and Ranches," *Be a Better Reader Series,* Foundation A, Prentice Hall, 1968).

Peter said, "You can't do it, Babs. You will get scared if you do." "No I won't," said Babs. "Yes, you will. You will get scared and cry," said Peter (Mae Knight Clark, *Lands of Pleasure,* Macmillan, California State Department of Education, 1969).

The Little Miss Muffet syndrome, which depicts females as helpless, easily frightened, and dreadfully dull, occurs over and over again in the literature. If one compares this image, which crystallizes in the formative years of child development, with the potential of women in adulthood, it becomes apparent that both male and female have difficulty in participating in equal sharing dialogues at the professional level. Males who have grown up learning dialogues such as are in children's books today are not able to listen to a female in adult life. Males paralyze when a rare female makes a constructive suggestion. Likewise females are trained not to take their share, or hold their own in decision-making interchange. There are no linguistic models in this early literature for females to take active parts in the dialogue nor for males to respond with dignified acceptance and a willingness to listen. With such indoctrination as this, is it any wonder, then, that doctors don't permit women on the surgical team and women scientists are excluded from projects and from the laboratory, where a female is thought to be useless or a nuisance?

It must also be realized that in some sense male stereotypes are also projected in these books. Future research could be undertaken on these aspects: Is a male permitted to be a whole person? Is he permitted the whole range of emotions that all human beings should have in their repertoire? Must he always be aggressive? Must he always be taller than the females in his circle? Is he allowed to make mistakes and still be accepted?

It is likely that the discrimination and obtrusive imbalance which occurs in the books is unintentional for the most part. But, as Vincent says, this does not mitigate its destructiveness. The results may be of much wider consequence than one might imagine. One of the studies (Anon., "A Feminist Look . . .") asks, "Is depression in the adult woman perhaps linked to the painful suppression of so many sparks of life?" It cannot be said, moreover, that all this treatment is out-of-awareness. For example, Nilsen reports that in a course entitled "Writing for Children" the instructor advised: "The wise author writes about boys, thereby insuring himself a maximum audience, since only girls will read a book about a girl, but both boys and girls will read about a boy." And Nilsen reports that the prize-winning *Island of the Blue Dolphins* was initially rejected by a publisher who wanted the heroine changed to a hero.

In order not to end on a blue note, it might be well to point out that remedies are in the offing. The National Organization for Women (NOW) initiated a bibliography[10] of children's books showing females in nonstereotyped roles — females "who assume a balanced role during the growing-up process. Traits such as physical capability, resourcefulness, creativity, assertiveness, ingenuity, adventuresomeness, and leadership are emphasized, in addition to literary quality." Thousands of copies of this bibliography have been sold, and authors are already writing material which is more equitable to both male and female. We might expect, then, that the new dialogues will take other forms and that "A Ride on a Sled," the story of Joan and Bill, might sound something like this:

> . . . *Joan then spoke up, "It's my turn to steer, Bill. Hang on, 'cause we're going a new way!"*

---

10. Anon., *Little Miss Muffet Fights Back*, comp. by Feminists on Children's Media (P.O. Box 4315, Grand Central Station, New York 10017), p. 48.

REFERENCES
SOURCES AND SELECTED BIBLIOGRAPHY

Anon., "A feminist look at children's books," by the Feminists on Children's Literature, *School Library Journal* (January 1971), pp. 19-24.

Anon., "Little Miss Muffet fights back," *School Library Journal* (November 1970), pp. 11, 14.

Anon., *Little Miss Muffet Fights Back,* comp. by Feminists on Children's Media, P.O. Box 4315, Grand Central Station, New York, N.Y. 10017.

Gardner, JoAnn, "Sesame Street and sex-role stereotypes," *Women: A Journal of Liberation* 1.3 (Spring 1970).

Heyn, Leah, "Children's books," *Women; A Journal of Liberation* 1.1 (Fall 1969), pp. 22-25.

Honigmann, John J., *Personality in Culture.* New York: Harper and Row, 1967, pp. 203-205.

Howe, Florence, "Liberated Chinese primers: (let's write some too)," *Women: A Journal of Liberation* 2.1 (Fall 1970), pp. 33-34.

Meade, Marion, "Miss Muffet must go: a mother fights back," *Woman's Day* (March 1971), pp. 64-65, 85-86.

Anon., *Report of the Advisory Commission on the Status of Women, California Women,* "Textbooks," p. 16, 1971.

Anon., "Sex role stereotyping in elementary school readers," pp. 13-18 in *Report on sex bias in the public schools,* NOW, New York City, 1971.

Anon., "Sugar and spice," editorial, *School Library Journal* (January 1971), p. 5.

Child, Irwin L., Elmer H. Potter, and Estelle M. Levine, "Children's textbooks and personality development," *Psychological Monographs* 60.3 (1946), p. 54.

Eliasberg, Ann, "Are you hurting your daughter without knowing it?" *Family Circle* (February 1971), pp. 38, 76-77.

Fisher, Elizabeth, "Children's books: The second sex, junior division," *The New York Times Book Review,* Part II (May 24, 1970), pp. 6, 44.

Frisof, Jamie Kelem, "Textbooks and channeling," *Women: A Journal of Liberation* 1.1 (Fall 1969), pp. 26-28.

Miles, Betty, "Harmful lessons little girls learn in school," *Redbook* (March 1971), pp. 86, 168-69.

Nilsen, Alleen Pace, "Women in children's literature," *College English* 32.8 (May 1971), pp. 918-926.

Schlaffer, Maria, "Sexual politics: Junior division," *All You Can Eat,* reprinted in *Sherwood Forest: Orange County People's Press* 1.20 (October 1970), p. 10.

Stavn, Diane Gersoni, "The skirts in fiction about boys: a maxi mess," *School Library Journal* Book Review (January 1971), pp. 66-70.

Stefflre, Buford, "Run, Mama, run: women workers in elementary readers," *Vocational Guidance Quarterly* 18.2 (December 1969), pp. 99-102.

U'Ren, Marjorie, "Sexual discrimination in the elementary textbooks" (unpublished manuscript, 14 p.), to be published in 51%: *The Case for Women's Liberation,* Basic Books.

Vincent, Gail Ann, "Sex differences in children's textbooks: a study in the socialization of the female," (unpublished manuscript, 20 p.).

Worley, Stinson E., "Developmental task situations in stories," *The Reading Teacher* 21.2 (November 1967), pp. 145-48.

6

In this frequently cited study, a forerunner of other similar reports, 1260 men and women responded to thirty four individual statements from the Inventory of Feminine Values developed by the authors. Responses were organized into the major categories of Attitude Toward Work and Accomplishment, Attitude Toward Marriage, Attitude Toward Child-Rearing, and Characteristics of Self.

Although women did not rate themselves in accordance with the typical female stereotype, they believed that males desired women who embodied this stereotyped sex role. Ironically, men's ratings of their ideal woman was very close to the women's self-ratings — balanced between active and passive components.

The real difficulty seems to lie in being able to perceive clearly what the other sex is looking for. This represents a very important finding. The two sexes are not polarized in their perceptions of woman's role, but only in their misperception of each other's perception. Men tend to give women conflicting cues making clear-cut perception of their views difficult. Better communication between the sexes as to each other's desires about the female role is essential.

Steinmann and Fox have used this technique cross-culturally as well as at several different time periods. The results are essentially the same, although women perceive themselves and the ideal woman as more active than they did several years ago.

Male-Female Perceptions of the Female Role in the United States*

Anne Steinmann and David J. Fox

A. INTRODUCTION

For some time now, there has been considerable discussion in both lay and professional circles about the problems faced by women in our changing society. Many authorities of varying degrees of expertness have voiced their opinions on this subject. However, these discussions, although often quite heated and involved, have been remarkably data-free. The current research was undertaken to obtain empirical data on the perception of the female role in terms of two basic questions: first, how do women view themselves, considering themselves as they are, as they would like to be, and as they think men would like them to be; and second, how do men see their ideal woman?

Two hypotheses were tested. The first hypothesis was that despite differences in socioeconomic class, ethnic or racial background, level of education, occupational or professional status, American women share certain values in relation to their roles in and out of the family, and that, specifically, they share a perceived conflict between the level of activity and independence they would like and the much lower level of activity they believe men would prefer them to have. The second hypothesis was that American men verbalize a level of activity they desire for women not different from that level of activity that women say they perceive for themselves.[1]

---

*From *The Journal of Psychology*, 1966, 64, 265-76. Footnotes have been renumbered.
1. Current extensions of the study are intended to test these hypotheses in countries other than the United States.

TABLE 1

MEANS AND STANDARD DEVIATIONS FOR SELF-PERCEPTION, IDEAL WOMAN, AND MAN'S IDEAL WOMAN (FOR FEMALE RESPONDENTS); AND MAN'S IDEAL WOMAN (FOR MALE RESPONDENTS), BY SAMPLE

Sample	Number		Female respondents						Male respondents	
			Self-perception		Own ideal		Man's ideal woman		Ideal woman	
	F	M	$\bar{X}^a$	sd	$\bar{X}$	sd	$\bar{X}$	sd	$\bar{X}$	sd
Undergraduates										
Public	96	75	+1.0	11.38	+4.6	13.82	−20.3	14.67	+9.3	8.22
Private (moderate cost)	51	**	+1.5	9.92	+3.6	14.43	−17.4	14.41	*	*
Private (expensive)	68	*	−6.6	11.13	−6.2	14.32	−22.8	14.17	*	*
Physicians	46	50	+5.0	7.81	+3.6	8.23	−13.8	15.64	+2.2	9.49
Lawyers	83	101	+7.6	12.32	+4.5	14.79	−23.0	16.63	−1.0	14.73
Artists	56	53	+8.6	11.03	+5.2	14.61	−16.8	18.15	+3.8	7.91
Business women	53	*	+3.4	10.50	+0.3	12.36	−15.8	17.22	*	*
Members of philanthropic organizations	65	64	+2.1	5.69	**	**	−13.9	12.01	−1.3	11.87
Nurses	218	*	+2.9	5.23	+2.2	10.32	−19.8	15.36	*	*
Negro professionals	91	80	+6.7	12.03	+0.9	16.26	−22.8	17.44	+4.1	13.72
Total	827	423								

a Other-achieving (intrafamily) = minus (−); self-achieving (extrafamily) = plus (+).
* No male sample.
** No data available from this sample for this form.

B. SUBJECTS

This paper is based on data from ten cluster samples totalling 837 American women, and six cluster samples totalling 423 American men. The samples (indicated in Table 1) include college undergraduates, physicians, lawyers, artists, working women and their husbands, nurses, and Negro professional men and women. Respondents were both Negro and white, and the noncollege respondents had all received a high-school education. The age range among both female and male samples was wide—ranging from the late teens to the seventies—although a majority were under forty. At the time these data were collected all respondents were residents of New York City, but many of the graduate students were temporary residents and among the professionals several had taken up residence within the past five years. In terms of birthplace, the respondents represented the several geographic regions of the United States, with the largest proportion born in the Northeast, Midwest, and Southeast. While religion specifically was not requested on the Personal Data form used, informal observation indicates that the samples included a reasonable cross section of Catholics, Jews, and Protestants. These were cluster samples selected because of availability and are not presented as random samplings of any groupings within the culture.

C. PROCEDURE

The instrument used for this study is the Inventory of Feminine Values. The Inventory consists of thirty four statements, each of which expresses a particular value or value judgment related to women's activities and satisfactions. The respondent indicates the strength of her or his agreement or disagreement to each statement on a five-point scale, ranging from "completely agree" to "completely disagree," through the midpoint of "I have no opinion."

Seventeen of the thirty four items are considered to provide a respondent with the opportunity to delineate a family-oriented woman who sees her own satisfactions coming second after those of her husband and family, and who sees her family responsibilities as taking precedence over any potential personal occupational activity. Marriage, child-rearing, and succorant nurturing are the main avenues of this woman's achievement. The other seventeen items delineate a self-achieving woman who considers her own satisfactions equally important with those of her husband and family and wishes opportunities to realize any latent ability or talent that she might have. The score on the Inventory represents the difference in strength of agreement to the intrafamily and extrafamily items. A respondent who took identical but opposite positions would have a score of zero; a respondent who consistently took the strongest possible passive position would have a score of -68, and a score of +68 if the strongest possible active position was taken. Positive scores between zero and +68 represent intermediate degrees of an active, self-achieving orientation, while negative scores between zero and -68 represent intermediate degrees of a group or family orientation.

The reliability of the Inventory has been estimated through the split-half technique, and when corrected through the Spearman-Brown procedure is .81. The items have face validity in that they are generally accepted conotations, but for further verification they also have been submitted to validation by seven judges who were asked to verify the classification of each item as intra- or extrafamily oriented. All items included in the current Inventory were unanimously agreed on by the judges.

Three forms of the Inventory were used in previously reported research with females.[2] Each form included the same thirty four items in varied order. Female subjects were asked to respond to the items in terms of how they themselves felt (Form SP), how their own ideal woman felt (Form WOI), and in terms of man's ideal woman; i.e., how they thought men would want women to respond (Form WMI).

In the research for this paper on male perception of the female role, male subjects were given a form of the Inventory that asks them to respond to the items as their ideal woman would (Form MI). Overall data from both women and men will be presented first; then the items will be organized into clusters of woman's satisfactions and activities and examined from each of four areas: (a) work and accomplishment, (b) marriage, (c) child-rearing, and (d) characteristics of the self.

---

2. A. Steinmann, J. Levy, and D. J. Fox, "Self-concept of college women compared with their concept of ideal woman and men's ideal woman," *J. Counsel Psychol.*, 1964, 2 (4), 370-74.

D. RESULTS

As noted, the data to test the first hypothesis about the homogeneity of female perceptions have already been reported.[3] Summarized briefly, these data support the first hypothesis: women *did* share a set of values. Although there was a variety of response within each sample, the average response pattern was the same: most women delineated a self-perception relatively balanced between strivings of self-realization, development, and achievement through their own potentialities—that is, extrafamily strivings—and self-realization and fulfillment by indirection, through permissive nurturing and other-achieving or intrafamily strivings. Women's ideal woman generally was similar to their self-perception, also balanced between self-achieving and other-achieving strivings. Their ideal was slightly more active than the self. However, their perception of man's ideal woman was a woman with little of the self-assertion and self-achievement they reported in themselves or in their ideal woman. Women saw man's ideal woman as significantly more accepting and permissive than their own self-perception of a subordinate role in both personal development and women's place in the familiar structure.

Table 1 presents, for review, these data from the samples of women. In self-perception, all the groups except the undergraduates attending an expensive private college reported somewhat self-achieving self-perceptions, with the artists' mean of +8.6 the strongest. It is these data, where nine of the ten separate means in Table 1 are within eight points from the zero midpoint, that support the conclusion that the respondents had self-perceptions with elements of both extrafamily, self-achieving, and intrafamily, other-achieving strivings, somewhat overbalanced toward the active or self-achieving satisfactions. It is well to note that every respondent studied in her self-perception had elements of both group and individual strivings, and no respondent ever scored within twenty points of the maximum, plus or minus 68. The standard deviations, of course, reflect the fact that there was considerable variability within this generalization.

The ideal woman delineated by these female respondents was slightly more self-achieving than the self-perception for seven of the nine samples where data were available, and so indicates that the composite ideal woman tends to be even more balanced than the self-perceptions between self-activating and other-activating

---

3. Ibid.

strivings. Typically, the discrepancy between self-perception and ideal woman is about two points, with the largest discrepancy evidenced in the sample of Negro professionals. Here, the discrepancy was 5.8 points.

The dramatic shift in the data occurs in the women's perception of man's ideal woman. Here all the samples delineated a *strongly* family-oriented woman, considerably more so in every instance than either their own self-perceptions or their perceptions of ideal woman. In ten of the eleven samples, only a few respondents indicated an active woman when speaking of man's ideal. Thus, on the average, while female respondents delineated a somewhat self-achieving self-perception and a slightly less self-achieving ideal woman, they attributed to men a strongly family-oriented ideal woman.

Table 1 also presents the new data on men's perception of their ideal woman. It is obvious that all six samples of men delineated an ideal woman relatively balanced between active and permissive elements.[4] Four of the samples were slightly on the active side of zero, and the other two slightly on the opposite side of zero. The discrepancy between the ideal woman men say they want and the ideal woman that women attribute to them is consistent in every comparison (ranging from 12.6 points for members of philanthropic organizations to 29.6 for public college undergraduates), and is always, always statistically significant at the .01 level. Moreover, the ideal woman men delineate is not significantly different from the women's own self-perceptions.

When the items themselves are studied in a second level of analysis and the female ideal and the ideal woman described by men compared, there was the same[5] response pattern for twenty nine of the thirty four items. Minor disagreement occurred in five items; of these, four were in the personal characteristic area, and only one item might be called a male-female item: whether it was woman's responsibility to make marriage work. Two-thirds of the men said that their ideal woman would not believe it was woman's responsibility to make marriage work. The women, however, were divided on this issue. Half of the women said that their ideal woman *would* believe it was woman's responsibility, the other half noted that their ideal woman did not think that a working marriage *was* woman's responsibility.

---

4. It is important to note that this discussion is considering relative positions on a continuum, not absolutes.

5. Response patterns were considered the "same" when they had the same modal response; they were considered "different" when they had different modal responses.

TABLE 2
MODAL RESPONSE PATTERN FOR MAN'S IDEAL WOMAN,
BY SEX, MODAL PATTERN, AND PER CENT

Paraphrase of item	Same response pattern			Different response pattern		
	Type[a]	Male %	Female %	Male Type %		Female Type %
I. Attitude Toward Work and Accomplishment as Woman, Wife, and Mother						
1. Would rather be famous than have affection*	D	81	89			
2. One attains satisfactions through one's own efforts	A	76	51			
3. Like to create something**				A	76	B 43-35
4. Capable woman has duty to be active				A	71	B 49-37
5. Woman who works cannot be as good a mother**				D	67	A 51
6. Unattractive women are most ambitious				A	55	B 47-35
7. Working mother can be as good a mother***				A	52	D 55
II. Attitude Toward Marriage both as a Goal for the Single Woman, and in Terms of the Husband-Wife Relationship						
8. Like to marry a man I look up to	A	80	91			
9. Encouragement greatest contribution of wife	A	68	78			
10. Conflict between fulfillment as woman and individual	D	68	60			
11. Better to marry person below her ideal than remain unmarried	D	68	51			
12. Ambitions should be subordinated to family	A	64	82			
13. Rather not marry than sacrifice beliefs	D	61	67			

Table 2 presents data on the similarity of response pattern on what women *thought* men wanted in an ideal woman and man's expressed concept of his ideal woman. In contrast to the agreement on 29 of the 34 items when each sex described its own ideal woman, this comparison of item response patterns for male ideal and the ideal woman attributed to them indicates the same response pattern for only fifteen items of the thirty four. Thus there

TABLE 2 (*continued*)

Paraphrase of item	Type^a	Same response pattern Male %	Same response pattern Female %	Different response pattern Male Type	%	Different response pattern Female Type	%
14. Make more concessions to husband's wishes	A	53	77				
15. Unfair that women have to compromise ideals				B	44-42	D	71
16. Marriage and children should take precedence for woman**				B	49-39	A	78
17. Husband who is sole provider will be more ambitious				B	36-47	A	64
18. Wife's opinion as important as husband's				A	70	B	44-49
19. Married woman should not crave personal success				D	66	A	69
20. Woman more responsible for success of marriage				D	64	A	58
21. Woman's place is in the home				D	51	A	66
III. Attitude Toward Child-Rearing in Terms of Importance and Practices							
22. Not sure joys of motherhood make up for sacrifices	D	63	75				
23. Main goal of life is well-adjusted children	A	55	75				
24. Would rear children to believe in equality of sexes				A	57	B	37-43
IV. Characteristics of Self in Terms of Interpersonal and Social Qualities and Behavior Particularly Toward Authority and Leadership							
25. I develop and express ideas energetically	A	86	67				
26. I am oblivious to the feelings of others	A	82	80				
27. Capable of putting myself in background	A	75	89				
28. Feel I can accept nothing from others	D	71	78				

was a different response pattern for the remaining nineteen items. Table 2 organizes the items into the four major areas noted earlier. Within each area, the items presented first are those in which the response pattern for male and female was the same. Those for

TABLE 2 (*continued*)

Paraphrase of item	Type[a]	Same response pattern		Different response pattern			
		Male %	Female %	Male Type	%	Female Type	%
29. I prefer to listen rather than to talk				B	48-32	A	73
30. Too concerned with how I impress people				B	38-48	D	54
31. I argue against people in authority				A	67	D	56
32. I am more concerned with my personal development				A	65	B	39-48
33. I try to act in accordance with other's feelings				D	56	A	69
34. I drift into a position of leadership				A	55	B	25-47

[a] A = agree, D = disagree, and B = bimodal.
* May also be considered in Category II.
** May also be considered in Category IV.
*** May also be considered in Category III.

which the response pattern was different are listed next.

Throughout Table 2, the letter "A" is used to represent a pattern in which the majority of the respondents agreed with the item. The letter "D" is used when the majority of the respondents disagreed with the item. The letter "B" is used to indicate what the authors consider the bimodal response, in which a majority of the respondents neither agreed nor disagreed. For each pattern, the proportions are also given.

In an examination of Table 2, in Section I—Attitude Toward Work and Accomplishment, one notes that both sexes agreed that man's ideal woman would prefer the constant affection of one man to admiration throughout the nation, and would believe that one's greatest satisfactions are obtained through one's own efforts. For the five other items that had different response patterns, it is of interest that on all five there *was* a modal response from the males, but for females there was a bimodal response for three, and a weak modal response for the other two. Thus, females as a group had no clear response pattern to these items.

Section II includes the largest cluster of items, fourteen, on attitude toward marriage. For half of the items, men and women had the same response pattern with the greatest agreement that man's ideal woman would want to marry a man to whom she could really look up.

This and the other six items on which the mode is the same paint a picture of a woman subordinate to her family, making more concessions than she expects from this husband, to whom she "really looks up" and for whom her encouragement is her greatest contribution, yet who feels no conflict between fulfillment as a woman and as an individual.

In the seven items in this area on which American men and women had different response patterns, the difference comes because, on these seven, women continued to attribute a subservient orientation to man's ideal, while the men did not. Should married women crave personal success? Men said their ideal woman would say "yes." Women said she would say "no." Is a woman more responsible than a man for the success of marriage? For men, their ideal woman would say "no"; women said she *would* feel more responsible. Similarly, concerning whether or not a wife's opinion should be as important as the husband's, whether a woman's place is in the home, whether it is unfair that women have to compromise their ideals, and whether marriage and children should take precedence for women, these American men took a relatively liberal position, while the American women felt that man's ideal woman would definitely take the family-oriented point of view.

In Section III, attitude toward child-rearing, two more concepts were added to the intrafamily cluster on which both men and women agreed: that the main goal of a woman's life is to raise well-adjusted children, and that the joys of motherhood make up for the sacrifices. Of interest for future generations is the fact that men saw their ideal woman as rearing children to believe in the equality of the sexes.

Section IV, with items dealing with characteristics of the self, includes references toward attitudes concerning authority and leadership, and two of them point up the paradox in much of these data: both men and women agreed that a woman should not only be capable of putting herself in the background and working for a person whom she admires, but also that she should be energetic in the development and expression of her ideas. This contradiction in attitude reveals, at least, that both the men and women agreed in their ambivalent attitude.

E. CONCLUSIONS AND IMPLICATIONS

What conclusions may be drawn from these data? It appears that certain rather definite statements may be made within the limitations of both instrument and samples. In examining Table 1, one pattern in the data is very clear: in all samples, these American women said, "I am pretty much what I would like to be, but I am not what men would like me to be." This pattern, moreover, is one wherein women attributed to men a strongly family-oriented ideal woman. On the other hand, American men, when questioned, stated that their ideal woman had a balance of intrafamily and extrafamily feelings. The discrepancy between the family-oriented, permissive woman that women believed men desired and the ideal woman that men actually delineated may be accounted for in at least four ways. In responding as they do: (a) both men and women were telling the truth, and the data reflect serious lack of communication; (b) women were projecting what they really might be feeling and what they would like men to believe; (c) men were *talking* a current liberal stereotype and may neither believe nor behave as they talked; and (d) when the men espoused a liberal concept of woman's role, they were exposing an ambivalence that may or may not be the result of their own use of projection and denial of an active role.

New research now under way is intended to test which of these four interpretations is the most sensible explanation of the discrepancy. However, at this time it is possible to state that, in the eyes of these American women, American men desired a type of woman that women had no wish to be. The discrepancy between ideas is so great, the gap is so wide and deep that even more than a lack of understanding this discrepancy suggests a real lack of communication between men and women. Evidently both men and women do not understand each one's desires as to what role a woman should assume.

In Table 2, in an examination of the specific items, certain points stand out clearly. First, men, in many respects, *were* delineating a more liberal point of view than the women attributed to them; but second, there was an internal contradiction in the responses of the men, a conceptual ambivalence.

Consider first the men's "liberal" responses. For example, at least 70 percent of the men said their ideal woman would believe that a capable woman has the duty to be active and that their ideal woman would like to create something important, and also that a wife's opinion is as important as the husband's opinion. In each of these instances, the women did not think that a man's ideal woman would think this way. There is real conflict within these perceptions.

But was the men's "liberal" perception of an ideal woman consistently liberal? Actually, the liberal expressions seem to be elicited by the global items. The men said that a woman should be "active" outside the family, have "responsibility," use her "talents," "create," "fulfill" herself. However, when men were asked, "What do you think about marriage and children as the most important aspects of a woman's life?" the men's liberality was not so clear. They split, a clear note of ambiguity. One might hypothesize that on a generalization level, men did accept woman's avenues of fulfillment, but when they were asked, "Does this mean that woman's own work, woman's own self-realization, might be at some time the most important aspect of her life?" these men answered, "No."

The women, in a sense, may have been more realistic than the men. They did not go along even with generalities, although they were split on some. Note the bimodal responses in Section II to items on whether a capable woman has a duty to be active or to create something important or whether attractive women are more ambitious than unattractive women. Here we see ambivalence, too, within the women's perception of men's ideal woman.

But this ambivalence seems different from what we have described as the internal contradiction ambivalence of men. As a group men gave clear modes, but these modes often conflicted in concept: i.e., the liberal position men took on global items *versus* the relatively traditional position they took on specific items. In contrast, the women were ambivalent as a group, reflected in the bimodal responses just cited. This group ambivalence suggests that the American women studied often did not have any clear perception of what men want in a woman. But if men *are* paradoxical and *are* feeding contradictory cues to women, obviously the women would not know how men think, which would give rise to the bimodal pattern for women. The data suggest men are saying to women, "Yes, you are very bright and with this brightness you should do something," but at the point when the women stir themselves and do "something," the men add, "but you can't do what you're doing because of the kids." The woman then says to herself, "What does this man want me to do?" Obviously, she is going to be uncertain.

Perhaps there is a suggestion here that at this time, in this "gray new world,"[6] both men and women are rejecting each one's desires as to what role they should assume.

---

6. Tom Wicker, "A Melancholy Link to Yesterday," *New York Times,* August 31, 1966.

7

Helen Hacker, now in the Sociology Department at Adelphi University, was one of the first to depict women as a minority group. Her original article, reproduced here, was first published in the October 1951 issue of Social Forces. She notes that women were not a numerical minority, but were singled out for unequal and discriminatory treatment. In effect, they had minority-group status. In the early 1950s it was indeed a rarity for anyone to be concerned with the stereotyped role and treatment of women.

In the paper written over twenty years later for this volume, Hacker notes how difficult it was to get the first paper published, almost three years. Today it has become a classic, frequently reproduced in various collections of readings for the social sciences. It has also touched off other similar evaluations of women's role, including Hacker's own updating of this material.

In the earlier paper, Hacker specifies the similarities between women and other minority groups, particularly blacks. She points out that women frequently display many of the psychological characteristics ascribed to other minorities. These include inferiority feelings, self-criticism, and what amounts to almost a separate subculture. Hacker makes special mention of the "marginal woman" who suffers conflict as she is torn between accepting and rejecting traditional roles.

In her more recent paper, Hacker notes the growth of women's groups and interest in women's roles, which she feels is part of, as well as influenced by, the general unrest in our society.

Hacker states that the parallel between women and blacks is still valid after twenty years. She feels that the separatist theme some radical women's groups are stressing is only a transitional phase. Most activist women want to modify their traditional roles and not break off all ties with men. However, Hacker points out that the majority of American women still don't want a change in traditional sex roles, although Hacker says they must be forced to be free.

These two articles show what has happened to women's status during the past twenty years.

Women as a Minority Group*

Helen Mayer Hacker

Although sociological literature reveals scattered references to women as a minority group, comparable in certain respects to racial, ethnic, and national minorities, no systematic investigation has been undertaken as to what extent the term "minority group" is applicable to women. That there has been little serious consideration of women as a minority group among sociologists is manifested in the recently issued index to *The American Journal of Sociology,* wherein under the heading of "Minority Groups" there appears: "See Jews; Morale; Negro; Races and Nationalities; Religious Groups; Sects." There is no cross-reference to women, but such reference is found under the heading "Family."

Yet it may well be that regarding women as a minority group may be productive of fresh insights and suggest leads for further research. The purpose of this paper is to apply to women some portion of that body of sociological theory and methodology customarily used for investigating such minority groups as Negroes, Jews, immigrants, etc. It may be anticipated that not only will principles already established in the field of intergroup relations contribute to our understanding of women, but that in the process of modifying traditional concepts and theories to fit the special case of women new viewpoints for the fruitful reexamination of other minority groups will emerge.

In defining the term "minority group," the presence of discrimination is the identifying factor. As Louis Wirth[1] has pointed out, "minority group" is not a statistical concept, nor need it denote an alien group. Indeed for the present discussion I have adopted his definition: "A minority group is any group of people who because of their physical or cultural characteristics, are singled out from the others in the society in which they live for differential and unequal treatment, and who therefore regard themselves as objects of collective discrimination." It is apparent that this definition includes both objective and subjective characteristics of a minority group: the fact of discrimination and the awareness of discrimination, with attendant reactions to that

---

*From *Social Forces,* vol. 30, October 1951.

1. Louis Wirth, "The Problem of Minority Groups," in *The Science of Man in the World Crisis,* ed. Ralph Linton (1945), p. 347.

awareness. A person who on the basis of his group affiliation is denied full participation in those opportunities which the value system of his culture extends to all members of the society satisfies the objective criterion, but there are various circumstances which may prevent him from fulfilling the subjective criterion.

In the first place, a person may be unaware of the extent to which his group membership influences the way others treat him. He may have formally dissolved all ties with the group in question and fondly imagine his identity is different from what others hold it to be. Consequently, he interprets their behavior toward him solely in terms of his individual characteristics. Or, less likely, he may be conscious of his membership in a certain group but not be aware of the general disesteem with which the group is regarded. A final possibility is that he may belong in a category which he does not realize has group significance. An example here might be a speech peculiarity which has come to have unpleasant connotations in the minds of others. Or a lower class child with no conception of "class as culture" may not understand how his manners act as cues in eliciting the dislike of his middle-class teacher. The foregoing cases all assume that the person believes in equal opportunities for all in the sense that one's group affiliation should not affect his role in the larger society. We turn now to a consideration of situations in which this assumption is not made.

It is frequently the case that a person knows that because of his group affiliation he receives differential treatment, but feels that this treatment is warranted by the distinctive characteristics of his group. A Negro may believe that there are significant differences between whites and Negroes which justify a different role in life for the Negro. A child may accept the fact that physical differences between him and an adult require his going to bed earlier than they do. A Sudra knows that his lot in life has been cast by divine fiat, and he does not expect the perquisites of a Brahmin. A woman does not wish for the rights and duties of men. In all these situations, clearly, the person does not regard himself as an "object of collective discrimination."

For the two types presented above: (1) those who do not know that they are being discriminated against on a group basis; and (2) those who acknowledge the propriety of differential treatment on a group basis, the subjective attributes of a minority group member are lacking. They feel no minority group consciousness, harbor no resentment, and, hence, cannot properly be said to belong in a minority group. Although the term "minority group" is inapplicable to both types, the term "minority-group status" may be substituted. This term is used to categorize persons who are denied rights to which they are entitled according to the value system of the observer. An observer who is a firm adherent of the democratic ideology will often consider persons to occupy a minority-group status who are well accommodated to their subordinate roles.

No empirical study of the frequency of minority-group feelings among women has yet been made, but common observation would suggest that consciously at least, few women believe themselves to be members of a minority group in the way in which some Negroes, Jews, Italians, etc., may so conceive themselves. There are, of course, many sex-conscious women, known to a past generation as feminists, who are filled with resentment at the discriminations they fancy are directed against their sex. Today some of these may be found in the National Woman's Party which since 1923 has been carrying on a campaign for the passage of the Equal Rights Amendment. This amendment, in contrast to the compromise bill recently passed by Congress, would at one stroke wipe out all existing legislation which differentiates in any way between men and women, even when such legislation is designed for the special protection of women. The proponents of the Equal Rights Amendment hold the position that women will never achieve equal rights until they abjure all privileges based on what they consider to be only presumptive sex differences.

Then there are women enrolled in women's clubs, women's auxiliaries of men's organizations, women's professional and educational associations who seemingly believe that women have special interests to follow or unique contributions to make. The latter might reject the appellation of minority group, but their behavior testifies to their awareness of women as a distinct group in our society, either overriding differences of class, occupation, religion, or ethnic identification, or specialized within these categories. Yet the number of women who participate in "women's affairs" even in the United States, the classic land of associations, is so small that one cannot easily say that the majority of women display minority-group consciousness. However, documentation, as well as a measuring instrument, is likewise lacking for minority consciousness in other groups.

Still women often manifest many of the psychological characteristics which have been imputed to self-conscious minority groups. Kurt Lewin[2] has pointed to group self-hatred as a frequent reaction of the minority group member to his group affiliation. This feeling is exhibited in the person's tendency to denigrate other members of the group, to accept the dominant group's stereotyped conception of them, and to indulge in "mea culpa"

2. Kurt Lewin, "Self-Hatred Among Jews," *Contemporary Jewish Record,* IV (1941), 219-232

breast-beating. He may seek to exclude himself from the average of his group, or he may point the finger of scorn at himself. Since a person's conception of himself is based on the defining gestures of others, it is unlikely that members of a minority group can wholly escape personality distortion. Constant reiteration of one's inferiority must often lead to its acceptance as a fact.

Certainly women have not been immune to the formulations of the "female character" throughout the ages. From those, to us, deluded creatures who confessed to witchcraft to modern sophisticates who speak disparagingly of the cattiness and disloyalty of women, women reveal their introjection of prevailing attitudes toward them. Like those minority groups whose self-castigation outdoes dominant group derision of them, women frequently exceed men in the violence of their vituperations of their sex. They are more severe in moral judgments, especially in sexual matters. A line of self-criticism may be traced from Hannah More, a blue-stocking herself, to Dr. Marynia Farnham, who lays most of the world's ills at women's door. Women express themselves as disliking other women, as preferring to work under men, and as finding exclusively female gatherings repugnant. The *Fortune* polls conducted in 1946 show that women, more than men, have misgivings concerning women's participation in industry, the professions, and civic life. And more than one-fourth of women wish they had been born in the opposite sex![3]

Militating against a feeling of group identification on the part of women is a differential factor in their socialization. Members of a minority group are frequently socialized within their own group. Personality development is more largely a resultant of intra- than inter-group interaction. The conception of his role formed by a Negro or a Jew or a second-generation immigrant is greatly dependent upon the definitions offered by members of his own group, on their attitudes and behavior toward him. Ignoring for the moment class differences within the group, the minority group person does not suffer discrimination from members of his own group. But only rarely does a woman experience this type of group belongingness. Her interactions with members of the opposite sex may be as frequent as her relationships with members of her own sex. Women's conceptions of themselves, therefore, spring as much from their intimate relationships with men as with women. Although this consideration might seem to limit the applicability to women of research findings on minority groups, conversely, it may

---

3. *Fortune,* September 1946, p. 5.

suggest investigation to seek out useful parallels in the socialization of women, on the one hand, and the socialization of ethnics living in neighborhoods of heterogeneous population, on the other.

Even though the sense of group identification is not so conspicuous in women as in racial and ethnic minorities, they, like these others, tend to develop a separate sub-culture. Women have their own language, comparable to the argot of the underworld and professional groups. It may not extend to a completely separate dialect as has been discovered in some preliterate groups, but there are words and idioms employed chiefly by women. Only the acculturated male can enter into the conversation of the beauty parlor, the exclusive shop, the bridge table, or the kitchen. In contrast to men's interest in physical health, safety, money, and sex, women attach greater importance to attractiveness, personality, home, family, and other people.[4] How much of the "woman's world" is predicated on their relationship to men is too difficult a question to discuss here. It is still a controversial point whether the values and behavior patterns of other minority groups, such as the Negroes, represent an immanent development, or are oriented chiefly toward the rejecting world. A content analysis contrasting the speech of "housewives" and "career women," for example, or a comparative analysis of the speech of men and women of similar occupational status might be one test of this hypothesis.

We must return now to the original question of the aptness of the designation of minority group for women. It has been indicated that women fail to present in full force the subjective attributes commonly associated with minority groups. That is, they lack a sense of group identification and do not harbor feelings of being treated unfairly because of their sex membership. Can it then be said that women have a minority-group status on our society? The answer to this question depends upon the values of the observer whether within or outside the group—just as is true in the case of any group of persons who, on the basis of putative differential characteristics, are denied access to some statuses in the social system of their society. If we assume that there are no differences attributable to sex membership as such that would justify casting men and women in different social roles, it can readily be shown that women do occupy a minority-group status in our society.

---

4. P. M. Symonds, "Changes in Sex Differences in Problems and Interests of Adolescents with Increasing Age," *Journal of Genetic Psychology,* 50 (1937), pp. 83-89, as referred to by Georgene H. Seward, *Sex and the Social Order* (1946), pp. 237-238.

Helen Mayer Hacker

MINORITY-GROUP STATUS OF WOMEN

Formal discriminations against women are too well-known for any but the most summary description. In general they take the form of being barred from certain activities, or, if admitted, being treated unequally. Discriminations against women may be viewed as arising from the generally ascribed status "female" and from the specially ascribed statuses of "wife," "mother," and "sister." (To meet the possible objection that "wife" and "mother" represent assumed, rather than ascribed, statuses, may I point out that what is important here is that these statuses carry ascribed expectations which are only ancillary in the minds of those who assume them.)

As female, in the economic sphere, women are largely confined to sedentary, monotonous work under the supervision of men, and are treated unequally with regard to pay, promotion, and responsibility. With the exceptions of teaching, nursing, social service, and library work, in which they do not hold a proportionate number of supervisory positions and are often occupationally segregated from men, they make a poor showing in the professions. Although they own 80 percent of the nation's wealth, they do not sit on the boards of directors of great corporations. Educational opportunities are likewise unequal. Professional schools, such as architecture and medicine, apply quotas. Women's colleges are frequently inferior to men's. In co-educational schools women's participation in campus activities is limited. As citizens, women are often barred from jury service and public office. Even when they are admitted to the apparatus to political parties, they are subordinated to men. Socially, women have less freedom of movement, and are permitted fewer deviations in the proprieties of dress, speech, manners. In social intercourse they are confined to a narrower range of personality expression.

In the specially ascribed status of wife, a woman—in several States—has no exclusive right to her earnings, is discriminated against in employment, must take the domicile of her husband, and in general must meet the social expectation of subordination to her husband's interests. As a mother, she may not have the guardianship of her children, bears the chief stigma in the case of an illegitimate child, is rarely given leave of absence for pregnancy. As a sister, she frequently suffers unequal distribution of domestic duties between herself and her brother, must yield preference to him in obtaining an education, and in such other psychic and material gratifications as cars, trips, and living away from home.

WOMAN: DEPENDENT OR INDEPENDENT VARIABLE?

If it is conceded that women have a minority-group status, what may be learned from applying to women various theoretical constructs in the field of intergroup relations?

SOCIAL DISTANCE BETWEEN MEN AND WOMEN

One instrument of diagnostic value is the measurement of social distance between dominant and minority group. But we have seen that one important difference between women and other minorities is that women's attitudes and self-conceptions are conditioned more largely by interaction with both minority and dominant group members. Before measuring social distance, therefore, a continuum might be constructed of the frequency and extent of women's interaction with men, with the poles conceptualized as ideal types. One extreme would represent a complete "ghetto" status, the woman whose contacts with men were of the most secondary kind. At the other extreme shall we put the woman who has prolonged and repeated associations with men, but only in those situations in which sex awareness plays a prominent role, or the woman who enters into a variety of relationships with men in which her sex identity is to a large extent irrelevant? The decision would depend on the type of scale used.

This question raises the problem of the criterion of social distance to be employed in such a scale. Is it more profitable to use we-feeling, felt interdependence, degree of communication, or degrees of separation in status? Social distance tests as applied to relationships between other dominant and minority groups have for the most part adopted prestige criteria as their basis. The assumption is that the type of situation into which one is willing to enter with average members of another group reflects one's estimate of the status of the group relative to one's own. When the tested group is a sex group rather than a racial, national, religious, or economic one, several important differences in the use and interpretation of the scale must be noted:

1. Only two groups are involved: men and women. Thus, the test indicates the amount of homogeneity or we-feeling only according to the attribute of sex. If men are a primary group, there are not many groups to be ranked secondary, tertiary, etc. with respect to them, but only one group, women, whose social distance cannot be calculated relative to other groups.

2. Lundberg[5] suggests the possibility of a group of Catholics

---

5. George A. Lundberg, *Foundations of Sociology* (1939), p. 319.

registering a smaller social distance to Moslems than to Catholics. In such an event the group of Catholics, from any sociological viewpoint, would be classified as Moslems. If women expressed less social distance to men than to women, should they then be classified sociologically as men? Perhaps no more so than the legendary Negro who, when requested to move to the colored section of the train, replied, "Boss, I'se done resigned from the colored race," should be classified as white. It is likely, however, that the group identification of many women in our society is with men. The feminists were charged with wanting to be men, since they associated male physical characteristics with masculine social privileges. A similar statement can be made about men who show greater social distance to other men than to women.

Social distance may be measured from the standpoint of the minority group or the dominant group with different results. In point of fact, tension often arises when one group feels less social distance than the other. A type case here is the persistent suitor who underestimates his desired sweetheart's feeling of social distance toward him.

3. In social distance tests the assumption is made of an orderly progression—although not necessarily by equal intervals—in the scale. That is, it is not likely that a person would express willingness to have members of a given group as his neighbors, while simultaneously voicing the desire to have them excluded from his country. On all scales marriage represents the minimum social distance, and implies willingness for associations on all levels of lesser intimacy. May the customary scale be applied to men and women? If we take the expressed attitude of many men and women not to marry, we may say that they have feelings of social distance toward the opposite sex, and in this situation the usual order of the scale may be preserved.

In our culture, however, men who wish to marry must perforce marry women, and even if they accept this relationship, they may still wish to limit their association with women in other situations. The male physician may not care for the addition of female physicians to his hospital staff. The male poker player may be thrown off his game if women participate. A damper may be put upon the hunting expedition if women come along. The average man may not wish to consult a woman lawyer. And so on. In these cases it seems apparent that the steps in the social distance scale must be reversed. Men will accept women at the supposed level of greatest intimacy while rejecting them at lower levels.

But before concluding that a different scale must be constructed when the dominant group attitude toward a minority group which is being tested is that of men toward women, the question may be raised as to whether marriage in fact represents the point of minimum social distance. It may not imply anything but physical intimacy and work accommodation, as was frequently true in non-individuated societies, such as preliterate groups and the household economy of the Middle Ages, or marriages of convenience in the European upper class. Even in our own democratic society where marriage is supposedly based on romantic love there may be little communication between the partners in marriage. The Lynds[6] report the absence of real companionship between husband and wife in Middletown. Women have been known to say that although they have been married for twenty years, their husband is still a stranger to them. There is a quatrain of Thoreau's that goes:

> Each moment as we drew nearer to each
> A stern respect withheld us farther yet
> So that we seemed beyond each other's reach
> And less acquainted than when first we met.

Part of the explanation may be found in the subordination of wives to husbands in our culture, which is expressed in the separate spheres of activity for men and women. A recent advertisement in a magazine of national circulation depicts a pensive husband seated by his knitting wife, with the caption, "Sometimes a man has moods his wife cannot understand." In this case the husband is worried about a pension plan for his employees. The assumption is that the wife, knowing nothing of the business world, cannot take the role of her husband in this matter.

The presence of love does not in itself argue for either equality of status or fullness of communication. We may love those who are either inferior or superior to us, and we may love persons whom we do not understand. The supreme literary examples of passion without communication are found in Proust's portrayal of Swann's obsession with Odette, the narrator's infatuation with the elusive Albertine, and, of course, Dante's longing for Beatrice.

In the light of these considerations concerning the relationships between men and women, some doubt may be cast on the propriety of placing marriage on the positive extreme of the social distance scale with respect to ethnic and religious minority groups. Since inequalities of status are preserved in marriage, a dominant group member may be willing to marry a member of a group which, in general, he would not wish admitted to his club. The

---

6. Robert S. and Helen M. Lynd, *Middletown* (1929), p. 120, and *Middletown in Transition* (1937), p. 176.

social distance scale which uses marriage as a sign of an extreme degree of acceptance is inadequate for appreciating the position of women, and perhaps for other minority groups as well. The relationships among similarity of status, communication as a measure of intimacy, and love must be clarified before social distance tests can be applied usefully to attitudes between men and women.

CASTE-CLASS CONFLICT

Is the separation between males and females in our society a caste line? Folsom[7] suggests that it is, and Myrdal[8] in his well-known Appendix 5 considers the parallel between the position of and feelings toward women and Negroes in our society. The relation between women and Negroes is historical, as well as analogical. In the seventeenth century the legal status of Negro servants was borrowed from that of women and children, who were under the patria potestas, and until the Civil War there was considerable cooperation between the Abolitionist and woman suffrage movements. According to Myrdal, the problems of both groups are resultants of the transition from a pre-industrial, paternalistic scheme of life to individualistic, industrial capitalism. Obvious similarities in the status of women and Negroes are indicated in Chart 1.

CHART 1. CASTELIKE STATUS OF WOMEN AND NEGROES

NEGROES	WOMEN
1. HIGH SOCIAL VISIBILITY	
a. Skin color, other "racial" characteristics	a. Secondary sex characteristics
b. (Sometimes) distinctive dress—bandana, flashy clothes	b. Distinctive dress, skirts, etc.
2. ASCRIBED ATTRIBUTES	
a. Inferior intelligence, smaller brain, less convoluted, scarcity of geniuses	a. ditto
b. More free in instinctual gratifications. More emotional, "primitive" and childlike. Imagined sexual prowess envied.	b. Irresponsible, inconsistent, emotionally unstable. Lack strong super-ego

7. Joseph Kirk Folsom, *The Family and Democratic Society* (1943), pp. 623-624.

8. Gunnar Myrdal, *An American Dilemma* (1944), pp. 1073-1078.

CHART 1—*concluded*

NEGROES	WOMEN
	Women as "temptresses."
c. Common stereotype "inferior"	c. "Weaker"

3. RATIONALIZATIONS OF STATUS

a. Thought all right in his place	a. Woman's place is in the home
b. Myth of contented Negro	b. Myth of contented woman—"feminine" woman is happy in subordinate role

4. ACCOMMODATION ATTITUDES

a. Supplicatory whining intonation of voice	a. Rising inflection, smiles, laughs, downward glances
b. Deferential manner	b. Flattering manner
c. Concealment of real feelings	c. "Feminine wiles"
d. Outwit "white folks"	d. Outwit "menfolk"
e. Careful study of points at which dominant group is susceptible to influence	e. ditto
f. Fake appeals for directives; show of ignorance	f. Appearance of helplessness

5. DISCRIMINATIONS

a. Limitations on education—should fit "place" in society	a. ditto
b. Confined to traditional jobs—barred from supervisory positions. Their competition feared. No family precedents for new aspirations	b. ditto
c. Deprived of political importance	c. ditto
d. Social and professional segregation	d. ditto
e. More vulnerable to criticism	e. e.g. conduct in bars.

6. SIMILAR PROBLEMS

a. Roles not clearly defined, but in flux as result of social change. Conflict between achieved status and ascribed status

While these similarities in the situation of women and Negroes may lead to increased understanding of their social roles, account must also be taken of differences which impose qualifications on the comparison of the two groups. Most importantly, the influence of marriage as a social elevator for women, but not for Negroes, must be considered. Obvious, too, is the greater importance of women to the dominant group, despite the economic, sexual, and prestige gains which Negroes afford the white South. Ambivalence is probably more marked in the attitude of white males toward women than toward Negroes. The "war of the sexes" is only an expression of men's and women's vital need of each other. Again, there is greater polarization in the relationship between men and women. Negroes, although they have borne the brunt of anti-minority group feeling in this country, do not constitute the only racial or ethnic minority, but there are only two sexes. And, although we have seen that social distance exists between men and women, it is not to be compared with the social segregation of Negroes.

At the present time, of course, Negroes suffer far greater discrimination than women, but since the latter's problems are rooted in a biological reality less susceptible to cultural manipulation, they prove more lasting. Women's privileges exceed those of Negroes. Protective attitudes toward Negroes have faded into abeyance, even in the South, but most boys are still taught to take care of girls, and many evidences of male chivalry remain. The factor of class introduces variations here. The middle-class Negro endures frustrations largely without the rewards of his white class peer, but the lower class Negro is still absolved from many responsibilities. The reverse holds true for women. Notwithstanding these and other differences between the position of women and Negroes, the similarities are sufficient to render research on either group applicable in some fashion to the other.

Exemplary of the possible usefulness of applying the caste principle to women is viewing some of the confusion surrounding women's roles as reflecting a conflict between class and caste status. Such a conflict is present in the thinking and feeling of both dominant and minority groups toward upper class Negroes and educated women. Should a woman judge be treated with the respect due a judge or the gallantry accorded a woman? The extent to which the rights and duties of one role permeate other roles so as to cause a role conflict has been treated elsewhere by the writer.[9] Lower class Negroes who have acquired dominant group

---

9. Helen M. Hacker, Towards a Definition of Role Conflict in Modern Woman (unpublished manuscript).

attitudes toward the Negro resent upper-class Negro pretensions to superiority. Similarly, domestic women may feel the career woman is neglecting the duties of her proper station.

Parallels in adjustment of women and Negroes to the class-caste conflict may also be noted. Point 4, "Accommodation Attitudes," of the foregoing chart indicates the kinds of behavior displayed by members of both groups who accept their caste status. Many "sophisticated" women are retreating from emancipation with the support of psychoanalytic derivations.[10] David Riesman has recently provided an interesting discussion of changes "in the denigration by American women of their own sex" in which he explains their new submissiveness as in part a reaction to the weakness of men in the contemporary world.[11] "Parallelism" and "Negroidism" which accept a racially-restricted economy reflect allied tendencies in the Negro group.

Role segmentation as a mode of adjustment is illustrated by Negroes who indulge in occasional passing and women who vary their behavior according to their definition of the situation. An example of the latter is the case of the woman lawyer who, after losing a case before a judge who was also her husband, said she would appeal the case, and added, "The judge can lay down the law at home, but I'll argue with him in court."

A third type of reaction is to fight for recognition of class status. Negro race leaders seek greater prerogatives for Negroes. Feminist women, acting either through organizations or as individuals, push for public disavowal of any differential treatment of men and women.

RACE RELATIONS CYCLE

The "race relations cycle," as defined by Robert E. Park,[12] describes the social processes of reduction in tension and increase of communication in the relations between two or more groups who are living in a common territory under a single political or

---

10. As furnished by such books as Helene Deutsch, *The Psychology of Women* (1944-1945), and Ferdinand Lundberg and Marynia F. Farnham, *Modern Woman: The Lost Sex* (1947).

11. David Riesman, "The Saving Remnant: An Examination of Character Structure," *Years of the Modern: An American Appraisal,* ed. John W. Chase (1949), pp. 139-40.

12. Robert E. Park, "Our Racial Frontier on the Pacific," *The Survey Graphic,* 56, (May 1, 1926), pp. 192-196.

economic system. The sequence of competition, conflict, accommodation, and assimilation may also occur when social change introduces dissociative forces into an assimilated group or causes accommodated groups to seek new definitions of the situation.[13] The ethnic or nationality characteristics of the groups involved are not essential to the cycle. In a complex industrialized society groups are constantly forming and re-forming on the basis of new interests and new identities. Women, of course, have always possessed a sex-identification though perhaps not a group awareness. Today they represent a previously accommodated group which is endeavoring to modify the relationships between the sexes in the home, in work, and in the community.

The sex relations cycle bears important similarities to the race relations cycle. In the wake of the Industrial Revolution, as women acquired industrial, business, and professional skills, they increasingly sought employment in competition with men. Men were quick to perceive them as a rival group and made use of economic, legal, and ideological weapons to eliminate or reduce their competition. They excluded women from the trade unions, made contracts with employers to prevent their hiring women, passed laws restricting the employment of married women, caricatured the working woman, and carried on ceaseless propaganda to return women to the home or keep them there. Since the days of the suffragettes there has been no overt conflict between men and women on a group basis. Rather than conflict, the dissociative process between the sexes is that of contravention,[14] a type of opposition intermediate between competition and conflict. According to Wiese and Becker, it includes rebuffing, repulsing, working against, hindering, protesting, obstructing, restraining, and upsetting another's plans.

The present contravention of the sexes, arising from women's competition with men, is manifested in the discriminations against women, as well as in the doubts and uncertainties expressed concerning women's character, abilities, motives. The processes of competition and contravention are continually giving way to accommodation in the relationships between men and women. Like other minority groups, women have sought a protected position, a niche in the economy which they could occupy, and, like other minority groups, they have found these positions in new occupations in which dominant group members had not yet

---

13. William Ogburn and Meyer Nimkoff, *Sociology* (2d ed., 1950), p. 187.

14. Howard Becker, *Systematic Sociology on the Basis of the "Beziehungslehre" and "Gebildelehre" of Leopold von Wiese* (1932), pp. 263-268.

established themselves and in old occupations which they no longer wanted. When women entered fields which represented an extension of services in the home (except medicine!), they encountered least opposition. Evidence is accumulating, however, that women are becoming dissatisfied with the employment conditions of the great women-employing occupations and present accommodations are threatened.

What would assimilation of men and women mean? Park and Burgess in their classic text define assimilation as "a process of interpenetration and fusion in which persons and groups acquire the memories, sentiments, and attitudes of other persons or groups, and, by sharing their experiences and history, are incorporated with them in a cultural life." If accommodation is characterized by secondary contacts, assimilation holds the promise of primary contacts. If men and women were truly assimilated, we would find no cleavages of interest along sex lines. The special provinces of men and women would be abolished. Women's pages would disappear from the newspaper and women's magazines from the stands. All special women's organizations would pass into limbo. The sports page and racing news would be read indifferently by men and women. Interest in cookery and interior decoration would follow individual rather than sex lines. Women's talk would be no different from men's talk, and frank and full communication would obtain between the sexes.

THE MARGINAL WOMAN

Group relationships are reflected in personal adjustments. Arising out of the present contravention of the sexes is the marginal woman, torn between rejection and acceptance of traditional roles and attributes. Uncertain of the ground on which she stands, subjected to conflicting cultural expectations, the marginal woman suffers the psychological ravages of instability, conflict, self-hate, anxiety, and resentment.

In applying the concept of marginality to women, the term "role" must be substituted for that of "group."[15] Many of the traditional devices for creating role differentiation among boys and girls, such as dress, manners, activities, have been de-emphasized in modern urban middle class homes. The small girl who wears a play suit, plays games with boys and girls together, attends a co-

15. Kurt Lewin, *Resolving Social Conflicts* (1948), p. 181.

duties in the home may have differed little for herself and her brother. But in high school or perhaps not until college she finds herself called upon to play a new role. Benedict[16] has called attention to discontinuities in the life cycle, and the fact that these continuities in cultural conditioning take a greater toll of girls than of boys is revealed in test scores showing neuroticism and introversion.[17] In adolescence girls find the frank, spontaneous behavior toward the neighboring sex no longer rewarding. High educational school, may have little awareness of sexual differentiation until the approach of adolescence. Parental expectations in the matters of scholarship, conduct toward others, grades are more likely to elicit anxiety than praise from parents, especially mothers, who seem more pleased if male callers are frequent. There are subtle indications that to remain home with a good book on a Saturday night is a fate worse than death. But even if the die is successfully cast for popularity, all problems are not solved. Girls are encouraged to heighten their sexual attractiveness, but to abjure sexual expression.

Assuming new roles in adolescence does not mean the complete relinquishing of old ones. Scholarship, while not so vital as for the boy, is still important, but must be maintained discreetly and without obvious effort. Mirra Komarovsky[18] has supplied statements of Barnard College girls of the conflicting expectations of their elders. Even more than to the boy is the "all-round" ideal held up to girls, and it is not always possible to integrate the roles of good date, good daughter, good sorority sister, good student, good friend, and good citizen. The superior achievements of college men over college women bear witness to the crippling division of energies among women. Part of the explanation may lie in women's having interiorized cultural notions of feminine inferiority in certain fields, and even the most self-confident or most defensive woman may be filled with doubt as to whether she can do productive work.

It may be expected that as differences in privileges between men and women decrease, the frequency of marginal women will increase. Widening opportunities for women will call forth a growing number of women capable of performing roles formerly reserved for men, but whose acceptance in these new roles may well remain

---

16. Ruth Benedict, "Continuities and Discontinuities in Cultural Conditioning," *Psychiatry*, 1 (1938), pp. 161-167.

17. Georgene H. Seward, *op. cit.*, pp. 239-240.

18. Mirra Komarovsky, "Cultural Contradictions and Sex Roles," *The American Journal of Sociology*, LII (November 1946), 184-189.

uncertain and problematic. This hypothesis is in accord with Arnold Green's[19] recent critical reexamination of the marginal man concept in which he points out that it is those Negroes and second-generation immigrants whose values and behavior most approximate those of the dominant majority who experience the most severe personal crises. He believes that the classical marginal man symptoms appear only when a person striving to leave the racial or ethnic group into which he was born is deeply identified with the family of orientation and is met with grudging, uncertain, and unpredictable acceptance, rather than with absolute rejection, by the group he is attempting to join, and also that he is committed to success-careerism. Analogically, one would expect to find that women who display marginal symptoms are psychologically bound to the family of orientation in which they experienced the imperatives of both the traditional and new feminine roles, and are seeking to expand the occupational (or other) areas open to women rather than those who content themselves with established fields. Concretely, one might suppose women engineers to have greater personality problems than women librarians.

Other avenues of investigation suggested by the minority group approach can only be mentioned. What social types arise as personal adjustments to sex status? What can be done in the way of experimental modification of the attitudes of men and women toward each other and themselves? What hypotheses of inter-group relations may be tested in regard to men and women? For example, is it true that as women approach the cultural standards of men, they are perceived as a threat and tensions increase? Of what significance are regional and community variations in the treatment of and degree of participation permitted women, mindful here that women share responsibility with men for the perpetuation of attitudes toward women? This paper is exploratory in suggesting the enhanced possibilities of fruitful analysis, if women are included in the minority group corpus, particularly with reference to such concepts and techniques as group belongingness, socialization of the minority group child, cultural differences, social distance tests, conflict between class and caste status, race relations cycle, and marginality. I believe that the concept of the marginal woman should be especially productive, and am now engaged in an empirical study of role conflicts in professional women.

19. Arnold Green, "A Re-Examination of the Marginal Man Concept," *Social Forces,* 26 (December 1947), pp. 167-171.

7 (continued)

Women as a Minority Group
Twenty Years Later

More than twenty years ago I wrote a paper called "Women As a Minority Group," which aroused so much interest that it took almost three years to get it published. Included among the suggestions put forth for revising it by some leading sociologists were that it might be more important to consider the stupid as a minority group; more fruitful to examine women-in-minorities, such as Yankee women, Negro women, Italian, Jewish, Nisei, or French-Canadian women; that the extent to which this concept was utilized by left-wing movements in Europe in the first quarter of the century should be explored. Following its publication in *Social Forces* in the fall of 1951, I carefully treasured the handful of requests for reprints. Last year, however, when I requested a reversion of copyright from *Social Forces,* the editors replied that regretably their financial situation was too precarious to part with the rights to one of their best money-makers.

In the intervening years I wrote my doctoral dissertation[1] (an earlier dissertation proposal, a study of women ministers entitled *Petticoats in the Pulpit,* had been rejected by Columbia) on attitudes toward working wives which nobody wanted to publish, a few more articles on role conflicts of modern women, a small discourse on men's problems called "The New Burdens of Masculinity," tried unsuccessfully to introduce a course on women at both Hunter College and the New School for Social Research, and styled myself a specialist in sex roles. But the general atmosphere seemed to be one of "mostly quiet on the female front." True, there were conferences on the special problems of educating women, a few anguished cries from suburbia, a dribble of books exhorting women to reimmerse themselves in femininity, a couple of which I reviewed for professional journals, or on how to over-

---

1. One amusing index of the change in the climate of opinion that has taken place is that the *American Journal of Sociology* rejected it in 1950 as too "polemical and journalistic," while the Roszaks in their *Masculine and Feminine* refer to its "professional, impersonal tone."

come the difficulties of combining homemaking and a job, mostly parttime, and a small band of female emancipators who struggled on without making much of an impression on the consciousness of female college students, who continued to vote overwhelmingly for marriage first when queried on this subject in my family classes. Even Betty Friedan's *The Feminine Mystique,* published in 1963, did not immediately cause the smoldering in the domestic bushes to leap into flame. Then in 1967 my friend Pauli Murray told me that the National Organization for Women was being formed and suggested that I become a charter member. At the time it impressed me as quite a radical organization, even though it was quite willing to admit men in equal partnership with women. Though I do not wish to minimize NOW's accomplishments in its formative years, the organization by no means had become a household word by the time I left for India in the late summer of 1969 to be a visiting professor of sociology at Bangalore University.

You can imagine, then, my re-entry shock in the fall of 1970, when I found the woman's movement in full swing, that I had been drafted to teach a course at Adelphi with the simple title "Women's Liberation," in which sweet young things were waxing passionate about women being an oppressed majority. Braless girls in overalls and miners' boots presented a strange contrast to the demure students in south India, who when asked to say something in class would often just chew on a corner of their saris in a state of complete confusion and embarrassment. I thought of Indian women doctors who at the age of thirty-five would not dream of getting married without the consent of their brothers. I remembered escorting students home who had come to visit me, if they stayed after nightfall, because no respectable Indian woman would walk on the street alone at night. What more, I asked myself—after this long acclimatization to India—can American women want? They have the most freedom, highest prestige, the most equality— if not dominance—in the home of any women in the world. Well, I found out what they wanted. To finish the unfinished revolution that the suffragists had begun, to remake the masculine world from top to bottom. Not since those days has this country seen such organized mass action. Parades, demonstrations, picket lines, sit-ins to desexigate help-wanted ads, to fight discrimination in getting and holding jobs and promotion, to consign the outer trappings of woman as sex object to the trash can, to combat degrading portrayals of women in advertising and the mass media, to give to women the control of their own bodies in striking down abortion laws, to pass the Equal Rights amendment, to revise marriage contracts, to explore alternative family forms. I arrived home just after the August 26, 1970, demonstration, in commemoration of the fiftieth anniversary of the ratification of the Nineteenth Amendment for women's suffrage, in New York City, in which the euphoria of "sisterhood is powerful" ran high. I remember the trinity of slogans for that day: right to abortion, day care centers, and equal pay for equal work. What had happened to set women in motion?

The sociologist Lewis Coser has written that members of his profession were caught unaware by the rise of black power because of their too great emphasis on a consensus model of society and neglect of the conflict theory of Marxism. I ask myself what deficiencies in my social outlook could account for my surprise at the resurgence of feminism, even though I had predicted it. One difference between the current woman's liberation movement and that of the suffragists seems to lie in the *esprit de corps* of the protagonists. My stereotype of the early feminists is that they were lone rebels in youth and joined forces with other women only in their mature years. Later on you will see why I stress the matter of age. The modern movement, in contrast, took off with the revolt of young radical women college students against being relegated to Jimmy Higgins work in the SDS and carrying out the traditional female functions of note-taking, coffee-serving, and sexual relief. They resented not being admitted to positions of power and leadership. "Make policy, not coffee," "Make war, not love." Black women too had to do a bit of ego swallowing to accept Stokely Carmichael's non-missionary ad-monition that the proper position of women in the black struggle was prone. Perhaps, though, we do not need a special sociological theory to account for the upsurgence of women, but can place it in the general social context of the conflicts of an affluent society riddled with poverty, fighting a disastrous and immoral war, losing faith in a business civilization, impatient at closing the gap between aspiration and achievement—to mention in a most general and oversimplified way the kind of social climate that gave rise to the civil rights movement and black nationalism, student rebellion, hippies and other counterculturists, the peace movement, the rediscovery of ethnicity. No doubt the present women's liberation movement is part and parcel of the general upheavals in our society, as well as being sparked by them.

It is not my purpose here, though, to explain the new feminism as a social movement, or to answer the question of what women really want. Rather I would like to talk about some ways in which my old paper would have to be revised in the light of contemporary happenings and to tell you about some changes in my own thinking on the woman question.

As some of you may recall, my article "Women as a Minority

Group" built upon the familiar analogy between women and blacks,[2] and despite the dramatic changes in both groups and Betty Friedan's rejection of this comparison, the parallels remain. Now some twenty years ago I did not say that women *were* a minority group, but that they had, from the viewpoint of a believer in the democratic creed, a minority-group status—that is, that although they suffered discrimination, most women were accommodated to their subordinate status. One might say that prior to emancipation Negroes too constituted an oppressed rather than a minority group. There is no need to dwell on the heightening of black consciousness, the search for ethnic roots, and the growth into a subculture, the return on a different level to the "separate but equal" slogan. The Negro's morale has soared since Arnold Rose's book of that title appeared in 1949. Although I discussed the question of social distance between men and women and the kind of homosociality that flowed from segregated sex roles, my main emphasis was that women, unlike other minority groups, were "together but unequal" in that they lived with the master race. Far from having a sense of group identification or wanting to sever their ties with men, most women were engaged in a continual competition with each other for the favorable attention of men. Of course, in the early years of the century some women were willing to sacrifice marriage in the interests of a career and felt there was an inherent conflict, in the trite phrase, between being a person and being a woman. But in the process they renounced their sexuality. Their decision to escape the domestic trap was facilitated by the Victorian view that celibacy was not a particularly deprived state for women. As William O'Neill says in his book *The Woman Movement,* "Even if a woman was denied children, she was also spared the coarse and painful means by which they came into being—processes especially repugnant to women of taste and sensibility." Radical feminists in the nineteenth century may have espoused free love as a way of breaking domestic fetters, but orthodox feminists rejected this view, feeling that emphasis on women's sexual role forged the chain that bound them to home and family—and indeed the increased awareness of female sexuality that developed in the 1920s resulted in the teenage marriages and the baby boom of the 1940's and 1950s, O'Neill continues.

Women who worked, according to Ruth Hartley, viewed their

2. The Negro-woman analogy, of course, leaves the black woman in an anomalous position. Does she experience "the positive effects of the double negative"? Are race consciousness and sex consciousness incompatible for her? The special situation of the black woman is too complex for discussion here, but is treated in my forthcoming book on the sociology of gender.

jobs as helping the family, an extension of the wife and mother role. The Adlerian feminine protest of the working wife was that even if I work like a man, I am still a woman—and of course a desirable sex object. Now, following the black lead, we seem to have come full circle. Radical feminists, like Ti-Grace Atkinson, say women have no need of men. If sex becomes too pressing, turn to self-help. Can we expect the emergence of a female nationalism calling for the creation of an Amazon state within our borders? Even if there can be no back-to-Africa movement for women, if we can credit Elizabeth Gould Davis, author of *The First Sex,* women might bend their efforts to raising submerged Atlantis where a superior female civilization once held sway. At any rate this new separatist movement, like its black counterpart, may represent only a transitional phase pending integration on an equal basis. In the meantime these radicals do not see the problem today as how to modify family institutions to fit in with economic ones, not how both men and women may be enabled to combine home and family with a job, but instead call for the abolition of the family and the virtual elimination of parenthood.

For the time being many women want a place of refuge, if not from men, at least from marriage, while seeking their feminine identities. What kind of definition will come from female studies and the rewriting of history from a feminine point of view? This may involve the recasting of evolutionary theory to account for the distinctive features of *Femina sapiens* in terms of reproductive needs in the first aquarian age (*vide* Elaine Morgan, *The Descent of Woman*), the excavation of her as (feminine form of hero) long buried by masculine prejudice, the identification of mute, inglorious feminine Miltons and guiltless Cromwells whose talents were never fostered, the glorification of female contributions that were not of the sort to leave any record, or the rehabilitation of lost matriarchies. Will such an immersion lead to an authentic female ethnicity or clarify the goals of the woman's struggle? It is not likely that these women in pursuit of what is unique about themselves will discover that it is the womb. Whether the future holds any distinctive life styles for men and women or any complementarity of the sexes remains to be seen.

The radical separatist theme is a relatively minor motif in the current orchestration of the woman's movement. Most liberationist groups are content to call for a modification of traditional roles rather than a complete breaking off of relationships with men. They seek to move the minds of the majority of American women who have no wish to be liberated. It is indeed understandable that older women whose lives have followed the traditional pattern of domesticity have little or nothing to gain from the liberation movement, but rather are threatened by a devaluation of their status as homemakers and mothers. (Indeed zero population growth may have disastrous psychological consequences for women.) At this point in their lives attractive options are not open to them. Similarly, unless one is stirred by a spark of divine discontent, it is difficult to resist the enormous appeal of being given social approval for a dependent, secure status protected from competition. (Even though women may have been unable to monopolize any significant sectors of industry, they have had the monopoly of their homes and families.) The child in all of us enjoys being lazy and slothful, savoring the present moment, and being treasured for ourselves rather than having to pit our achievements against those of others. And when one considers the deep and pervasive programming of women by all the socializing agents of parents, peers, counselors, mass media, etc., it is not surprising that the mass of American women is not unambivalently for a radical change in sex roles.

But the point I want to make here is that this outlook is shared by professional and business women. Indeed, it has been remarked that some of the most successful women executives and writers are unfriendly to the women's liberation movement. Most notorious are the members of the Pussycat League, founded by an attorney, advertising consultant, and a rich housewife, who believe that "looking, cooking, and smelling good for men are our major responsibilities and result in more than equal rights for us."

We need not, however, go to the self-proclaimed opponents of woman's liberation to find women who may be suspected of having mixed feelings about extending educational and economic opportunities to all women; they may even be harbored within the movement. This matter of vested interest is the second theme in the continuation of the class-caste parallel between women and blacks. In his article "Human, All Too Human," which appeared in the January 1947 issue of *Survey Graphic,* the noted black sociologist E. Franklin Frazier describes the stake that middle- and upper-class Negroes have in segregated institutions that protect them from floundering in the wide sea of white competition. Negroes had reason to fear white competition because past discrimination had resulted in their being educated in inferior schools. Although Frazier acknowledges the dependence of a tiny Negro upper class on the black masses who serve as their clients, customers, and servants, he feels that only the short-run interests of Negro professional and business persons lie in segregation. Full integration of blacks into American life and provision of equal opportunity would free their successors from this fear. Frazier, though, focuses on white competition. When the walls of segregation come tumbling down, more blacks would be able to compete effectively with those blacks already at the top. Similarly, it can be said that equal rights will increase the competition that achievement-oriented women will have to face from other women. They may well lose their privileged position. Even those women who have renounced sexual competition with women may now have to suffer economic and social defeat as well. Such women may have succumbed to the male flattery of being told that they think like a man, are free from feminine emotionalism and illogicality, are one of the few women acceptable in otherwise all-male gatherings, much like the "understanding" woman at a male homosexual party. It is standard in the blue-collar class and a feature of middle-class dinner parties for guests to break up into homosocial groups. A recent article in the *New York Times* recounts the resentment expressed by female guests to some Washington hostesses about this practice. The men apparently are less eager to join the ladies for their after-dinner liquers. The professional woman particularly often disdains joining the distaff side where the talk presumably centers on children, servants, fashions, recipes, and other traditionally feminine topics and goes with the men to talk business, politics, professional gossip, developments in their common field, etc. Her sex gives her a special piquancy and status in the men's group. Especially at university functions do women professors speak scornfully of faculty wives, while enjoying the kind of deference they may get from them. If in the future the number of women who are "just a housewife" dwindles, no special cachet will attach to the intellectual woman vis-a-vis both men and women. When tokenism ends, women too will then founder in the sea of female competition. Middle-aged women who have struggeled to a modest success may feel resentful of younger women for whom the path has been smoothed.

Although the ambivalence of a few favored women is understandable, they must also realize that they are still kept at a competitive disadvantage with men, and can attain equality only if, to paraphrase Debs, they choose to rise not above their sex, but with it. In their own self-interest they must strive to kick their sisters out of the doll's house. "Equal pay for equal work" is a slogan to which almost everyone gives lip service. The fact is, though, that women can never achieve equality with men as long as there are any differences in the social expectations for the two sexes, as long as any protected or sheltered role is open to women, but not to man. Or, in terms of the obligatory aspects of the wife-mother role, women cannot realize equality if they continue to bear by themselves the main responsibility for the care of home and children. If the work role remains an additional option for women, and equal sharing in homemaking and child care is not required of men, the present sexual division of labor will not be seriously challenged. So long as women's acceptance in the world of work is predicated upon their having discharged their primary obligation in regard to home and children, their emancipation remains conditional. They will continue to grow up looking to marriage rather than an occupation as their livelihood. With the husband-father regarded as the main source of support, men will receive higher wages than women for the same work. Although economic theory may postulate a marginal productivity basis for wages, sentimental factors have always entered into their determination, and particularly for men a concealed needs principle reflecting their role as family provider. Differential wages for men and women are further justified in the employer's eyes by special costs associated with female employees, stemming from the primacy of their homemaking and child-guardian role, such as higher turnover, higher absenteeism, lower ambitions, etc.

When we look at the feminine role in terms of privileges rather than obligations, this argument implies that women can no longer enjoy the luxury of choice. The dominant liberal ideology here and abroad continues to call for two roles for women, but not for men. Day care centers, special educational programs, and collective services to lighten domestic burdens are viewed as measures to help women, but not men, add a work life to their home life. Those who espouse a libertarian, pluralistic *Weltanschauung* may be tempted to endorse the possibility of at least one sex's having two strings to its bow. The exemption from success in the occupational world, however, no longer conduces to psychological comfort in a society in which achievement values are dominant, but may rather lead to vacillation, insecurity, and regret. The woman's problem of not knowing which way to jump may be more stressful than the man's problem of seeing how far he can jump.[3] The lower level of aspiration, which is a frequent outcome of woman's minuet between home and job, partially justifies and reinforces the discriminations they encounter in the opportunity structure. Thus a vicious circle is formed, similar to Myrdal's theory with regard to Negroes in our society. Women do not prepare for certain vocations because they know they will have to be much better than a man to succeed in them, and because of their lack of dedication

---

3. The "damned if you do and damned if you don't" plight of modern American women is documented in my doctoral dissertation, *"A Functional Approach to the Gainful Employment of Married Women,* Columbia University, 1961. See especially Chapter IV, "The Problem of Identification."

and commitment, they are given even less of a chance. The vicious circle can be converted into a benign one only when the key function of a husband is no longer that of provider and that of the wife to be homemaker and mother.

At the risk of belaboring the obvious, it must be insisted that no direct assault on discrimination against women, whether it be legislative, stricter law enforcement, court action, persuasion both gentle and violent, can succeed so long as men appear to represent a better investment than women and the probability remains that a man's salary is more likely to pay for the spouse's domestic services than a woman's. This position represents a change in my own thinking. Years ago at Hunter College when I used to present a ten-point plan for the reconstruction of family life, I would plead for social arrangements to implement the wife's option to work — or, as Alva Myrdal put it, the right of the working woman to marry and have children. My first plank stated: "Men and women, according to individual preference and mutual agreement, will work full-time in the home, full-time in a profession, or some division of time between the two." The catch here is that if most couples elected to follow the traditional pattern, fundamental change in discriminatory attitudes toward women could not be anticipated. If women are ever to achieve equality with men — and the "if" calls attention to the fact that the function of the sociologist is not to impose values, but only to expose inconsistencies among values and between means and ends — work must become as mandatory for women as it is for men, or, conversely, it will be socially acceptable for some men not to work. My objection is not to the possibility that one spouse will make the living while the other makes the life, but only to the cultural assumption that the stay-at-home person or secondary breadwinner will be the wife. The role of housewife must be abolished, unless the role of househusband can gain equal favor.

The alternative of such a reversal of traditional roles is not considered even by seemingly sophisticated analysts of the "woman question." Morton Hunt,[4] for example, writing in *Playboy* magazine in 1970, acknowledges the frustrations and unfairness of the disrupted second-rate career pattern associated with women's "two roles," but goes only so far as to consider the possibility of husband and wife sharing equally in all things, a solution he rejects as denying career advancement to both spouses and resulting in inefficient performance of household tasks.

The sharing of roles by husband and wife, however, as the way

---

4. Morton Hunt, "Up Against the Wall, Male Chauvinist Pig," in *Women's Liberation,* ed. Michael E. Adelstein and Jean G. Pival. New York: St. Martin's Press, 1972), p. 49.

to free women for work outside the home is the method congenial to advanced, democratic capitalist societies, such as Sweden. Marxist ideology prefers the transfer of domestic tasks to outside agencies, but so far this method has not been successful. Owing to military and economic exigencies, the Soviet Union has had to default on the creation of social services, and, since Russian men resist participating in the maintenance of the home, Russian women carry a double burden. Although women in the kibbutzim in Israel were largely relieved of cooking, cleaning, and child care for their own families, they wound up being relegated to these activities for the settlement as a whole.

Perhaps some compromise between the socialist and capitalist methods can be followed in the United States. That is, redefinitions of marital roles will break down the sexual division of labor within the home. At the same time, the personnel involved in providing collective services for those families that wish to take advantage of them will be recruited from both sexes. For families preferring to have one parent stay at home, the cost of child care can be shared by the community in the form of child allowances and other stipends.

Thus we have reviewed three currents in the woman's movement which to some degree have their black counterparts. First, female separatism is even less viable than black nationalism. Second, the vested interests of privileged women in the status quo must be recognized and overcome. Third, the kind of feminine self-image that lowers aspiration and permits the acceptance of a dependent status, similar to the defeatist attitudes of other minority groups, must be countered directly by changing the ideological messages that women receive, and indirectly by creating the social conditions that enable women to avail themselves of their equality. Concurrently, men too can be relieved of some burdens of masculinity. Certainly the emotional re-education of men and women will have to go hand in hand with social engineering in enlarging the repertory of life styles open to members of both sexes.

SUGGESTED PAPERS AND PROJECTS

Papers

1. Review evidence for sex-role stereotypes in children's literature.
2. Discuss the use of sex-related pronouns in the English language.
3. Discuss uses of personal space by males and females, e.g., who sits next to whom, who touches whom, who interrupts whom, etc.
4. Compare women to members of minority groups—similarities and differences.

Projects

1. Go to the library, choose three books at random from the children's section, and look for sex-role stereotyping. Look at the illustrations. Who are the subjects and what are they doing?
2. List ten synonyms for males and ten for females. Discuss the differences between the two lists.
3. Interview five males and five females (different individuals in class can choose different age subjects) and ask them to give ten traits describing themselves.
5. Present a series of one sentence or so autobiographical descriptions to two groups. Reverse the sex of the subject described in either group. Ask groups to complete story and note differences in endings from group to group.
7. Choose three different time periods of TV viewing time. Note whether the nature or content of the material, obvious or not, changes depending on the time of the day and the expected female audience the station expects.
8. Compare and contrast the images of men and women projected by *Cosmopolitan, Playboy,* and *Ms.*
9a. Look at boxes containing boys' and girls' toys. Who is portrayed in the box? What are they doing?
 b. Describe the kinds of prizes found in cereal boxes.

ADDITIONAL REFERENCES

Allport, G. *The nature of prejudice.* New York: Doubleday, 1958. Traits due to victimization, chap. 9.

Broverman, I. R.; Vogel, S. R.; Broverman, D. M.; Clarkson, F. E.; and Rosenkrantz, P. S. Sex-role stereotypes: A current appraisal. *Journal of Social Issues,* 1972, *28*(2), 59-78.

Campbell, D. P. The SVIB M-F Scales: Must we ignore feminine aversions for carburetors? Paper presented at the 80th annual convention of the American Psychological Association, Honolulu, September 1972.

Cattell, R. B., and Lawson, E. D. Sex differences in small group performance. *Journal of Social Psychology,* 1962, *58,* 141-45.

Clarkson, P. E.; Vogel, S. R.; Broverman, I. K.; and Broverman, D. M. Family size and sex role stereotypes. *Science,* 1970, *167,* 390-92.

Dalstrom, E., ed. *The changing roles of men and women.* London: Duckworth, 1967.

Deaux, K. To err is humanizing: But sex makes a difference. *Representative Research in Social Psychology,* 1972, *3,* 20-28.

——— and Emswiller, I. Explanations of successful performance on sex-linked tasks: What's skill for the male is luck for the female. *Journal of Personality and Social Psychology,* 1974, *29,* 80-85.

Denmark, F. L., and Guttentag, M. The effect of college attendance on women: Changes in self-concept and evaluation of student role. *Journal of Social Psychology,* 1966, *69,* 155-58.

——— and ———. Dissonance in the self-concepts and educational concepts of college and non-college oriented women. *Journal of Counseling Psychology,* 1967, *17,* 113-15.

Ehrlich, C. The male sociologists' burden: The place of women in marriage and family texts. *Journal of Marriage and the Family,* 1971, *33*, 421-30.

Fidell, L. S. Covert sex discrimination: Against women as subjects for research. Paper presented at the 80th annual convention of the American Psychological Association, Honolulu, September 1972.

Friedan, B. *The feminine mystique.* New York: Norton, 1963.

Goldberg, P. Are women prejudiced against women? *Transaction,* 1968, *5*(5), 28-30.

Gump, J. P. A comparative analysis of black and white female sex-role attitudes. Paper presented at the 80th annual convention of the American Psychological Association, Honolulu, September 1972.

Harris, S. Influence of subject and experimenter sex in psychological research. *Journal of Consulting and Clinical Psychology,* 1971, *37,* 291-94.

Helson, R. The changing image of the career woman. *Journal of Social Issues,* 1972, *28,* 33-46.

Komarovsky, M. Cultural contradictions and sex roles. *American Journal of Sociology,* 1946, *52,* 184-89.

— — —. Functional analysis of sex roles. *American Sociological Review,* 1950, *15,* 508-516.

Lefkowitz, M. The women's magazine short-story heroine in 1957 and 1967. *Journalism Quarterly,* 1969, *46,* 364-66.

Liebert, R.; McCall, R.; and Hanratty, M. Effects of sex-typed information on children's toy preferences. *Journal of Genetic Psychology,* 1971, *119,* 133-36.

McDonald, R. I., and Cynther, H. D. Relationship of self- and ideal-self descriptions with sex, race, and class in southern adolescents. *Journal of Personality and Social Psychology,* 1965, *1,* 85-88.

Pilisuk, M.; Skolnick, P.; and Overstreet, E. Predicting cooperation from the two sexes in a conflict situation. *Journal of Personality and Social Psychology,* 1968, *10,* 35-43.

McKee, J. P., and Sherriff, A. C. The differential evaluation of males and females. *Journal of Personality,* 1957, *25,* 356-71.

Sistrunk, F., and McDavid, J. W. Sex variable in conforming behavior. *Journal of Personality and Social Psychology,* 1971, *17,* 200-207.

Slater, P. E. Role differences in small groups. *American Sociological Review,* 1955, *20,* 300-310.

Smith, R. W. Covert discrimination against women as colleagues. Paper presented at the 80th annual convention of the American Psychological Association, Honolulu, September 1972.

Steinmann, A.; Fox, D. J.; and Farkas, R. Male and female perceptions of male sex roles. *Proceedings of the American Psychological Association,* 1968, *8,* 421-22.

Unger, R. K.; Raymond, B. J.; and Levine, S. Are women discriminated against? Sometimes. *International Journal of Group Tensions,* 1974, *4,* (in press).

Vinacke, W. E., and Bond, J. R. Coalitions in mixed-sex triads. *Sociometry,* 1961, *24,* 61-75.

Section II

How The Therapist Looks at Women

8 Introduction

Consideration of women has not been ignored by the psychotherapist or psychoanalyst. In fact, until recently psychoanalysts were the only scholars who paid any significant attention to women. Their views have influenced many current investigators who attempt to extend or refute their approach. Without any empirical foundation women have been analyzed, described, and assigned to an inferior position since the time of Freud. Freud's system focused on biological reasons for their lower status, ignoring cultural and social factors [1927].

Such views were deeply rooted in Freud's observations of women, although they merely seemed to reflect the given status of the nineteenth century middle-class woman rather than being based on any scientific evidence. Freud and his followers had an impact not only on therapists and mental health workers up to the present time, but on twentieth-century thought in general. Unfortunately, these unscientific views served to perpetuate the myth of women as a devalued group.

Freud emphasized both the castration complex and penis envy as basic determinants of personality development. His theory proposes that "anatomy is destiny" with the female clearly the loser since she obviously lacks a penis and cannot encounter the Oedipal struggle. Freud presents his case within the framework of the Oedipus complex. A girl resolves the Oedipus complex by replacing her wish for a penis with her wish for a child. Consequently, the female's course of development is different from the male's and the resultant superego is weaker. Her eventual goal will be to marry someone like her father.

In the development of the female ego Freud argues that woman becomes aware early in life that she cannot compete with boys. He maintains that from the moment women see a penis they want one. They try to deny that they are "castrated." Freud assumes that having a penis is superior to not having one, and, therefore woman develops a sense of inferiority, sharing the contempt for man for lacking this important part of the anatomy.

As if this is not enough. Freud also attacks the clitoris; he states that clitoral masturbation is masculine and that "abolition of clitoris sexuality is a necessary pre-condition for the development of femininity" (1927, p. 139).

Other theorists, even though they de-emphasize some of Freud's basic personality determinants, still follow in Freud's footsteps in terms of their view of women.

Thus Bruno Bettleheim (in Weisstein, 1969) sees women as wanting to be good wives and mothers: "We must stand with the realization that, as much as women want to be good scientists or engineers, they want first and foremost to be womanly companions of men and to be mothers" (p. 20).

Erik Erikson (1964) also defines women in terms of their relationship to men. Woman is seen as different from man, but her self-concept depends upon him. Her identity is defined not only in terms of the man she marries, but is already defined in terms of the man/men by whom she would like to be sought.

Erikson's paper is within the "anatomy is destiny" clique, although he feels that the existence of a "productive inner bodily space" is more of a reality than the "missing organ" concept of Freud. He "proves" over and over again that it is the "inner space" that determines a woman's character structure, her personality, her goals. And *since a woman is never not a woman* (a point he stresses over and over again), she must deal with this factor or not fulfill herself.

He says that her role should not be competitive with men's roles, since she is a totally different person. She is inner-directed, he is outer-directed, and she should do work that would make use of her special sensitivity and her helping nature. He uses his testing on children at the University of California to prove his point.

Erikson describes a study in which boys and girls are observed during play behavior; the children are constructing a "scene" with various figures representing men, women, policemen, and so on, as well as blocks, autos, and the like. He finds that statistically significant differences exist between the sexes; the boys are concerned with constructing "outer space" while the girls are more concerned with "inner space." He goes on to point out that the play space seems to parallel the "morphology of genital differentiation."

Erikson also speaks of a woman's need to have her inner space filled in order to be fulfilled. To be truly "feminine" a woman must be "receptive," in contrast to the man who must be "actively penetrating" in order to be "masculine." In a very gentle, very supportive way Erikson comes to the same conclusion as Freud.

Even Erich Fromm, a theorist who emphasizes the importance and often devastating effects that cultural values and the social milieu can have on personal growth, defines personality in bipolar sex-related terms. According to Fromm, masculinity is characterized by the qualities of penetration, guidance, activity, discipline, and adventurousness. On the other hand, he sees the feminine character as possessing such qualities as productive receptivity, protectiveness, realism, endurance, and motherliness (1956).

Although certain women psychoanalysts such as Helene Deutsch (1944) were also followers of Freud, other analysts, especially Horney (1967) and Thompson (1964), criticized these negative views of women and argued against his concept of penis envy. They objected to a psychology of women considered only from a masculine viewpoint.

The need for a more equitable psychology of women has also been noted by Shainess (1969), Chesler (1971), and Laws (1970). Both Shainess and Chesler note that most of the concepts about women were formulated by men and accepted by women. Chesler examines the problem of mental illness in women and the role that psychotherapy plays in maintaining the traditional male-female status positions. A female psychiatric patient remains within the "female culture," which encourages a sense of worthlessness and dependency. More women than men suffer some form of mental illness. Chesler notes the preponderance of male therapists both in psychology and psychiatry, and wonders how men who generally have a sexist view of women can treat those who come to them seeking a refuge from the oppression of a male-dominated society. She suggests that male clinicians stop treating women altogether because the patient-therapist relationship is one more power relationship in which the woman submits to a dominant male authority figure. Laws makes a plea for more studies and data about women. Empirical research would be invaluable.

Very few therapists have been guided by these criticisms. A recent study by Broverman et al. (1970) indicates that even present-day practicing clinicians view mental health in terms of a double standard. Thus the healthy male was seen as significantly different from the healthy female by psychologists, psychiatrists, and social workers, both male and female. In addition, the healthy adult, sex unspecified, was seen in terms of the male stereotype. This finding really puts the female into a conflict situation, for in order to be a healthy female and adjusted within her ascribed sex category, the woman is forced to be abnormal according to general mental health standards. The survey indicated that the healthy woman differed from the healthy male

. . . by being more submissive, less independent, less adventurous, more easily influenced, less aggressive, less competitive, more excitable in minor crises, having their feelings more easily hurt, being more emotional, more conceited about their appearance, less objective, and disliking math and science (pp. 4-5).

Few theorists would see such an individual as constructively oriented or self-actualizing.

Broverman et al. see this double standard on the part of clinicians as stemming possibly from an adjustment view of health. Perhaps it is healthy for women (and therapists) to embrace the above stereotype because that is what society expects of them. On the other hand, it is healthy for men to pursue the generally accepted standard of mental health because this is consistent with their social reality. Fromm (1956), Szasz (1961), and others have suggested that the concept of mental health is a culturally conditioned one. Many individuals have been warped in the name of mental health; many more were labeled abnormal because they deviated from such a social norm.

But such a double standard of mental health is not conducive to personal growth for women, so perhaps we must strive for maladjusted deviants.

Although most present-day feminist therapists (a small but increasing number) challenge traditional theories and traditional practitioners, there exists basically only a plethora of criticism, with a corresponding shortage of clearly stated new theoretical views.

One such view comes from a present-day Freudian, B. Wolman. Not all Freudians subscribe to Freud's views on women, and Wolman in his paper "Between Men and Women" criticizes Freud for an overemphasis on sexuality. He feels that the basic drive in humans is a struggle for survival and not sex. The latter is not only secondary, but is also colored by this drive for survival. Therefore, such issues as who shall rule over whom are part of the struggle for survival. Historically, men subjected women with their greater physical strength and they brainwashed women to accept this. Therefore, Wolman feels that penis envy is the result of man's physical superiority, not the cause. He feels Freud's observations were correct, that in the Victorian era it meant something to be a man—i.e., to be somebody—but that his interpretations were incorrect.

Wolman notes that today many men wish to be women. Breast envy is quite common. Both breast and penis symbolize the power structure, and sexuality becomes the carrier for survival in terms of feelings of superiority and inferiority. The interrelations between men and women are based on this idea of survival.

A quite different view is presented by Mundy; Mundy believes that the symptoms of depression, guilt, or passive-aggressive maneuvers that a woman often presents to a therapist are the result of rage—a rage caused by the contradictions between role and self, the impossibility of her ever fulfilling the cultural ideal (which states that a women is pleasant, never unhappy, and so on) in terms of her actual feelings about her activities. These contradictions produce low self-esteem with consequent feelings of frustration and anger. Women may protect themselves against the consequences by avoiding the occasion of anger through narcotic drugs, social withdrawal, mental withdrawal into fugue states, excessive sleeping or eating, etc. Some women do explode with their anger but divert it into a reinforcement of their femininity by attacking those who attack the feminine model, e.g. mothers who punish girls' aggression more than boys'. A woman who allows her anger to surface may feel guilty and sick. She may then attempt to focus on the feeling rather than the cause, and thus try to stop feeling angry rather than do anything directly to change the provoking situation.

Mundy considers it essential for the therapist to treat the rage; to have the woman acknowledge its presence in all of its manifestations, and to see that it is justified. The woman needs the reassurance that she can be openly aggressive without losing her femininity. In fact, that it is far more dangerous to repress her anger. The therapist must aid in the expression of this rage rather than attempt to reduce it.

Torrey (1971) reverses the orthodox Freudian view of women by stating that it is the man who envies the woman's ability to have children. His penis is a substitute in his unconscious mind for "The baby they can never have all their own." Men fear female equality because they feel it will result in eventual superiority of women— because women possess the power of procreation. In fact, Torrey blames patriarchy and male chauvinism on man's wish to have a baby and fear of the woman's power of procreation. Thus he must dominate the woman and keep her within the confines of the family; the baby must have his name. This is his way of having a baby. "To compensate for his lack of procreativity, the male exaggerates his role in sublimated creativity."

Riess (1971) tries to illustrate changes needed in theory and practice in order to establish a new psychology for the new women. He starts by summarizing the orthodox or Freudian view, then proceeds to undermine Freud's assumption of bisexuality by pointing out that from conception to the fifth week of life all embryos are feminine; the male is the deviant pattern. Reiss then attacks the "myth" of the superiority of vaginal orgasms, citing evidence from Master and Johnson's work. He states that vaginal orgasms are possible only through stimulation of the clitoris. Moreover, the clitoris (he says) is unique; its only function is pleasure. Hence it is not a penis analog.

Finally, he says that the "typical" feminine traits of sub-missiveness, receptivity, and passivity can be seen as inevitable defenses against the male's resentment of his inability to satisfy the unsatisfiable.

Perhaps these new approaches as well as others that are being developed will serve to revolutionize psychotherapy for women and make them truly independent. More importantly, new models of women may emerge which cast doubt on many dubious but accepted cultural givens of today.

REFERENCES

Broverman, I. K.; Broverman, D. M.; Clarkson, F. E.; Rosenkrantz, P. S.; and Vogel, S. R. Sex-role stereotypes and clinical judgments of mental health. *Journal of Consulting and Clinical Psychology,* 1970, *34,* 1-7.

Chesler, P. Women psychiatric and psychotherapeutic patients. *Journal of Marriage and the Family,* 1971, *33,* 746-59.

Deutsch, H. *The psychology of women,* 2 vols. New York: Grune & Stratton, 1944.

Erikson, E. H. Inner and outer space: Reflections on womanhood. *Daedalus,* 1964, *93,* 582-606.

Freud, S. Some psychological consequences of the anatomical distinction between the sexes. *International Journal of Psychoanalysis,* 1927, *8,* 133-43.

Fromm, E. *The art of loving.* New York: Harper & Row, 1956.

Horney, K. *Collected writings.* In H. Kelman (Ed.), *Feminine psychology.* New York: Norton, 1967.

Laws, J. L. The social psychology of women: Shibboleths and lacunae. Pittsburgh: Know, Inc., May 1970. Paper originally presented at the meeting of the American Psychological Association, Washington, D.C., September 1969.

Riess, B. F.new psychology of women or a psychology for the new woman, active or passive. Paper presented at the meeting of the Eastern Psychological Association, New York, April 1971.

Shainess, N. Images of woman: Past and present, overt and obscured. *American Journal of Psychotherapy,* 1969, *23,* 77-97.

Szasz, T. The myth of mental illness. New York: Harper & Row, 1961.

Thompson, C. M. *On women.* New York: New American Library, 1964.

Torrey, J. W. Psychoanalysis: A feminist revision. Paper presented at the conference Problems and Solutions: The Women's Liberation Movement, Bridgeport, Conn., March 1971.

Weisstein, N. Woman as nigger. *Psychology Today,* October 1969, pp. 20ff.

9

Freud, with his tremendous impact on much of the twentieth-century thinking in general and psychology in particular, did not fail to capture attention with his views on women. In fact, present-day feminist therapists, both male and female, started their viable movement as a protest against the thinking and formulations of Freud. Never empirical, Freud did believe that human psychology had as an important component some biological base. However, he did not have the knowledge, the vast amount of information known in the biological sciences today. He was also unwittingly influenced by the middle-class Victorian society of Vienna—ignoring differences in acculturation over time and from one place to another.

In this paper Freud tries to argue that women are incomplete, i.e., their sexual apparatus is inferior or "mutilated" as compared to men. They see the penis of a brother or playmate and recognize it as superior to their own small organ. As a result of this anatomical inferiority, as well as their less developed libidinal development, women never quite reach up to par—par being the level at which men function. When a woman realizes that the lack of a penis is not a personal punishment, she begins to share the contempt felt by men for her sex.

Freud also notes how the Oedipus complex raises more problems for girls than for boys, since girls abandon the mother, who is their original love object, and take the father on as the love object. This is one of the consequences of penis envy. For the female, penis equals child. Keeping this objective in sight, she takes her father as love-object and her mother becomes the object of her jealousy. Freud believed that a woman's character formation depended on how she handled penis envy. In any case, this problem will stymie her thgoughout life.

Althrough Freud admitted to speculation and a lack of a fully developed theory regarding women, nevertheless he promulgated these views to which most present-day therapists basically still adhere.

Some Psychological Consequences of the Anatomical Distinction Between the Sexes*

Sigmund Freud

In my own writings and in those of my followers more and more stress is laid upon the necessity for carrying the analyses of neurotics back into the remotest period of their childhood, the time at which sexual life reaches the climax of its early development. It is only by examining the first manifestations of the patient's innate instinctual constitution and the effects of his earliest experiences that we can accurately gauge the motive forces that have led to his neurosis and can be secure against the errors into which we might be tempted by the degree to which they have become remodelled and overlaid in adult life. This requirement is not only of theoreitcal but also of practical importance, for it distinguishes our efforts from the work of those physicians whose interests are focussed exclusively upon therapeutic results and who employ analytic methods but only up to a certain point. An analysis of early childhood such as we are considering is tedious and laborious and makes demands both upon the physician and upon the patient which cannot always be met. Moreover it leads us into dark regions where there are as yet no sign posts. Indeed, analysts may feel reassured, I think, that there is no risk of their work becoming mechanical and so of losing its interest during the next few decades.

In the following pages I bring forward some findings of analytical research which would be of great importance if they could be proved to apply universally. Why do I not postpone publication of them until further experience has given me the necessary proof, if such proof is obtainable? Because the conditions under which I work have undergone a change, with implications which I cannot disguise. Formerly I was never one of those who are unable to hold back what seems to be a new discovery until it has been either confirmed or corrected. My *Traumdeutung* and my 'Fragment of an Analysis of a Case of Hysteria' (the case of Dora) were suppressed by me — if not for the nine years enjoined by Horace — at all events for four or five years before I allowed them to be published.

---

*From the *International Journal of Psychoanalysis, 8,* 1927, 133- 42.

But in those days I had unlimited time before me and material poured in upon me in such quantities that fresh experiences were hardly to be escaped. Moreover I was the only worker in a new field, so that my reticence involved no danger to myself and no risk of loss to others.

But now everything has changed. The time before me is limited. The whole of it is no longer spent in working, so that my opportunities for making fresh observations are not so numerous. If I think I see something new, I am uncertain whether I can wait for it to be confirmed. And further, everything that is to be seen upon the surface has already been exhausted; what remains has to be slowly and laboriously dragged up from the depths. Finally, I am no longer alone. An eager crowd of fellow-workers is ready to make use of what is unfinished or doubtful, and I can leave them that part of the work which I should otherwise have done myself. On this occasion, therefore, I feel justified in publishing something which stands in urgent need of confirmation before its value or lack of value can be decided.

In examining the earliest mental shapes assumed by the sexual life of children we have been in the habit of taking as the subject of our investigations the male child, the little boy. With little girls, so we have supposed, things must be similar, though in some way or other they must nevertheless be different. The point in their development at which this difference lay could not clearly be determined.

In boys the situation of the Oedipus complex is the first stage that can be recognized with certainty. It is easy to understand, because at that stage a child retains the same object which it previously cathected with its pre-genital libido during the preceding period while it was being suckled and nursed. The further fact that in this situation it regards its father as a disturbing rival and would like to get rid of him and take his place is a straightforward consequence of the actual state of affairs. I have shown elsewhere[1] how the Oedipus attitude in little boys belongs to the phallic phase, and how it succumbs to the fear of castration, that is, to narcissistic interest in their own genitals. The matter is made more difficult to grasp by the complicating circumstance that even in boys the Oedipus complex has a double orientation, active and passive, in accordance with their bisexual constitution; the boy also wants to take his mother's place as the love-object of his father — a fact which we describe as the feminine attitude.

As regards what precedes the Oedipus complex in boys we are far from complete clarity. We know that this prehistoric period

1. 'The Passing of the OEdipus Complex' (1924), *Collected Papers,* Vol. II.

includes an identification of an affectionate sort with the boy's father, an identification which is still free from any sense of rivalry in regard to his mother. Another element of this stage is invariably, I believe, a masturbatory stimulation of the genitals, the onanism of early childhood, the more or less violent suppression of which by the persons in charge of the child sets the castration complex in action. It is to be assumed that this onanism is attached to the Oedipus complex and serves as a discharge for the sexual ex- citation belonging to it. It is, however, uncertain whether the onanism has this character from the first, or whether on the other hand it makes its first appearance spontaneously as an 'organ activity' and is only brought into relation with the Oedipus complex at some later date; this second possibility is by far the more probable. Another doubtful question is the part played by bed- wetting and by the breaking of that habit through the intervention of educational measures. We are inclined to adopt the simple generalization that continued bed-wetting is a result of onanism and that its suppression is regarded by boys as an inhibition of their genital activity, that is, as having the meaning of a threat of castration: but whether we are always right in supposing this remains to be seen. Finally, analysis shows us in a shadowy way how the fact of a child at a very early age listening to its parents copulating may set up its first sexual excitation, and how that event may, owing to its after-effects, act as a starting-point for the child's whole sexual development. Onanism, together with the two attitudes in the Oedipus complex, later on become attached to this impression, the child having subsequently interpreted its meaning. It is impossible, however, to suppose that these observations of coitus are of universal occurrence, so that at this point we are faced with the problem of 'primal phantasies.' Thus the history of what precedes the Oedipus complex even in boys, raises all of these questions to be sifted and explained; and there is the further problem of whether we are to suppose that the process invariably follows the same course, or whether a great variety of different preliminary stages may not converge upon the same final situation.

In little girls the Oedipus complex raises one problem more than in boys. In both cases the mother is the original object; and there is no cause for surprise that boys retain that object in the Oedipus complex. But how does it happen that girls abandon it and instead take their father as an object? In pursuing this question I have been able to reach some conclusions which may throw some light upon what precedes the Oedipus relation in girls.

Every analyst has come across certain women who cling with especial intensity and tenacity to the bond with their father and to the wish in which it culminates of having a child by him. We have good reason to suppose that the same wish-phantasy was also the motive force of their infantile onanism, and it is easy to form an impression that at this point we have been brought up against an elementary and unanalysable fact of infantile sexual life. But a thorough analysis of these very cases brings something different to light; namely, that here there is a long history previous to the Oedipus complex, and that the complex is in some respects a secondary formation.

The old children's doctor Lindner once remarked[2] that a child discovers the genital zones (the penis or the clitoris) as a source of pleasure during the period at which it indulges in sucking for pleasure (thumb-sucking). I shall leave it an open question whether it is really true that the child takes the newly found source of pleasure in exchange for the recent loss of its mother's nipple—a possibility to which later phantasies (fellatio) seem to point. Be that as it may, the genital zone is discovered at some time or other, and there seems no justification for attributing any mental content to its first stimulations. But the first step in the phallic phase which begins in this way is not the linking-up of the onanism with the object-cathexes of the Oedipus situation, but a momentous discovery which it is the lot of little girls to make. They notice the penis of a brother or playmate, strikingly visible and of large proportions, at once recognize it as the superior counterpart of their own small and inconscpicuous organ, and from that time forward fall a victim to penis-envy.

There is an interesting contrast between the behaviour of the two sexes. In the analogous situation, when a little boy first catches sight of a girl's genital region, he begins by showing irresolution and lack of interest; he sees nothing or disowns what he has seen, he softens it down or looks about for expedients to bring it into line with his expectations. It is not until later, when some threat of castration has obtained a hold upon him, that the observation becomes important to him: if he then recollects or repeats it, it arouses a terrible storm of emotion to him and forces him to believe in the reality of the threat which he has hitherto laughed at. This combination of circumstances leads to two reactions, which may become fixed and will in that case, whether separately or together or in conjunction with other factors, permanently determine the boy's relations to women; horror at the mutilated creature or triumphant contempt for her. These developments, however, belong to the future, though not to a very remote one.

The little girl behaves differently. She makes her judgment and

---

2. Cf. *Drei Abhandlungen zur Sexualtheorie.*

her decision in a flash. She has seen it and knows that she is without it and wants to have it.[3]

From this point there branches off what has been named the masculinity complex of women, which may put great difficulties in the way of their regular development towards femininity, if it cannot be got over soon enough. The hope of some day obtaining a penis in spite of everything and so of becoming like a man may persist to an incredibly late age and may become a motive for the strangest and otherwise unaccountable actions. Or again, a process may set in which might be described as a 'denial,' a process which in the mental life of children seems neither uncommon nor very dangerous but which in an adult would mean the beginning of a psychosis. Thus a girl may refuse to accept the fact of being castrated, may harden herself in the conviction that she *does* possess a penis and may subsequently be compelled to behave as though she were a man.

The psychological consequences of penis-envy, insofar as it does not become absorbed in the reaction-formation of the masculinity complex, are various and far-reaching. After a woman has become aware of the wound to her narcissism, she develops, like a scar, a sense of inferiority. When she has passed beyond her first attempt at explaining her lack of a penis as being a punishment personal to herself and has realized that that sex character is a universal one, she begins to share the contempt felt by men for a sex which is the lesser in so important a respect, and, so far at least as maintaining this judgment is concerned, she clings obstinately to being like a man.[4]

---

3. This is an opportunity for correcting a statement which I made many years ago. I believed that the sexual interest of children, unlike that of pubescents, was aroused, not by the difference between the sexes, but by the problem of where babies come from. We now see that, at all events with girls, this is certainly not the case. With boys it may no doubt happen sometimes one way and sometimes the other; or with both sexes chance experiences may determine the event.

4. In my first critical account of the 'History of the Psycho-Analytic Movement', written in 1913 (*Collected Papers,* Vol. I.), I recognized that this fact represents the core of truth contained in Adler's theory. That theory makes no bones about explaining the whole world by this single point ('organ-inferiority', the masculine protest, breaking away from the feminine line of development) and prides itself upon having in this way robbed sexuality of its importance and put the desire for power in its place. Thus the only organ which could claim without any ambiguity to be called 'inferior' would be the clitoris. On the other hand, one hears of analysts who boast that, though they have worked for dozens of years, they have never found a sign of the existence of a castration complex. We must bow our heads in recognition of the greatness of this achievement, even though it is only a negative one, a piece of virtuosity in the art of overlooking and misconceiving. The two theories form an interesting pair of opposites: in one of them not a trace of a castration complex, in the other nothing at all but its effects.

Even after penis-envy has abandoned its true object it continues to exist: by an easy displacement it persists in the character-quality of *jealousy*. Of course jealousy is not limited to one sex and has a wider foundation than this, but I am of opinion that it plays a far larger part in the mental life of women than of men and that that is because it is enormously reinforced from the direction of displaced penis-envy. While I was still unaware of this source of jealousy, I was considering the phantasy 'a child is being beaten' which occurs so commonly in girls, and constructed a first phase for it in which its meaning was that another child, a rival of whom the subject was jealous, was to be beaten.[5] This phantasy seems to be a relic of the phallic period in girls. The peculiar rigidity which struck me so much in the monotonous formula 'a child is being beaten' can probably be interpreted in a special way. The child which is being beaten (or caressed) may at bottom be nothing more nor less than the clitoris itself, so that at its very lowest level the statement will contain a confession of masturbation, which has remained attached to the content of the formula from its beginning in the phallic phase up to the present time.

A third consequence of penis-envy seems to be a loosening of the girl's relation with her mother as a love-object. The situation as a whole is not very clear, but it can be seen that in the end the girl's mother, who sent her into the world so insufficiently equipped, is almost always held responsible for her lack of a penis. The way in which this comes about historically is often that soon after the girl has discovered that her genitals are unsatisfactory she begins to show jealousy of another child on the ground that her mother is fonder of it than of her, which serves as a reason for her giving up her affectionate relation to her mother. It will fit with this if the child which has been preferred by her mother is made into the first object of the beating-phantasy which comes to a head in masturbation.

There is yet another surprising effect of penis-envy, or of the discovery of the inferiority of the clitoris, wich is undoubtedly the most important of all. In the past I had often formed an impression that in general women tolerate masturbation worse than men, that they more frequently fight against it and that they are unable to make use of it in circumstances in which a man would seize upon it as a refuge without any hesitation. Experience would no doubt elicit innumerable exceptions to this statement, if we attempted to turn it into a rule. The reactions of human individuals of both sexes are of course made up of masculine and feminine traits. But it appeared nevertheless as though masturbation were further

---

5 . 'A Child is being Beaten' (1919), *Collected Papers,* Vol. II.

removed from the nature of women than of men, and the solution of the problem could be assisted by the reflection that masturbation, at all events of the clitoris, is a masculine activity, and that the aboliton of clitoris sexuality is a necessary pre-condition for the development of femininity. Analyses of the remote phallic period have now taught me that in girls, soon after the first signs of penis-envy, an intense current of feeling against onanism makes its appearance which cannot be attributed exclusively to the educational influence of the persons in charge of the child. This impulse is clearly a forerunner of the wave of repression which at puberty will do away with a large amount of the girl's masculine sexuality in order to make room for the development of her femininity. It may happen that this first opposition to auto-erotic stimulation fails to attain its end. And this was in fact the case in the instances which I analysed. The conflict continued, and both then and later the girl did everything she could to free herself from the compulsion to masturbate. Many of the later manifestations of sexual life in women remain unintelligible unless this powerful motive is recognized.

I cannot explain the opposition which is raised in this way by little girls to phallic onanism except by supposing that there is some concurrent factor which turns her violently against that pleasurable activity. Such a factor lies close at hand in the narcissistic soreness which is bound up with penis-envy, the girl's reflection that after all this is a point on which she cannot compete with boys and that it would therefore be best for her to give up the idea of doing so. Thus the little girl's recognition of the anatomical distinction between the sexes forces her away from masculinity and masculine onanism on to new lines which lead to the development of femininity.

So far there has been no question of the Oedipus complex, nor has it up to this point played any part. But now the girl's libido slips into a new position by means — there is no other way of putting it — of the equation 'penis = child.' She gives up her wish for a penis and puts in place of it a wish for a child; and *with this object in view* she takes her father as a love-object. Her mother becomes the object of her jealousy. The girl has turned into a little woman. If I am to credit a single exaggerated analytic instance, this new situation can give rise to physical sensations which would have to be regarded as a premature awakening of the female genital apparatus. If the girl's tie with her father comes to grief later on and has to be abandoned, it may give place to an identification with him and the girl may thus return to her masculinity complex and perhaps remain fixated in it.

I have now said the essence of what I had to say: I will stop, therefore, and cast an eye over our findings. We have gained some insight into the history of what precedes the Oedipus complex in girls. The corresponding period in boys is more or less unknown. In girls the Oedipus complex is a secondary formation. The operations of the castration complex precede it and prepare for it. As regards the relation between the Oedipus and castration complexes there is a fundamental contrast between the two sexes. *Whereas in boys the Oedipus complex succumbs to the castration complex,*[6] *in girls it is made possible and led up to by the castration complex.* This contradiction is cleared up if we reflect that the castration complex always operates in the sense dictated by its subject matter; it inhibits and limits masculinity and encourages femininity. The difference between the sexual development of men and women at the stage we have been considering is an intelligible consequence of the anatomical distinction between their genitals and of the mental situation involved in it; it corresponds to the difference between a castration that has been carried out and one that has merely been threatened. In their essentials, therefore, our findings are something self-evident that it should have been possible to foresee.

The Oedipus complex, however, is such an important thing that the manner in which one enters and leaves it cannot be without its effects. In boys (as I have shown at length in the paper to which I have just referred and to which all of my present remarks are closely related) the complex is not simply repressed, it is literally smashed to pieces by the shock of threatened castration. Its libidinal cathexes are abandoned, desexualized and in part sublimated: its objects are incorporated into the ego, where they form the nucleus of the super-ego and give this new formation its characteristic qualities. In normal, or rather, in ideal cases the Oedipus complex exists no longer, even in the unconscious; the super-ego has become its heir. Since the penis (in Fercenczi's sense) owes its extraordinarily high narcissistic cathexis to its organic significance for the propagation of the species, the catastrophe of the Oedipus complex (the abandonment of incest and institution of conscience and morality) may be regarded as a victory of the race over the individual. This is an interesting point of view when one considers that neurosis is based upon a struggle of the ego against the demands of the sexual function. But to leave the standpoint of individual psychology is not likely to help very much in clarifying an already complicated situation.

In girls the motive for the destruction of the Oedipus complex is lacking. Castration has already had its effect, which was to force the child into the situation of the Oedipus complex. Thus the

6. 'The Passing of the OEdipus Complex' (1924), *Collected Papers,* Vol. II.

Oedipus complex escapes the fate which it meets with in boys: it may either be slowly abandoned or got rid of by repression, or its effects may persist far into what is for women a normal mental life. I cannot escape the notion (though I hesitate to give it expression) that for women the level of what is ethically normal is different from what it is in men. Their super-ego is never so inexorable, so impersonal, so independent of its emotional origins as we require it to be in men. Character-traits which critics of every epoch have brought up against women—that they show less sense of justice than men, that they are less ready to submit to the great necessities of life, that they are more often influenced in their judgments by feelings of affection or hostility—all of these would be amply accounted for by the modification in the formation of their super-ego which we have already inferred. We must not allow ourselves to be deflected from such judgments by the denials of the feminists, who are anxious to force us to admit complete equality in the position and worth of the sexes: but we shall, of course, willingly agree that the majority of men are also far behind the masculine ideal and that all human individuals, as a result of their bisexual disposition and of cross-inheritance, combine in themselves both masculine and feminine characteristics, so that pure masculinity and femininity remain theoretical constructions of uncertain content.

I am inclined to set some value on the considerations I have brought forward upon the psychological consequences of the anatomical distinction between the sexes. I am aware, however, that this opinion can only be maintained if my findings, which are based on a handful of cases, turn out to have general validity and to be typical. If not, they would remain as a contribution to our knowledge of the different paths along which sexual life develops.

In the valuable and comprehensive studies upon the masculinity and castration complex in women by Abraham, Horney and Helene Deutsch [7] there is much that touches closely upon what I have written but nothing that coincides with it completely, so that here again I feel justified in publishing this paper.

---

7. Abraham, 'Manifestations of the Female Castration Complex' (1921), *Selected Papers;* Horney, 'On the Genesis of the Castration Complex in Women' (1923), International Journal of Psychoanalysis, Vol. VI., 4; Helene Deutsch, *Psychoanalyse der weiblichen Sexualfunktionen,* Vienna, 1925.

10

Chesler's interesting article points out that there are more female than male mental patients. Both black and white women are significantly more likely to have experienced a nervous breakdown or felt as if they were going to have one. Other symptoms of mental illness more likely to be experienced by women than men are nervousness, insomnia, and nightmares. These symptoms can also be found in female children. Chesler notes that males are more likely to reflect destructive hostility toward each other; females are more likely to express a self-critical and often self-destructive set of attitudes.

Chesler suggests that the reason more women than men are involved in psychotherapy is because it is one of the only two socially approved institutions [the other being marriage] for middle-class women. She claims both institutions isolate women from each other, both emphasize individual rather than collective solutions to women's unhappiness, and both are based on a woman's helplessness and dependence on a strong male authority figure. Both institutions allow a woman to express and diffuse her anger by experiencing it as a form of emotional illness. Each woman believes her symptoms are unique to her, are her own fault, and is unaware that they are really a result of social oppression.

Chesler provocatively suggests that male therapists stop treating women altogether, since the power relationship in which the woman submits to a dominant male authority is not conducive to the development of independence, or even a healthy dependence in the woman. Unfortunately, women prefer male therapists because they respect their competence and authority, feel more comfortable with them, and because they mistrust women both as authorities and as people.

Women as Psychiatric and Psychotherapeutic Patients*

Phyllis Chesler

This paper presents a feminist interpretation of mental illness based on national statistics, mental health surveys, psychological and sociological experiments, psychological analytic theories and practices, and on an original study. An analysis of NIMH statistics revealed that 125,351 more women than men have been psychiatrically hospitalized from 1964-1968. From 1950-1968, 223,268 more women than men were hospitalized in state mental asylums. Female patients generally outnumber males in private treatment, and both significantly prefer a male rather than a female therapist. These facts are discussed as one of the effects of sex-role stereotyping and the oppression of women.

Like all sciences and valuations, the psychology of women has hitherto been considered only from the point of view of men. It is inevitable that the man's position of advantage should cause objective validity to be attributed to his subjective, affective relations to women . . . the question then is how far analytical psychology also, when its researches have women for their object, is under the spell of this way of thinking (Horney, 1926).

Although Karen Horney wrote this in 1926, very few psychiatrists and psychologists seem to have agreed with and been guided by her words. Female psychology is still being viewed from a masculine point of view. Contemporary psychiatric and psychological theories and practices both reflect and influence our culture's politically naive understanding and emotionally brutal treatment of women. Female unhappiness is viewed and "treated" as a problem of individual pathology, no matter how many other female patients (or non-patients) are similarly unhappy—and this by men who have studiously bypassed the objective fact of female oppression. Woman's inability to adjust to or to be contented by feminine roles has been considered as a deviation from "natural" female psychology rather than as a criticism of such roles.

---

*From the *Journal of Marriage and the Family,* November 1971

I do not wish to imply that female unhappiness is a myth conjured up by men; it is very real. One of the ways white, middle-class women in America attempt to handle this unhappiness is through psychotherapy. They enter private therapy just as they enter marriage—with a sense of urgency and desperation. Also, black and white women of all classes, particularly unmarried women, comprise the largest group of psychiatrically hospitalized and "treated" Americans. This paper will present the following analysis:

1. that for a number of reasons, women behave in the manner labeled "mentally ill" more often and more easily than men do; that their "mental illness" is mainly self-destructive; and that they are punished for their self-destructive behavior, either by the brutal and impersonal custodial care given them in mental asylums, or by the relationships they have with most (but not all) clinicians, who implicitly encourage them to blame themselves or to take responsibility for their unhappiness in order to be "cured."

2. that both psychotherapy and marriage, the two major socially approved institutions for white, middle-class women, function similarly, i.e., as vehicles for personal "salvation" through the presence of an understanding and benevolent (male) authority. In female culture, not being married, or being unhappily married, is experienced as an "illness" which psychotherapy can, hopefully, cure.

This paper will discuss the following questions: What are some of the facts about women as psychiatric or psychotherapy patients in America. What "symptoms" do they present? Why are more women involved, either voluntarily or involuntarily with mental health professionals than are men? Who are the psychotherapists in America and what are their views about women? What practical implications does this discussion have for women who are in a psychotherapeutic relationship?

GENERAL STATISTICS

A study published in 1970 by the U.S. Department of Health, Education, and Welfare (Table I) indicated that in both the black and white populations significantly more women than men reported having suffered nervous breakdowns, having felt impending nervous breakdowns,[1] psychological inertia and dizziness.

---

1. At all age levels.

WOMAN: DEPENDENT OR INDEPENDENT VARIABLE?

TABLE 1. SYMPTOM RATES BY SEX, SEX AND AGE, AND SEX AND RACE

Symptom and sex	Total 18-79 years	Age 18-24 years	25-34 years	35-44 years	45-54 years	55-64 years	65-74 years	75-79 years	Race White	Negro
Nervous breakdown										
Male	3.2	1.3	1.8	3.5	3.0	5.4	5.4	1.5	3.2	2.8
Female	6.4	1.0	3.6	5.0	7.3	12.7	10.7	13.1	6.0	10.4
Felt impending nervous breakdown										
Male	7.7	6.9	7.4	8.6	11.7	6.4	3.1	2.2	7.7	8.2
Female	17.5	14.6	21.6	19.3	18.8	14.5	13.8	10.2	17.8	16.1
Nervousness										
Male	45.1	43.5	47.5	51.9	48.1	37.7	36.6	30.2	47.2	31.3
Female	70.6	61.4	74.4	75.0	72.5	72.6	62.9	65.6	73.2	55.2
Inertia										
Male	16.8	17.2	16.1	17.6	16.3	16.9	18.2	12.1	16.9	17.1
Female	32.5	31.0	34.0	35.2	31.1	29.7	31.9	35.6	33.1	29.5
Insomnia										
Male	23.5	20.4	16.7	20.8	26.8	27.0	35.9	26.5	24.1	20.4
Female	40.4	28.0	33.5	33.7	42.8	53.8	59.0	51.0	40.9	38.9
Trembling Hands										
Male	7.0	7.6	6.5	5.4	5.7	8.8	10.0	8.5	6.9	7.1
Female	10.9	10.4	12.2	12.1	10.6	9.3	9.2	13.0	10.6	12.3
Nightmares										
Male	7.6	5.7	9.4	7.7	7.7	8.2	5.8	6.5	6.9	13.0
Female	12.4	12.8	15.8	14.7	9.9	7.5	11.6	11.8	12.3	14.3
Perspiring hands										
Male	17.0	23.2	24.9	17.7	14.7	11.0	7.9	3.0	17.0	16.8
Female	21.4	28.6	27.7	24.2	19.6	15.0	9.2	5.9	22.2	16.0
Fainting										
Male	16.9	17.6	15.7	15.7	18.1	17.3	17.8	17.2	17.5	13.8
Female	29.1	28.5	33.2	29.9	27.0	26.2	29.7	24.8	30.4	20.5
Headaches										
Male	13.7	13.0	12.8	13.8	15.2	15.6	11.3	10.0	13.8	11.9
Female	27.8	24.0	31.6	29.6	29.5	25.9	24.2	19.3	27.5	30.9
Dizziness										
Male	7.1	6.3	3.0	5.0	7.6	10.7	12.8	14.3	6.9	9.2
Female	10.9	8.4	9.5	8.5	10.1	14.3	16.9	16.6	10.3	15.7
Heart palpitations										
Male	3.7	3.3	2.0	2.1	3.9	7.2	6.4	1.5	3.6	4.8
Female	5.8	1.7	3.1	4.7	6.2	9.7	10.4	14.8	5.7	6.4
SCALE MEAN VALUE										
Male										
White	1.70	1.72	1.70	1.72	1.78	1.69	1.66	1.19	1.70	....
Negro	1.55	1.25	1.03	1.37	1.79	1.87	2.23	2.99	....	1.55
Female										
White	2.88	2.61	3.07	2.93	2.89	2.86	2.82	2.80	2.88	....
Negro	2.65	1.91	2.61	2.60	2.52	3.27	3.79	2.62	....	2.65

Both black and white women also reported higher rates than men for the following symptoms: nervousness, insomnia, trembling hands, nightmares, fainting and headaches. White women who were never married reported fewer symptoms than white married or separated women. These findings are essentially in agreement with an earlier study published in 1960, by the Joint Commission on Mental Health and Illness. The Commission reported the following information for non-hospitalized American adults: (1) Greater distress and symptoms are reported by women than by men in all adjustment areas. They report more disturbances in general adjustment, in their self-perception, and in their marital and parental functioning. This sex difference is most marked at the younger age intervals. (2) A feeling of impending breakdown is reported more frequently by divorced and separated females than by any other group of either sex. (3) The unmarried (whether single, separated, divorced or widowed) have a greater potential for psychological distress than do the married. (4) While the sexes did not differ in the *frequency* with which they reported "unhappiness," the women reported more worry, fear of breakdown, and need for help. (Gurin, Veroff and Feld, 1960).

What such studies do not make clear, is how many of these "psychologically distressed" women are involved in any form of psychiatric or psychological treatment. Other studies have attempted to do this. William Schofield (1963) found that the average psychiatrist sees significantly more female than male patients. A study published in 1965 reported that female patients outnumbered male patients 3:2 in private psychiatric treatment (Buhn, Conwell and Hurley, 1965). Statistics for public and private psychiatric hospitalization in America do exist and of course, are controversial. However, statistical studies have indicated certain trends. According to NIMH statistics 125,351 more women than men were psychiatrically hospitalized and/or treated on an outpatient basis from 1964 through 1968. These facilities include general hospitals, private hospitals, state and county hospitals, outpatient clinics, Veterans' Administration hospitals and outpatient clinics, and excludes all private psychotherapeutic treatment. Between 1950 and 1968, 223,268 more women than men were hospitalized in state and county mental hospitals. Earlier studies have reported that admission rates to both public and private psychiatric hospitals are significantly higher for women than men (Maltzberg, 1959). Unmarried people (single, divorced or widowed) of both sexes are disproportionately represented among the psychiatrically hospitalized (Dayton, 1940; Sigler and Phillips, 1960). Thus, while according to the 1970 HEW report, single, white women in the general population report less psychological distress than married or separated white women, (Srole, 1962) women (as well as men) who are psychiatrically *hospitalized* tend to be unmarried.

Private psychotherapy, like marriage, is an integral part of middle class female culture. Patients entering private therapy betray significantly different attitudes towards men and women therapists. A number of them indicate that they feel sex is important in the therapeutic relationship by voluntarily requesting a therapist of a particular sex.

I have recently completed a study of 1,001 middle-income clinic outpatients (538 women and 463 men) who sought therapeutic treatment in New York City from 1965 to 1969. Patient variables, such as sex, marital status, age, religion, occupation, and so forth, were related to patient requests for a male or a female therapist at the time of the initial interview. These findings are based on a sample of 258 people (159 women and 99 men) who voluntarily requested either a male or a female therapist or who voluntarily stated that they had no sex-of-therapist preference. Twenty-four percent of the 538 women and 14 percent of the 463 men requested a therapist specifically by sex. The findings were as follows:

1. Sixty-six percent of the patients were single and 72% were under 30. Whether male or female, they significantly requested a male rather than a female therapis. ($x^2 = 17.2$ p $<$ .001.) This preference was significantly related to marital status in women ($x^2 = 12.6$ p $<$.02) but not in men ($x^2 = 4.4$ n.s.). Specifically, single women prefer a male therapist significantly more than a female therapist and significantly more than having no sex-preference at all ($x^2 = 21.7 <$ .001). This suggests that a woman may be seeking psychotherapy for very different reasons than a man; and that these reasons are probably related to or strictly determined by her relationship (or lack of one) to a man. The number of requests for female therapists was approximately equal to the number of "no preference" requests for both men and women. Age, rather than marital status, was a significant determinant of sex-of-therapist preference for men ($x^2 = 39.7$ p $<$.001) but not for women ($x^2 = 2.5$). Specifically, men under 30 prefer male therapists. Single women, under or over 30, of any religion, requested male therapists more often than married or divorced women did. Legally married women (N $=$ 21) requested female therapists more often than any of the other sample groups. Age and marital status were independent for men ($x^2 = 23.4$) and for women ($x^2 = 16.5$).

2. While all of the male patients regardless of their marital status requested male therapists rather than female therapists, some differential trends did exist. A higher percentage of divorced men

Phyllis Chesler

TABLE 2. PERCENTAGE DISTRIBUTION OF PATIENT THERAPIST
PREFERENCE, MARITAL STATUS, AGE, AND RELIGION

	Women (N=159)	Men (N=99)	Total (N=258)
Therapist preference	%	%	%
Male	49	40	45
Female	31	25	29
None	20	35	26
Marital Status			
Single	69	63	
Married/living with someone	17	24	
Divorced/separated	14	13	
Age			
Under 30	75	69	
Over 30	25	31	

	Women (N=59)				Men (N=99)			
Religion:	Jewish %	Catholic %	Protestant %	None %	Jewish %	Catholic %	Protestant %	None %
	40	19	16	25	41	22	14	23

(53 percent) requested male therapists, as compared with either divorced women (53 percent vs. 35 percent), married women (53 percent vs. 41 percent), married men (53 percent vs. 25 percent), or single men (53 percent vs. 44 percent). There was a significant relation between a male patient's request for a male therapist and his age (under thirty) and his religion: Specifically, 63 percent of the Jewish male patients (who composed 40 percent of the entire male sample and 73 percent of whom were under thirty) requested male therapists—a higher percentage than in any other group.

3. Some of the most frequent reasons given by male patients for requesting male therapists were: greater respect for a man's mind; general discomfort with and mistrust of women; and specific embarrassment about "cursing" or discussing sexual matters, such as impotence, with a woman.[2] Some of the most common reasons given by female patients for requesting male therapists were: greater respect for and confidence in a man's competence and authority; feeling generally more comfortable with and relating better to men than to women; and specific fear and mistrust of women as authorities and as people, a reason sometimes combined with statements about dislike of the patients' own mothers.[3]

2. One wonders why women are not equally "embarrassed" about discussing their impotence (frigidity) with male therapists.

3. This, as well as the significantly greater female preference for a male therapist, supports Goldberg's 1968 findings of female antifemale prejudice. See P. Goldberg, "Are women prejudiced against women," *Trans-action*, April 1968, pp. 28-30.

TABLE 3. THE RELATIONSHIP BETWEEN THERAPIST PREFERENCE AND
PATIENT MARITAL STATUS

	Female Preference			Male Preference		
Marital Status: Therapist Preference	Male %	Female %	None %	Male %	Female %	None %
Single	54	30	16	44	28	29
Married/living with someone	41	37	22	25	25	50
Divorced	35	26	39	53	23	23

In general, both men and women stated that they trusted and respected men—as people and as authorities—more than they did women, whom they generally mistrusted or feared.

Patients who requested a female therapist generally gave fewer reasons for their preference; one over-thirty woman stated that "only a female would understand another female's problems"; another woman stated that she sees "all males as someone to conquer" and is "less open to being honest with them." Almost all of the male patients who *gave reasons* for requesting a female therapist were homosexual. Their main reasons involved expectations of being "sexually attracted" to a male therapist, which they thought would distract or upset them. One nonhomosexual patient felt he would be too "competitive" with a male therapist.

4. Thirty-six percent of the male and 37 percent of the female patients reported generally unclassifiable symptoms during the initial clinic interview. Thirty-one percent of the female and 15 percent of the male patients reported depression as their reason for seeking therapy; 25 percent of the male and seven percent of the female patients reported active homosexuality; 15 percent of the female and 14 percent of the male patients reported anxiety; eight percent of the female and seven percent of the male patients reported sexual impotence; four percent of the male and three percent of the female patients reported drug or alcoholic addiction. The fact that at least twice as many female as male patients report depression, and almost four times as many male as female patients report homosexuality accords with previous findings and with national statistics.

5. Male and female patients remained in therapy for approximately equal lengths of time (an average of 31 weeks for males and 28 weeks for females). However, those men who requested male therapists remained in therapy longer than any other patient group (an average of 42 weeks compared to an

average of 30 weeks for females requesting a male therapist; an average of 34 weeks for male and 31 weeks for female patients requesting a female therapist; an average of 12 weeks for male and 17 weeks for female patients with a stated "no preference").

In other words, male patients who requested (and who generally received) a male therapist remained in treatment longer than their female counterparts. Perhaps one of the reasons for this is that women often get married and then turn to their husbands (or boy friends) as authorities or protectors, whereas men generally do not turn to their wives or girl friends as authorities, but rather as nurturing mother-surrogates, domestics, sex objects, and perhaps, as friends. They usually do not turn to women for expert advice; hence, when they decide they need this kind of help, they tend to remain in therapy with a male therapist. Female patients, on the other hand, can transfer their needs for protection or salvation from one man to another. Ultimately, a female patient or wife will be disappointed in her husband's or therapist's mothering or saving capacities and will continue the search for salvation *through a man* elsewhere.

PRESENTING SYMPTOMS

Studies of childhood behavior problems have indicated that boys are most often referred to child guidance clinics for aggressive, destructive (antisocial), and competitive behavior; girls are referred for personality problems, such as excessive fears and worries, shyness, timidity, lack of self-confidence, and feelings of inferiority (MacFarlane *et al.*, 1954; Phillips, 1956; Gilbert, 1957; Peterson, 1961; Terman and Tyler, 1954). This should be compared with adult male and female psychiatric symptomatology: "the symptoms of men are also much more likely to reflect a destructive hostility toward others, as well as a pathological self-indulgence . . . Women's symptoms, on the other hand, express a harsh, self-critical, self-depriving and often self-destructive set of attitudes" (Phillips, 1969). A study comparing the symptoms of male and female mental hospital patients, found male patients significantly more assaultive than females and more prone to indulge their impulses in socially deviant ways like robbery, rape, drinking, and homosexuality (Zigler and Phillips, 1960). Female patients were more often found to be self-deprecatory, depressed, perplexed, suffering from suicidal thoughts, or making actual suicidal attempts (U.S. Department Justice, 1969).

According to T. Szasz (1961), symptoms such as these are

"indirect forms of communication" and usually indicate a "slave psychology": "Social oppression in any form, and its manifestations are varied, among them being . . . poverty . . . racial, religious, or sexual discrimination . . . must therefore be regarded as prime determinants of indirect communication of all kinds (e.g. hysteria)."

At one point in *The Myth of Mental Illness* Szasz refers to the "dread of happiness" that seems to afflict all people involved in the "Judaeo-Christian ethic." Although he is not talking about women particularly, his analysis seems especially relevant to our discussion of female psychiatric symptomatology:

> In general, the open acknowledgment of satisfaction is feared only in situations of relative oppression (e.g., all-suffering wife vis-a-vis domineering husband). The experiences of satisfaction (joy, contentment) are inhibited lest they lead to an augmentation of one's burden . . . *the fear of acknowledging satisfaction is a characteristic feature of slave psychology.* (emphasis added)
>
> The 'properly exploited' slave is forced to labor until he shows signs of fatigue or exhaustion. Completion of his task does not signify that his work is finished and that he may rest. At the same time, even though his task is unfinished, he may be able to influence his master to stop driving him—and to let him rest—if he exhibits signs of imminent collapse. Such signs may be genuine or contrived. Exhibiting signs of fatigue or exhaustion—irrespective of whether they are genuine or contrived (e.g., 'being on strike' against one's boss)—is likely to induce a feeling of fatigue or exhaustion in the actor. I believe that this is the mechanism responsible for the great majority of so-called chronic fatigue states. Most of these were formerly called 'neurasthenia,' a term rarely nowadays used. Chronic fatigue or a feeling of lifelessness and exhaustion are still frequently encountered in clinical practice.
>
> Psychoanalytically, they are considered 'character symptoms.' Many of these patients are unconsciously 'on strike' against persons (actual or internal) to whom they relate with subservience and against whom they wage an unending and unsuccessful covert rebellion (Szasz, 1961).

The analogy between "slave" and "woman" is by no means a perfect one. Women have been conceptualized (Engels, 1942) as the first group to be enslaved by another group, and therefore, in some sense, as the prototypes for all subsequent forms of enslavement (along class or racial lines). Women are still conditioned to exhibit the signs and "symptoms" of slavery (in Szasz' sense), and *this* is what our culture, and our clinicians, recognize as "mental illness." When men exhibit "female" behavior they too are viewed, or view themselves, as "mentally ill." When women exhibit "male" behavior they too are often viewed as "mentally ill" (lesbians, "aggressive" career-women, "promiscuous" women, etc.). In general, men are conditioned to behave aggressively or "criminally." If they are poor or black men, they will often commit acts that will lead to jail, or to institutions for the "criminally insane." If they are white or wealthy men they will usually proceed with business and war as usual. They are not apt to receive or bestow upon themselves the "mental illness" label.

WHY ARE THERE MORE FEMALE PATIENTS?

Psychiatrists and psychologists have traditionally described the signs and symptoms of various kinds of real and felt oppression as mental illness. Women often manifest these signs, not only because they are oppressed in an objective sense, but also because the sex role (stereotype) to which they are conditioned is composed of just such signs. For example, Phillips and Segal (1969) report that when the number of physical and psychiatric illnesses were held constant for a group of New England women and men, the women were more likely to seek medical and psychiatric care. They suggest that women seek psychiatric help because the social role of women allows them to display emotional and physical distress more easily than men. "Sensitive or emotional behavior is more tolerated in women, to the point of aberration, while self-assertive, aggressive, vigorous physical demonstrations are more tolerated among men."

Women who are hospitalized, either voluntarily or involuntarily remain within the "female culture" which encourages and enforces a sense of worthlessness and dependency. Male mental patients are "punished" more than male convicts in that *all* mental patients are treated as women (as infantile, untrustworthy, "emotional," etc.).

It may be that more women than men are involved in psychotherapy because it — along with marriage — is one of the only two socially approved institutions for middle class women. That these two institutions bear a strong similarity to each other is highly significant. For most women the psychotherapeutic encounter is just one more instance of an unequal relationship, just one more opportunity to be rewarded for expressing distress and to be "helped" by being (expertly) dominated. Both psychotherapy and marriage isolate women from each other; both emphasize individual rather than collective solutions to woman's unhappiness; both are based on a woman's helplessness and dependence on a stronger male authority figure; both may, in fact, be viewed as reenactments of a little girl's relation to her father in a patriarchal society (Foucault, 1967); both control and oppress women similarly—yet, at the same time, are the two safest havens for women in a society that offers them no others.

Both psychotherapy and marriage enable women to safely express and defuse their anger by experiencing it as a form of emotional illness, by translating it into hysterical symptoms: frigidity, chronic depression, phobias, and the like. Each woman as patient thinks these symptoms are unique and are her own fault. She is neurotic, rather than oppressed. She wants from a psychotherapist what she wants—and often cannot get—from a husband: attention, understanding, merciful relief, a *personal solution*—in the arms of the right husband, on the couch of the right therapist (Steinem, 1970). The institutions of therapy and marriage not only mirror each other, they support each other. This is probably not a coincidence, but is rather an expression of the American economic system's need for geographic and psychological mobility, i.e., for young, upwardly mobile "couples" to "survive," to remain more or less intact in a succession of alien and anonymous urban locations, while they carry out the function of socializing children.

The institution of psychotherapy may be used by many women as a way of keeping a bad marriage together, or as a way of terminating it in order to form a good marriage. Some women, especially young and single women, may use psychotherapy as a way of learning how to catch a husband by practicing with a male therapist. Women probably spend more time during a therapy session talking about their husbands or boy friends—or lack of them—than they do talking about their lack of an independent identity or their relations to other women.

The institutions of psychotherapy and marriage both encourage women to talk—often endlessly—rather than to act (except in their socially prearranged roles as passive women or patient). In marriage the talking is usually of an indirect and rather inarticulate nature. Open expressions of rage are too dangerous, and too ineffective for the isolated and economically dependent women. Most often, such "kitchen" declarations end in tears, self-blame, and in the husband's graciously agreeing with his wife that she was "not herself." Even control of a simple—but serious—conversation is usually impossible for most wives when several men, including their husbands, are present. The wife-women talk to each other, or they listen silently to a group of women talking; even if there are a number of women talking and only one man present, the man will question the women, perhaps patiently, perhaps not, but always in order to ultimately control the conversation from a superior position.

In psychotherapy the patient-woman is encouraged—in fact directed—to talk, by a therapist who is expected or perceived to be as superior or objective. The traditional therapist may be viewed as ultimately controlling what the patient says through a subtle system of rewards (attention, interpretations, and so forth) or rewards withheld—but, most ultimately, controlling in the sense that he is attempting to bring his patient to terms with the female role, i.e., to an admission and acceptance of dependency. Traditionally, the psychotherapist has ignored the objective facts of female oppression. Thus, in every sense, the female patient is still not having a "real" conversation—either with her husband or her therapist. But how is it possible to have a "real" conversation with those who directly profit from her oppression? She would be laughed at, viewed as silly or crazy, and if she persisted, removed from her job—as secretary or wife, perhaps even as patient.

Psychotherapeutic talking is indirect in the sense that it does not immediately or even ultimately involve the woman in any reality-based confrontations with the self. It is also indirect in that words-—*any* words—are permitted, so long as certain actions of consequence are totally avoided (such as not paying one's bills).

WHO ARE THE PSYCHOTHERAPISTS AND WHAT ARE THEIR VIEWS ABOUT WOMEN?

Contemporary psychotherapists, like ghetto schoolteachers, do not study themselves or question their own motives or values as easily or as frequently as they do those of their "neurotic" patients or their "culturally deprived" pupils. However, in a 1960 study Schofield (1963) found that 90 percent of psychiatrists were male; that psychologists were predominantly males, in a ratio of two to one; and that social workers (the least prestigious and least well-paying of the three professional categories) were predominantly females, in a ratio of two to one. The psychologists and psychiatrists were about the same age, an average of forty-four

years; the social workers' average age was thirty-eight. Less than
five percent of the psychiatrists were single; 10 percent of the
psychologists, six percent of the social workers, and one percent
of the psychiatrists were divorced. In other words, the majority of
psychiatrists and psychologists are middle-aged married men,
probably white, whose personal backgrounds were seen by
Schofield as containing "pressure toward upward social mobility."
In 1960 the American Psychiatric Association totaled 10,000 male
and 983 female members.

What must further be realized is that these predominantly male
clinicians are involved in a political institution that has taken a
certain traditional view of women. A great deal has been written
about the covertly or overtly patriarchal, autocratic, and coercive
values and techniques of psychotherapy (e.g., Goffman, 1961;
Szasz, 1961; Bart, 1971; Scheff, 1966). Freud believed that the
psychoanalyst-patient relationship must be that of "a superior and
a subordinate." The psychotherapist has been seen—by his critics
as well as by his patients—as a surrogate parent (father or mother),
saviour, lover, expert, and teacher—all roles that foster "submission, dependency, and infantilism" in the patient: roles that
imply the therapist's omniscient and benevolent superiority and the
patient's inferiority (Freud, 1914). (Szasz has remarked on the
dubious value of such a role for the patient and the "undeniable"
value of such a role for the "helper.") Practicing psychotherapists
have been criticized for treating unhappiness as a disease
(whenever it is accompanied by an appropriately high verbal and
financial output); for behaving as if the psychotherapeutic
philosophy or method can cure ethical and political problems; for
teaching people that their unhappiness (or neurosis) can be
alleviated through individual rather than collective efforts; for
encouraging and legitimizing the urban middle-class tendency
toward moral irresponsibility and passivity; for discouraging
emotionally deprived persons from seeking "acceptance,
dependence and security in the more normal and accessible
channels of friendship" (Schofield, 1963). Finally, the institution of
psychotherapy has been viewed as a form of social and political
control that offers those who can pay for it temporary relief, the
illusion of control, and a self-indulgent sense of self-knowledge;
and that punishes those who cannot pay by labeling their
unhappiness as psychotic or dangerous, thereby helping society
consign them to asylums where custodial care (rather than
therapeutic illusions) is provided.

These criticisms, of course, apply to both male and female
therapy patients. However, the institution of psychotherapy differentially and adversely affects women to the extent to which it is

similar to marriage, and insofar as it takes its powerfully socialized cues from Freud and his male and female disciples (Helene Deutsch, Marie Bonaparte, Marynia Farnham, Bruno Bettleheim, Erik Erikson, Joseph Rheingold), viewing woman as essentially "breeders and bearers," as potentially warm-hearted creatures, but more often as simply cranky children with uteri, forever mourning the loss of male organs and male identity. Woman's fulfillment has been couched — inevitably and eternally — in terms of marriage, children, and the vaginal orgasm.[4]

In her 1926 essay entitled "The Flight from Womahood," Karen Horney says:

> The present, analytical picture of feminine development (whether that picture be correct or not) differs in no case by a hair's breadth from the typical ideas that the boy has of the girl.

We are familiar with the ideas that the boy entertains. I will therefore only sketch them in a few succinct phrases, and for the sake of comparison will place in a parallel column our ideas of the development of women.

The Boy's Ideas	Our Psychoanalytic Ideas of Feminine Development
Naive assumption that girls as well as boys possess a penis	For both sexes it is only the male genital which plays any part
Realization of the absence of the penis	Sad discovery of the absence of the penis
Idea that the girl is a castrated, mutilated boy	Belief of the girl that she once possessed a penis and lost it by castration
Belief that the girl has suffered punishment that also threatens him	Castration is conceived of as the infliction of punishment
The girl is regarded as inferior	The girl regards herself as inferior. Penis envy

---

4. The traditional psychoanalytic theories about women, especially Freud's, have been well and fully criticized by Karen Horney, Simone de Beauvoir, Clara Thompson, Natalie Shainess, Betty Friedan, Albert Adler, Thomas Szasz, and Harry Stack Sullivan.

The boy is unable to imagine how the girl can ever get over this loss or envy	The girl never gets over the sense of deficiency and inferiority and has constantly to master afresh her desire to be a man
The boy dreads her envy.	The girl desires throughout life to avenge herself on the man for possessing something which she lacks [5]

The subject of women seems to elicit the most extraordinary and yet authoritative pronouncements from many "sensitive" psychoanalysts:

Sigmund Freud:

(Women) refuse to accept the fact of being castrated and have the hope of someday obtaining a penis in spite of everything . . . I cannot escape the notion (though I hesitate to give it expression) that for woman the level of what is ethically normal is different from what it is in man. We must not allow ourselves to be deflected from such conclusions by the denials of the feminists who are anxious to force us to regard the two sexes as completely equal in position and worth (1956).

We say also of women that their social interests are weaker than those of men and that their capacity for the sublimation of their interests is less . . . the difficult development which leads to femininity [seems to] exhaust all the possibilities of the individual (1933).

Erik Erikson:

. . . young women often ask whether they can 'have an

---

5. Freud's indirect rejoinder, made in his 1931 essay entitled "Female Sexuality," is as follows: It is to be anticipated that male analysts with feminist sympathies, and our women analysts also will disagree with what I have said here. They will hardly fail to object that such notions have their origin in the man's "masculinity complex," and are meant to justify theoretically his innate propensity to disparage and suppress women. But this sort of psychoanalytic argument reminds us here, as it so often does, of Dostoevsky's famous 'knife that cuts both ways.' The opponents of those who reason thus will for their part think it quite comprehensible that members of the female sex should refuse to accept a notion that appears to gainsay their eagerly coveted equality with men. The use of analysis as a weapon of controversy obviously leads to no decision.

identity' before they know whom they will marry and for whom they will make a home. Granted that something in the young woman's identity must keep itself open for the peculiarities of the man to be joined and of the children to be brought up, I think that much of a young woman's identity is already defined in her kind of attractiveness and in the selectivity of her search for the man (or men) by whom she wishes to be sought (1964).

Bruno Bettelheim:

. . . as much as women want to be good scientists and engineers, they want first and foremost, to be womanly companions of men and to be mothers (1965).

Joseph Rheingold:

. . . woman is nurturance . . . anatomy decrees the life of a woman . . . When women grow up without dread of their biological functions and without subversion by feminist doctrines and therefore enter upon motherhood with a sense of fulfillment and altruistic sentiment we shall attain the goal of a good life and a secure world in which to live (1964).

These are all familiar views of women. But their affirmation by experts indirectly strengthened such views among men and *directly* tyrannized women, particularly American middle-class women, through the institution of psychotherapy and the tyranny of published "expert" opinion, stressing the importance of the mother for healthy child development. In their view, lack of—or superabundance of—mother love causes neurotic, criminal, psychiatric, and psychopathic children!

Most child development research, like most birth control research, has centered around women, not men: for this is "women's work," for which she is totally responsible, which is "never done," and for which, in a wage-labor economy, she is never directly paid. She does it for love and is amply rewarded—in the writings of Freud *et al.*

The headaches, fatigue, chronic depression, frigidity, "paranoia," and overwhelming sense of inferiority that therapists have recorded about their female patients have not been analyzed in any remotely accurate terms. The real oppression (and sexual repression) of women remains unknown to the analysts, for the most part. Such symptoms have not been viewed by most therapists as "indirect communications" that reflect a "slave psychology.'' Instead, such symptoms have been viewed as hysterical and neurotic productions, as underhanded domestic tyrannies manufactured by spiteful, selfpitying, and generally unpleasant women whose *inability to be happy as women* probably stems from unresolved penis envy, an unresolved Electra (or female Oedipal) complex, or from general, intractable female stubborness.

In a rereading of some of Freud's early case histories of female ''hysterics,'' particularly his *Case of Dora* (1952), what is remarkable is not his brilliance or his relative sympathy for the female ''hysterics,'' rather, it is his tone: cold, intellectual detective-like, controlling, sexually Victorian. He really does not like his ''intelligent'' eighteen-year-old patient. For example, he says:

> For several days on end she identified herself with her mother by means of slight symptoms and peculiarities of manner, which gave her an opportunity for some really remarkable achievements in the direction of intolerable behavior.

The mother has been diagnosed, unseen, by Freud, as having ''housewife's psychosis.''

L. Simon reviews the plight of Dora:

> . . . she (Dora) had been brought to Freud by her father for treatment of . . . tussis nervosa, aphonia, depression, and taedium vitae.' Despite the ominous sound of these Latinisms it should be noted that Dora was not in the midst of symptom crisis at the time she was brought to Freud, and there is at least room for argument as to whether these could be legitimately described as symptoms at all. If there was a crisis, it was clearly the father's. Nevertheless, Freud related the development of these 'symptoms' to two traumatic sexual experiences Dora had had with Mr. K., a friend of the family. Freud eventually came to explain the symptoms as expressions of her disguised sexual desire for Mr. K., which he saw, in turn, as derived from feelings she held toward her father. Freud attempted, via his interpretations, to put Dora in closer touch with her own unconscious impulses.
>
> . . . Indeed, the case study could still stand as an exemplary effort were it not for a single, but major, problem having to do with the realities of Dora's life. For throughout his therapeutic examination of Dora's unconscious Freud also knew that she was the bait in a monstrous sexual

bargain her father had concocted. This man, who during an earlier period in his life had contracted syphilis and apparently infected his wife . . . was now involved in an affair with the wife of Mr. K. There is clear evidence that her father was using Dora to appease Mr. K., and that Freud was fully aware of this . . . At one point Freud states: 'Her father was himself partly responsible for her present danger for he had handed her over to this strange man in the interests of his own love-affair.' But despite this reality, despite his full knowledge of her father's predilections, Freud insisted on examining Dora's difficulties from a strictly intrapsychic point of view, ignoring the manner in which her father was using her, and denying that her accurate perception of the situation was germane.

. . . Freud appears to accept fully the willingness of these men to sexually exploit the women around them. One even finds the imagery of capitalism creeping into his metapsychology. Freud's work with Dora may be viewed as an attempt to deal with the exploitation of women that characterized that historical period without even an admission of the fact of its existence. We may conclude that Freud's failure with Dora was a function of his inappropriate level of conceptualization and intervention. He saw that she was suffering, but instead of attempting to deal with the conditions of her life he chose—because he shared in her exploitation—to work within the confines of her ego (1970).

Although Freud eventually conceded (but not to Dora) that her insights into her family situation were correct, he still concluded that these insights could not make her "happy," Freud's own insights—based on self-reproach, rather than on Dora's reproaching of those around her—would hopefully help her discover her own penis envy and Electra complex; somehow this would magically help her to adjust to, or at least to accept, her only alternative in life: housewife's psychosis. If Dora had not left treatment (which Freud views as an act of revenge), her cure, presumably would have involved her regaining (through desperation and self-hypnosis) a grateful respect for her patriarch-father; loving and perhaps serving him for years to come; or getting married and performing these service functions for a husband or surrogate-patriarch.[6]

---

6. Freud was not the only one who disliked Dora. Twenty-four years later, as a forty-two-year-old married woman, Dora was referred to another psychiatrist, Felix Deutsch, for "hysterical" symptoms. Let me quote his description of her:

WOMAN: DEPENDENT OR INDEPENDENT VARIABLE?

Szasz (1961) comments on the "hysterical" symptoms of another of Freud's female patients, Anna O., who fell "ill" while nursing her father.

Anna O. thus started to play the hysterical game from a position of distasteful submission: she functioned as an oppressed, unpaid, sick-nurse, who was coerced to be helpful by the very helplessness of a (bodily) sick patient. The women in Anna O.'s position were—as are their counterparts today, who feel similarly entrapped by their small children—insufficiently aware of what they valued in life and of how their own ideas of what they valued affected their conduct. For example, young middle-class women in Freud's day considered it their duty to take care of their sick fathers. They treasured the value that it was their role to take care of father when he was sick. Hiring a professional servant or nurse for this job would have created a conflict for them, because it would have symbolized to them as well as to others that they did not love ('care for') their fathers. Notice how similar this is to the dilemma in which many contemporary women find themselves, not, however, in relation to their fathers, but rather in relation to their young children. Today, married women are generally expected to

---

The patient then started a tirade about her husband's indifference toward her offerings and how unfortunate her marital life had been . . . this led her to talk about her own frustrated love life and her frigidity . . . resentfully she expressed her conviction that her husband had been unfaithful to her . . . tearfully she denounced men in general as selfish, demanding, and ungiving . . . (she recalled that) her father has been unfaithful even to her mother . . . she talked mainly about her relationship to her mother, of her unhappy childhood because of her mother's exaggerated cleanliness . . . and her lack of affection for her . . . she finally spoke with pride about her *brother's* career, but she had little hope that her *son* would follow in his footsteps . . . more than 30 years have elapsed since my visit at Dora's sickbed . . . from (an) informant I learned the additional pertinent facts about the fate of Dora . . . she clung to (her son) with the same reproachful demands she made on her husband, who had died of a coronary disease— *slighted and tortured by her almost paranoid behavior, strangely enough, he had preferred to die . . . rather than divorce her. Without question only a man of this type could have been chosen by Dora for a husband. At the time of her analytic treatment she had stated unequivocally 'men are all so detestable that I would rather not marry. This is my revenge.' Thus, her marriage had served only to cover up her distaste of men . . . (Dora's) death from a cancer of the colon, which was diagnosed too late for a successful operation, seemed a blessing to those who were close to her. She had been, as my informant phrased it, 'one of the most repulsive hysterics' he had ever met.*

My italics. Felix Deutsch, A footnote to Freud's 'Fragment of an analysis of a case of hysteria,' *The Psychoanalytic Quarterly*, 1957, 26.

156

take care of their children; they are not supposed to delegate this task to others. The 'old folks' can be placed in a home: it is all right to delegate their care to hired help. This is an exact reversal of the social situation which prevailed in upper middle-class European circles until the First World War and even after it. Then, children were often cared for by hired help, while parents were taken care of by their children, now fully grown.

To Freud, it was to Anna's "great sorrow" that she was no longer "allowed to continue nursing the patient."

We may wonder to what extent contemporary psychotherapists still view women as Freud did, either because they believe his theories, or because they are men first and so-called objective professionals second: it may still be in their personal and class interest to (quite unmaliciously) remain "Freudian" in their treatment of women. Two studies relate to this question.

As part of Schofield's 1960 study, each of the psychotherapists were asked to indicate the characteristics of his "ideal" patient, "that is, the kind of patient with whom you feel you are efficient and effective in your therapy." Schofield reports that "for those psychotherapists who did express a sex preference, a preference for females was predominant in all three professional groups." The margin of preference for female patients was largest in the sample of psychiatrists, nearly two-thirds of this group claiming the female patients as "ideal".[7] From 60 to 70 percent of each of the therapist groups place the ideal patient's age in the twenty to forty year range. Very rarely do representatives of any of the three disciplines express a preference for a patient with a graduate degree (M.A., M.D., Ph.D.).

Summarizing his findings, Schofield suggests that the efforts of most clinical practitioners are "restricted" to those clients who present the Yavis syndrome—youthful, attractive, verbal, intelligent, and successful. And, we may add, hopefully female.

A recent study by Broverman et al. (1970) supports the hypothesis that most clinicians still view their female patients as Freud viewed his. Seventy-nine clinicians (forty-six male and thirty-three female psychiatrists, psychologists, and social workers) completed a sex-role stereotype questionnaire. The questionnaire consists of 122 bipolar items, each of which describe a particular behavior or trait. For example:

---

7. Less than one-third of the psychiatrists and one-fourth of the psychologists expressed a preferred sex in their ideal patient.

very subjective . . . very objective
not at all aggressive . . . very aggressive

The clinicians were instructed to check off those traits that represent healthy male, healthy female, or healthy adult (sex unspecified) behavior. Both male and female clinicians had different standards of mental health for men and women. Their concepts of healthy mature men do not differ significantly from their concepts of healthy mature adults, but their concepts of healthy mature women do differ significantly from those for men or for healthy adults. Finally, what is judged healthy for adults, sex unspecified, and for adult males, is in general highly correlated with previous studies of social desirability as perceived by non-professional subjects.

It is clear that for a woman to be healthy she must "adjust" to and accept the behavioral norms for her sex even though these kinds of behavior are generally regarded as less socially desirable. As the authors themselves remark, "This constellation seems a most unusual way of describing any mature, healthy individual."

Obviously, the ethic of mental health is masculine in our culture. Women are perceived as childlike or childish, as *alien* to most male therapists. It is therefore especially interesting that some clinicians, especially psychiatrists prefer female patients. Perhaps their preference makes good sense; a male therapist may receive a real psychological "service" from his female patient: namely, the experience of controlling and feeling superior to a female being upon whom he has projected many of his own forbidden longings for dependency, emotionality, and subjectivity and from whom, as a superior expert, as a doctor, he is protected as he cannot be from his mother, wife, or girl friend. And he earns money to boot!

SOME POLEMICAL CONCLUSIONS AND SUGGESTIONS

Private psychoanalysis or psychotherapy is a commodity available to those women who can buy it, that is, to women whose fathers, husbands, or boy friends can help them pay for it.[8] Like the Calvinist elect, those women who can *afford* treatment are already "saved." Even if they are never happy, never free, they will

---

8. There are many women who spend most of their salary on their "shrink," and who live with men or with their parents, usually under infantilizing conditions, in order to do so. One wonders who exactly, and how many at that, can pay for private psychoanalytic or psychotherapeutic treatment — treatment that costs anywhere from

be slow to rebel against their psychological and economic dependence on men. One look at their less-privileged (poor, black, and/or unmarried) sisters' position is enough to keep them silent and more or less gratefully in line. The less-privileged women have no real or psychological silks to smooth down over, to disguise, their unhappiness; they have no class to be "better than." As they sit facing the walls, in factories, offices, whorehouses, ghetto apartments, and mental asylums, at least *one* thing they must conclude is that "happiness" is on sale in America—but not at a price they can afford. They are poor. They do not have to be bought off with illusions; they only have to be controlled.

Lower-class and unmarried middle-class women do have access to free or sliding-scale clinics, where, as a rule, they will meet once a week with minimally experienced psychotherapists. I am not suggesting that *maximally* experienced psychotherapists have acquired any expertise in salvation that will benefit the poor and/or unmarried woman. I am merely pointing out that the poor woman receives what is generally considered to be "lesser" treatment.

Given these facts—that psychotherapy is a commodity purchasable, by the rich and most indirectly (in the form of psychiatric incarceration) inflicted on the poor; that as an institution, it socially controls the minds and bodies of middle-class women via the adjustment-to-marriage ideal and the minds and bodies of poor and single women via psychiatric incarceration; and that most clinicians, like most people in a patriarchal society, have deeply antifemale biases—it is difficult for me to make practical suggestions about "improving" therapeutic treatment. If marriage in a patriarchal society is analyzed as the major institution of female oppression, it is logically bizarre to present husbands with helpful hints on how to make their wives "happier." Nevertheless, wives, private patients, and the inmates of mental asylums already exist in large numbers. Therefore, I will make several helpful suggestions regarding woman, "mental illness," and psychotherapy.

Male psychologists, psychiatrists, and social workers must realize that as scientists they know nothing about women; their expertise, their diagnoses, even their sympathy is damaging, and oppressive to women. Male clinicians should stop treating women altogether, however much this may hurt their wallets and/or sense of benevolent authority. For most women the psychotherapeutic encounter is just one more power relationship in which they submit to a dominant authority figure. I wonder how well such a structure can encourage independence—or healthy dependence—in a

fifteen to fifty dollars per session, two to five times a week, for anywhere from two to five years. None but a small urban minority can afford such treatment at its supposed "best."

woman. I wonder what a woman can learn from a male therapist (however well-intentioned) whose own values are sexist? How free from the dictates of a sexist society can a female as patient be with a male therapist? How much can a male therapist empathize with a female patient? In *Human Sexual Inadequacy* (1970) Masters and Johnson state that their research supported unequivocally the "premise that no man will ever fully understand a woman's sexual function or dysfunction . . . (and the same is true for women) . . . it helps immeasurably for a distressed, relatively inarticulate or emotionally unstable wife to have available a female co-therapist to interpret what she is saying and even what she is attempting unsuccessfully to express to the uncomprehending husband and often to the male co-therapist as well." I would go one step further here and ask: what if the female cotherapist is male-oriented, as much of a sexist as her male counterpart? What if the female therapist has never realized that she is oppressed as a woman? What if the female therapist views marriage and children as sufficient fulfillment for women—except herself?

What "therapeutic" suggestions can I make? Obviously, if "mental illness" does exist, it is not effectively or humanely cured or even isolated in the psychiatric hospital. If it doesn't exist, psychiatric hospitals function as political prisons—for the aged, the young, the unmarried, the poor, the black, and the female. Private treatment for those who can afford it probably serves as a sub-stitute family or friendship institution, and very occasionally, as a legitimate form of religion (that of self-knowledge). However, at its best, if such private treatment does not incorporate a feminist awareness, female patients cannot, by definition, get "better."

REFERENCES

Bart, P. 1971 "The myth of a value free psychotherapy." In Wendell Bell and James May (eds.), Sociology and the Future. New York: Russell Sage Foundation.

Bettelheim, B. 1965 "The commitment required of a woman entering a scientific profession in present day American society." Woman and the Scientific Professions. Cambridge, Mass.

Broverman, I. K., et al. 1970 "Sex role stereotypes and clinical judgments of mental health." Journal of Consulting and Clinical Psychology 34.

Buhn, A. K., M. Conwell, and P. Hurley 1965 "Survey of private psychiatric practice." Archives of General Psychiatry 12.

Dayton, M. A. 1940 New Facts on Mental Disorders. Springfield, Ill.: Charles C. Thomas.

Engels, F. 1942 The Origins of Family, Private Property, and the State, New York: International Publishers.

Erikson, E. H. 1964 "Inner and outer space: Reflections on womanhood." Daedalus 93.

Foucault, M. 1967 Madness and Civilization. New York: Mentor Books.

Freud, S. 1914 "On the history of the psychoanalytic movement." Collected Papers 1.

― ― ― . 1933 New Introductory Lectures in Psychoanalysis. New York: W. W. Norton.

― ― ― . 1952 Case of Dora: An Analysis of a Case of Hysteria. New York; W. W. Norton.

Gilbert, G. M. 1957 "A survey of 'referral problems in metropolitan child guidance centers'." Journal of Clinical Psychology 13.

Gurin, G., J. Veroff, and S. Feld. 1960 Americans View Their Mental Health. New York: Basic Books.

Horney, K. 1967 "The flight from womanhood." In H. Kelman (ed.), Femimine Psychology. New York: W. W. Norton.

MacFarlane, J. et al. 1954 A Developmental Study of the Behavior Problems of Normal Children Between Twenty-One Months and Thirteen Years. Berkeley: University of California Press.

Maltzberg, B. 1959 "Important statistical data about mental illness." In S. Arieti (ed.), American Handbook of Psychiatry. New York: Basic Books.

Masters, W. H., and V. E. Johnson. 1970 Human Sexual Inadequacy. Boston: Little, Brown.

Petersen, D. R. 1961 "Behavior problems of middle childhood." Journal of Consulting Psychology 25.

Phillips, D. L., and B. E. Segal. 1969 "Sexual status and psychiatric symptoms." American Sociological Review 34.

Phillips, L. 1956 "Cultural versus intrapsychic factors in childhood behavior problem referrals." Journal of Clinical Psychology 12.

— — —. 1969 "A social view of psychopathology." In P. London and D. Rosenhan (eds.), Abnormal psychology. New York: Holt, Rinehart & Winston.

Pollack, E. S., R. W. Redick, and C. A. Taube. 1968 "The application of census socioeconomic and familial data to the study of morbidity from mental disorders." American Journal of Public Health 58 (1).

Rheingold, J. 1964 The Fear of Being a Woman. New York: Grune & Stratton.

Scheff, T. J. 1966 Being Mentally Ill: A Sociological Theory. Chicago: Aldine.

Schofield, W. 1963 Psychotherapy: The Purchase of Friendship. Englewood Cliffs, N. J.: Prentice-Hall.

Simon, L. J. 1970 "The political unconscious of psychology: Clinical psychology and social change." Unpublished manuscript.

Srole, L., et al. 1962 Mental Health in the Metropolis: Midtown Manhattan Study. New York: McGraw-Hill.

Steinem, G. 1970 "Laboratory for love styles." New York Magazine (February).

Szasz, T. T. 1961 The Myth of Mental Illness. New York: Harper & Row.

Termna, L. M., and L. E. Tyler. 1954 "Psychological sex differences." In L. Carmichael (ed.), Manual of Child Psychology. New York: John Wiley.

U. S. Department of Health, Education and Welfare 1970. Selected Symptoms of Psychological Distress. Washington, D.C.: U.S. Department of Health, Education and Welfare, Public Health Services, and Mental Health Administration.

U.S. Department of Justice 1970. Uniform Crime Reports— 1969. Washington, D.C.: U.S. Department of Justice, August 13.

Zigler, E., and L. Phillips. 1960 "Social effectiveness and symptomatic behaviors." Journal of Abnormal and Social Psychology.

11

Despite growing awareness of sex-role stereotypes, and despite criticisms of Freud and other therapists in terms of their sexist views of women, this study clearly shows the effect of these stereotypes on recent [1970] judgments of mental health. The negative reaction of feminist therapists to traditional psychotherapy is strengthened by the finding reported in the following study that men and women psychologists, psychiatrists, and social workers alike make a clear-cut distinction between the healthy man and the healthy woman. The healthy woman is more submissive, less independent, less aggressive, less competitive, more emotional, and more concerned with her appearance than is the healthy man. Even more damaging than this already negative assessment of women is the finding that the healthy male is not seen as different from the healthy adult [sex unspecified], whereas the adult and feminine concepts of health do differ significantly.

This double standard probably reflects the fact that clinicians expect women to adjust to a particular social role, i.e., that deemed desirable and acceptable by society for her sex. By accepting these stereotypes, clinicians help to perpetuate them, fostering conformity and restricting the choices open to women.

The authors point out that clinicians should carefully reexamine and revise their attitudes about sex role stereotypes and should learn to view mental health in terms of development of individual potential. Perhaps clinicians should be given special training in this and be made aware of the superficial slickness but long-term problems created by adherence to culturally determined sexual stereotypes.

This article should be "must" reading for clinicians, potential clinicians, patients and potential patients, as well as all those concerned with the treatment of women in therapy situations.

Sex-Role Stereotypes and Clinical Judgments of Mental Health*

Inge K. Broverman, Donald M. Broverman,
Frank E. Clarkson, Paul S. Rosenkrantz,
and Susan R. Vogel

A sex-role Stereotype Questionnaire consisting of 122 bipolar items was given to actively functioning clinicians with one of three sets of instructions: To describe a healthy, mature, socially competent (a) adult, sex unspecified, (b) a man, or (c) a woman. It was hypothesized that clinical judgments about the characteristics of healthy individuals would differ as a function of sex of person judged, and furthermore, that these differences in clinical judgments would parallel stereotypic sex-role differences. A second hypothesis predicted that behaviors and characteristics judged healthy for an adult, sex unspecified, which are presumed to reflect an ideal standard of health, will resemble behaviors judged healthy for men, but differ from behaviors judged healthy for women. Both hypotheses were confirmed. Possible reasons for and the effects of this double standard of health are discussed.

Evidence of the existence of sex-role stereotypes, that is, highly consensual norms and beliefs about the differing characteristics of men and women, is abundantly present in the literature (Anastasi & Foley, 1949; Fernberger, 1948; Komarovsky, 1950; McKee & Sherriffs, 1957; Seward, 1946; Seward & Larson, 1968; Wylie, 1961; Rosenkrantz, Vogel, Bee, Broverman, & Broverman, 1968). Similarly, the differential valuations of behaviors and characteristics stereotypically ascribed to men and women are well established (Kitay, 1940; Lynn, 1959; McKee & Sherriffs, 1959; Rosenkrantz et al., 1968; White, 1950), that is, stereotypically masculine traits are more often perceived as socially desirable than are attributes which are stereotypically feminine. The literature also indicates that the social desirabilities of behaviors are positively related to the clinical ratings of these same behaviors in terms of "normality-abnormality" (Cowen, 1961), "adjustment" (Wiener,

*From *Journal of Consulting and Clinical Psychology*, 1970, 34(1), 1–7.

I.K. Broverman, D.M. Broverman, Clarkson, Rosenkrantz, and Vogel

Blumberg, Segman, & Cooper, 1959), and "health-sickness" (Kogan, Quinn, Ax, & Ripley, 1957).

Given the realtionships existing between masculine versus feminine characteristics and social desirability, on the one hand, and between mental health and social desirability on the other, it seems reasonable to expect that clinicians will maintain parallel distinctions in their concepts of what, behaviorally, is healthy or pathological when considering men versus women. More specifically, particular behaviors and characteristics may be thought indicative of pathology in members of one sex, but not pathological in members of the opposite sex.

The present paper, then, tests the hypothesis that clinical judgments about the traits characterizing healthy, mature individuals will differ as a function of the sex of the person judged. Furthermore, these differences in clinical judgments are expected to parallel the stereotypic sex-role differences previously reported (Rosenkrantz et al., 1968).

Finally, the present paper hypothesizes that behavioral attributes which are regarded as healthy for an adult, sex unspecified, and thus presumably viewed from an idea, absolute standpoint, will more often be considered by clinicians as healthy or appropriate for men than for women. This hypothesis derives from the assumption that abstract notions of health will tend to be more influenced by the greater social value of masculine stereotypic characteristics than by the lesser valued feminine stereotypic characteristics.

The authors are suggesting, then, that a double standard of health exists wherein ideal concepts of health for a mature adult, sex unspecified, are meant primarily for men, less so for women.

METHOD

Subjects

Seventy-nine clinically-trained psychologists, psychiatrists, or social workers (46 men, 33 women) served as Ss. Of these, 31 men and 18 women had PhD or MD degrees. The Ss were all actively functioning in clinical settings. The ages varied between 23 and 55 years and experience ranged from internship to extensive professional experience.

Instrument

The authors have developed a Stereotype Questionnaire which is described in detail elsewhere (Rosenkrantz et al., 1968). Briefly, the questionnaire consists of 122 bipolar items each of which describes, with an adjective or a short phrase, a particular behavior trait or characteristic such as:

Very aggressive   Not at all aggressive

Doesn't hide emotions at all   Always hides emotions

One pole of each item can be characterized as typically masculine, the other as typically feminine (Rosenkrantz et al., 1968). On 41 items, 70% or better agreement occurred as to which pole characterizes men or women, respectively, in both a sample of college men and in a sample of college women (Rosenkrantz et al., 1968). These items have been classified as "stereotypic."

The questionnaire used in the present study differs slightly from the original questionnaire. Seven original items seemed to reflect adolescent concerns with sex, for example, "Very proud of sexual ability . . . not at all concerned with sexual ability." These items were replaced by seven more general items. Since three of the discarded items were stereotypic, the present questionnaire contains only 38 stereotypic items. These items are shown in Table 1.

Finally, in a prior study, judgments have been obtained from samples of Ss as to which pole of each item represents the more socially desirable behavior or trait for an adult individual in general, regardless of sex. On 27 of the 38 stereotypic items, the masculine pole is more socially desirable (male-valued items), and on the remaining 11 stereotypic items, the feminine pole is the more socially desirable one (female-valued items).

Instructions

The clinicians were given the 122-item questionnaire with one of three sets of instructions, "male," "female," or "adult." Seventeen men and 10 women were given the "male" instructions which stated "Think of normal, adult men and then indicate on each item the pole to which a mature, healthy, socially competent adult man would be closer." The Ss were asked to look at the opposing poles of each item in terms of directions rather than extremes of behavior. Another 14 men and 12 women were given "female" instructions, that is, they were asked to describe a "mature, healthy, socially competent adult woman." Finally, 15 men and 11 women were given "adult" instructions. These Ss were asked to describe a "healthy, mature, socially competent adult person" (sex unspecified). Responses to these "adult" instructions may be considered indicative of "ideal" health patterns, without respect to sex.

Scores

Although Ss responded to all 122 items, only the stereotypic items, which reflect highly concensual, clear distinctions between men and women, as perceived by lay people were anlayzed. The questionnaires were scored by counting the number of Ss that marked each pole of each stereotypic item, within each set of instructions. Since some Ss occasionally left an item blank, the proportion of Ss marking each pole was computed for each item. Two types of scores were developed: "agreement" scores and "health" scores.

The agreement scores consisted of the proportion of Ss on that pole of each item which was marked by the majority of the Ss. Three agreement scores for each item were computed; namely, a "masculinity agreement score" based on Ss receiving the "male" instructions, a "femininity agreement score," and an "adult agreement score" derived from the Ss receiving the "female" and "adult" instructions, respectively.

The health scores are based on the assumption that the pole which the majority of the clinicians consider to be healthy for an adult, independent of sex, reflects an ideal standard of health. Hence, the proportion of Ss with either male or female instructions who marked that pole of an item which was most often designated as healthy for an adult was taken as a "health" score. Thus, two health scores were computed for each of the stereotypic items: a "masculinity health score" from Ss with "male" instructions, and a "femininity health score" from Ss with "female" instructions.

RESULTS

Sex Differences in Subject Responses

The masculinity, femininity, and adult health and agreement scores of the male clinicians were first compared to the comparable scores of the female clinicians via *t* tests. None of these *t* tests were significant (the probability levels ranged from .25 to .90). Since the male and female Ss did not differ significantly in any way, all further analyses were performed with the samples of men and women combined.

CLINICAL JUDGMENTS OF MENTAL HEALTH

TABLE 1

MALE-VALUED AND FEMALE-VALUED STEREOTYPIC ITEMS

Feminine pole	Masculine pole
Male-valued items	
Not at all aggressive	Very aggressive

Not at all independent	Very independent
Very emotional	Not at all emotional
Does not hide emotions at all	Almost always hides emotions
Very subjective	Very objective
Very easily influenced	Not at all easily influenced
Very submissive	Very dominant
Dislikes math and science very much	Likes math and science very much
Very excitable in a minor crisis	Not at all excitable in a minor crisis
Very passive	Very active
Not at all competitive	Very competitive
Very illogical	Very logical
Very home oriented	Very worldly
Not at all skilled in business	Very skilled in business
Very sneaky	Very direct
Does not know the way of the world	Knows the way of the world
Feelings easily hurt	Feelings not easily hurt
Not at all adventurous	Very adventurous
Has difficulty making decisions	Can make decisions easily
Cries very easily	Never cries
Almost never acts as a leader	Almost always acts as a leader
Not at all self-confident	Very self-confident
Very uncomfortable about being aggressive	Not at all uncomfortable about being aggressive
Not at all ambitious	Very ambitious
Unable to separate feelings from ideas	Easily able to separate feelings from ideas
Very dependent	Not at all dependent
Very conceited about appearance	Never conceited about appearance

Female-valued items

Very talkative	Not at all talkative
Very tactful	Very blunt
Very gentle	Very rough
Very aware of feelings of others	Not at all aware of feelings of others
Very religious	Not at all religious
Very interested in own appearance	Not at all interested in own appearance
Very neat in habits	Very sloppy in habits
Very quiet	Very loud
Very strong need for security	Very little need for security
Enjoys art and literature very much	Does not enjoy art and literature at all
Easily expresses tender feelings	Does not express tender feelings at all

Agreement Scores

The means and sigmas of the adult, masculinity, and femininity agreement scores across the 38 stereotypic items are shown in Table 2. For each of these three scores, the average proportion of Ss agreeing as to which pole reflects the more healthy behavior or trait is significantly greater than the .50 agreement one would expect by chance. Thus, the average masculinity agreement score is .831 ($z = 3.15$, $p < .001$), the average femininity agreement score is .763 ($z = 2.68$, $p < .005$), and the average adult agreement score is .866 ($z = 3.73$, $p < .001$). These means indicate that on the stereotypic items clinicians strongly agree on the behaviors and attributes which characterize a healthy man, a healthy woman, or a healthy adult independent of sex, respectively.

TABLE 2

MEANS AND STANDARD DEVIATIONS FOR ADULT,
MASCULINITY, AND FEMININITY AGREEMENT
SCORES ON 38 STEREOTYPIC ITEMS

Agreement score	M	SD	Deviation from chance	
			Z	p
Adult	.866	.116	3.73	< .001
Masculinity	.831	.122	3.15	< .001
Femininity	.763	.164	2.68	< .005

Relationship Between Clinical Judgments of Health and Student Judgments of Social Desirability

Other studies indicate that social desirability is related to clinical judgments of mental health (Cowen, 1961; Kogan et al., 1957; Wiener et al., 1959). The relation between social desirability and clinical judgment was tested in the present data by comparing the previous established socially desirable poles of the stereotypic items (Rosenkrantz et al., 1968) to the poles of those items which the clinicians judged to be the healthier and more mature for an *adult*. Table 3 shows that the relationship is, as predicted, highly significant ($X^2 = 23.64$, $p < .001$). The present data, then, confirm the previously reported relationships that social desirability, as perceived by nonprofessional Ss, is strongly related to professional concepts of mental health.

The four items on which there is disagreement between health and social desirability ratings are: to be emotional; not to hide emotions; to be religious, to have a very strong need for security. The first two items are considered to be healthy for adults by clinicians but not by students; the second two items have the reverse pattern of ratings.

TABLE 3

CHI-SQUARE ANALYSIS OF SOCIAL DESIRABILITY
VERSUS ADULT HEALTH SCORES ON
38 STEREOTYPIC ITEMS

Item	Pole elected by majority of clinicians for healthy adults
Socially desirable pole	34
Socially undesirable pole	4

Note.—$\chi^2 = 23.64$, $p < .001$.

Sex-Role Stereotype and Masculinity versus Femininity Health Scores

On 27 of the 38 stereotypic items, the male pole is perceived as more socially desirable by a sample of college students (male-valued items); while on 11 items, the feminine pole is seen as more socially desirable (female-valued items). A hypothesis of this paper is that the masculinity health scores will tend to be greater than the femininity health scores on the male-valued items, while the femininity health scores will tend to be greater than the masculinity health scores on the female-valued items. In other words, the relationship of the clinicians' judgments of health for men and women are expected to parallel the relationship between stereotypic sex-role behaviors and social desirability. The data support the hypothesis. Thus, on 25 of the 27 male-valued items, the masculinity health score exceeds the femininity health score; while 7 of the 11 female-valued items have higher femininity health socres than masculinity health scores. On four of the female-valued items, the masculinity health scores exceeds the femininity health score. The chi-square derived from these data is 10.73 $(df = 1, p<.001)$. This result indicates that clinicians tend to consider socially desirable masculine characteristics more often as healthy for men than for women. On the other hand, only about half of the socially desirable feminine characteristics are considered more often as healthy for women rather than for men.

On the face of it, the finding that clinicians tend to ascribe male-valued stereotypic traits more often to healthy men than to healthy women may seem trite. However, an examination of the content of these items suggests that this trite-seeming phenomenon conceals a powerful, negative assessment of women. For instance, among these items, clinicians are more likely to suggest that healthy women differ from healthy men by being more submissive, less independent, less adventurous, more easily influenced, less aggressive, less competitive, more excitable in minor crises, having their feelings more easily hurt, being more emotional, more conceited about their appearance, less objective, and disliking math and science. This constellation seems a most unusual way of describing any mature, healthy individual.

Mean Differences between Masculinity Health Scores and Femininity Health Scores

The above chi-square analysis reports a significant pattern of differences between masculine and feminine health scores in relationship to the stereotypic items. It is possible, however, that the differences, while in a consistent, predictable direction, actually are trivial in magnitude. A t test, performed between the means of the masculinity and femininity health scores, yielded a t of 2.16 $(p \leq 05)$, indicating that the mean masculinity health score (.827) differed significantly from the mean femininity health score (.747). Thus, despite massive agreement about the health dimension per se men and women appear to be located at significantly different points along this well-defined dimension of health.

Concepts of the Healthy Adult versus Concepts of Healthy Men and Healthy Women

Another hypothesis of this paper is that the concepts of health for a sex-unspecified adult, and for a man, will not differ, but that the concepts of health for women will differ significantly from those of the adult.

This hypothesis was tested by performing t tests between the adult agreement scores versus the masculinity and femininity health scores. Table 4 indicates, as predicted, that the adult and masculine concepts of health do not differ significantly $(t = 1.38, p > .10)$, whereas, a significant difference does exist between the concepts of health for adults versus females $(t = 3.33, p < .01)$.

These results, then, confirm the hypothesis that a double standard of health exists for men and women, that is, the general standard of health is actually applied only to men, while healthy women are perceived as significantly less healthy by adult standards.

TABLE 4

RELATION OF ADULT HEALTH SCORES TO MASCULINITY
HEALTH SCORES AND TO FEMININITY HEALTH
SCORES ON 38 STEREOTYPIC ITEMS

Health score	M	SD
Masculinity	.827	.130
		$t = 1.38^*$
Adult	.866	.115
		$t = 3.33^{**}$
Femininity	747	.187

* $df = 74$, $p > .05$.
** $df = 74$, $p < .01$.

DISCUSSION

The results of the present study indicate that high agreement exists among clinicians as to the attributes characterizing healthy adult men, healthy adult women, and healthy adults, sex unspecified. This agreement, furthermore, holds for both men and women clinicians. The results of this study also support the hypotheses that (a) clinicians have different concepts of health for men and women and (b) these differences parallel the sex-role stereotypes prevalent in our society.

Although no control for the theoretical orientation of the clinicians was attempted, it is unlikely that a particular theoretical orientation was disproportionately represented in the sample. A counterindication is that the clinicians' concepts of health for a mature adult are strongly related to the concepts of social desirability held by college students. This positive relationship between social desirability and concepts of health replicates findings by a number of other investigators (Cowen, 1961; Kogan et al., 1957; Wiener et al., 1959).

The clinicians' concepts of a healthy, mature man do not differ significantly from their concepts of a healthy adult. However, the clinicans' concepts of a mature healthy woman do differ significantly from their adult health concepts. Clinicians are significantly less likely to attribute traits which characterize healthy adults to a woman than they are likely to attribute these traits to a healthy man.

Speculation about the reasons for and the effects of this double standard of health and its ramifications seems appropriate. In the first place, men and women do differ biologically, and these biological differences appear to be reflected behaviorally, with each sex being more effective in certain behaviors (Broverman, Klaiber, Kobayashi, & Vogel, 1968). However, we know of no evidence indicating that these biologically-based behaviors are the basis of the attributes stereotypically attributed to men and to women. Even if biological factors did contribute to the formation of the sex-role stereotypes, enormous overlap undoubtedly exists between the sexes with respect to such traits as logical ability, objectivity, independence, etc., that is, a great many women undoubtedly possess these characteristics to a greater degree than do many men. In addition, variation in these traits within each sex is certainly great. In view of the within-sex variability, and the overlap between sexes, it seems inappropriate to apply different standards of health to men compared to women on purely biological grounds.

More likely the double standard of health for men and women stems from the clinicians' acceptance of an "adjustment" notion of health, for example, health consists of a good adjustment to one's environment. In our society, men and women are systematically trained, practically from birth on, to fulfill different social roles. An adjustment notion of health, plus the existence of differential norms of male and female behavior in our society, automatically lead to a double standard of health. Thus, for a woman to be healthy, from an adjustment viewpoint, she must adjust to and accept the behavioral norms for her sex, even though these behaviors are generally less socially desirable and considered to be less healthy for the generalized competent, mature adult.

By way of analogy, one could argue that a black person who conformed to the "pre-civil rights" southern Negro stereotype, that is, a docile, unambitious, childlike, etc., person, was well adjusted to his environment and, therefore, a healthy and mature adult. Our recent history testifies to the bankruptcy of this concept. Alternative definitions of mental health and maturity are implied by concepts of innate drives toward self-actualization, toward mastery of the environment, and toward fulfillment of one's potential (Allport, 1955; Bühler, 1959; Erikson, 1950; Maslow, 1954; Rogers, 1951). Such innate drives, in both blacks and women, are certainly in conflict with becoming adjusted to a social environment with associated restrictive stereotypes. Acceptance of an adjustment notion of health, then, places women in the conflictual position of having to decide whether to exhibit those positive characteristics considered desirable for men and adults, and thus have their "femininity" questioned, that is, be deviant in terms of being a woman; or to behave in the prescribed feminine manner, accept second-class adult status, and possibly live a lie to boot.

Another problem with the adjustment notion of health lies in the conflict between the overt laws and ethics existing in our society versus the covert but real customs and mores which significantly shape an individual's behavior. Thus, while American society continually emphasizes equality of opportunity and freedom of choice, social pressures toward conformity to the sex-role stereotypes tend to restrict the actual career choices open to women, and, to a lesser extent, men. A girl who wants to become an engineer or business executive, or a boy who aspires to a career as a ballet dancer or a nurse, will at least encounter raised eyebrows. More likely, considerable obstacles will be put in the path of each by parents, teachers, and counselors.

We are not suggesting that it is the clinicians who pose this dilemma for women. Rather, we see the judgments of our sample of clinicians as merely reflecting the sex-role stereotypes, and the differing valuations of these stereotypes, prevalent in our society. It is the attitudes of our society that create the difficulty. However, the present study does provide evidence that clinicians do accept these sex-role stereotypes, at least implicitly, and, by so doing, help to perpetuate the stereotypes. Therapists should be concerned about whether the influence of the sex-role stereotypes on their professional activities acts to reinforce social and intrapsychic conflict. Clinicians undoubtedly exert an influence on social standards and attitudes beyond that of other groups. This influence arises not only from their effect on many individuals through conventional clinical functioning, but also out of their role as "expert" which leads to consultation to governmental and private agencies of all kinds, as well as guidance of the general public.

It may be worthwhile for clinicians to critically examine their attitudes concerning sex-role stereotypes, as well as their position with respect to an adjustment notion of health. The cause of mental health may be better served if both men and women are encouraged toward maximum realization of individual potential, rather than to an adjustment to existing restrictive sex roles.

REFERENCES

Allport, G. W. *Becoming.* Princeton: Yale University Press, 1955.

Anastasia, A., and Foley, J. P., Jr. *Differential psychology.* New York: Macmillan, 1949.

Broverman, D. M.; Klaiber, E. L.,; Kobayashi, Y.; and Vogel, W. Roles of activation and inhibition in sex differences in cognitive abilities. *Psychological Review,* 1968, *75,* 23-50.

Bühler, C. Theoretical observations about life's basic tendencies. *American Journal of Psychotherapy,* 1959, *13,* 561-581.

Cowen, E. L. The social desirability of trait descriptive terms: Preliminary norms and sex differences. *Journal of Social Psychology,* 1961, *53,* 225-233.

Erikson, E. H. *Childhood and society.* New York: Norton, 1950.

Fernberger, S. W. Persistence of stereotypes concerning sex differences. *Journal of Abnormal and Social Psychology,* 1948, *43,* 97-101.

Kitay, P. M. A comparison of the sexes in their attitudes and beliefs about women. *Sociometry,* 1940, *34,* 399-407.

Kogan, W. S.; Quinn, R.; Ax, A. F.; and Ripley, H. S. Some methodological problems in the quantification of clinical assessment by Q array. *Journal of Consulting Psychology,* 1957, *21,* 57-62.

Komarovsky, M. Functional analysis of sex roles. *American Sociological Review,* 1950, *15,* 508-516.

Lynn, D. B. A note on sex differences in the development of masculine and feminine identification. *Psychological Review,* 1959, *66,* 126-135.

Maslow, A. H. *Motivation and personality.* New York: Harper, 1954.

McKee, J. P., and Sherriffs, A. C. The differential evaluation of males and females. *Journal of Personality,* 1957, *25,* 356-371.

McKee, J. P., and Sherriffs, A. C. Men's and women's beliefs, ideals, and self-concepts. *American Journal of Sociology,* 1959, *64,* 356-363.

Rogers, C. R. *Client-centered therapy: Its current practice, implications, and theory.* Boston: Houghton Mifflin, 1951.

Rosenkrantz, P.; Vogel, S.; Bee, H.; Broverman, I.; and Broverman, D. Sex-role stereotypes and self-concepts in college students. *Journal of Consulting and Clinical Psychology,* 1968, *32,* 287-295.

Seward, G. H. *Sex and the social order.* New York: McGraw-Hill, 1946.

Seward, G. H., and Larson, W. R. Adolescent concepts of social sex roles in the United States and the two Germanies. *Human Development,* 1968, *11,* 217-248.

White, L., Jr. *Educating our daughters.* New York: Harper, 1950.

Wiener, M.; Blumberg, A.; Segman, S.; and Cooper, A. A. Judgment of adjustment by psychologists, psychiatric social workers, and college students, and its relationship to social desirability. *Journal of Abnormal Social Psychology,* 1959, *59,* 315-321.

Wylie, R. *The self concept.* Lincoln: University of Nebraska Press, 1961.

12

Benjamin Wolman is a faculty member in the Department of Psychology at Long Island University and a practicing clinician in New York City. Wolman considers himself a Freudian, but he disagrees with Freud's views on woman.

Wolman says power and the struggle for survival constitute the main drive of individuals, not sexuality. Male domination was biological, but based on man's superior physical strength and women's fertility, not based on the penis and vagina as such. Given these biological differences, the drive for survival explained many facets of the male-female relationship. The penis, the most obvious sign of masculinity, became a symbol of power.

Women were brainwashed as well as subjugated into accepting an inferior role. What Freud called "penis envy," Wolman calls a wish not for a sexual tool but for fatherly power. It reflects a protest against male domination and is not universal. However, for the women in Freud's circles, penis envy was a general phenomenon.

Wolman's theories are based on longitudinal studies from his clinical practice. He reports that "penis envy" is much more common among his older women patients, brought up with a traditional, controlling father, than with his younger women patients, brought up in families where this father supremacy didn't exist. Wolman also notes that in families where maternal authority is strong, some of his male patients wish to be women and display what he terms "breast envy."

To sum up, Wolman postulates the importance of power and survival as a basic drive, but whether this quest for power results in so called penis envy, breast envy, or neither one depends on the sociocultural setting, not merely on biological sex characteristics. Does this theory reflect a more feminist, less sexist approach to therapy for women? According to Wolman it does.

Between Men and Women

Benjamin B. Wolman

THEORETICAL PREMISES

One need not fall prey to anthropomorphism and ascribe human characteristics to the entire organic nature, but neither should one sterilize human behavior to make it resemble minerals or electrons. Whatever occurs in the world follows certain general laws, such as Newton's Laws of Gravitation and Einstein's $E = mc^2$. These general laws of inorganic nature apply also to the organic one, but the organic nature is subject to several new laws nonapplicable to the inorganic world; consider oxidation, metabolism, and growth. Moreover, as new species evolve, the new and intricate processes are determined by a set of entirely new and more complex laws. Thus, any reductionism that aims at presenting the totality of data of human behavior in terms of elementary biology, or tries to explain biology in terms of nuclear physics, does not do justice to either science.

FIGHT FOR SURVIVAL

One of the outstanding features of organic life is that life comes to an end. The unmistakable fact of death of the individual organism does not imply at all the end of organic life as such, for several organic processes continue in dead organisms. Moreover, while there is no evidence that the organic nature in general or any particular species resists annihilation, there is no doubt that practically all zoological organisms fight for survival and react to threats by fight or flight.

Darwin's laws of fight for survival and survival of the fittest do not apply to the entire nature or even to the entire organic nature. Darwinism is applicable to several zoological species and introduces a teleological or hormic element despite Darwin's avowed mechanistic determinism. One may, though, console oneself by saying that the apparent intent to stay alive does not contradict determinism. Any purposive behavior can be interpreted in the context of causal chain by posing the question why a certain organism sets a certain goal or acts in a goal-directed manner. There is no indication, however, that nature as such displays such a tendency.

The assumption that fight for survival is the main force in most if not all higher organisms led Darwin to the postulation of two innate drives, the instinct of survival of the species and the instinct of survival of the individual. Several scientists, among them Sigmund Freud, followed in Darwin's footsteps. Freud (1887-1902) originally postulated ego instincts related to the survival of the individual and libido instincts related to the survival of the species. Since all higher species procreate in a sexual manner, sexuality was believed to serve the survival of the species.

In the "Three Essays on Sexuality" (1905) Freud clearly distinguished between procreation and human sexual drive. The human sexual drive was freed by Freud from the procreative bind provided by Judaism and Christianity; Freud established the sexual drive as an independent and all-important motivating factor related to the search for pleasure. Freud's libido has become the single greatest driving force and the determining factor in psychological growth and development from birth to maturity. Freud's theory of psychosexual development included most aspects of human behavior, and the development stages of the libido was presented as the key factor in personality structure. Terms such as the "oral character," "polymorphous pervert," "object love," etc. bear witness to the all-important role ascribed by Freud to sexuality in personality development and human relations (Deutsch, 1945; Freud, 1898, 1931; Wolman, 1968).

THE PRIMACY OF SURVIVAL

The present essay is an attempt to prove that Freud's ideas were based on observations of a *particular* phenomenon in a *particular* cultural, historical setting, and they must be revisited and viewed in a broader perspective of biological and sociocultural factors. The biological factors have to be stated in terms of the *primacy* of the fight for survival and its universality, thus presenting sexuality as a second-order issue greatly colored by the primary biological drive for survival. The sociocultural factors will be related to the ever changing morals and mores and to the inevitably limited empirical studies.

POWER AND ACCEPTANCE

The fight for survival is apparently the most general biological law. All living creatures fear death, but as far as we know, human beings are the only ones capable of imagining, thinking, and anticipating real or unreal dangers. With the exception of ants, squirrels, and a few other species, most animals seek food only when they are hungry, and are unable to anticipate future shortages. No animals wage preventive wars or spend their entire life accumulating possessions they cannot possibly use, nor do any animals worry about remote or nonexisting threats to their lives.

Human beings seem to be the only species obsessed with the fear of not having enough to eat or of falling prey to their real or imaginary enemies. Fear of dangers makes one wish to be able to overcome them. Thus, the strongest human motive is, necessarily, the desire of being strong. If survival is the archlaw of nature, the urge for power is its necessary corollary.

Let us define "power" as the ability to defend oneself against enemies and to get food. Obviously the amount of power is measured by one's chances for survival. An organism is strong when it is endowed with tools and weapons that provide food and protect it against enemies; an organism is weak when it is poorly equipped. The peak of power is called omnipotence. An omnipotent being has all the power, that is, it can satisfy all its needs and ward off all threats. It cannot die of starvation or be killed by its enemies. Obviously omnipotence necessarily includes immortality. Living organisms operate on a continuum of greater or lesser amounts of power; the less power, the greater is the threat to their lives; the more power they have, the better the chance for survival. Death is the zero point of power; dead organisms cannot do anything.

Power can be used in two directions: it can help others to satisfy their needs or it can prevent their satisfaction. When one uses one's power for helping others, he is called by them friendly; when he hurts them, he is hostile. Let us call these two directions in which power can be used positive (friendly) and negative (hostile) acceptance.

One can present power and acceptance on quasi-Cartesian coordinates:

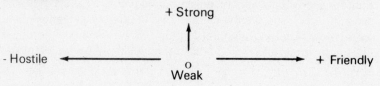

180

Power starts from zero to absolute omnipotence; acceptance is marked plus if friendly and minus if hostile (Wolman, 1956).

My assumption is that the striving for power is a derivative from the general drive for survival, which I call *lust for life*. Most of human actions are a direct outcome or indirect derivative of the lust for life, and those actions that do not seem to be related to survival are colored by this fundamental drive. The care for one's health and physical strength and prowess is a clear expression of the lust for life. Accumulation of property, production of food, housing, and clothing, the arms race and building fortunes and many other behavioral patterns represent overt and observable acts of this all-important drive.

Being strong may not suffice for warding off enemies, and one may try to *look strong* in order to win allies and deter enemies. Showing off power may serve as a useful and economical method in the fight for survival (Wolman, 1973).

MALE-FEMALE POWER RELATIONS

The fear of enemies and the need for allies is apparently the main reason for hostile and friendly feelings respectively. Undoubtedly, all interactional patterns, including the male-female relationships, are influenced by power and acceptance determinants. In the past and in present times the male-female relationships have been a mixture of economic cooperation, sexual attraction, display of force, domineering, dependence, aggression, alliance, and occasional tenderness. There is little if any evidence for the beautiful Upanishad myth quoted by Freud in "Beyond the Pleasure Principle," which assumed that

> the first human being on earth, Atman, felt no delight. Therefore a man who is lonely feels no delight. He wished for a second. He was as large as man and wife together. He then made this his Self to fall in two, and hence arose husband and wife. Therefore Yagnavalkya said: "We two are thus (each of us) like half a shell! Therefore, the void which was there is filled by the wife," [Freud, 1920, p. 58.]

Neither biology nor anthropology confirms such a complementarity, though there is no reason to exclude the possibility that some men and some women complement one another. Moreover, according to the Indian myth, it was the man Atman who had the need for a companion, and male superiority was set

181

thus in a subtle yet distinct manner.

Also the Hebrew myth of Adam and Eve seems to be a manmade story. The Bible tells that the man, Adam, was created first, despite the well-known fact that all men were born of women. Eve was a part of his body. Medieval Christian philosophers argued that women have no soul, for there is no mention of God giving a soul to Eve. And when the time of expulsion from the Garden of Eden came, God himself had to tell Eve: "He shalt rule over thee." Apparently, Adam needed an outside authority to impose his rule over the woman.

PHYLOGENETIC CONSIDERATIONS

Freud noticed that

> from the earliest times it was muscular strength that decided who owned things or whose will should prevail. Muscular strength was soon supplemented by the use of tools; the winner was the one who had the better weapons or who used them more skillfully. From the moment at which weapons were introduced, intellectual superiority already began to replace brute muscular strength; but the first purpose of the fight remained the same" [1932, pp. 274-75].

I maintain that the same reasoning applies to male-female relationships. With rare exceptions, described by Evans-Pritchard (1967), Mead (1949), Murdock (1949), and others, in practically all prehistorical and ancient societies men subjugated women. Women were pieces of property to be robbed or bought, used or abused. In badly underpopulated areas, women were a useful commodity. The ancient Romans raped the Sabine women, and practiced *ius vitae necisque* (the right of life and death) over their women and children. In ancient Hebrew the word *baal* stands for both owner and husband.

There were two sources of this male domination. The first was related to men's *physical strength,* and the second to *women's fertility.* These two biological factors need not be overlooked by researchers and social planners, for no matter how much one believes in equal rights for all people, one must not assume that an oversimplified egalitarianism and disregard of factual differences are conducive to democractic planning.

The fact that survival has always been the main preoccupation of mankind explains many aspects of the male-female relationship. Hunting and fighting against other human beings required maximum physical strength. Small wonder that many ancient tribes killed weak, sickly, and deformed neonates, and some others eliminated the old and infirm. It is therefore not surprising that men assumed or usurped the leader's role in primitive societies where physical prowess was the most important factor in the struggle for survival (Engels, 1965; Kardiner, 1939).

Female fertility was almost as important as the struggle for survival. In a primitive economy based on the number of working hands, one's wealth largely depended on the number of children one had. Prior to the system of mass slavery, production of children was one of the fundamental factors in an economy. With the advent of mass slavery in the era of the decline of the Roman Empire, the size of the family shrank and the incidence of homosexuality rose sharply.

In earlier times, in the shepherd type and early farming economies, having children was one of the most productive aspects of an economy. In the poorly populated lands only those who had many children had enough labor force for tending the herds, tilling the soil, and fighting off the neighbors. According to the Bible, the Lord promised Abraham that his progeny (the Chosen People) would be as numerous as the stars in the sky and the sand on the seashore. Such a promise would be a mixed blessing today.

There are, however, clear biological differences in the roles of men and women in reproduction. At best, a woman can produce fifteen to twenty children in her lifetime, but hardly any woman can provide adequate care for all her children. A man can fertilize several women, and if he possesses a large number of women, he can produce an army. Thus polygyny was not determined by male superiority or other differences between the mentality of men and women, but mainly by the difference in their respective roles in the reproductive process. Moreover, mothers and expectant mothers necessarily depended on their male partners for food and protection against enemies. The subjugation of women by men was not a product of psychological differences, but was brought about by a particular socioeconomic system where physical force was at a premium and child-bearing women could not provide food and shelter for themselves (Engels, 1960).

Power thus became the symbol of masculinity, and prophets and poets praised the virtues of being a male. The Latin word *virtus* (virtue) is derived from the word *vir*, which means a man. The Hebrew *gibbor* (hero) and *g'vurah* (courage) are derivatives of *gever* (male). In practically all languages *homo* (human being) is synonymous with an adult male. Wisdom, courage, leadership, and responsibility have been ascribed to men, despite the obvious fact that such a generalization flew in the face of evidence.

Rationalization (distortion of reality in defense of self-esteem) is probably older than rational thinking, for in all times cowardly, sheepish, submissive, and stupid men by far outnumber the brave, leading, self-assured, and wise men.

The innumerable cases of heroic women have been played down, partly silenced and often totally denied. The very same virtues praised in men were discouraged and ridiculed in women: brave, aggressive, and wise women were branded as pushy, arrogant, competing with men, and therefore nonfeminine. Cowardly men have been ridiculed as being "feminine," and brave women have been ostrasized for being "masculine." The owners of slaves have always preferred submissive, subservient, and dull slaves.

PENIS-PROUD MALES

The male sexual organ is undoubtedly the most obvious sign of masculinity. Besides being a source of sensual pleasure comparable to the tongue and palate, the penis has become a symbol of power. The penis has never played any outstanding role in the struggle for survival, but it has played a unique and spectacular role in procuring the feeling of power. The so-called virility, he-man feeling, male pride and other terms referring to the man's ability to sleep with women and produce children have been glorified as symbols of power. Small wonder that men took such a pride in this child-producing tool. I doubt whether male dogs, horses, bulls, and apes derive any pride at all from their mounting, inserting, and copulating proficiency, but human beings, thanks to their ability for symbolic thinking, have accepted the penis and its potency as symbols of virility and creativity. Such a correspondence was never proven.

The human species in its earliest gloomy, hungry, and danger-fraught origins had good reason for developing the myth of male pride and male supremacy. Eunuchs, impotents, and sexually passive males were ridiculed and ostrasized for they were of little help to their tribe, which badly needed speedy and abundant production of workers and warriors. Troubadours and other poets described the hero who fought bravely against enemies and conquered (that is fertilized) many women. Sexual achievements were praised for valid economic and military reasons, and all primitive religions adored the gods-fathers with erected penises ready for action.

DUAL STANDARDS

The ingenious Romans knew that they could defeat their enemies in combat but they could not rule them by sheer force. The very survival of male domination depended on brainwashing of their female slaves. Men, the *Herrenvolk,* enjoyed all freedoms and especially sexual freedom. In peace or at war men felt free to "conquer" (physically) any woman they could lay a hand on, but women were supposed to be faithful to their permanent or temporary users. Promiscuity in men was hailed as a great virtue and a noble sign of virility. Poets and troubadours glorified the great achievements of Don Juans, and every king and ruler, starting with the ancient Egyptian and Judean kings until the great French Revolution, was surrounded by a host of courtesans and ladies-in-waiting.

Women were not only subjugated but also brainwashed into a gracious acceptance of their subordinated role. They were told that to be feminine meant not to compete with men in intelligence, industry, initiative, maturity, and courage. The ideal woman as the men presented her was a strange mixture of infant-mother images. When men were in one of their artificially fanned heroic moods, their women were expected to be as soft, gentle, submissive, and obedient as an infant in a crib. Whenever men were tired, defeated, and hurt, their women were expected to act the sympathetic, affectionate, soothing, ever present and ever caring mother.

This brainwashing encompassed every aspect of a girl's life from cradle to grave. A little girl was told she must not act in a free, expressive manner as her brothers did. As she was growing up, all male-controlled educational systems trained her for her future role as man's toy, joy, and caretaker. She was not allowed to have her own desires and ambitions, and her thinking was as constricted as the toes of Chinese girls; obviously men feared that free-thinking and ambitious slaves might rebel and run away. Woe to a woman who dared to express her sexual desires! Pious medieval monks invented perverse-sadistic tortures for "women-witches" who were believed to have slept with no one else but the poor devils. The famous *"Malleus maleficarum* (witches' hammer) is a magnificent monument of projecting masculine perversions, combining blatant pornography with saintly rationalizations.

WOMAN: DEPENDENT OR INDEPENDENT VARIABLE?

PENIS ENVY

It took Freud's genius to discover what others tried to hide. Many little girls wished they were boys, for this was the only, though imaginery, way of escaping discrimination and subservience. Young men could go whereever they pleased, talk to whoever they wished to, and choose the occupation they liked, but a girl was her father's slave until he agreed to transfer her to her future husband. Marriage was, in a way, the only way of escaping father's tyranny, but the marital oath committed the woman to love, honor, and obey her new master. Most women preferred new masters to old ones, and some of them somehow managed to outsmart their marital partners.

In the Victorian era, marriage was the only socially acceptable avenue for women. Unmarried women were ridiculed, ostrasized, and blamed for remaining single. When a girl was unhappy being a girl and preferred an active and independent life pattern, she was called tomboy, amazon, and masculine, and to be feminine meant to cruise between infantile dependence and motherly worries. When a woman refused to accept the three great feminine Ks, *Kuche, Kirche, Kinder* (kitchen, church, and children), she was treated as an outcast.

In Freud's time masculinity and femininity could have been described as follows:

> When you say "masculine" you mean as a rule "active," and when you say "feminine" you mean passive. . . . The male sexual cell is active and mobile; it seeks out the female one, while the latter is stationary and waits passively. This behavior of the elementary organism of sex is more or less a model of the behavior of the individuals of each sex in sexual intercourse. The male pursues the female for the purpose of sexual unity, seizes her and pushes his way into her [Freud, 1932, p. 156].

Freud did not invent penis envy, but discovered this fairly widespread phenomenon. It stands to reason that the more restrictions were imposed on girls, the more frequent was the wish to escape the yoke by a magic switching to the opposite sex. Some of my female patients dreamed about switching the railroad tracks.

Penis envy was never a general feeling common to all women at all times; certainly the Tschambuli or Arapesh women never had any reason for such an envy. Arapesh men and women shared household and child-rearing responsibilities, and the Tschambuli women were the dominating sex (Murdock, 1949).

Freud's clinical observations of penis envy in women who were reared in an atmosphere of discrimination and subjugation must be interpreted in light of another hypothesis brought forward by Freud, the tendency of the child to identify with the "strong aggressor" (Fenichal, 1945). In patriarchal families, the father was the absolute ruler, and the male and female children were proud to identify with the father rather than the mother. All of Freud's writings stress the preference for a masculine father-based superego (Freud, 1938).

One must therefore interpret penis envy in girls not as an envy of their little brothers or playmates but rather as a wish for the possession of the large fatherly penis, and with it the *fatherly power*. Penis envy does not seem to be a general and universal element of female psychology but should be perceived as the *feminine protest against male domination*. The penis, as the cherished symbol of power, was envied by women not because it was a sexual tool, for their vaginas can undoubtedly procure as much and often more sensual pleasure than the penis; it was the penis as the *power symbol* that elicited the well-understood envy feelings (Horney, 1937; Kelman, 1967; Millett, 1970).

THE MOTHER-WHORE COMPLEX

One can readily invoke socioeconomic reasons for the subjugation of women in olden times and explain the currently ongoing rebellion of women in terms of the technological development. There is, however, an important aspect of the male-female relationship which escapes such an interpretation, namely the mother-whore complex, that is, the idealization and debasement of women by men.

The reasons for this ambivalent attitude go beyond economic exigency.

All men, whether they like it or not, were carried, born, and fed by women through the periods of conception, pregnancy, birth, infancy, and many years thereafter. Not all men resent this fact; thus whatever will be said below concerning the mother-whore complex does not bear the stamp of generality.

For every human being, male and female alike, the mother is the prototype of a *friendly power*. The mother is the main, if not the only, source of life, and the bulwark of survival. The adoration of mother is ontogenetically typical for all infants, and phylogenetically typical for periods of oppression and despair. The

187

adoration of the Holy Mother is a case in point.

One seeks support of a friendly power as long as one feels weak and expects to receive unconditional support, but such an ideal relationship may not last very long. Infants "love" the "good" mother who unconditionally satisfies their wishes but they hate the same mother whenever she refuses to meet their demands. Ambivalent feelings toward powerful protectors are an inevitable product of dependence and rebellion against being weak and dependent. Welfare recipients do not waste love on their benefactors, and poor relatives often resent their wealthy supporters.

The ambivalent feeling toward the mother is shared by little boys and little girls, and this ambivalence has been perpetuated throughout generations, taking on various forms and shapes. Rarely if ever a woman resolved her antimother feelings, and in Freud's times it was acceptable for young women to displace hatred on their mothers-in-law. Freud interpreted this phenomenon as a residue of the castration complex; the symbolic loss of a penis represented a loss of power and dominance, and of the privileged male status.

The boys' ambivalent feelings toward the mother has been usually channeled into a mother-whore complex. Even most cowardly and ineffectual men can play the role of a strong man and discharge brute force toward someone weaker than themselves. Women were the choice target, and male-controlled public opinion was and perhaps still is in favor of the "masculine assertion" toward women and children (Lederer, 1968; Unger, 1973).

The possession of a penis has given men an additional tool to use in humiliating women and in self-aggrandizement. The sexual act as such is neither particularly beautiful nor ugly; like almost everything else in human life, it can be practiced in a most lofty and most base manner, but the allegedly aggressive and domineering act of insertion was often represented as a debasement of women.

The ambivalent male attitude toward women has been immortalized in poetry and in obscenity. Poets sang songs of the beautiful godlike creatures they admired and desired, while uninspired and less sophisticated men used colorful terms to denote their disrespect for whatever one can do with women. This polarization has been well expressed in the medieval adoration of the mother image, the Holy Virgin (she must stay a virgin to become holy), and the malicious persecution of women under the guise of witchcraft. Even today, in colloquial Italian the expression *porca Madonna* (Madonna the pig) conveys the simple message: even the Virgin was an abominable creature.

Benjamin B. Wolman

THE EMANCIPATION OF WOMEN

Errors die hard and the owl of wisdom is a notorious latecomer. The demand for equal rights for women came one century later than it was due. The emancipation of women was started by men themselves for not too noble reasons: men needed women to work for them. Such an occurrence does not represent a significant deviation from other historical occurrences. Christians were liberated by a Roman Emperor, Jews by the French Revolution, and Russian workers assumed power under the leadership of a scion of an aristocratic family.

The industrial Revolution with its insatiable need for working hands pulled out thousands of women from hearth and crib. The decline of the feudal system and the rapidly diminished role played by agriculture forced large masses of women into the open labor markets of the budding capitalist economy.

Women's participation in the production and distribution of goods, that is in the economic struggle for survival, has irrevocably changed their psychosocial roles. The masculine role of provider, which was the backbone of the traditional male-dominated family structure, began to crack, and presently it is heading toward a hitherto unknown crisis (Ackerman, 1958).

The erosion of the traditional male-female relationship started in the lowest and the highest social classes. The middle classes have been notoriously the bullwark of conservatism, and Freud's patients came from highly conservative middle-class families where fathers exercised an absolute power. Thus penis envy was probably an almost general phenomenon among Freud's female patients.

The present-day family constellation deprived the father of his authority but it did not replace it by any other authority. One can't help wondering what will happen in our times to the Oedipus complex, the latency period, and the whole area of male-female relationships, but as things stand today, the balance of power is no longer on one side only. Modern women have destroyed the myth of their intellectual inferiority and denied, in vivo, the assumption of their either cherub or witch personality.

THE CHANGING PATTERNS

Not all men love women, nor do all men hate them, nor does the one attitude exclude the other. This relationship is not necessarily reciprocal, but neither is the female-male relationship diametrically different from the male-female attitudes. There has been a good deal of speculation and little factual knowledge concerning the characteristics of the two sexes and their interaction, though this area of behavior is secondary in importance to breadwinning behavior only. From the inception of sexual reproduction, that is since the times when females began to bear children (males never did), the child versus mother relationship has been the first social and emotional experience in everyone's life. The first prenatal impressions are the intrauterine ones; the first serious shock of separation is childbirth; the first sensations of hunger, thirst, satiation, comfort, warmth, and security are experienced in the context of child-mother relationships.

Several psychoanalytically oriented research workers, among them Anna Freud, Sybel Escalona, Marianne Kris, and Katherine Wolff, have embarked upon validating Freud's ideas concerning early childhood. Some psychoanalysts, notably Otto Rank and Melanie Klein, developed speculative hypotheses concerning the earliest psychological experiences. Most of these studies and hypothetic descriptions of those earliest interindividual relationships are inevitably based on *ex post facto* findings, for the ability for verbal communication develops at a much later stage, and experimental studies similar to those practiced in comparative psychology are unthinkable in human beings. Even purely descriptive studies such as those conducted by the Soviet pedologists in the third and fourth decades of our century and by several American psychologists, starting with J. B. Watson and A. Gesell, are neither too precise nor too enlightening, simply because a tender age is not too conducive to objective research.

My own study of the topic represents a series of *ex post facto,* party longitudinal case studies related to psychotherapeutic practice. Some of my patients communicated feelings and attitudes that reached far back into infancy. Hardly anyone had clear recollections of their first two years of life, but the analysis of the dreams and anxiety states presented fertile ground for inferential hypotheses.

BREAST ENVY

This sociological structure has inevitably brought new psychological phenomena. Neonates still need tender loving care, and their feelings of security (and power) depend on being accepted by the parents. However, today's toddlers and preschool children fear their fathers much less than previous generations did. Rarely a mother threatens the child to tell on him to the father; in a great many of the cases I saw in clinical practice, maternal authority was equal to or greater than the paternal.

In view of these psychosocial changes, I have not been surprised to notice that some of my male patients had dreams indicative of their wish to be women. In some dreams the breasts appeared as the cherished possession, and the confusion of penis and breast has been quite frequent.

On the basis of my clinical observations, I venture to hypothesize that neither men nor women can completely resolve their Oedipal involvements, whether the positive ones (with the parent of the opposite sex) or the negative (with the parent of the same sex). Some residuum of the "first love" for the parent or the parent substitute seems to remain forever in almost all people.

While there is a good deal of evidence concerning the universality of the Oedipal involvement (though it is necessarily different in different cultures), one may doubt the universality of penis envy. In twenty years of clinical practice in this country, I had a great many women patients. Going through my case reports, I arrived at the conclusion that penis envy was more frequent among the older generation of women, brought up in traditional father-controlled families with a clear male supremacy, then in the younger generation of women brought up in families with a tenuous or nonexistent father supremacy. Freud's observation of identification with the stronger parental figure seems to have been corroborated by my cases.

The male wish to be a woman was noticed by some psychoanalysts a long time ago. Fenichel (1945, p. 336) noticed that many men who are not homosexual at all identify with their mothers and later with their girl friends. In some cases, feminine men deny that becoming a girl may mean the loss of the penis and "they try to stress the fact that they actually have a penis while acting as though they were girls; thus they are girls with penises."

The gradually increasing incidence of breast-envy requires further study. At the present time, all that could be said is a sociocultural speculation. It seems that many ideas, theories, and even empirical studies have been influenced by the sociocultural setting. For instance, Terman and Miles found in 1936 that men are self-assertive and aggressive while women are compassionate and sympathetic. But these were the ideas of the thirties. Today, some studies indicate that aggressiveness is not limited to one sex only (Bernard, 1971).

REFERENCES

Ackerman, N. W. *The psychodynamics of family life.* New York: Basic Books, 1958.

Bernard, S. Aggression in women. In J. Agel (ed.), *The radical therapist.* New York: Ballatine Books, 1971.

Deutsch, H. *The psychology of women,* 2 vols. New York: Grune & Stratton, 1945.

Engels, F. *The origin of the family, private property and the state.* Moscow: Foreign Languages Publishing House, 1960.

Epstein, C. F. *Women's place.* Berkeley: University of California Press, 1971.

Evans-Pritchard, E. E. *The position of women in primitive societies.* New York: Free Press, 1965.

Fenichel, O. *Psychoanalytic theory of neurosis.* New York: Norton, 1945.

Freud, S. *The origins of psychoanalysis: Letters to Wilhelm Fliess, drafts and notes* (1887-1902). New York: Basic Books, 1954.

— — —. Sexuality in the etiology of neurosis (1898). *Standard edition,* vol. 1, 1962, pp. 263-86.

— — —. Female sexuality (1931). *Standard edition,* vol. 21, pp. 225-43.

— — —. *An outline of psychoanalysis* (1938). New York: Norton, 1949.

— — —. *New introductory lectures on psychoanalysis* (1932). New York: NOrton, 1933.

— — —. Beyond the pleasure principle (1920). *Standard edition,* vol. 18, pp. 7-64.

— — —. Three essays on sexuality (1905). *Standard edition,* vol. 7, pp. 130-245.

Horney, K. *The neurotic personality of our time.* New York: Norton, 1937.

Kardiner, A. *The individual and His Society.* New York: Columbia University Press, 1939.

Kelman, H., ed. *Feminine psychology.* New York: Norton, 1967.

Lederer, W. *The fear of women.* New York: Harcourt Brace Jovanovich, 1968.

Mead, M. *Male and female.* New York: Morrow, 1949.

Millett, K. *sexual politics.* New York: Doubleday, 1970.

Murdock, G. *Social structure.* New York: Macmillan, 1949.

Terman, L. M., and Miles, C. C. *Sex and personality.* New York: McGraw-Hill, 1936.

Unger, R. K. Are women discriminated against? *International Journal of Group Tensions,* 1973, *4,* 71-81.

Wolman, B. B. *The unconscious mind: The meaning of*

Freudian psychology. Englewood Cliffs, N.J.: Prentice-Hall, 1968.

— — —. Leadership and group dynamics. *Journal of Social Psychology,* 1956, *43,* 11-25.

— — —. Call no man normal: New ideas on mental disorders. New York: International Universities Press, 1973.

13

Jean Mundy is a faculty member at Long Island University and a practicing psychologist in New York. She is a feminist and active in women's groups. Mundy's views of women are quite different from those of her colleague Wolman, although they too have emerged from working with women in her practice. They are not based on empirical data.

Mundy feels that because of the role conflicts and contradictions that women have to contend with, they harbor a great deal of anger. Because of cultural standards, they must either repress this rage, converting it unconsciously into other symptoms, or use the anger to attack those who attack the "feminine" model. If they do express anger, they feel guilty and sick, focusing on the feeling rather than on the provoking situation. Passivity can become both a demand and an expression of rage.

Mundy says that the first step in therapy is for the patient to acknowledge her rage. The therapist must help the patient realize it is all right for her to express her anger and that there may even be advantages in being openly aggressive. Expressing her feelings and not tranquilizing them is important for the woman. Only in this way can she really derive help and be set free.

It is impossible to say that this theory fits the needs of all therapists for all women. Empirical evidence in support of this or any of the theories is unavailable. However, Mundy's views as well as those of Wolman and other therapists reflect a trend toward pro-women and antitraditional views. Not all therapists see all women in the light of the traditional sex stereotypes and models.

Women In Rage: A Psychological Look at the Helpless Heroine

Jean Mundy

When one wants or is expected to belong to a group, and the requirements for membership appear to be contradictory, con- fusion results. Men who try to be masculine and women who try to be feminine according to contemporary cultural dictates may find themselves trying to reconcile opposites. The male tries to be strong but silent, tender but tough (see Ruitenbeek, 1967). The female tries to be helpless but helpful in an attempt to reconcile the antithetic positions of "naturally passive" but "naturally" a competent mother. Diametrically opposed qualities are attributed to each of the sex roles. To resolve the dilemma, the individual may switch from one mode of behavior to another in rapid succession, or even try two modes simultaneously.

Conflicts are generated in men and women in most cultures. This paper will give an overview of the psychological repercussions of one conflict induced by our culture: passivity verses activity. Though the psychology of men has much in common with the psychology of women, this conflict is of particular importance to the psychology of women because women are often taught that it is not feminine to be very active. Women are likely to inhibit direct expression of aggression in particular, and because of such inhibition are likely to harbor more anger than men, and express this anger in self-defeating ways.

Being expected to live up to a contradictory model is one of the causes of rage. In this chapter I shall first sketch one source of anger embedded in the cultural expectations (myths) associated with becoming a woman. When direct expression of rage is blocked, as it often is in women who believe the expression to be unfeminine, other indirect expressions occur. These indirect ex- pressions subsequently complicate social relationships.

Second, the core of this paper will be a discussion of some of the forms that rage may take in the lives of women who seek therapy. These examples are not logically distinct, nor do they represent progressive degrees of pathology or point to a coherent theory. They are highlighted here because they contain the common

196

denominator, aggression. The main types are (*a*) physical disorders, (*b*) sexual behavir disorders, (*c*) social disorders, and (*d*) agitated depression.

Finally, a recommendation is made that the therapist do everything possible to help the woman become aware of the aggressive components of her behavior. With new awareness, and acceptance of activity as appropriate behavior for a woman, she may be free to express constructively both her desire to be passive and her desire to be active.

ONE SOURCE OF RAGE IN WOMEN: ROLE CONFLICT

The inherently contradictary models of Eve, the source of sin and death in the world, and Mary, the paradigm of perfect virtue and renewed life, may have sprung from the biological functions of women. Because womenibleed periodically (a sign of dying to the primitive) and give birth, they are taken to be both the source of death and of life. Karen Horney (1932), states that men fear women because the mystery of motherhood is the mystery of mysteries, the source of life itself and hence of all religious feelings and awe. Briffault (1927), states that it is a universal doctrine that evil, sin, and death were brought into this world by women.

Lederer, in his book *The fear of women* (1968) relates the fear more directly to the menstruating function. The desire to counter this "death" force resulted in superstitious isolation of woman during the monthly flow, and even isolation of all objects touched by her. The force was seen as so powerful in some that it could kill at remote distances. He cites many fascinating examples, such as the Australian aborigine who, upon discovering that his wife had lain on his blanket at her menstrual period, killed her and then died of terror himself within a fortnight. Primitive man realized that when a woman bled, new life did not develop, and this condition was assumed to be contagious.

> Among the Bribri Indians of Costa Rica a menstruous woman may only eat from banana leaves, which, when she has done with them, she throws away in some sequestered spot; for were a cow to find them, and eat them, the animal would waste away and perish. And if anyone drank out of the same cup after her, he would surely die [Lederer, p. 27]

The anthropological material magnifies the situation by dramatizing the problems. Listening to the not-so-primitive woman, one still hears the Eve and Mary aspects of the cycle. Eve "bleeds" from having eaten the fruit of the apple tree and is cursed with shame, guilt, and death. Mary, on the other hand, gives "virgin birth" to God himself, accentuating the powerful life-giving (reproductive) aspects of femininity.

In modern times, a girl may learn to focus on the life-giving or the death aspects of menstruation. The veil of secrecy tends to create negative (guilty) attitudes. She may well be huddled into a corner by her mother, or if her mother can't face it, her ill-informed friends or older relatives may tell her in hushed tones about the curse that will fall upon her every month because of her crime of being a woman. The older women stress the need for cleanliness— which is impossible to attain—and the girl is told to expect pain during her sickness. Above all, she is warned to keep her menstruation a secret.

Or the life force (Mary) may be accentuated. The girl is told that her menstruation is a joyous occasion, a sign that her body is now prepared for her role as a mother. So what if it is something of a nuisance? Like all other aspects of motherhood, the joy menstruation brings is well worth the bother. If then the period comes and the girl finds it less than a joy, she will wonder what is the matter with her and may develop a gnawing suspicion that she is somewhat less than a woman. For Eve to be Mary is indeed difficult in the midst of severe cramps!

When identity is challenged, one compensates by exaggerating whatever the culture identifies as acceptable traits. Boys, for example, may concentrate on physical size and wear shoulder pads and boots to appear larger, while girls spend time "making up" to look pretty as a picture. These devices are a boost to the morale, but unfortunately helplessness is somewhat identified as feminine and girls may deliberately cultivate passivity even when it destroys competence. For example, it is a well-known fact that competence in math declines in many girls as they reach puberty, not because of some strange late maturating recessive gene but because of their discovery that math is "masculine." Girls learn how to wait for help in order to fit the stereotype of Sleeping Beauty. When the girl becomes a woman and discovers that she is also expected to be a competent wife, active housewife, and independent mother, her attempts to break out of the helpless female role produce behavior ranging from the comic to the tragic.

Accentuating the feminine is not restricted to women who doubt their basic orientation but is found in almost all women. We are social beings, and fulfill at least part of our needs by being members of many large and small groups. As members of a group, we are expected to behave like the others in that group. This kind of tracking by identification with a group begins early and never ends. Grouping by gender is the largest and earliest group to which an individual is assigned. Even at the diaper pin stage, the difference is noticeable, and is reinforced by differential treatment. There are basic biological differences, of course, but it is the culture that develops personality differences between the sexes early in life.

In fact, even before birth, the parents are likely to emphasize sex roles. "Boys kick harder than girls" is used to make predictions about the gender of the fetus in the womb. The correct prediction gives the parents a head start in providing the appropriate, socially approved environment — the nursery is redone in pink or blue.

Male/female is a universal tracking device, though no two cultures fully agree on the corresponding masculine/feminine qualities, or the degree of overlap tolerated. People who are difficult to classify generate anxiety in themselves and others and are often the victims of intolerance and even punishment. The person who is unable or unwilling to be classified may well be cast out from the community and excluded from the interchange of goods, services, and love. No pigeonhole means no pigeon.

To adapt to one's cultural milieu is essential, and thus men and women learn strategies to cope with contradictions in the traditional models. Some styles of life are essentially functional while others are self-defeating. Those who are unable to reconcile the role contradictions develop low self-esteem, with the consequent frustration and anger.

Woman has no monopoly on rage, but as the cultural standard generally precludes overt assertion, she will display a greater range of covert manifestations, displacements, denial mechanisms, and symptoms than people who are following the male model. (Whenever men are denied opportunities for direct assertion, for instance, when they are governed by hostile superior officers, the same picture emerges.)

Both male and female scream the vital cry when in pain. A woman may try to scream quietly in order to avoid stepping out of role. Shocked by her own "unfeminine" anger, she feels guilty and sick. She concludes that when she is angry, there must be something wrong with her. She may then attempt to focus on the feeling rather than on the cause and try to stop feeling angry, rather than do anything directly to change the provoking situation. Again, the model may heighten the problem for she may mistakenly believe that women must always be passive.

It's a rare woman who can be very active in the "man's world" without doubting her own femininity. The societal sanctions against outbursts of energy or long-term ambition in women are too great for most women to bear. To protect themselves against the consequences of displays of rage, women generally suppress or divert it. One psychological "solution" is a disengaging action that avoids the occasions of anger. Narcotic drugs, alcohol, social withdrawal, mental withdrawal into fugue states, preoccupation with sensations or altered states of perception (delusions, illusions, hallucinations), excessive sleeping, even excessive eating can be used to dull the awareness of the outside world. Or one can distort the manifestations of the feelings until they are outside most conscious awareness, and only appear in disguised form, such as in projective techniques (personality measuring devices developed by psychologists) and dreams.

Some women do explode with their anger, but divert it into a reinforcement of their femininity by attacking in "self-defense" those people who attack the feminine model. There are many examples to choose from outside the therapy session. Shirley Bernard in her article "Aggression in Women" (1971) reports a Stanford University study that showed that mothers punished their five-year-old daughters for being aggressive, whereas aggression in sons of the same age was encouraged. Ironically, the mothers used very aggressive methods to punish their daughters. Apparently women feel justified in attacking a girl who is unfeminine. The mother may let out all the stops, but because she is defending the stereotype of femity she can be overtly aggressive and—in this case—reinforce her identification.

Women attack their own children who fail to live up to the model, and other women as well. Splinter groups occur when women caucus. Each small group is eager to defend their version of the feminine model. The parents attack the childless teachers, the married ones find fault with the singles, the working women threaten the unemployed. Women who have succeeded in the "man's world" are not supported, but are seen as enemies who have turned traitor. Those who have spent their lives working out a difficult compromise are not about to cheer someone who seems to have found an easier solution. It seems that the major socially approved opportunity for a woman to be aggressive is when she is defending her claim to membership in the generic club: woman.

PHYSICAL DISORDERS

Little will be said here about *explosions* of rage, because in the psychotherapist's arena one feels mostly the *implosions.* Even more destructive, psychologically speaking, is directing the anger inward. This is comparable to building a bomb and then dropping it in your own lap. It results in some form of depression, neurosis, psychosis, alcoholism, as well as gradual and dramatic suicides.

When I asked students in my classes at Long Island University, "What happens when you get angry?" almost all the women reported that they could not attack the provoking cause directly and so they substituted something else, or someone else, or themselves, and attacked that instead. One girl wrote of a chronic skin condition that was connected to thwarted rage.

> When my father would fly into rages at me and call me names like "stupid," I would get so mad I chose not to speak to him at all. My mother would react by not reacting; she would pretend that nothing was going on and would thus give support to my father. Once when I couldn't stand it anymore I ripped a favorite blouse of mine and tore apart beads I had cherished and then locked myself in the bathroom and cried. I have a bad skin condition and when I get upset it itches, and I scratch it and it breaks out worse. When I was 13 I reached puberty and began menstruating, and it was then that my skin was at its worst and covered practically my whole body.

This last phrase, which seems to omit the word "rash" as an oversight, could be taken to mean her new feminine skin covered practically her whole body, while throughout her statement one can find examples of role conflict as the source of anger.

Germaine Greer expresses a similar kind of frustration from displaying anger. Note that here, too, the blocked expression of anger has long-lasting consequences—this time, a sleepless night.

> . . . I was rapping with some terrible American tourist—with him and his wife and their friends—and he escorted me up the stairs to the level our apartments were on. He put his arm around my waist, and I thought, "What are you doing that for?" But I wasn't going to start screaming—he wasn't raping me.
>
> When we got to the top of the stairs, he went to kiss me and I put my face down like a child being kissed goodnight for bed. And without a word, without any indication, in a curious, cold and calculating way he put his hand on my breast—and I thought, "I'll kill you." Because he'd just invaded, taken a liberty not granted and there wasn't anything I could do about it.
>
> I couldn't speak, I was so angry—my throat closed up as if

I were being strangled—and later I told a friend of mine that if I'd had a machete I'd have killed him. I lay in bed all that night, just burning with anger—thinking "I'll make him pay for that, I'll make him beg my pardon"] "Female sexuality: what it is—and what it isn't," *Mademoiselle*, July 1971, p. 116-117].

Unexpressed anger can be a contributing cause to even more altered physical states—seizures. Rosa, an outpatient in a mental hospital clinic, was unable to work and had to be helped by welfare payments. She was employed for three years in a restaurant but her boss used to "scream a lot" and "make me nervous." She began having epileptic-like seizures at the rate of about twice a month. She eventually lost her position. She reports that she "gets all excited and cries" and falls down and hurts herself when she collides with furniture. Instead of screaming, she bites her tongue, which prevents her from eating for days after and consequently damages her own physical health.

The Gestalt theorist Fritz Perls gives an even more extreme example of aggression turned inward:

A girl has been deserted by her lover. . . . Her first reaction is "I shall kill him because he left me. If I can't have him nobody else shall." . . . But then her aggression turns into suffering. "I can't live without him, life is too painful. I want to escape, die." The wish to kill has turned into the wish to die [*Ego, hunger, and aggression,* 1961, p. 222].

The aggression toward the lover is still present in the suicidal action, for the patient believes that if she kills herself he will be unhappy for the rest of his life.

Katherine, the heroine of the film *Jules and Jim,* manages to kill both herself and her lover. Throughout the movie she has buried her rage under a cover of sweetness, melancholy, and erratic behavior. At the end she dresses carefully with hat and gloves and smiles serenely while she drives both herself and her ex-lover to death by drowning.

Sometimes it is not one's own death but the death of the fetus that becomes the substitute target for aggression. Benedek in "The Psychobiology of Pregnancy" (1970) points out case after case of furious hatred of mothers for their unborn children. Benedek states:

Women fantasy about harboring a cancerous growth, a gnawing animal, or even a monster. Such fantasies, alien to the ego and often in traumatic contrast to the woman's wish for pregnancy and motherhood, activate grave anxiety frequently experienced as losing her mind. . . . Having become painfully aware of her fear of and hostility toward her unborn child, the anxiety might lead to severe phobic defenses against the sense of inadequancy in her motherliness [p. 145].

Benedek concludes that the intense emotional state of the mother can, if prolonged, actually affect the nutritional health of the offspring as well as the mother.

The occurrence of nausea and vomiting—commonly called morning sickness—has been linked to the degree of emotional stress during pregnancy. In our culture the mother's role conflict, her feelings about giving up her own helplessness in order to care for the baby, and her own rage are some of the factors in the production of physical discomfort. In some cultures pregnancy discomfort does not exist. Margaret Mead found that only 14 percent of Navaho women had "morning sickness," and those 14 percent differed from the other Navaho women in that they had learned to speak English from the missionaries. One wonders if attitudes were taught along with the English.

In a psychological study of thirty six normal New York mothers, Zuckerberg (1972) found that not one was free of negative emotions. Those who insisted that their pregnancy was "idyllic" and who would not admit to any anger had the greatest number of psychosomatic symptoms. Being enraged is bad for one's health, but being enraged and denying it is worse. These were not minor emotions; concern about death of self was mentioned by thirty of the thirty-six.

Expectant mothers project their fear of rage onto the infant and show obsessive concern that the baby will die. To assess projection, Dr. Zuckerberg asked her group to write a story about a picture of a pregnant woman standing near two men. Here are the stories written by two of the potential mothers:

(1) A woman was leaving her doctor's office. She was very disturbed. Her doctor told her that her baby was dead. She didn't know what to do. She walked blindly into the street, noticing no one. A car came and ran her over. She was dead. That was the end of her troubles.

(2) This lady appears to be at an art exhibit. She is aware that both the young man in front of her and the old man on the side are watching her. She's wondering what they are thinking. He's probably thinking that she really should take better care of herself as far as her appearance is concerned. The older man is

probably feeling a little melancholy. As for the woman herself, she is feeling very content. She's enjoying the warm feeling that she experiences. She's really glad that she's going to have a baby.

When the two women were compared, the second was found to have a significantly greater number of psychosomatic symptoms. The double messages sent to her from the culture—that she is made to be a mother yet must hide her pregnant body—are a source of confusing disturbances. Women are not expected to express angry feelings about pregnancy, and must displace their aggression. When the angry feelings emerge to consciousness, they frighten the owner, causing self-doubt.

Helene Deutsch (1945) found that the cause of difficulties with nursing often lies in the woman's own aggressions, which make her feel "like a wild beast during lactation." The failure of the suckling function represents an attempt to escape, not in order to protect herself, but chiefly in order to protect the child against the dangers of her aggression.

Rage may also contribute to the intensity of the common menstrual "cramps." The "curse" myth is promulgated by women and the womb is a likely target for displacement of anger. It is comforting to have a cause—even the wrong one—to blame for our ill feeling. People are prone to believe anything rather than engage in a long, difficult search for logical explanations. It is too anxiety-provoking to admit that the unknown is unknowable, which is why peculiar psychological theories (like strange religions) can gain adherents. When a woman feels emotionally upset, the monthly cycle makes an illogical but culturally accepted excuse for her feelings. Premenstrual, postmenstrual, and midmenstrual blues leave very few days for which one must be held personally accountable. Having found an impersonal "cause," one is free to indulge onself, and no man will argue. Others are quick to accept this scapegoat to end the search for a personal or interpersonal villain and exonerate themselves.

There is yet another advantage to blaming the uterus and "knowing" the cause of all unhappiness is the cycle. One can gain the ever important illusion of control over one's emotions by rituals, or the pill, or other manufactured products that "guarantee carefree freedom." The ads suggest that using their products will finally make you glad you are a woman.

Some woman turn to hysterectomies in a vain attempt to eradicate the psychological "cause" of their frustration. Another alternative, nonsurgical X-ray castration, is not painful or expensive, but physicians are reluctant to perform this procedure because of the well-known ambivalence of women regarding that important symbol of their role, the womb. Physicians are familiar with the loud demand to be free of the monthly cramps followed by the loud wail, "What possible good am I now that I've had my hysterectomy?"

SEXUAL BEHAVIOR DISORDERS

Sexual activity is microcosmic; the person's feeling and actions during sexual intercourse usually reflect their adopted social roles and interpersonal attitudes. Occasionally, role reversals occur—the repressed aspects of one's personality emerge. A very passive individual may become quite aggressive or even vice versa, which is of even greater interest to the therapist. Only a few examples will be considered here, and the discussion of these is restricted to problems of role conflict and expressions of rage.

An unmarried woman executive, near the top of a million-dollar business, was raped at knifepoint by a man who first tied up the friend who had walked her home for protection. The woman afterward came to me for psychotherapy, not because of murderous rages against the rapist, but for a suicidal depression. Her depression came about because while submitting to him she became sexually excited and enjoyed parts of the experiences in the midst of her terror. Her cry was not "How could he?" but "How could I?"

Aggression often promotes sexual excitement, and sexual excitement aggression. Another one of the notable exceptions to the proscription against female aggression is encouraging women to fight against male sexual advances. A woman may try to resist, but psychologically, this has the effect of increasing the sexual excitement of both. She encourages him by discouraging him.

There are several psychological components to this seemingly self-defeating behavior. Because fighting by resisting is socially acceptable for a woman, she avoids the guilt that comes from overt aggression as well as some of the guilt that she is conditioned to feel from having sex with someone she doesn't love.

A woman's early response to being raped is often fear that her mother will find out. Eastman, in his study of "First Intercourse" (*Sexual Behavior,* March 1972), found that *during* the first act of sexual intercourse the girl's principal concern was pregnancy (62 percent), what parents might think (55 percent), what friends might think (34 percent), and what school officials might think (9 percent). Adding together what parents, friends and school officials might think results in a total of 99 percent of the girls (28 percent of the boys). Even while being raped at knifepoint it is likely that a woman is going to behave in ways that she hopes will gain approval from the significant people in her life. Even under these critical circumstances she is going to try to live up to her expected role.

The woman executive in the case mentioned earlier advanced in her career by squelching her passive side. She had remained unmarried partly because she saw marriage as a "giving in." But the passivity that she was striving to put down was still in her unconscious and broke through under these traumatic circumstances. Hence the depression, not over the sexual activity, but with the confrontation with her own feelings. "How could I?" includes the question of how she could have squelched her potential as a wife and mother.

The guilt that a woman feels when she becomes overtly aggressive (unless fighting for designated female causes such as motherhood) is such a burden that it is avoided by creating scapegoats to suit the occasion. If she can provoke the other person into behaving like a monster, she feels justified in attacking the "monster." But much to the dismay of all, she will burst into tears if the "monster" counter attacks or threatens to leave her.

In sexual behavior, passive-active conflicts are often expressed as frigidity or refusal to become involved. A variation of the latter is having so many "affairs" that one is really not involved in any. The refusal to become involved sometimes masquerades as religious belief or scientific objectivity. By putting others on a pedestal or under a microscope, one can avoid real contact. The worship can be praise or fear — on one's knees one cannot look people in the eye. Whether one throws stones or petals, they are thrown from a distance. By labeling human relationships a "mystery," one avoids confrontation.

Withholding sexual gratification as an expression of anger is often subtle. Rather than open defiance one finds approach-avoidance cycles. Appearances of "togetherness" are really "separate but equal." Women often win the war by leaving the field. Space is mapped out and lines drawn, usually labeled "his" and "hers." What appears to be cooperation is often competition.

Homosexual behavior has as many dynamics as heterosexual, but for the purposes of this paper it is sufficient to point out that some lesbian activity is an attempt to resolve the passive-active role conflicts, and may occasionally be an expression of aggression against others. One woman explained to me that she "gets even" with her M.D. husband, who is too involved with his practice to attend to her in the way that she desires, by using his car with M.D. plates to rendezvous with a female lover. She relishes the fantasies of what his professional colleagues and his patients would think if they knew the real reason his car was parked for this "house call." Another woman who announced to her kaffeeklatsch circle that she was thinking of "going gay" was astonished to hear several of them say, "Well, it serves him right!"

SOCIAL DISORDERS

If withholding sexual gratification is not sufficient for expressing rage, rage may be expressed by withholding other desired qualities or activities. Withholding moral support or the laundry may be forms of aggression subtle enough to avoid retaliation. Complaints are parried with "How do you expect me to get all my work done around here?" Dinner may be well served but the potatoes cold. Protesters are accused of "not appreciating my efforts." The variations are as many as the number of angry women. Having accepted helplessness as a life style, they find it easy to exaggerate this into incompetence.

Of interest to the psychologist is the fact that this mechanism can be an unconscious maneuver of omnipotence. If "no one helps me" then perhaps "I don't need any help," or "he cannot help me anyway because he is useless." By doing the work of other people instead of one's own, one can "prove" superiority to others ("I can do what they cannot") and inconvenience them at the same time by being the weak link in the chain of household activity. Looking stupid while actually being competent is another version of being aggressive while appearing passive. The woman may preclude more demands being made on her by claiming that the present ones are so taxing, and simultaneously showing up the "opposition" by making their hard work seem wasted effort.

The patient who cannot cooperate because of a phobia may be expressing both helplessness and omnipotence simultaneously. One patient, a neurotic, was unable to do her share as a volunteer to help care for the church because she "might spread germs around the altar." She believed that her germs might start an epidemic, so that the hundreds of people who came to services there and received communion from the priest might get sick and die. Her phobia kept her from many activities that she claimed she would have enjoyed, such as eating out in restaurants with her husband. She was helpless, but what power her little germs had, greater than the power of God represented by the altar! Phobias may replace myths in the modern generation; phobias create an illusion of powerful forces as work.

The same kind of magical thinking often underlies intractable guilt. "It's all my fault" can be reread as "Look how much power I have, I am responsible for so much."

The woman may fight against her feelings of passivity by becoming unduly sensitive to any offer of help. Offers are felt as orders or demands. The woman who uses her helplessness as a demand may suspect genuine offers of assistance to be sabotaged. "Don't tell me what to do" is usually accompanied by nagging. An endless series of silly demands are made, often predicted by statements about one's own weakness. She demands concessions for her weakness, and tries to balance her own feelings of being controlled by controlling others.

Dependence can be exaggerated until it becomes both a demand and an expression of rage. But there is a dangerous boomerang effect. After convincing others that she must be cared for, she feels more vulnerable because she is at their mercy. The feeling of utter helplessness generates panic from impotence and a desire for compensatory power. Pauline, the silent-screen heroine, tied to the railroad track by a villain, is utterly helpless, but her very precarious state stirs the hero to her rescue. One presumes they live happily ever after. But in real life the heroine may continue to make demands that no hero can fill. She hints that only a great man can fill her great needs, and so he makes supreme efforts for a time. Often the needs are not spelled out — "It would spoil it if I told you. You have to guess." "Get me anything" may be a come-on, so that if he fails to get the "right" gift it is rejected. The giver as well as the taker then feels personally inadequate.

A new pool of anxiety and guilt is created from which both parties to these passive-active manipulations can draw. If the other person is low in self-esteem, he will attempt to build up his ego by offering more gifts or services, until far more than he can offer comfortably is presented, often with demands that it be accepted. Then it is snapped up with a cursory "You shouldn't, but O.K. if you want it that way." The game has not ended, however, until the gift is lost, thrown away, or given to a nondeserving person. The life style of dependence precludes ever making a profit and thereby becoming somewhat independent. Further, the gift must be destroyed because it is a reminder of the impotence that generated it. And finally, there is the Robin Hood rule: profiting from a gift that was ill-gotten promotes shame, which can be removed only by giving the gift away.

AGITATED DEPRESSION

Depression probably has as many meanings and ramifications as sexual behavior. Here we will restrict the analysis to aspects of depression which are related to passive-active behavior and feelings of rage. Depression is often anger turned inward against the self.

Depression, like disposing of the prized gift, can be "proof" of guilt or that I did not commit a crime, for if I did I would be profiting from it — enjoying it — rather than crying. Depression can be used to avoid the guilt that comes from feeling angry, and interestingly enough, can be used to avoid expressing more anger. Depression saps strength; the person cannot fight. Physical functions are so slowed that no energy is available. Depression may actually prevent a person from committing suicide because of inability to mobilize a plan of action. Murder, also, can be forestalled because one is too weak to kill.

Bonime's description of the depressed (1959) highlights this inability to carry out a plan.

> Indecisiveness suspends constructive action, and perfectionism either exaggerates the task hopelessly beyond a conceivable initiation of effort or dissipates all the available time and energy in the completion of small fragments of a full and responsible program.
>
> A housewife, for example, gets nothing done while trying to decide what task to tackle first, or she neglects marketing, meals and clothes, while she exhausts herself and squanders the day in making everything in the bathroom gleam perfectly [p. 247].

Compulsive activity may well be a device to prevent the occurrence of some other tabooed activity, and in some cases to prevent the acting out of rage. The obsession may use up all the time until the person collapses into a state of enforced inactivity. Angry depressions are often manifested by irresponsibility, but the conflict produces fatigue. Fatigue is so common in our society that it is mistaken as normal. To patients who are afraid of freedom, fatigue seems to be preferable. Discouragement, lethargy, boredom, lapses of concentration, poor memory, escapes into television (soap operas provide a good share of misfortune falling on the heroes), and endless meaningless telephone calls all serve to block the direct expression of rage. The list continues with food fads and preoccupation with nonsensical (and therefore safe)

209

activity of the latest fad.

Inactivity is not normal; the body struggles to manifest some life, but relentless pacing in circles (avoiding goal-directed efforts), hand wringing, and repetitious gestures are the only actions allowable. Doing while not doing, quiet rages and active depressions are manifested simultaneously. Having tried her best to live up to the cultural expectation and its promise of being accepted into the group with love, the woman may discover that she still isn't happy. Admitting that she might have made a mistake seems worse than trying to live with the mistake, and after a fruitless search for "what's wrong" she may finally seek help from a therapist.

PSYCHOTHERAPY

Psychotherapy is no place to hide. The first step in therapy is to acknowledge the rage and all of its peculiar manifestations. "Were you angry?" or "Are you angry?" may be helpful in drawing out the individual's attention to her feelings in the psychotherapy session. To be able to accept her feelings she may need the reassurance that she can do so and still be a feminine woman (I point out Liz, Sophia, and Catherine to counteract Cinderella, Snow White, and Sleeping Beauty). She may find it hard to admit to anger without assurance that she is still lovable. The expectation of drastic punishment for initiating aggressive action is another hidden demon. One needs to learn that retaliation is no longer forthcoming, that punishments leveled in childhood were indeed severe, but of minor importance now.

Accepting her hostile intentions may temporarily raise overwhelming feelings of guilt, but this is a necessary consequence of accepting responsibility for one's own action. To leave the safety of appearing helpless and defenseless requires courage. To make it easier to accept her real power and the control she is exerting on herself and others, the therapist can clarify the psychological fact that many punishments are self-induced and unnecessary. The woman must learn that it is all right to feel angry, that there are some advantages to being openly active, and, that even aggression can be useful.

Because the therapist is not afraid of the woman's anger, she learns not to be afraid of it herself. Often the person in the therapeutic chair fears that she will do irreparable harm or even murder if she lets any of the anger out. She needs to understand that repression is also dangerous. Reassurance is needed that her controls are as strong as her emotions. The answer to "I'd like to strangle him" is "Yes, but you never have." Sometimes humor is the quickest way through the morass. The obsessive compulsive phobic woman mentioned earlier, who thought her germs would kill, finally acknowledged that it was her policeman husband that she was ambivalent about killing. The therapist, in a moment of exasperation, told her that she would have to boil the gun free of germs before she could use it. Since then, her husband has noticed that she giggles whenever she spies his gun and he is grateful for this change of temper.

Sometimes, however, the rage is too deeply buried for any standard psychotherapeutic short cuts, and the woman in therapy must have time to hear the voice of her own anger. In some cases the direct query about the anger brings a categorical denial: "I'm never mad." Individuals who resist complex explanations coming from the therapist might be able to accept messages from their own dreams. Most people can accept being told, "You are everything in your dream, you wrote it, you act in it, it all represents something about you. The dream is a record of your actions and feelings." The individual may then be instructed on how to recollect and record the dreams, and interpret them herself, with caution. While years of training are necessary for analytical dream analysis, the method published by Piotrowski, in part, can be learned rather quickly by the intelligent woman. Piotrowski (1971) stresses that nouns need not be universally equated with rigid symbolic meanings but that each dreamer has a personal lexicon that requires diligent search by therapist and patient together. He looks rather to the *action* in the dream as characteristic of the dreamer. For example, if a dreamer related, "I turned off the radio," then she frequently avoids or ignores stimuli in general, not just radio stations. However, Piotrowski would not have the person associate to "radio" because he has found that associations to the dream lack the validity that is offered in the uncensored dream. He has also found that the more similar the characters in the dream are to the dreamer, the more acceptable is the action of those characters to her, and conversely, the less similar, the less acceptable. People can learn to apply this system to their own dreams in order to gain visual images of their unrecognized feelings. Eventually, insights are gleaned.

For example, a woman professor who categorically denied for some time that she had ever been angry in her life saw through her own passive disguise of the anger after it was brought to light by the following dream:

I was showing a video tape to an audience. I wanted to show

them a holocaust, or volcano erupting, but I couldn't find the right place on the tape, so I played popular songs instead.

She believed that she did not have violent emotions in her repertoire, but in fact revealed her hidden feelings under the guise of light and popular patter. She thought she was passive when she was covertly aggressive. After examining the action in the dream she recognized that her usual "witty" sarcasm in the classroom was comparable to the volcano letting off steam, and was basically quite hostile. For a teacher to be unable to find the right place from which to present a lecture would create a feeling of impotence, which she covers up by "playing." She also realized that her desire to "erupt" sprang from feelings of lacking something essential required to carry out her role. She learned more, much more, about herself from a study of this dream and others and began to trust her own feelings as well as the therapist.

Having brought the anger into the light of day and having the individual accept the existence of aggressive urges, the next step is to tease out the general passive-active behavior patterns. The therapist may lead the individual to reflect on their developmental history to point out the long-term development. Some women are aided by requesting written autobiographies from them or fill-in questionnaires of salient points. The behavior patterns being manifested now, which are the source of personal difficulties, were probably quite effective when the woman was a young girl. The individual is understandably reluctant to give up patterns that once were rewarded and must be helped to find new ones. New choices need be made. Sorting out the contribution of others and one's own part in the regeneration of problem situations is essential. The woman in therapy needs to learn the difference between finding fault and finding causes. The probe to assess the precise degree of blame—often seen in marital therapy—is a waste of time. Assuming that everyone shares in the guilt allows us to go on to remedies.

Rather than continue to deny rage, the patient should permit the anger to find the appropriate target and not be displaced to innocent by-standers. Hostile aggression—the wish to kill—must be turned to instrumental aggression—the wish to survive. The woman should learn not to attack blindly men, other women, her own children, or her own body, but to attack the real life problems and processes that are frustrating. Encouraging her to find real ways to meet her needs is more productive than tranquilizing her feelings. One can begin with feelings but must end with action. Rage is a form of involvement, and after all, rage is much to be preferred to alienation, schizophrenic withdrawal, or the aftereffects of lobotomy. The latter reduces rage by "making a hole in your skull and removing the work of centuries" (E. B. White, in *The second tree from the corner,* 1935, p. 82). Better yet, let us raise the woman in rage to a woman in action.

Banking on the natural survival mechanisms in all of us, the therapist can help the woman in distress to use her energy, including that unleashed by rage, for her own constructive purposes. Learning how to covert forms of passive-active behavior are self-destructive and have produced psychosomatic, sexual, and social disorders is usually sufficient motivation for change. Therapy may begin in an office but ends only when a new identity and patterns of relating are established outside the therapy sessions. Effective feminine action follows after the woman has exorcised her "curse."

REFERENCES

Beard, M. R. *Woman as force in history.* New York: Collier Books, 1946.

Benedek, T. The psychobiology of pregnancy. In J. E. Anthony and T. Benedek, *Parenthood: Its psychology and psychopathology.* Boston: Little, Brown, 1970.

Bernard, S. Aggression in women. In J. Agel, *The radical therapist.* New York: Ballantine Books, 1971, pp. 188-91.

Bonime, W. The psychodynamics of neurotic depression. In S. Arieti (Ed.), *American handbook of psychiatry,* vol. 3, chap. 18. New York: Basic Books, 1959.

Briffault, R. *The mothers.* New York: Macmillan, 1927.

Deutsch, H. *Psychology of women,* vol. 2. New York: Grune & Stratton, 1945.

Eastman, W. F. First intercourse. In *Sexual Behavior,* March 1972, pp. 22-27.

Greer, G., et al. Female sexuality: what it is—and what it isn't. *Mademoiselle,* July 1971, pp. 108-117.

Horney, K. The dread of women. *International Journal of Psychoanalysis,* 1932, *13,* 384.

Lederer, W. *The fear of women.* New York: Harcourt Brace, 1968.

Mead, M. Cultural patterning of prenatal behavior. In S. Richardson & A. Guttmacher, *Childbearing, its social and psychological aspects.* New York: Williams & Wilkins, 1967.

Perls, F. S. *Ego, hunger, and aggression.* New York: Vintage Books, 1961.

Piotrowski, Z. A. A rational explanation of the irrational: Freud's and Jung's own dreams reinterpreted. *Journal of Personality Assessment,* 1971, 35, 504-523.

Roche, H. P. *Jules and Jim.* New York: Avon Press, 1967.

Ruitenbeek, H. M. *The male myth.* New York: Dell, 1967.

White, E. B. *The second tree from the corner.* New York: Harper, 1935.

Zuckerberg, J. An exploration into the feminine role conflict and bodily symptomatology in pregnancy. Unpublished doctoral dissertation, Long Island University, 1972.

SUGGESTED PAPERS AND PROJECTS

Papers

1. Do women have the personality characteristics of members of minority groups?
2. Discuss the Freudian view of feminine personality and its derivatives.
3. How does the feminist therapist view women?
4. How many women are hospitalized and why?

Projects

1. Interview five males and five females. Have them list the adjectives that seem most appropriate to either the healthy man, healthy woman, or healthy person. Have class members compare adjective lists.
2. Pick three clinical psychology testbooks and examine the way they treat women.
3. Interview a therapist of each sex. See what their conception of appropriate sex roles is.
4. Read Sylvia Plath's *The Bell Jar.* What is the protagonist's attitude toward therapy and visa versa?

ADDITIONAL REFERENCES

Bonaparte, M. *Female sexuality.* New York: Grove Press, 1962.

Chesler, P. *Women and madness.* Garden City, N.Y.: Doubleday, 1972.

Freud, S. Femininity: Lecture 33 in *New introductory lectures on psychoanalysis.* New York: Norton, 1965.

Harding, M. E. (Ed.) *The way of all women.* New York: C. G. Jung Foundation for Analytical Psychology, 1970.

Horney, K. *New ways in psychoanalysis.* New York: Norton, 1939.

Section III

The Development of Sex Differences and Sex Roles

14 Introduction

Can one validly predict some aspects of the behavior of a child on the basis of his or her sex alone? If sex differences in psychology or behavior exist, at what age do these differences become manifest? What factors, biological or cultural, are responsible for the emergence of sex differences in behavior?

There is a great deal of controversy about the existence of sex differences in early childhood. There have been a large number of both positive and negative findings relating to the same aspects of behavior. Maccoby and Jacklin (1971) have reviewed the findings in a paper presented to the American Psychological Association which is currently being revised for publication. They have concentrated on research that has appeared since Maccoby's book on the development of sex differences was published in 1967. They assert that no consistent sex differences have unequivocably been shown to exist in the following supposedly sex-characteristic areas of behavior: dependency, attachment to the mother, and activity level. It is probably true that girls are more sensitive to external stimuli than boys. One stereotype about early sex differences in behavior appears to be correct: males are considerably more aggressive than females under almost all conditions studied. Sex differences in aggressive behavior apparently predate the child's awareness of what sex she or he is. They appear as early in life as such behavior can be observed.

Maccoby and Jacklin state the requirements that should be met before sex-characteristic behavior can be considered to be biologically based. The behavior must (1) be cross-culturally universal, (2) appear early in life, (3) be found in higher primates as well as humans, and (4) be susceptible to biochemical manipulation such as hormone administration. The greater potentiality of males for aggression meets these criteria.

Once the child becomes aware of his or her own sex, behavior may become contaminated by this awareness; e.g., the child may modify his or her behavior according to cultural expectations. Therefore, the age at which the child acquires knowledge of his or her sex becomes critical in determining which of the many sex differences that emerge as the child becomes older are biologically rather than culturally based. Brown (1957, 1958) has suggested that a majority of children can distinguish between the sexes by three years of age. Therefore, there is only a limited period during which rather directly biologically based behavior may be observed.

There are many problems in defining what is meant by the ability to distinguish one's own sex. Both Brown (1958) and Lynn (1959) have attempted to clarify the terms most often used in research on the development of sex roles. Lynn especially has attempted to differentiate the terms "sex-role identification," "sex-role preference," and "sex-role adoption." He defines "sex-role preference" as "the desire to adopt the behavior associated with one sex or the other, or the perception of such behavior as preferable or more desirable." Such preferences are measured by having children choose objects, pictures, or behaviors characteristic of one sex or the other. "Sex-role adoption" takes note of behaviors that may be sexually specific, but not necessarily part of a sexual preference. For example, a girl may wear pants because it is convenient or expedient to do so, but still prefer a feminine role. The term "sex-role identification" is reserved for the incorporation of behavior that is specific to a given sex and of the unconscious reactions characteristic of that sex. Identification is considered to be an implicit process. It is often measured by means of projective techniques.

Confusion over the use of the term "identification" is rife. It may refer to (1) behavior: the child acts in the manner of the parent; (2) motive: the child is disposed to act like the parent; (3) process: the mechanisms through which behaviors and motives are learned (Bronfenbrenner, 1960). Some of these usages are susceptible to measurement and some are not. Lack of clarity has even led some psycholgists to suggest doing away with the term altogether. However, the concept of identification is of too much theoretical and historical interest to be easily ignored.

When identification is operationally defined it is usually in terms of response similarity or perceived similarity. Either children and their parents fill out similar tests of personality and comparisons are made between them, or the child responds twice to a questionnaire, once as self and once as parent. Occasionally a knowledgeable observer may fill out the questionnaire for both the child and the parents. Responses studied to determine the degree of the child's identification with the maternal and paternal parent are not limited only to those related to sex-role.

Unclear terminology is one of the major complications in attempting to understand sex-role research. The definition of the term "sex-role" is itself unclear (Angrist, 1969). Like identification, it is sometimes used to refer to observable behavior, sometimes to refer to expectations for behavior, and sometimes for some combination thereof. For our purposes "sex-role" is defined in a very general way as any behavior, attitudes, or expectations that appear to characterize one sex more than the other. Realization of one's sex-role develops gradually through the first three years of life and probably shows developmental changes throughout adolescence (Kohlberg and Zigler, 1967). Boys and girls acquire different aspects of their sex-role at different rates. In fact, the timing of proper sex identification for the different sexes is an important theoretical issue.

Most theories of sex-role learning differ on the way the process of identification produces different psychosexual orientations in the two sexes. Classical psychoanalytic theory stresses the existence of a motivational force of considerable power which compels the child to become like the parent (Bronfenbrenner, 1960). Such a force has "instinct-like" properties. The classical Freudian position postulates that girls experience greater difficulty than boys in developing appropriate sexual identification because of their envy of the male organ. It also postulates that girls have to overcome a homosexual hurdle in identifying with the model who is their first love object.

Psychoanalytic theory focuses on the role of the fear of punishment during the socialization process. Children attempt to "defend against the aggressor" by acquiring his or her characteristics. However, it is not clear why the same-sexed parent is identified with more by the child. In fact, it has been suggested that masculine identification is as essential for "normal" femininity as for masculinity (Johnson, 1963). The modern analytic view also downplays the role of penis envy in sex-role differentiation. Robertiello (1970) asserts that although under normal circumstances a girl will note the difference between herself and boys, she will not feel inferior because of it.

The psychoanalytic view differs from most other theories of sex-role development in its predictions about the timing of sex awareness for boys and girls. Since the theory states that the process of identification is more complicated for girls than for boys, it predicts that awareness of one's own sex will occur later for girls than for boys. A number of studies have been designed to test this prediction (Brown, 1957, 1958; Lynn, 1959; Ward, 1969). These studies take the position that early closeness to the mother gives girls an initial advantage in learning proper identification. Boys, rather than girls, have the more complex process since they must shift their identification away from the mother. Therefore, they predict that proper sex identification will take place earlier for girls.

Lynn's (1959) paper exemplifies studies based upon a social

learning theory of identification in contrast to psychoanalytic theory. He postulates that boys must shift to masculine identification despite the relative absence of male models. Both males and females have the same stereotyped views of the characteristics of the two sexes. Boys learn their masculine identification via the reinforcement of culturally prescribed behavior. Girls, on the other hand, have the presence of a specific female model—their mothers. It is predicted that girls will be more like their mothers than boys will be like their fathers. These results are supported by evidence from Gray and Klaus (1956) and Ward (1969).

Lynn also suggests that the early advantage in identification for girls is counterbalanced by later living in our masculine-oriented culture. "The superior position and privileged status of the male permeates nearly every aspect, major and minor, of our social life. The gadgets and prizes in boxes of breakfast cereal, for example, commonly have a strong masculine rather than feminine appeal" (Brown, 1958, p. 235). Measures of sex preference rather than sex identification indicate that girls prefer the male sex-role long after they have adopted their own. More than 50 percent of children of both sexes find socially assigned homemaking tasks distasteful (Hartley, 1961).

There are a number of methodological problems implicit in social learning theory. Many of the studies make use of the It Scale for Children (Brown, 1957), which has been criticized on the grounds that the supposedly neutral figure is easily interpreted as being male. If girls actually do perceive the figure as male, it would account for the continued high preference girls seem to show for the male sex-role. Additional methodological problems concern the various measures of sex-role identification, preference, and adoption. Ward (1969) indicates that these measures are independent of each other and seem to operate differently for boys and girls. It is not clear, however, what aspects of sex-role each method measures.

Other problems of social learning theory are actually more general than its ability to explain differential sex-role development. All theories of learning have difficulty separating learning (or some other inferred process) and performance. An example, specific to the study of sex-role differences, is the explanation that the greater preference that girls seem to show for the male sex-role is a reflection of the greater latitude given to girls in sex-role development (Brown, 1958). Girls are permitted more overt behaviors characteristic of the opposite sex than boys. There are many more "tomboys" than "sissies." Girls may wear masculine clothing, have masculine names and toys without censure, although the reverse is not true for boys.

The range of behavior within each sex is also very wide. Just because girls are less apt to express aggression does not mean they are incapable of doing so. Bandura (1965) found that although boys were much more likely to imitate an aggressive model, both boys and girls imitated to the same extent if reinforced for doing so. Maccoby and Jacklin (1971) cite a number of studies indicating that a given environmental condition may affect girls and boys differently. It is possible that the motivations and reinforcements affecting sex-specific behavior may be different for the two sexes.

The nature of the reinforcement also tends to be unclear in many of these studies. Social learning theory hypothesizes that parents differentially reinforce boys and girls for behaviors deemed appropriate to their own sex. Girls are rewarded, or at least less punished, for dependent behavior. Boys are rewarded, or less punished, for aggressive behavior. Rothbart and Maccoby (1966) attempted to determine whether parents actually do reinforce culturally prescribed sex differences. They recorded a child's voice that was ambiguous with respect to sex in a number of situations requiring parental intervention. The fathers and mothers of nursery school children (half of whom were told the voice was male and half that it was female) were asked to indicate what responses they would make in each situation. The situations involved dependency, aggression, and autonomy.

They found, surprisingly, that neither the sex of the parent nor the sex of the child was critical. What was significant was the interaction between them. Parents showed greater permissiveness toward a child whose sex was opposite to their own. For example, fathers were more permissive toward girls and mothers were more permissive toward boys. Parents with a high degree of sex-role differentiation of their own showed this effect to a greater extent than those with low sex-role differentiation.

If this experiment is a valid model of the true life situation, children of either sex receive inconsistent reinforcement from their parents. Since sex differences in aggressive behavior appear well before other sources of reinforcement come into play, it is difficult to understand how social learning theory can account for Rothbart and Maccoby's results. A possible explanation is that differential treatment of boys and girls occurs without the awareness of the individuals involved. Girl and boy babies may receive different handling, wear different clothes, and be given different toys. Goldberg and Lewis (1969) observed that mothers talked to and handled girl babies more than boy babies. Another difference may be parental use of sex-appropriate verbal appellations (Hartley, 1964).

The nature of the parent-parent and parent-child relationship may also be of importance. Psychoanalytic theory as modified by Parsons stresses the importance of parental power in the development of sex-role identification. The child identifies with the parent because he is powerful in his ability to dispense both rewards and punishments. Thus, this theory predicts that children of either sex will find it easier to identify with the more powerful parent.

Hetherington (1965) attempted to investigate the effect of the sex of the dominant parent upon sex-role preference, parent-child similarity, and the child's imitation of a parental figure. She found that the dominance of the parent significantly affected only the sex-role preferences of boys. Boys from mother-dominated homes showed a lower degree of male sex-role preference and lower father-son similarity than boys from father-dominated homes. Parental dominance did not affect sex-role preference in girls or mother-daughter similarity. Father dominance, however, did increase father-daughter similarity. The children showed increased similarity to the dominant parent even in non-sex-typed traits. The study provides evidence for the psychoanalytic view that "identification with the aggressor" is important in sex-role learning, but indicates that this process is more important for boys than for girls.

One of the major problems of theories involving social power is the way such power is perceived. There have been a great many studies of children's perceptions of their parents' behavior. Although families presumably differ as to who wields various kinds of power, studies indicate that, in general, mothers are perceived as being more nurturant and controlling through indirect covert means by both boys and girls (Droppleman and Schaefer, 1963). However, there have not yet been studies providing clear evidence that there is a veridical relationship between perceived and actual attitudes and the actual use of power within families. Kohlberg and Zigler (1967) have suggested a cognitive-developmental approach to sexual identification which is partially derived from Piaget's work. To psychologists, it may bear an analogous resemblance to the James-Lange theory of emotion. In opposition to social learning theory, they assert that the child acquires awareness of his or her own sex from anatomical makeup and then selects behaviors compatible with this physical reality. Behavior appropriate to his or her own sex is motivated and reinforced by a need for structured reality and the maintenance of self-esteem. Thus, rather than the social environment acting passively upon children by way of culturally biased rewards and punishments, they actively select components from the environment in line with their cognition of their own sex. Preferential attachment for the same sex parent stems from the basic sex-role identity; it does not cause it.

The cognitive-developmental view provides some original ideas on the development of sex differences, but few empirical studies based upon this theory have been performed. One prediction that distinguishes this theory from psychoanalytic and social learning theories is that of a relationship between IQ and sex-role learning. Bright children (especially boys) are found to be maturationally advanced over average children in sex-role development (Kohlberg and Zigler, 1967). For example, average children of ten showed a pattern of sex-role preferences and identification roughly similar to that of their bright seven-year-old mental counterparts. Average children of six to seven showed a pattern similar to bright four-year-olds.

Kohlberg and Zigler assert that these findings support their theory. However, they have demonstrated only correlations, not determined causalities. Since social learning studies have not controlled for intelligence, it is not clear that sex-role learning is unaffected by IQ. The question of what is intelligence, especially in relation to sex-role development, is also relevant here.

When one discusses psychological issues, one usually expects to find two sides of a disagreement. The area of sex-role development, however, contains at least four theoretical positions: the classical Freudian or neo-Freudian position, psychoanalytic positions based upon social power, social learning theory, and the cognitive-developmental approach. As we have discussed earlier, these theories have generated differential predictions concerning (1) the age at which each sex acquires its proper sex-role, (2) the role and nature of the reinforcement of sex differences and psychosexual identity, (3) the role of parental dominance in the acquisition of proper sex-roles, and (4) the effect of IQ upon the acquisition of sex-roles. None of these theories seems to be completely accurate. Part of the difficulty lies in the complex nature of the problems and the difficulties of measurement in this area.

Most studies of masculinity-femininity at every age level employ questionnaires of some sort whose purpose is difficult to disguise. When individuals describe behavior that is related to sex-role, it is difficult to determine whether they are indicating their own preferences or referring to culturally prescribed roles. There is no reason to expect a strong relationship between the sex-role one attributes to oneself and the actual similarity of one's behavior to that characteristic of one sex or the other. In fact, Nichols (1962) constructed several ingenious scales on sex differences: a Subtle Scale composed of items showing sex differences that people are generally not aware of; a Stereotype Scale composed of items showing no sex difference, but for which there is a general expectation of one; and an Obvious Scale composed of items showing sex differences of which people are generally aware. He tested the relationships between the three scales and found a strong negative relationship between the Subtle and Stereotype Scales; e.g., there was a negative relationship between the way people describe their behavior as typical of their own sex and the way they describe it when they are unaware of its sex-related character.

Perhaps what is needed in this area is a marriage of cultural anthropology and psychology. Weithorn (1972) points out that studies of cultural contributions to the development of sex-roles are confounded both by cultural bias (the way one views another culture is conditioned by one's own) and cultural "inurement" (the way one views one's own culture is also conditioned by it). For example, the failure of Soviet and kibbutz "experiments in sex-role equality" are often explained as indicating that biological differences between the sexes cannot be ignored. Weithorn points out that in these experiments the female is always cast in the masculine role while men are not encouraged to do feminine jobs. She asserts that "biological differences cannot be ignored in the division of labor, but neither should they be subverted to use as excuses for suppression and disenfranchisement."

Weithorn enumerates the biological differences that may be particularly relevant to the development of sex differences in all cultures: (1) the male is larger and stronger than the female; (2) only the female can bear and nurture the infant; (3) maternity is absolutely determinable, while paternity is not; (4) the male can be more reproductively prolific than the female. She also points out that the temperamental differences among cultures are often much greater than the differences between men and women within a culture. She suggests that the focus should be on which enculturation patterns serve to suppress particular behaviors in one sex while enhancing them in the other.

There are a number of psychological questions that need to be answered cross-culturally. For example, findings in the United States indicate that both men and women regard males more favorably than females (McKee and Sherriffs, 1959); both sexes prefer to have a male child (Hammer, 1970), and males with high male-role identification have higher self-esteem than females with either high or low female-role identification (Connell and Johnson, 1970). Findings related to sex-role stereotypes will be discussed extensively in another section, but it would be valuable to know whether such findings hold up in other societies with greater diversity of social organization than our own.

Other questions that should be examined cross-culturally are:

Are males more susceptible to psychological and psychosexual disturbances in other societies, as they are in our own? How similar are sex-role preferences of children to those of adults in various cultures? What are the qualitative and quantitative differences in the modes of expression permitted the different sexes? One would like to see the universality of various theoretical positions on sex-role development tested. More naturalistic observational studies of mother-child relationships in various cultures similar to those done on primates would also be useful.

Another topic of interest involves the implications for change in sex roles in the future. Is sexual identity as irreversible as is usually thought? Lansky (1964) has found that fathers who have sons but no girls have a more female sexual identification than fathers who have daughters but no sons. It is difficult to understand how a feminine identification would tend to produce male offspring, so it is likely that this finding suggests that identification changes are possible even in adulthood. Vogel et al. (1970) have also shown that sex-role preferences may be altered by environmental events — in this case, maternal employment.

Is a new cultural pattern emerging in the United States? Many students of the subject suggest that male and female role differences are disappearing as the two sexes show increasing similarity in educational experiences, flexibility of household tasks, increases in the kind and number of outside jobs held by women, and the use of "unisex" apparel. Barry (1969), however, has recently taken the position (on the basis of data collected in his classic study of cross-cultural differences in sex roles [Barry, Bacon, and Child, 1957]) that cultures that emphasize conformity and collective family structures show the greatest amount of sex-role differences. Weithorn (1972) points out that we cannot legislate changes in attitudes about sex roles. Nonconscious assumptions about a woman's "natural" talents (or lack of them) are at least as prevalent among women as they are among men (Bem and Bem, 1970).

How can one resolve the nature-nurture argument on sex differences? We can do so partly by taking the interactional position that some aspects of sex roles are biologically based and some culturally conditioned. Various cultures differentially reinforce biological predispositions, often in the same way, because there are biological characteristics common to all human beings. Proponents of biological causality must recognize the wide range of biological differences between individuals even of of the same sex.

It is possible that biological and cultural factors interact differently in males and females. Bem and Bem (1970) cite a study by

WOMAN: DEPENDENT OR INDEPENDENT VARIABLE?

Gottesman in 1963 which showed that there was a genetic basis for dominance and submission personality characteristics, but only in males. They take this finding to imply that only males in our culture are given enough latitude for their biological differences to shine through. However, it is possible that Gottesman's finding implies that the genetic bases of dominance and submission are different for males and females. Evidence on sex differences in cognitive function (which will be discussed extensively in another section) indicates that females mature faster than males. IQ is correlated with different motor and personality characteristics in male infants than in female infants (Moss and Kagan, 1958). The only conclusion possible today is that some sex differences do indeed exist, but that their origin is still an open question.

REFERENCES

Angrist, S. S. The study of sex roles. *Journal of Social Issues,* 1969, *25*, 215-32.

Bandura, A. Influence of models' reinforcement contingencies on the acquisition of imitative responses. *Journal of Personality and Social Psychology,* 1965, *1*, 589- 95.

Barry, H. Cross-cultural perspectives on how to minimize the adverse effects of sex differentiation. Paper presented at the Symposium on Behavioral Sciences of the American Psychological Association, Washington, D.C., September 1969.

Barry, H.; Bacon, M.K.; and Child, I. L. A cross-cultural survey of some sex differences in socialization. *Journal of Abnormal and Social Psychology,* 1957, *55*, 327-32.

Bem, S. L., & Bem, D. J. Case study of a non-conscious ideology: Training the woman to know her place. In D. J. Bem (Ed.), *Beliefs, attitudes, and human affairs.* Belmont, Calif.: Brooks-Cole, 1970.

Bronfenbrenner, U. Freudian theories of identification and their derivatives. *Child Development,* 1960, *31*, 15-40.

Brown, D. G. Masculinity-femininity development in children. *Journal of Consulting Psychology,* 1957, *21*, 197-202.

— — —. Sex-role development in a changing culture. *Psychological Bulletin,* 1958, *55*, 232-42.

Connell, D. M. and Johnson, J. E. Relationship between sex-role identification and self-esteem in early adolescents. *Developmental Psychology,* 1970, *3*, 268.

Droppleman, L.F., and Schaefer, E. S. Boys' and girls' reports of maternal and paternal behavior. *Journal of Abnormal and Social Psychology,* 1963, *67*, 648-54.

Goldberg, S., and Lewis, M. Play behavior in the year-old infant: Early sex differences. *Child Development,* 1969, *40*, 21-31.

Gray, S. W., and Klaus, R. The assessment of parental identification. *Genetic Psychology Monographs,* 1956, *54*, 87-114.

Hammer, M. Preference for a male child: Cultural factor. *Journal of Individual Psychology,* 1970, *26*, 54-56.

Hartley, R. E. Current patterns in sex roles: Children's perspectives. *Journal of National Association of Women's Deans and Counselors,* 1961, 25, 3-13.

— — —. A developmental view of female sex-role differentiation and identification. *Merrill-Palmer Quarterly,* 1964, *10*, 3-16.

Hetherington, E. M. A developmental study of the effects of sex of the dominant parent on sex-role preference, identification, and imitation in children. *Journal of Personality and Social Psychology,* 1965, *2.,* 188-94.

Johnson, M. M. Sex-role learning in the nuclear family. *Child Development,* 1963, *34*, 319-33.

Kohlberg, L., and Zigler, E. The impact of cognitive maturity on the development of sex-role attitudes in the years 4-8. *Genetic Psychology Monographs,* 1967, *75,* 89-165.

Lansky, L. M. The family structure also affects the model: Sex-role identification in parents of preschool children. *Merrill-Palmer Quarterly,* 1964, *10*, 39-50.

Lynn, D. B. A note on sex differences in the development of masculine and feminine identification. *Psychological Review,* 1959, *66*, 126-35.

Maccoby, E.E., and Jacklin, C. N. Sex differences and their implications for sex roles. Paper presented at the 79th meeting of the American Psychological Association, Washington, D.C., September 1971.

McKee, J. P., and Sherriffs, A. C. Men's and women's beliefs, ideals and self-concepts. *American Journal of Sociology,* 1959, *64*, 356-63.

Moss, H. A., and Kagan, J. Maternal influences on early IQ scores. *Psychological Reports,* 1958, *4,* 655-61.

Nichols, R. C. Subtle, obvious and stereotype measures of masculinity-femininity. *Educational and Psychological Measurement,* 1962, *22*, 449-61.

Robertiello, R. C. Penis envy. *Psychotherapy: Theory, Research, and Practice,* 1970, 7, 204-205.

Rothbart, M. K., and Maccoby, E. E. Parents' differential reactions to sons and daughters. *Journal of Personality and Social Psychology,* 1966, *4,* 237-43.

Vogel, S. R.; Broverman, I. K.; Broverman, D. M.; and Clarkson, F. E. Maternal employment and perception of sex roles among college students. *Developmental Psychology,* 1970, *3,* 384-91.

Ward, W. D. Process of sex-role development. *Developmental Psychology,* 1969, *1*, 163-68.

15

Lynn has provided an excellent review paper that differentiates between the classical Freudian position and the social learning position on masculine and feminine identification. These theories make different predictions on the rate at which each sex acquires its proper sex-role. Although Lynn discusses and provides data on these predictions, his real contribution is to point out one of the major problems of research in the area: the lack of good operational definitions of the terms used. Thus Lynn distinguishes between sex-role identification on one hand and sex-role preference and sex role adoption on the other.

Different measures may be utilized to identify idfferent components of sex roles. These various components may not be closely correlated with each other. For example, a girl may show proper identification with her own sex but prefer the masculine role because of its higher prestige. A boy may adopt masculine characteristics, but unconsciously identify with his mother.

Lynn's paper attempts to clarify apparently contradictory findings on sex-role development. He suggests that measures depending upon the choice of male vs. female objects should be considered identification tests. He suggests that there are developmental changes in these measures which are different for males and females. Both sexes initially identify with the mother, but boys shift toward identification with the male role. Females are more likely to show preference for an adoption of the opposite sex-role than males, and this tendency increases with age. Lynn believes these developmental trends are largely the result of culturally determined rewards and punishments.

A Note on Sex Differences in the Development of Masculine and Feminine Identification*

David B. Lynn

The purpose of this note is to contribute to the theoretical formulation of sex differences in the development of masculine and feminine identification, and to review research findings relevant to this formulation. The concept of identification has held a prominent position not only in psychoanalysis, but also in other psychological theories (Cava & Rausch, 1952; Fenichel, 1945; Lazowick, 1955; Martin, 1954; Mowrer, 1953; Sanford, 1955; Stokes, 1950; Tiller, 1958; Tolman, 1943). Sanford said of the term "identification":

> A term that can be employed in so many different ways and that, as Tolman says, has been accepted by most psychologists and sociologists, could hardly mean anything very precise. It might be proposed, quite seriously, that we give up the term "identification" altogether. . . . We must in any case specify "what kind" [of identification] . . . (Sanford, 1955, p. 107).

In this paper an attempt is made to comply with Sanford's latter suggestion rather than throw out the term "identification" altogether. Such widespread use of the term suggests, if nothing more, its potential utility with adequate clarification.

The present formulation differs from the classical Freudian position which postulates that girls experience greater difficulty than boys in developing appropriate sexual identification because of their envy of the gential organ possessed by little boys. It also differs from the Freudian position that, because the girl has the same-sex parent (the mother) as her first love-object, she must therefore overcome a homosexual hurdle in developing same-sex identification (Fenichel, 1945). The position taken in this paper is in agreement with those who hold that, on the contrary, the early

---

*From *Psychological Review,* 1959, *66* (2), 126-35. Footnotes have been renumbered.

closeness of the girl to the same-sex parent (the mother) gives her an initial advantage in progressing toward appropriate identification (Brown, 1956; Mowrer, 1953). This initial advantage is thought to be counterbalanced, to a large extent, by later learning experiences in this maculine-oriented culture.

Before developing this formulation further, let us differentiate the concept of identification from other similar concepts. Brown (1956) clarified the concept of sex-role identification considerably by contrasting it to *sex-role preference.* Sex-role preference refers to the desire to adopt the behavior associated with one sex or the other, or the perception of such behavior as preferable or more desirable. This concept has been measured by simply asking Ss whether they have ever wished to be of the opposite sex (Fortune survey, 1946; Gallup, 1955; Terman, 1938). It has also been measured by having children state their preference for objects, or pictures of objects, characteristic of one sex or the other (Brown: 1956, 1957; Rabban, 1950). Let us add the concept of *sex-role adoption.* This concept refers to the actual adoption of behavior characteristic of one sex or the other, not simply the desire to adopt such behavior. Women, for example, sometimes wear clothes usually associated with males, e.g., trousers. Men sometimes become beauty operators, a vocation usually associated with women. This concept refers to one's overt behavior, not to one's sex-role preference. An individual may, for example, *adopt* behavior characteristic of his own sex because it is expedient to do so, not because he *prefers* doing so. Sex-role preference is, to this extent, irrelevant to this particular concept. The sex role one actually incorporates, i.e., the role one identifies with, may, in some cases, also be irrelevant to sex-role adoption.

Sex-role identification is reserved to refer to the actual incorporation of the role of a given sex, and to the unconscious reactions characteristic of that role. Thus, a person may be identified with the opposite sex, but for expediency adopt much of the behavior characteristic of his own sex. He may even prefer the role of his own sex, although identified with the opposite-sex role. One would expect such a person, being identified with the opposite sex, to have many unconscious reactions characteristic of the opposite-sex role despite his adopting much of the behavior characteristic of the same-sex role. On the other hand, the woman who, on appropriate occasions, adopts aspects characteristic of the opposite-sex role, such as wearing trousers or wearing short hair, is certainly not necessarily identified with the male role. Thus, *sex-role adoption* refers to overt behavior characteristic of a given sex, and *sex-role identification* refers to a more basic process characteristic of a given sex. Sex-role identification is much more

233

difficult to measure than sex-role preference or adoption. Attempts have been made to measure what is here referred to as sex-role identification through projective techniques, such as human figure drawings (Brown & Tolor, 1957; Jolles, 1952; Morris, 1955; Tiller, 1958; Tolor, 1955; Weider & Noller: 1950, 1953), and through measuring the similarity between responses of parents and their children (Gray & Klaus, 1956; Lazowick, 1955).

It is probably true that most individuals may be said to prefer, adopt, and identify with their own sex role. Most psychologists associate psychological disturbances with a lack of harmony among aspects of an individual's sex role. With the present conceptual scheme a variety of combinations are theoretically possible, e.g., a person might identify with and adopt the pattern of his own sex, but still prefer the opposite-sex role. On the other hand, a person might identify with the opposite-sex role, adopt the behavior of his own sex, and also consciously prefer the same-sex role, etc. These sex-role definitions should become better clarified in the body of the paper.

THEORETICAL FORMULATIONS

Before stating specific hypotheses let us briefly formulate the position taken in this paper concerning the development of masculine and feminine identification. The developmental processes, as presented here, are not considered inevitable nor universal. If these processes are appropriately described for the U.S. culture of today, they may not fit a significantly altered U.S. culture of the future. Moreover, if these processes are appropriately described for the U.S. culture, they may, nevertheless, be inappropriate to many other cultures. Cross-cultural studies should help verify and amplify the hypotheses presented in this paper.

First, it is assumed that the process of identification follows the laws of learning. Next, it is postulated that, for both male and female infants, learning to identify with the mother (or the person playing the mother-role) is among the earliest learning experiences. In this formulation, it is considered one of the major sex differences in the development of identification that the boy must shift from his initial identification with the mother to identification with the masculine role, whereas the girl need make no such shift.

The shift from mother to masculine identification is begun when the boy discovers that he somehow does not belong in the same sex-category as the mother, but rather as the father; that he is no longer almost completely in a woman's world characterized by the maternal care received during infancy, but is now increasingly in a man's world. It is true that in early childhood, as well as in infancy, the child's life is mainly peopled with women rather than men, but the ideology of our culture in general, and the demands made on the little boy in particular, are masculine in nature. Despite the shortage of male models, a somewhat stereotyped and conventional masculine role is nonetheless rather clearly spelled out for him. A study by Sherriffs and Jarrett (1953) indicated that men and women share the same stereotypes about the two sexes. They found that ". . . virtually no behavior or quality escapes inclusion in either a male or female 'stereotype,' and that these stereotypes are substantially the same whether held by men or women" (Sherriffs & Jarrett, 1953, p. 161).

If the boy behaves like a "little man," say by not crying when hurt, this "brave" behavior is reinforced. Perhaps he is rewarded by being called "Mommy's nice little man." If, on the other hand, he does not behave in a masculine-stereotyped fashion, say he cries when hurt, this behavior may be negatively reinforced, e.g., by being called a sissy. If he behaves in a feminine-stereotyped fashion, say by playing with dolls beyond a certain age, he may be similarly ridiculed. Moreover, he is rewarded simply for having been born masculine through countless privileges accorded males but not females. The boy learns to prefer the masculine role to the feminine one, to adopt the masculine role, and, in time, to identify with it. Sex-role identification, being a more deeply rooted process than either sex-role preference or sex-role adoption, is consequently more slowly changed. However, through the reinforcement of the culture's highly developed system of rewards and punishment, the boy's early learned identification with the mother eventually weakens and becomes more or less replaced by the later learned identification with a culturally defined, somewhat stereotyped masculine role.

The development of the appropriate sex-role identification for the girl is considered, in many ways, the converse of that for the boy. When the girl leaves infancy she goes from a woman's world of mother care to a man's world. Being feminine, she thus moves from a same-sex- to an opposite-sex oriented world, whereas the boy, conversely, moves from an opposite-sex-oriented to a same-sex-oriented world. Unlike the situation for the boy, whose sex role is well spelled out for him, the girl, upon leaving infancy, does not receive adequate reinforcement through distinct rewards for adopting the feminine role, and definite punishment for adopting the masculine one. On the contrary, she is, in a sense, punished simply for being born female, whereas the boy is rewarded simply

235

for being born male. Findings in *Patterns of Child Rearing,* by Sears et al. (1957), support the suggestion that the girl is, in a way, punished for being female. The girls were found to be treated less permissively than boys and more conformity was demanded of them. Hubert and Britton (1957) also found mothers of boys to be less strict with them, expect less understanding of rules, and to allow more activity. The girl quickly learns to prefer the masculine role since our culture, despite definite changes is still masculine-centered and masculine-oriented, and offers the male many privileges and much prestige not accorded the female. As Brown pointed out,

> The superior position and privileged status of the male permeates nearly every aspect, minor and major, of our social life. The gadgets and prizes in boxes of breakfast cereal, for example, commonly have a strong masculine rather than feminine appeal. And the most basic social institutions perpetuate this pattern of masculine aggrandizement. Thus, the Judeo-Christian faiths involve worshipping God, a "Father," rather than a "Mother," and Christ, a "Son," rather than a "Daughter" (Brown, 1958, p. 235).

Smith (1939) found results to suggest that children, as they grow older, increasingly learn to give males prestige. Smith asked children from eight to 15 to vote on whether boys or girls had desirable and undesirable traits. He found: (*a*) with increase in age, boys have a progressively poorer relative opinion of girls, and girls have a progressively better relative opinion of boys; (*b*) with increase in age, boys have a progressively better opinion of themselves, and girls have a progressively poorer opinion of themselves. Kitay (1940) found that women share with men the prejudices prevailing in our culture against their own sex.

Not only does the girl learn to prefer the masculine role because of its many advantages, but she, unlike the boy, is not given the degree of negative reinforcement for adopting certain aspects of the opposite-sex role. Although restricted in many ways more than boys, girls are nevertheless allowed more freedom than boys in opposite-sex role adoption. For a girl to be a tomboy does not involve the censure that results when a boy is a sissy. Girls may wear masculine clothing (shirts, trousers), but boys may not wear feminine clothing (skirts, dresses). Girls may play with toys typically associated with boys (cars, trucks, erector sets, guns), but boys are discouraged from playing with feminine toys (dolls, tea sets).

Data from two national sample interview studies of adolescents, reported by Douvan (1957a, 1957b), suggest that the role for the adolescent girl is very poorly defined by the culture. Since she is typically not yet married, the adolescent girl cannot play her primary role of wife and mother. Furthermore, the culture discourages her from taking action to realize this primary role. The female is not supposed to take the major initiative in choosing a mate. She must, to a large extent, be chosen as a mate rather than actively choosing. Moreover, because her primary goal is marriage and family, the girl's vocational plans do not imply the same career commitment that the boy's vocational plans imply for him. Douvan concludes that "girls . . . can do little about the central aspect of feminine identity before marriage" (1957b, p. 190).

The girl, however, has the same-sex parental model for identification (the mother) with her more than the boy has the same-sex parental model (the father) with him. Both boys and girls usually spend more time with their mothers than with their fathers. They see the mother engaging in many activities, and under many circumstances in which they do not see the father. There is much incidental learning which takes places from such contact with the mother. Although both boys and girls doubtless learn a great deal in this incidental fashion, it is only the girls, not the boys, who can, later on at the appropriate time, apply such latent learning in a direct fashion in their lives. The boys, being separated more from their fathers than girls from their mothers, tend to identify with the steroetype of the masculine role which the culture in general, not simply the father in particular, spells out for them. The girl, on the other hand, tends to identify with aspects of her own mother's role specifically.

However, the girl is still affected by many cultural pressures despite the fact that she need not shift identification, and despite the physical presence of the mother during her development. In this formulation it is predicted that the prestige and privileges afforded males but not females, and the lack of punishment for adopting aspects of the masculine role, have a slow, corrosive, weakening effect on the girl's feminine identification. Conversely, the prestige and privileges accorded the male, the rewards offered for adopting the masculine role, and the punishment for not doing so, are predicted to have a strengthing effect on the boy's masculine identification.

HYPOTHESES

The following hypotheses emerge from this formulation:

1. The young boy's same-sex identification is at first not very firm because of the shift from mother to masculine identification. On the other hand, the young girl, because she need make no such shift in identification, is relatively firm in her initial feminine identification. However, the culture reinforces the boy in developing masculine identification much more adequately than it does the girl in developing feminine identification. *Consequently, with increasing age, males become relatively more firmly identified with the masculine role and females relatively less firmly identified with the feminine role.*

2. The culture offers higher prestige and more advantages to the male than to the female. *Consequently, a larger proportion of females than males will show preference for the role of the opposite sex.*

3. Not only is the male role accorded more prestige than the female role, but boys are more likely to be punished than girls for adopting aspects of the opposite-sex role. *Therefore, a higher proportion of females than males adopt aspects of the role of the opposite sex.*

4. The girl has the same-sex parent (the mother) with her more than the boy has the same-sex parent (the father) with him as a model for identification. However, a stereotyped sort of masculine role is spelled out rather clearly for the boys by the culture. *Consequently, males tend to identify with a cultural stereotype of the masculine role, whereas females tend to identify with aspects of their own mothers' role specifically.*

TEST OF HYPOTHESES

Let us now see how consistently these hypotheses fit previous findings and whether this formulation helps clarify seeming contradictions.

If Hypothesis 1 is valid, that with increasing age, boys become relatively more firmly identified with the masculine role and girls relatively less firmly identified with the female role, and assuming that figure drawings constitute an adequate measure of identification, then this hypothesized trend should be reflected in the sex of the figure drawn first. The data do seem, in fact, to support this hypothesis. Brown and Tolor (1957) reviewed a number of studies on human figure drawings. The studies on figure drawings with children (Jolles, 1952; Morris, 1955; Tolor & Tolor, 1955; Weider & Noller: 1950, 1953) show that, with younger children, a higher proportion of girls than boys drew the same-sex figure first, and with older children this trend is reversed, and a larger proportion of boys than girls drew the same-sex figure first. A study by Jolles (1952), using a wide age range, might be specifically cited in this regard. Jolles found that with children between five and 12, a significantly higher proportion of younger boys drew the opposite-sex figure first than did older boys. A significant higher proportion of 11- and 12-year-old girls drew the opposite-sex figure first than did boys of the same age.

Lynn and Sawrey,[1] in an unpublished study in which eight- and nine-year-old Norwegian children were asked to draw a family (in contrast to drawing a person), found that a higher proportion of girls than boys drew the same-sex parent figure first, largest, and in most detail.

Despite the fact that with younger children a higher proportion of girls than boys drew the same-sex figure first, studies with adults consistently show a higher proportion of men than women drawing the same-sex figure first. Brown and Tolor (1957) combined findings from several studies of figure drawings with college Ss and found that 91% of the men drew the male figure first while only 67% of the women drew the female figure first.

Thus, the findings on figure drawings support the hypothesis that with increasing age males become more firmly same-sex identified and females relatively less firmly same-sex identified. However, Brown and Tolor (1957) found evidence leading them to suggest that human figure drawings may be an adequate test of identification. Confidence in the validity of this hypothesis must await substantiation through further research findings.

In this formulation it is considered one thing to show a sex-role preference, and quite another to form a sex-role identification. Hypothesis 2 predicts that, because of higher prestige and greater privileges accorded the masculine role, a higher proportion of females than males will show opposite-sex-role preference. In this connection Rabban (1950) asked 300 children between 30 months and eight years of age to choose the toys they liked best from a number of toys. Some of the toys were judged to be typically associated with boys and others with girls. All of the Ss were also asked to pick a doll which resembled them most and to indicate the sex of the doll. In addition, they were asked whether they would like to be a "mama" or "daddy" when they grow up. The results showed no significant differences between three-year-old children, but otherwise boys showed significantly more masculine preferences than girls feminine preferences.

Brown (1957) administered the It Scale for Children to 303 boys

---

1. Lynn, D. B., and Sawrey, W. L. Sex differences in the personality development of Norwegian children.

and 310 girls between the ages of approximately 5 ½ and 11 ½. The It scale is composed of pictures of various objects and figures typical of and associated with the role of one sex in contrast to the other. A card with a child-figure drawing on it, referred to as "It," is used by having each S make choices for It. Brown found that boys showed a much stronger preference for the masculine role than girls for the feminine role, particularly in all grades below the fifth. He found that girls at the kindergarten level showed a preference pattern characterized by relatively equal preference for masculine and feminine elements, and girls from the first grade through the fourth grade showed a stronger preference for the masculine role than for the feminine role. In contrast to girls in all earlier grade levels, girls in the fifth grade showed a predominant preference for the feminine role.

The Lynn Structured Doll Play Test (Lynn: 1955, 1957a, 1957b; Lynn & Lynn, in press; Lynn & Sawrey, in press; Tiller, 1958) was used in the study of 80 eight- and nine-year-old Norwegian children mentioned above in connection with an unpublished study by Lynn and Sawrey. The Structured Doll Play Test (SDP) is a projective test in which the S is presented with dolls representing family and peer group figures in a series of typical family and peer group situations. The S resolves these situations through doll play. One of the SDP situations required the S to choose either the boy or girl doll as the one for the ego-doll to play with. The results showed a significantly higher proportion of girls choosing the boy doll (the opposite-sex child doll) than the girl doll (the same-sex child doll). Thus, despite the fact that these same Norwegian girls had drawn the same-sex parent figure first, largest, and in most detail, they nevertheless showed a preference for the opposite-sex child doll.

These results are consistent with studies of sex-role preference in adults in which men and women were asked whether they had ever wished to belong to the opposite sex. These studies show that below 5% of adult males as contrasted to as high as 31% of adult females recall consciously having been aware of the desire to be of the opposite sex (Fortune survey, 1946; Gallup, 1955; Terman, 1938).

Thus, the research findings in general support the hypothesis that more females prefer the masculine sex role than males the feminine role.

Hypothesis 3 predicts that more females not only prefer, but also adopt the masculine role than males do the feminine role. Emmerich (in press) used a structured doll play interview with 31 Ss between 3 ½ and 5 years of age. Emmerich measured the degree of similarity between the S's conception of his parent's nurturance-control attitude and the S's own nurturance-control attitude. The

*S*s parent's nurturance-control attitude was indicated by the doll play fantasy of the parent doll's actions toward a child doll. The *S*s own nurturance-control attitude was indicated by the fantasy of the child doll's actions toward a baby doll. The degree of similarity between the parent's and *S*'s attitude was the difference between the parent doll's and the child doll's nurturance-control scores. In the present conceptual framework this is considered a measure of fantasied sex-role adoption. Emmerich found that only the boys but not the girls showed a significant tendency to select the same-sex parent as a model more than the opposite-sex parent. Thus, the boys adopted (in fantasy) the father role more closely than they did the mother role. In this way the hypothesis tended to be supported, at least for young children.

As was pointed out above, the mother is typically with the children more than the father is, thus making herself available as a model for identification more frequently than the father. Largely for this reason, Hypothesis 4 predicts that males tend to identify with a cultural stereotype of the masculine role whereas females tend to identify with aspects of their own mothers' role specifically. Gray and Klaus (1956) did a study relevant to this hypothesis, using responses to a sentence completion test and to the Allport-Vernon-Lindzey Study of Values filled out by 34 female and 28 male college students, their parents, and by the students as they believed their mothers and fathers would respond. They found much more similarity between the women and their mothers than between the men and their fathers, both as tested and as perceived.

Hypothesis 4 was also supported in a study by Lazowick (1955). The *S*s in this study were 30 college students. These *S*s and their mothers and fathers were required to rate concepts, e.g., "myself," "father," "mother," etc. The degree of similarity between "meanings" of each concept as rated by *S*s and their parents was then determined. It was found that the similarity between fathers and their own children was not significantly greater than between fathers and children randomly matched. On the other hand, the similarity between mothers and their own children was greater than between mothers and children randomly matched.

Thus, despite the fact that data on figure drawings suggest that more men are same-sex identified than women, these results suggest that women are more closely identified with aspects of the role of their own same-sex parent (mother) specifically than men are with their own same-sex parent (father).

What are some of the ways this theoretical formulation may clarify seemingly contradictory or confusing findings? This paper reviewed studies showing that a higher proportion of girls than

241

boys chose objects and pictures of objects characteristically considered masculine (Brown: 1956, 1957; Rabban, 1950); and yet, in the study by Lynn and Sawrey, a higher proportion of eight-year-old girls than boys drew the same-sex parent figure first, largest, and in most detail. These findings are very confusing if the term "identification" is used in connection with both the operations "sex-role object choice" and "parent drawings." The differentiation suggested by Brown (1956), and also used in this formulation, between sex-role preference and sex-role identification may eliminate the contradiction in these results. The studies of choice of masculine and feminine objects are considered, in this formulation, studies of *sex-role preference;* whereas the studies of figure drawings are considered studies of *sex-role identification.*

The results in which a higher proportion of adult males than females drew the same-sex figure first are in seeming contradiction with data reviewed showing a closer similarity between responses of women and their mothers' responses, than of men and their fathers' responses (Gray & Klaus, 1956). The contradiction is removed by the hypothesis that the male identifies with a stereotype of the masculine role, and the female with her mother's role specifically.

The data showing that females responded with more similarity to their own mothers' responses than males to their fathers' responses (Gray & Klaus, 1956) may also seem to contradict the data in the study by Emmerich (in press) in which young boys, but not girls, showed a significant tendency to select the same-sex parent as a model more than the opposite-sex parent. There is, however, a great deal of difference between the operations involved in these two studies, viz. in the *S*'s *fantasy* of the father doll's actions (Emmerich, in press), and the *actual* responses of real fathers to the materials used in the study by Gray and Klaus (1956). In the framework of the present formulation the boys in the doll play study *adopted,* in fantasy, the father role significantly more closely than they did the mother role; whereas in the study of Gray and Klaus the adult males did not *identify* as closely with their own fathers' role as the women with their own mothers' role.

SUMMARY

The purpose of this note is to contribute to the theoretical formulation of sex differences in the development of masculine and feminine identification, and review research findings relevant to this formulation.

There was a differentiation made among the concepts of *sex-role preference, sex-role adoption,* and *sex-role identification.*

The process of identification was assumed to follow the laws of learning. Both male and female infants were hypothesized to learn to identify with the mother. Boys, but not girls, must shift from this initial identification with the mother to masculine identification. Despite the fact that the girl need not shift her identification, and despite the physical presence of the mother during her development, the girl is still affected by many cultural pressures. The prestige and privileges offered males but not females, and the lack of punishment for adopting aspects of the masculine role, are predicted to have a slow, corrosive, weakening effect on the girl's feminine identification. Conversely, the prestige and privileges accorded the male, the culture's systematic rewards for adopting the masculine role, and punishment for not doing so, strengthen the boy's masculine identification.

The following hypotheses emerged:

1. With increasing age, males become relatively more firmly identified with the masculine role, and females relatively less firmly identified with the feminine role.

2. A larger proportion of females than males will show preference for the role of the opposite sex.

3. A higher proportion of females than males adopt aspects of the role of the opposite sex.

4. Males tend to identify with a cultural stereotype of the masculine role, whereas females tend to identify with aspects of their own mothers' role specifically.

These hypotheses were generally supported by the research findings which were reviewed. This formulation may help clarify previously confusing and seemingly contradictory data.

REFERENCES

Brown, D. G. Sex-role preference in young children. *Psychol. Monogr.*, 1956, *70*, No. 14 (Whole No. 421).

Brown, D. G. Masculinity-femininity development in children. *J. consult. Psychol.*, 1957, *21*, 197-202.

Brown, D. G. Sex-role development in a changing culture. *Psychol. Bull.*, 1958, *55*, 232-242.

Brown, D. G., & Tolor, A. Human figure drawings as indicators of sexual identification and inversion. *Percept. mot. Skills,* 1957, *7*, 199-211 (Monogr. Suppl. 3).

Cava, E. L., & Rausch, H. L. Identification and the adolescent boy's perception of his father. *J. abnorm. soc. Psychol.,* 1952, *47*, 855-856.

Douvan, Elizabeth. Character processes in adolescence. Paper read at the American Psychological Association, New York, August 1957. (a).

Douvan, Elizabeth. Independence and identity in adolescence. *Children,* 1957, *4*, 186-190. (b).

Emmerich, W. A study of parental identification in young children. *Genet. Pscyhol. Monogr.,* in press.

Fenichel, O. *The psychoanalytic theory of neurosis.* New York: Norton, 1945.

Fortune Survey. *Fortune,* August 1946.

Gallup, G. *Gallup poll.* Princeton: Audience Research Inc., June 1955.

Gray, Susan W., & Klaus, R. The assessment of parental identification. *Genet. Psychol. Monogr.,* 1956, *54*, 87-109.

Hubert, M. A. G., & Britton, J. H. Attitudes and practices of mothers rearing their children from birth to the age of two years. *J. Home Econ.,* 1957, *49*, 208-223.

Jolles, I. A study of the validity of some hypotheses for the qualitative interpretation of the H-T-P for children of elementary school age: I. Sexual identification. *J. clin. Psychol.,* 1952, *8*, 113-118.

Kitay, P. M. A comparison of the sexes in their attitudes and beliefs about women: A study of prestige groups. *Sociometry,* 1940, *3*, 399-407.

Lazowick, L. M. On the nature of identification. *J. abnorm. soc. Psychol.,* 1955, *51*, 175-183.

Lynn, D. B. Development and validation of a structured doll play test for children. *Quart. Bull. Indiana Univer. Med. Ctr.,* Jan. 1955.

Lynn, D. B. Father-absence and personality development of children in Norwegian sailor families. Paper read at the Midwestern Psychological Association, Chicago, April 1957. (a)

Lynn, D. B. *Structure Doll Play Test manual.* Unpublished manuscript (mimeo.), Indiana Univer. Med. Sch. Library, Indianapolis, Indiana, 1957. (b)

Lynn, D.B., and Lynn, Rosalie. The Structured Doll Play Test as a projective technique for use with children. *J. proj. Tech.,* in press.

Lynn, D.B., and Sawrey, W.L. The effects of father-absence on Norwegian boys and girls. *J. abnorm. soc. Psychol.,* in press.

Martin, W. E. Learning theory and identification: III. The development of values in children. *J. genet. Psychol.,* 1954, *84*, 211-217.

Morris, W. W. Ontogenetic changes in adolescence reflected by the Drawing-Human-Figures Techniques. *Amer. J. Orthopsychiat.,* 1955, *25,* 720-728.

Mowrer, O. H. *Psychotherapy: Theory and research.* New York: Ronald Press, 1953.

Rabban, M. Sex-role identification in young children in two diverse social groups. *Genet. Psychol. Monogr.,* 1950, *42,* 81-158.

Sanford, N. The dynamics of identification. *Psychol. Rev.,* 1955, *62,* 106-118.

Sears, R. R., Maccoby, E. E., & Levin, H. *Patterns of child rearing.* Evanston, Ill.: Row, Peterson, 1957.

Sherriffs, A. C., and Jarrett, R. F. Sex differences in attitudes about sex differences. *J. Psychol.,* 1953, *35,* 161-168.

Smith, S. Age and sex differences in children's opinion concerning sex differences. *J. genet. Psychol., 1939, 54, 17-25.*

Stokes, *S. M. An inquiry into the concept of identification. J. genet. Psychol.,* 1950, *77,* 163-189.

Terman, L. M. *Psychological factors in marital happiness.* New York: McGraw-Hill, 1938.

Tiller, P. O. Father absence and personality development of children in sailor families. *Nordisk Psykologi's Monogr.,* 1958, Ser. No. 9.

Tolman, E. C. Identification and the post-war world. *J. abnorm. soc. Psychol.,* 1943, *38,* 141-148.

Tolor, A., and Tolor, B. Judgment of children's popularity from their human figure drawings. *J. proj. Tech.,* 1955, 19, 170-176.

Weider, A., and Noller, P.A. Objective studies of children's drawings of human figures. I Sex awareness and socio-economic level. *J. clin. Psychol.,* 1950, *6,* 319-325.

Weider, A., and Noller, P.A. Objective studies of children's drawings of human figures. II. Sex, age, intelligence, *J. clin. Psychol.,* 1953, *9,* 20-23.

16

If one assumes that sex roles are the result of social learning, it becomes necessary to find the source of the rewards and punishments which define the properties of the "proper" role for the child. The obvious place to look for such influences is the parental reaction to the social behavior of the child. Rothbart and Maccoby have provided a well-controlled empirical study designed to determine whether mothers and fathers react differentially to the behavior of children depending upon the sex of the child. The parents' attitudes toward sex-role differentiation was also investigated.

If sex-role characteristic behavior is selectively reinforced by the parents, one would expect to find that dependent behaviors were less reinforced for females. The experimenters used a sexually ambiguous child's voice as a stimulus and a number of life-like social situations involving dependency, aggression and autonomy. They did not find any differences in behavior dependent upon either the parents' or the child's sex alone. Instead, they found that fathers were more permissive toward female children in all situations and mothers were more permissive toward male children. Attitudes toward sex-role did not affect this behavior. In this paper, Rothbart and Maccoby suggest that since sex differences in parental reinforcement of sex characteristic behavior are inconsistent, such behaviors may be differentiated because of a strong biological component.

Although this study is a very interesting one, generalizations on the basis of it must be limited. As Rothbart and Maccoby themselves note, the population may have been a highly self-selected one—parents whose children were enrolled in a parent-education nursery school. Moreover, the subjects were aware that they were being studied, thus, their behavior may not have been characteristic of their usual reactions to similar social situations. Nevertheless, the study provides some interesting data on sex of parent x sex of child interactions which deserve further investigation.

Parents' Differential Reactions to Sons and Daughters*

Mary K. Rothbart and Eleanor E. Maccoby

This study investigated parents' reactions to a child's voice as a function of (a) sex of parent, and (b) sex of child. Using as a stimulus a child's voice that was ambiguous with respect to sex, 1 group of parents was told they were hearing a boy's voice, another that they were hearing a girl's voice. A pattern of results emerged with fathers showing generally greater permissiveness toward girls than boys for both dependency and aggression, and with mothers showing greater permissiveness toward boys than girls. Parents' sex-role differentiation scores as measured by a questionnaire were also found to relate to their responses to the child's voice, but the expectation that high-differentiation parents would show a stronger tendency to promote stereotyped sex-role behavior in the child was not upheld.

The existence of sex differences in psychological functioning has been repeatedly documented in psychological literature. Often the differences have been unexpected and have taken complex forms (Oetzel, in press). Any theory of sex typing that attempts to understand the sources of these differences must consider the possible effects of differential parent pressures occurring as a function of the sex of the child. Few studies have as yet explored the nature of differential parent behaviors toward boys and girls, and any complete study of this kind would have to consider sex of parents as another important source of variation. The present study therefore attempts to examine parent behavior toward a child as a function of (a) sex of the parent, and (b) sex of the child.

Previous studies of mother-father differences in treatment of boys and girls have been of two major types. The first involves children's perceptions of their parents' behavior; the second involves parents' perception of their own behavior and attitudes toward their children. Numerous studies of children's perceptions

---

* From *Journal of Personality and Social Psychology,* 1966, *4*(3), 337-43.

of their parents have been carried out, and the literature is summarized and briefly criticized by Droppleman and Schaeffer (1963). Considering only studies with preadolescent children, a common finding has been that both boys and girls "prefer" the mother to the father and find her friendlier and easier to get along with (Hawkes, Burchinal, and Gardner, 1957; Kagan, 1956; Simpson, 1935).

Cross-sex findings suggesting an interaction between sex of parent and sex of child have also been reported. When Simpson (1935) questioned children ranging in ages from 5 to 9, the boys said they were punished (spanked) more by their fathers than their mothers. Girls said mothers spanked them more, but the inference from their projective responses was that the father punished more. Kagan and Lemkin (1960) interviewed children ages 3-8 and found few sex differences in reports of parent practices. Both boys and girls reported that the opposite-sex parent "kissed the most." Girls saw the father as more punitive and affectionate than the mother, while boys saw him only as more punitive. Kagan (1956) interviewed first-, second-, and third-grade children on four issues: Who (the mother or the father) would be on the child's side in an argument; who punishes; who is the boss of the house; who is more feared. With children of all ages combined, there was little cross-sex difference in response. When the younger and older children were treated separately, the older children showed a consistent tendency to see the same-sex parent as less benevolent and more frustrating.

In studies involving parents rather than children, Aberle and Naegele (1952) and Tasch (1952) used only fathers as subjects. Fathers reported different expectations for sons and daughters and said that they participated in different activities with their sons than with their daughters. Sears, Maccoby, and Levin (1957) used only mothers as subjects, interviewing at length mothers of nursery school children. Mothers reported that they permit more aggressiveness from boys when it is directed toward parents and children outside the family, no difference in permissiveness of aggression against siblings. No differences in severity of punishment for aggression nor in permissiveness for dependency were found. Mothers reported they did most of the disciplining of both sexes, but that the father took a larger role in disciplining his son when both parents were at home. In a study with both parents, Goodenough (1957) found that mothers were less concerned about their child's appropriate sex typing than were fathers. Fathers also reported they were actively involved in implementing sex typing of their children, while mothers reported they did not consciously attempt to influence sex typing.

WOMAN: DEPENDENT OR INDEPENDENT VARIABLE?

Emmerich (1962) gave questionnaires for assessing nurturance and restrictiveness to parents of children ages 6-10, defining nurturance as reward for positive behavior and dependency, and restrictiveness as punishment for negative behavior. The two scales were combined as a measure of power. Mothers were found to be more nurturant and less restrictive toward children of both sexes. A marked trend was also found for fathers to exert more power toward their sons than their daughters, and a similar but less powerful trend for mothers to exert more power toward their daughters than toward their sons. Emmerich's data are suggestive of differences between mothers and fathers in their treatment of boys and girls, but only on a very general dimension. The questions asked of parents were also quite amorphous, for example, rating the extent to which he compliments his daughter "when she does what she knows she should do," or gives her "something at the time she wants it."

The present experiment is an attempt to study parents' reactions to specific child behaviors, including some regarded as sex typed, for example, dependency and aggression.

We are also interested in a test of hypothesis proposed by social learning theorists to account for sex differences in behavior. Mischel (in press) suggests:

> The greater incidence of dependent behaviors for girls than boys, and the reverse situation with respect to physically aggressive behavior, seems directly explicable in social learning terms. Dependent behaviors are less rewarded for males, physically aggressive behaviors are less rewarded for females in our culture, and, consequently there are mean differences between the sexes in the frequency of such behaviors after the first few years of life.

Assuming that the family constitutes the major "culture" to which the preschool child is exposed, we might predict from this learning-theory interpretation that both parents would consistently reinforce dependency more strongly in girls and aggression more strongly in boys. The present study is designed to test this prediction.

Parents were put in a hypothetical situation with a child and were asked to record their immediate reactions to what the child said and did. To avoid the additional variables that would compound an adult's reaction to an actual boy or girl, the recorded voice of a single child constituted the stimulus material. The voices of a number of 4-year-olds were recorded, and one was chosen which judges could not readily identify as to sex. Some of the parents were informed that it was a boy's voice, some that it was a girl's voice, and differences in their responses were examined. A questionnaire was also used to measure the extent to which a parent differentiates between the sexes by either (a) feeling boys and girls are different on selected characteristics, or (b) feeling boys and girls *should* differ on these characteristics. It was hypothesized that parents showing high differentiation between boys and girls would show greater differences in reaction to the boy's voice compared with the girl's voice than would parents who differentiated little between the sexes.

METHOD

This study was preceded by an initial individual testing of 58 mothers. A small pilot group of both mothers and fathers was then tested in a group-administered procedure, and the coding categories and questionnaire were revised. The final testing involved both fathers and mothers in a group administration.

Selection of the Stimulus Voice

The child speaker was chosen by recording nine nursery school children reciting a prepared script. Six adult judges rated the sex of each child after hearing the tape recordings. The voice selected (that of a boy) was judged to be a boy by half the judges and a girl by the other half. In the actual study, none of the parent subjects questioned the sex attributed to the voice they heard.

The statements comprising the script were adaptations of actual statements of 3- and 4-year-old children recorded in the same locality approximately a year before the final study. An attempt was made to make the script as realistic as possible, and a number of mothers in the individually administered pretest remarked that the recorded child sounded very much like their own nursery school child.

Subjects

Subjects were 98 mothers and 32 fathers of children enrolled in a parent-education nursery school. These parents came from a range of socioeconomic status levels, with a concentration of upper-middle-class families.

Of these parents, 60 mothers and 21 fathers were told that the voice was a girl's, 38 mothers and 11 fathers that it was a boy's.

251

WOMAN: DEPENDENT OR INDEPENDENT VARIABLE?

The reason for a larger number of parents hearing the girl's than the boy's voice was that only the number of parents expected to attend had been matched according to sex and age of the nursery school child and assigned to the two groups. More parents attended than had been anticipated, and the extra parents all heard the girl's voice.

The group hearing the boy's voice and the group hearing the girl's voice proved to be matched according to sex of nursery school age child, but it was later found that the two groups were not well matched with respect to whether the parent had children of only one or of both sexes. Our sample was divided according to this variable, and no differences in a direction that would influence our results were found.

Presentation of the Stimulus Voice

Parents were tested in four separate groups (fathers-girl's voice, fathers-boy's voice, mothers-girl's voice, mothers-boy's voice), with female experimenters. Each experimenter introduced the parents to the situation represented by the tape-recorded voice. The subject was asked to imagine that he (or she) was at home reading, with his 4-year-old boy, Johnny (or girl, Susan), playing with a puzzle in an adjacent room. With the child is the 1-year-old baby. Subjects were asked to give their immediate reactions to the 4-year-old's statements by writing down what they would say or do in response to each statement. The child's statements were as follows. (Due to some lack of clarity in the tape, each statement of the child was repeated by the experimenter to assure that it was understood by all subjects.)

1. Daddy (or Mommy), come look at my puzzle.
2. Daddy, help me.
3. Does this piece go here?
4. Baby, you can't play with me. You're too little.
5. Tell him he can't play with my puzzle—it's mine!
6. Leave my puzzle alone or I'll hit you in the head!
7. I don't like this game—I'm gonna break it!
8. I don't like this game. It's a stupid game. You're stupid, Daddy.
9. Ow! Baby stepped on my hand!
10. Daddy—it hurts.
11. Daddy, get me another puzzle.
12. It's not raining now—I'm going across the street and play.

After each statement, the experimenter stopped the tape while subjects recorded their reactions.

Parents' responses were coded for each item, and items were grouped according to 7 different scales: Help Seeking (Items 1, 2, 3, 11), Comfort Seeking (9, 10), Dependency (Help and Comfort Seeking scales combined), Aggression (6a, 7a, 8a), Allowing Child to Stop Game (7, 8), Siding with Child versus Baby (4, 5, 6), and Autonomy (12). Scores on all scales ranged generally from permissiveness for the child (low score) to nonpermissiveness for the child's actions (high score). For example, in response to the child's statement 9 ("Ow! Baby stepped on my hand!"), a rating of high comfort was given to the response, "Here, Mommy will kiss it," while a rating of low comfort was given to the response, "Keep your hand away from the baby's food." In response to Statement 5 ("Tell him he can't play with my puzzle—it's mine!"), a parent who said, "That's right. Let's find the baby something else," was rated as siding with the child. A response of "Johnny, let your brother help you" was rated as siding with the baby. All protocols were coded by one rater, and 25 were coded independently by a second rater. Reliabilities ranged from .83 to 1.00, with a mean scale correlation of .90.

Questionnaire

The parent questionnaire, administered immediately after the tape-recorded script, measured two aspects of parents' attitudes about sex differences. Part 1 asked parents' opinions about differences they felt actually existed between boys and girls. The items included were taken from statements given by mothers to open-ended interview questions about sex differences from the files of the Sears et al. (1957) study. The format for the questionnaire was adapted from Sherriffs and Jarrett (1953). A sample from the 40-item list is as follows:

More likely to be obedient are: __ __ __ .
G B X

Here, G represents girls, B boys, and X no sex differences. The measure of sex-role differentiation for this part of the scale was the total number of X responses, with a large number of X responses indicating low sex-role differentiation.

Part 2 of the questionnaire measured what differences parents felt *should* exist between boys and girls. Boys and girls were rated separately on how important it was to the parent that his child be described by each characteristic. A sample item is:

Very impor- tant *not* to	Fairly impor- tant *not* to	Unimportant to	Fairly impor- tant to	Very impor- tant to	
					be obedient.

TABLE 1

MOTHERS' AND FATHERS' REACTIONS TO BOY'S VERSUS GIRL'S VOICE

Voice	Help Seeking (High score-refuses help)		Comfort Seeking (High score-refuses)		Dependency (High score-refuses)		Aggression (High score-does not permit)	
	Mothers	Fathers	Mothers	Fathers	Mothers	Fathers	Mothers	Fathers
Boy's								
M	8.71	8.45	4.24	5.82	12.95	14.18	4.95	5.64
SD	1.71	1.51	1.73	2.18	2.32	2.92	1.29	2.16
N	38	11	38	11	38	11	37	11
Girl's								
M	9.15	8.39	5.02	4.84	14.17	13.12	4.91	4.86
SD	1.93	1.61	1.86	1.56	3.05	2.55	1.32	1.62
N	59	18	59	19	59	17	56	21

	Allowing Child to Stop Game (High score-does not)		Siding With Child versus Baby (High score-sides with baby)		Autonomy (High score-does not permit)		Aggression toward Parent (High score-does not permit)	
	Mothers	Fathers	Mothers	Fathers	Mothers	Fathers	Mothers	Fathers
Boy's								
M	3.62	4.18	6.13	7.64	1.97	2.27	1.59	2.27
SD	1.09	1.17	1.43	1.43	.64	.64	1.76	1.01
N	37	11	37	11	37	11	38	11
Girl's								
M	4.00	3.62	6.76	6.20	2.10	2.40	1.75	1.67
SD	1.09	1.16	1.47	1.61	.47	.60	1.16	1.11
N	57	21	59	19	60	20	60	21

Note.—Mean scores,

254

As a measure of sex-role differentiation for Part 2 of the questionnaire, absolute differences between ratings of an item's importance for girls and importance for boys were summed. The higher this difference (D) score, the higher the sex-role differentiation that was indicated.

RESULTS

Parents' Response to the Child's Voice

When the direction of differences for all scales are considered, a general trend emerges. Mothers tend to be more permissive for the boy's voice and fathers more permissive for the girl's voice (see Table 1). While only one main effect was significant (Scale 7— fathers allowed more autonomy than mothers, $p < .05$), interactions were significant for Scale 2 (Comfort Seeking, $p < .05$), Scale 3 (Dependency, $.05 < p < .10$), Scale 5 (Allowing Child to Stop Game, $.05 < p < .10$), and Scale 6 (Siding with Child versus Baby, $p < .01$) as shown in Table 2. On all of these scales, the interaction was in the direction of mothers showing more permissiveness and positive attention to their sons than to their daughters, fathers showing more permissiveness and positive attention to their daughters than to their sons.

Our failure to find a significant interaction for the Aggression scale was somewhat surprising, since in the initial pilot study we had found a strong tendency for mothers to allow more aggression from their sons than from their daughters. In the pilot study, our

TABLE 2

SUMMARY OF ANALYSES OF VARIANCE INTERACTION
TESTS BETWEEN SEX OF PARENT
AND SEX OF CHILD'S VOICE

Variable	Interaction (MS)[a]	Error (MS)	F
Help Seeking	1.81	3.24	.56
Comfort Seeking	16.29	3.28	4.97**
Dependency	27.06	7.67	3.53*
Aggression	3.13	2.11	1.48
Allowing Child to Stop Game	5.54	1.31	3.70*
Siding with Child versus Baby	24.94	2.16	11.55***
Autonomy	.04	.32	.12
Aggression toward Parent	4.02	1.02	3.94**

* $p < .10, df = 1/121, 1/122.$
** $p < .05, df = 1/123, 1/125.$
*** $p < .01, df = 1/123.$

measure of aggression had been composed chiefly of aggression directed against the parent. For this reason, Item 8*a* (Aggression toward Parent) was examined separately from the rest of the Aggression scale. Item 8*a* showed a significant interaction ($p < .05$), with fathers allowing more aggression from their daughters than from their sons and mothers allowing more aggression from their sons than from their daughters.

Questionnaire

Parent's X scores on the questionnaire (extent to which parent felt differences *do* exist between boys and girls) were correlated with parents' D scores (extent to which parent felt differences *should* exist between boys and girls). The correlation between X and D scores for mothers was $-.53$; the correlation for fathers was $-.40$. Since a high D score and a low X score both represent high sex-role differentiation, these findings indicate a positive correlation between the two measures.

There were no significant differences between mothers' and fathers' sex-role differentiation scores, but parents who had heard the girl's voice tended to have higher sex-role differentiation scores than parents who had heard the boy's voice. This trend appeared in mothers' X and D scores and in fathers' D scores, but was significant only for mothers' D scores ($p < .05$). This finding is difficult to explain, and it suggests that questionnaire scores may be influenced by situational variables.

Finally, parents with high sex-role differentiation scores were separated from parents with low sex-role differentiation scores. Both X and D scores for mothers and fathers were standardized, and divided approximately at the median for the high-and low-differentiation groups. Since not all parents received the questionnaire, *Ns* for the fathers' group were quite small. Parents' responses to the child's voice were then compared, with the expectation that high-differentiation parents would show larger differences between their treatment of boys and girls than would low-differentiation parents. It was also expected that these differences would be in the direction of promoting sex-typed behavior. The first part of this prediction received some support in this study; the second part did not. When scores for all scales were standardized and summed for each subject, giving a general permissiveness score toward the child, high-differentiation parents tended to show greater permissiveness to the opposite-sex child (see Table 3). High sex-role differentiation parents showed larger differences between treatment of boys and girls than did low-differentiation parents for fathers separated on the basis of D scores (p .02) and for mothers separated on the basis of X scores ($p <$ .05). The differences were in the same direction but not significant for mothers separated according to D scores and fathers separated according to X scores.

In testing the hypothesis that differences would run in a sex-stereotyped direction, parents' responses on the Dependency and Aggression scales were more closely examined. On the basis of all parents' responses to the D questionnaire, it was expected that

TABLE 3

MEAN STANDARD SCORES REPRESENTING DEGREE
OF OVERALL PERMISSIVENESS FOR HIGH-
AND LOW-DIFFERENTIATION PARENTS

	Mothers		Fathers	
Voice	High diff.	Low diff.	High diff.	Low diff.
	Groups assigned according to D scores			
Boy's				
M	48.74	47.72	56.75	50.92
SD	4.90	2.15	2.40	4.74
N	15	12	5	6
Girl's				
M	53.05	49.23	47.63	50.48
SD	5.45	4.09	4.49	4.57
N	10	11	8	9
	Groups assigned according to X scores			
Boy's				
M	48.62	48.52	55.15	53.05
SD	4.53	3.95	2.78	4.67
N	14	15	7	4
Girl's				
M	53.26	47.60	49.93	49.90
SD	4.81	5.12	3.85	4.52
N	11	9	9	10

Note.—High scores = nonpermissiveness.

high-differentiation parents would act to promote dependency in girls and assertiveness in boys. When these scales are examined, however, the differences seem rather to be for high-differentiation parents to show greater relative permissiveness to the opposite-sex child than low-differentiation parents. These differences were significant only in Scales 1 and 3 for mothers separated according to D scores (high-differentiation mothers more permissive of dependency in boys, $p <$ .05 for both scales), and Scale 3 for fathers separated according to X scores (high-differentiation fathers more permissive of dependency in girls, $p <$ .05). The direction of these results suggests that high-differentiation parents do not necessarily promote sex-role stereotypes; they rather show an intensification of the kinds of differences found for parents as a whole. When the scores of all high-differentiation parents (regardless of which voice they heard) were compared with those of low-differentiation parents, there was an additional tendency for low-differentiation parents to show more general permissiveness than high-differentiation parents, but in no case was this difference significant.

DISCUSSION

Although previous studies have found clear differences between the behavior of mothers and fathers independent of the sex of the child, the present study found only one difference (permissiveness for autonomy) to be independent of the child's sex. A source of this discrepancy may be that earlier studies relied on verbal reports of children and parents; these reports might be expected to be influenced by the cultural stereotypes of the mother and the father. The present study differed from the earlier ones in that a measure more closely approaching the behavior of a parent in an actual situation was used. Also, the fact that the fathers in this study were attending a meeting concerning their children indicates an involvement with the child that may not be found in the father population as a whole.

Another interesting discrepancy exists between some of the current findings and the predictions expected on the basis of common-sense notions of sex typing. For example, the mothers in this study were more likely to allow aggression toward themselves from their boys, as expected in sex-role stereotypes, but they were also more acceptant of comfort seeking in their sons than in their daughters, an entirely unexpected finding. Fathers, on the other hand, were more acceptant of their daughters' comfort seeking, but also allowed more aggression to be directed toward themselves from their daughters than from their sons. In short, the sex of parent seems to be a better predictor of his differential response to boys and girls than does a sex-role stereotype.

This finding presents some difficulties for the social learning theory interpretation of sex differences outlined at the beginning of this paper (Mischel, in press). Rather than consistent reinforcement of sex-typed behavior by both parents, inconsistency between parents seems to be the rule, and while a parent may treat his child in a manner consistent with the cultural stereotype in one area of behavior, in another he may not.

It is, of course, possible that the only reinforcement counter to the cultural stereotype comes from the child's parents, and that reinforcement from other sources serves to counteract inconsistent parental pressures. It is also possible that parents shift their reinforcing behaviors as their children become older. These possibilities might apply to sex differences in dependency, which seem to emerge late enough to be affected by influences outside the home or later shifts in parental behavior. However, sex differences in aggression have been observed early, while the family is still the primary influence, and our findings fail to support the interpretation that differential reinforcement from both parents is of a kind to promote these differences at this early age level. Perhaps there is a biological component in these sex differences which is of importance either in its own right or in interaction with socialization practices.

There are several possible sources of the cross-sex interaction. In instances of permissiveness for the child's dependent behavior, the parent may be simply responding to the young child as a member of the opposite sex, reacting more favorably to the actions of the child who most resembles his marital partner. Or, reflecting the other side of the Oedipal coin, the parent may react less favorably to the same-sex child because of feelings of rivalry with this child. Another hypothesis, this one concerned with parents' differential responses to negative behavior in the child, suggests that parents may tend to punish the expression of impulses that they do not allow in themselves. As a child, the parent has been punished for certain actions and thoughts, and he may react negatively when he sees expression of these actions and thoughts in his child. When the child is of the same sex as himself, the parent may be more strongly reminded of the situation in which he had been punished, and more negative feelings are evoked. The parent is therefore more likely to punish the same-sex child for negative actions than the opposite-sex child.

This list of possibilities suggests that family interaction springs from multiple motivations, and that any tendency parents may have to reinforce culturally stereotypic behavior in their children may be outweighed by other determinants of their behavior. Parent behavior, then, may not always be consistent with preparing children for the social roles they will fill. Indeed, the child may acquire some aspects of his appropriate role behavior in spite of, rather than because of, what at least one of his parents does as a reinforcing agent.

Although the questionnaire results are by no means conclusive, they suggest a pattern of differences for high-differentiation parents that is simply a stronger statement of the general findings of the study. Perhaps parents with high-differentiation scores are more aware of the differences that distinguish their sons and daughters, but tend to react in a sex-specific way to these sex differences rather than actively promoting sex-typed behavior in their children.

Parents taking the questionnaire for the most part had fairly low sex-role differentiation scores. If this study were replicated with a lower-class sample of parents, we would expect a wider range of sex-role differentiation scores and even stronger interaction effects than were found in this study.

REFERENCES

Aberle, D.F., and Naegele, K.D. Middle class fathers' occupational role and attitudes toward children. *American Journal of Orthopsychiatry,* 1952, *22,* 366-378.

Droppleman, L.F., and Schaeffer, E.S. Boys' and girls' reports of maternal and paternal behavior. *Journal of Abnormal and Social Psychology,* 1963, *67,* 648-654.

Emmerich, W. Variations in the parent role as a function of the parent's sex and the child's sex and age. *Merrill-Palmer Quarterly,* 1962, *8,* 3-11.

Goodenough, E. W. Interest in persons as an aspect of sex differences in the early years. *Genetic Psychology Monographs,* 1957, *55,* 287-323.

Hawkes, G.R., Burchinal, L.G., and Gardner, B. Pre-adolescents' views of some of their relations with their parents. *Child Development,* 1957, *28,* 393-399.

Kagan, J. The child's perception of the parent. *Journal of Abnormal and Social Psychology,* 1956, *53,* 257-258.

Kagan, J., and Lemkin, I. The child's differential perception of parental attributes. *Journal of Abnormal and Social Psychology,* 1960, *61,* 440-447.

Mischel, W. A social learning view of sex differences in behavior. In E. E. Maccoby (Ed.), *The development of sex differences.* Stanford: Stanford University Press, 1966, in press.

Oetzel, R. M. Selected bibliography on sex differences. In E. E. Maccoby (Ed.), *The development of sex differences.* Stanford: Stanford University Press, 1966, in press.

Sears, R.R., Maccoby, E.E., and Levin, H. *Patterns of child rearing.* Evanston, Ill.: Row, Peterson, 1957.

Sherriffs, A.C., and Jarrett, R.F. Sex differences in attitudes about sex differences. *Journal of Psychology,* 1953, *35, 161-168.*

Simpson, M. Parent preferences of young children. Teachers College of Columbia University Contributions to Education, 1935, No. 652.

Tasch, R. G. The role of the father in the family. *Journal of Experimental Education,* 1952, *20,* 319-361.

17

Laboratory studies of parental behavior toward a child are not, by their very nature, able to take into consideration the social makeup of the family. Many psychoanalytically based theories have stressed the fear of punishment as a major factor in the child's development of a sex role. They suggest that the child identifies with the parent because of his powerful ability to dispense both rewards and punishments.

Hetherington has attempted to verify empirically the role of parental power in the development of various components of the sex role. She suggests that if parental power is important, then the child should tend to identify with and prefer the role of the dominant parent regardless of the sex either of that parent or of the child. Her data indicate partial confirmation of her hypotheses. Boys from mother-dominant homes show persistent disruption of male sex-role identification. Girls from father-dominant homes, however, have appropriate sex-role identification and preference. She suggests that the psychoanalytic notion of "identification with the aggressor" is appropriate for boys, but less so for girls. Her data may indicate that sex-role development in males and females is controlled by different factors.

A Developmental Study of the Effects of Sex of the Dominant Parent on Sex-Role Preference, Identification, and Imitation in Children*

E. Mavis Hetherington

This study investigated the effects of sex of the dominant

* From *Journal of Personality and Social Psychology*, 1965, *2*, 188-94.

parent on sex-role preferences, parent-child similarity, and the childs' imitation of the parent in 3 age groups. Parental dominance was found to facilitate imitation in both boys and girls. Maternal dominance was related to disruption in the formation of masculine sex-role preferences in boys and low father-son similarity. Parental dominance had little effect on sex-role preferences in girls or in mother-daughter similarity, but paternal dominance was related to increased father-daughter similarity.

Most theories of identification agree that identification is based on a process or processes whereby the child through imitation, modeling, or introjection acquires traits, characteristics, and values similar to the parent. In normal development the boy is assumed to identify with the father, and the girl with the mother which results in the preference for and adoption of appropriate sex-role behavior. Psychoanalytic theory has stressed the role of fear of punishment and identification with the aggressor, while learning theory has stressed the facilitating effects of reward in promoting iden-tification. A third theory (Parsons, 1955) has emphasized the importance of total parental power in the development of iden-tification. According to Parsons, the child identifies with the parent because he is powerful in his ability to dispense both rewards and punishments. Several recent experiments support the position that parental power or dominance plays a major role in identification (Hetherington & Brackbill, 1963; Mussen & Distler, 1959).

In identifying with parents, children may acquire traits and values which are particularly characteristic of either male or female roles in our society. This would be directly related to the formation of sex-role preferences. They may also imitate parental behaviors which are not sex typed but which are equally appropriate in males and females. It would be expected that the rate of development and type of sex-role preference would be related not only to parental behavior but also to social pressures to conform, and the status of a given sex in the culture. Parent-child similarity in traits which are not sex typed should have fewer extra familial social sanctions bearing on them and therefore should be more directly and consistently related to reinforcements and imitative models provided by the parents. Since the child has relatively few social contacts outside the family in the preschool years it would be expected that identification on both sex-typed and non-sex-typed measures would be closely related to family power structure in 4-

and 5-year-old children. However in older children sex-typed behaviors should be increasingly influenced by social norms. Boys will be encouraged by peers and adults outside the family to develop masculine sex-role preferences and girls feminine sex-role preferences and these preferences should therefore be less directly related to parental dominance in older than in younger children. It would also be predicted that because of the greater prestige and privileges of males in our culture, girls will be slower and less consistent in developing appropriate sex-role preferences than boys (Brown, 1956, 1958). In contrast parent-child similarity on non-sex-typed traits should be closely related to parental dominance in both preschool and school aged boys and girls. This similarity would be expected to increase with age as identification is more fully established.

If children identify with the dominant parent and this parent is the same sex as the child this should facilitate the development of normal sex-role preferences. If the dominant parent is the opposite sex of the child this should strengthen cross-sex identification and may retard the development of normal sex-role preferences. This disruption in identification and sex-role preferences should be particularly marked in boys from mother-dominant homes since the acquiescing father supplies a socially inappropriate model for the son. In contrast, girls from father-dominant homes at least have parental models whose power relationships are appropriate for their culturally defined sex roles. Although it could be argued that a dominant mother does not provide a normal sex-role model for girls, maternal dominance may not preclude the mother having other feminine traits with which a daughter will identify.

If imitation is involved in identification, childrens' performance on an experimental task involving imitation of the parents and a measure of parent-child personality similarity should be positively related. Past research (Bandura, 1962; McDavid, 1959) suggests that although children tend to imitate the most powerful model there is a greater readiness for both boys and girls to imitate a male model. Thus children should imitate and have personality traits similar to the most dominant parent, particularly if it is the father. The findings of McDavid also suggest that girls will imitate increasingly with age while boys will imitate less.

The present study investigated the effects of parental dominance on sex-role preferences, parent-child trait similarity, and imitation of boys and girls of three different age levels.

265

METHOD

Subjects

Subjects were three groups of 36 boys and 36 girls ages 4-5, 6-8, and 9-11 enrolled in nursery schools or in elementary schools in a public-school system. Half of the boys and girls in each group came from mother-dominant homes and half from father-dominant homes.

Experimenters

Half of the subjects in each condition were run by male experimenters and half by female experimenters. Since no experimenter differences were found in a preliminary analysis of the data, this variable was not considered in the final analysis.

Parental Dominance Measure

The parental dominance measure was adapted from a procedure by Farina (1960). Farina's problem situations were modified to make them more suitable for all age levels in the present study. Each parent was seen individually in a quiet room in his own home. He was read 12 hypothetical problem situations involving child behavior and asked how he would handle them when he was by himself. Both parents were then brought together and asked to arrive at a compatible solution on handling these childrens' problems. The discussion of each problem continued until both parents said the terminating signal "agreed." The experimenter participated only minimally in the discussion in order to clarify scoring responses. All interviews were tape-recorded and scored later.

The scoring procedure was identical with that used by Farina (1960) which involved seven indices of parental dominance. If six of the seven indices indicated paternal dominance the family was classified as father dominant; if six of the indices indicated maternal dominance the family was classified as mother dominant. A total of 326 couples were run in order to obtain the 108 mother dominant and 108 father dominant families for the study.

Procedure

The study was comprised of three procedures: the It Scale for

Children (ITSC; Brown, 1956), a parent-child similarity task, and an imitation task.

ITSC

The ITSC, a projective test of sex-role preference, was administered to each subject at school. In this test the child is presented with a drawing of an ambiguous child figure referred to as "It," and is asked to choose what It would like in a series of 36 picture cards of objects and figures identified with masculine or feminine roles. Scores can range from 0, exclusively feminine choices, to 84, exclusively masculine choices. It is assumed that "the child will project himself or herself into the It-figure on the basis of his or her own sex-role preference, and will attribute to It the child's own role preference [Brown, 1956, p. 5]."

Parent-Child Similarity Measure

A list of 130 adjectives was given to 10 advanced education students who were asked to categorize the adjectives as more characteristic of males, or females, or as neutral (equally applicable to both sexes). They were also asked to check whether each adjective was descriptive of the behavior of children or adults or both. Forty adjectives which had been rated as neutral by 90% of the judges and as descriptive of both adults and children by all were included in the final list (e.g., friendly, honest, imaginative, humorous, pleasant, capable, etc.). These adjectives appeared to give a broad view of non-sex-typed personality traits.

Parents were asked to give the name of someone who knew them well enough to rate them on the adjective check list. Different raters were used for each parent. The lists were sent to the raters with assurances of the confidentiality of the responses and were returned by mail to the experimenter. If the list was not returned in 2 weeks, raters were contacted by phone. Eleven of the raters refused to cooperate and others suggested by the parents were substituted. Children were rated on the same list by their teachers. In an attempt to control for response bias raters were asked to mark 15 adjectives which were most like the ratee X, 15 which were most unlike the ratee O, and to leave 10 blank.

The procedure was repeated on 45 of the families 1 month later. The test-retest reliabilities were .82 for ratings of mothers, .86 for fathers, and .79 for children.

Similarity scores were based on the number of identical responses in the mother and child, and father and child lists. Two blanks, X-X or O-O pairings on an item were scored as similar.

WOMAN: DEPENDENT OR INDEPENDENT VARIABLE?

Imitation Task

Each child was run in his home on the imitation task twice, once with each parent as a model. The child was instructed that he and his parent were participating in a study attempting to evaluate what things people think are prettiest. While the child watched, the parent, who had been coached before the experimental session, was asked to indicate by pointing and naming which picture in each of 20 pairs of pictures he thought was prettiest. The parent repeated this procedure three times consistently selecting the predetermined prettiest pictures. The child then went through the series once selecting the pictures he thought were prettiest. One month later the same procedure was repeated with the other parent and a second series of pictures. Order of presentation of list

TABLE 1

ANALYSIS OF VARIANCE OF ITSC SCORES

Source	df	MS	F
Parental dominance (D)	1	1,247.07	4.67*
Sex of child (S)	1	32,047.04	120.03**
Age (A)	2	2,055.70	7.70**
D × S	1	4,329.12	16.21**
D × A	2	265.29	<1
S × A	2	6,520.29	24.47**
D × S × A	2	154.92	<1
Error	204	267.00	
Total	215		

* $p < .05$.
** $p < .01$.

and parent models was balanced for male and female children. An imitation measure of number of similar responses was derived for mother-child and father-child.

RESULTS

Separate analyses of variance were run on ITSC scores, parent-child similarity measures, and parent-child imitation scores. Differences between means were tested by Duncan multiple range tests; those reported are significant at $p < .05$.

Sex-Role Preference

The summary of an analysis of variance of ITSC scores for all subjects is presented in Table 1. As was expected, parental

268

dominance influenced sex-role preference. More appropriate sex-role preferences occurred when the father is dominant than when the mother is dominant. Duncan range tests indicated that the differences in sex-role preferences for girls from mother- and father-dominant homes were nonsignificant, however these differences for boys were significant at all ages. Mother dominance was related to less masculine sex-role preferences in boys.

As predicted, girls were later in developing feminine sex-role preferences than were boys in masculine sex-role preferences. Boys at age 4-5 had already developed a preference for the masculine role which continued and increased slightly but nonsignificantly through ages 9-11. In contrast, girls showed a significant increase in preference for the feminine role in the age 9-11 group. The means and standard deviations of ITSC scores for the three age groups of boys and girls from mother- and father-dominant homes are summarized in Table 2. A high score indicates masculine sex-role preferences.

TABLE 2

MEANS AND STANDARD DEVIATIONS OF ITSC SCORES

Ages	Mother dominant				Father dominant			
	Boys		Girls		Boys		Girls	
	M	SD	M	SD	M	SD	M	SD
4–5	52.4	14.3	41.8	15.9	67.3	13.1	44.8	16.9
6–8	53.7	22.3	55.1	14.3	66.9	14.9	44.6	16.1
9–11	61.0	20.9	24.1	15.9	74.2	12.7	19.1	15.9

Parent-Child Similarity

A summary of the analysis of variance of mother-child and father-child similarity measures obtained from the adjective check list ratings by friends and teachers is presented in Table 3. Duncan range tests indicates that 4- and 5-year-old children obtained lower parent-child similarity ratings than the two older groups who did not differ from one another.

Dominance played an important role in parent-child similarity. Children tended to be more similar to the dominant parent than the passive parent. Mother dominance appeared to inhibit father-child similarity. This similarity was lower than mother-child similarity in father-dominant homes. The disrupted identification of boys was again particularly marked in mother-dominant homes. In father-dominant homes the boy identified significantly more with the father than the mother, however in mother-dominant homes this relation was reversed. In fact, the mother-son similarity in mother-dominant homes did not differ from the father-son similarity in father-dominant homes.

In contrast, girls in father-dominant homes identified equally strongly with both parents.

Also their mother-daughter similarity did not differ from that in mother-dominant homes. On the other hand, girls in mother-dominant homes identified notably more with mother than father. The father-daughter similarity scores in mother-dominant homes

TABLE 3

ANALYSIS OF VARIANCE OF PARENT-CHILD
SIMILARITY SCORES

Source	df	MS	F
Parental dominance (D)	1	498.38	18.06**
Sex of child (S)	1	2.38	<1
Age (A)	2	273.17	9.90**
D × S	1	107.98	3.91*
D × A	2	29.82	1.08
S × A	2	58.42	2.13
S × D × A	2	15.91	<1
Error (a)	204	27.59	
Similarity (Sim)	1	564.90	20.43**
Sim × D	1	2,380.08	86.08**
Sim × S	1	630.74	22.81**
Sim × A	2	23.85	<1
Sim × D × S	1	158.92	5.75*
Sim × D × A	2	59.55	2.15
Sim × S × A	2	39.82	1.44
Sim × D × S × A	2	52.78	1.91
Error (b)	204	27.65	
Total	431		

* $p < .05$.
** $p < .01$.

were significantly lower than similarity scores in any other group. The means and standard deviations of parent-child similarity scores for all groups are summarized in Table 4.

TABLE 4

MEANS AND STANDARD DEVIATIONS OF PARENT-CHILD SIMILARITY SCORES

	Mother dominant						Father dominant					
Ages:	4–5		6–8		9–11		4–5		6–8		9–11	
Similarity	M	SD	M	SD	M	SD	M	SD	M	SD	M	SD
Mother-daughter	19.1	5.3	19.8	4.5	21.9	5.8	18.7	5.3	21.1	4.3	20.1	5.9
Mother-son	16.9	6.1	20.4	6.1	23.3	5.3	15.8	6.0	15.2	4.3	15.3	4.5
Father-daughter	11.6	4.1	12.0	4.6	12.7	3.6	18.2	5.8	19.5	6.0	18.3	6.3
Father-son	12.1	4.4	16.2	4.5	15.0	4.3	17.6	6.8	23.3	5.4	23.6	4.8

Parent-Child Imitation

A summary of the results of the analysis of variance of imitation scores is presented in Table 5. In the childs' imitation of the parent, as in sex-pole preferences and parent-child similarity, parental dominance was a significant factor. Children of both sexes imitated the dominant parent more than the passive parent. The prediction that children would imitate the father more than the mother was not confirmed. There were no significant differences between imitation of the dominant mothers and fathers, or between passive mothers and fathers. As was expected on the basis of past research, girls imitated more than boys; however no differential trends with age for the two sexes were found. The means and standard deviations of imitation scores are presented in Table 6.

TABLE 5

ANALYSIS OF VARIANCE OF PARENT-CHILD
IMITATION SCORES

Source	df	MS	F
Parental dominance (D)	1	1.12	<1
Sex of child (S)	1	108.00	10.58**
Age (A)	2	5.56	<1
D × S	1	.01	<1
D × A	2	20.10	1.97
S × A	2	24.02	2.35
D × S × A	2	4.97	<1
Error (a)	204	10.21	
Imitation (I)	1	1.56	<1
I × D	1	560.34	58.30**
I × S	1	15.57	1.62
I × A	2	23.16	2.41
I × D × S	1	6.25	<1
I × D × A	2	4.89	<1
I × S × A	2	3.71	<1
I × D × S × A	2	7.50	<1
Error (b)	204	9.61	
Total	431		

* $p < .05$.
** $p < .01$.

Relations Among Measures

The ITSC scores, father-child and mother-child similarity measures, and father-child and mother-child imitation scores were correlated separately for boys and girls in mother- and father-dominant homes for each age group. The results suggest that these measures are meaningfully related only for older girls from father-dominant homes. In this group, girls who imitate their mother are rated as being similar to them on the adjective check list ($r = .58$, $p < .01$) and have feminine sex-role preferences ($r = -$

TABLE 6

MEANS AND STANDARD DEVIATIONS OF PARENT-CHILD IMITATION SCORES

| | Mother dominant | | | | | | Father dominant | | | | | |
| | 4–5 | | 6–8 | | 9–11 | | 4–5 | | 6–8 | | 9–11 | |
Imitation	M	SD	M	SD	M	SD	M	SD	M	SD	M	SD
Mother-daughter	13.3	3.4	13.4	3.7	14.7	3.1	11.7	2.6	11.3	3.6	10.7	3.8
Mother-son	12.3	3.2	12.0	2.6	12.3	4.5	10.9	2.8	10.1	3.8	9.1	2.9
Father-daughter	10.1	3.1	11.2	3.0	11.8	2.8	11.8	3.1	14.2	3.1	14.4	3.2
Father-son	10.1	2.8	10.8	3.1	11.1	2.9	13.1	2.8	12.8	3.1	11.9	3.7

.68, $p < .01$). When these girls have feminine sex-role preferences they are rated as similar to their mothers ($r = -.67$, $p < .01$), when they have masculine sex-role preferences they are rated as similar to their fathers ($r = .42$, $p < .05$). It appears that in homes where parents serve as culturally appropriate sex-role models with the father more dominant than the mother, girls' feminine sex-role preferences are closely related to imitation of the mother and similarity to the parents on other traits which are not sexually defined.

In contrast, there are few systematic or meaningful relationships for girls from mother-dominant homes or for boys from either mother- or father-dominant homes. There was a tendency for parent-child imitation to be related to parent-child similarity in these groups, but there was little relationship between sex-role preference and the other measures. In fact, for boys there were no significant correlations between the ITSC and any other measures at any age.

DISCUSSION

The results appear to support partially a theory of identification based on parental power. Parental dominance influenced children in imitation of parents, sex-role preferences, and similarity to parents in non-sex-typed traits. Inversions of the normal parental dominance pattern were related to more disruption in the identification of boys than of girls. Boys from mother-dominant homes acquired non-sex-typed traits like the mother and also more feminine sex-role preferences than boys from father-dominant homes. Contrary to expectations these differences in sex-role preferences were present at ages 4-5 and were sustained through ages 9-11. The predicted decrease in the relationship between sex-

272

role preference and parental dominance with age did not occur. It appears that later social pressures on boys to acquire masculine preferences do not adequately counteract the early developed more feminine preferences of boys in mother-dominant homes. The prediction of an increasing similarity of the child and dominant parent on non-sex-typed traits with age is supported. This similarity is significantly less in 4- and 5-year-olds than in older children. Since the period from 3 to 6 years is considered to be a critical formative one in which identification is rapidly changing and growing, this increase in similarity following the preschool years might be anticipated. After this marked increase in identification, a stabilizing of identification on non-sex-typed traits appears to occur early in the school aged years.

It was surprising that girls from mother- and father-dominant homes showed no difference in sex-role preference at any age, since it might be assumed that a dominant mother offers her daughter a rather "unfeminine" role model. However, it should be remembered that the measure of maternal dominance in this study was one of dominance relative to the spouse and not to other members of her own sex. Thus a mother could be more dominant than a passive husband and still not be dominant or "unfeminine" relative to other women. The significance of parental dominance relative to other members of the same sex remains to be investigated. It is possible that since the feminine role in our culture is less well defined, less highly valued (Lynn, 1959; McKee & Sherriffs, 1957), and later acquired than the male role, these factors attenuate any differences due to maternal dominance.

It could be argued that lack of appropriate paternal dominance rather than the presence of maternal dominance led to the obtained findings. If boys and girls initially both identify with the mother, the socially appropriate sex-role behavior of paternal dominance may be necessary to facilitate the shift in identification models for the boy. Since normal identification for girls involves sustaining and intensifying the mother-child relationship, father dominance may contribute only to cross-sex identification and do little to disrupt the girls' primary identification. Social pressures may also encourage the child to identify with the like-sexed parent unless his behavior is culturally inappropriate. Since the feminine role is less well defined than the masculine role, either dominant or passive behavior in mothers may be regarded as more acceptable than passivity in fathers. Evidence for this is provided not only by the different results for boys and girls on the ITSC, but also by the parent-child similarity on traits not influenced by sex typing. Paternal dominance facilitated cross-sex identification in girls but did not disturb like-sex identification. Thus the mother-daughter and father-daughter similarity in father-dominant homes, and mother-daughter similarity in mother-dominant homes did not differ significantly. However, neither the sons nor daughters in mother-dominant homes identified with the passive father.

This interpretation of the role of dominance in identification appears to be consistent with the psychoanalytic stress on the great importance of "identification with the aggressor" in boys' identification, and its lesser importance in the identification of girls.

REFERENCES

Bandura, A. Social learning through imitation. In M. R. Jones (Ed.), *Nebraska symposium on motivation: 1962.* Lincoln: Univer. Nebraska Press, 1962. Pp. 211-269.

Brown, D.G. Sex-role preference in young children. *Psychological Monographs,* 1956, 70 (14, Whole No. 421).

Brown, D. G. Sex role development in a changing culture. *Psychological Bulletin,* 1958, *55,* 232-242.

Farina, A. Patterns of role dominance and conflict in parents of schizophrenic patients. *Journal of Abnormal and Social Psychology,* 1960, *61,* 31-38.

Hetherington, E. Mavis, & Brackbill, Yvonne. Etiology and covariation of obstinacy, orderliness and parsimony in young children. *Child Development,* 1963, *34,* 919-944.

Lynn, D. B. A note on sex differences in the development of masculine and feminine identification. *Psychological Review,* 1959, *66,* 126-135.

McDavid, J.W. Imitative behavior in preschool children. *Psychological Monographs,* 1959, *73* (16, Whole No. 486).

McKee, J. P., & Sherriffs, A. C. The differential evaluation of males and females. *Journal of Personality,* 1957, *25,* 356-371.

Mussen, P., and Distler, L. Masculinity, identification, and father-son relationships. *Journal of Abnormal and Social Psychology.*

Parsons, T. Family structure and the socialization of the child. In T. Parsons and R.F. Bales (Eds.), *Family, socialization, and interaction process.* Glencoe, Ill.: Free Press, 1955. Pp. 35-131.

18

The question of whether sex roles are primarily biologically or primarily socially determined is still largely unresolved. One of the great problems is that experimental manipulation is nearly impossible. Therefore, researchers must search for situations in which the desired manipulations have already occurred. In the case of sex-role differences, one common method is to study various cultures that have different prescriptions for behavior appropriate to the two sexes.

Weithorn has reviewed some of the literature in this area and points out a number of important considerations that must be kept in mind when considering data of this sort. Weithorn's most important point is that differences are probably not simply the result of historical accident. Certain behaviors are regarded as male-characteristic in almost all cultures studied, while some behaviors are regarded as female-characteristic. Male-characteristic behaviors are usually related to the superior strength and speed of the male. Female-characteristic behaviors are related to child-bearing and nurturance. These differences are biologically based, and thus various cultures do not represent independent solutions to similar social conditions.

Weighorn also points out the lack of "conceptual equivalences" which may lead to biases in the gathering and treatment of the data. It is rare to find two societies in which the same questions have been asked and answered. Examination of one's own culture may be biased because of "culture inurement". Important data may be overlooked because beliefs concerning them pervade the culture. The investigator may not even be aware that there is a question to be asked.

Weithorn points out that "social experiments" involving equality of the sexes have not actually been performed. All these experiments—for example, the kibbutz—involve the female performing the masculine role, but not the other way round. The basic biological differences between the sexes have been ignored. She suggests that with present changes in technology, population control, and so on, a situation exists today which for the first time may lead to equivalent sex roles for males and females.

Woman's Role in Cross-Cultural Perspective

Corinne J. Weithorn

Our society is changing rapidly. One of the consequences of this rapid change is the reevaluation of many cultural institutions, not the least of which is the role of woman. Women have been seeking to improve their status for a long time but the emphasis of the present struggle is not on women per se; it is on the relationship between men and women. While the traditional thrust of feminist movements has been to gain equality for women and to broaden the scope of their activities in the world of men, this new movement questions the validity of the masculine model as a basis for women's rights. In so doing, it strikes at the very core of many assumptions about the differences between men and women and urges changes not only in women's roles, but in men's roles as well.

These pressures for change focus on three aspects of traditional male-female relationships: (1) assumptions about differences in the temperamental qualities of men and women and the expectations for behavior based on those assumptions, (2) the division of labor wherein women assume the responsibility for domestic chores and men assume the responsibility for providing sustenance, and (3) male dominance in law and custom.

THE CROSS-CULTURAL PERSPECTIVE

How much change is possible? Present-day literature is filled with arguments pro and con the question of whether existing relationships are determined by sex-linked biological inheritance or by enculturation. Cross-cultural data provide a perspective that can illuminate these discussions. Such data enable comparisons among cultures with respect to similarities and differences in male-female relationships. Societies exist as a result of human effort to adapt biological capabilities to environmental circumstances. The extent to which there are similarities in women's status throughout diverse cultures would indicate whether that status is an inevitable consequence of that adaptation. Cross-cultural research on the relationships between the sexes should attempt to determine whether those relationships reflect sex-linked biological inheritance, the extent to which they are adaptive to existing conditions, and the extent to which they are anachronistic vestiges of adaptation to no longer existing circumstances.

SOME PROBLEMS OF CROSS-CULTURAL DATA

There are a number of problems to be encountered in using ethnological studies to compare specific aspects of human behavior. The first of these, which has been referred to as lack of "conceptual equivalence" (Sears, 1961), occurs because field studies of primitive peoples have been made by individuals of different professional disciplines, with differing orientations and objectives. Behaviors that may have been considered important objects of study by some may have been totally ignored or given cursory treatment by others. The second problem is that the accuracy of the material may be questionable. In many studies tribal informants were the primary sources of information. They answered questions for the ethnographer, who in turn interpreted the material for the reader. As to this sort of reportage, Otto Klineberg (1949) has stated:

> When an anthropologist tells us about culture patterns and their relationship to individual behavior, we would also like to know, and this is what we miss in these studies: Does *everybody* do this? Is this the sort of thing people *should* do or what they *actually* do? Do *you* do this? Do you *always* do this? [Klineberg, p. 136].

A third problem is that ethnographer bias about the nature of customs and behaviors can result in selectivity of the material that is presented. It also can result in editorializations that tend to support a point of view, but which obscure the original data. For example, in some societies it is customary for a man to marry the widow and adopt the children of his deceased brother. This practice often has been interpreted as a way of ensuring the protection of the widow and her offspring. However, another viewpoint might characterize this practice as enslavement of the widow, as in Sullerot's (1970) comment on the custom: "Thus in Greece, Israel and India the widow was part of the husband's estate and was left to his eldest male relative like chattel" (Sullerot, p. 21).

277

WOMAN: DEPENDENT OR INDEPENDENT VARIABLE?

The problem of maintaining objectivity about cultures is not confined to studies of alien societies. Just as ethnographers experience a form of culture shock when they encounter life styles and cultures vastly different from their own, so students of contemporary culture experience what might be called culture inurement. Lack of insight about one's own culture can prevent objective analysis; important data may be overlooked or minimized because they are not consonant with belief. It is culture inurement that is the object of attention in the consciousness-raising groups of the contemporary women's liberation movement.

Despite all of the difficulties inherent in comparison of cultures based on diverse and unequivalent data, it still is possible to sort out some of the patterns that have emerged with respect to the status of women.

HUMAN SOCIETIES

Humans live together in groups that share rules and regulations governing behavior. In all known societies, men and women assume different roles, although these roles vary greatly from one society to another. The prehistory of human society can only be inferred from fragmented archeological evidence. Nevertheless, it is possible to use a broad theoretical framework from which certain assumptions may be made.

Each sex has a set of inherited biological characteristics that have evolved as a means of ensuring survival and reproduction. Customs, traditions, and role functions within groups have developed as a result of efforts to adapt these biological characteristics to the exigencies of ecologic and economic survival. Among the biological differences between men and women which have significance in the development of societies, the following have particular relevance to the three areas in which the relationships between men and women currently are being explored: (1) the male is stronger and larger than the female; (2) only the female can carry and nurture the infant; (3) maternity is absolutely determinable, while paternity is not; and (4) the male can be more prolific than the female, since he can continue to reproduce during the gestation period of each of his offspring.

The first two of these biological differences seem directly related to the way in which the division of labor has developed. The third and fourth, however, seem related to the development of family structure and the dominance hierarchy, although the precise nature of that relationship can be complicated by many factors.

Corinne J. Weithorn

DIFFERENCES IN TEMPERAMENTAL QUALITIES

Women generally are presumed to be more passive, dependent, and "instinctively" nurturant than men, while men are considered to be more aggressive than women. The important question relating to these temperamental differences is whether they are due to sex-linked biological inheritance or to early enculturation. Ultimately the answer will come more definitively from scientific data about genetic endowment and the effects of hormonal and endocrinological factors on behavior. Presently, knowledge in this area is scanty, although one recent study can be offered to support the notion that gender identification is principally a matter of enculturation. That study focused on nineteen hermaphrodites who had been assigned gender roles opposite to their chromatin pattern. The individuals who had been assigned to their lifelong gender prior to the age of three readily developed the role expectancies and behaviors of that gender. The authors interpreted that result as follows:

> We conclude that an individual's gender role and orientation as a boy or girl, man or woman does not have an innate, preformed instinctive basis as some theorists have maintained. Instead, the evidence supports the view that psychological sex is undifferentiated at birth—a sexual neutrality, one might say—and that the individual becomes psychologically differentiated as masculine or feminine in the course of the many experiences of growing up [Hampson, (1965) p. 119].

The importance of early training in the determination of personality patterns and temperamental qualities also is evident in cross-cultural data. The differences in temperamental qualities among cultures often are much greater than the differences between men and women in any given culture.

The notion of "masculine" and "feminine" temperaments was specifically explored by Margaret Mead in her study of three New Guinea tribes (1935). Of the Arapesh and Mundugumor tribes, she states:

> Two of these tribes have no idea that men and women are different in temperament. They allow them different economic and religious roles, different skills, different vulnerabilities to evil, magic and supernatural in-

279

fluences . . . But any idea that temperamental traits of the order of dominance, malleability are inalienably associated with one sex (as opposed to the other) is entirely lacking" [p. xiv].

All three of the tribes are patrilineal and polygynous and share common origins of folklore and religious practice, although each tribe has introduced its own modifications. However, the resemblances end there. Among the Arapesh, a nonviolent, gentle people, both mother and father have nurturing responsibilities. The attitude of the Arapesh to paternal responsibility is described in the following passage:

The minute day-by-day care of little children, with its routines, its exasperations, its wails of misery that cannot be correctly interpreted, these are as congenial to the Arapesh men as they are to the Arapesh women. And in recognition of this care, as well as in recognition of the father's initial contribution, if one comments upon a middle-aged man as good-looking, the people answer: 'Good-looking? Y-e-s. But you should have seen him before he bore all those children." [p. 39].

Among the Arapesh, population control is achieved in a manner appropriate to the gentle, nonaggressive nature of the people. Infanticide is rare; instead, both mother and father are forbidden to have sexual relations for a year after the birth of their child, and this restriction pertains to relations between the father and his other wives as well.

Just as Arapesh men and women share the same temperamental qualities, so the Mundugumor men and women have a common set of personality traits. But the latter are a distrustful, aggressive, rivalrous people who are rejecting toward children. Property rights pass from a parent to the opposite-sexed child, so that parents and their same-sexed children become alienated from each other. In fact, hostility, suspicion, and lack of cooperative effort not only characterize parent-child relationships, but prevail in every social institution. Wives are bought by the transfer of a sister to the bride's family and fathers may even exchange their own daughters for a young wife for themselves. Paradoxically, this chattel-like position of women makes them more desirable commodities as infants.

The relationship of the child-rearing practices of the Mundugumors to their adult temperaments are suggested clearly in the following paragraph:

Mundugumor women suckle their children standing up, supporting the child with one hand in a position that strains the mother's arm and pinions the arms of the child. There is none of the mother's dallying or sensuous pleasure in feeding her child that occurs among the Arapesh. Nor is the child permitted to prolong his meal by any playful fondling of his own or his mother's body. He is kept firmly to his major task of absorbing enough food so that he will stop crying and consent to be put back in his basket. The minute he stops suckling for a moment, he is returned to his prison. Children, therefore, develop a very definite, purposive fighting attitude, holding firmly to the nipple and sucking milk as rapidly and vigorously as possible. They frequently choke from swallowing too fast; the choking angers the mother and infuriates the child, thus further turning the suckling situation into one characterized by anger and struggle rather than by affection and reassurance [Mead, 1935, pp. 195-96].

In the third society, the Tchambuli, men and women have very different temperamental qualities, but the Tchambuli society is filled with paradoxes. Though patrilineal, the true source of power resides with women because of an intricate kinship system. Temperamentally, men were found to be more unstable, vain, neurotic, and emotionally subservient. "Men . . . are dependent on the security given them by women and even in sex activity looking to women to give them the leads" [Mead, 1935, p. 263].

The Tchambuli society is an artistic one and the education of the Tchambuli male consists of the gradual revelation of the male-kept secrets of their artistry. However, these secrets are given grudgingly by the older men, for it is the secrecy with which they are concerned, rather than with the illumination of the young. Thus, while the Tchambuli girl quickly is absorbed into the society of women, the Tchambuli boy frequently is ignored.

He is left about upon the edges of his society, a little too old for the women and a little too young for the men. . . . This period of three, sometimes four years in the lives of the boys sets up habits that prevail throughout their lives. A sense of neglect, of exclusion settles over them [Mead, 1935, p. 267].

Thus, in one tribe, both men and women are gentle and nurturant, in another, neither sex possesses these qualities, and in a third, the temperamental qualities of the men are very much like those frequently attributed to women in contemporary society. Margaret Mead comments:

If these temperamental attitudes which we have traditionally regarded as feminine—such as passivity, responsiveness, and a willingness to cherish children—can so easily be set up as a masculine pattern in one tribe and in another be outlawed for the majority of men, we no longer have any basis for regarding such aspects of behavior as sex-linked. . . . The material suggests that we may say that many, if not all of the personality traits which we have called masculine or feminine, are as lightly linked to sex as are the clothing, the manner and the form of headdress that a society at a given period assigns to either sex [p. 280].

This study and other cross-cultural comparisons (Whiting and Child, 1953) strongly suggest that temperamental differences between the sexes are primarily a matter of enculturation. American psychologists, concerned with contemporary society, have studied levels of aggression and dependency in children (Levin and Sears 1956; Sears et al., 1953; Sears et al., 1957). Generally, it has been found that parental expectations differ for boys and girls and that behaviors are differentially reinforced. However, many of the studies on the relationship of child-rearing practices and temperamental qualities in children have yielded equivocal results, or results in which there were so many interacting variables that it was difficult to focus on specific relationships. Moreover, even when results clearly are supportive of the dependence of temperament on socialization practices, it still is not possible to exclude the contribution of sex-linked biological inheritance.

Are women "instinctively" nurturant? The place of humans in the animal world suggests the possibility that buried deep within us may be undiscovered instinctive behaviors. However, the sense of smell upon which much of the instinctive nurturance of infrahuman species is based, and which is more highly developed in lower mammalian forms, is relatively weak in humans. Nevertheless, the debate continues and belief in one or the other basis for woman's nurturing role is evident in most discussions. Consider the contrast in points of view of the following contemporary authors. The first statement was made in a discussion of the disillusionment of many women with life on the Israeli kibbutz:

. . . it is quite possible that after the frontier-like conditions of Kibbutz existence have nearly disappeared and after some of the "non-feminine" demands upon women have been relaxed, their "maternal" or "instinctive" needs for nurturance of children and for passivity vis a vis the male reassert themselves and demand opportunity for expression [Rabin, 1970, p. 304].

The second statement appeared originally in an article by Eva Moberg and is quoted in full by Rita Liljestrom (1970) in her discussion of the role of women in Sweden:

Actually, there is no biological connection whatsoever between the function of giving birth to and nursing a child and the function of washing its clothes, preparing its food and trying to bring it up to be a good and harmonious person [p. 203].

The question of biological predisposition versus enculturation with respect to nurturance has centered essentially on women. The evidence from cross-cultural research strongly suggests that human males are capable of being highly nurturant and that human females are capable of being nonnurturant and rejecting. Perhaps the focus of study should be the extent to which enculturation patterns serve to suppress nurturance tendencies in boys, while enhancing them in girls. Nurturance may be a universal human proclivity, capable of being developed in individuals of either sex.

THE DIVISION OF LABOR

As is the case with all anthropoids, human males protect females and children. In human society, males also provide food (Mead, 1949). Primarily, women care for the young, gather and prepare the food, and take care of other domestic chores. In the study of primitive societies it is possible to see the direct relationship between biological differences in men and women and the division of labor: man's greater strength and size better equipped him to perform more strenuous activities such as hunting and building, while woman's exclusive ability to carry and nurture the young kept her home-bound. According to D'Andrade (1966), the development of all divisions of labor in primitive societies took place as the result of activities directly related to these biological sex differences. He states: "The thesis to be considered . . . is that the division of labor by sex comes about as a result of generalization from activities directly related to physical sex differences to activities only indirectly related to these differences" (p. 178).

This thesis is logical and amply supported by the analysis offered

(Murdock, 1935) of labor assignments in a variety of primitive cultures. Thus, for example, weapon-making by men, while not requiring physical strength, is a logical extension of the hunting and fighting responsibilities, while the gathering and preparation of food by women is a logical extension of their home-bound child nurturance functions.

In pre-industrial societies, families lived in small, circumscribed areas and production of goods for sale and sustenance was largely a family affair. Men and women worked together, although the types of work differed. As technology developed, the production of goods was removed from the home, but it was difficult for women to move out into the world of industry and yet attend to the domestic labor that was their responsibility. As the technology produced "labor'saving" devices for the home, women began to have the time and freedom to enter the now male-dominated industrial and business community. A woman was able to do this, however, only to the extent that she was able to combine management of her domestic responsibilities with the requirements of her employment.

This slow progression of events took place wherever societies changed as the result of gradual adaptation to new economic conditions. However, in some countries, such as the Soviet Union, old traditions and attitudes were discarded precipitously and replaced with new, ideologically based concepts. One of the precepts of the Communist revolution was that the labor market was to be occupied equally by men and women. Women were exhorted to become contributing and active participants in the industrial and agricultural work of the economy.

Field and Flynn (1970) describe four types of Soviet women depicted in the Communist party literature, two with positive characteristics and two with negative characteristics. The most laudable existence for a woman was to be a Comrade Positive. Such a woman willingly and easily occupied her rightful place in the working world. Second to her was the Comrade Willing, who had the inclination to work but who somehow had not been able to organize her domestic life well enough to accomplish this worthy goal. The Comrade Reluctant, a negative type, had lazy, bourgeois notions of woman's role but was partially redeemed by the fact that she had some conflict about her opinions and felt some remorse about her idleness. The Comrade Parasitic, however, not only was lazy and disinclined to work, but felt neither remorse nor shame.

The Soviet notion of equality for women in the division of labor suffered from one essential drawback. The concept of female equality was cast in the masculine model and, while women were encouraged and welcomed into the labor force, men were not encouraged to participate in domestic chores. Field and Flynn describe this state of affairs as follows:

> Women, like men, are expected to put in a full day's work at the office, in the plant or in the field, but Soviet men, jealous of their masculinity and spoiled by their indulgent mothers and submissive sisters, refuse to help their wives in their household duties. What would the neighbors say if they saw him washing dishes or making beds? No wonder, then, that some Soviet women have taken to complaining in the newspapers that they are asked to work just as hard as their husbands on the job, but that at home their husbands will not lift a finger to help (p. 276).

Thus the double burden of home care and outside employment engendered the same role conflicts in Soviet women as in Western women. This problem became the subject of discussion in the Soviet Union in the 1950s. Suggestions for ameliorating the situation included reserving lighter work for women, making work schedules for mothers more flexible, reducing women's domestic load through more child-care and food-preparation centers, and softening attitudes about women's obligation to work. None of these suggestions, however, contained even the remotest suggestion that men might be encouraged to share domestic responsibilities.

The kibbutz in Israel presents another example of an ideologically based society in which the emancipation of women clearly was expressed as a paramount goal. The Israeli kibbutz was exclusively an agricultural society in which the family structure was but part of a total communal structure. Although the nuclear family was preserved, rearing and education of children was provided for by the kibbutz as a whole. Every individual shared in the total cooperative effort. The failure of the ideology with respect to the status of women has been documented by Melford Spiro (1956).

One of the specific aims of the kibbutz was to alter the role of the women—to "abrogate the traditional dependence of the female on the male, of the wife on her husband." Interestingly, the essential biological difference between the sexes—woman's exclusive ability to carry and nurture children—was considered to be the "biological tragedy of woman." Thus, one of the goals of communal life was to free her from her domestic chores so as to enable her to become the equal of man. These domestic chores were to be relegated to the communal kitchens, laundries, nurseries, etc. Clearly the direction and scope of these strivings were based on the masculine model and, as such, were destined to fail. Many of the dissatisfactions of the kibbutz woman related to the fact that her new role was too physically strenuous. Moreover, the communal domestic facilities apparently did not ameliorate the "biological tragedy of woman." The following passage by Spiro reveals why:

> In view of its emphasis on the economic equality of the sexes, how is it that the women have not become "rooted" in the economic life of the kibbutz? It has already been noted that when the vattikim first settled on the land, there was no sexual division of labor. Women, like men, worked in the fields and drove tractors; men, like women, worked in the kitchen and the laundry. Men and women, it was assumed, were equal and could perform their jobs equally well. It was soon discovered, however, that men and women were not equal. For obvious biological reasons women were compelled at times to take temporary leave from that physical labor of which they were capable. A pregnant woman, for example, could not work too long, even in the vegetable garden, and a nursing mother had to work near the Infant's House in order to be able to feed her child. Hence, as the kibbutz grew older and the birth rate increased, more and more women were forced to leave the "productive" branches of the economy and enter its service branches. But as they left the productive branches it was necessary that their places be filled, and they were filled by men. The result was that the women found themselves in the same jobs from which they were supposed to have been emancipated— cooking, cleaning, laundering, teaching, caring for children, etc. In short, they have not been freed from the "yoke" of domestic responsibilities." [Spiro, 1956, p. 225].

It would seem that division of labor premised on the two basic biological differences between the sexes—man's greater strength and woman's reproductive and nurturance functions—has not been abrogated in any society of which we have knowledge. In primitive societies, division of labor is most closely related to adaptation of biological differences to survival. In contemporary Western societies, the variety of cultural institutions relating to sex roles have evolved at different rates of speed. The result is that the woman, freer of domestic chores than ever before, finds herself fighting her way into the man's world and cajoling the man into hers. In the Soviet Union and on the Israeli kibbutz, the notion of equality was cast in the masculine model by an ideology that ignored the basic biological differences between the sexes.

Perhaps the whole struggle to realign male-female relationships in the area of division of labor would be better served if the concept of "equal" were not interchanged with the concept of "equitable." Biological differences cannot be ignored in the division of labor, but neither should they be subverted to use as excuses for suppression and disenfranchisement.

LEGAL ENFRANCHISEMENT AND DOMINANCE PATTERNS

In most contemporary societies, women do not have the same legal rights as men and their social and economic status is lower than that of men. These patterns also are discernible in primitive societies. There are more patrilineal than matrilineal families and more patriarchies than matriarchies; in societies where infanticide is practiced, it is female infanticide; the folklore and mythology of many cultures is replete with images of women as evil temptresses, seducers, and witches; in most religions it is the man who is the guardian of the faith, be it in the rituals of primitive society or at the alters of contemporary houses of worship. Of course, there are societies where one or another of these situations does not obtain. Anthropologists suggest that at some periods and in some places, a totally different order of dominance may have prevailed (Petros, 1963). However, those cultures frequently are inferred to have existed or are presented as sketchily documented historical antecedents to present forms of society.

There is much greater diversity of social organization in primitive society than in contemporary society. Primitive peoples developed many ways of dealing with sexual and familial relationships. Marriage, for example, takes many forms: monogamy, in which a single pair bond is established; polygyny, in which one man has many wives; polyandry, in which one woman has many husbands, all of whom share kinship relationships with the offspring, and polyandrogyny, in which several men marry several women. This last form is but one step removed from promiscuity, which may have been the earliest behavior pattern. It must be assumed that those institutions that survived did so because they best enabled humans to adapt to their environments. It is likely that there may have been other forms of communal living which were nonadaptive and thus did not endure.

Biological differences of man's greater strength and woman's nurturance functions were very much a part of the development of societies. However, two other biological differences are more closely related to the development of legal and social institutions pertaining to the dominance order between men and women. One is the indeterminate nature of paternity and the other is man's greater prolificacy. It is possible to trace many patterns of male-female dominance to these two biological differences.

Each society has dealt differently with the problems of man's need to establish his paternity and to transmit his property. The lines of authority and passage of property rights are not always related to marriage forms in primitive society, at least not in any predictable way. For example, in matrilineal societies in Eastern New Guinea, male dominance is very much in evidence, even though property passes through the mother. However, the dominant male in a child's life is his maternal uncle. Consanguinity is the primary bond and a man's descendents are his sister's children (Malinowski, 1929). In a sense, this form of dominance and succession seems directly related to the need to adapt to the problem of indeterminate paternity and thus may be a relic of an earlier form of that society.

The Khasas are a polyandrous society that is both patriarchal and patrilineal. (Petros, 1963). Among these people, a woman is considered inferior and serves many husbands, all of whom usually share some kinship bond and maintain the state of polyandry as a means of preserving their fraternity and sharing their limited property—too meager to be divided among them. Polyandry frequently is a direct concomitant of female infanticide, which occurs most often in economically marginal societies as a means of population control. Since man has greater potential prolificacy, reduction of the number of males would have far less impact on population control than reduction of the number of females.

Not all polyandrous societies are male dominant, although reports of matriarchies are less well documented. The Cashibos in Peru have been described as a matriarchal, polyandrous society in which women not only ruled, but selected their many simultaneous husbands and discarded them at will (Petros, 1963). In the Marquesa Islands polyandry was practiced as part of the pattern of primogeniture. An eldest child of either sex was in a position of power and possessed property so he or she could afford several spouses (Kardiner, 1939).

Despite the variety of marriage forms, all primitive societies have carefully elaborated structures governing kinship, marriage, and dominance patterns. In preliterate socieities it is not always possible to distinguish between law and custom, but in literate cultures the distinction is made even though the laws very often are merely institutionalizations of prevailing customs. In both law and custom, however, women usually have considerably more restrictions placed on them with respect to personal and sexual freedom. These restrictions usually are associated with their reproductive role (Ford, 1970). Harsh penalties for female adultery do indeed become a theme in patrilineal societies, while male dalliance is less severely punished. Sullerot (1970) suggests that these restrictions were associated with the acquisition of private property, and consequently with the need to safeguard the succession of the property through the establishment of paternity.

In contemporary society, the legal status of women has been changing in fairly predictable relationship to the degree of industrialization, although the pace of the change is strongly dependent on the culture and traditions of the region. Thus there are differences in the legal status of women in different countries at any given moment. While the trend in legal enfranchisement is unmistakable, its realization is impeded by resistance on the parts of both men and women to changes in culturally determined roles. Consider, for example, the number of notable American women who, when asked to comment on women's liberation, reply, "Well, I certainly agree with equal pay for equal work and legal equality, but some of those other things. . . ." Indeed, those "other things" are the attacks on the deeply enculturated attitudes and traditional role expectancies regarding women. Jessie Bernard (1968) has stated this conflict as follows: ". . . the issues which concern the modern generation have to do with personal, private, even sexual rights rather than legal, political and economic rights" (p. 3).

Changes in attitudes and traditional role expectancies lag behind changes in legal structure for several reasons. First, legal enfranchisement frequently represents a superimposition of new laws on a society that is not culturally ready for them. In those areas where industrialization and urbanization have created new economic exigencies, old patterns have eroded, but the more rural areas have resisted change. Second, the nature and strength of the original customs strongly influence the extent to which legal changes will be accepted. Third, many attitudes and cultural practices whose origins are obscure have been incorporated into religious dogma, which renders them impervious to change; it is easier to change manmade laws than those that have divine attribution. In primitive societies those practices that no longer seem to be logical or to have survival value frequently are accounted for as supernatural taboo. Similarly, in contemporary culture, religion has preserved and immobilized attitudes regarding women. This point is made succinctly by Unger (1968, p. 77) in her discussion of the role of women in Islamic countries: ". . . the Islamic religion . . . cloaks the painful condition . . . [of women] in theological casuistry. As apologies for immutability, these factors present an obstacle to evolution."

The theme of male domination exists throughout the Judaic,

Moslem, and Oriental cultures (Sullerot, 1970). Christianity presumably introduced the concept of freedom for all, including women, but the extent to which this freedom was realized was another matter. Dicta put forth by St. Paul indicated that woman, like Eve, was a temptress who could be saved only through a life of purity and fidelity (Seward, 1970). Thus throughout history the degree to which women have obtained and then taken advantage of legal enfranchisement has been a function of earlier cultural beliefs and their encapsulation in religious dogma. In those countries where custom can be traced to original Moorish, Arabic, Judaic, and Oriental influences, where male domination and patriarchy were strong, women's rights have been realized far more slowly than in those countries whose cultural origins were in northern and western Europe.

A corollary of the pattern of male dominance in the Near and Far Eastern cultures is the strength of mother-son bonds relative to husband-wife bonds. Only through motherhood is a woman of these cultures able to achieve any status at all. Spinellis et al. (1970, p. 303) describe the state of the contemporary Greek woman: ". . . despised and suspected as a woman, she is revered, trusted, respected and obeyed as a mother." Similarly, among certain groups in India, a childless woman is regarded as a sorceress (Mintern and Hitchcock, 1963). Once she achieves motherhood, however, provided that she has sons, she attains a position of respect and status never before accorded her.

> The subordinate status of women is further emphasized by the custom that women must crouch on the floor and pull their saris over their faces when in the presence of their husband or any man older than their husband. The custom is so pervasive that young women usually cover their faces even in front of older, low-caste serving men. This is a sign of respect for the man's status. Covering the face in the presence of one's husband is also a sign of respect for his mother, another of the customs designed to protect the mother-son relationship from being threatened by the son's attachment to his wife" [p. 240].

Strong male dominance also is the cultural pattern in Latin America, as a result of the combined influence of the *machismo* tradition of the Spanish *conquistadores* and Catholic church dicta of inherent male rights and divine purity (Williamson, 1970). Womanly virtues are considered to be humility, patience, forbearance, and childbearing.

The status of women in the more Western and northern

European countries historically was more emancipated. Women were neither secluded nor enjoined from property rights. They played a more active role in religious, political, and economic life (Sullerot, 1970). The superimposition of religious dogma on the freer cultural attitudes about women resulted in different interpretations of that dogma. To the combination of these forces must be added the effects of more rapid industrialization in those areas. Although less restricted than her southern and eastern sisters, the northern European woman was more fortunate only in degree, since inferiority in the dominance hierarchy and the legal codes also was her lot.

HOW IT HAPPENED

It might be assumed that in early tribal life, offspring represented a valued asset to man since they could provide support and help in his struggle with other men and in his efforts to survive within his environment. In order to enlarge the number of kinsmen, he would have to secure for himself the certainty of paternity which nature had denied him. Consequently, man sought to assure himself of that paternity by making rules and regulations that would reduce the chances of his wife's consorting with other men. These rules and regulations served to delimit the freedom of the woman, whose maternity was indisputable. In order to ensure that his wife did not attract other men, he either isolated her in a harem, limited her freedom in the society of men, or partially hid their charms by the use of face veils or *sheitls* (the wigs worn by married Orthodox Jewish women). Implicit in this need to seclude one's wife is that, if given half a chance, she would make a break for sexual freedom. Thus the notion of woman as seductress and temptress becomes a parallel theme to that of suppression. This notion also enabled man to project his own sexual yearnings onto woman and thus to absolve himself of culpability.

How did the pervasiveness of women's inferior status come about? Why did they let it happen? Perhaps they contracted for the sustenance and protection that their lesser physical strength and her reproductive function prevented them from obtaining for themselves. After all, their survival directly depended on the sustenance provided by man, while man's survival only indirectly rested on woman's nurturance of the young. It is true that the origins of the attitudes and structures that comprise the dominance hierarchy and the legal status of women are complex and obscure. Conjecture and inference play important roles in the search for these origins. It is not conjecture, however, to observe that now that strength no longer is a requisite for survival, pregnancy no longer a necessary consequence of sexual activity, and the infant no longer dependent on the mother's breast, women are demanding a revised contract, one more adaptive to survival in contemporary society.

REFERENCES

Bernard, Jessie. The status of women in modern patterns of culture. *Annals of the American Academy of Political and Social Science,* 1968, vol. 375.

D'Andrade, Roy G. Sex differences and cultural institutions. In *The development of sex differences,* (Ed.) E.E. Maccoby. Stanford: Stanford University Press, 1966.

Field, Mark G., and Flynn, Karin I. Worker, mother, housewife: Soviet woman today. In *Sex roles in changing society,* (Eds.) G. H. Seward and R. C. Williamson. New York: Random House, 1970.

Ford, Clellan S. Some primitive societies. In *Sex roles in changing society,* (Eds.) G. H. Seward and R. C. Williamson. New York: Random House, 1970.

Hampson, John L. Determinants of psychological sex orientation. In *Conference on sex and behavior,* (Ed.) F. Beach. New York: Wiley, 1965.

Kardiner, Abram. *The individual and his society.* New York: Columbia University Press, 1939.

Klineberg, Otto. Recent Studies of National Character, in *Culture and personality,* (Eds.) S. Stansteld and M. Smith. New York: Basic Books, 1949.

Levin, H., and Sears, Robert R. Identification with parents as a determinant of doll play aggression. *Child Development,* 1956, *27,* 135-53.

Liljestrom, Rita. The Swedish model. In *Sex Roles in changing society,* ed. G. H. Seward and R. C. Williamson. New York: Random House, 1970.

Majundar, D. N. *Himalayan polyandry.* New York: Asia Publishing House, 1962.

Malinowski, Bronislaw. *The sexual life of savages.* New York: Halcyon House, 1929.

Mead, Margaret. *Sex and temperament in three primitive societies.* New York: Morrow, 1935.

———. *Male and female.* New York: Morrow, 1949.

Minturn, Leigh, and Hitchcock, John. The Rajputs of Phalapur, India. In *Six cultures: Studies in child rearing,* ed. B. B. Whiting. New York: Wiley, 1963.

Murdock, G. P., Comparative data on the division of labor by sex. *Social Forces,* 1935, *15,* 551-53.

Petros, Prince of Greece. *A study of polyandry.* The Hague: Mouton, 1963.

Rabin, A. I. The sexes: Ideology and reality in the Israeli kibbutz. In *Sex roles in changing society,* (Eds.) G.H. Seward and R. C. Williamson. New York: Random House, 1970.

Sears, Robert R. Transcultural variables and conceptual equivalence. In *Studying personality cross-culturally,* (Ed.)

B. Kaplan. Evanston, Ill.: Row, Peterson, 1961.

———. Development of gender role. *Conference on sex and behavior,* (Ed.) F. Beach. New York: Wiley, 1965.

———; Whiting, John; Nowlis, V., and Sears, P. Some childrearing antecedents of aggression and dependency in young children. *Genetic Psychology Monograph,* 1953, No. *47,* pp. 135-234.

———; Maccoby, Eleanor E., and Levin, H. *Patterns of child rearing.* Evanston, Ill.: Row, Peterson, 1957.

Seward, Georgene. Sex roles ancient to modern. In *Sex roles in changing society,* (Eds.) G.H. Seward and R. C. Williamson. New York: Random House, 1970.

Spinellis, C. D.; Vassiliou, Vasso; and Vassiliou, George. Milieu development and male-female roles in contemporary Greece. In *Sex roles in changing society,* (Eds.) G. H. Seward and R. C. Williamson. New York: Random House, 1970.

Spiro, Melford. *Kibbutz: Venture in Utopia.* Cambridge: Harvard University Press, 1956.

Sullerot, Eveline. *Woman, society, and change.* New York: McGraw-Hill, 1970.

Unger, Baraet Zeki. Women in the Middle East and North Africa and universal suffrage. In *Annals of the American Academy of Political and Social Science,* 1968, *375.*

Whiting, John Wesley and Child, Irvin. *Child training and personality.* New Haven: Yale University Press, 1953.

Williamson, Robert C. Role themes in Latin America. In *Sex roles in changing society,* (Eds.) G.H. Seward and R.C. Williamson. New York: Random House, 1970.

ADDITIONAL REFERENCES

Bardwick, J., and Douvan, E. Ambivalence: The socialization of women. In V. Gornick and B. K. Moran (Eds.), *Woman in sexist society.* New York: Basic Books, 1971.

Chodorow, N. A cross-cultural examination of the socialization of males and females. In V. Gornick and B. K. Moran (Eds.), *Woman in sexist society.* New York: Basic Books, 1971.

Coser, R., and Rodoff, G. Women in the occupational world: Social disruption and conflict. *Social Problems,* 1971, *18,* 535-54.

Douvan, E. Sex differences in adolescent character processes. *Merrill-Palmer Quarterly,* 1960, *6,* 203-211.

——— and Adelson, J. *The adolescent experience.* New York: Wiley, 1966.

Emmerich, W. Socialization and sex-role development. In P. Baltes and K. Schaie (Eds.), *Life-span developmental psychology: Personality and socialization.* New York: Academic Press, 1973.

Epstein, C. F. *Woman's place: Options and limits in professional careers.* Berkeley: University of California Press, 1970.

Erikson, E. *Identity, youth and crisis,* chap. 7. New York: Norton, 1968.

Henry, J. *Culture against man.* New York: Random House, 1963.

Kagan, J. Acquisitions and significance of sex typing and sex role identity. In M. Hoffman and L. Hoffman (Eds.), *Review of child development research,* vol. 1, New York: Russell Sage Foundation, 1964.

— — —. The emergence of sex differences. *School Review,* 1972, *80*, 229-40.

Laosa, L. M., and Brophy, J. E. Sex and birth order interaction in measures of sex typing and affiliation in kindergarten children. *Proceedings of the 78th Annual Convention of the American Psychological Association,* 1970, *5*, 363-64.

Lewis, M. Parents and children: Sex role development. *School Review,* 1972, *80*, 229-40.

Liebert, R. M.; McCall, R. B.; and Hanratty, M. A. Effects of sex-typed information on children's toy preferences. *Journal of General Psychology,* 1971, *119*, 133-36.

Lynn, D. B. Determinants of intellectual growth in women. *School Review,* 1972, *80*, 241-60.

Maccoby, E. (Ed.) *The development of sex differences.* Stanford: Stanford University Press, 1966.

SUGGESTED PAPERS AND PROJECTS

Papers:

1. What are the psychological assumptions about boys and girls in child psychology textbooks?
2. Prepare a cross cultural analysis of sex-role socialization.
3. Discuss the sex-role socialization trends in the United States.
4. Discuss the mother-infant relationship and its effect upon later sex-typed behavior of the young.

Projects:

1. *Ask five boys* and five girls what they want to be when they grow up.
2. Pretend you are a new parent. Describe your baby.
3. Interview several parents of school-age children. The parent of at least one boy and one girl must be included in the sample. Ask whether the children were sent to nursery school, at what age they walked to school alone, and at what age they could sleep away from home. (Note the limitations of the method involving reminiscence.)
4. Observe mother-child interactions in a playground. How are autonomy and dependence reinforced? Is there a sex difference?

Section IV

Sex Differences in Cognitive Functions

19 Introduction

There are well over a thousand studies of psychological sex differences. Even if one limits oneself to those involving sex differences in cognition, it is obviously imposiible to review more than a fraction. Oetzel (1966) provided an extensive bibliography of studies on sex differences. If one summarizes her data with regard to sex differences in cognitive function, one finds that there is a 4:1 ratio of studies showing a female advantage over males in verbal skills and a 3:1 ratio of sudies indicating a male advantage over females in problem solving and numerical and spatial skills. A search of the literature since 1965 shows little change in this pattern of sex differences.

Sex differences in favor of girls' language development appear as soon as children show true speech (McCarthy, 1953). Girls say their first word earlier, articulate more clearly and at an earlier age, use sentences earlier, and use longer, more fluent sentences than boys. Boys catch up by about age ten in vocabulary and reading, but remain consistently inferior to girls in tests of grammar, spelling, and word fluency.

During the preschool years girls learn significantly more letter names than boys, although boys seem to learn number names as well as girls (Iversen, Silberberg and Silberberg, 1970). From the early grades on boys show superior performance in tasks involving spatial and analytic ability, although there are no differences between the sexes in computational skill during the school years. Little can be said regarding the differential performance of boys and girls on intelligence tests rather than measures of achievement because those items upon which the two sexes consistently perform differently are usually eliminated. Studies of adult performance on various subtests of the Wechsler Adult Intelligence Scale (WAIS), however, indicate that males show superior performance on information, arithmetic, block design, and picture arrangement, while females are superior on the digit symbol subtest (Shaw, 1965).

Unfortunately, most of the data in this area come from correlational descriptive studies rather than manipulated variable experiments. Attempts to dichotomize behavior into male vs.

female traits tend to obscure the correlational nature of most of the data. Individuals show more or less of a particular trait, not all, or none of it. Dichotomizing the data also tends to obscure the great overlap in masculine and feminine characteristics. Females who score high in a particular trait are much more similar to males who score high than to females who score low in that characteristic. Correlational studies describe the properties of populations, not those of any particular individual.

It is probably necessary to manipulate cognitive processes within individuals directly rather than to rely on large-scale cross-subject analysis. However, there is a major problem in the determination of what manipulations will be effective. Theoretical and empirical studies of sex differences in cognitive function differ widely on the nature of both the factors that cause sex differences and those that will change sexual differentiation once it is present. Hypotheses on the nature of the operative factors range from almost totally physiological theories to those that stress only the social environment of the individual.

Broverman and his associates (1968) present an extensive review of the literature in support of their position that sex differences in cognitive abilities reflect sex-related differences in physiology. They cite evidence that indicates females are superior to males on simple overlearned perceptual-motor tasks. Males, on the other hand, are superior to females on complex tasks requiring inhibition of immediate responses to obvious stimuli in favor of responses to less obvious stimuli (cognitive restructuring). They suggest that these sex differences can be found across many species and that they are related to the different "setting" of the adrenergic activating (sympathetic nervous system) and cholinergic inhibitory (parasympathetic nervous system) in the two sexes. They suggest that estrogen is a more potent CNS excitant than androgen, and thus females are more activated or less inhibited than males. Such activation would facilitate learning of simple tasks, but would retard performance when inhibition is necessary.

Broverman et al.'s paper cites a great deal of evidence both physiological and psychological in nature. Many of the data are correlational in nature with the deficits already suggested previously. For example, their physiological theory does not account for the large overlap in the cognitive abilities of males and females. In fact, there is a positive relationship between subtests of the Wechsler Intelligence Scale for Children (WISC) and WAIS, so that an individual of either sex who does well or poorly on one part of the test will tend to perform in a similar manner on other parts of the test, whether verbal or cognitive-analytic in nature.

There is also no direct evidence that inhibition of complex

cognitive functions involves any part of the autonomic nervous system. This system does function in response to stress and anxiety. The learning tasks that Broverman et al. associate with sex differences are also affected by level of anxiety. The learning of simple tasks is enhanced and complex ones impaired by increases in anxiety level. High IQ is negatively correlated with anxiety in females and positively correlated with anxiety in males (Kagan and Moss, 1962). It is possible that what Broverman and his associates are describing as a sex-related neural difference is really a sex-related difference in anxiety level. Such an explanation appears to deal more parsimoniously with their data and takes other information into account as well. It is difficult to understand how a theory based upon the differential physiological effects of various sex hormones can account for the large number of prepubertal sex differences found.

Parlee (1972) has presented an exhaustive critique of Broverman et. (1968). Her paper should be read because the large number of studiés cited by Broverman and his associates and the massive amounts of physiological and neurological terminology utilized by them may make their position appear to be more "scientific" than it is—especially for those not well-versed in the field of physiological psychology. Unfortunately, her critique appeared four years after the original paper and may be overlooked by those who read the earlier study.

Parlee points out that Broverman and his associates may have been too simplistic in differentiating inhibitory, perceptual-restructuring tasks (at which males excel) for simple, perceptual-motor tasks (at which females excel). In order to do so, for example, they have characterized all verbal and reading tasks in which females consistently perform better than males as requiring *only* simple perceptual-motor skills. Parlee also points out (as we have above) that the relationship between cognitive function and the activity of the autonomic nervous system has not yet been empirically demonstrated. "without in any way casting doubt on the relevance of animal research to human psychology, it seems fair to say that an argument that depends upon an analogy between spontaneous motor activity in rats and reading speed in humans leaves much to be desired (p. 182)."

She suggests that the authors of the theory may also be confused about the neurophysiological relationship between the parasympathetic nervous system and acetylcholine activity. Despite the fact that the term "Cholinergic" is often applied to parasympathetic neural activity, acetylcholine is also found as a neurotransmitter in the sympathetic nervous system. In sum, she charges that Broverman et. al.'s conclusions represent "another in a series of purportedly objectively scientifically empty statements on the topic of sex differences (p. 184)."

Other physiologically based theories stress the differential rates of cognitive maturation of the two sexes. Girls may be developmentally advanced compared to boys as early as the sixth month of life. They display more sustained attention to visual stimuli and prefer more varied and novel auditory patterns than boys at both six and thirteen months of age (Kagan and Lewis, 1965). Correlations between the child's IQ and parents' IQ or educational level are significant at a much younger age for girls than for boys (Honzik, 1963; Werner, 1969; Reppucci, 1971). For girls the relationship may be significant as early as twenty months of age as compared to five years for boys.

Reppucci (1971) has recently done a study demonstrating the effect that illustrates some of the difficulties of interpreting the data. He found that girls' performance on all cognitive tasks (both verbal and analytic) was more closely correlated with their father's educational level than with their mother's. Thus it is not likely that identification with the mother provides the basis for the earlier onset of parent-child resemblance in cognitive function for girls. It has been suggested that the effect may be due to the greater cooperativeness of little girls, but this too may be a function of greater maturity of the CNS.

The earlier developmental maturity of girls may aid in the modification of their responses by environmental stimuli. Girls are assumed to be more susceptible to environmental manipulation at an earlier age than boys. However, it is also possible that educational level affects the way daughters are treated, but not sons. Developmental differences, moreover, do not seem to be able to account for sex differences in analytic or spatial tasks.

Sherman (1967) and Keogh (1971) suggest that males and females differ in their use of cognitive strategies. Sherman presents an extensive review of the literature in support of her contention that key measures of analytic-cognitive processes such as the rod and frame test and embedded figures tasks are substantially related to space perception and therefore sex biased. She suggests that female performance on spatial tasks is inferior to that of males even when there is no conflict with visual field and no analysis involved. Females show no impairment on analytic tasks involving verbal material. She asserts that the use of terms such as "analytical cognitive approach" implies a generality that has not been established.

Sherman cites evidence to suggest that a genetic sex difference in visualization may account for differences in such tasks as block sorting, discrimination of hidden figures, and the ability to perceive the position of an object independent of its surroundings. Spatial visualization has rarely if ever been controlled for, and such a control might eliminate sex differences entirely.

There is much evidence to suggest a physiological basis for sex differences in spatial visualization. Stafford (1961) has suggested that spatial visualization is carried as a recessive gene on the X chromosome. Therefore, it would be more likely to make its presence known in males than in females. Money and Alexander (1966) have demonstrated an extreme form of space-form blindness in individuals with Turner's syndrome (an XO genetic constitution). Lansdell, (1962, 1964) has indicated that there are differential impairments involving design preferences in the two sexes following neurosurgery.

Although Sherman and Broverman and his associates have very different positions on the genesis of sex differences in cognitive performance, they all suggest that there may be an inverse relationship between verbal ability and problem-solving ability. Sherman takes a kind of "as the twig is bent, so the tree will grow" position. Slight predispositional differences in young girls and boys might take on greater importance with age and different experiences. Verbally precocious girls will tend to continue to try to find verbal solutions for problems involving space perception. A study by Maier and Casselman (1970) has provided support for the use of different cognitive strategies by males and females. Even the matching of scores on the mathematics section of the SAT did not remove sex differences in problem-solving ability. In fact, females with high math aptitude scores accounted for most of the differences between the sexes. The authors suggest that qualitative differences in cognitive styles are present even between highly able boys and girls. Data from split-brain work in man (Gazzaniga, Bogen, and Sperry, 1965) has indicated that the dominant hemisphere for speech is opposite that for visualization. As of today, however, there are few data on the differential use of the two hemispheres by males and females.

Keogh (1971) presents some empirical verification of the use of different cognitive strategies by boys and girls. She shows that boys do significantly better than girls in tasks involving pattern walking, but not in pattern drawing. Boys, unlike girls, improve their walked copy of geometric figures as more visual cues became available in the environment. Distribution of objective scores overlapped for the two sexes, but not by much. Boys and girls also showed consistent subjective differences in their styles of pattern walking. Boys made precise corners and angles and were accurate in starting and stopping patterns. Girls were more hesitant and imprecise. Since there was no difference between the sexes in copying patterns by drawing, it is hard to account for these differences in terms of motivation.

Sherman accounts for much of the difference between the sexes in terms of differential opportunity to learn skills in those areas where differences are found. Boys spend more time in building models, driving cars, and reading maps than girls. There is no evidence, however, that the two sexes receive differential practice on visualization tasks. Even if behavior is sex-role differentiated, we are left with a "chicken or the egg" problem. Do children engage in certain activities because they are reinforced by society for doing so or because such activities are more readily reinforced due to physiological predispositions?

A number of investigators have attempted to analyze cognitive differences in terms of sex-role expectations. Stereotyping of sex roles has been discussed in several other sections. The relationship between cognitive functions and sex roles has been excellently reviewed by Maccoby (1966) and will be discussed only briefly here. There are several major arguments against a simplistic relationship between a child and his or her same-sexed parent. We lack data on any differential treatment of young children. Some sex differences appear before a child is aware of what sex he or she is, while others do not appear until the child has been exposed to a large number of sources of influence in addition to his or her parents. Some sex-related behaviors do not appear to be readily accessible to imitation. For example, how can spelling or largely covert reasoning and analytic ability be directly imitated by the child? Lastly, some sex differences first appear late in school life when differential experience is assumed to be minimal.

Assumptions of minimal experiential differences between boys and girls during the school years are probably unwarranted. Shinedling and Pedersen (1970) present evidence of complex relationships between the sex of the teacher, the sex of the student, and the subject being studied. They found that males performed significantly less well under female than under male teachers when verbal material was studied. Pedersen and his associates suggest that cultural expectancies and experimenter bias effects operate in both the classroom and under testing conditions.

Pedersen, Shinedling, and Johnson (1968) carefully studied the effect of examiner, sequence of subtests, and sex of subject on performance on various arithmetic subtests of the WISC. The WISC is supposed to be relatively insensitive to extraneous variables. They found that female subjects gave significantly outstanding performances when tested by female examiners. Their study also indicated that the subjects were affected differently depending upon whether a male or a female examiner tested them first. Pedersen and his associates conclude that the predominance of male math teachers and female English teachers in our society may be producing an educational artifact in terms of sex-related aptitudes.

A number of studies present data that indicate that a self-fulfilling prophecy effect (Rosenthal, 1966) may be operating in the area of sex differences in performance which is similar to that operating for racial and socioeconomic differences in performance. Wylie (1963) indicated that white girls, blacks, and children of low socioeconomic status made more modest estimates of their own abilities than white boys, whites, and children of high socioeconomic status. Low test anxious subjects performed better on problem solving tasks than high anxious subjects, and these differences were particularly strong for females (Russell and Sarason, 1965). Females have, in general, a higher anxiety level than males (Maccoby, 1966). Cultural expectations with regard to problem-solving abilities combined with higher levels of test anxiety could produce most of the female deficiencies in problem solving, especially since most testers are male.

Experiments designed to improve the problem-solving abilities of women have produced mixed results. "Women may derive comfort from the fact that under certain conditions they performed as well as men" (Hoffman and Meier, 1966, p. 382). The sex variable in problem-solving performance is not subject to simple generalizations. For example, under standard motivational conditions women performed better when a female examiner conducted the test, but under conditions designed to enhance motivation (a pep talk) their performance was enhanced by a male examiner and impaired by a female examiner. The relationship of women to other women, particularly in areas involving competence and power, is a complex one. It may be that a motivational pep talk was perceived as sexist and patronizing when uttered by a woman, or it may have aroused more anxiety than the same talk by a male.

Hoffman and Maier suggest that the standard problem situation that involves no particular motivation, male-oriented problems, and male examiners would tend to produce inferior performance in women. Their manipulations did not produce any long-lasting change, but they were encouraged that attitudes developed during eighteen years of socialization could be affected even briefly by their relatively simple manipulations. In a note of caution, however, Maier (Maier and Casselman, 1970) points out that his studies of thirty three years ago and today still show similar sex differences despite increasing similarity in the training of the two sexes.

Probably the best way to avoid the problems involved in dichotomizing behavior into masculine and feminine would be to find manipulations that change cognitive facilities in subjects of both sexes. To date, no such manipulations have been successful. Bieri (1960) has suggested that the way to study sex differences is to analyze behavioral differences within each sex in terms of personality variables that, while common to both sexes, may be considered to be closely related to either the masculine or feminine sex role. Among such characteristics that have been studied are parental identification, acceptance of authority, passivity, anxiety, aggression, etc. The results have been inconsistent, but tend to indicate that the same factors have different effects for the two sexes. Studies that do not consider the sex of the subject when subjecting them to "equivalent" manipulations may be attempting to compare apples and oranges. Cognitive processes may have different etiologies in males and females. They may be affected differently by what appear to be the same environmental conditions. It has been suggested to one of the authors, tongue in cheek, that we will not be able to resolve the issue of sex differences in cognition until we can study a series of identical twins, one of each sex, in the same environment.

It cannot be overemphasized that there is more overlap between males and females than there are differences between them. In fact, cross-sexual identification is positively correlated with IQ for both males and females (Kagan and Moss, 1962). A major problem in the area of cognitive differenceshis the question of whether different implies inferior. Henshel (1971) has analyzed traditional sources of bias in the study of masculinity-femininity. She points out that since what constitutes male vs. female traits is determined by our culture (which is both overtly and covertly antifeminist), masculine traits are those that are highly valued. Feminine attributes are comprised of nonattributes——the absence of those attributed to males.

One becomes aware of the cultural bias in psychology as one studies the literature on cognitive differences. Most studies concentrate on problem solving, analytic thinking, etc., despite the fact that learning disorders are three to ten times more frequent for boys than girls (Bentzen, 1963). Bentzen has suggested that the male preponderance of such disorders is due to the stress of responding to societal demands that do not provide for the maturational difference between boys and girls. Nevertheless, few studies have concerned themselves with the factors associated with verbal precocity in girls.

In conclusion, it is important to keep in mind that if we keep referring to the literature as competent scientists should, we may be building on dated standards and realities. We still do not know how much of sex differences in cognitive function is "real" and how much is the result of unwitting biases in the studies. "Sexist" is not yet an "in" term among established or leading researchers. "It is at times not even known to exist as it is so inextricably and finely meshed in our institutions, values, and attitudes" (Henshel, 1971, p. 14).

REFERENCES

Bentzen, F. Sex ratios in learning and behavior disorders. *American Journal of Orthopsychiatry,* 1963, *33,* 92-98.

Bieri, J. Parental identification, acceptance of authority, and within sex differences in cognitive behavior. *Journal of Abnormal and Social Psychology,* 1960, *60,* 76-79.

Broverman, D.M.; Klaiber, E.L.; Kobayashi, Y., and Vogel, W. Roles of activation and inhibition in sex differences in cognitive abilities. *Psychological Review,* 1968, *75,* 23-50.

Gazzaniga, M.S.; Bogen, J.E., and Sperry, R.W. Observations on visual perception after disconnection of the cerebral hemispheres in man. *Brain,* 1965, *88,* 221-36.

Henshel, A. Anti-feminist bias in traditional measurements of masculinity-feminity. Paper presented at the meeting of the National Council on Family Relations, Estes Park, Colorado, 1971.

Hoffman, L.E., and Maier, N.R. Social factors influencing problem solving in women. *Journal of Personality and Social Psychology,* 1966, *4,* 382-90.

Honzik, M. P. A sex difference in the age of onset of the parent-child resemblances in intelligence. *Journal of Educational Psychology,* 1963, *54,* 231-37.

Iversen, I.A.; Silberberg, N.E.; and Silberberg, M.C. Sex differences in knowledge of letter and number names in kindergarten. *Perceptual and Motor Skills,* 1970, *31,* 79-85.

Kagan, J., and Lewis, M. Studies of attention in the human infant. *Merrill-Palmer Quarterly,* 1965, *11,* 95-127.

Kagan, J., and Moss, H.A. *Birth to maturity.* New York: Wiley, 1962.

Keogh, B. K. Pattern copying under three conditions of an expanded spatial field. *developmental Psychology,* 1971, *4,* 25-31.

Lansdell, H.A. a sex difference in effect of temporal lobe neurosurgery on design preference. *Nature,* 1962, *194,* 852-54.

— — —. Sex differences in hemispheric asymmetries of the human brain. *Nature,* 1964, *203,* 550.

McCarthy, D. Some possible explanations of sex differences in language development and disorders. *Journal of Psychology,* 1953, *35,* 155-60.

Maccoby, e.E. Sex differences in intellectual functioning. In E.E. Maccoby (Ed.), *The development of sex differences,* Stanford: Stanford University Press, 1966.

Maier, N.R.F., and Casselman, G.C. The SAT as a measure of problem-solving ability in males and females. *Psychological Reports,* 1970, *26,* 927-39.

Money, J., and Alexander, D. Turner's syndrome: Further demonstration of the presence of specific cognitional deficiencies. *Journal of Medical Genetics,* 1966, *3,* 47-48:

Oetzel, R.M. Annotated bibliography. In E.E. Maccoby (Ed.), *The development of sex differences.* Stanford: Stanford University Press, 1967.

Parlee, M.B. Comments on "Role of activation and inhibition in sex differences in cognitive abilities". *Psychological review,* 1972, *79,* 180-84.

Pedersen, D.M., Shinedling, M.M., and Johnson D.L. Effects of sex examiner and subject on children's quantitative test performance. *Journal of personality and Social Psychology,* 1968, *10,* 251-54.

Reppucci, N. D. Parental education, sex differences, and performance on cognitive tasks among two-year-old children. *Developmental Psychology,* 1971, *4,* 248-53.

Rosenthal, R. *Experimenter effects in behavioral research.* New York: Appleton-Century-Crofts, 1966.

Russell, D. G. and Sarason, I. G. Test anxiety, sex and experimental conditions in relation to anagram solution. *Journal of Personality and Social Psychology,* 1965, *1,* 493-96.

Shaw, D. J. Sexual bias in the WAIS. *Journal of Consulting Psychology,* 1965, *29,* 590-91.

Sherman, J. a. Problem of sex differences in space perception and aspects of intellectual functioning. *Psychological Review,* 1967, *74,* 290-99.

Shinedling, M. M., and Pedersen, D. M. Effects of sex of teacher and student on children's gain in quantitative and verbal performance. *Journal of Psychology,* 1970, *76,* 79-84.

Stafford, R. E. Sex differences in spatial visualization as evidence of sex-linked inheritance. *Perceptual and Motor Skills,* 1961, *13,* 428.

Werner E. E. Sex differences in correlations between children's IQ's and measures of parental ability and environmental ratings. *Developmental Psychology,* 1969, *1,* 280-85.

Wylie, R. C. Children's estimates of their schoolwork ability as a function of sex, race and socioeconomic level. *Journal of Personality,* 1963, *31,* 203-224.

20

Since Broverman has participated in a number of studies on what might be termed "sexism" among clinical psychologists and on sex stereotyping among college students, it is surprising that he is the chief author of a paper that stresses an innate, physiological approach to sex differences in cognitive abilities. This extensive review surveys a large number of studies that the authors feel indicate that females are superior to males on simple motor tasks while males are superior to females on tasks requiring inhibition or perceptual restructuring. They suggest that the sex differences are due to the differential effects of estrogen and androgen upon the central nervous system. They suggest that estrogen has an excitory effect upon the autonomic nervous system, thus enhancing the learning of simple tasks while detracting from tasks requiring inhibition.

Although Broverman and his associates probably did not mean to sound so, the paper has a more "sexist" bias than most of the other studies in the area. What is especially noticeable is that they have tended to ignore evidence that there is a tremendous overlap in the cognitive abilities of males and females. Moreover, they dismiss as relatively irrelevant the information that specific cognitive abilities are correlated with each other so that an individual, male or female, who scores high on some subtests of a general intelligence test will tend to score high on all of the subtests.

It seems to us that a more economical explanation of cognitive differences between males and females, where they exist, may be in terms of differences in anxiety level. Maccoby in her excellent book The Development of Sex Differences[1] has discussed sex differences in anxiety extensively. There is much evidence to indicate that females have higher anxiety levels in test-taking performance than males. Studies in learning have shown that anxiety tends to improve learning on simple tasks and retard complex ones.[2] Thus, individuals who score high on the Taylor Manifest

---

1. E. E. Maccoby. Sex differences in intellectual functioning. In *The Development of Sex Differences,* Ed. E. E. Maccoby, pp. 25-55. Stanford University Press, 1966.

2. E. R. Hilgard and D. G. Marquis. *Conditioning and Learning.* New York: Appleton-Century-Crofts, 1940.

Anxiety Scale [MAS] condition more rapidly in simple Pavlovian procedures such as eyelid conditioning, but perform more poorly than low scorers on the MAS on tasks requiring a choice among a number of alternative responses.

Despite the orientation of the study, the paper contains a great deal of interesting information about the kinds of manipulations and measures used to study cognitive differences. It also raises a number of questions that could be studied experimentally. For example, during the menstrual cycle, pregnancy, and post-menopause, levels of estrogen are very different. In the same women, studied at intervals during these periods, is there variation in cognitive performance that is different for simple vs. complex tasks? How do hormonal treatments affect the cognitive performance of males vs. female animals? Are such treatments effective throughout the lifetime of the organism or only during certain critical periods? How does one account for prepubertal sex differences in cognition?

Roles of Activation and Inhibition in Sex Differences in Cognitive Abilities*

Donald M. Broverman, Edward L. Klaiber, Yutaka Kobayashi, and William Vogel

A hypothesis that known sex differences in cognitive abilities reflect sex-related differences in physiology is offered. Females surpass males on simple, overlearned, perceptual-motor tasks; males excel on more complex tasks requiring an inhibition of immediate responses to obvious stimulus attributes in favor of responses to less obvious stimulus attributes. It is hypothesized that these sex differences are reflections of differences in relationships between adrenergic activating and cholinergic inhibitory neural processes, which, in turn, are sensitive to the "sex" hormones, androgens and estrogens. Studies of

*From *Psychological Review*, 1968, 75 (1), 23-50. Footnotes have been renumbered.

the effects of drug and hormone administrations on these behaviors, and of sex hormones on adrenergic and cholinergic neuro-transmitters are examined. Implications for cross-sectional correlative analyses of cognitive organization are discussed.

Interest in the relationship of biochemical processes to mental events has increased greatly in recent years. The therapeutic effectiveness of the tranquilizing drugs in mental illness has focused attention, in particular, on the relationship of the catecholamines and adrenergic processes to behavior; while the stimulating studies of Krech and his colleagues (Rosenzweig, Krech, & Bennett, 1960) and Carlton (1963) have called attention to the roles of acetylcholine and cholinergic processes in learning phenomena. There has been no attempt to date, however, to utilize the findings of these studies to explain individual differences in the cognitive functioning of the normal, nonpathological human. It is towards this task, the construction of a biological framework within which normal human individual differences in certain mental abilities may be conceptualized, that the present paper is directed.

The mental abilities with which we are concerned are those in which known sex differences occur, that is, simple, perceptual-motor tasks in which females excel; and more complex tasks which require a reorganizing of stimulus elements, in which males excel (Anastasi & Foley, 1949). These sex differences are customarily attributed to differences in child rearing accorded the two sexes. We believe, on the other hand, that the phenomena may be more adequately explained in terms of the physiological differences existing between the sexes. Specifically, we hypothesize that the sex differences in cognitive abilities are reflections of differences in relationships between adrenergic activating and cholinergic inhibitory neural processes, which, in turn, are sensitive to the gonadal steroid "sex" hormones, androgens and estrogens. Support for these hypotheses will be derived from examination of the results of studies of the effects on behaviors of drugs which manipulate adrenergic and cholinergic processes, studies in which behaviors are manipulated by hormones, and studies in which hormones are used to manipulate components of the adrenergic and cholinergic neural cycles.

While we have a strong research interest in cognitive sex differences per se, we feel that the general arguments of this paper may be brought to bear upon a much wider domain of behavioral phenomena such as those induced by stress, and the developmental changes accompanying adolescence and old age. The specific case of sex differences in cognitive abilities was selected, mainly, because it is a much-explored area in which broad agreement exists as to the nature of the basic phenomena.

Finally, we believe that acceptance of the hypothesis of a physiological basis for cognitive sex differences raises serious difficulties for traditional correlative or factor-analytic approaches to the assessment of cognitive organization. The viewpoint advocated by this paper is that the functional relationships involved in cognitive organization cannot be properly ascertained by a cross-sectional analysis of abilities, but, rather, require assessments of the changes in relationships between abilities within individuals which are induced by pertinent organismic changes such as variations in hormone levels, the administration of drugs, and so on. Each of these considerations is elaborated upon below.

SEX DIFFERENCES IN ABILITIES

Two well-established differences between males and females in cognitive abilities are: (a) the superiority of females over males in tasks requiring relatively simple perceptual-motor associations; and (b) the superiority of males over females in certain tasks requiring suppression of responses to immediately obvious stimulus attributes of the task in favor of responses to other, not immediately obvious, stimulus attributes, that is, inhibitory perceptual-restructuring tasks.

Simple Perceptual-Motor Tasks

Females have been reported to exceed males in speed of color naming in both young children (Staples, 1932) and young adults (Stroop, 1935). Females also exceed males on clerical aptitude tests which require rapid perception of details and frequent shifts of attention (Paterson & Andrew, 1946). The clerical superiority of females has been found to be present from the fifth grade through the senior year of high school (Paterson & Andrew, 1946; Schneidler & Paterson, 1942). Feminine superiorities in both children and adults have been reported on the Digit Symbol Subtest of the WISC, WAIS, and Wechsler Bellevue Intelligence Tests (Gainer, 1962; Miele, 1958; Norman, 1953). The Digit Symbol task also requires rapid perception and frequent shifts of attention.

Young girls exceed young boys in tasks of fine manual dexterity (Gesell, Halverson, Thompson, Ilg, Castner, Ames, & Amatruda, 1940; McNemar, 1942) just as adult women exceed adult men in this attribute (Tiffin & Asher, 1948).

Although not commonly thought of as perceptual-motor behaviors, speech and reading do involve these functions. For example, speech involves the motoric coordination of the vocal apparatus: the tongue, larynx, diaphragm, etc., while reading involves perceptual scanning, recognition of letter patterns, etc. While the coordinations involved in speech and reading are initially difficult for the young child, they normally become effortless and automatic after a period of sustained practice. As with other simple perceptual-motor behaviors, females are superior to males from childhood through adulthood in verbal functions (McCarthy, 1930; Terman, 1946) and in reading (Samuels, 1943). The incidence of speech and reading pathologies is also significantly lower in females than males (Bennett, 1938; Schnell, 1946, 1947).

In short, evidence exists that females exceed males in tasks that require rapid, skillful, repetition, articulation, or coordination of "lightweight," over-learned responses (perceptual responses, small muscle movements, simple perceptual-motor coordinations).

Inhibitory Perceptual-Restructuring Tasks

A difference in favor of the male sex has been consistently reported on tasks which require subjects (Ss) to separate certain stimulus attributes from the field in which they are embedded. The Gottschaldt Figures, in which Ss must find a simple pattern embedded within a more complex pattern, are good paradigms of these tasks. Thurstone (1944, p. 111) described his "flexibility of closure" factor, which was best defined by the Gottschaldt Figures, as reflecting "freedom from Gestaltbindung" or "the ability to shake off one set in order to take a new one."

Another widely used perceptual-restructuring task is the Rod and Frame Test which requires S to adjust a luminescent rod to the vertical in a darkened room when the rod is within a tilted luminiscent square frame. "For successful performance of this task the subject must 'extract' the rod from the tilted frame through reference to body position [Witkin, Lewis, Hertzman, Machover, Meissner, & Wapner, 1954, p. 25]," that is, inhibit the influence of the frame.

A long list of studies indicates that males are superior to females on the Rod and Frame Test of Perception, and/or Gottschaldt Figures (Andrieux, 1955; Bennett, 1956; Bieri, Bradburn, & Galinsky, 1958; Carden, 1958; Chateau, 1959; Fink, 1959; Franks, 1956; Miller, 1953; Newbigging, 1952, 1954; Seder, 1957; Wit, 1955; Young, 1957; Zukmann, 1957).

Perceptual-restructuring is also a requirement in many other tasks, though perhaps to a lesser degree than in the Gottschaldt

315

and the Rod and Frame Tests. For instance, in the widely used Kohs Blocks Test (Kohs, 1923) *S*s are required to reduce the given perceptual pattern to parts corresponding to blocks. On many assembly tasks *S*s are required to see parts as they would appear in a larger pattern for task solution. Spatial tests typically require *S*s to see stimulus elements as they would appear in a different position in space, while mazes require *S* to ascertain whether or not an alley does indeed lead to his goal versus ending up in a not-immediately-apparent cul-de-sac. Each of these tasks requires *S*s to put aside or inhibit an immediate response to obvious stimulus attributes in favor of responses to less obvious stimulus relationships.

Sex differences in favor of males have been reported in each of these tasks. For instance, boys have been found to exceed girls significantly in counting partially hidden blocks from pictures (McNemar, 1942), assembling objects (Anastasi & Foley, 1949), and solving mazes (Porteus, 1918). A Scottish investigation included 444 boys and 439 girls of the same age and not differing in overall IQ (MacMeeken, 1939). The boys did significantly better than the girls on a battery of tests consisting of a form board, a manikin to be assembled, two picture completion tests, cube construction, and the Kohs Blocks ($CR = 3.74$, $p < .001$).

Empirically, the Witkin Gottschaldt Figures (Witkin, 1950), Kohs Blocks, Rod and Frame, Porteus Mazes (Porteus, 1950), and WAIS Object Assembly Subtest (Wechsler, 1955) have been reported to belong to the same cognitive factor (Gardner, Jackson, & Messick, 1960; Podell & Phillips, 1959; Witkin, Dyk, Faterson, Goodenough, & Karp, 1962).

The literature consistently indicates, then, that males exceed females in ability to perform tasks requiring perceptual inhibition and restructuring.

The different patterns of abilities in the two sexes are usually interpreted as reflections of culturally prescribed sex differences in child training procedures. Girls, for instance, may be rewarded more than boys for the development of routine, repetitive households skills such as sewing, knitting, washing dishes, etc.; while boys may be encouraged more to develop the analytical skills valued in the adult male world of business and science (Anastasi & Foley, 1949). However, different cultural rewards seem inadequate as explanations of sex differences in ease of conditioning of a simple response with minimal, if any, cultural relevance, that is, the eye blink. A feminine superiority in eyelid conditioning has been reported in 18 out of 19 studies, with the differences significant in eight of the studies (Spence & Spence, 1966).

Similarly, the cultural reward hypothesis has difficulty in explaining greater feminine acuity in sensory thresholds, such as in hearing (Corso, 1959) and taste (Soltan & Bracken, 1958).

The cultural reward hypothesis is also inadequate to explain analogous sex differences in subhuman species such as the rat or chicken. Just as human females condition more rapidly than males (Spence & Spence, 1966), so have female rats been reported to condition more rapidly than male rats (Irwin, 1964).

Running in activity wheels by rodents requires quick reflex actions, split-second timing, and skillful coordination (Kavanau & Brant, 1965). Rodents give preference to this skilled activity since they run more in wheels than they do in straight runways (Brant & Kavanau, 1964); and more in wheels with hurdles, or in square wheels than in conventional round wheels (Kavanau & Brant, 1965). Female rats indulge in this skilled activity significantly more than male rats (Hitchcock, 1925). Female rats also evidence more spontaneous exploratory activity than male rats (Simmel, Cheney, & Landy, 1965).

Also, just as human males are more adept at performing tasks requiring inhibition and restructuring that human females, so are male rats apparently superior to female rats in an analogous task; that is, the maze. Empirically, maze-bright rats tend to develop spatial or directional "hypotheses" about maze solutions; while maze-dull rats rely more on visual cues (Krechevsky, 1933). Rats achieve spatial hypotheses, according to Rosenzweig, Krech, and Bennett (1960), by ignoring dominant visual cues and adopting the less obvious hypothesis of location in space. The ability of rats to inhibit simple perceptual responses in favor of more complex but less obvious spatial relationships, then, is related to maze-brightness.

Several studies have reported that male rats learn mazes faster than female rats (Hubbert, 1915; McNemar & Stone, 1932; Sadovnikova-Koltzova, 1929; Tryon, 1931). Although Tomilin and Stone (1933), in a careful, well-controlled study, concluded no sex differences in *general* learning ability in rats, they also reported that male rats, in each of two independent samples, did significantly better than females on an elevated maze. Only one study reports females to be superior to males in maze learning (Corey, 1930). Tomilin and Stone (1933) criticized Corey's (1930) study as having employed inadequate hunger motivation (4 hours deprivation), noting that the number of trials required to reach mastery grossly exceeded other studies employing the same or similar mazes. Hence, the weight of evidence supports the proposition that male rats perform in mazes better than female rats.

Finally, female chickens have been reported to be less able to maintain conditioned inhibitory responses than male chickens (Zielinski, 1960).

It appears, then, that sex differences in simple perceptual-motor versus inhibitory perceptual-restructuring tasks extend across species. The cultural reward hypothesis of cognitive sex differences, therefore, has difficulty in explaining human sex differences in ease of conditioning of culturally nonrelevant responses, human sex differences in sensory thresholds, and sex differences in animals which seem to parallel sex differences in human abilities. Hence, entertainment of an alternative hypothesis, wherein both human and animal sex differences in the above behaviors are considered to be physiological in origin, seems warranted. More concretely, the hypothesis of this paper is that human sex differences in cognitive abilities, in ease of conditioning, and in sensory thresholds, as well as animal sex differences in behavior, are reflections of the balance between the activating influence of central adrenergic processes and the inhibitory influence of central cholinergic processes, which, in turn, are influenced by gonadal steroid "sex" hormones. Before proceeding to a discussion of the physiology involved, however, a more careful consideration of the attributes of those behaviors which differentiate males and females seems desirable.

CLASSIFICATION OF TASKS

The classification of tasks on which known sex differences occur into simple perceptual-motor versus inhibitory-restructuring tasks has been based, essentially, on face validities of the tasks involved. In defense of this procedure, it may be pointed out that a degree of consensuality exists on this matter in the sex differences literature (Anastasi & Foley, 1949; Thurstone, 1944; Witkin et al., 1962). However, the present paper has added behaviors in which sex differences exist that may not be easily classified by this scheme, for example, eyelid conditioning, sensory thresholds, or spontaneous activity in rats. Hence, before examining the psychopharmacological literature, which adds still further to the varieties of behaviors to be considered, it is necessary to develop a more comprehensive and explicit set of classification criteria.

Attributes of Behaviors in Which Females Are Superior

The behaviors in which females are superior to males seem to have the following attributes:

1. The behaviors appear to be based mainly upon past experience or learning, as opposed to problem solving of novel or

318

thresholds represent an extreme of this attribute; but other more obviously learned behaviors such as typing, color naming, or difficult tasks. Thus, color naming, talking, reading, etc., are based upon extensive previous experience.

2. As a result of extensive prior practice, the behaviors appear to involve minimal mediation by higher cognitive processes. Sensory conditioning are termed skilled or well-acquired as they move towards reflexive automatic responses.

3. The behaviors typically involve fine coordinations of small muscles with perceptual and attentional processes, such as in typing or reading, rather than coordination of large muscle movements as in athletics.

4. Finally, the behaviors are evaluated in terms of the speed and accuracy of repetitive responses, as in color naming, rather than in terms of production of new responses or "insight," as in maze solutions.

Table 1 lists the behaviors considered in the following sections that seem to possess the above attributes.

TABLE 1

SIMPLE OVERLEARNED REPETITIVE BEHAVIORS MEASURED IN TERMS OF SPEED, ACCURACY, OR FREQUENCY OF OCCURRENCE AND WHICH REQUIRE MINIMAL CENTRAL MEDIATION

Humans
  Speed of naming colors
  Speed of canceling numbers
  Reading speed
  Coding speed (digit symbol task)
  Tapping speed
  Writing speed
  Walking
  Typing
  Simple calculations
  Eye-blink conditioning
  Discrimination of letter series
  Letter canceling
  Auditory pitch discrimination
  Visual acuity
  Critical flicker fusion

Animals
  Spontaneous activity (wheel)

Spontaneous activity (open field)
Speed of conditioning
Rate of conditioned responses

Attributes of Behaviors in Which Males Are Superior

The behaviors in which males are superior to females seem to be characterized by the following:

1. The behaviors involve an inhibition or delay of initial response tendencies to obvious stimulus attributes in favor of responses to less obvious stimulus attributes, as in the Embedded Figures Test.

2. The behaviors seem to involve extensive mediation of higher processes as opposed to automatic or reflexive stimulus response connections.

3. Finally, the behaviors are evaluated in terms of the production of solutions to novel tasks or situations, such as assembling parts of a puzzle or object, as opposed to speed or accuracy of repetitive responses.

Table 2 lists behaviors to be considered in subsequent sections that seem to possess these attributes.

The position of this paper is that the two classes of behaviors listed in Tables 1 and 2 are affected in opposite ways by manipulations of the balance between the adrenergic and cholinergic central nervous systems. Attributes of these nervous systems are discussed below.

Adrenergic-Cholinergic Antagonisms and Cognitive Functioning

The adrenergic autonomic nervous system is often referred to as the sympathetic autonomic nervous system, while the cholinergic autonomic nervous system is frequently referred to as the parasympathetic nervous system. The sympathetic and parasympathetic autonomic nervous systems are frequently in competition and the final effect then depends upon the relationship between the momentary activity of the two systems. For instance, sympathetic nerves tend to enlarge, while parasympathetic nerves tend to contract the pupil of the eye (Fulton, 1949).

TABLE 2

Complex Behaviors Requiring Problem
Solving, Delay, or Reversal of Usual Habits

Humans

Temporal judgment (delayed responses)
Mirror tracing
Maze performance
Ability to retard overpracticed motor movements
Discriminant reaction time
Habit reversal, counting backwards

Animals

Delayed responses (conditioned inhibition)
Maze learning
Alternation of reinforced responses
Habit reversal

The adrenergic nervous system is considered to have a mobilizing function in preparation for action, while the cholinergic system is thought to work towards protection, conservation, and relaxation of the organism when action is not required (Fulton, 1949).

Hess (1954) emphasized the role of subcortical portions of the central nervous system in the regulation of sympathetic and parasympathetic peripheral activity. Hess (1954) termed the adrenergic subcortical system "ergotropic" since it controls motor activity, sensory reactivity, wakefulness, alertness, etc.; while the cholinergic subcortical system was termed "trophotropic" since it promotes sleep, inhibition of activity, relaxation, etc. Antagonisms between the ergotropic and trophotropic subcortical systems in their regulation of certain behaviors were also described by Hess; for example, the degree of wakefulness and motor activity were described as resultants of the competing systems. Activation in this paper, then, will refer, physiologically, to activity of the central adrenergic nervous system: and, behaviorally, to a predominance of ergotropic over trophotropic behaviors. Inhibition will refer, physiologically, to activity of the central cholinergic nervous system; and, behaviorally, to a diminution of ergotropic behaviors in favor of trophotropic behaviors.

It is our hypothesis, then, that the same ergotropic functions that facilitate wakefulness and sensory reactivity also facilitate performances of simple perceptual-motor tasks. Similarly, we hypothesize that the same trophotropic functions that promote relaxation and sleep also contribute to the cognitive ability to delay initial response tendencies to obvious stimulus attributes, in favor of responses to other, less obvious stimulus relationships. These hypotheses span two quite disparate areas of function, that is, central autonomic versus intellectual functioning. However, if evidence can be mustered in their support, the embodied concepts would considerably increase our understanding of the relationship between physiology and human abilities.

Substances Affecting the Sympathetic Nervous System

The sympathetic nervous system was termed "adrenergic" because epinephrine, an amine secreted by the adrenals, was once thought to be the neural transmitter of the system. Later work indicated that several amines are probably involved in the neural transmission of the sympathetic system. Dopamine and norepinephrine, for instance, are believed to facilitate neural transmission in the "ergotropic" portion of the old brain. Norepinephrine applied to the medial preoptic region of the brain produces alertness and motor hyperactivity (Hernandez-Peon & Chavez-Ibarra, 1963).

The amine gamma-aminobutyric acid is believed to aid in the repolarization of sympathetic neurons after neural discharge and so facilitate rapid repeated firing of the neuron (Roberts, Wein, & Simonsen, 1964).

Adrenal secretions of epinephrine into the peripheral bloodstream are thought to stimulate centers in the hypothalamus as well as the reticular activating system, thus alerting the organism (Rothballer, 1959), although epinephrine does not, itself, penetrate cortical brain tissue.

Monoamine oxidase (MAO) is an enzyme thought to be primarily responsible for the metabolic inactivation of cellular stores of norepinephrine and dopamine (Kopin, 1964).

Iproniazid, an "energizing" drug used in the treatment of depression, inhibits MAO activity, thereby allowing stores of norepinephrine and dopamine to accumulate and so induce behavioral activity (Kopin, 1964).

Caffeine, perhaps the most widely used pharmacological stimulant, is believed to induce sympathetic stimulation by the same physiological route as norephinephrine, that is, an ability to increase the activity of an energy-releasing enzyme, 3', 5'-AMP in tissues, although caffeine and norepinephrine achieve this effect in different ways (Ritchie, 1965).

Amphetamine (benzedrine sulfate), another widely used stimulant or "pep" pill, is thought to achieve its effects by inducing a release of norepinephrine (Stein, 1964).

Reserpine, a "tranquilizing" drug, is believed to sedate through the depletion of norepinephrine levels in adrenergic tissues, while chlorpromazine, another tranquilizer, is thought to sedate by blocking the neural amine receptors, although not affecting amine levels, and so preventing amine activity (Stein, 1964). Empirically, it has been observed that the depletion of norepinephrine and dopamine brain levels through the administration of reserpine results in stupor, while the return of activity, alertness, etc., corresponds with the time of recovery of satisfactory amine levels in both rabbits (Spector, 1963) and cats (Wada, Wrinch, Hill, McGeer, & McGeer, 1963).

Substances Affecting the Parasympathetic System

The peripheral parasympathetic nervous system is called "cholinergic" because acetylcholine (ACh) is thought to be the neural transmitting substance of the system (Fulton, 1949). Recent studies now suggest that ACh is also involved in the neural transmission of the central portion of the parasympathetic nervous system. For instance, Hernandez-Peon and Chavez-Ibarra (1963) induced sleep in cats by implanting ACh crystals in the hypothalamus.

Released ACh is metabolically inactivated by the enzyme acetylcholinesterase. Physostigmine and eserine are drugs which inhibit acetylcholinesterase, thus prolonging and enhancing the physiological activity of ACh (Goodman & Gilman, 1965).

Atropine and scopolamine, on the other hand, block the action of ACh (Carlton, 1963). The effects of ACh, then, can be either enhanced or depressed by the appropriate drugs. For instance, sleep induced by electrical stimulation of the lateral preoptic region was enhanced by the injection of physostigmine, whereas injections of atropine prevented the induction of sleep by electrical stimulation in the same area (Hernandez-Peon & Chavez-Ibarra, 1963).

TABLE 3

Substances Which Result in Either Increased Activation or Increased Inhibition via Adrenergic or Cholinergic Stimulation or Depression

Increased activation		Increased inhibition	
Adrenergic stimulation	Cholinergic depression	Adrenergic depression	Cholinergic stimulation
Epinephrine Dopamine Norepinephrine Glutamic acid Gamma-amino-buteric acid Amphetamine (benzedrine sulfate) Caffeine Iproniazid	Atropine Scopolamine Cholinesterase Pentamethonium-iodide	Reserpine Chlorpromazine Monoamine oxidase	Eserine Physostigmine Acetylcholine

Separate neural activating and inhibitory processes exist, then, and each is susceptible to independent augmentation or diminution by specific drugs. Accordingly, the balance between activating and inhibitory processes may be altered in either direction by changes in either process; for example, a shift in the direction of greater probability of sympathetic response may be induced either by an increase in activation or a decrease in inhibition. The results in either case should be similar.

Table 3 lists the various substances with which this paper is concerned that produce either increased activation or increased inhibition via either adrenergic or cholinergic stimulation or depression.

We now propose that the relationship between simple per-ceptual-motor and inhibitory perceptual-restructuring tasks, may be, in part, a function of the balance between the activating in-fluence of the sympathetic, and the inhibitory tendencies of the parasympathetic subcortical nervous systems. Hence, it is hypothesized that an alteration in the activation-inhibition balance in the direction of greater activation, either by the administration of substances which stimulate the sympathetic nervous system, or which depress the parasympathetic nervous system, will tend to facilitate simple perceptual-motor task performances and impair performances of inhibitory perceptual-restructuring tasks. Con-versely, an alteration of the activation-inhibition balance in the direction of greater inhibition, either by the administration of substances which reduce activation or which augment inhibition, will tend to impair simple perceptual-motor task performances, and enhance performances of perceptual-restructuring tasks. These theoretical expectations are listed in Table 4.

TABLE 4

HYPOTHESES CONCERNING THE EFFECTS OF STIMULATION AND DEPRESSION OF
ADRENERGIC AND CHOLINERGIC NERVOUS SYSTEMS ON SIMPLE PERCEPTUAL–
MOTOR AND PERCEPTUAL–RESTRUCTURING TASK PERFORMANCES

	Increased activation		Increased inhibition	
	Adrenergic stimulation	Cholinergic depression	Adrenergic depression	Cholinergic stimulation
Simple perceptual-motor tasks	improvement	improvement	impairment	impairment
Perceptual-restructuring tasks	impairment	impairment	improvement	improvement

Psychopharmacological evidence relating to each of the hypotheses listed in Table 4 is considered below.

EFFECTS OF SUBSTANCES WHICH STIMULATE THE ADRENERGIC NERVOUS SYSTEM

The activation-inhibition balance may be altered in the direction of greater activation by stimulating the adrenergic nervous system. Sympathetic stimulants, then, should facilitate manners of simple perceptual-motor tasks and impair performances of inhibitory perceptual-restructuring tasks.

Simple Perceptual-Motor Tasks

The sympathomimetic stimulant amphetamine has been reported to improve performances of simple perceptual-motor tasks such as speed of naming color hues (Callaway & Stone, 1960), rate of canceling numbers (Adler, Burkhardt, Ivy, & Atkinson, 1950; Lehmann & Csank, 1957; Tyler, 1947), and reading speed (Florey & Gilbert, 1943; Lebensohn & Sullivan, 1944). Amphetamine also improves sensory functioning such as visual acuity (Lebensohn & Sullivan, 1944), pitch discrimination (Thurlow, 1946), and critical flicker-fusion frequency (Adler et al., 1950; Lehmann & Csank, 1957; Simonson & Enzer, 1941).

Amphetamines have been reported to improve performances on tasks requiring the rapid use of hands and fingers such as tapping speed (Lehmann & Csank, 1957; Simonson & Enzer, 1941) and writing speed (Nash, 1962); as well as the rates of spontaneous motor activity in both humans (Golla, Blackburn, & Graham, 1940) and rats (Mirsky, White, & O'Dell, 1959; Zieve, 1937).

Amphetamines increased the rate of eye-blink conditioning in humans (Franks & Trouton, 1958), and barpress conditioning in rats (Skinner & Heron, 1937; Wentink, 1938).

The stimulant caffeine has been reported to increase the speed of typing, color naming, simple calculations, and tapping in humans (Hollingworth, 1912), and bar-pressing in rats (Skinner & Heron, 1937).

Finally, the administration of glutamic acid, the precursor of the amine gamma-aminobutyric acid, has been reported to improve the ability of normal adults to perform simple tasks (Muller, 1955) Schwobel & Tamm, 1952).

An abundance of evidence exists, then, in support of the notion that the experimental augmentation of activating processes

325

facilitates performances of the class of behaviors in which females appear to be superior to males.

Inhibitory Perceptual-Restructuring Tasks

Substances which stimulate the sympathetic nervous system should, according to the argument of this paper, impair performances of tasks that require inhibition or delay of otherwise prepotent responses.

Pavlov (1927) observed long ago that the administration of the sympathetic stimulant caffeine disrupts conditioned inhibition, for example, a dog conditioned to wait 15 seconds after the ringing of a bell before he receives food will normally not salivate until the 15 seconds are almost passed. Injection of caffeine destroys the conditioned ability of the dog to delay salivation. Salivation then occurs immediately upon the ringing of the bell. This is a clear example of the antagonistic relationship between activating and inhibitory processes. Similarly, Hollingworth (1912) reported that caffeine impaired discrimination reaction times in human *S*s. The impairment, according to Hollingworth (1912), was ". . . . accompanied by a great number of false reactions. The false reactions appear to be caused by a preliminary briskness produced by the caffeine, and the retardation in reaction time caused by a voluntary caution in the attempt to eliminate the false reactions [p. 120]." Impairments of discriminative reaction time by caffeine have also been reported by Cheney (1935, 1936).

The stimulant amphetamine, administered to rats, disrupted previously conditioned temporal patterns of barpressing behavior by causing the rats to press too soon (Carlton, 1961; Sidman, 1956). A similar acceleration of temporal judgment after amphetamines in humans has been reported by Dews and Morse (1958).

After administering amphetamines to air-crew men, Davis (1947) reports, "When one activity competes with another and separate responses have to be made to more than one stimulus at much the same time, the effects of the drug tend to be unfavorable and behavior disorganized [p. 43]." Davis (1947) also stated that the amphetamines led to impulsive and inappropriate activity when *S* performed constraining duties.

Carlton (1961) reported that amphetamine induced a greater number of errors in rats who had to alternate the pushing of two levers for rewards, that is, inhibit the tendency to repeat the preceding reinforced response.

Both amphetamine (benzedrine) and caffeine have been

reported to impair maze learning in rats (Dispensa & Barrett, 1941; Lashley, 1917; Minkowsky, 1939), while iproniazid administration, which results in heightened norepinephrine levels, impaired maze learning in mice (Woolley & van der Hoeven, 1963).

Impairments of human performance by stimulants were also reported by Ellson, Fuller, and Urmston (1950) who, after administering glutamic acid (the precursor of the amine GABA) to retardates, reported an increase in "errors of overimpulsivity" on a mirror-tracing task. The mirror-tracing task requires that a sensory response (the mirror image) be inhibited in favor of a conceptual response (the internal reversal of the sensory image). Chambers and Zabarenko (1956) also reported an increase in impulsive errors on a standard intelligence test in retardates treated with glutamic acid.

Finally, epinephrine administered intravenously impaired the ability of normal humans to write slowly (Basowitz, Korchin, Oken, Goldstein, & Gussack, 1956).

The above evidence supports the hypothesis that increased activation impairs performances of tasks that require cognitive inhibition. More important, the above indicates that the same experimental manipulation, that is, augmentation of sympathetic nervous activity, has the opposing effects of improving the ability to perform simple perceptual-motor tasks, on which females tend to be superior, and impairing the ability to perform tasks requiring inhibition or perceptual-restructuring, on which males tend to be superior.

EFFECTS OF SUBSTANCES WHICH DEPRESS PARASYMPATHETIC FUNCTIONING

The activation-inhibition balance may also be altered in the direction of greater activation by depressing the inhibitory cholinergic parasympathetic nervous system. Anticholinergic drugs, then, should have effects on abilities parallel to those of the previously considered stimulants, that is, anticholinergic drugs should facilitate performances of simple perceptual-motor tasks and impair performances of perceptual-restructuring tasks.

Simple Perceptual-Motor Tasks

Intramuscular injections of the anticholinergic drugs atropine and scopolamine, like the stimulant amphetamine, have been observed to increase: the amount of open field activity (Tapp, 1965); spontaneous activity in wheels (Frommel & Fleury, 1960; Meyers, Roberts, Riciputi, & Domino, 1964; Tripod, 1957); and rates of conditioned responses in rats (Carlton, 1961). Intraventricular injections of atropine caused increased motor activity in cats (Feldberg & Sherwood, 1954b). Finally, both cholinesterase (an enzyme which inactivates acetylcholine) and pentamethonium iodide, an acetylcholine blocking agent, injected intraventricularly induced activity in catatonic schizophrenics (Sherwood, 1952).

This evidence is consistent with the proposition that an increase in the activation balance via diminution of the inhibitory processes leads to increased output of simple perceptual-motor behaviors.

Perceptual-Restructuring or Inhibitory Tasks

Drugs which depress parasympathetic nervous system function, thus increasing the dominance of the activating sympathetic system, should impair performances of perceptual-restructuring or inhibitory tasks.

The anticholinergic drug atropine has been reported to impair the ability of rats to learn a maze (Whitehouse, 1959).

Both atropine and scopolamine, like the previously considered amphetamine, induced a greater number of errors in rats on Carlton's (1961) lever-switching task.

Finally, atropine, like amphetamine, impairs conditioned inhibition by causing rats to bar-press too soon on a fixed interval schedule of reinforcement (Carlton, 1961).

In general, then, the anticholinergic drugs produce behavioral effects similar to those of the sympathomimetic stimulants, that is, they facilitate simple perceptual-motor tasks and impair performances of tasks requiring inhibition.

EFFECTS OF SUBSTANCES WHICH
DEPRESS SYMPATHETIC FUNCTIONING

Simple Perceptual-Motor Tasks

Substances which decrease activating processes by depressing the sympathetic nervous system should impair performances of simple perceptual-motor tasks. The literature provides evidence in support of this hypothesis. For instance, the administration to humans of chlorpromazine (CPZ), a drug believed to depress sympathetic nervous functioning by blocking neural amine activity (Stein, 1964), has been reported to slow tapping speed and impair flicker fusion (Lehmann & Csank, 1957). CPZ adversely affected the performance of the WAIS Digit Symbol Subtest (Kornetsky, Humphries, & Evarts, 1957) and impaired the efficiency of continuous performance in which *S* must discriminate all X's and Y's preceded by A's from a series of rapidly presented letters, a task thought to measure, primarily, alertness or attentiveness (Primac, Mirsky, & Rosvold, 1957).

CPZ administered to rats reduces the rate of spontaneous motor activity (Mirsky et al., 1959).

Uhr (1960), after reviewing the effects of CPZ and reserpine (an amine depletor) on performance, concluded that they "impair speeded, coordinated psychomotor and simple perceptual skills." Thus, there is good reason to believe that depression of adrenergic sympathetic nervous system impairs simple perceptual-motor functioning.

Inhibitory Perceptual-Restructuring Tasks

Depressed functioning of the activating sympathetic nervous system should facilitate the performance of inhibitory perceptual-restructuring tasks.

CPZ generally slows performances. However, CPZ speeded the performance of a task involving overlearned habits (counting from 1 to 20), when the task had to be performed backwards, that is, when the prepotent habit of counting forwards had to be inhibited (Shatin, Rockmore, & Funk, 1956). Presumably, CPZ reduced the degree of sympathetic activation of responses to the highly overpracticed habit of counting forwards, thus facilitating a reversal of that procedure, that is, counting backwards.

Although Helper, Wilcott, and Garfield (1963) found that the administration of CPZ to mental retardates generally worsened their performances on intelligence tests, they also found a reduction of "Q" type errors on the Porteus Maze Test. "Q" errors are described by Porteus (1950) as errors of carelessness or impulsiveness, that is, lack of appropriate inhibition.

Gonzalez and Ross (1961) trained rats to jump through doors associated with different stimuli. Rats treated with CPZ were better able to reverse their jumping habit when the differentiating stimuli were reversed in significance than were control rats. This task also requires the inhibition of a previously conditioned response to sensory stimuli.

Reserpine, an amine depletor, facilitated maze learning in mice (Woolley & van der Hoeven, 1963).

Finally, Scheckel (1962) reported that low (.003 mg/kg) doses of CPZ facilitated the ability of monkeys to make correct delayed responses, while larger (1 mg/kg) doses decreased this ability. Apparently facilitation on inhibitory restructuring tasks by CPZ requires that CPZ be concentrated enough to lower activation, but not so concentrated that it impairs functioning in general.

Evidence exists in the literature, then, supporting the proposition that a tilting of the activation-inhibition balance towards greater inhibition by depressing the activating sympathetic nervous system facilitates performances of inhibitory tasks.

EFFECTS OF SUBSTANCES WHICH AUGMENT PARASYMPATHETIC NERVOUS FUNCTIONS

Substances which augment parasympathetic nervous function should alter the activation-inhibition balance in the direction of greater inhibition and, therefore, impair performances on simple perceptual-motor tasks and facilitate performances of inhibitory perceptual-restructuring tasks.

Simple Perceptual-Motor Tasks

Eserine blocks the activity of acetylcholinesterase, the enzyme that inactivates ACh. Eserine, then, causes a rise in ACh levels and, presumably, an increase in the parasympathetic antagonism of the sympathetic nervous system. Feldberg and Sherwood (1954a) reported that intraventricular injections of eserine induced a massive inhibition of motor activity, but no decrease in muscle tonus in cats, that is, the injected cat would maintain whatever position its limbs were placed in. A very strong stimulus, such as a loud noise, momentarily activated the cat, after which it again froze its posture. Similar results were obtained with intraventricular injections of ACh (Feldberg & Sherwood, 1954b).

Pryor (1964) reported that Tryon's S_1 "maze-bright" strain of rats tends to be spontaneously less active than Tryon's S_3 "maze dull" strain. The S_1 strain has been reported to have higher brain levels of ACh than the S_3 strain (Rosenzweig, Krech, & Bennett, 1960).

This evidence, though scant, is consistent and conforms to the expectation: Substances which augment the parasympathetic nervous system tend to diminish simple perceptual-motor behaviors.

Perceptual-Restructuring Tasks

Augmentation of the parasympathetic nervous system should facilitate the performance of inhibitory perceptual-restructuring tasks. Whitehouse (1959) reports that the administration of eserine, which increases ACh, increased the ability of rats to master a T maze.

Rosenzweig et al. (1960) have reported that animals with naturally high ACh levels in the brain also learn mazes more rapidly than animals with low brain ACh levels.

Again, the evidence, though meager, consistently supports the notion that augmentation of the parasympathetic nervous system tends to facilitate the performances of perceptual-restructuring tasks.

Evidence from psychopharmacological studies exists, then, in support of each of the hypotheses concerning the effects of adrenergic and cholinergic stimulation and depression on performance of simple perceptual-motor and perceptual-restructuring tasks. Each experimental manipulation of the adrenergic and cholinergic systems tends to produce opposite effects on performances of the two types of tasks. These studies support the notion that a functional inverse relationship exists between the neural and cognitive processes related to simple perceptual-motor and perceptual-restructuring tasks which, in turn, represent salient differences in the cognitive functioning of the two sexes. The hormonal evidence relating to this cognitive difference is examined in the next section.

STEROID "SEX" HORMONES AND THE ACTIVATION-INHIBITION BALANCE

This paper hypothesizes (*a*) that females are more activated, or less inhibited, than males, and (*b*) that this sex difference in activation-inhibition balance is due to differences in the levels of the steroid "sex" hormones, estrogens and androgens, typical of each sex. Hormone behavior studies support this hypothesis. Studies involving estrogens, the hormones associated primarily with female characteristics, will be reviewed first, followed by the studies involving androgens, the "male" hormones.

ESTROGENS AND
THE ACTIVATION-INHIBITION BALANCE

Human females exceed human males on simple perceptual-motor tasks. The same sex difference in analogous behaviors, that is, spontaneous motor activity, is true in rats. Female rats are spontaneously more active than male rats (Hitchcock, 1925). A series of studies have firmly linked estrogens causally to this difference in rats. Thus, female rats were observed to be most active at the day of estrus when estrogen effects are maximal (Slonaker, 1924; Wang, 1923, 1924). Peak activity at time of estrus has also been reported in the sow (Altmann, 1941) and in the human female at mid-cycle, the usual time of ovulation (Billings, 1939). The removal of the ovaries results in a 60-95% drop in activity in rats (Wang, 1923; Richter, 1927); while injections of estrone (an estrogen) increased the activity levels of both spayed female rats (Young & Fish, 1945), and normal adult and senile male rats (Hoskins & Bevin, 1941). The weights of the ovaries in adult female rats, corrected for body weight, have been reported to be significantly positively correlated with spontaneous activity by Riss, Burstein, Johnson, and Lutz (1959).

Finally, the latency of conditioned responses was found to be least at time of estrus in the sow (Altmann, 1941).

The above studies indicate that estrogens tend to increase activation, or decrease inhibition in rats, the sow, and, possibly, the human.

Similar conclusions about the effect of estrogens can be reached from studies of the effects of this hormone on an abnormal brain state, that is, convulsability. Convulsions may indicate overexcitation or lack of inhibition. Mature female rats have been reported to be more convulsion-prone from electric shock than male rats of the same age and strain (Woolley, Timiras, Rosenzweig, Krech, & Bennett, 1961).

Consulsability varies in female rats with the estrous cycle, reaching a peak prepuberally (Woolley & Timiras, 1962a). Intact mature females were found more convulsable than mature female rats who were ovariectomized pre-puberally (Woolley & Timiras, 1962b). Finally, administration of synthetic estrogens was observed to increase convulsability in both female and male rats (Woolley et al., 1961; Woolley & Timiras, 1962a, 1962b).

Estrogen, then, consistently alters the activation-inhibition balance in favor of greater activation.

ANDROGENS AND
THE ACTIVATION-INHIBITION BALANCE

The relationship of androgens to the activation-inhibition balance is more complicated than that of estrogen. Since males are apparently less activated or more inhibitory than females, it would be ideal if androgens could be shown to reduce activation and increase inhibition. This is not the case. In fact, the reverse seems to be correct: Within the normally occurring physiological range, androgens also seem to increase activation, although to a lesser extent than estrogens.

Removal of the testes, the organ which produces most of the androgen in the male, reduces the activity level of adult male rats significantly below that of intact male rats (Hoskins, 1925; Richter, 1933). The effect is proportional to the amount of testicular tissue removed (Gans, 1927), and has been reversed by implanting testicular tissue in male castrate rats (Richter & Wislocki, 1928). The activity of goldfish was increased 400% by a diet of dried ram's testicle (Stanley & Teacher, 1931). Riss et al. (1959) report positive, but marginally significant ($p < .10$) correlations between the testicle weight of adult male rats, corrected for body weight, and spontaneous activity.

Studies in our laboratories indicate that doses of testosterone (the most potent androgen) injected into castrated male rats facilitate operant conditioning of a fixed-ratio bar-press task. Two groups of 10 experimental male rats, castrated at 21 days of age, received either .0125 or .025 mg. testosterone propionate in oil daily for 14 days. The experimental rats conditioned significantly faster than 10 similar rats receiving a lower (.00625 mg.) dose level of testosterone [$F = 6.72$; p .02]; and faster than 10 similar rats receiving only oil injections [$F = 8.02$; p .01]. Rats receiving higher dose levels of testosterone did not differ significantly in their rate of conditioning from the rats receiving oil only, or the lower does levels of testosterone. This latter finding is in agreement with a study by Heller [1932] who reported that massive injections of testicular extracts with known androgenic activity into castrated male rats did not restore the rats to previous activity levels. The reason for this curvilinear effect of androgens is not understood.

Injections of testosterone into castrate human males increased the ability to perceive flicker (Simonson, Kearns, & Enzer, 1941), an ability which is augmented by sympathetic stimulants such as amphetamine and impaired by sympathetic depressants such as chlorpromazine (Lehmann & Csank, 1957).

Recently, an "Automatization Cognitive Style," defined as

greater ability to perform simple perceptual-motor tasks, such as object naming, color naming, etc., than ability to perform inhibitory, perceptual-restructuring tasks, such as the Gottschaldt Figures, has been examined in relationship to physical development in adolescent and young adult males (Broverman, Broverman, Vogel, Palmer, & Klaiber, 1964). Ss with relatively superior abilities on simple perceptual-motor tasks ("Strong Automatizers") may be considered to be activation dominant, while Ss with relatively superior abilities on inhibitory perceptual-restructuring tasks ("Weak Automatizers") may be considered to be inhibition dominant. The Strong Automatizers appeared to have more androgenized physiques than the Weak Automatizers. In a follow-up study, Strong Automatizers were found to have larger biceps and chests, and to have better pubic hair development than Ss with "weak Automatization" cognitive styles (Klaiber, Broverman, & Kobayashi, 1967). These physical attributes are interpretable as the effects of androgens on physical development (Dorfman & Shipley, 1956; Joss, Zuppinger, & Sobel, 1963; Tanner, 1962). Twenty-four hour urinary excretions of 17-ketosteroids, an often-used clinical measure of androgen levels (Dorfman & Shipley, 1956), have also been found positively correlated ($r = .421$; $p < .01$) to the Automatization Cognitive Style in 38 adult males selected to represent extremes of androgenicity (Klaiber et al., 1967), and again in 42 randomly selected soldiers ($r = .356$; $p < .05$), that is, Strong Automatizers tended to have greater 24-hour urinary 17-ketosteroid excretions than Weak Automatizers. Hence, the evidence suggests that androgen levels in males are positively related to a behavioral expression of the activation-inhibition balance. Moreover, individual differences in simple perceptual-motor versus inhibitory perceptual-restructuring tasks within each sex may be due to individual differences in gonadal "sex" hormone levels.

ESTROGENS VERSUS ANDROGENS AS ACTIVATING AGENTS

The available evidence persistently suggests that estrogens are more potent activating agents than are androgens. Thus, females, both human and animal, appear to be more behaviorally activated, or less able to inhibit, than males. Ovarian transplants raised the activity level of castrated male rats to that of intact females (Wang, Richter, & Guttmacher, 1925), while ovariectomies reduced female rat activity into or below male rat activity ranges (Richter, 1927; Wang, 1923). The cognitive activation-inhibition differences between sexes in both animals and humans, therefore, may be primarily due to sex differences in estrogens.

Mechanisms by which steroid "sex" hormones may affect the sympathetic and parasympathetic nervous systems are discussed below.

STEROID "SEX" HORMONES AND THE SYMPATHETIC NERVOUS SYSTEM

The various monoamines, for example, norepinephrine, which facilitate neural transmission in the adrenergic sympathetic nervous system are inactivated, primarily, by the enzyme monoamine oxidase (MAO). The levels of neural stores of the monoamines are controlled, in part, by neural MAO activity. Generally, it is assumed that high levels of MAO activity are associated with low levels of cellular norepinephrine and reduced behavioral activity, while low levels of MAO are associated with high levels of norepinephrine and heightened behavioral activity (Kopin, 1964). Behavioral activity, then, is normally considered to be positively related to norepinephrine, and negatively related to MAO activity.[1]

ESTROGENS AND MONOAMINE OXIDASE (MAO)

Estrogen appears to affect MAO activity, as indicated by the following studies.

Ovariectomy of female rats produced a rise in hypothalamic MAO activity (Kobayashi, Kobayashi, Kato, & Minaguchi, 1964b). Estrogens administered to ovariectomized rats yielded hypothalamic MAO activity levels which were significantly lower than ovariectomized rats not receiving estrogen treatment (Kobayashi, Kobayashi, Kato, & Minaguchi, 1966).

Kobayashi et al. (1964b) have also reported that MAO activity varies in the hypothalamus of the female rat as a function of the estrous cycle. MAO activity was found to be lower at the day of

---

1. Kopin (1966) has pointed out that *chronically* low MAO activity results in decreased adrenergic functioning due to the accumulation of "false" neurotransmitters that are normally metabolized by MAO. The "false" neurotransmitters, which are relatively ineffective as neuro-activators, displace norepinephine from cellular binding sites where they proceed to act as inefficient neurotransmitters.

estrus than on the proestrus (previous) day. In contrast, Zolovick, Pearse, Boehlke, and Elefthiou (1966) have recently reported MAO activity in the rat hypothalamus tends to be highest at time of estrus.

More recently, measuring MAO activity in female rat hypothalami, Kamberi and Kobayashi[2] have reported rapid changes in hypothalamic MAO on the proestrus day with a peak at 10 AM and a low at 6 PM. These points represent the extremes of hypothalamic MAO activity throughout the estrous cycle. The estrus day was characterized by moderate levels of MAO activity. Thus, the contradictory results of Kobayashi et al. (1964b) versus Zolovick et al. (1966) may be due to slight but significant differences in the times at which hypothalamic MAO was measured.

Plasma MAO activity in regularly ovulating women also varies significantly with the menstrual cycle, and the plasma MAO activity of amenorheic women, which was significantly greater than that of normal women, returned to a normal range after estrogen therapy (Klaiber, Kobayashi, & Broverman, 1967).

Thus, estrogens appear to influence MAO activity in both animals and humans.

ANDROGENS AND MONOAMINE OXIDASE (MAO)

Androgens also appear to influence MAO activity, as indicated below.

Zeller[3] has reported that castration of male rats raised the level of brain MAO activity, while injections of androgens in castrated male rats yielded brain MAO activity levels comparable to intact rats. In vitro experiments in our laboratories indicate that testosterone (the most potent androgen) depresses MAO activity in rat hypothalamic tissue.

Significant negative correlations in normal males were reported between plasma MAO activity and 24-hour urinary 17-ketosteroid excretions, an indirect clinical index of androgen levels which contain both adrenal and testicular androgen metabolites (Klaiber et al., 1967). We have again observed significant negative correlations between urinary 17-ketosteroid excretions and plasma MAO activity in a more recent study involving 42 soldiers. Hence, it appears that androgens also tend to lower MAO activity in humans

2. I. Kamberi and Y. Kobayashi, personal communication, April, 1967.

3. E. A. Zeller, personal communication, May, 1965.

and, presumably, thereby increase amine levels in the activating sympathetic nervous system.

Both androgens and estrogens, then, appear to influence MAO in animals and humans. The ability of the "sex" hormones to influence MAO, in turn, provides a rational mechanism for explaining the apparent activation effects of these hormones.

STEROID "SEX" HORMONES AND THE PARASYMPATHETIC NERVOUS SYSTEM

Perhaps the best evidence in support of a central nervous system "sex" steroid-cholinergic relationship derives from reports that castrations in both male (Kobayashi, Kobayashi, Kato, & Minaguchi, 1963) and female (Kobayashi, Kobayashi, Kato, & Minaguchi, 1964a) rats are followed by rises in hypothalamic choline acetylase, the enzyme primarily responsible for the synthesis of acetylcholine (Hebb, 1957). It is possible that the decreased behavioral activity following castration may be, in part, a function of increased inhibition stemming from heightened production of acetylcholine in the hypothalamus following castration. Estrogens administered to ovariectomized female rats produce returns to normal levels of both behavioral activity (Young & Fish, 1945), and hypothalamic choline acetylase (Kobayashi et al., 1964a). On the other hand, testosterone administered to ovariectomized female rats caused, not a drop, but a further rise in choline acetylase (Kobayashi et al., 1964a). Parallel testosterone-choline acetylase studies with male rats have not been reported.

Both androgen and estrogen deficiencies induced by castration, then, appear to induce rises in acetylcholine synthesis. Estrogen administration, at least, reverses this effect. Thus, while the precise relationships of the steroid "sex" hormones to the acetylcholine cycle need further clarification, there can be no doubt that such relationships do exist.

ESTROGENS VERSUS ANDROGENS AS NEURAL ACTIVATORS

Estrogens and androgens appear to differ in their effects on the sympathetic and parasympathetic nervous system in two ways, both of which could result in females being more activated than males.

337

First, as noted above, estrogens inhibited the activity of choline acetylase, the enzyme which synthesizes acetylcholine, in the rat hypothalamus, but testosterone did not (Kobayashi et al., 1964a). This difference should tend to produce less trophotropic behavior, and less cognitive inhibition, in females than males.

Second, estrogens appear to be more potent MAO inhibitors than androgens. Thus, Wurtman and Axelrod (1963) report that the livers of female rats have significantly lower levels of MAO activity than livers of male rats. Injections of estrogens lowered the liver MAO activity levels of the male rats to the levels of female rats. Injections of androgens into intact female rats, however, resulted in an elevation of the low female liver MAO activity levels up into the male range. The elevation of MAO activity by androgens in this case, however, may have been due to the disruptive effect of androgens on ovarian secretions of estrogens. Wurtman and Axelrod (1963) reported that the testosterone-injected female rats had small uteri and an absence of vaginal estrus. Thus, the tendency of MAO to rise due to an absence of estrogen may have exceeded the MAO inhibition induced by the injected androgens.

The apparent greater ability of estrogens, compared to androgens, to inhibit MAO activity, then, may also contribute to the greater activation of females compared to males.

In any event, it is obvious that both androgens and estrogens exert influences on components of both the adrenergic and cholinergic neural cycles. While more work is needed to further clarify the precise physiological effects of the two hormones on the neural cycles, it is clear that rational physiological explanations of cognitive sex differences are not only possible, but probable.

STEROID HORMONES AND THE "BLOOD-BRAIN BARRIER"

The arguments of this paper require that the gonadal steroid "sex" hormones affect central nervous processes. On the other hand, it is generally thought that steroid molecules do not cross the "blood-brain barrier." The "blood-brain barrier" with respect to steroids, however, does not include many of the visceral portions of the subcortical old brain. For instance, radioactivity from tagged estrogens is readily taken up by the hypothalamic, preoptic, and other portions of the sub-cortex (Gorski & Whalen, 1966); while concentrations of cortisol, another steroid hormone, have been found to be 10 times greater in hypothalamic tissues than in plasma (Henkin & Bartter, 1966). Hence, the "blood-brain barrier" does not seem to be an obstacle to the arguments presented in this paper.

DISCUSSION

The psychopharmacological studies provide strong evidence of an inverse relationship between the physiological processes underlying simple perceptual-motor abilities and those physiological processes contributing to performances of inhibitory restructuring tasks. Each pharmacological manipulation, that is, adrenergic stimulation, adrenergic depression, cholinergic stimulation, and cholinergic depression, produced opposite effects on the two abilities. These findings support the hypothesis that variations in performances of simple perceptual-motor and inhibitory restructuring tasks are behavioral representations of the balance between adrenergic and cholinergic neural processes.

The behavioral studies involving the steroid "sex" hormones, androgens and estrogens, support the notion that these "sex" hormones influence activation and inhibition processes, both in animals and humans.

Finally, the steroid-enzyme studies provide rational mechanisms by which steroids may influence neural activation and inhibition processes which, in turn, affect behavior.

There seems ample reason, then, to conclude that the sex differences in performances of simple perceptual-motor and inhibitory restructuring tasks are related, in part at least, to the differential effects of the "sex" steroid hormones on activation and inhibition neural processes.

Implications of Physiological Hypothesis of Sex Differences for the Assessment of Cognitive Organization

If the proposition that performances of simple perceptual-motor and inhibitory restructuring tasks are reflections of the balance between adrenergic activating and cholinergic inhibitory neural processes is accepted, then it is pertinent to ask why negative correlations between these abilities are not observed, since a given adrenergic versus cholinergic balance apparently exerts opposite effects on the two sets of behaviors. As Thurstone (1935) pointed out, abilities exist, in nature, in a "positive manifold," that is, all abilities tend to be positively interrelated. Positive correlations have also been reported between simple perceptual-motor and inhibitory restructuring tasks (Podell & Phillips, 1959).

339

The resolution of this difficulty may involve individual differences in general level of ability, "g," which apply equally to performances of simple perceptual-motor and inhibitory restructuring tasks. Adding or subtracting the same "g" component to the performance of simple perceptual-motor and inhibitory restructuring tasks of each individual could easily induce a greater amount of positive covariance between the two tasks than the activation versus inhibition induced negative covariance. Elimination of the "g" factor through "ipsatization" of scores, that is, expressing individual scores as deviations from the individual's general level of performance, has consistently produced bipolar factors in which simple perceptual-motor and inhibitory restructuring tasks are contrasted (Broverman, 1964), and which are related in the expected directions to physical indices of androgen stimulation (Broverman et al., 1964). However, since the removal of "g" variance, either by ipsatization or by standard factor extraction procedures, tends to artifactually induce negative relationships in the residual variance (MacAndrew & Forgy, 1963; Ross, 1963), such oppositions between abilities have been necessarily interpreted cautiously as statistical rather than functional expressions of relationships between abilities. Unfortunately, no unambiguous statistical method of demonstrating inverse relationships between abilities in the presence of an overriding "g" factor exists. On the other hand, the evidence in the present paper suggests that the positive relationships typically observed between abilities (Thurstone, 1935) should also be interpreted cautiously since they may reflect the dominant influence of a large "g" component which, in effect, is acting as a suppressor variable on other lesser, but physiologically interpretable and important, negative relationships.

The resolution of this methodological impasse seems to require either experimental manipulations of factors which differentially affect abilities, as exemplified by the various drug studies cited in this paper; or else an examination of changes in relationships between abilities that vary as a function of known physiological differences, such as physiological sex differences. Numerous other variations in physiological states invite such examinations. For instance, epinephrine inducing psychological stress situations ought to differentially affect simple perceptual-motor versus inhibitory restructuring tasks, that is, the activating effect of epinephrine ought to facilitate performances of simple perceptual-motor tasks and impair performances of inhibitory restructuring tasks. Many studies exist in support of this expectation, that is, facilitation by stress of simple perceptual-motor tasks has been reported by Gates and Rissland (1923); Lazarus and Eriksen (1952);

Steisel and Cohen (1951); Vogel, Baker, and Lazarus (1958); Vogel, Raymond, and Lazarus (1959); while stress impairments of performances of tasks requiring a reorganization or restructuring of stimuli have been reported by Hamilton (1916); Maier, Glaser, and Klee (1940); Cowen (1952a, 1952b); Ross, Rupel, and Grant (1952); Vogel, et al., (1959); Castaneda (1956); Castaneda and Palermo (1955); Palermo (1957).

Another situation involving well-known physiological and performance changes is the effect of aging, with its fall-off in gonadal steroid production and decrements in simple perceptual-motor tasks, but maintenance of complex verbal abilities (Welford, 1958). Similarly, the onset of adolescence with its concommitant increase in gonadal "sex" steroid production; the menopause with its abrupt cessation of gonadal steroid production; the menstrual cycle with its rhythmic variation in steroid production; and the seasonal changes in temperature with their concommitant changes in the production of hormones required to maintain thermal equilibrium, each affords opportunities for investigations of changing relationships between abilities within individuals. Closer attention to differential changes across abilities in each of the above instances may yield increased understanding of the relationships between mental processes.

Finally, simple perceptual-motor versus inhibitory restructuring abilities need not be the only intrapsychic cognitive antagonism. In principle, numerous intrapsychic antagonisms may exist. The developmental psychologists (Piaget, 1950; Werner, 1957) have suggested that mental development consists of the subordination and integration of ontogenetically early, phylogenetically primitive processes to developmentally later more complex processes. In this case, the argument of the present paper concerning the relationship of simple perceptual-motor and inhibitory restructuring processes could be applied to all stages of development, that is, the more vigorous a given lower-level function, the more difficult is it to inhibit and subordinate the lower function to a specific higher-level function whose emergence requires the subordination of the lower-level process. For instance, the stronger the perceptual responses (either perceptual-motor, or perceptual-restructuring) to a stimulus, the more difficult it may be to drop these relatively concrete modes of response in favor of more abstract, conceptual, or symbolic responses. At each stage of development a dynamic opposition between achieved abilities and emerging superordinate abilities may take place. The varying outcomes of these contests in different individuals may underlie the consistent bipolar factors of abilities found in the within-individual variance of abilities (Broverman, 1964; Burt, 1940; Moursy, 1952).

WOMAN: DEPENDENT OR INDEPENDENT VARIABLE?

It is the contention of this paper, then, that progress in the understanding of cognitive processes may be facilitated by paying greater attention to differences in relationships between abilities that vary as a function of differences in internal organismic states.

REFERENCES

Adler, H. F., Burkhardt, W. L., Ivy, A. C., & Atkinson, A. J. Effect of various drugs on psychomotor performance at ground level and at simulated altitudes of 18,000 feet in a low pressure chamber. *Journal of Aviation Medicine,* 1950, *21*, 221-236.

Altmann, M. Interrelations of the sex cycle and behavior of the sow. *Journal of Comparative Psychology,* 1941, *31*, 481.

Anastasi, A., & Foley, J. P. *Differential psychology.* New York: Macmillan, 1949.

Andrieux, C. Contribution a l'etude des differences entre hommes at femmes dans la perception spatiale. *L'Annee Psychologique,* 1955, *55*, 41-60.

Basowitz, H., Korchin, S. J., Oken, D., Goldstein, M. S., & Gussack, H. Anxiety and performance changes with a minimal dose of epinephrine. *Archives of Neurology and Psychiatry,* 1956, *76*, 98-105.

Bennett, C. C. An inquiry into the genesis of poor reading. *Teachers College, Columbia University, Contribution to Education,* 1938, *755*, 139.

Bennett, D. H. Perception of the upright in relation to body image. *Journal of Mental Science,* 1956, *102*, 487-506.

Bieri, J., Bradburn, W. M., & Galinsky, M. D. Sex differences in perceptual behavior. *Journal of Personality,* 1958, *26*, 1-12.

Billings, E. G. The occurrence of cyclic variations in motor activity in relation to the menstrual cycle in the human female, *Johns Hopkins Hospital Bulletin,* 1939, *54*, 440-454.

Brant, D. H., & Kavanau, J. L. 'Unrewarded' exploration and learning of complex mazes by wild and domestic mice. *Nature,* 1964, *204*, 267-268.

Broverman, D. M. Generality and behavioral correlates of cognitive styles. *Journal of Consulting Psychology,* 1964, *28*, 487-500.

Broverman, D. M., Broverman, I. K., Vogel, W., Palmer, R. D., & Klaiber, E. L. The automatization cognitive style and physical development. *Child Development,* 1964, *35*, 1343-1359.

Burt, C. *The factors of the mind.* London: University of London Press, 1940.

Callaway, E., III, & Stone, G. Re-evaluating focus of attention. In L. Uhr & J. D. Miller (Eds.), *Drugs and behavior.* New York: Wiley, 1960, Pp. 393-398.

Carden, J. A. Field dependence, anxiety, and sociometric status in children. Unpublished master's thesis, University of Texas, 1958.

Carlton, P. L. Some effects of scopolamine, atropine, and amphetamine in three behavioral situations. *Pharmacologist,* 1961, *3*, 60.

Carlton, P. L. Cholinergic mechanisms in the control of behavior by the brain. *Psychological Review,* 1963, *70*, 19-39.

Castaneda, A. Effects of stress on complex learning and performance. *Journal of Experimental Psychology,* 1956, *52*, 9-12.

— — —, A., & Palermo, D. S. Psychomotor performance as a function of amount of training and stress. *Journal of Experimental Psychology,* 1955, *50*, 175-179.

Chambers, G. S., & Zabarenko, R. N. Effects of glutamic acid and social stimulation in mental deficiency. *Journal of Abnormal and Social Psychology,* 1956, *53*, 315-320.

Chateau, J. Le test de structuration spatiale. *Le Travail Humain,* 1959, *22*, 281-297.

Cheney, R. H. Comparative effect of caffeine per se and a caffeine beverage (coffee) upon the reaction time in normal young adults. *Journal of Pharmacology,* 1935, *53*, 304-313.

Cheney, R. H. Reaction time behavior after caffeine and coffee consumption. *Journal of Experimental Psychology,* 1936, *19*, 357-369.

Corey, S. M. Sex differences in maze learning by white rats. *Journal of Comparative Psychology,* 1930, *10*, 333-338.

Corso, J. F. Age and sex differences in pure-tone thresholds. *Journal of the Acoustical Society of America,* 1959, *31*, 498-

Cowen, E. L. The influence of varying degrees of psychological stress on problem-solving rigidity. *Journal of Abnormal and Social Psychology,* 1952, *47*, 512-519. (a)

— — —. Stress reduction and problem-solving rigidity. *Journal of Consulting Psychology,* 1952, *16*, 425-428. (b)

Davis, D. R. Psychomotor effects of analeptics and their relation to fatigue phenomena in air crew. *British Medical* 1947, *5*, 43-45.

Dews, P. B., & Morse, W. H. Some observations on an operant in human subject and its modification by dextro amphetamine. *Journal of the Experimental Analysis of Behavior,* 1958, *1*, 359-364.

Dispensa, J., & Barrett, M. E. The effect of amphetamine (benzedrine) sulfate on maze performance of the albino rat. *Journal of Psychology,* 1941, *11*, 397-410.

Dorfman, R. L., & Shipley, R. A. *Androgens.* New York: Wiley, 1956.

Ellson, D. G., Fuller, P. R., & Urmston, R. G. The influence of glutamic acid on test behavior. *Science,* 1950, *112*, 248-250.

Feldberg, W., & Sherwood, S. L. Behavior of cats after intraventricular injections of eserine and DFP. *Journal of Physiology,* 1954, *125*, 488-500. (a)

— — —, & — — —. Injections of drugs into the lateral ventricle of the cat. *Journal of physiology,* 1954, *123*, 148-167. (b)

Fink, D. M. Sex differences in perceptual tasks in relation to selected personality variables. Unpublished doctoral dissertation, Rutgers University, 1959.

Florey, C. D., & Gilbert , J. The effects of benzedrine sulfate and caffeine citrate on the efficiency of college students. *Journal of Applied Psychology,* 1943, *27*, 121-134.

Franks, C. M. Differences determinees par le personalite dans la perception visuelle de la verticalite. *Revue de Psychologie Appliquee,* 1956, *6*, 235-246.

— — —, & Trouton, D. Effects of amobarbital sodium and dexamphetamine sulfate on the conditioning of the eyeblink response. *Journal of Comparative and Physiological Psychology,* 1958, *51*, 220-222.

Frommel, E., & Fleury, C. Du paradoxe du mecanisme de la potentialisation de l'effet dormitif des barbituriques par la belladone. *Medicina Experimentalis* (Basel), 1960, *3*, 257-263.

Fulton, J. F. *Physiology of the nervous system.* (3rd ed.) New York: Oxford University Press, 1949.

Gainer, W.L. The ability of the WISC subtests to discriminate between boys and girls of average intelligence. *California Journal of Educational Research,* 1962, *13*, 9-16.

Gans, H.M. Studies on vigor. XIV. Effect of fractional castration on voluntary activity of male albino rats. *Endocrinology,* 1927, *11*, 145-148.

Gardner, R.W., Jackson, D.N., & Messick, S.J. Personality organization in cognitive controls and intellectual abilities. *Psychological Issues,* 1960, *2* (Whole No. 8).

Gates, G.S., & Rissland, L.Q. The effect of encouragement and discouragement upon performance. *Journal of Educational Psychology,* 1923, *14*, 21-26.

Gesell, A., Halverson, H.M., Thompson, H., Ilg, F.L., Castner, B.M., Ames, L.B., & Amatruda, C.S. *The first five years of life: A guide to the study of the preschool child.* New York: Harper, 1940.

Golla, F.L., Blackburn, J.M., & Graham, S. A comparison between some of the effects of isomyn (benzedrine) and of methylisomyn. *Journal of Mental Science,* 1940, *86*, 48-59.

Gonzalez, R.C., & Ross, S. The effects of chlorpromazine on the course of discrimination-reversal learning in the rat. *Journal of Comparative and Physiological Psychology,* 1961, *54*, 645-648.

Goodman, L. S., & Gilman, A. (Eds.) *The pharmacological basis of therapeutics.* New York: Macmillan, 1965.

Gorski, R.A., & Whalen, R.E. (Eds.) *Brain and behavior, Vol. III: The brain and gonadal function.* UCLA Forum in Medical Sciences, No. 3. Los Angeles: University of California Press, 1966.

Hamilton, G.V. A study of perseverance reactions in primates and rodents. *Behavior Monograph,* 1916, *3*, No. 13.

Hebb, C.O. Biochemical evidence for neural function of acetylcholine. *Physiological Reviews,* 1957, *37*, 196-220.

Heller, R.E. Spontaneous activity in male rats in relation to testis hormone. *Endocrinology,* 1932, *16*, 626-632.

Helper, M.M., Wilcott, R.C., & Garfield, S.L. Effects of chlorpromazine on learning and related processes in emotionally disturbed children. *Journal of Consulting Psychology,* 1963, *27*, 1-9.

Henkin, R.I., & Bartter, F.C. The presence of corticosterone and cortisol in the central and peripheral nervous system of the cat. Paper presented at the 48th meeting of the Endocrine Society, Chicago, June 20, 1966.

Hernandez-Peon, R., & Chavez-Ibarra, G. Sleep induced by electrical or chemical stimulation of the forebrain. In R. Hernandez-Peon (Ed.), *The physiological basis of mental activity.* New York: Elsevier, 1963. Pp. 188-198.

Hess, W.R. *Diencephalon, autonomic and extrapyramidal functions.* New York: Grune & Stratton, 1954.

Hitchcock, F.A. Studies in vigor. V. The comparative activity of male and female albino rats. *American Journal of Physiology,* 1925, *75*, 205-210.

Hollingworth, H.L. The influence of caffeine on mental and motor efficiency. *Archives of Psychology, New York,* 1912, *3* (Whole No. 22), 1-166.

Hoskins, R.G. Studies on vigor. II. The effect of castration on voluntary activity. *American Journal of Physiology,* 1925, *72*, 324-330.

– – – & Bevin, S. The effect of fractionated chorionic gonadotropic extract on spontaneous activity and weight of elderly male rats. *Endocrinology,* 1941, *27*, 929-931.

Hubbert, H.B. The effect of age on habit formation in the albino rat. *Behavior Monograph,* 1915, *2*, 1-55.

Irwin, S. Extrapolation from animals to men: Strain and sex differences. In H. Steinberg, A.V.S. de Reuck, & J. Knight (Eds.), *Ciba symposium on animal behaviour and drug action.* London: Churchhill. P. 426.

Joss, E.E., Zuppinger, K.A., & Sobel, E.H. Effect of testosterone propionate and methyl testosterone on growth and skeletal maturation in rats. *Endocrinology,* 1963, *72,* 123-130.

Kavanau, J.L., & Brant, D.H. Wheel running preferences of peromyscus. *Nature,* 1965, *208* (5010), 597-598.

Klaiber, E.L., Broverman, D.M., & Kobayashi, Y. The automatization cognitive style, androgens, and monoamine oxidase. *Psychopharmacologia,* 1967, in press.

— — —, Kobayashi, Y., & Broverman, D. M. Plasma monoamine oxidase (MAO) activity in ovulating and amenorheic women. Paper presented at the 49th meeting of the Endocrine Society, Miami, June, 1967.

Kobayashi, T., Kobayashi, T., Kato, J., & Minaguchi, H. Fluctuations in choline acetylase activity in hypothalamus of rat during estrous cycle and after castration. *Endocrinologia Japonica,* 1963, *10,* 175-182.

— — —, Kobayashi, T., Kato, J., & Minaguchi, H. Effects of sex steroids on the choline acetylase activity in the hypothalamus of female rats. *Endocrinologia Japonica,* 1964, *11,* 9-18 (a).

— — —, — — —, — — —, & — — —. Fluctuations in monoamine oxidase activity in the hypothalamus of rat during the estrous cycle and after castration. *Endocrinologia Japonica,* 1964, *11,* 283-290.

Kobayashi, T., Kobayashi, T., Kato, J., & Minaguchi, H. Cholinergic and adrenergic mechanisms in the female rat hypothalamus with special reference to feedback of ovarian steroid hormones. In G. Pincus, T. Nakao, & J. Tait (Eds.), *Steroid dynamics.* New York & London: Academic Press, 1966. Pp. 305-307.

Kohs, S.C. *Intelligence measurement.* New York: Macmillan, 1923.

Kopin, I.J. Storage and metabolism of catecholamines: The role of monoamine oxidase. *Pharmacological Review,* 1964, *16,* 179-191.

— — —. The role of false transmitters in the action of monoamine oxidase inhibitors. In R.A. Cohen (Chm.), Symposium on false neurochemical transmitters. *Annals of Internal Medecine,* 1966, *65,* 359-360.

Kornetsky, C., Humphries, O., & Evarts, E.V. Comparison of psychological effects of certain centrally acting drugs in man. *A.M.A. Archives of Neurology and Psychiatry,* 1957, *77,* 318-324.

Krechevsky, I. Hereditary nature of "hypotheses." *Journal of Comparative Psychology,* 1933, *16,* 99-116.

Lashley, K.S. The effects of strychnine and caffeine upon the rate of learning. *Psychobiology,* 1917, *1*, 141-169.

Lazarus, R.S., & Eriksen, C.W. Psychological stress and its personality correlates: Part I. The effects of failure stress upon skilled performance. *Journal of Experimental Psychology,* 1952, *43*, 100-105.

Lebensohn, J.E., & Sullivan, R.R. Temporary stimulation of emmetropic visual acuity. *U.S. Naval Medical Bulletin,* 1944, *43*, 90-95.

Lehmann, H.E., & Csank, J. Differential screening of phrenotropic agents in man: Psychophysiologic test data. *Journal of Clinical and Experimental Psychopathology,* 1957, *18*, 222-235.

MacAndrew, C., & Forgy, E. A note on the effects of score transformations in Q and R factor analysis techniques. *Psychological Review,* 1963, *70*, 116-118.

MacMeeken, A.M. *The intelligence of a representative group of Scottish children.* London: University of London Press, 1939.

Maier, N.R., Glaser, N.M., & Klee, J.B. Studies of abnormal behavior in the rat: III. The development of behavior fixations through frustration. *Journal of Experimental Psychology,* 1940, *26*, 521-546.

McCarthy, D. The language development of the preschool child. *University of Minnesota Institute of Child Welfare Monograph,* 1930, *4*, 174.

McNemar, Q. *The revision of the Stanford-Binet scale: An analysis of the standardization data.* Boston: Houghton Mifflin, 1942.

———, & Stone, C. P. The sex difference in rats on three learning tasks. *Journal of Comparative Psychology,* 1932, *14*, 171-180.

Meyers, B., Roberts, K.H., Riciputi, R.H., & Domino, E.F. Some effects of muscarinic cholinergic blocking drugs on behavior and the electrocorticogram. *Psychopharmacologia,* 1964, *5*, 289-300.

Miele, J.A. Sex differences in intelligence: The relationship of sex to intelligence as measured by the Wechsler Adult Intelligence Scale and the Wechsler Intelligence Scale for Children. *Dissertation Abstracts,* 1958, *18*, 2213.

Miller, A.S. An investigation of some hypothetical relationships of rigidity and strength and speed of perceptual closure. Unpublished doctoral dissertation, University of California, 1953.

Minkowsky, W.L. The effect of benzedrine sulphate upon learning. *Journal of Comparative Psychology,* 1939, *28*, 349-360.

Mirsky, J.H., White, H.D., & O'Dell, T.B. Central nervous system depressant effects of some indolylethylpyridines. *Journal of Pharmacology and Experimental Therapy,* 1959, *125*, 122-127.

Moursy, E.M. The hierarchical organization of cognitive levels. *British Journal of Psychology,* 1952, *5*, 151-180.

Muller, R. Psychologische Wirkwerte der kristallinen L (+) Glutaminsaure, der Gamma-Aminobuttersaure und komplexer Erweisze. *Arzneimittel Forschung,* 1955, *5*, 1-12.

Nash, H. Psychologic effects of amphetamines and barbiturates. *Journal of Nervous and Mental Disease,* 1962, *134*, 203-217.

Newbigging, P.L. Individual differences in the effects of subjective and objective organising factors on perception. Unpublished doctoral dissertation, University College, University of London, 1952.

— — —. The relationship between reversible perspective and embedded figures. *Canadian Journal of Psychology,* 1954, *8,* 204-208.

Norman, R.D. Sex differences and other aspects of young superior adult performance on the Wechsler Bellevue. *Journal of Consulting Psychology,* 1953, *17*, 411-418.

Palermo, D.S. Proactive interference and facilitation as a function of amount of training and stress. *Journal of Experimental Psychology,* 1957, *53*, 293-296.

Paterson, D.G., & Andrew, D.M. *Manual for the Minnesota Vocational Test for Clerical Workers.* New York: Psychological Corporation, 1946.

Pavlov, I.P. *Conditioned reflexes.* Oxford: Clarendon Press, 1927.

Piaget, J. *The psychology of intelligence.* New York: Harcourt, Brace, 1950.

Podell, J.E., & Phillips, L. A developmental analysis of cognition as observed in dimensions of Rorschach and objective test performance. *Journal of Personality,* 1959, *27*, 439-463.

Porteus, S.D. The measurement of intelligence: 643 children examined by the Binet and Porteus tests. *Journal of Educational Psychology,* 1918, *9*, 13-31.

— — —. *The Porteus maze test and intelligence.* Palo Alto, Calif.: Pacific Books, 1950.

Primac, D.W., Mirsky, A.F., & Rosvold, H.E. Effects of centrally acting drugs on two tests of brain damage. *Archives of Neurology and Psychiatry,* 1957, *77*, 328-332.

Pryor, G.T. Brain serotonin and behavior in selected strains of rats. Unpublished doctoral dissertation, University of California, 1964.

Richter, C.P. Animal behavior and internal drives. *Quarterly Review of Biology,* 1927, *2*, 307-343.

―――. The effect of early gonadectomy on the gross bodily activity of rats. *Endocrinology,* 1933, *17*, 445-450.

―――, & Wislocki, G.B. Activity studies on castrated male and female rats with testicular grafts, in correlation with histological studies of the grafts. *American Journal of Physiology,* 1928, *86*, 651-660.

Riss, W., Burstein, S.D., Johnson, R.W., & Lutz, A. Morphologic correlates of endocrine and running acitivity. *Journal of Comparative and Physiological Psychology,* 1959, *52*, 618-620.

Ritchie, J.M. Central nervous system stimulants. II. The xanthines. In L.S. Goodman & A. Gilman (Eds.), *The pharmacological basis of therapeutics.* New York: Macmillan, 1965. Pp. 354-366.

Roberts, E., Wein, J., & Simonsen, D.G. Gamma-aminobutyric acid, vitamin B6, and neuronal function―A speculative hypothesis. In R.S. Harris, I.G. Wool, & J.A. Loraine (Eds.), *Vitamins and hormones.* New York: Academic Press, 1964. Pp. 264-274.

Rosenzweig, M.R., Krech, D., & Bennett, E.L. A search for relations between brain chemistry and behavior. *Psychological Bulletin,* 1960, *57*, 476-492.

Ross, B.M., Rupel, J.W., & Grant, D.A. Effects of personal, impersonal, and physical stress upon cognitive behavior in a card sorting problem. *Journal of Abnormal and Social Psychology,* 1952, *47*, 546-551.

Ross, J. The relation between test and person factors. *Psychological Review,* 1963, *70*, 432-443.

Rothballer, A.B. The effects of catecholamines on the central nervous system. *Pharmacological Review,* 1959, *11*, 494.

Sadovnikova-Koltzova, M.P. Genetische analyse des temperamentes der ratten. *Zeitschrift fur Induktive Abstammungsund Verebungslehre,* 1929, *49*, 131-145.

Samuels, F. Sex differences in reading achievement. *Journal of Educational Research,* 1943, *36*, 594-603.

Scheckel, C.L. Effects of chlorpromazine and chlordiazepoxide on delayed matching in the monkey measured by a self-adjusting procedure. *American Psychologist,* 1962, *17*, 398.

Schneidler, G.R., & Paterson, D.G. Sex differences in clerical aptitude. *Journal of Educational Psychology,* 1942, *33*, 303-309.

Schnell, H. Sex differences in relation to stuttering: Part I. *Journal of Speech Disorders,* 1946, *11*, 277-298.

―――. Sex differences in relation to stuttering: Part II. *Journal of Speech Disorders,* 1947, *12*, 23-38.

Schwobel, G., & Tamm, J. Reaktionszeitmessunger bei Glutaminsaurezufuhr. *Klinische Wochenschrift,* 1952, *30,* 750-755.

Seder, J.A. The origin of differences in extent of independence in children: Developmental factors in perceptual field dependence. Unpublished bachelor's thesis, Radcliffe College, 1957.

Shatin, L., Rockmore, L., & Funk, I.C. Response of psychiatric patients to massive doses of thorazine. II. Psychological test performance and comparative drug evaluation. *Psychiatric Quarterly,* 1956, *30,* 402-416.

Sherwood, S.L. Intraventricular medication in catatonic stupor. *Brain,* 1952, *75,* 68-75.

Sidman, M. Drug-behavior interaction. *Annals of the New York Academy of Sciences,* 1956, *65,* 282-302.

Simmel, E.C., Cheney, J.H., & Landy, E. Visual vs. locomotor response effects on satiation to novel stimuli: A sex difference in rats. *Psychological Reports,* 1965, *16,* 893-896.

Simonson, E., & Enzer, N. The effect of amphetamine (benzedrine) sulfate on the state of motor centers. *Journal of Experimental Psychology,* 1941, *29,* 517-523.

———, Kearns, W. M., & Enzer, N. Effect of oral administration of methyltestosterone on fatigue in eunuchoids and castrates. *Endocrinology,* 1941, *28,* 506-512.

Skinner, B.F., & Heron, W.T. Effects of caffeine and benzedrine upon conditioning and extinction. *Psychological Record,* 1937, *1,* 340-346.

Slonaker, J.R. The effects of pubescence, oestration, and menopause on the voluntary activity of the albino rat. *American Journal of Physiology,* 1924, *68,* 294-315.

Soltan, H.C., & Bracken, S.E. The relation of sex to taste reactions for P.T.C., sodium benzoate and four "standards." *Journal of Heredity,* 1958, *49,* 280-284.

Spector, S. Monoamine oxidase in control of brain serotonin and norepinephrine content. *Annals of the New York Academy of Sciences,* 1963, *107,* 856-864.

Spence, K.W., & Spence, J.T. Sex and anxiety differences in eyelid conditioning. *Psychological Bulletin,* 1966, *65,* 137-142.

Stanley, L.L., & Teacher, G.L. Activity of goldfish on testicular substance diet. *Endocrinology,* 1931, *15,* 55-56.

Staples, R. The responses of infants to color. *Journal of Experimental Psychology,* 1932, *15,* 119-141.

Stein, L. Self-stimulation of the brain and the central stimulant action of amphetamine. *Federation Proceedings,* 1964, *23,* 836-850.

Steisel, I.M., & Cohen, B.D. The effects of two degrees of failure on level of aspiration and performance. *Journal of Abnormal and Social Psychology,* 1951, *46,* 79-82.

Stroop, J.R. Studies of interference in serial verbal reactions. *Journal of Experimental Psychology,* 1935, *18,* 643-672.

Tanner, J.M. *Growth at adolescence* (2nd ed.) Oxford: Blackwell, 1962.

Tapp, J.L. Cholinergic mechanisms in operant responding. *Journal of Comparative and Physiological Psychology,* 1965, *59,* 469-472.

Terman, L.M. Psychological sex differences. In L. Carmichael (Ed.), *Manual of child psychology.* New York: Wiley, 1946. Pp. 954-1000.

Thurlow, W.R. The perception of pitch of high frequencies. *American Psychologist,* 1946, *1,* 255.

Thurstone, L. L. *The vectors of mind.* Chicago: University of Chicago Press, 1935.

– – –. *A factorial study of perception.* Chicago: University of Chicago Press, 1944.

Tiffin, J., & Asher, E.J. The Purdue pegboard: Norms and studies of reliability and validity. *Journal of Applied Psychology,* 1948, *32,* 234-247.

Tomilin, M.I., & Stone, C.P. Sex differences in learning abilities of albino rats. *Journal of Comparative Psychology,* 1933, *16,* 207-229.

Tripod, J. Caracterisation generale des effets pharmacodynamiques de substances psychotropiques. In S. Garattini & V. Ghetti (Eds.), *Psychotropic drugs.* Amsterdam: Elsevier, 1957. Pp. 437-447.

Tryon, R.C. Studies in individual differences in maze ability. II. The determination of individual differences by age, weight, sex, and pigmentation. *Journal of Comparative Psychology,* 1931, *12,* 1-22.

Tyler, D.B. The effect of amphetamine sulfate and some barbiturates on the fatigue produced by prolonged wakefulness. *American Journal of Physiology,* 1947, *150,* 253-262.

Uhr, L. Objectively measured behavioral effects of psychoactive drugs. In L. Uhr & J.G. Miller (Eds.), *Drugs and behavior.* New York: Wiley, 1960. Pp. 610-633.

Vogel, W., Baker, R.W., & Lazarus, R.S. The role of motivation in psychological stress. *Journal of Abnormal and Social Psychology,* 1958, *56,* 105-112.

– – –, Raymond, S., & Lazarus, R. S. Intrinsic motivation and psychological stress. *Journal of Abnormal and Social Psychology,* 1959, *58,* 225-233.

Wada, J.A., Wrinch, J., Hill, D., McGeer, P.L., & McGeer, E.G. Central aromatic amine levels and behavior. *Archives of Neurology,* 1963, *9,* 81-89.

Wang, G.H. Relation between "spontaneous" activity and oestrus cycle in the white rat. *Comparative Psychology Monograph,* 1923, *2* (Whole No. 6).

― ― ―. A sexual activity rhythm in the female rat. *American Naturalist,* 1924, *58,* 36-42.

Wang, G.H., Richter, C.P., & Guttmacher, A.F. Activity studies of male castrated rats with ovarian transplants, and correlation of the activity with the histology of the grafts. *American Journal of Physiology,* 1925, *73,* 581-598.

Wechsler, D. *Wechsler adult intelligence scale.* New York: Psychological Corporation, 1955.

Welford, A.T. *Ageing and human skill.* London: Oxford University Press, 1958.

Wentink, E.A. The effects of certain drugs and hormones upon conditioning. *Journal of Experimental Psychology,* 1938, *22,* 150-163.

Werner, H. *Comparative psychology of mental development.* New York: International Universities Press, 1957.

Whitehouse, J.M. The effects of physostigmine and atropine on discrimination learning in the rat. Unpublished doctoral dissertation, University of Colorado, 1959.

Wit, O.C. Sex differences in perception. Unpublished master's thesis, University of Utrecht, 1955.

Witkin, H.A. Individual differences in ease of perception of embedded figures. *Journal of Personality,* 1950, *19,* 1-15.

― ― ―, Dyk, R. B., Faterson, H. F., Goodenough, D. R., & Karp, S. A. *Psychological differentiation.* New York: Wiley, 1962.

― ― ―, Lewis, H.B., Hertzman, M., Machover, K., Meissner, P. B., & Wapner, S. *Personality through perception.* New York: Harper, 1954.

Woolley, D.E., & Timiras, P.S. Estrous and circadian periodicity and electroshock convulsions in rats. *American Journal of Physiology,* 1962, *202,* 379. (a)

― ― ―, & Timiras, P. S. The gonad-brain relationship: Effects of female sex hormones on electroshock convulsions in the rat. 'Endocrinology, 1962, *70,* 196. (b)

― ― ―, ― ― ― & Rosenzweig, M. R., Krech, D., & Bennett, E. L. Sex and strain differences in electroshock convulsions of the rat. *Nature,* 1961, *190,* 515.

― ― ―, & Van der Hoeven, T. Alteration in learning ability caused by changes in cerebral serotonin and cathecholamines *Science,* 1963, *139,* 610-611.

Wurtman, R.J., & Axelrod, J. Sex steroids, cardiac 3h-norepinephrine, and tissue monoamine oxidase levels in the rat. *Biochemical Pharmacoloqv,* 1963. *12.,* 1417-1419.

Young, H.H., Jr. Personality test correlates or orientation to the vertical: A test of Witkin's field-dependency hypothesis. Unpublished doctoral dissertation, University of Texas, 1957.

Young, W.C., & Fish, W.R. The ovarian hormones and spontaneous running activity in the female rat. *Endocrinology*, 1945, *36*, 181-189.

Zielinski, K. Studies on higher nervous activity in chickens: II. The effect of sex on conditioned excitatory and inhibitory alimentary reflexes. *Acta Biologiae Experimentalis,* Warsaw, 1960; *20*, 79-90.

Zieve, L. Effect of benzedrine on activity. *Psychological Record,* 1937, *1*, 393.

Zolovick, A.J., Pearse, R., Boehlke, K.W., & Eleftheriou, B.E. Monoamine oxidase activity in various parts of the rat brain during the estrous cycle. *Science,* 1966, *154*, 649.

Zukmann, L. Hysteric compulsive factors in perceptual organization. Unpublished doctoral dissertation, New School for Social Research, 1957.

21

Parlee has criticized Broverman et al.'s hypothesis that sex differences in cognitive abilities are a reflection of sex-related differences in physiology; e.g., that an excitatory effect upon the autonomic nervous system is produced by estrogen and an inhibitory effect uopn that system is produced by androgen. They theorize that this tipping of the balance of the autonomic nervous system toward excitation in femаies induces their advantage in simple perceptual-motor learning. On the other hand, tipping toward inhibition in males induces advantages in behaviors involving cognitive restructuring; e.g., behavior in which ignoring obvious stimulus attributes is beneficial for learning.

Parlee criticizes this hypothesis on three bases. [1] She suggests that their review and classification of the literature on sex differences in cognitive ability is simplistic and arbitrarily selective. [2] There is no direct evidence on the relationship between neurophysiological function and human cognitive abilities. [3] The authors may have made an error in their proposed mechanism of the way sex differences in cognition might be biochemically mediated. They seem to suggest that acetylcholine is the only neurochemical transmitter present in the parasympathetic nervous system and that noradrenaline is the only transmitter present in the sympathetic nervous system. Her review of their research demonstrates how work that is apparently scientifically accurate may actually reflect prejudices, assumptions, and overgeneralizations typical of the study of cerebral sex differences.

Comments on "Roles of Activation and Inhibition in Sex Differences in Cognitive Abilities*

Mary B. Parlee

The hypothesis of D. M. Broverman, E. L. Klaiber, Y. Kobayshi, and W. Vogel that "known sex differences in cognitive abilities reflect sex-related differences in physiology" is criticized on the grounds that (a) their review and classification of the literature on sex differences in cognitive abilities is inadequate because it is selective, and arbitrarily characterizes those facts which it does include, (b) the pharmacological studies cited in support of their thesis involve behaviors which are at best tangentially related to human cognitive abilities and rely for their relevance on some dubious cross-species analogies, and (c) the authors have made, and defended, a factual error in citing evidence for an important part of their proposed mechanism by which "sex" hormones might affect autonomic activity.

Singer and Montgomery (1969) commented on one aspect of the article by Broverman, Klaiber, Kobayashi, and Vogel (1968) entitled "Roles of activation and inhibition in sex differences in cognitive abilities." In their reply to these remarks, Broverman, Klaiber, Kobayashi, and Vogel (1969) noted that Singer and Montgomery had been concerned with only part of the argument, and that they "have not challenged, or even commented upon, the major bodies of evidence presented in our paper [p. 328]." In view of the importance of and increasing work on the topic of sex differences in cognitive functioning, it seems worthwhile to consider in more detail some of the other difficulties in Broverman et al.'s (1968) paper.

---

* From *Psychological Review*, 1972, 79 (2), 180-84.

Broverman et al. (1968) offer the hypothesis that "known sex differences in cognitive abilities reflect sex-related differences in physiology [p. 23]." This is a strong claim. If true, it would represent a major advance toward the goal of linking psychological functions with their physiological concomitants and would offer a partial explanation of one of the most pervasive phenomena in psychology. What follows is a brief summary of their argument, followed by a more detailed evaluation and analysis of the evidence on which it is based.

Broverman et al. (1968) begin with a review of the psychological literature on sex differences in cognitive ability and categorize the results into those tasks at which men have been found to excel and those at which women excel. They characterize the tasks on which men do better as those "more complex tasks requiring an inhibition of immediate responses to obvious stimulus attributes in favor of responses to less obvious stimulus attributes [p. 23]" and the tasks on which women's performance is better as "simple, overlearned, perceptual-motor tasks [p. 23]." The key concept of inhibition as used above is related to the "inhibitory" function of the parasympathetic division of the autonomic nervous system, and the behavioral consequences of chemically altering the balance between the sympathetic and parasympathetic nervous systems are discussed to show that parasympathetic dominance is associated with the ability to perform the inhibitory, perceptual-restructuring tasks (the kind at which men excel) and sympathetic dominance with perceptual-motor tasks (at which women surpass men). The authors then seek to establish that the "sex" hormones, androgens and estrogens, affect the balance between activation and inhibition (the vagueness of this formulation is recognized and is considered below), and they discuss possible indirect mechanisms by which androgens and estrogens might affect the autonomic nervous system (with, in their view, the androgens favoring parasympathetic and the estrogens sympathetic dominance). Thus their argument seems to be that sex differences in hormonal patterns produce sex differences in the balance of sympathetic and parasympathetic activity which produce sex differences on cognitive tasks; androgens, secreted by the male testes, favor the parasympathetic dominance necessary for the more "complex" ("inhibitory restructuring") tasks, while estrogens, secreted by the female ovaries, promote the sympathetic dominance which facilitates performance on "simple, overlearned, perceptual-motor tasks." Let us look at this argument more closely.

WOMAN: DEPENDENT OR INDEPENDENT VARIABLE?

REVIEW AND CLASSIFICATION OF LITERATURE ON SEX DIFFERENCES IN COGNITIVE ABILITIES

Of the several comprehensive reviews of the literature on human sex differences that are available (Anastasi, 1958; Garai & Scheinfeld, 1968; Maccoby, 1966; Tyler, 1965), all support the generalization that adult males perform better on mathematical and spatial tasks and adult women on verbal and perceptual-motor tasks. These reviews document the wide variety of studies on which these generalizations are based; they make no attempt, however, to abstract a factor of similarity among the types of performance at which each sex excels. Broverman et al. undertake the theoretically important task of making such an abstraction, and in so doing do not attempt to provide an exhaustive account of known sex differences, but rather a classification of certain cognitive tasks according to criteria which they have established for distinguishing between the tasks at which each sex excels. While the organization and tone of their article tend to suggest that their review of the sex differences literature is more comprehensive than it is, and that the classification of the tasks at which males and females excel was induced from the available data, it is clear from a comparison with other reviews that the studies they classify into two categories (Tables 1 and 2 of their article) were selected according to the hypotheses which they present as inductive generalizations or conclusions. In no other way could the authors arrive at a class of tasks at which females are superior which could be characterized as meeting the criteria of "simple overlearned repetitive behaviors measured in terms of speed, accuracy, or frequency of occurrence and which require minimal central [i.e., cognitive] mediation [p. 28]." since it ignores the large body of evidence (summarized in Oetzel, 1966, and elsewhere) showing that females surpass males on almost all measures on language performance. Surely it is inadequate to claim that verbal fluency, vocabulary size, grammatical sensitivity, etc., "involve minimal mediation by higher cognitive processes [p. 28]." Yet the authors make just this claim reasoning that "Although not commonly thought of as perceptual-motor behaviors, speech and reading do involve these functions [p. 25]" and that, therefore, there is no conceptual confusion in a statement like "As with other simple perceptual-motor behaviors, females are superior to males from childhood through adulthood in verbal functions [p. 25]." Their discussion of "The behaviors [not "some of the behaviors"] in which females are superior to males . . . [p. 28]" refers to a list which includes only "reading speed."

Properly employed, the hypothetico-deductive method is essential to scientific theory construction, and its use in the Broverman et al. case is not in question. What is questionable, however, is their use of prior hypotheses (in this case the criteria for classification) to select supporting data (here, various studies of sex differences) in such a way that evidence which directly contradicts the hypotheses is ignored.

Apart from the difficulties of dealing with a restricted range of data, there is also some problem with the way Broverman et al. characterize the common factor underlying the performance of those tasks on which they report males to surpass females. They state that these tasks require "suppression of responses to immediately obvious stimulus attributes of the task in favor of responses to other, not immediately obvious, stimulus attributes . . . [p. 24]" (what these attributes—obvious or nonobvious—are is never made clear). This abstraction and description of the common underlying ability is very similar to the description by Witkin, Lewis, Hertzman, Machover, Meissner, and Wapner (1954) and Witkin, Dyk, Faterson, Goodenough, and Karp (1962) of the ability underlying males' performance on the Gottschaldt hidden figures, rod-and-frame, and other similar tasks, and Witkin et al.'s (1954) discussion of the Rorschach (inkblot) test clearly illustrates the difficulties with this characterization. Thus, while Witkin et al. (1954, p. 477) describe performance on the hidden figures test as depending on the ability to perceptually restructure ("break up") the drawing or to inhibit the response to the whole configuration (so as to concentrate on those parts relevant to the search for the hidden figure), they also speak of the subject's "passive acceptance" and response to a single feature of the inkblot rather than his "actively attempting to provide an integration of form [1954, p. 207]" of the whole figure. There seems to be an unresolved contradiction here. Does the ability to respond to part of a complex perceptual whole involve "passive acceptance" or the presumably more active "perceptual-restructuring?" Is response to the whole configuration a lack of inhibition of the "immediately obvious" stimulus characteristics or an "integration of form?" While these questions could be put into a form which could be tested empirically, this has not yet been done, and the inconsistency which they presently illustrate brings into question the description of certain tasks as "inhibitory restructuring" without further refinement and clarification of the concept.

Thus Broverman et al.'s (1968) review and classification of the literature on sex differences in cognitive abilities seems to be selectively designed to support their hypothesis as to the criteria or attributes which distinguish cognitive tasks on which males and females excel. Their selection leads them to ignore or distort contradictory evidence (as in the case of their characterization of the tasks at which women surpass men) and to support an unclear conception of the tasks on which males are superior.

RELATION OF COGNITIVE FUNCTIONS TO THE ACTIVITY OF THE AUTONOMIC NERVOUS SYSTEM

In adducing evidence to support their proposal that "the relationship between simple perceptual-motor and inhibitory perceptual-restructuring tasks, may be, in part a function of the balance between the activating influence of the sympathetic, and the inhibitory tendencies of the parasympathetic subcortical nervous system [p. 31]," Broverman et al. (1968) rely on studies of the behavioral consequences of chemically stimulating or depressing one or the other branches of the autonomic nervous system. The logic of their argument is unexceptionable: they look at the effects of substances which stimulate/depress the sympathetic/parasympathetic nervous systems on both kinds of tasks. They seek to establish the hypotheses that "the same ergotropic functions [those mediated by the sympathetic nervous system] that facilitate wakefulness and sensory reactivity also facilitate performances of simple perceptual-motor tasks [p. 29]" and that "The same trophotropic functions [those mediated by the parasympathetic nervous system] that promote relaxation and sleep also contribute to the cognitive ability to delay initial response tendencies to obvious stimulus attributes in favor of responses to other, less obvious stimulus relationships [p. 29]." (Elsewhere these cognitive abilites which are associated with "sleep and relaxation"—as opposed to "wakefulness and sensory reactivity"—are characterized as behaviors "involving extensive mediation of higher processes" and which involve "the production of solutions to novel tasks or situations [p. 28].") The evidence for these hypotheses, however, is slim.

Even granting that some operationally clear-cut categorization of human cognitive abilities into perceptual-motor and perceptual-restructuring could be achieved, Broverman et al. in many cases fail to show that the kinds of behaviors which are affected by chemically altering the sympathetic-parasympathetic balance fall

Mary B. Parlee

into one or the other of these categories. For example, in the section on the effects of depressing parasympathetic function on simple perceptual-motor tasks (a manipulation predicted by their hypothesis to improve performance), they cite increased open field activity, spontaneous activity in wheels, and rates of conditioned responses in rats, and motor activity in cats as "eviden- ce . . . consistent with the proposition that an increase in the activation balance via a diminution of the inhibitory processes leads to increased output of simple perceptual-motor behaviors [p. 34]." Their notion of the appropriate extension of these sorts of animal data to human cognitive performance is illustrated else- where as follows: "Human females exceed human males on simple perceptual-motor tasks. The same sex difference in analogous behaviors, that is, spontaneous motor activity, is true in rats pp. 37]." Without in any way casting doubt on the relevance of animal research to human psychology, it seems fair to say that an argument that depends on an analogy between spontaneous motor activity in rats and reading speed in humans leaves much to be desired. Some examples of "perceptual-restructuring" tasks affected by chemical manipulation and cited in support of their hypothesis include alternate pushing of two levers (rats), writing slowly, temporal judgment, performance on a mirror tracing task, and "errors of overimpulsivity" in retardates.

Frequently, it seems that the studies cited by the authors in support of their hypotheses, qualify as evidence only on the assumption that the terms "activation" and "inhibition" have parallel meanings in psychology and neurophysiology: that, for example, the "inhibitory" activity of the parasympathetic nervous system is comparable to Pavlov's "conditioned inhibition," that "activation" caused by the sympathetic nervous system is reflected in spontaneous motor "activity," etc. Even granting the possibility of a simple one-to-one relation between psychological and neural processes, this sort of argument would be deficient in view of the fact that "activation" and "inhibition" can have several meanings in both psychology and neurophysiology. To take but a few examples, "activation" can refer in neurophysiology to the triggering by a neuron of other neurons or an effector, to the massive neural activity resulting from stimulation of the "reticular activating system," or to the pattern of autonomic changes resulting from stimulation of the sympathetic nervous system. In addition to the "inhibitory" action of one neuron on the firing rate of another, the "inhibitory" functions of the parasympathetic nervous system include increased activation of the digestive tract. And certainly "inhibition" has more than one meaning in psychology. The authors recognize that their hypotheses "span two quite disparate areas of function, that is, central autonomic versus intellectual functioning [pp. 29-30]," but they nevertheless fail to deal explicitly, not to say rigorously, with the problems this involves.

Thus although Broverman et al.'s argument proceeds through all the appropriate headings, the evidence for their repeated assertions of their thesis (first as hypothesis, then as conclusion at the beginning and end of almost every section) is inadequate to support their conclusion that a functional relationship exists between activation/inhibition or adrenergic/cholinergic neural processes or sympathetic/parasympathetic activity and the kinds of cognitive tasks listed in Tables 1 and 2 or described in the text as perceptual-motor and perceptual-restructuring.

RELATION OF ANDROGENS AND ESTROGENS TO THE "ACTIVATION-INHIBITION" BALANCE

This final phase of Broverman et al.'s argument seeks to establish a connection between estrogens and androgens, sympathetic/parasympathetic balance, and cognitive performance. They cite evidence from "rats, the sow, and, possibly, the human [p. 37]" indicating that estrogens are related to "activity" in the sense of spontaneous motor activity, and that androgens are also related to spontaneous activity (in rats and goldfish), but to a lesser extent than estrogens. This sort of evidence of the effects of hormones on the "behavioral expression of the activation-inhibition balance [p. 39]" leads them to think that "the cognitive activation-inhibition differences between the sexes in both animals and humans, therefore, may be primarily due to sex differences in estrogens [p.39]." (As passages such as these illustrate, it is not clear that the authors consistently use "activation-inhibition balance" as either a psychological construct or a neurological process. In fact, they stipulatively define activation and inhibition as having both behavioral and neurological referents, and their argument seems to rely heavily on a blurring of the distinction between the two.)

While the authors have not, at this point in their argument, actually equated "activation-inhibition balance" with sympathetic-parasympathetic balance, the paper requires a very careful reading in order to avoid the inference that they are the same. When the authors do turn direftly to a consideration of possible mechanisms by which androgens and estrogens could affect the parasympathetic and sympathetic nervous systems, respectively, they suggest that the hormone effects are mediated through their influence on the enzymes which control the available stores of the two transmitter substances for the autonomic nervous system. Specifically, their proposal is that the enzyme monoamine oxidase "provides a rational mechanism for explaining the apparent activation effects of these ["Sex"] hormones [p. 40]" since it both regulates the amount of adrenaline available as a transmitter substance in the sympathetic nervous system and is itself influenced by both androgens and estrogens. In the section of "Steroid 'Sex' Hormones and the Parasympathetic Nervous System," the authors cite as "perhaps the best evidence]p. 40]" of hormonal effects the fact that the concentration of choline acetylase, an enzyme involved in regulating the amount of acetylcholine available as a transmitter substance, rises in the hypothalamus of castrated rats. Apparently Broverman et al. are unaware of the fact that while adrenergic and sympathetic, cholinergic and parasympathetic are often used loosely as synonymous terms, the transmitter substance in the preganglionic (central) portion of the sympathetic nervous system is acetylcholine (Ruch & Fulton, 1960, p. 228). "Sex" hormone effects on choline acetylase concentrations in the hypothalamus, therefore, do not constitute evidence — indirect or otherwise — of hormonal effects on the *balance* between sympathetic/parasympathetic activity, which is the general point they are trying to establish. They offer no other evidence that "sex" hormones have any effect on the activity of the parasympathetic nervous system. (When Singer & Montgomery, 1969, commented on the nonidentity of cholinergic-parasympathetic and adrenergic-sympathetic, Boverman et al., 1969, replied that these were "arbitrary problems of definition [p. 328]." This, of course, is true. In the context of the Broverman et al. paper, however, it is clear that authors must be ignorant of the factual point that the sympathetic nervous system does involve cholinergic transmission, since they have cited increased hypothalamic choline acetylase as evidence that sex hormones affect the parasympathetic nervous system. It is simply false for them to say that "No part of our argument needs to be altered, regardless of which terminology is employed [p. 329]." Their argument needs to be altered in light of the factual distinction embodied in a precise use of the terms sympathetic/parasympathetic and adrenergic/cholinergic.)

In the final section of their paper, Broverman et al. (1968) note that the "simple perceptual-motor versus inhibitory restructuring abilities need not be the only intrapsychic cognitive antagonism [p. 43]." With reference to the thesis (Piaget, 1950; Werner, 1957) that

363

ontogenetic development, like phylogenetic evolution, involves integration and subordination of "primitive" mental processes to more "complex" ones, they suggest that the argument they have developed "could be applied to all stages of development [p. 43]." (One suspects that a more forthright exposition of the implications of this notion might be found in Funke (1968) where it was suggested that females constititue a "semi-human" missing link in the evolutionary passage from anthropoid ape to man (cf. human).)

In sum, Broverman et al. "feel that the general arguments of this paper may be brought to bear upon a much wider domain of behavioral phenomena . . . [p. 24]." Considering the nature and relevance of the evidence on which their arguments rest, such a generalization of their thesis seems at best premature. As it stands, their conclusion represents another in a series of purportedly objective, scientifically empty statements on the topic of sex differences. As Ellis (1934) has said.

The history of opinion regarding the cerebral sexual dif-ference forms a painful page in scientific annals. It is full of prejudices, assumptions, fallacies, over-hasty generalizations. The unscientific have had a predilection for this subject; and men of science seem to have lost the scientific spirit when they approached the study of its seat [p. 119].

REFERENCES

Anastasi, A. *Differential psychology.* (3rd ed.) New York: Macmillan, 1958.

Broverman, D. M., Klaiber, E. L., Kobayashi, Y., & Vogel, W. Roles of activation and inhibition in sex differences in cognitive abilities. *Psychological Review,* 1968, *75*, 23-50.

Broverman, D. M., Klaiber, E. L., Kobayashi, Y., & Vogel, W. Reply to the "comment" by Singer and Montgomery on "Roles of activation and inhibition in sex differences in cognitive abilities." *Psychological Review,* 1969, *76*, 328-331.

Ellis, H. *Man and woman.* (8th ed.) London: A. & C. Black, 1934. Cited in A. Montagu, *The natural superiority of women.* (Rev. ed.) London: Collier-Macmillan Ltd., 1968. P. 62.

Funke, M. *Are women human?* Cited in A. Montagu, *The natural superiority of women.* (Rev. ed.) London: Collier-Macmillan Ltd., 1968. P. 62.

Garai, J. E., & Scheinfeld A. Sex differences in mental and behavioral traits. *Genetic Psychology Monographs,* 1968, *77*(2), 169-299.

Maccoby, E. E. Sex differences in intellectual functioning. In E. E. Maccoby (Ed.), *The development of sex differences.* Stanford: Stanford University Press, 1966.

Oetzel, R. M. Annotated bibliography. In E. E. Maccoby (Ed.), *The development of sex differences.* Stanford: Stanford University Press, 1966.

Piaget, J. *The psychology of intelligence.* New York: Harcourt, Brace, 1950.

Ruch, T. C., & Fulton, J. F. (Eds.) *Medical physiology and biophysics.* Philadelphia: W. B. Saunders, 1960.

Singer, G., & Montgomery, R. B. Comment on roles of activation and inhibition in sex differences in cognitive abilities. *Psychological Review,* 1969, *76*, 325-327.

Tyler, L. E. *The psychology of human differences.* (3rd ed.) New York: Appleton-Century-Crofts, 1965.

Werner, H. *Comparative psychology of mental development.* New York: International Universities Press, 1957.

Witkin, H. A., Lewis, H. B., Hertzman, M., Machover, K., Meissner, P. B., & Wapner, S. *Personality through perception.* New York: Harper, 1954.

Witkin, H. A., Dyk, R. B., Faterson, H., Goodenough, D. R., & Karp, S. A. *Psychological differentiation.* New York: Wiley, 1962.

22

Repucci's study, unlike many included in this volume, represents a relatively limited empirical study of a specific issue: the more rapid cognitive development of girls than boys. A number of previous studies have demonstrated that girls show a correlation with the IQ and/or educational level of their parents at a much earlier age than boys. It has been suggested that girls, because of their faster maturational development, are much more susceptible to environmental influences at an early age than boys. Hence, they show the effects of their parents' intelligence at an earlier age than boys. Reppucci's study indicates that sex differences in cognition, related to parental factors, are present in children as young as two years of age. It illustrates the difficulty in attempting to dichotomize the sex differences into either physiological or environmental factors.

Parental Education, Sex Differences, and Performance on Cognitive Tasks Among Two-Year-Old Children*

N. Dickon Reppucci

The relation between sex of child, parental educational level, and performance on three different types of cognitive tasks—two vocabulary tasks, an embedded figures task, and a two-choice discrimination task—was

* From *Developmental Psychology*, 1971, 4 (2), 248-53. Footnotes have been renumbered.

investigated among forty-eight 2-year-old children. It was expected that parental education would be positively related to superior performance on all of the tasks for girls but unrelated for boys. The results confirmed this expectation.

Parental education level and sex differences in the overt behavior and problem-solving strategies of preschool and school age children have been investigated and debated for many years. There are intriguing questions concerning the origins and early manifestations of these differences and many have wondered how early these differences can be detected.

The acceleration of girls over boys in physiological and physical development is well documented (Anastasi, 1958; Bayley, 1950). The developmental acceleration of girls also has been noted in intellectual spheres. During childhood, girls are advanced relative to boys in all aspects of language: age of onset, vocabulary size, number of phoneme types, etc. (Irwin & Chen, 1946; Maccoby, 1966; McCarthy, 1930). In recent years, evidence has been accumulating to indicate that certain experiential factors affect girls more than boys. Bayley (1966) reported typically higher correlations between parental education and indexes of cognitive abilities for girls than for boys. Likewise, Honzik (1963) noted an increasingly positive correlation between the child's IQ and the parents' education with age, the girls' correlations becoming statistically significant around age 3 years, while boys' correlations were not significant until age 5. The inference is that experiences associated with parental education are affecting the girls more and earlier than the boys.

As part of a larger investigation related to individual differences in the consideration of information (Reppucci, 1970), it was possible to investigate the relation between sex, parental education level, and performance on three different types of cognitive tasks among 2-year-old children. It was expected that parental education would be positively related to superior performance on all of the tasks for girls but unrelated for boys.

METHOD

Subjects

The subjects for this study were 48 white children, 24 boys and 24 girls, aged 27 months who were originally recruited by advertisements in one of the local newspapers as part of an extensive longitudinal study being conducted by Jerome Kagan and his associates. The children were seen as close to 27 months from their date of birth as possible within 14 days. With the exception of one child who was accompanied by her older sister (the child's chief caretaker because of the mother's paralytic condition) all children came to the laboratory with their mothers. Mean parental education level was determined by the following metric: 6 = postcollege, 5 = college degree, 4 = part college, 3 = high school diploma, 2 = ninth grade completed, and 1 = ninth grade not completed. Children from all educational levels were represented in the sample. For girls, the mean parental education level was 4.0; for boys, it was 3.5. This difference was not significant. For girls, the range was from 1.5 to 6.0; for boys from 1.0 to 5.5. When mother's and father's educational levels were analyzed separately, there were no significant differences between the boys and the girls. Finally, the product-moment correlation coefficients between the educational levels of the father-mother pairs for the boys and for the girls were .72 ($p < .01$) and .50 ($p < .01$), respectively.

Experimenters[1]

A single trained woman experimenter administered both of the laboratory tasks to all children. Two other trained women experimenters administered the vocabulary tasks in the home. Although there is evidence for a Sex of the Experimenter X Sex of the Children interaction effect between the ages of 4 and 7 years (Gewirtz, 1954; Gerwirtz & Baer, 1958; Stevenson, 1961), only female experimenters were used in the present investigation for two reasons. First, Stevenson (1961) demonstrated that a female experimenter is a more effective social reinforcer with children of both sexes under 4 years of age than is a male experimenter. Thus, the use of a female experimenter for young preschool children maximizes the effectiveness of the reinforcement for these children. Second, it is a known fact that the behavior of young children is commonly played for women administrators and judges.

Procedure

The experimenter administered the first two tasks in a large playroom which had one-way mirrors. The child had become accustomed to the room by playing with toys during a 30-minute

---

1. The author is grateful to Judith Jordan, Janet Levine, and Susannah Sak, who were the experimenters in this study.

play session. The mother was always present.

Embedded figures task. The experimenter presented the child with a picture of a girl and taught him to touch the figure. Next, while keeping this model within the child's view, she presented him with a series of backgrounds with the figure embedded in them. The child's task was to find and touch the figure. Following the initial learning, the experimenter showed the child six sets of embedded figures, each consisting of a model and three embeddings of the model. The first three sets were relatively easy discrimination tasks consisting of a dog, horse, and bird in backgrounds containing a number of colored figures that looked progressively more like the model as the difficulty increased. The final three sets were schematic drawings of a cat, car, and flower embedded in black and white line backgrounds. If possible, at least one response to each embedding was obtained. Only two children failed to complete at least the first four sets. The number of errors for each response was recorded on an Esterline-Angus event recorder by an observer behind the one-way mirrors. The mean interobserver reliability coefficient for 10 children on errors was .99.

Two-choice discrimination task. The experimenter told the child they were going to play a game with candy (M&Ms). An apparatus which had two cups in the front below two white plastic encasements was used. Each encasement contained both a red and yellow light which were invisible unless turned on. The experimenter controlled the lighting and could turn on any single light or any combination of lights. Each time the child touched the yellow light first, he was rewarded with an M&M which was delivered in the cup below the correct light. Once the experimenter felt confident that the child had learned the discrimination, she used a fixed schedule for alternating stimuli, in which the most probable chance score would be 50 percent correct (Gellermann, 1933). This schedule was continued until the child had five *consecutively* correct trials or had stopped playing the game. Each response was recorded on the Esterline-Angus event recorder by the observer. The percentage of errors was calculated for each child. The mean interobserver reliability coefficient for 10 children was .99. Recording difficulties caused the elimination of 5 children.

Vocabulary recognition and vocabulary naming tasks. Within 1 week of the time of the laboratory session, another experimenter made a home visit. She administered a vocabulary recognition and a vocabulary naming test. The vocabulary recognition test was composed of 22 items in which the child had to choose among three alternatives. She presented the child with three colored pictures, each on a 6 X 3-1/2 inch laminated card, and asked him to touch one of them, for example, pictures of a knife, fork, and

N. Dickon Reppucci

spoon were presented and the child was asked to touch the fork. Full credit was given only when the child touched the correct picture first, and half credit only if he touched the correct picture second.

The vocabulary naming test was administered next. This test was composed of 15 items in which a single colored picture on a 6 X 3-1/2 inch laminated card was shown to the child. The experimenter asked the child, "What is this?" Examples of the items were a key, a policeman, and a zipper. Full credit was given only when the child responded accurately first. Half credit was given if, after an initial incorrect response, the child responded accurately or if any answer was close to accuracy, for example, "coffee" or "broken" for a broken coffee cup, "man for a policeman, "light" for a light socket. Maximum possible scores on the vocabulary recognition and naming tests were 22 and 15, respectively.

RESULTS

Parental education level was investigated by sex in relation to five performance variables from the four different tasks. The variables were total number of correct responses on each of the vocabulary tests, percentage of errors on the two-choice discrimination task, and mean number of errors and percentage of trials on which the child ever pointed to the correct figure on the embedded figures task. (The two measures on the embedded figures task were used because it would be possible for a child to be accurate 100 percent of the time but make many errors since the accuracy score was based on the child ever being correct.) The correlation matrices for these variables and mean parental education are presented in Table 1.

For girls, all of the variables were highly intercorrelated; for boys, only the two vocabulary scores were related. Mean parental education level was significantly related to performance on all of the tasks for girls and unrelated for boys. There were no mean differences between boys and girls on any of these variables.

In order to examine parental education level in more detail, each of the five performance variables was correlated with the mothers' and the father' education levels separately. These results are presented in Table 2.

Again, boys' performance was essentially unrelated to parental educational level, whereas girls' performance was related to each of the parents' educational levels. Interestingly, girls' performance

TABLE 1

PRODUCT-MOMENT CORRELATION COEFFICIENTS BETWEEN MEAN PARENTAL EDUCATION AND MEASURES OF COGNITIVE PERFORMANCE AMONG 27-MONTH-OLD CHILDREN

Variable	Vocabulary recognition	Vocabulary naming	% accurate responses (EFT)[a]	Mean no. errors (EFT)	% errors on two-choice discrimination task
			Girls		
Mean parental education	.65**	.48**	.55**	−.36	−.57**
Vocabulary recognition	—	.68**	.56**	−.42	−.71**
Vocabulary naming	—	—	.55**	−.52*	−.55**
% accurate responses (EFT)	—	—	—	−.44*	−.64**
Mean no. errors (EFT)	—	—	—	—	.49*
			Boys		
Mean parental education	.30	.19	−.13	.28	−.33
Vocabulary recognition	—	.74**	.29	−.18	.08
Vocabulary naming	—	—	.20	.07	.32
% accurate responses (EFT)	—	—	—	−.22	−.30
Mean no. errors (EFT)	—	—	—	—	−.08

[a] Percentage of trials on which the child ever pointed to the correct figure on the embedded figures task (EFT).
* $p < .05$, two-tailed test.
** $p < .01$, two-tailed test.

TABLE 2

PRODUCT-MOMENT CORRELATION COEFFICIENTS BETWEEN PARENTAL EDUCATIONAL LEVELS AND MEASURES OF COGNITIVE PERFORMANCE AMONG 27-MONTH-OLD CHILDREN

Variable	Vocabulary recognition	Vocabulary naming	% accurate responses (EFT)a	Mean no. errors (EFT)	% errors on two-choice discrimination task
			Girls		
Mother's education	.37	.36	.45*	−.42*	−.20
Father's education	.72**	.49*	.52**	−.32	−.71**
			Boys		
Mother's education	.31	.17	−.07	.08	−.38
Father's education	.25	.18	−.16	.41	−.22

a Percentage of trials on which the child ever pointed to the correct figure on the embedded figures task (EFT).

* $p < .05$, two-tailed test.

** $p < .01$, two-tailed test.

TABLE 3

Correlation Coefficients between Measures of Cognitive Performance among 27-Month-Old Girls and the Educational Level of Their More Educated Parent with the Father's Education Level Partialed Out

Variable	Vocabulary recognition	Vocabulary naming	% accurate responses (EFT)[a]	Mean no. errors (EFT)	% errors on two-choice discrimination task
Educational level	−.09	.24	.11	−.04	−.58*

[a] Percentage of trials on which the child ever pointed to the correct figure on the embedded figures task (EFT).

* p < .01, two-tailed test.

was correlated more highly with fathers' educational level than with mothers'.

Finally, in an attempt to determine whether or not it is fathers who have more influence than mothers on girls' performance, or, alternatively, whether it is the more educated parent who exercises the influence, partial correlation coefficients were computed (see Table 3).

In only one case was there a significant correlation, that is, higher educational level, per se, was related to the precentage of errors on the two-choice discrimination task. However, an analysis of the difference between this correlation and the correlation between fathers' educational level and the percentage of errors on the two-choice discrimination task indicated that the fathers' educational level tended to exert the more important effect ($T = 1.80$, $p<.10$).Thus, the results support the finding that fathers' educational level has a major influence on girls' cognitive performance.

DISCUSSION

The findings clearly support the hypothesis that parental education is related to performance on cognitive tasks among 2-year-old girls but not among 2-year-old boys. The stronger association between parental education and cognitive performance for girls has at least two possible interpretations. Girls may be biologically and psychologically more differentiated than boys due to girls' general developmental maturity relative to boys'. The general developmental maturity may aid in the modification of girls' responses by environmental contingencies, which would mean that differential experience in the world is more faithfully reflected in the behavior of girls. Thus, we might expect a more consistent relation among girls between specific experiences that are presumed to promote cognitive performance.

An alternative explanation, which is not inconsistent with the first, requires no biological assumptions. It assumes that parental education level has an influence on the way mothers and fathers treat their daughters but no influence on the way they treat their sons. Levine, Fishman, and Kagan (1967) provide some evidence for this interpretation. These investigators found that mothers with higher educational levels vocalized more in response to their 4-month-old daughters' vocalizations than mothers with lower educational levels. In addition, and perhaps equally important, they found no differences in the way mothers with various educational levels treated their 4-month-old sons. Thus it may be that the familiar idea, "boys will be boys," influences parents, regardless of educational attainment, to treat their sons in a similar fashion.

Whatever the explanation, the results of the present study indicate that as early as 27 months of age vocabulary level and other types of cognitive performance among girls are influenced by parental education level. These results, in conjunction with those of Honzik (1963) and Bayley (1966), strengthen the conviction that girls are more susceptible to environmental influence than boys and affected by it earlier.

A final point which deserves comment is the accentuated relations between girls' cognitive performance and fathers' educational attainment found in this investigation. For the most part, research on parent-child interactions during early development has been concentrated almost exclusively on the mother-child relationship. This is most probably based on the assumption that the child's chief caretaker, usually the mother, will have the most significant effect upon the child's early development. While this assumption may be correct, it has neglected investigation of the interaction between the child and other significant figures in his life, in particular the father. It may be that there are broader social class discrepancies in fathers' behavior toward their children than among mothers'; thus, fathers' differential behaviors assume a greater significance in determining differences in the child's cognitive development. One suggested direction for future research is the systematic investigation of the father-child relationship, for example, natural observation of the father's behavior toward his child. Such investigation may help to unravel the mysteries of differential development.

REFERENCES

Anastasi, A. *Differential psychology.* (3rd ed.) New York: Macmillan, 1958.

Bayley, N. *Studies in the development of young children.* Berkeley: University of California Press, 1950.

Bayley, N. Developmental problems of the mentally retarded child. In I. Phillips (Ed.), *Prevention and treatment of mental retardation.* New York: Basic Books, 1966.

Gellerman, L. W. Chance orders of alternating stimuli in visual discrimination experiments. *Journal of Genetic Psychology,* 1933, *42*, 206-208.

Gewirtz, J. L. Three determinants of attention-seeking in young children. *Monographs of the Society for Research in Child Development,* 1954, *19* (2, Serial No. 59).

——— Baer, D. M. The effect of brief social deprivation on behaviors for a social reinforcer. *Journal of Abnormal and Social Psychology, 1958, 56,* 49-56.

Honzik, M. P. A sex difference in the age of onset of the parent-child resemblance in intelligence. *Journal of Educational Psychology,* 1963, *54,* 231-237.

Irwin, O. C., & Chen, H. P. Development of speech during infancy: Curve of phonemic types. *Journal of Experimental Psychology,* 1946, *36*, 431-436.

Levine, J., Fishman, C., & Kagan, J. Sex of child and social class as determinants of maternal behavior. Paper presented at the meeting of the American Orthopsychiatry Association, Washington, D. C., March 1967.

Maccoby, E. E. Sex differences in intellectual functioning. In E. E. Maccoby (Ed.), *The development of sex differences.* Stanford: Stanford University Press, 1966.

McCarthy, D. Language development of the preschool child. *Institute of Child Welfare Monograph,* 1930, No. 4.

Repucci, N. D. Individual differences in the consideration of information among two-year-old children. *Developmental Psychology,* 1970, *2*, 240-246.

Stevenson, H. W. Social reinforcement with children as a function of CA, sex of E, and sex of S. *Journal of Abnormal and Social Psychology,* 1961, *63*, 147-154.

23

Sherman's review represents another view of the basis for sex differences in cognitive function. She concentrates on differences in space perception between males and females. She suggests that key measures of analytic cognitive function such as the embedded figures task and the rod and frame task are substantially related to space perception and therefore are sex-biased. She cites evidence that females show inferior performance on spatial tasks even when there is no conflict with the visual field and no analysis required. On the other hand, there is no impairment of cognitive analysis when verbal materials are employed.

Sherman suggests that sex differences in spatial perception may be based, at least in part, on differential practice on tasks requiring spatial visualization. Boys spend more time in building models, driving cars, reading maps, etc. than girls. However, there is no good empirical evidence that such sex differences exist. Evidence from other cultures would also be necessary. Even if such differential practice effects exist, we are left with the problem whether the "sex-appropriate" behavior is reinforced by the society or self-selected by children because it is more easily reinforced. There is evidence [including some cited by Sherman himself] that spatial perception may have a physiological basis. Again, it is likely that an interaction of physiological and environmental factors is responsible for those sex differences in cognition which do exist.

Problem of Sex Differences in Space Perception and Aspects of Intellectual Functioning

Julia A. Sherman

Key measures of analytical cognitive approach are sub-

*From *Psychological Review*, 1967, *74*, 290-299.

stantially related to space perception, and therefore are sex biased. Consequently a conclusion of sex differences in analytical ability based on these data appears unwarranted. The construct of analytical cognitive approach, itself, appears questionable. Space perception also appears to be a relevant variable to control in studies of sex differences in geometric and mathematical problem solving. A causal explanation of the development of sex differences in spatial perception is presented based partly on differential practice. Other causal explanations of sex differences in analytical approach are discussed and an attempt is made to accommodate them within this framework.

The thesis of this article is that sex differences in spatial perception have been neglected as an explanation of sex differences in various aspects of intellectual functioning. It seems important to draw attention to this omission since findings of sex differences in intellectual functioning are being widely cited and uncritically accepted. They are part of the data being used to make educational decisions.

The most glaring example of failure to consider the role of space perception occurs in the interpretation of the findings of sex differences in analytical approach. This nearly always boils down to differences in performance on the Rod and Frame Test (RFT), the Embedded Figures Test (EFT), or some other spatial task. While broader questions might be raised, this discussion will be limited to only those aspects of the problem that directly relate to sex differences. Other explanations of sex differences in analytical approach will be considered.

The possible role of space perception in contributing to other sex differences in intellectual functioning will be noted. Finally, in order to provide additional perspective and insight into the causality of this sex difference, an attempt will be made to sketch the main factors responsible for the development of sex differences in space perception.

ANALYTICAL COGNITIVE APPROACH

Sex differences have been repeatedly reported on some of the tasks used to measure the analytical cognitive approach (Witkin, Dyk, Faterson, Goodenough, & Karp, 1962). Women have been described as accepting the field more passively than men, being more field-dependent or global as opposed to field-independent or analytical in their style of cognition. Perceiving in an analytical way is said to involve experiencing items as discrete from their backgrounds. It reflects ability to overcome the influence of an embedding context. The two most popular measures of field dependence, EFT and RFT, involve visual space perception. While significant sex differences have been obtained with these tasks, other measures of field dependence which have been used, such as rotator-match brightness constancy, paper-square-match brightness constancy, or body steadiness, do not involve visual space perception and do not show sex differences of a significant amount (Witkin, Lewis, Hertzman, Machover, Meissner, & Wapner, 1954). RFT and EFT also seem to relate better to other variables (Witkin et al., 1954). Most of the research on analytical cognitive approach has used tasks of space perception.

The Spatial Character of EFT and RFT

Several studies provide documentation confirming the spatial character of these tasks. Thurstone (1944) reported correlations of .411 and .429 between two different forms of the Gottschaldt Figures Test, similar to Witkin's EFT, and the Primary Mental Abilities (PMA) Space Test. These three tests and a block design test all showed high saturations on the same Factor A, with sex loading .26 on the same factor, males achieving a superior performance.

Podell and Phillips (1959) did a cluster analysis of the results of a wide variety of tests using a small sample of 32 male subjects. The Gottschaldt Figures Test correlated .77 with Witkin's version of the EFT which in turn correlated .29 with the PMA Space Test. These three tests and others clustered together on Dimension I, which these authors call spatial decontexualization. They were unable to replicate these findings on a second small male sample.

Gardner, Jackson, and Messick (1960) performed a factor analysis of the test results of 63 female subjects. Included among the tests were RFT, EFT, Spatial Orientation, Part V of the Guilford-Zimmerman Aptitude Survey, and Thurstone's Cards Test, also a spatial test. EFT correlated .53 with the Spatial Orientation Test and .33 with the Cards Test. RFT correlated .35 with the Spatial Orientation Test and .04 with the Cards Test. All correlations but the last were significant at least at the .05 level. Significant correlations were also reported between the two Thurstone versions of the Gottschaldt Figures Test and the Witkin EFT and RFT. All five tests loaded together on the same factor. On the basis of their results, Gardner and his colleagues rejected the term field-dependence-independence in favor of field articulation. They concluded (a) that the results provide clear evidence that the field articulation control principle is relevant to the space factors of flexibility of closure, spatial relations, and spatial orientation, and (b) that distinctions among these supposedly different abilities were not apparent in their sample.

It is not possible to review the complex literature on space perception here. It should be noted, however, that while the researchers on space perception have not been in agreement about the number and names of space factors, Werdelin (1961), in a careful review of the literature, concluded that all the space factors are closely related. Michael, Guilford, Fruchter, and Zimmerman (1957) made a similar point.

Sex Differences in Space Perception

A major difficulty with the predominant use of spatial tasks in measuring analytical approach is the fact that girls and women have an inferior performance on spatial tasks even when there is no conflict with a visual field and no analysis required. This sex difference has been repeatedly found and is well known. The evidence will not be repeated here since very competent reviews are available (Anastasi, 1958; Fruchter, 1954; Sandstrom, 1953; Tyler, 1965; Werdelin, 1961). The difference has been reported on all spatial factors, but Werdelin (1961) concluded that it may be limited to visualization. What differences are found probably depends a great deal on how thoroughly the two groups are matched. Sex differences are not commonly found until the early school years (Maccoby, 1966). Fruchter (1954), stated that the spatial abilities mature between 11 and 15. Witkin and his co-workers (Witkin et al., 1954) reported consistent sex differences only at age 17 and after. The developmental curve of field independence closely parallels that of spatial ability (Gardner et al., 1960). An increment in the sex difference apparently occurs in adolescence.

It would seem that the empirical results of sex differences in analytic approach or field dependence might be explainable without any reference to field, without any need to infer a passive approach to the field, globality, or lack of analytical skill. The fallacy involved is similar to concluding that women are more analytical than men based on findings of superior female ability to decontexualize the red and green figures on the Isihara Color Blindness Test.

Use of a term such as analytical cognitive approach implies a generality which has by no means been established. Not only is it difficult to discriminate from the space factors, but it appears unrelated to the verbal area. Witkin and his colleagues (Witkin et al., 1962) reluctantly concluded, contrary to their hypothesis, that verbal tasks and tasks involving configurational stimuli seem to exploit different skills. Whether one considers the underlying sex difference to be in space perception or in analytical cognition is more than a matter of semantics or even of parsimony. The spatial explanation permits a logical, testable explanation of the development of this sex difference capable of subsuming other hypotheses within its frame. This will be elucidated later in this article.

Other Explanations

There have been several attempts to explain the sex differences in analytical field approach, but none considered differential spatial ability. Witkin et al. (1954) concluded that the sex differences in their findings were cultural in origin. They cited the tremendous overlapping in the male and female score distributions, and the fact that the sex differences only reached consistent significance at a time when sex role differentiation becomes more pronounced. Witkin and his co-workers (Witkin et al., 1962) have suggested, and Maccoby (1966) has elaborated, an interpretation based on the greater dependency and conformity of women. Bieri, Bradburn, and Galinsky (1958) concluded that sex differences on EFT are attributable to the superior mathematical ability of males as measured by the Scholastic Aptitude Test. These explanations may possibly be accommodated within the framework of the spatial hypothesis, as will be made clear.

OTHER ASPECTS OF INTELLECTUAL FUNCTIONING

Stable and reliable sex differences have also been reported in solving problems of geometry and mathematical reasoning (Tyler, 1965). In discussing sex differences in intelligence, there has been a tendency to lump together evidence from studies of problem solving and analytical cognitive approach, for example by Maccoby (1966). Problem-solving tasks and tests of higher mathematics often involve geometry. Thus it seems appropriate to comment on these other abilities, though separately, since the case for the role of space perception is different in each instance.

Insofar as geometry is concerned, Werdelin (1961) has established the importance of spatial perception in performance of geometric problems. He matched 143 male-female pairs in age, social class, reasoning, verbal, and number abilities. Examining the remaining sex differences in performance on a wide variety of tests, he concluded that the sex differences are attributable to inferior female skill in the space factor of visualization. He hypothesized that the sex differences do not occur on items in which visual organization is easily comprehended and which are to be manipulated as given, but on those in which the organization and reorganization aspect are exaggerated. Sex differences were less among the students schooled together, suggesting experience as a factor in producing the difference.

In the case of mathematical problem solving, Guilford, Green, and Christensen (1951) concluded that spatial visualization contributes to solution of problems, and French (1951, 1955) concluded that it promotes successful achievement in mathematics. There is, however, no direct evidence that the sex difference in mathematical problem solving is a function of failure to control for the sex difference in spatial visualization.

The closest approximation of control of the spatial visualization variable in a study of sex differences in problem solving is the study of Sweeney (1953). He found to his surprise that matching groups on the Flags Test, a test of spatial relations, proved to be as good a control for eliminating sex differences in problem solving as matching for mathematics. Had he matched for visualization rather than for spatial relations, he might have been able to eliminate the sex difference entirely. There is no intention to imply that spatial visualization is the only variable that can produce a sex difference in mathematical problem solving. Interest and motivation are important factors (Carey, 1955; Milton, 1958), and of course any study of this topic needs to control a host of factors that are not specifically related to sex. The point is that spatial visualization is a variable to be controlled. It should now be clear how the hypothesis that sex differences in mathematical ability account for sex differences in performance on the EFT (Bieri et al., 1958) might be subsumed within the spatial hypothesis. Sex differences in spatial skill may account for both.

An Illustration

An example of the gathering momentum of overgeneralization is the study of Kagan, Moss, and Sigel (1963). It has been cited as extending the evidence for global versus analytical cognitive style correlates to a broader range of tasks beyond the more directly perceptual. They concluded that males show a stronger analytic attitude than females. The only statistically significant finding of sex difference reported involved learning nonsense syllables associated with geometrical figures, a sex-biased task. On a sorting task used to measure abstraction, the categories defining the quality of abstraction were highly arbitrary, as Riley Gardner pointed out in a critique attached to the Kagan et al. (1963) paper. While boys scored higher than girls by these standards, there was no indication that the differences were statistically significant. To bolster their case, the authors cited Wechsler (1958), referring to the slight but statistically significant superiority of males on the Block Design subtest and the Picture Completion subtest of the Wechsler Adult Intelligence Scale. While it seems reasonable to say that the Block Design subtest involves analysis, it is very much a spatial task, and the Picture Completion subtest hardly seems to qualify as a test of analytical attitude at all (Cohen, 1959). Thus the findings of sex differences stem basically from spatial tasks and the evidence appears far from sufficient to warrant their general conclusion of sex differences in analytical attitude.

DIFFERENTIAL PRACTICE AS A KEY TO CAUSATION

Evidence of Learning of Spatial Perception

Stafford (1961) concluded that spatial visualization has a hereditary component which is transmitted by a recessive gene carried on the X chromosome. Thus the aptitutde would appear more often in men. While the role of innate factors is not yet clear, Gibson (1953) and Santos and Murphy (1960) came to the general conclusion that perceptual learning does occur. It seems likely that the sex difference in spatial perception may be traced in part to differential learning.

Ironically enough, Witkin (1948) found that training, which was largely didactic, significantly decreased the visual dependence of a group of women on a spatial orientation task. This same task was among those which Witkin later labeled measures of analytical approach. Witkin never followed the lead of this preliminary study because the subjects reported that the correct response still seemed wrong. Witkin therefore concluded that their cognitive approach had not changed. Many scientists find a change in performance more convincing evidence than phenomenological report. However, it would be interesting to know what the subjects would have reported had they been trained to the asymptote of their ability.

The study of Elliott and McMichael (1963) is similar in that the training methods were largely didactic with even fewer actual trials of practice. They used two groups of seven subjects each. One group received only didactic training while the other group received some practice as well. Only the latter group showed a significant decrease in field dependence on the RFT, but it was transient. More intensive and systematic efforts to condition the underlying behaviors may yield less ambiguous findings.

Brinkmann (1966) pointed out that ordinary school curriculum offerings are not always effective in developing spatial visualization (Brown, 1954; Mendicino, 1958; Ranucci, 1952). Like Van Voorhis (1941), he emphasized estimation and visualization in his training procedures and was able to demonstrate significant improvement in performance on a spatial perception measure. One of two matched groups of eighth-grade pupils, 13 girls and 14 boys in each group, received programmed learning for 3 weeks. The program consisted of 505 items illustrating selected concepts of geometry and materials for tactual-kinesthetic visual feedback. The program was presented during the regular period of mathematics; the control group continued with the usual instruction. Comparison of the pre-post testing scores on Form A of the Differential Aptitude, Space Relations Test, showed an increase in the experimental group significant at the .001 level. Use of the experimental program involved less reliance on the teacher. Those children who felt that the teacher taught better, possibly the more dependent ones, gained significantly less from the experimental program. This is consistent with the findings cited by Maccoby (1966) of the negative relationship between dependency and development of field independence. Brinkmann did not present data comparing the sexes on the pretesting. On the basis of the posttest raw scores, he concluded that there was no appreciable difference, and that girls can at least hold their own when provided opportunity to learn. At this age, however, spatial abilities have not fully matured, and the sex difference is probably not so great as later on. A study such as this using larger numbers of males and females of an older age would be of great value.

The data of Blade and Watson (1955) are also relevant. After the first year of engineering studies, they found average gains of nearly 1 sigma in the scores of engineering students (mostly men) on the College Entrance Examination Board Spatial Relations Tests. Gains for engineering students were significantly greater than for students in other studies, or for a group of potential students refused admission and not pursuing studies in the interim between testings. Freshmen with the 10 highest and 10 lowest scores on the spatial test greatly differed in previous course work related to spatial perception such as mechanical drawing. There were even greater differences in the frequency of jobs and hobbies of a mechanical or technical nature, which of course involve much spatial work. The relationship of such courses, hobbies, and jobs to conventional masculine role expectations should be obvious.

Considering the large gains accomplished as an incidental by-product of the engineering curriculum, it may be inferred that there were many males far from the asymptote of their ability in spatial perception. It may also be inferred that the gap in a group of females would be much greater.

Differential Practice

Because of the unknowns involved in assuming what is relevant activity in increasing spatial skill, it is difficult to know whether the sexes do in fact receive differential practice. It must be remembered, however, that even during the ages of greatest sex difference, the score distributions greatly overlap, and the sex difference is often slight. It may be that even moderate overall differences in practice would be sufficient to create this effect. While experimental studies will be needed to verify this hypothesis, it is interesting to note the number of plausibly spatial activities that are sex-typed.

As Witkin and his co-workers (Witkin et al., 1954) pointed out, the increased disparity at about age 17 in field independence, and presumably performance on spatial tasks, occurs at a time of increasing sex-role differentiation. Very few girls are found in the high school classes of mechanical drawing, analytical geometry, and shop. Spare-time activities of tinkering with the car, sports, model building, driving a car, direction finding, and map reading are sex-typed and might also be sources of differential practice. When one considers the number of hours an interested boy may spend in such activities, it is easy to see how sex differences could develop. During most adult years, the academic, vocational, and avocational differences between the sexes as a whole are at least as great.

Even before the adolescent sex role divergence, there are probably relevant differences. Boys as a group spend more time in aiming activities and games, model construction, building with blocks and later with other materials. It seems very likely that these activities are involved in the development of spatial skills. The causal mix of innate, cultural, and learned factors probably varies from person to person, but the Blade and Watson (1955) and Brinkmann (1966) findings indicate that it is unwise to assume that all children normally have the experiences which will fully develop their spatial skills.

Differential learning by virtue of sex-typed activities is consistent with the findings cited by Maccoby (1966) that cross-sex typing is associated with optimal intellectual development in women. It is also consistent with the substantial amount of evidence which she

387

cited showing a correlation, but not necessarily a causal relationship, between less analytical skill and dependency and conformity. Independent, nonconforming women would be more likely to pursue activities contrary to cultural sex-role expectations. In natural situations, several factors tend to be present together: dependency, fearfulness, less exploration, increased time with the mother, increased verbal skill, decreased spatial skill, and, for girls, conventional sex typing. For this reason, experimental approaches appear most likely to provide clarification.

Inhelder' View

Inhelder's view (Tanner & Inhelder, 1958) appears to be consonant with the thesis developed in this essay. She pointed out that while boys and girls of the same age do not show a difference in logical functioning, they do show a difference in formation of spatial representation, that is the transformation and development of geometric solids.. This might serve as a preadaptation or prerequisite for later development. A slight difference in young children might thus take on greater importance with age and be increased by differential experiences. Inhelder reported that children with richer possibilities of manipulation and visual tactile exploration have better spatial representation. In her opinion, the mental image in its spatial form is originally the interiorization of the movements of exploration. Boys, at least by preschool age, show more muscular reactivity, that is, restless, vigorous overt activity, than girls (Anastasi, 1958). It appears likely that this extra activity includes a differential in movements of exploration.

Other Factors

While differential learning is regarded a very important factor, other factors may well be ordinarily involved in the causal chain of events. The possible roles of inheritance, conformity, and cross-sex typing have already been mentioned. In her discussion of the development of sex differences in intellectual functioning, Maccoby (1966) has discounted a great variety of explanations as insufficient. Each is indeed insufficient by itself, but she has erred in trying to place too much weight on any one argument.

For example, girls as a group are more verbally precocious than boys. Boys are genetically larger and stronger, and they are more active than girls (Anastasi, 1958). The girls talk somewhat earlier than boys, but even more important is their superior articulation. At 24 months McCarthy (1943) found that 78 percent of a girl's speech was comprehensible compared to only 49 percent of a boy's speech. The boys didn't entirely catch up until age 4. Satisfying needs by use of social communication mediated by words is a prominent early alternative for girls. The boys, unable to communicate so effectively, may use their superior musculature to get what they want. Less able to control and be controlled by verbal means, the stage could already be set for sex differentials in active exploration and problem solution by action rather than words. Dependency could grow out of the verbal, social bent, and could also increase this trend for both sexes.

The twig having been bent to reliance on a verbal, socially mediated approach to problems, spatial skills may not be exercised and developed in girls. As already outlined, this trend would be supported and increased by the cultural sex-typing of activities. McCall (1953) made a comparative factor study of the scores of 451 eighth-grade pupils on 31 subtests covering verbal, number, and space factors. He found that on tasks of space perception the girls used their verbal ability while the boys did not. The girls, as is consistent with previous findings (Tyler, 1965), were superior to boys in verbal ability At this age, boys showed averagely well-developed verbal, number, and space abilities while girls excelled only in verbal ability, scoring below boys on the other two factors. McCall hypothesized that girls excel in verbal ability in early years, but that boys tend to catch up in school. Boys by their versatility then begin to excel girls.

A corollary for boys of the bent twig hypothesis is that action, nonverbal approaches may more easily become fixed, with the result that verbal, socially-mediated behavior fails to develop adequately. A full exposition of the evidence for this corollary is beyond the scope of this paper. Suffice it to note that the greater frequency of such an outcome in males is consistent with the greater frequency of aggressive behavior problems in boys and men, less interest in people, less dependency, less verbal fluency, and more problems in speech and reading (Anastasi, 1958; Tyler, 1965).

IMPLICATIONS AND CONCLUSIONS

Key measures of analytical cognitive approach are substantially related to space perception, and are therefore sex biased. Consequently a conclusion of sex differences in analytical ability based on these data appears unwarranted. Controls for differential spatial skill are needed in these studies and in studies of sex differences in geometric and mathematical problem solving. The question of the degree to which spatial skill can be learned has a potential significance beyond explaining results of studies in analytical cognitive approach. To the extent to which it is a factor in more complex mental functions, the way may be opened for improved remedial education.

Although the main focus of this article has been on sex differences, the evidence considered and the arguments developed tend to cast doubt on the adequacy of the construct of analytical cognitive approach. It should be noted that only that portion of the research of Witkin and his colleagues that deals with spatial measures, sex differences, and sex-typed personality differences is subject to the criticisms brought out in this article. Witkin's early research is not so expansive in its conclusions. The path of increasing overgeneralization may be traced in the terms used. The phenomenon which was described as visual independence in 1948 (Witkin, 1948), became field independence in 1954 (Witkin et al., 1954), analytical cognitive approach in 1962 (Witkin et al., 1962), and analytical ability in 1966 (Maccoby, 1966).

To summarize the main points of the critique: (a) Key measures of this construct do not appear differentiable from the spatial factors; (b) the term analytical consequently implies an unwarranted generality, especially since the construct appears unrelated to the verbal area; (c) the link between sex, sex roles, and spatial skill could account for a considerable part of the relationship between personality variables and performance on the perceptual tasks. It could also account for the fact that such correlations are higher with the spatial measures (Witkin et al., 1954). The impressive stability of the field independence measures (Witkin et al., 1954) could occur because they are related to sex-typing which itself is very stable.

Perhaps this latter point, (c), bears further explication. If skill on spatial tasks is learned to an important extent, and if the opportunities for learning are sex-typed, then feminine males would be less likely to engage in male sex-typed activities which develop spatial skills. Thus, generally speaking, male sex-typing would promote field independence; female sex-typing would promote field dependence. Individuals low in analytical field approach do in fact show characteristics more typical of women than men. These include less achievement motivation, more dependency, less aggressiveness, more interest in people, and poorer performance on the Block Design subtest of the Wechsler tests than on the Vocabulary subtest (Witkin et al., 1962). It appears highly likely that these relationships are mediated by sex-typed spatial learning, and would be greatly reduced by controlling for spatial ability or, as Blade and Watson (1955) prefer to say, achievement in spatial perception.

390

REFERENCES

Anastasi, A. *Differential psychology; individual and group differences in behavior.* (3rd ed.) New York: Macmillan, 1958.

Bieri, J., Bradburn, W., & Galinsky, M. D. Sex differences in perceptual behavior. *Journal of Personality,* 1958, *26*, 1-12.

Blade, M., & Watson, W. S. Increase in spatial visualization test scores during engineering study. *Psychological Monographs,* 1955, *69* (12, Whole No. 397).

Brinkmann, E. H. Programmed instruction as a technique for improving spatial visualization. *Journal of Applied Psychology,* 1966, *50,* 179-184.

Brown, F. R. The effect of an experimental course in geometry on ability to visualize in three dimensions. Unpublished doctoral dissertation, University of Illinois, 1954.

Carey, G. L. Reduction of sex differences in problem solving by improvement of attitude through group discussion. Unpublished doctoral dissertation, Stanford University, 1955.

Cohen, J. A factorial structure of the WISC at ages 7-6, 10-6 and 13-6. *Journal of Consulting Psychology,* 1959, *23*, 285-299.

Elliott, R., & McMichael, R. E. Effects of specific training on frame dependence. *Perceptual and Motor Skills,* 1963, *17*, 363-367.

French, J. W. The West Point tryout of the guidance battery. (Research Bulletin 51-12) Princeton: Educational Testing Service, 1951.

_ _ _ The West Point tryout of the guidance battery, part 2. (Research Bulletin 55-6) Princeton: Educational Testing Service, 1955.

Fruchter, B. Measurement of spatial abilities: History and background. *Educational and Psychological Measurement,* 1954, *14*, 387-395.

Gardner, R. W., Jackson, D. N., & Messick, S. J. Personality organization in cognitive controls and intellectual abilities. *Psychological Issues,* 1960, *2* (Whole No. 8).

Gibson, E. J. Improvement in perceptual judgments as a function of controlled practice or training. *Psychological Bulletin,* 1953, *50*, 401-431.

Guilford, J. P., Green, R. F., & Christensen, P. R. A factor analytic study of reasoning abilities. II Administration of tests and analysis of results. Report No. 3, 1951. University of Southern California, Psychology Laboratory.

WOMAN: DEPENDENT OR INDEPENDENT VARIABLE?

Kagan, J., Moss, H. A., & Sigel, I. E. The psychological significance of styles of conceptualization. In J. C. Wright & J. Kagan (Eds.), Basic cognitive processes in children. *Monographs of the Society for Research in Child Development,* 1963, *28*, No. 2.

Maccoby, E. E. Sex differences in intellectual functioning. In E. E. Maccoby (Ed.), *The development of sex differences.* Palo Alto, California: Stanford University Press, 1966. Pp. 25-55.

McCall, J. R. *Sex differences in intelligence: A comparative factor study.* Washington: Catholic University Press, 1955.

McCarthy, D. Language development of the preschool child. In R. G. Barker, J. S. Kounin, & H. F. Wright (Eds.), *Child behavior and development.* New York & London McGraw-Hill, 1943. Pp. 107-128.

Mendicino, L. Mechanical reasoning and space perception: Native capacity or experience. *Personnel and Guidance Journal,* 1958, *36*, 335-338.

Michael, W. G., Guilford, J. P., Fruchter, B., & Zimmerman, W. S. The description of spatial-visualization abilities. *Educational and Psychological Measurement,* 1957, *17*, 185-199.

Milton, G. A. Five studies of the relation between sex role identification and achievement in problem solving. Technical Report No. 3, December, 1958, Yale University, Department of Psychology, Department of Industrial Administration.

Podell, J. E., & Phillips, L. A developmental analysis of cognition as observed in dimensions of Rorschach and objective test performance. *Journal of Personality,* 1959, *27*, 439-463.

Ranucci, E. R. The effect of the study of solid geometry on certain aspects of space perception abilities. Unpublished doctoral dissertation, Teachers College, Columbia University, 1952.

Sandstrom, E. I. Sex differences in localization and orientation. *Acta Psychologica,* 1953, *9*, 82-96.

Santos, J. F., & Murphy, G. An odyssey in perceptual learning. *Bulletin of the Menninger Clinic,* 1960, *24*, 6-17.

Stafford, R. E. Sex differences in spatial visualization as evidence of sex-linked inheritance. *Perceptual and Motor Skills,* 1961, *13*, 428.

Sweeney, E. J. Sex differences in problem-solving. Technical Report No. 1, December 1, 1953, Stanford University. (Doctoral dissertation submitted to Stanford University, 1953.)

392

Tanner, J. M., & Inhelder, B. (Eds.), *Discussions on child development.* New York: International Universities Press, 1958.

Thurstone, L. L. *A factorial study of perception.* Chicago: University of Chicago Press, 1944.

Tyler, L. E. *The psychology of human differences.* New York: Appleton-Century-Crofts, 1965.

Van Voorhis, W. R. The improvement of space perception ability by training. Unpublished doctoral dissertation, Pennsylvania State University, 1941.

Wechsler, D. *The measurement and appraisal of adult intelligence.* (4th ed.) Baltimore: Williams & Wilkins, 1958.

Werdelin, I. *Geometrical ability and the space factors in boys and girls.* Lund, Sweden: University of Lund, 1961.

Witkin, H. A. The effect of training and of structural aids on performance in three tests of space orientation. Report No. 80, 1948. Washington: Division of Research, Civil Aeronautics Association.

Witkin, H. A., Dyk, R. B., Faterson, G. E., Goodenough, D. R., & Karp, S. A. *Psychological differentiation.* New York: Wiley, 1962.

Witkin, H. A., Lewis, H. B., Hertzman, M., Machover, K., Meissner, P. B., & Wapner, S. *Personality through perception.* New York: Harper & Row, 1954.

24

Keogh's paper is a relatively simple empirical study demonstrating that sex differences in perceptual strategies in the organization of space exist. It is interesting in that she has compared pattern drawing and pattern walking under different conditions in the same individuals. She finds that girls' performance as compared to that of boys is impaired only in pattern walkin, e.g., copying by walking a geometric design drawn on an index card which was clearly visible to the child at all times. Keogh found qualitative as well as quantitative differences between the performances of boys and girls. She makes no attempt to determine the etiology of these differences, but suggests that the simplicity of the task and the obvious differences in the manner in which it is performed by the two sexes suggests quite different perceptual strategies in boys and girls.

Pattern Copying Under Three Conditions of an Expanded Spatial Field*

Barbara K. Keogh

One hundred and thirty-five children (CAs 8-9) copied patterns by drawing and by walking in an expanded spatial field under three conditions: no defined reference points, reference points, and reference points plus visual tracking cues. Drawing differences among groups were nonsignificant. Boys were significantly better than girls in reproducing patterns by walking under two of three walking

* From *Developmental Psychology*, 1971, 4 (1) 25-31.

conditions. Boys improved in pattern walking across conditions as more visual cues were available; girls did not. Differences were reflected in objective scores and in styles of pattern walking. Findings suggest a sex difference in perceptual strategies in the organization of space.

Considerable evidence regarding development of visuo-motor and spatial organization has come from studies of drawing and copying ability. Most pattern copying tasks are conducted within a limited and structured spatial field. Preliminary studies of pattern reproduction in an expanded spatial field revealed facets of visuo-motor organization not elicited by traditional pattern copying measures (Keogh & Keogh, 1968).

Keogh and Keogh (1967) studied ability of English school boys to copy patterns by walking them on a large unmarked floor, so that children made gross motor representations of what was perceived visually. Such a task requires definition of reference points within the expanded field, and adjustment of these reference points to changing body positions as design parts are completed. There was steady improvement in ability to walk patterns from ages 6 through 8. Young children and mentally retarded children had difficulty with pattern walking, often became confused or disoriented, and made distorted and inaccurate copies of simple stimulus patterns. Previous work on pattern walking was limited to performance of boys under a single walking condition with simple patterns as stimuli.

The present study was designed (a) to compare the ability of boys and girls to reproduce patterns by walking, (b) to investigate pattern walking performance when complexity of the stimulus patterns was increased, and (c) to consider the effect of differing amounts of available visual cues on pattern walking performance. Patterns were walked under conditions of no defined reference points, defined reference points, and reference points plus visual tracking cues.

METHOD

Sample

Subjects were drawn from the total population of third- and fourth-grade classes in one suburban southern California elementary school. The total sample of 135 subjects contained 52 third-grade boys, 23 fourth-grade boys, 37 third-grade girls, and 23 fourth-grade girls. Twelve boys and 10 girls were nonwhite. Children with known sensory, motor, or intellectual defects were excluded. Subjects were randomly assigned to one of three experimental groups, taking into account representation by age, grade level, classroom, and race. Twenty-five boys and 20 girls were in each experimental group. Chronological age means and standard deviations by groups were 106.28 (4.09), 106.12 (6.09), 106.72 (5.36 months for boys, and 107.15 (5.99), 107.00 (6.17), and 108.65 (5.95) months for girls. There were no significant differences among groups in CA.

Procedure

Subjects were seen individually and asked to make pencil copies of 10 designs on 8-1/2 X 11 inch white paper, one design per page. Patterns are shown in the order of presentation in Figure 1. The last 5 more complex patterns are combinations of the first 5 simple patterns. Before beginning the test patterns, each subject copied the circle as a practice design. Patterns were presented on 8 X 8 inch cards which were visible to the subject while he drew. There was no time limit. Each child's method of copying was recorded by an investigator while the child drew. The investigator copied the child's drawing on a separate piece of paper, indicating the order and direction of lines composing the drawing.

Within a week after drawing the designs, each subject was seen again individually and asked to make the patterns by walking. Designs were presented singly in the same order as drawn. The subjects walked the patterns under one of three conditions.

Walking Method A (Floor)

Subjects were tested in a large, empty, school cafeteria. Floors were unmarked. No reference points on floor or walls, starting or

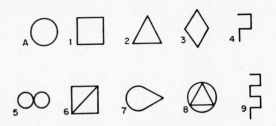

397

stopping points, nor restrictions on space to be used were indicated. The child was asked to pretend that the floor was a large piece of paper and that he had sticky paint on the bottom of his shoes; thus, wherever he walked he would leave a mark, so he could draw a picture by walking. Designs were held so the child could see them at all times as he walked. The circle was used as a practice design. Great care was taken to ensure that the child understood the task. If the subject appeared confused, the task was reexplained, and he was allowed to do the circle another time. All subjects walked the circle successfully. Reproduction of the design was recorded on a separate score sheet by a second investigator while the child walked. The form of the child's walked pattern was drawn, and the order and direction of lines indicated.

Walking Method B (Mat)

The same instructions and procedures were followed as in Method A, except the patterns were walked on a 9 X 9 foot plain linoleum mat. Reference points were not identified and the child could start the pattern from any point on the mat.

Walking Method C (Sand)

Similar procedures were followed as in Methods A and B except that patterns were walked on a 9 X 9 foot sand box. The sand box was level with surrounding asphalt in a kindergarten play yard. The sand was raked smooth after each trial so that footprints were visible when the child walked.

All drawn and walked patterns were scored 1 to 4, 1 representing an extremely poor, unrecognizable copy; 4 an accurate copy. Walked patterns were scored at the time of walking according to characteristics of the walked copy, not the style of walking. Three scores were obtained: a subtotal of simple designs (1-4), a subtotal of complex designs (5-9), and a total of all nine designs. The practice design (circle) was not scored. Girls' walked patterns were recorded and scored by two observers independently. All data were collected to the children's school during regular school hours.

RESULTS

Data were organized to consider questions of interscorer reliability, the effects of differing experimental conditions on pattern walking, comparisons and relationships of pattern drawing and pattern walking scores, and sex differences in pattern copying.

Interscorer Reliability

Two observers independently recorded and scored the walked patterns of the 60 girls. Interrater reliability for the sums of the four simple patterns, the five complex patterns, and total pattern scores were computed with Pearson *r*. For the floor group, coefficients of correlation were .70, .81, and .79 for the simple, complex, and total pattern walking scores, respectively. Comparable values of *r* were .76, .89, and .87 and .85, .86, and .90 for the Mat and Sand groups, respectively ($p = .01$). Interscorer reliabilities for individual designs ranged from .27 to .93. Design 4 was the least reliably rated, Pearson $r = .27$, .75, and .65 for Floor, Mat, and Sand conditions, respectively. With the exception of Design 4 under the Floor condition, all interrater reliabilities were statistically significant ($p = .01$).

Effects of Conditions

Pattern drawing and pattern walking scores were first analyzed separately for boys and girls with a one-way analysis of variance according to experimental conditions. Pattern drawing occurred under the same conditions for all subjects and groups. As anticipated, *F* values were nonsignificant for all pattern drawing comparisons within sex. The three subgroups of boys were comparable in pattern drawing scores, as were the three subgroups of girls.

Pattern walking comparisons among conditions differed for boys and for girls. Means, standard deviations, and *F* values were found for complex and total walking scores. Values of *t* for between-group comparisons on complex walking scores were significant for Floor and Mat conditions ($t = 2.18$, $p = .05$), and for Floor and Sand conditions ($t = 3.51$, $p = .01$). Comparable *t* values for total walking scores were 1.56 ($p = .10$) and 2.99 ($p = .01$). Differences between Mat and Sand conditions were nonsignificant although favoring the Sand group. Boys improved in walking performance across conditions of Floor, Mat, and Sand. For girls, all comparisons of pattern walking performance yielded nonsignificant *F* values. In contrast boys, girls did not improve significantly in pattern walking according to conditions of Floor, Mat, or Sand.

TABLE 1

MEANS, STANDARD DEVIATIONS, AND F VALUES FOR COMPARISONS OF BOYS' AND GIRLS' PATTERN WALKING BY CONDITIONS

Group	Floor	Mat	Sand	F	df
Boys					
Simple					
M	12.60	12.84	13.44	1.26	2/72
SD	1.98	2.17	1.58		
Complex					
M	12.20	13.72	14.64	6.06*	2/72
SD	2.52	2.34	2.64		
Total					
M	24.80	26.56	28.08	4.40*	2/72
SD	3.76	4.05	3.91		
Girls					
Simple					
M	11.05	10.95	11.25	.175	2/57
SD	1.28	1.43	2.07		
Complex					
M	12.35	12.75	12.85	.325	2/57
SD	1.79	2.05	2.35		
Total					
M	23.40	23.70	24.10	.203	2/57
SD	2.62	3.31	4.30		

Note.—N = 25 boys in each condition; N = 20 girls in each condition.
* $p < .01$.

Drawing and Walking Performance

Comparisons of drawing and walking scores were made separately for boys and girls with a correlated t formula (Guilford, 1950). Findings are summarized in Tables 2 and 3. For boys, there were no significant differences between simple drawing and walking scores under any condition. For complex designs and total designs, however, drawn patterns were significantly better than walked patterns when the walking occurred on the floor or the mat. No differences were found when designs were walked on the sand.

Examination of Table 3 reveals that for girls, drawn patterns were better than walked patterns under all conditions. Eight of nine t values were significant beyond the .01 level.

Relationships Between Drawing and Walking

Product-moment coefficients of correlation between walking and drawing scores were computed for simple, complex, and total scores. Computations were based on ratings of one observer who recorded and scored all walked patterns. For boys under the Floor condition, coefficients were .48 and .53 ($p = .05$) for drawn and walked simple and total scores, respectively. For girls under the Sand condition, coefficients were .48, .54, and .62 ($p<.05$) for simple, complex, and total designs, respectively. No other relationships between drawn and walked scores were significant.

Comparisons of Boys and Girls

To determine possible effects of experimental conditions and sex on pattern copying performance, a 2 (Sex) X 3 (Walking Conditions) analysis of variance was performed on drawing and walking scores for simple pattern total, complex pattern total, and total pattern copying scores.

The main effect of sex was significant for all pattern walking comparisons. The F values were 36.13 ($df = 1/129$, $p = .01$) for total simple designs, 4.68 ($df = 1/129$, $p = .05$) for total complex designs, and 18.09 ($df = 1/129$, $p = .01$) for total designs. Effect of conditions was significant for the sum of complex designs ($F = 4.59$, $df = 2/129$, $p = .05$). No interaction was significant. Values of t for comparisons of boys and girls by conditions are found in Table 4. With the exception of complex designs walked on the floor, boys were favored in all comparisons.

Main effects of sex and conditions were nonsignificant for all pattern drawing scores. Interaction of sex and condition was

TABLE 2

MEANS, STANDARD DEVIATIONS, AND t VALUES FOR BOYS' DRAWN AND WALKED
PATTERNS BY EXPERIMENTAL CONDITIONS

Condition	Drawn		Walked		t
	M	SD	M	SD	
Floor					
Simple	12.92	1.73	12.60	1.98	.84
Complex	15.40	1.78	12.20	2.52	6.25***
Total	28.32	2.87	24.80	3.76	5.33***
Mat					
Simple	13.16	1.11	12.84	2.17	.67
Complex	15.04	1.99	13.72	2.71	2.41**
Total	28.20	2.71	26.56	4.05	1.97*
Sand					
Simple	13.44	1.45	13.44	1.58	.00
Complex	15.08	1.87	14.64	2.65	.69
Total	28.52	2.63	28.08	3.91	.47

Note.—N = 25 in each condition.
* $p < .10$.
** $p < .05$.
*** $p < .001$.

TABLE 3

MEANS, STANDARD DEVIATIONS, AND *t* VALUES FOR COMPARISONS OF GIRLS' DRAWN AND WALKED PATTERNS BY EXPERIMENTAL CONDITIONS

Condition	Drawn		Walked		*t*
	M	SD	M	SD	
Floor					
Simple	13.00	.86	11.05	1.28	6.09**
Complex	15.40	1.31	12.35	1.79	6.49**
Total	28.40	1.71	23.40	2.62	8.77**
Mat					
Simple	13.10	1.55	10.95	1.43	4.39**
Complex	15.20	1.80	12.75	2.05	5.10**
Total	28.30	2.81	23.70	3.31	5.48**
Sand					
Simple	12.15	1.60	11.25	2.07	2.00*
Complex	14.65	1.87	12.85	2.35	3.75**
Total	26.80	3.04	24.10	4.30	3.46**

Note.—N = 20 in each condition.
* p < .10.
** p < .01.

significant for simple pattern drawing ($F = 3.14$, $df = 2/129$, $p = .05$). Although there were no significant differences in drawing scores by sex for the Floor and Mat groups, girls in the Sand Walking group were the poorest pattern drawers of all six groups, a finding which may reflect a sampling bias. Based on results of the Sand Walking groups, an analysis of covariance with simple drawing as the covariate and simple, complex, and total walking scores as dependent variables yielded significant F values for the covariate effect ($F = 10.63$, 15.68, 51.58, $df = 1/128$, $p = .01$,

TABLE 4

MEANS, STANDARD DEVIATIONS, AND t VALUES FOR
COMPARISONS OF BOYS' AND GIRLS' WALKED
PATTERNS BY CONDITIONS

Condition	Boys	Girls	t
Floor			
Simple			
M	12.60	11.05	1.96***
SD	1.98	1.28	
Complex			
M	12.20	12.35	.22
SD	2.52	1.79	
Total			
M	24.80	23.40	1.38
SD	3.76	2.62	
Mat			
Simple			
M	12.84	10.95	3.28***
SD	2.17	1.43	
Complex			
M	13.72	12.75	1.43
SD	2.34	2.05	
Total			
M	26.56	23.70	2.49**
SD	4.05	3.31	
Sand			
Simple			
M	13.44	11.25	3.93***
SD	1.58	2.07	
Complex			
M	14.64	12.85	2.32
SD	2.64	2.35	
Total			
M	28.08	24.10	3.20***
SD	3.91	4.10	

Note.—$N = 25$ boys in each condition; $N = 20$ girls in each condition.
* $p < .05$.
** $p < .02$.
*** $p < .01$.

respectively). Although simple drawing was a significant covariate, the main effect of sex on pattern walking was confirmed for the simple and total walking comparisons ($F = 32.16$ and 8.24, $df = 1/128$, $p = .01$). The effect of condition on complex walking was also supported ($F = 5.59$, $df = 2/128$, $p = .01$). No interaction was significant.

DISCUSSION

Two major findings warrant discussion. First, boys were better than girls in ability to make patterns by walking in an expanded spatial field. Second, boys improved in pattern walking under conditions of increased visual cues, girls did not.

Distributions of objective scores overlapped, in that a few boys were poor walkers and a few girls were good walkers. However, consistent subjective differences in styles of walking were apparent. Boys made precise angles and corners, were accurate in starting and stopping points, and indicated clearly when a pattern was completed. Boys appeared to make complex patterns in subunits, completing one design part and pausing or stopping before beginning the next part. Girls walked hesitantly, made rounded corners and imprecise angles, starting and stopping points were not coordinated, and patterns were left incomplete. Girls appeared more investigator than task oriented. In contrast to boys who walked patterns in parts or sections, many girls attempted to walk patterns in one continuous line. Pattern 6 was often walked as a figure 8, and Pattern 8 frequently made as a single unit, rather than as a separate triangle within a circle.

Pattern walking performance of boys and girls is consistent with findings of other investigators who report sex differences in spatial organization favoring boys (Howard & Templeton, 1966; Lord, 1941; Mellone, 1944; Money, 1965). Further sex differences in task orientation, sensitivity to adults, and the like have been described (Maccoby, 1966). Such motivational or attitudinal factors might influence performance in pattern copying. However, sex differences were found only in pattern walking, not drawing, so it is difficult to account for the discrepancies in performance on the basis of motivation alone.

The pattern walking task was unique for all subjects, but because of its major motor component may have been less comfortable for girls than for boys. Appealingly simple, this interpretation is not consistent with the findings under the three walking conditions. As all children could walk well, differences in pattern walking appear more closely related to styles of perceptual

405

organization than to motor components. Witkin, Dyk, Paterson, Goodenough, and Karp (1962) have related sex differences in perceptual style to a field dependence-independence dimension, and suggest that girls are more global than analytic in perceptual style. Global perception may be an adequate strategy for the organization of stimuli within a limited spatial field, but an analytic style may be more effective for structuring three-dimensional space. Pattern walking requires abstraction and organization of parts from an embedding field, and appears to be another correlate of field dependence-independence.

It should be emphasized that differences in performance of boys and girls increased as more visual cues were available. Apparently, boys attended to and used relevant cues in solving the task, whereas, girls did not. An attending hypothesis (Zeaman & House, 1963) has been proposed to explain the poor pattern walking performance of retarded children (Keogh, 1969). However, subjects in the present study were of normal intelligence, and no differences were found in pattern drawing or pattern walking under the condition at least cues. Differences were observed as more cues were available.

Perceptual style and cue selection are obviously interrelated and influence the organization of space in relation to self. Reproduction of patterns by walking elicits a wide range of individual differences in this regard. The simplicity of the task and the observed difference in the manner in which patterns were walked suggest that boys and girls use different perceptual strategies in the organization of space.

Guilford, J. P. *Fundamental statistics in psychology and education.* New York: McGraw-Hill, 1950.

Howard, I. P., & Templeton, W. B. *Human spatial orientation.* London: Wiley, 1966.

Keogh, B. K. Pattern walking under three conditions of available visual cues. *American Journal of Mental Deficiency,* 1969, *74* , 376-381.

Keogh, B. K., & Keogh, J. F. Pattern copying and pattern walking performance of normal and educationally subnormal boys. *American Journal of Mental Deficiency,* 1967, *71*, 1009-1013.

Keogh, B. K., & Keogh, J. F. Pattern walking: A dimension of visuo-motor performance. *Exceptional Children,* 1968, *34*, 617-618.

Lord, F. E. A Study of spatial orientation of children. *Journal of Educational Research,* 1941, *34*, 481-505.

Maccoby, E. E. (Ed.) *The development of sex differences.* Stanford: Stanford University Press, 1966.

Mellone, M. A. A factorial study of picture tests for young children. *British Journal of Psychology,* 1944, *35* , 9-16.

Money, J. *A standardized road-map test of direction sense.* Baltimore: Johns Hopkins University Press, 1965.

Witkin, H., Dyk, R. B., Faterson, H. F., Goodenough, D. R., & Karp, S. A. *Psychological differentiation.* New York: Wiley, 1962.

Zeaman, D., & House, B. J. The role of attention in retardate discrimination learning. In N. R. Ellis (Ed.), *Handbook of mental deficiency.* New York: McGraw-Hill, 1963.

25

The study by Pedersen and his associates represents a more environmentally based approach to the bases of cognitive differences between the sexes than the papers heretofore discussed. The purpose of their study was to determine the effects of sex of the examiner upon the performance of male and female subjects on a mathematics test. They found that subjects performed best under examiners of their own sex and that female subjects gave outstandingly better performances when tested by females than when tested by males. The dependent variable used in this study was the WISC arithmetic subtest, which should have been relatively insensitive to extraneous variables.

The authors suggest that the predominance of male math teachers and female English teachers in our society may be producing an educational artifact in terms of sex-related aptitudes. Natural biasing affects the testing results without experimental manipulation. The study illustrates the difficulty of using previous possibly biased, studies as evidence for sex differences in cognitive functions.

Although the study gives data on possible sources of sex bias and experimenter effect which have been rarely discussed in the psychological literature, we should not let our positive evaluation of the findings blind us to its methodological flaws. The authors tend to make large generalizations from an N of only twenty four subjects [twelve of each sex]. This study is most unusual in that it has as many experimenters as subjects. Second, repeated presentations of the WISC arithmetic subtest to the same subjects may have produced peculiar practice effects, which were not analyzed. Nevertheless, the study illuminates one of the major dilemmas in the study of women. It is necessary to investigate previous research, but these previous studies contain many unanalyzable sources of possible bias.

Effects of Sex of Examiner and Subject on Children's Quantitative Test Performance*

Darhl M. Pedersen, Martin M. Shinedling, and Dee L. Johnson

24 examiners (12 males and 12 females) and 24 3rd-grade Ss (12 males and 12 females) participated in the experiment. Each of 4 distinct subsets by a corresponding distinct subset of 6 examiners (3 males and 3 females). 2 subsets of Ss were tested by the 3 male examiners 1st, the other 2 were tested by the females 1st. The sequence by which Ss were exposed to examiners within each sex was counterbalanced. A 2x2x2 analysis of variance with 2 between variables (Sequence and Sex of S) and 1 within variable (Sex of Examiner) was completed using the sum of the test scores obtained under the 3 male examiners and the 3 female examiners as the 2 dependent variable scores for each S. It was found that (a) the main effects for Sex of S and Sequence were not significant, (b) the main effect for Sex of Examiners was significant, and (c) 2 interaction effects—Sex of S/x/Sex of Examiner and Sequence/x/Sex of Examiner—were significant. Female examiners elicited higher scores across Sex of S than male examiners. The Ss performed best under examiners of the same sex.

Milton (1957) has stated that "during recent years, there has been an increased interest in the effects of nonintellectual processes upon problem-solving and thinking [p. 208]." It has been demonstrated by Milton and a number of other investigators that sex-role identification is an important nonintellectual factor related to problem-solving ability. Bieri (1960) showed that parental identification was related to sex differences in cognitive behavior. Kuckenberg (1963) compared boys whose fathers had been absent during their early years with boys whose fathers had been present. She found that the boys who did not have an opportunity to learn their sex role through identification with their fathers did not develop as great an interest in and knowledge of mathematics, which is a part of the male sex role. At maturity the mathematical aptitude scores were higher relative to verbal aptitude scores for

410

father-present boys than for father-absent boys. The mathematical aptitudes were especially low in cases where the father had left before his son's birth and was away as long as 2-3 years. It has been demonstrated that among third-grade students males are superior to females in mathematical ability (Heilman, 1933; Samuels, 1942; Stevenson, 1961). Bittner and Shinedling (1968) have demonstrated that at the third-grade level male examiners elicited better performance on Piaget's tasks related to the concept of conservation of substance than did female examiners.

The principal purpose of the present study was to determine the effect of sex of the examiner upon the performance of male and female subjects on a mathematics test. It was hypothesized that because of sex-role identification the mathematics test scores would be higher for both males and females when the examiner was a male than when the examiner was a female. It was also hypothesized that there would be a significant interaction effect between the sex of the examiner and the sex of the subject because of the superior performance of male subjects elicited by male examiners. Finally, it was hypothesized that male subjects would score higher on the mathematics test than females irrespective of the sex of the examiner.

METHOD

Subjects and Examiners

Two groups were involved in the experiment: subjects and examiners. The subjects consisted of 24 third-grade students (12 males and 12 female) who were chosen at random from a third-grade class in Rock Canyon Elementary School in Provo, Utah. The examiners consisted of 24 teacher education majors at Brigham Young University (12 male and 12 female) who volunteered to participate in the study.

Measuring Instrument

The Arithmetic subtest of the Wechsler Intelligence Scale for Children (WISC; Wechsler, 1949) was used to measure mathematical ability in this study for the following reasons: (a) The WISC is a standardized test which has good coefficients of validity and reliability (Jensen, 1965); (b) the Arithmetic subtest has an intercorrelation of .57 with the full-scale score and has a reliability coefficient of .63 at the 7 ½-year age level (Wechsler, 1949); (c) the WISC provides scaled scores for each subtest which permits a simple and rapid conversion of raw scores to standard scores; (d) the Arithmetic subtest is objectively scored; and (e) the Arithmetic subtest requires approximately 15 minutes to administer. This was an advantage because it permitted each testing period to last only approximately 1 ½ hours. A longer test would have required such a long testing period that at the third-grade level fatigue would have become a salient factor influencing test performance.

Design and Procedure

Each child was tested six times — three times by male examiners and three times by female examiners. To eliminate possible order effects involving examiner, two factors were counterbalanced — sex of examiner and examiners within each sex. To accomplish this each of four distinct subsets of six subjects was tested by a corresponding, distinct subset of six examiners. Each subset of subjects and examiners consisted of three males and three females. Two of the subsets of subjects were tested by three male examiners first and then by three female examiners. In the other

TABLE 1

ANALYSIS OF VARIANCE SUMMARY TABLE

Source	df	MS	F
Between Ss	23		
Sequence (A)	1	16.33	3.15
Sex of Ss (B)	1	21.33	4.12
A × B	1	1.33	.26
Error (b)	20	5.18	
Within Ss	24		
Sex of examiner (C)	1	114.08	7.73*
A × C	1	126.75	8.58**
B × C	1	200.08	13.50***
A × B × C	1	18.75	1.27
Error (w)	20	14.77	
Total	47		

* $p < .025$.
** $p < .01$.
*** $p < .005$.

two the order was reversed. Therefore, the sex of the examiners to which the subjects were first exposed was counterbalanced. Half of the subjects were tested by three male examiners followed by three female examiners. The other half were tested by three female examiners followed by three male examiners. Furthermore, the sequence by which subjects were exposed to the examiners of each sex was counterbalanced so that each of the six subjects in

Dahrl M. Pedersen, Martin M. Shinedling, and Dee L. Johnson

each subset experienced a unique sequence of testing by the six examiners assigned to that subset.

Each subset of subjects was tested during a separate session. Just prior to each experimental session the six assigned examiners were briefed for approximately 20 minutes on the administration of the WISC Arithmetic subtest and the general experimental procedures. The experimental sessions were conducted in a large room with six separate stations located far enough apart so that they were well isolated from one another. Neither the examiners nor the subjects were given any information concerning the purpose of the experiment.

Two scores were obtained for each subject. The first was the sum of his WISC Arithmetic subtest standard scores obtained under three male examiners. The second was the sum of his standard scores obtained under three female examiners. Therefore, a group of 12 male subjects and a group of 12 female subjects existed, each with a score obtained under male examiners and a score obtained under female examiners. The hypotheses were tested using a 2x2x2 mixed-design analysis of variance (Meyers, 1966) with two between variables (Sequence and Sex of Subject) and one within variable (Sex of Examiner).

RESULTS

The results of the 2x2x2 mixed-design analysis of variance of the effects of Sex of Examiner, effects of Sex of Subject, effects of Sequence, and their interactions are presented in Table 1. The Sex of Examiner main effect was significant at the .025 level. However, contrary to the prediction, female examiners elicited better performance than male examiners. This was primarily due to the outstanding performance of female subjects when tested by female examiners. Consider the following four means: male subjects tested by male examiners (35.75), male subjects tested by female examiners (34.75), female subjects tested by male examiners (33.00), and female subjects tested by female examiners (41.67). The interaction of Sex of Subject with Sex of Examiner was highly significant as predicted ($p < .005$). Individual comparisons among the four means were made using Sheffe's (1953) test. Female subjects tested by female examiners did significantly better than male subjects tested by female examiners ($p < .05$). Also, female subjects performed significantly better when tested by female examiners than when tested by male examiners ($p < .05$). However, although male subjects tended to perform better under

413

male examiners than under female examiners as was predicted, the difference was not significant. The hypothesis that male subjects would perform better than female subjects irrespective of the sex of the examiner was not confirmed. The Sex of Subject main effect failed to reach significance at the .05 level. The surprisingly good performance of female subjects with female examiners tended to mitigate against the predicted main effects. The Sequence main effect, that is, the order by which subjects were tested by the two sets of male and female examiners, was not significant. The Sequence x Sex of Examiner effect was significant ($p < .01$). However, the Sequence x Sex of Subject interaction effect was not significant.

DISCUSSION

Completion of this study was motivated in part by Rosenthal's (1963) research in the area of the experimenter variable. In general, previous experimenter variable studies have generated two important questions, one methodological and one empirical.

The methodological question concerns the experimental design used in many of the experimenter variable studies, that is, assigning subjects to experimenters so that subjects are nested under experimenters. The mixed-design analysis of variance used in this study yielded a more exact estimate of the experimenter effect. The present study has demonstrated that when subject effects are removed, the sex of experimenter is a significant variable.

The empirical question has to do with the extent of the natural bias of the experimenter in this culture. In many of the experimenter variable studies the expectancy of the experimenters was manipulated. These expectancies produced biases which led to significant effects. The present study attempted to determine whether natural biases which emerge from sex-role conceptions or expectations can manifest themselves through examiner effects in the testing of children. On the basis of the obtained results it would appear that natural biasing affects testing results without experimental manipulation. This evidence tends to warrant the generalization of Rosenthal's research to an area not yet explored.

Although it was predicted that males would perform better when tested by males than when tested by females, it was not predicted that females would perform better when tested by females than when tested by males. In fact, the female subjects did so much better when tested by female examiners that the Sex of Examiner main effect was in the direction of the female examiners eliciting the better test performance across sex of subjects.

The finding that the Sequence x Sex of Subject interaction was not significant but that the Sequence x Sex of Examiner interaction was significant replicates the finding by Bittner and Shinedling (1968), who tested third-grade subjects using one of Piaget's tasks. Testing each subject several times by several different examiners demonstrates that the subject performs differently as a function of the sex of the examiner. However, this finding is somewhat artifactual in that subjects are normally not tested repeatedly by examiners of different sex. While the findings indicate that subjects are affected differentially depending upon which sex of examiner tests them first, it is not an ecologically representative model of normal assessment procedures.

The demonstration of experimenter effects on the subjects' performance on the WISC Arithmetic subtest, which should be relatively insensitive to extraneous variables, suggests that even greater experimenter effects may occur with measurement instruments that are more sensitive to the effects of extraneous variables.

The findings also suggest an answer to Brown's (1965) question as to why males score higher than females on quantitative tests, and why females score higher than males on verbal tests. The present results showing that females perform better on a quantitative test when tested by females refers to a testing situation; it may be that the factors that produced this result also influence the performance of subjects in a mathematical learning situation. It is possible that the greater proportion of male mathematics teachers and the greater proportion of female English teachers could be producing an educational artifact in our society which tends to produce superior quantitative ability in males and superior verbal ability in females. It may be that one way to develop females who are more competent in mathematics is to produce more female mathematics teachers. However, this possibility can be checked only through appropriate additional research.

REFERENCES

Bieri, J. Parental identification, acceptance of authority, and within-sex differences in cognitive behavior. *Journal of Abnormal and Social Psychology,* 1960, *60,* 76-79.

Bittner, A. C., & Shinedling, M. M. A methodological investigation of Piaget's concept of conservation of substance. *Genetic Psychology Monographs,* 1968, *77,* 135-165.

Brown, R. *Social psychology.* New York: Free Press of Glencoe, 1965.

Heilman, J. D. Sex differences in intellectual abilities. *Journal of Educational Psychology,* 1933, *24,* 47-65.

Jensen, V. H. *Tests and their use in counseling.* Provo, Utah: Brigham Young University Press, 1965.

Kuckenberg, K. G. Effect of early father absence on scholastic aptitude. Unpublished doctoral disertation, Harvard University, 1963.

Milton, G. A. The effects of sex-role identification upon problem-solving skill. *Journal of Abnormal and Social Psychology,* 1957, *55,* 208-212.

Myers, J. L. *Fundamentals of experimental design.* Boston: Allen & Bacon, 1966.

Rosenthal, R. Experimenter attributes as determinants of subjects' responses. *Journal of Projective Techniques,* 1963, *27,* 324-331.

Samuels, F. Sex differences in reading achievement. *Journal of Educational Research,* 1942, *36,* 594-603.

Sheffe, H. A. A method for judging all possible contrasts in the analysis of variance. *Biometrika,* 1953, *40,* 87-104.

Stevenson, H. W. Social reinforcement with children as a function of CA, sex of *E,* and sex of *S. Journal of Abnormal and Social Psychology,* 1961, *63,* 147-154.

Wechsler, D. *Wechsler Intelligence Scale for Children: Manual.* New York: Psychological Corporation, 1949.

26

*This study represents an attempt to determine what factors
account for the relatively poor problem-solving performance
of women. Hoffman and Maier have examined a number of
social variables, sex of examiner, motivation, and masculine
versus feminine versions of problems. They found that each
variable produced some effects on some problems. They
suggest that the sex variable in problem-solving performance
is a complex one, not subject to simple generalizations.
However, under certain conditions women performed as well
as men.*

*Hoffman and Maier indicate that female performance
improves under the influence of immediate situational
determinants such as the discussion of feelings about such
tests, the composition of the group, the feminization of the
content of problems. They suggest that the performance
differences between the sexes may stem from attitudes
developed over years of socialization and that it is
encouraging that the negative effect can be reduced even for
a short time by such simple manipulations.*

Social Factors Influencing Problem Solving in Women*

L. Richard Hoffman and Norman R. F. Maier

A series of experiments were carried out in an attempt to
determine why the problem-solving performance of
women is relatively poorer than that of men. The 9
problems used were rather simple, and each had a correct
answer. The following experimental variables were tested:

*From *Journal of Personality and Social Psychology*, 1966, 4 (4), 382-90.
Footnotes have been renumbered.

(a) sex of E, (b) added motivation, and (c) masculine vs. feminine versions of problems. The results showed that each variable influences the results on some problems. Male Es' attempts to motivate Ss were successful on some problems, whereas the same attempt by female Es had a detrimental effect. Under standard motivation, women tended to perform better when a female E conducted the test. The importance of feminine vs. masculine versions of the problem showed inconsistent results, and the conclusions of previous research were not supported. The results demonstrate that the sex variable in problem-solving performance is a complex one and is not subject to simple generalizations. Women may derive comfort from the fact that under certain conditions they performed as well as men. Since the factor crucial in 1 problem situation was found to be irrelevant even in another similar problem, the authors were unable to classify problems into types in which females were at a disadvantage.

One of the most consistent findings in the psychological literature is the inferiority of women's problem-solving performance, especially on problems of the arithmetic reasoning type (e.g., Carey, 1958; Maier, 1933). The conclusion often reached is that this inferiority is a genetic one.

Recently, however, considerable evidence has been accumulated to suggest that social factors, both of an immediate and a long-term nature, can affect women's problem-solving effectiveness. A series of related studies has shown a positive relationship between success and various measures of masculine "sex-role identification," that is, the degree of identification with the male role even among women (Berry, 1958, 1959; Carey, 1958; Milton, 1959). The more masculine the person's interests and attitudes are, the more able he (or she) is in problem solving. Although these attitudes probably arise during socialization, especially in adolescence when boys and girls are developing appropriate sex identities, the striking sex differences in scores on these measures may still be due to basic biological propensities. However, the fact that there is considerable variation within each sex, and this variation also correlates with problem-solving performance, tends to indicate that social factors are operating.

Even more striking are the instances of improved performance by women under the influence of immediate situational changes Carey (1958) improved women's scores on a problem-solving test by conducting discussions of their feelings about such activities. Milton (1959) found that women did better on problems with feminine rather than masculine content in which the underlying logic was identical. Hoffman and Maier (1961) discovered that women were more effective in mixed-sex groups than in all-female groups in solving the horse-trading problem. Thus, while women's generally negative attitude toward problem solving seems to restrict their problem-solving performance, their ability to solve problems successfully has been revealed under certain circumstances.

The present study was designed to examine experimentally some of the conditions under which women would be motivated to improve their performance as compared to the standard experimental conditions. The standard experimental procedure involves a male experimenter who administers a set of problems phrased in masculine terms (Milton, 1959) with the instruction, "Solve as many as you can." What can be varied to motivate women to higher achievement?

A direct attempt to induce achievement motivation was ruled out in two grounds: (a) the failures of several researchers to arouse achievement motivation in American college women (McClelland, Atkinson, Clark, & Lowell 1953), and (b) the fact that the achievement motive is less salient in young women than are nurturant and affiliative motives (Douvan & Adelson, 1965). The Douvan and Adelson reports suggest that women might be more willing to work at solving problems if such work were seen as instrumental to satisfying nurturant or affiliative motives. Therefore, a talk was prepared to appeal to these motives for use in one experimental variation.

The sex of the experimenter was also varied. The literature on personality development suggests that same-sex identification is the common pattern for both sexes (Douvan & Adelson, 1965). Therefore, while women can feel comfortable in rejecting problem-solving as a masculine activity when a man conducts the experiment, they might become more involved with a female experimenter. On the other hand, the talk designed to arouse motivation might have different effects depending on the sex of the source. Douvan and Adelson (1965) suggest that males are appropriate objects to satisfy nurturant and affiliative motives in women, but the effect of a woman's attempt to arouse such motives is not clear.

A third variable, the sexual content of the problem, was also used in part of the experiment. Milton's (1959) demonstration that women did better on problems with feminine content persuaded us to include this variable with the others in attempting to maximize the improvement we could generate in women's problem-solving effectiveness.

METHOD

General Procedure

Subjects met to solve problems in groups of about 10-20 of the same sex. The experimenter announced that this was to be an experiment on problem solving *and gave them the motivational talk.* The experimenter then passed out a booklet to each subject which contained the problems. Identification data were recorded on the front page. *With some additional words of encouragement* the experimenter informed the subjects that they had 1 minute to solve the horse-trading problem[1] (Maier & Solem, 1952), which appeared on the second page. After 1 minute had elapsed, *the experimenter again encouraged the subjects* and gave them another 2 minutes to work on the problem again. At the end of 2 minutes the experimenter announced that there were eight additional problems in the booklet which they would have 32 minutes to solve. Subjects were permitted to solve these problems in any order and to go back to unsolved ones if they wished, but they were not permitted to return to the horse-trading problem. *The experimenter again encouraged the subjects before starting this final part of the session.* The italicized parts of the procedure were omitted in the control condition. The session was terminated after 32 minutes, the experiment was explained to the subjects, and answers were provided for problems when subjects requested them.

Problems

The eight problems included in the booklets, in addition to the horse-trading problem already mentioned, were selected from those used by Milton (1959) as reported in his technical report of sex-role identification (Milton, 1958). Since we had allotted only 1 hour for the experiment, we chose only the arithmetic and logical reasoning problems:[2] numbers 3, 5, 7, 9, 11, 13, 15, and 19. Half the subjects were given the masculine versions of these problems

---

1. The problem is as follows: "A man bought a horse for $60, sold it for $70, bought it back for $80 and then sold it for $90. How much money did the man make in the horse business&"

2. There were 10 such problems, but we found from pretesting them that 2 had different logics in the masculine and feminine forms and were, thus, not comparable. The feminine form of a third pair also differed from its masculine version, but we modified it to make it comparable and included it in the set of problems used. Problem 7 had the following two forms: (masculine) A snail starts at the bottom of a well

and the other half, the feminine versions. Only the standard form of the horse-trading problem was given to all subjects.

Experimenters

Two male and two female psychologists conducted the sessions.[3] The female experimenters ran sessions only with female subjects.

Motivational Talk

The following text was used as the basis for the experimenters' motivational talk:

I know that as soon as I mention problem solving to a group of women, many of you immediately react negatively, some even violently. Problem solving, you feel, is a job for men, not for women.

The results of our research seem to show that this is the case, because men usually do a better job in solving problems than women do. However, we know that under certain conditions, women are perfectly capable of solving the problems I am about to give you.

So I have gone out on a limb with my fellow psychologists. I have decided to show them that women are as good as or better than men! We already know that women live longer than men, are healthier than men, are generally better students, get better scores on intelligence tests, but when it comes to problem solving, you just don't do as well.

I thought they had me on this until last year when we ran an experiment using these same problems. This was an experiment with groups of men and women. It showed that women in these groups with men were able to solve the problems as well as the men did and far better than the women in all-female groups. It wasn't just a case of the women getting answers from the men, either. They did it on their own.

Whenever somebody talks about solving problems, most of you

---

12 feet deep and crawls up 4 feet each day. Each night, however, the poor thing slips back 3 feet. How long will it take the snail to reach the top of the well? (feminine) Jane is trying to lose 12 pounds so that she may try on a new dress. By careful dieting she loses 4 pounds each week. Each weekend, however, the poor girl gains back 3 pounds. How long will it take before she can try on the dress?
In both cases the answer is 9 on the assumption that the subject achieves the goal before "slipping back."

3. Richard Schmuck, Edith Pelz, and Margaret Hoffeller performed ably as experimenters, in addition to the first author.

react negatively. How did you feel when I announced this was a problem-solving experiment? "Problem solving is for men. I just don't like to solve problems. It's boring." But you solve problems all the time. You just don't call them problems. You decide when a dress is a good buy for the money or when meat is a good buy in the food market. This is the kind of problem we have for you today.

What I need is your help in showing my doubting friends that even in problem solving you are as good if not better than men. The problems you are going to get are the same ones we used in last year's experiment, so I know you can do them. All I ask is that you give them your whole-hearted attention.

Help me prove that women are just as good as or better than men.

The experimenters delivered the talk essentially as written, but since they neither read nor memorized it, modifications were made in the words used. The experimenters role played to the talk before they conducted the sessions.

Subjects were offered encouragement between parts of the session in the form of brief statements which reminded them that the problems could be done, that they could help the experimenter show that women were as good as men at problem solving, and to take it easy. The experimenters said these things in a supportive manner.

Subjects

Seventy-three men and 243 women (students in introductory psychology courses) solved both the horse-trading problem and the set of eight reasoning problems. An additional 62 men and 124 women solved the horse-trading problem with male experimenters, the women under motivated and control conditions.

RESULTS

The results will be presented in two sections: the horse-trading problem, and the other eight reasoning problems. The reasons for separating the two sets of results are: (a) A body of data has accumulated on the horse-trading problem which has shown both consistent sex differences and the effects of social factors on women's performance (Hoffman & Maier, 1961; Maier & Solem, 1952); (b) the horse-trading problem was administered first and apart from the other eight problems; and (c) a "feminine" version of the problem was missing from this part of the experiment.

L. Richard Hoffman and Norman R. F. Maier

Horse-Trading Problem[4]

Table 1 shows the usual significant and substantially better performance of men than women on the problem under standard

TABLE 1

COMPARISONS OF MEN AND WOMEN SUBJECTS WITH MALE EXPERIMENTERS
ON THE HORSE-TRADING PROBLEM UNDER STANDARD CONDITIONS

Percentages of correct solutions on:			
1st administration (1 min.)		2nd administration (2 min.)	
Men ($N = 135$)	Women ($N = 154$)	Men ($N = 135$)	Women ($N = 154$)
43.7	25.3	57.8	26.0
$\chi^2 = 10.81, df = 1, p < .01$		$\chi^2 = 30.17, df = 1, p < .001$	
Percentages repeating correct solutions on 2nd administration		Percentages of changes from incorrect to correct solutions	
Men ($N = 59$)[a]	Women ($N = 39$)[a]	Men ($N = 76$)[b]	Women ($N = 115$)[b]
96.6	74.4	27.6	9.6
$\chi^2 = 10.70, df = 1, p < .01$		$\chi^2 = 10.80, df = 1, p < .01$	

[a] N = number of subjects with correct initial solutions.
[b] N = number of subjects with incorrect initial solutions.

conditions. A significantly ($p < .01$) higher proportion of men than women (a) solved the problem correctly on both administrations, (b) answered correctly the second time if they were correct the first time, and (c) changed from an incorrect to a correct answer on the second administration. Thus, under the standard conditions with a male experimenter, men were more successful in solving this problem than were women.

Tables 2 and 3 show the effects on the proportions of correct answers for female subjects with sex of the experimenter varied under control and motivated conditions.[5] The only significant effect ($p < .02$) after the first minute (Table 2) was the better performance of women with female experimenters. The 35.0% of female subjects (combined control and motivated groups) under female experimenters who solved the problem correctly is not

---

4. The data from subjects who solved the horse-trading problem, but not the other eight problems, are included in these analyses, since the method of administration and the pattern of results were the same as for the other subjects. The larger N provides more stable estimates of the percentages obtained.

5. Although we cannot be certain that all subjects who received the motivational talk were appropriately motivated nor that control subjects were not motivated, we shall refer to the subjects who received the talk as "motivated."

423

significantly less than the 43.7% of correct male subjects (x^2 = 2.63, df = 1, p < .10, cf. Table 1). The motivational attempt, whether given by male or female experimenters, had no effect on performance.

On the second administration of the problem (after an additional 2 minutes), however, the effects of the motivational talk became evident, but in interaction with the sex of the experimenter who gave it (see Table 3). Male experimenters' motivational attempts succeeded in improving the percentage of correct solutions, compared to the control subjects (40.0% versus 26.0%), while the talk by the female experimenters appears to have had a negative impact on their subjects (33.7% versus 53.5%). Again, under control conditions, women with female experimenters did significantly better than they did with male experimenters (53.5% versus 26.0%) and about as well as the men (57.8%).

The interaction of the motivational conditions with the sex of the experimenter also appears in both analyses of the changes from the first to the second answers to the problem. With male experimenters a *higher* percentage of motivated than control subjects retained the correct solution once they had it (88.0% versus 74.4%) or changed from an incorrect to a correct answer (25.0% versus 9.6%). In contrast, with female experimenters a *smaller* percentage of motivated subjects than control retained the correct

TABLE 2

CORRECT SOLUTIONS BY FEMALE SUBJECTS WITH MALE
AND FEMALE EXPERIMENTERS UNDER TWO
MOTIVATIONAL CONDITIONS
(HORSE-TRADING PROBLEM: FIRST ADMINISTRATION)

Control female Ss		Motivated female Ss	
Male Es (N = 154)	Female Es (N = 99)	Male Es (N = 110)	Female Es (N = 104)
25.3%	39.4%	22.7%	30.8%

Partition of χ^2

Comparison	χ^2
Total	12.09*
Motivation (M) $\times$ Correct (C)	1.00
E Sex (E) $\times$ C	6.41*
M $\times$ E[a]	4.25
M $\times$ E $\times$ C	0.43

[a] The significance of this comparison (p < .05) is a chance artifact of the disproportionate assignment of subjects to conditions with different experimenters.
* p < .02, df's = 4, 1.

initial solution (78.1% versus 92.3%) or changed from incorrect to correct solutions (13.9% versus 28.3%).

Thus, both the change from male experimenter to female experimenter and the motivational attempt by male experimenters resulted in an improvement in women's performance compared to the standard conditions. Furthermore, the improvement resulting from the female experimenter produced performance equal to the men. The attempt by the female experimenters to motivate the women, however, failed to produce any overall improvement from the first to the second administration. In fact, the possibility that the talk had an unsettling effect is suggested by the relatively high percentage of women (21.9%) who abandoned their initially correct answers for incorrect ones.

Eight Reasoning Problems

Table 4 compares the mean number of "masculine" problems solved correctly by men and women under control conditions with male experimenters. Both an analysis of variance of the raw scores and an analysis of covariance, with mathematical aptitude scores as the covariate,[6] are shown.

TABLE 3

Correct Solutions by Female Subjects with Male and Female Experimenters under Two Motivational Conditions (Horse-Trading Problem: Second Administration)

Control female Ss		Motivated female Ss	
Male Es ($N = 154$)	Female Es ($N = 99$)	Male Es ($N = 110$)	Female Es ($N = 104$)
26.0%	53.5%	40.0%	33.7%

Partition of χ^2	
	χ^2
Comparison	
Total	20.15***
Motivation (M) $\times$ Correct (C)	0.00
E Sex (E) $\times$ C	6.62*
M $\times$ E[a]	4.25
M $\times$ E $\times$ C	9.28**

[a] The significance of this comparison ($p < .05$) is a chance artifact of the disproportionate assignment of subjects to conditions with different experimenters.
* $p < .02$, $df = 1$.
** $p < .01$, $df = 1$.
*** $p < .001$, $df = 4$.

---

6. All subjects had taken either the Graduate Record Examination or the

TABLE 4

CORRECT SOLUTIONS BY MEN AND WOMEN UNDER
CONTROL CONDITIONS WITH MALE EXPERIMENTERS
(EIGHT REASONING PROBLEMS, MASCULINE VERSIONS)

	Men (N = 35)	Women (N = 30)
Mean number solved	4.6	3.0
SD	1.90	1.91
Adjusted M[a]	4.0	3.1

Analysis of variance

Source	MS	F
Sex of S	41.35	12.16**
Error	3.40	

Analysis of covariance[a]

Source	MS	F
Sex of S	9.21	3.61
Error	2.55	

[a] Mathematical aptitude standard scores used as covariate and to adjust mean number correct. Regression estimate based on total sample.
** $p < .01$, $df = 1$.

The analysis of variance shows a significant difference ($p < .01$) between the sexes, favoring the men. When mathematical aptitude was controlled, however, the value of F was reduced below the .05 level of significance. The difference still favored the men, so there is room for improvement in the women's performance.

The results of the three-factor (sex of experimenter, motivation, problem content) attempt to improve the women's performance are shown in Table 5.

Although there is some suggestion in the analyses of variance and covariance of differences produced by the experimental variables, none of the F tests was significant at the .05 level. Overall there was little effect of the experimental variables and, certainly, no replication of the pattern of results shown for the horse-trading problem.

The most disappointing result was the failure to replicate Milton's (1959) finding that women did better on problems with

American Council on Education Test of Intelligence. The Mathematical and Quantitative scores, respectively, on these examinations were then converted, using University of Michigan norms, to standard scores, which served as covariate. Mathematical aptitude correlated .55 (p .01) with the number of problems solved correctly for the total sample. Male subjects had significantly higher mathematical aptitude scores than female subjects.

TABLE 5
CORRECT SOLUTIONS BY WOMEN TO EIGHT REASONING PROBLEMS

	Male Es (N = 30)				Female Es (N = 45)			
	Control		Motivated		Control		Motivated	
	Masculine version of problems	Feminine version of problems	Masculine version of problems	Feminine version of problems	Masculine version of problems	Feminine version of problems	Masculine version of problems	Feminine version of problems
M	3.0	2.6	2.8	3.6	3.0	3.0	3.1	3.0
SD	1.91	1.48	1.40	1.30	1.60	1.72	1.58	1.82
Adjusted M[a]	3.1	2.8	3.0	3.2	3.4	2.9	2.9	3.0

	Analysis of variance		Analysis of covariance[a]	
Source	MS	F	MS	F
Sex of E (E)	0.12		2.45	1.35
Motivation (M)	3.21	1.22	1.55	3.13
Problem content (P)	0.17		5.69	
E × M	1.85		0.40	
E × P	1.16		1.66	
E × M × P	7.76	2.94	0.84	
Error	2.64		1.82	

Note.—No F is significant at the .05 level. Ns were randomly reduced to permit the 3-factor analysis of variance.
[a] See footnote a, Table 4.

feminine than with masculine content. The analysis of covariance suggests, further, that they did less well on the feminine problems ($p < .10$) when mathematical aptitude was controlled. Furthermore, Table 6 shows that the men, too, found the feminine problems more difficult than the masculine ones ($p < .05$). Their performance on the feminine problems was reduced to the level of the women's performance on the masculine problems, but was slightly better ($p < .10$) than the women's performance on the feminine problems.

Although the overall results on the eight reasoning problems showed no effect of the experimental conditions, chi-square analyses were performed on each problem separately. These showed a variety of patterns of effects with no apparent underlying factor. Only one problem (Number 19) showed the same effects as the horse-trading problem, and two problems (Numbers 7 and 9) accounted for the greater difficulty of the feminine versions of the problems. Moreover, even the sex differences were not uniform. A significantly higher percentage of correct solutions by men than women occurred on only three problems, and on one problem the reverse was true.

DISCUSSION

The overall results of this experiment are, to say the least, confusing. The findings on the horse-trading problem support the thesis that a variety of social factors in the standard experimental situation tend to inhibit women's performance. Either a change from a male to a female experimenter or an appeal for help by a male experimenter would appear to arouse motives to stimulate effective performance, while the standard situation arouses motives which produce inferior performance. The same appeal from a female experimenter, however, has apparently little effect or even, in contrast to her mere presence, an actively inhibiting effect (cf. Table 3). The consistency of these results for both experimenters of each sex and their close approximation to results obtained in previous experiments (e.g., Hoffman & Maier, 1961) encourage us to believe that this experimental attempt to improve women's problem solving was successful. We therefore are tempted to suggest possible theoretical interpretations of the way the experimental variations affected the women's motivation.

Women's typically inferior performance on the horse-trading problem appears to be more a function of inappropriate motivation than lack of ability. The conditions of the standard experimental situation promote motivation to inhibit the full expression of true

TABLE 6

CORRECT SOLUTIONS BY MEN AND WOMEN TO EIGHT REASONING PROBLEMS
(MALE EXPERIMENTERS, CONTROL CONDITION ONLY)

	Male Ss		Female Ss	
	1	2	3	4
	Masculine version of problems ($N = 35$)	Feminine version of problems ($N = 35$)	Masculine version of problems ($N = 30$)	Feminine version of problems ($N = 35$)
Mean number solved	4.6	3.6	3.0	2.6
SD	1.90	1.73	1.91	1.42
Adjusted M^a	4.0	3.3	3.1	2.8

Analyses of variance

Source	1 vs. 2		2 vs. 3		2 vs. 4	
	MS	F	MS	F	MS	F
Treatment	18.52	7.38**	6.38	1.93	16.52	5.33**
Error	2.51		3.30		3.10	

Analyses of covariance

Source	1 vs. 2		2 vs. 3		2 vs. 4	
	MS	F	MS	F	MS	F
Treatment	9.03	4.61*	0.83	<1	8.35	3.44
Error	1.96		2.38		2.43	

a See footnote a, Table 4.
* $p < .05$, $df = 1$.
** $p < .01$, $df = 1$.

ability. The male experimenter's request to achieve in a masculine activity produces a conflict in women between conforming to authority and being feminine. Both the tone of delivery and the content of our experimental talk were designed specifically to make successful problem solving instrumental to the satisfaction of aroused nurturant and affiliative motives. If this attempt was successful, we suggest that the male experimenter's request for help resolves the conflict between the masculine problem-solving activity and being feminine, thus freeing the female subjects for more effective performance. Similarly, when the experimenter is a female, the problem-solving activity becomes feminine through identification, and no conflict is created to interfere with effective problem solving. When the female experimenter asks for help, however, a new conflict is established between affiliative motives and nurturant motives toward an inappropriate object, which conflict has an inhibiting effect.

A plausible alternative interpretation is possible if we consider the impact of the talk by male experimenters to have reduced the women's fear of failure by suggesting that they can solve the problems. The standard approach of the female experimenters could have the same consequences. Furthermore, the negative effects of the female experimenter's talk could be due to a further arousal of such fears. Some negative evidence on this point was obtained from a small sample of subjects with male experimenters in a lack of difference on the Alpert-Haber Achievement Anxiety Test between motivated and control conditions. However, since these data were not collected on the total sample, the results cannot be considered conclusive.

When, however, we consider the results for the set of eight reasoning problems, we find that they offer essentially negative evidence for the importance of social factors in female problem solving and raise questions about any simple interpretation. Furthermore, when the results for each of these problems separately are compared across conditions (as with the horse-trading problem), we find a variety of patterns emerging. One problem confirmed the horse-trading problem;other problems varied only according to the sex content of the problems; still others showed no differences at all, even between male and female subjects. In addition, no similarities were apparent in the types of problems (insight versus deductive or hard versus easy) or in the particular content of problems which showed similar patterns of results.

Thus, we may ask, "What explanation is there for these conflicting results?" Were the social factors effective only for the first 3 minutes in overcoming the women's negative attitudes, but then lost their force with the break in procedure between the horse-trading problem and the other eight problems? Since these attitudes were developed during 18 or more years of socialization, perhaps we should feel encouraged that we were able to reduce their negative effect even for such a short period.

Are these social factors important only for problems like the horse-trading problem, which require insight? This explanation seems unlikely, since a number of the other problems also require insight, but were not similarly affected by the experimental procedures.

Did the initial concentration on the horse-trading problem help to focus the impact of the experimental variations, which became more diffuse with a much longer time period? The latter method of administering the problems may also have encouraged the women to settle for the more obvious answers on the insight problems in order to conserve time for problems which they felt would take longer.

A last possibility, yet certainly a real one, is that the results for the horse-trading problem were merely fortuitous. We tend to reject this possibility in the light of the consistency of these results across the several experimenters and across the number of sessions conducted at different times.

Rather, we feel that the results of the present experiment are important in their demonstration of the complexity of problem-solving phenomena. Both the horse-trading problem and the set of eight reasoning problems have been employed in a variety of previous studies in which relationships with the subject's sex and/or with noncognitive factors in the subject have been demonstrated. The fact that when used in the same experiment the problems produced contrasting results indicates the need for caution in generalizing about sex differences in problem solving. The above list of possible explanations for the present results points to some of the variables which require more precise experimentalization to determine their separate and interactive effects. It is apparent that problem-solving performance in women is influenced by a number of variables, but only some of these operate for a given problem situation.

REFERENCES

Berry, P. C. an exploration of the interrelations among some nonintellectual predictors of achievement in problem solving. Technical Report No. 4, 1958, Yale University, Departments of Industrial Administration and Psychology, Contract Nonr 609-20, Office of Naval Research.

— — —. A second exploration of the interrelations among some nonintellectual predictors of achievement in problem solving. Technical Report No. 5, Yale University, 1959, Departments of Industrial Administration and Psychology, Contract Nonr 609-20, Office of Naval Research.

Carey, G. L. Sex differences in problem-solving performance as a function of attitude differences. *Journal of Abnormal and Social Psychology,* 1958, *56*, 256-260.

Douvan, E., & Adelson, J. B. *The adolescent experience.* New York: Wiley, 1965.

Hoffman, L. R., & Maier, N. R. F. Sex differences, sex composition, and group problem solving. *Journal of Abnormal and Social Psychology,* 1961, *63*, 453-456.

Maier, N. R. F. An aspect of human reasoning. *British Journal of Psychology,* 1933, *24*, 144-155.

Maier, N. R. F., & Solem, A. R. The contribution of a discussion leader to the quality of group thinking: The effective use of minority opinions. *Human Relations,* 1952, *5*, 277-288.

McClelland, D. C., Atkinson, J. W., Clark, R. A., & Lowell, E. L. *The achievement motive.* New York: Appleton-Century-Crofts, 1953.

Milton, G. A. Five studies of the relation between sex-role identification and achievement in problem solving. Technical Report No. 3, 1958, Yale University, Departments of Industrial Administration and Psychology, Contract Nonr 609-20, Office of Naval Research.

— — —. Sex differences in problem solving as a function of role appropriateness of the problem content. *Psychological Reports,* 1959, *5*, 705-708.

SUGGESTED PAPERS AND PROJECTS

Papers

1. Sex differences in cognitive function: nature vs. nurture.
2. Sex differences in language development: nature vs. nurture.
3. Sex differences as measured by intelligence tests.
4. The effect of the sex of the tester on psychological measurement.

Projects

1. Compute grade point averages separately for all courses taken with male professors as compared to female professors.
2. Spend a half hour each with a mother of a female and a mother of a male infant. Keep track of the time each mother spends talking to each child.
3. On a scale of 1 to 10 rank how anxious you are before taking an exam. Note sex differences in admitted anxiety. (Does the admission of anxiety demonstrate anxiety?)
4. Visit classes for children with learning disabilities. What sorts of impairments are found and what are their sex ratios?

ADDITIONAL REFERENCES

Dawson, J. L. M. Effects of sex hormones on cognitive style in rats and men. *Behavior Genetics,* 1972, *2*, 21-42.

Exline, R. Effects of need for affiliation, sex and the sight of others upon initial communications in problem solving groups. *Journal of Personality,* 1962, *30*, 541-56.

Hoffman, L. R., and Maier, N. R. F. Sex differences, sex composition and group problem solving. *Journal of Abnormal and Social Psychology,* 1961, *63*, 453-56.

Karabenick, S. Effect of sex of competitor on the performance of females following success. Paper presented at the 80th annual convention of the American Psychology Association, Honolulu, September 1972.

Koenig, F., Sulzer, J. L., and Hansche, W. J. Mother's mode of discipline and children's verbal ability. *Child Study Journal,* 1971, *2*, 19-22.

Lansdell, H., and Davie, J. C. Massa intermedia: Possible relation to intelligence. *Neuropsychologia,* 1972, *10*, 207-210.

Young, M. L. Age and sex differences in problem solving. *Journal of Gerontology,* 1971, *26*, 330-36.

Section V

Is There Psychosexual Neutrality at Birth?

27 Introduction

Is there psychosexual neutrality at birth? Or do potential or actual differences in behavior attributable to differences in genetic sex exist? When and how do such differences arise? Do differences between "male" and "female" nervous systems exist before environmental influences begin to exert their differential effects upon the two sexes?

There are a number of areas of investigation which are attempting to resolve the issues related to psychosexual development. These areas of investigation are: (1) injections of sex hormones or elimination of glandular structures in rats, guinea pigs, and monkeys before or just after birth; (2) clinical evaluation of humans with varying kinds of sexual disturbances in chromosomal makeup, gonadal structure, gonadal physiology, or psychological functioning; (3) observational studies of primate parent-child interactions from birth onward; (4) experimental studies of very young humans while they are still in a neutral hospital environment. The manner by which the data are obtained seems to determine to some extent the position that investigators take on the question of how much psychosexual differentiation exists at birth.

The position of many students of animal behavior (Young, Goy, and Phoenix, 1964; Harris, 1964; Levine, 1966; Diamond, 1968; Goy, 1970) may be summarized as follows. Experimental studies of hormone injections before or just after birth in a variety of species tend to indicate that androgen (the male sex hormone) present during a critical period of development (the timing of which varies with the species) directs the previously neutral or feminine central nervous system toward maleness. If no androgen is present during the critical period, the central nervous system becomes or remains female irrespective of the genetic sex of the organism. Reproductive behaviors are not the only behaviors affected by hormonal treatment. Sex differences in levels of activity, play behavior, and aggression are often found even in early childhood when measurements reveal. no differences in the kinds of or amounts of hormones circulating in the bloodstream. Thus the effects of prenatal or neonatal hormonal manipulation cannot be explained solely as an alteration in sensitivity of neural tissues to hormonal activation.

Distinctions between the sexes in terms of behavior are purely quantitative. No one has ever been able to agree upon a behavior that is unique to one sex or the other. The action of hormones on the developing nervous system is viewed as predetermining the levels of those behaviors that are considered to be sexually dimorphic, e.g., characteristic of either males or females.

One of the principal differences between male and female mammals is that females have a cyclic pattern of hormone release while males have a continuous release system. Although gonadal hormone release appears to be under the control of the pituitary, the "master gland" itself is not sexually differentiated. Pituitaries transplanted from males to females and vice versa regulate the sexual system of the animals to which they are transplanted in a perfectly normal manner; e.g., the pituitary from a male rat produces cyclic activity in a female. Whether a mammal will show a male or a female pattern seems to be determined by some characteristic of the central nervous system itself, possibly by centers in the hypothalamus.

Gonadal and neural sex may be independent in some organisms. The critical period for neural differentiation appears to be later than that for gonadal differentiation. Experimeters have produced chromosomal and morphological males (XY males with external male genitalia) who show female reproductive behavior such as lordosis (presentation of the genital area to the male) after being primed with female hormone at puberty. These males, who have been deprived of fetal androgen by castration before the critical period of neural differentiation, never show male behavior despite huge doses of male hormone at puberty. Chromosomal and morphological females, masculinized by doses of androgen during the critical period, will show complete male patterns of reproductive behavior after priming with male hormones at puberty. Male and female mammals not exposed to the hormones of the opposite sex during fetal life may show suppression of their normal sexual behavior if given huge doses of such hormones at puberty, but never complete reversal to the behavior of the opposite sex. Hormonal injection during the critical period of neural differentiation may also produce patterns of activity and social behavior characteristic of the sex opposite to that indicated by the makeup of the sex chromosomes.

Goy (1970) presents a review of his and others' recent findings on the way the hormones that are present during critical periods of development affect psychosexual differentiation. He asserts that nothing from either clinical human or experimental animal research contradicts the view that the female form and psychosexual orientation can develop in the absence of hormonal influences from the gonads. The hormones secreted by the fetal and neonatal ovary do not appear to be essential to the development of fairly complete sexual responsiveness.

Recent research indicates, on the other hand, that the male form and psychosexual orientation is dependent upon the presence of androgens during a critical period of development. The fact that "something must be added" to produce a male may account for the much larger percentage of defects in morphology and gender identity found in genetic males than in genetic females.

Goy's own research indicates that social behaviors that have no obvious relationship to reproduction, such as play and threat behaviors, are affected in masculinized female monkeys. He suggests that early hormonal influences predispose an individual to the acquisition of specific patterns of behavior and that neuronal structures that are not dependent upon the activational properties of hormones appear to be involved in the acquisition and maintenance of masculine social behavior.

Much information about psychosexual development has been derived from clinical observations of individuals with sexual abnormalities of varying kinds. These individuals manifest some degree of sexual ambiguity and are neither wholly male nor wholly female. They may differ from the "norm" in terms of (1) chromosomal sex—missing or excessive numbers of sex chromosomes; (2) gonadal sex—atrophied or ambiguous gonadal structures; (3) hormonal sex—usually excessive amounts of androgens; (4) external genital structure—sex organs that at birth appear to be of the sex opposite to that of the internal reproductive organs; (5) psychosexual identification—preference for or adoption of a sex role opposite to that of their own sex, or homosexuality.

The position of students of human sexual disturbances (Money, Hampson, and Hampson, 1957; Money, 1970; Money, 1971) may be summarized as follows. Potentialities for both male and female psychosexual identity and behavior exist in the human brain. Whatever may be the possible unlearned assistance from constitutional sources, the child's psychosexual identity is not written, unlearned, in the genetic code, the hormonal system, or the nervous system at birth. The child usually becomes conditioned to adhere to a model congruent with his or her anatomy at an early age—perhaps as young as the age of three. Under abnormal conditions, however, where there may be disagreement between internal and external sexual determinants, it is the sex of assignment and rearing that usually determines psychosexual identity.

Much research has been done on individuals with excessive

numbers of X chromosomes (XXY: Klinefelter's syndrome) or a reduced number of X chromosomes (XO: Turner's syndrome). Research is beginning to appear on individuals with an XYY gentic constitution. Generalizations from such individuals is difficult because they show an increased frequency of retardation, mental illness, and physical pathologies in addition to their sexual disturbances. However, investigators find that some individuals with Klinefelter's syndrome do not show increased feminization of psychosexual identity although there appears to be a weakening of masculine orientation in comparison to males with a normal XY complement. Individuals with Turner's syndrome show greater feminization of psychosexual identity than normal females. Money and Mittenthal (1970) hypothesize that this very complete feminine gender identity may be due to the fact that there is no gonadal development at all, and therefore no malelike hormonal effects upon the developing brain.

Another clinical source of data is the genetic female who suffers from an excessive amount of prenatal androgen due to adrenal hyperactivity or exposure during fetal life to an androgen-like drug. Such females are often born with external genitalia that appear male. When this condition is recognized at birth and the necessary hormonal and surgical corrections are immediately instituted, psychosexual identity still remains more like that of the opposite sex. The incidence of "tomboyism" is much higher than for control groups. There appears to be some residual effect of the male hormone on the developing brain. However, most of these individuals accept themselves as female if this is the sex of original assignment and rearing.

Money and his associates feel that convincing evidence of the power of social influences on gender identity comes from congenital hermaphrodites with the same degree of hermaphroditism, but with different sexes of assignment. Psychosexual differentiation takes place in accordance with the sex of assignment and rearing. Requests for sex reassignment are rare (Money, 1970). Money (1971, asserts that the conformity of most human hermaphrodites to their early sex of assignment is such that it can withstand even ugly virilization in a "girl" at puberty or breast development and erectile inadequacy in a "boy."

Money (1971, 1972) no longer holds a neutrality-at-birth theory, but feels that gender identity is the end product of a sequence of bipotential events. Bipotentiality is present in the chromosomes (XX or XY), in the fetal gonads (ovary or testes), in the external genitalia, and in the developing nervous system. At the beginning of each stage, the course of development can take a male or female path, but not after the critical period has ended. The vestiges of the sequence not developed may remain within the organism. For example, Fisher (1956) has been able to elicit both maternal and mounting behavior in the male rat by injecting small amounts of testosterone into the hypothalamus. Animals treated with anti-androgens during fetal life are capable of behaving as either normal males or females, depending upon the sex hormone then present in the bloodstream (Money and Ehrhardt, 1971).

Bipotentiality is probably resolved in favor of unipolar masculinity if androgens are present during the critical period of development. Feminine components of behavior are inhibited. However, the completeness of inhibition of female behavioral potential probably decreases as one ascends the phylogenetic scale. Money feels that the genetic code does not exhaustively program gender for human beings.

There are many problems in contrasting theoretical positions that stress a "nature vs. nurture" basis for psychosexual differentiation. Such a dichotomy is oversimplistic for this issue. Researchers who study human beings and those who study animals differ mainly in the weight they accord to experiential vs. hormonal influences. There is probably an interaction of congenital and social factors. A critical article by Diamond (1965) has pointed out some of the difficulties. (1) These theoretical positions have been derived from different methods of investigation on different organisms. (2) A demonstration that human beings are flexible in their psychosexual identification does not disprove the possibility that a "built-in" bias exists which may be overcome. (3) We are dealing with an interaction of genetic and experiential components, the relative contribution of which may vary with the particular behavior pattern and organism observed.

Unfortunately, Diamond's paper criticizes a theoretical position — psychosexual neutrality — which is no longer widely held. Nevertheless, he makes some major points that are worth reiterating. For example, he points out that the demonstration that hermaphroditic humans are flexible in their psychosexual orientation does not indicate that this is true for normal humans. "Acquiescence to a malassigned sex role does not by itself constitute 'correctness' of assignment" (Diamond, 1968).

One of the great problems in comparing theoretical positions on psychosexual differentiation is the great stress advocates of both physiological and environmental oriented theories place on clinical studies. One facet of the problem is that researchers of different theoretical positions agree neither on the clinical evidence nor on the interpretations that can be made from the data they do agree upon. A more general facet of the problem is the nature of clinical material. In general, individuals do not appear for treatment unless there is "something wrong with them." Thus we have no information on the number of individuals in the general population with the same physiological deficits who are functioning in a "normal" manner. One example of this lack of control data is the relatively high incidence of individuals with XYY chromosomal abnormalities found in the "normal" population after this abnormality became known.

The question of whether the central nervous system is "sexed" at birth is particularly interesting with reference to findings that show that psychosexual identity affects many behaviors in addition to those that directly involve reproduction. Sex differences have been reported in activity levels in rats (Levine, 1966), guinea pigs (Young, Goy, and Phoenix, 1964), primates (Mitchell, 1968; Goy, 1970) and humans (Pedersen and Bell, 1970). Male mammals show greater amounts of aggression as well as greater levels of activity than females. Newborn human females are found to be more responsive to sweet tastes and less willing to exert effort to obtain food than males (Nisbett and Gurwitz, 1970). In general, very young human females are more sensitive to environmental stimuli than males (Bell and Darling, 1965), while males show higher levels of motor activity, crying, and wakefulness.

It is possible that parental reactions to such early behavioral differences reinforce and amplify innate sexual differences. Observational studies of infant-mother interactions in primates (Mitchell, 1968; Mitchell and Brandt, 1970) may provide a model for the effect of the early environment upon the psychosexual differentiation of humans. Such studies indicate that female monkeys have more physical contact with their female young and restrain them more often than their male young. They played more frequently with their male young and withdrew from them more than from their female young. The higher activity and aggression levels of the male infants (they bit their mothers much more frequently than female infants) may have in part accounted for the decreased amount of maternal contact. Conversely, the decreased restraints and increased withdrawals of the mother may have promoted independence in the males. Bell (1968) has suggested that there are congenital differences in the behavior of human infants which may lead to differences in parental treatment. Mons (1967) has shown that male infants are more irritable than female infants and that by the twelfth week of life, mothers provided less social stimulation for male than for female infants. These data are correlational in nature. As far as we know, no careful studies have been done to determine whether an infant's irritability, regardless of sex, actually leads to decreased maternal contact.

Despite what appears to be overwhelming evidence of the

predisposition of psychosexual characteristics, there are considerable data that indicate that the environment plays a role in gender determination even in lower animals. Money and Ehrhardt (1971) have reviewed a large number of animal studies involving hormonal manipulations and, as might be expected from their theoretical position, cite a number of studies showing that sex-characteristic behavior such as aggression is sensitive to environmental effects for a long postnatal period. Ward (1972) has shown that prenatal stress can produce feminization of male rats. It has long been known (Rosenblatt and Aronson, 1958) that the effect of castration upon the sexual behavior of adult male cats depends upon the amount of sexual experience they have had previous to the operation.

Ramey (1972) gives a clear warning on the dangers of extrapolating from animal studies to human behavior. "Species differences are often profound and at the level of psychosexual responses, the extraordinary preeminence of the human neocortex makes a hash of the simplistic conclusions of many ethologists and anthropologists" (Ramey, 1972). The extent to which the neocortex is involved in sexual behavior is not clear even in lower mammals. It appears to be more important for male sexual behavior than for female and to increase in importance as one ascends the phylogenetic scale (Beach, 1947). Conversely, dependence on hormonal control may decrease. These generalizations hold only for the physical and perhaps the sensory aspects of reproductive behavior.

Little is known about neocortical involvement in sex-characteristic but nonreproductive behaviors or in gender identity. It is possible that genetic-endocrine-experiential contributions will be found to be species-specific, sex-specific, and even behavior-specific. The same behaviors may have different etiologies in different species or for the two sexes in the same species.

While there is yet no final answer to the problem of the origin of psychosexual differences between the sexes, the data seem to indicate that prenatal exposure to sex hormones in the course of fetal development produces characteristic behavioral predispositions in all mammals. Influences are not limited to effects upon sexual behavior in adulthood. However, despite the potentiating effect of androgen upon the central nervous system, human psychosexual identity and sexually dimorphic behaviors may be very plastic and may be molded and even reversed by social influences during early childhood.

Lastly, it must be stressed again that "male" and "female" behaviors, especially in higher primates, show a great deal of overlap. Unfortunately, the similarities between the sexes are less interesting to most investigators than the differences. The controversy about the nature of sex differences is similar in some ways to the ongoing controversy about the innate vs. environmental determinants of intelligence. For both issues, one can only reiterate that individual behavior cannot be predicted on the basis of group performance, whatever its etiology. The social roles of men and women must be related to individual needs — not to membership in a particular racial or sexual caste.

REFERENCES

Beach, F. A. A review of physiological and psychological studies of sexual behavior in mammals. *Physiological Review,* 1947, *27,* 240-307.

Bell,R.Q.A reinterpretation of the direction of effects in studies of socialization. *Psychological Review,* 1968, *75,* 81-95.

— — — and Darling, J. The prone head reaction in the human newborn: relationship with sex and tactile sensitivity. *Child Development,* 1965, *36,* 943-49.

Diamond, M. A critical evaluation of the ontogeny of human sexual behavior. *Quarterly Review of Biology,* 1965, *40,* 147-75.

— — —. Genetic-endocrine interactions and human psychosexuality. In M. Diamond (Ed.), *Perspectives in reproduction and sexual behavior.* Bloomington: Indiana University Press, 1968.

Fisher, A. E. Maternal and sexual behavior induced by intracranial chemical stimulation. *Science,* 1956, *124,* 228-29.

Goy, R. W. Early hormonal influences on the development of sexual and sex related behavior. In F. O. Schmitt (Ed.), *The neurosciences: second study program.* New York: Rockefeller University Press, 1970.

Harris, G. W. Sex hormones, brain development and brain function. *Endocrinology,* 1964, *75,* 627-48.

Levine, S. Sex differences in the brain. *Scientific American,* 1966, *214,* 84-90.

Mitchell, G. D. Attachment differences in male and female infant monkeys. *Child Development,* 1968, *39,* 611-20.

— — —, & Brandt, E. M. Behavioral differences related to experience of mother and sex of infant in the rhesus monkey. *Developmental Psychology,* 1970, *3,* 149.

Money, J. Sexual dimorphism and homosexual gender identity. *Psychological Bulletin, 1970, 74, 425-40.*

— — —. Sexually dimorphic behavior, normal and abnormal. In N. Kretchmer and D. N. Walcher (Eds.), *Environmental influences on genetic expression.* Washington, D.C.: U.S. Government Printing Office, 1971.

— — —. Determinants of human sexual identity and behavior. In C. J. Sager and H. S. Kaplan (Eds.), *Progress in group and family therapy.* New York: Brunner Mazel Publishers, 1972.

445

— — — and Ehrhardt, A. A. Fetal hormones and the brain: Effect on sexual dimorphism of behavior—a review. *Archives of Sexual Behavior,* 1971, *1,* 241-62.

— — —, Hampson, J. G., and Hampson, J. L. Imprinting and the establishment of gender role. *Archives of Neurology and Psychiatry,* 1957, *77,* 333-36.

— — — and Mittenthal, S. Lack of personality pathology in Turner's syndrome: Relation to cytogenetics, hormones and physique. *Behavior Genetics,* 1970, *1,* 43-56.

Mons, H. A. Sex, age, and stage as determinants of mother-infant interaction. *Merrill-Palmer Quarterly,* 1967, *13,* 19-36.

Nisbett, R. E., and Gurwitz, S. B. Weight, sex and the eating behavior of human newborns. *Journal of Comparative and Physiological Psychology,* 1970, *73,* 245-53.

Pedersen, F. A., and Bell, R. Q. Sex differences in preschool children without histories of complications of pregnancy and delivery. *Developmental Psychology,* 1970, *3,* 10-15.

Ramey, E. R. Sex hormones and executive ability: The successful woman. Symposium presented at the New York Academy of Sciences, New York, May 1972.

Rosenblatt, J. S., and Aronson, L. R. The decline of sexual behavior in male cats after castration with special reference to the role of prior sexual experience. *Behavior,* 1958, *12,* 285-338.

Ward, I. Prenatal stress feminizes and demasculinizes the behavior of males. *Science,* 1972, *175,* 82-84.

Young, W. C.; Goy, R. W.; and Phoenix, C. H. Hormones and sexual behavior. *Science,* 1964, *143,* 212-18.

28

This paper provides an up-to-date review of the findings in this area. The author is one of the researchers who pioneered the experimental studies on prenatal and neonatal hormonal effects upon sexual behavior. In 1964, Goy collaborated with Young and Phoenix on a survey article in Science entitled "Hormones and Sexual Behavior," which has been considered a landmark in the field. In his more recent article, included in this volume,.he summarizes some of the recent literature on human psychosexual development as well as findings from animal studies.

Goy has organized the somewhat confusing mass of research findings into two major categories. [1] Experimental approaches to the anhormonal case discusses the process of sexual development when the amount of fetal or neonatal androgen is reduced either by castration at birth or by a genetically based lack of cellular response to male hormones [testicular feminization]. Such interference tends to produce defective or absent male behavior. [2] Contributions of testicular hormones to development of behaviors characteristic of the male discusses changes in the sexual behavior of genetic females due to prenatal administration of androgens. Androgenized females show sex-characteristic behaviors at a level between that shown by genetic males and that shown by genetic females.

Recent evidence has indicated that absence of androgen for any reason during critical periods of development tends to produce psychosexual "females" despite genetic makeup while the presence of androgens produces "males" irrespective of genetic makeup. Goy makes the point that testosterone-treated females show malelike behavior patterns that are not limited to those relating directly to reproduction. These changes in social behavior are independent of gonadal secretions at the ages when these behaviors are being displayed.

This survey of recent research raises several issues. Goy points out the logical impossibility of completely separating genetic and endorcine contributions to psychosexual development. More empirically, his research has concerned itself with male-characteristic behaviors such as rough and tumble play, threat, and aggression. One would like to know *the effect of testosterone treatment on behaviors that appear more frequently among females, such as grooming. The reaction of masculinized females to infants as compared to normal males and females would also be of interest.*

Early Hormonal Influences on the Development of Sexual and Sex-Related Behavior*

Robert W. Goy

Under ideal conditions, the procedures for investigating the influences of early hormonal states on the development of behavior are simple and classical. The appropriate procedures involve removal or destruction of the endocrine gland (which is the only, or primary, source of particular hormones) so that the effects of development in the anhormonal state can be determined. In addition, replacement therapy with extracts of the gland or with pure synthetic forms of the hormone should be carried out to determine which of a variety of possible compounds most closely duplicates the effects of the glandular secretions. In actual practice, the problem of characterizing the hormonal influences on sexual development is more difficult to analyze. In part, the greater difficulty is attributable to the existence of two different endocrine glands (the ovary and the testis), each present in a distinctive genetic constitution. This situation poses a logical dilemma in the sense that we can never ask or answer the questions of what is the effect of ovariectomy in the genetic male or orchiectomy in the genetic female. Part of the difficulty also lies in the fact that our knowledge of the nature of the secretory products of these endocrine glands during early development is extremely limited. So limited, in fact, that it is questionable whether the principle of "replacement therapy" can be effectively applied to the analysis of the problem. To further complicate matters, the endocrine glands are not functional at all times in early development. Accordingly, experiments designed to test glandular influences will yield either negative or unparalleled results, unless they are carried out during those periods that are normally characterized by heightened levels

*From *The Neurosciences: Second Study Program,* ed. F. O. Schmitt, pp. 197-207. New York: Rockerfeller University Press, 1970.

of secretory activity.

These difficulties and complications do not pose any greater obstacle to the analysis of psychosexual differentiation than to the analysis of morphological differentiation. In the analysis of both problems, investigators have had to proceed by making certain assumptions and by using situations that are only approximations of the ideal case for endrocrinological studies. What follows in this presentation is a review of the literature on psychosexual differentiation within the context of the ideal case, while at the same time pointing out the limitations of the data and the nature of the assumptions underlying specific interpretations.

The effects of spontaneously occurring hormonal deficiencies during early development: the anhormonal case

In human development an event that prevents any gonad from forming rarely takes place. The condition is known clinically as Turner's Syndrome and characteristically it results in the development of a phenotypic female, who, because of the lack of gonads, fails to show the pubertal changes associated with gonadal activity at that time. Such individuals are not regarded as unfeminine at any time during their early development, and many cases are discovered only when they fail to manifest signs of puberty at the normal time. If treated with ovarian hormones during the period of adolescence, these individuals respond in a manner not measurably different from that of the normal female. Moreover, to the extent that the literature permits such a statement, the psychosexual orientation and libido of such individuals closely parallel those of the normal female. Individuals suffering from Turner's Syndrome, however, do not qualify as pure or ideal cases for demonstrating the effects of the development of the genetic female in the absence of an ovary. Such individuals are not genetic females (xx), nor are they genetic males (xy). The evidence available from karyotypes indicates that the majority of such cases possess only one sex chromosome. Presumably, karyotypes of the y-o variety fail to develop.

An animal case paralleling Turner's Syndrome was fortuitously discovered many years ago by F. A. Beach (1945). During a series of routine ovariectomies of female rats, Beach encountered one animal that contained no traces of ovarian or testicular tissue and that appeared phenotypically indistinguishable from normal females. When this subject was injected with suitable quantities of estrogen and progesterone, it responded by displaying the complete pattern of behavioral estrus characteristic of the normal female. The parallel with Turner's Syndrome is incomplete, however, as the genotype of this rat was never determined. Accordingly, we do not know whether the case demonstrates agonadal development of the genotypic male, female, or some other genotype.

From the literature on human beings, it is possible to approach the anhormonal case in a very indirect way. In another rare genetic anomaly, individuals incapable of responding to androgens have been identified. The genetic disorder in these instances is a disorder not of the sex chromosomes, but rather of the autosomes. As a result of this autosomal factor, the individual case may go undetected in the genetic female in whom physiological responses to androgens are relatively less important. Accordingly, the syndrome has been primarily associated with the genetic male. The association of the condition with the male genotype has given rise to an unfortunate misnomer for the condition, and it is known clinically as Testicular Feminization. In line with current views, however, the testis of these individuals is not feminizing nor does it secrete hormones which in their types or pattern resemble the hormones of the ovary. At least in the adult state of these individuals, the testes secrete amounts of androgens and estrogens that are within the range of normal genetic males. Nevertheless, as the clinical term implies, genetic males possessing the abnormal genes are indistinguishable from phenotypic females in their external appearance as well as in thier psychosexual orientation and libidinal interests. Interpretation of this clinical case as a demonstration of the effects of anhormonal development in the genotypic male requires specific assumptions. These are: (1) that the genetic disorder prevents or blocks responsiveness to androgens throughout all development, early as well as late; and (2) that the gonadal secretions during early development are essentially similar to those of the normal genetic male. Although no data exist which permit us to decide directly upon the validity of these assumptions, the normal-appearing testicular morphology and the absence of Mullerian-duct derivatives are indirectly supportive.

Cases of genetically determined disorders of sexual development in males occur spontaneously among lower mammals, but no studies have been carried out to assess the behavioral characteristics of afflicted individuals in adulthood. In a colony of rats maintained at Oklahoma City Medical Center, a high incidence of genital malformation and incomplete sexual differentiation occurs among genotypic males (Stanley and Gumbreck, 1964; Allison, 1965; Allison et al., 1965; Stanley et al., 1966). Experiments that would permit decisive interpretations of the nature of the disorder have not, however, been carried out. From the data available, decisions cannot be made as to whether the malformations are a result of insufficient androgen, insensitivity to normal amounts of androgen, or delayed formation of the gonad. In many cases, however, as in the human syndrome, individuals carrying the abnormal genes resemble females to varying degrees in their outward morphology.

The somatic manifestations of the abnormal gene actions are variable and present a continuum of effects. Allison et al. (1965) have described individuals completely devoid of any internal reproductive-tract structures. Externally they appear very feminine, with small vaginal orifices and nipples along the milk line. Much less severe examples of developmental aberration also are seen, in which the morphology is essentially masculine but the individuals are sterile.

Although the data summarized concerning spontaneous anomalies of sexual development are somewhat limited, nothing that has been described contradicts the view that the female form and psychosexual orientation can develop in the absence of hormonal influences from the gonads. Moreover, the development of the female pattern does not depend on a specific sexual genotype. Individuals that are genotypically XO or XY can and do develop (under specific circumstances) along lines as feminine as those characteristic of the normal female.

Experimental approaches to the anhormonal case

Studies of behavioral development have been restricted to gonadectomy during relatively late stages, compared with studies in experimental embryology. In addition, most, if not all, of the definitive behavioral studies have been carried out on the rat. In this species, studies of early gonadal activity permit some estimate to be made of testicular secretions present during the early period of development. Noumura et al. (1966) have shown that the testis develops the capacity to synthesize androgens as early as the thirteenth day of fetal development. In our laboratory, biochemical assays demonstrate that testosterone can be found in the peripheral blood of newborn rats and continues to be present in measurable amounts until about the tenth day after birth (Resko et al., 1968) (Figure 1). These results mean that castration of the male rat on the day of birth deprives the individual of testicular androgens only for a little more than half of the period that these hormones are normally present. Despite this relatively crude approximation of the anhormonal case, experiments conducted by Grady et al. (1965) demonstrated that castration during the neonatal period had profound effects of the sexual development of genotypic males. Individuals deprived of their testes at either one or five days of age developed behavioral characteristics normally present only in genotypic females of this species. When these males reached adult ages and were injected with estrogen and progesterone, they displayed lordosis (the posture of the receptive female) in response to mounting by normal males. Males castrated at 10 days of age or later showed little or no tendency to display lordosis under comparable conditions of testing (Table 1). As illustrated in Table I, males castrated on the day of birth displayed lordosis which more closely resembled that displayed by normal

TABLE I

Means of the mean copulatory quotients of castrated male rats receiving estradiol benzoate and progesterone

(Numbers in parentheses are the per cent of tests during which the experimental subjects were mounted.*)

Groups	N, Ss	3.3 μg.	N, Ss	6.6 μg.
Spayed females	9	.452 (97)	7	.787 (100)
Day-1 males	8	.301 (88)	7	.572 (100)
Day-5 males	8	.253 (78)	6	.183 (96)
Day-10 males	5	.000 (75)	6	.028 (88)
Day-20 males	7	.003 (79)	7	.056 (89)
Day-30 males	7	.000 (71)	7	.085 (89)
Day-50 males	8	.000 (84)	7	.053 (96)
Day-90 males	7	.000 (78)	7	.038 (100)

* Data adapted from Grady et al., 1965.

females than did any other group.

When males castrated at these early ages are allowed to mature and are then injected with testosterone propionate, the pattern of sexual behavior is characterized by frequent mounting behavior, but intromission and ejaculation are either absent or infrequent (Beach and Holz, 1946; Grady et al., 1965). The investigators who have studied this problem most closely have repeatedly pointed to inadequacies of phallic development as one of the possible reasons for the general failure of early castrates to display intromission and ejaculation despite injection of high doses of testosterone in adulthood. The theoretical question with regard to whether the perinatal testis contributes to the development of male sexual behavior by altering central neural mechanisms or by altering the peripheral effector apparatus has not been answered experimentally. Since the initial study by Grady et al. (1965), the technical problems that stand in the way of a direct answer have not been overcome, and the neutrality of their position in regard to

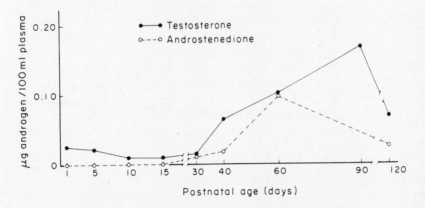

FIGURE 1   Concentration of testosterone in pooled samples of peripheral plasma obtained from independent groups of male rats at different postnatal ages. (From data published by Resko et al., 1968; Figure previously published in Goy, 1968.)

these alternatives has had to be maintained. In a very recent re-examining of the same problem, Beach et al. (1969) restated this position:

> A choice between these alternatives (i.e. influences on central neural structures vs. peripheral effector structures, RWG) cannot be made on the basis of the present evidence, but they are not mutually exclusive and the most conservative hypothesis would seem to be that both types of effect are important.

The male hamster, as does the male rat, undergoes extensive psychosexual differentiation during the early postnatal period. Accordingly, it can provide comparative data bearing on the general question of the behavioral characteristics which develop in the absence of the testis during a period of development that is critical for psychosexual differentiation. Eaton (1969) has recently studied male hamsters castrated on the day of birth. As in the rat, such males develop an expression of the lordosis response closely resembling that of the normal female. When given estrogen and progesterone in adulthood, lordosis lasting for 267 out of a possible 300 seconds could be elicited readily by the sniffing behavior of a sexually active, normal male. The corresponding data for normal females was 290 out of 300 seconds.

Investigations of the genetic female are less satisfactory than those of the male from the point of view of providing evidence that early ovariectomy results in a state of hormonal deprivation. No direct biochemical measurements exist to support the notion that the ovary is active endocrinologically during fetal or neonatal life in the female rat or any other mammal. Although data have been collected showing that ovariectomy soon after birth leads to pituitary changes suggestive of a loss of negative feedback, the specific hormone involved in this feedback has never been identified.

If hormones secreted by the neonatal ovary contribute to female sexuality, as some investigators have postulated (A. A. Gerall, J. B. Dunlap, and C. N. Thomas, personal communication), they are not essential to the development of fairly complete sexual responsiveness. Adult female rats, ovariectomized on the day of birth, display vigorous lordosis patterns when the proper ovarian hormones are supplied by injection (Wilson and Young, 1941). Moreover, ovariectomy on the day of birth does not prevent the development of some behaviors that can be stimulated by testosterone in adulthood. When such females are injected with testosterone propionate, they display marked augmentation of mounting when paired with receptive female partners (Harris and Levine, 1965; Gerall and Ward, 1966; Whalen et al., 1969). The ability of the genetic female rat to display increased frequencies of mounting behavior during testosterone treatment in adulthood does not depend, however, on removal of the ovary on the day of birth. A common finding among lower mammals is that mounting occurs spontaneously in many females and that testosterone will stimulate mounting activity in intact adult females or in females spayed as adults (Beach and Rasquin, 1942; Goy and Young, 1958; Pheonix et al., 1959; Gerall and Ward, 1966; Young, 1961).

The results obtained from these experimental studies are consistent with the interpretation of the spontaneous occurrences of gonadless development. Including the special case of Testicular Feminization, in which autosomal genetic factors prevent responsiveness to androgens, all cases of development in an early environment deficient either in gonadal hormones or in the physiological actions of the hormones are associated with the retention and elaboration of neural systems that mediate behavior characteristic of the normal genetic female. This generalization holds true whether we are considering mounting behavior of the normal female and its stimulation by a variety of hormones in adulthood, or are considering lordosis responses and their stimulation by estrogen and progesterone. Just as the consequences of development in the anhormonal environment are not limited to a particular form of behavior, so, too, they are not restricted to a particular sexual genotype. Both the genetic male and the genetic female develop along parallel, if not entirely identical, lines when deprived of their gonads. In short, both genetic sexes develop in a manner which so far has not been distinguished from that of a normal female, but which differs markedly from that of a normally differentiated male.

CONTRIBUTIONS OF TESTICULAR HORMONES TO THE DEVELOPMENT OF BEHAVIORAL TRAITS CHARACTERISTIC OF THE MALE

The experiments reviewed so far show that testicular secretions contribute to the suppression or loss of the lordosis reflex, which otherwise develops in genetic male rats. Such an effect on the sexual behavior repertoire may be regarded as one of the contributions the early testis makes to the development of a male psychosexual orientation in this species. But this effect of testicular hormone early in development is not limited to the genotypic male. When female rats or guinea pigs are treated with testosterone propionate at the proper times in early life, the development of lordosis can be markedly interfered with, or in some cases prevented entirely (Phoenix et al., 1959; Barraclough and Gorski, 1962; Harris and Levine, 1965; Goy et al., 1962; Harris, 1964; Goy et al., 1964). The female guinea pig and rat differ markedly in the length of the gestational interval, which lasts for 68 days in the former and only 21 days in the latter. Corresponding to this difference in the length of prenatal life, the developmental period during which testosterone propionate is effective in suppressing the development of lordosis differs in the two species. For the genetic female guinea pig, testosterone is maximally effective when it is administered between the thirtieth and fortieth days of *prenatal life.* For the rat, in contrast, the maximally effective period for androgenic suppression is during the first five days of *postnatal life.*

Suppression of the development of lordosis can be effected by a wide variety of gonadal steroids including estradiol (Feder and

Whalen, 1965; Levine and Mullins, 1966), androstenedione (Stern, 1969), and progesterone (Diamond and Wong, 1969). It is unlikely that all these hormones are involved in the normal testicular suppression of lordosis, for the quantity of each hormone that must be injected greatly exceeds that which could be expected to result from normal secretory activity. In contrast to the other hormones mentioned, estradiol is known to interfere with the development of male copulatory behavior (Whalen, 1964). Nevertheless, the experiments demonstrate that the developmental period when the testis is normally active can be viewed as a period of sensitivity to a broad spectrum of steroids, and each may make a different contribution to development.

Possibilities exist for the production of a wide variety of psychosexual abnormalities when the array of testicular hormones is considered singly and in various combinations. One recent example deserves special attention because of its possible relevance to the etiology of male homosexuality. During the 10 to 20 days of life immediately after birth, testosterone is the principal, if not the only, androgen present in the testis and peripheral blood of the male rat (Resko et al., 1968). There is substantial evidence supporting the interpretation that the presence of this hormone accounts for the suppression of such feminine characteristics as lordosis and the augmentation of such male characteristics as mounting, intromission, and ejaculation as the organism develops. When the testis is removed at birth, however, and androstenedione in critical dosages is the only androgen provided during this developmental period, a unique set of behavioral traits characterize the adult (Goldfoot, et al., 1969).

Such genetically male individuals develop normal male genitalia as well as mounting, intromission, and ejaculation behavior, but their over-all masculinity is incomplete. The development of lordosis is not suppressed by androstenedione in the amounts administered by Goldfoot et al., and accordingly the adult pattern includes the retention of behavioral traits that are normally characteristic of genetic females. The parallelism to homosexuality is illustrated not by the retention of lordosis per se, but by the implication that specific hormonal conditions permit the retention of broadly defined feminine characters while, at the same time, contributing to the formation of normal male genitalia. Inasmuch as androstenedione is a normal biosynthetic precursor of testosterone, any genetic disturbance that prevents the final formation of testosterone could contribute to the formation of morphologically phenotypic males with psychosexual abnormalities marked by the retention of feminine characters.

The genotypic female has been widely used as a subject to demonstrate the influence of early testosterone on the development of behaviors normally characteristic of the male. In the first demonstration of these effects to come from our laboratory, evidence was presented for an augmentation of mounting behavior in the female guinea pig that was independent of any hormonal stimulation in adulthood and that represented a permanent change in the behavior of these treated females. Corresponding effects have been reported for female hamsters (Crossley and Swanson, 1968) and some strains of female rats treated with testosterone propionate during the neonatal period (Harris and Levine, 1962; Gerall and Ward, 1966; Nadler, 1969) but not for others (Whalen et al., 1969). An additional aspect of the effects of early androgen was brought out in our first study by the demonstration that treated females showed a heightened sensitivity to testosterone propionate in adulthood. When both normal and treated females were injected with identical amounts of testosterone propionate, the treated females showed a more rapid rise in the rate of mounting displayed in standardized tests as well as a higher over-all frequency of mounting. Comparable results were obtained when prenatally treated and normal females were given daily testosterone from birth to 70 days of age. Again, the treated females developed mounting behavior more rapidly and to a higher level of expression than females not treated prior to birth (Goy et al., 1967). In more recent studies of the genetic female rat, Gerall and Ward (1966) and Ward (1969) have demonstrated that, if treatment of genetic females with testosterone propionate is begun before birth and continued for a short time into the neonatal period, the sexual behavior pattern can be almost completely reversed. Females treated in this way display the complete male copulatory pattern, including intromission and ejaculation, when given additional testosterone propionate in adulthood.

Throughout our work with the effects of testosterone given at early stages of development, we have believed that it is important to show that the behavioral outcomes were not attributable to toxic or other pharmacological effects of the hormone. For this purpose, the behavior of sibling males treated identically has formed a part of our studies (Phoenix et al., 1959). In no case has early testosterone in the doses we administered altered the behavior of treated males compared with normal males. Inasmuch as a damaging effect of excessive testosteone during early development has been reported in earlier work (Wilson and Wilson, 1943), behavioral measures demonstrating that treated males are behaviorally normal takes on a special importance.

457

WOMAN: DEPENDENT OR INDEPENDENT VARIABLE?

Masculine patterns of social behavior are influenced by early androgen

The effects of early testosterone propionate on the development of masculine patterns of responses are not limited to aspects of sexual behavior. Swanson (1967) has shown masculinizing effects of perinatal androgen on the open-field behavior of female hamsters, and Bronson and Desjardins (1968) have demonstrated comparable influences of androgen on the fighting and aggressive behaviors of mice. The results with fighting behavior in mice are entirely consistent with the view that early androgen has an organizing action on the nervous system in the sense that androgens in adulthood modify or augment aggressive behavior only in males, not in females (Beeman, 1947; Tollman and King, 1956).

So long as effects could be shown only for behaviors that form a part of the male and female sexual repertoire, or for behavioral traits requiring the actions of hormones in adulthood, a possible interpretation was that the primary effect of early androgen was an alteration of the sensitivity of the neural tissues to specific hormones. Such an interpretation is not inaccurate as it applies to sexual behaviors or to the fighting behavior of mice, but, for the past five years, C.H. Phoenix and I have been studying the development of behaviors that dictate the need for a broader view of the actions of early androgen. We have chosen to study the social behavior of young rhesus monkeys for a demonstration of these broad effects. The primary reason for this choice was that studies by Rosenblum (1961) and Harlow (1965) had demonstrated that patterns of infant and juvenile social interactions unrelated to sexual behavior were sexually dimorphic in this species. Studies we have conducted confirm these earlier reports for five different kinds of social interactions observed under our standardized conditions. For each of the five behaviors the distinction between the sexes is purely quantitative, rather than qualitative. That is, no behavior that is unique to one sex has been identified. In addition, all the behaviors we have studied are displayed much more frequently by males than by females.

In these experiments, genetic female monkeys were treated for varying periods of time beginning on day 39 of gestational age through the day 69 or day 105 of the average 168-day gestation period. In the monkey, which, like the guinea pig, is a long-gestation species, the critical period for psychosexual differentiation appears to be prior to birth rather than after birth, as it

458

is in the rat and hamster. Testosterone propionate dissolved in oil was injected intramuscularly into the mother and reached the fetuses via placental circulation. After weaning, usually at three months of age, the treated females were randomly assigned to groups containing normal males, castrated males, normal females, or combinations of these various subjects. The frequency with which these testosterone-treated females displayed patterns of threatening, play initiation, rough-and-tumble play, and chasing play are illustrated in Figures 2, 3, 4, and 5, respectively. The data are presented for four consecutive series of observations, which represent samples of behavior during the first, second, third, and fourth years of life. Comparable data for normal males and females are depicted in the same Figures. For all the behaviors illustrated, males differ significantly from females, and the treated females are intermediate.

The differences between the sexes in social behavior patterns are independent of gonadal secretions at the ages when these behaviors are being displayed. Although testicular secretory activity has been assayed biochemically and shown to be at low level during the infant and juvenile periods (Resko, 1967), low levels are not essential to the display of these behaviors in the genetic male. Conversely, low levels of ovarian activity play no measurable role in suppressing or diminishing the frequency with which these behaviors are displayed by the normal genetic female. The data presented in Table II demonstrate that castration of the male rhesus on the day of birth does not prevent the display of these social behaviors at frequencies characteristic of the normal intact male. Correspondingly, ovariectomy on the day of birth does not facilitate the display of these "masculine" behaviors by the genetic female.

The mounting of rhesus males is a complex behavior that develops gradually with maturation and depends in part on social experience (Mason, 1961; Harlow, 1961, 1965). During the infant, juvenile, and adolescent periods, the mounting of rhesus monkeys shifts gradually from the infantile pattern of standing at the partner's rear or side to the mature pattern of clasping the partner's ankles or legs with the feet. The age at which the mature double-foot-clasp mount is first displayed by males under our conditions of rearing and observation is extremely variable, ranging from eight months to as much as three years of age. The possibility exists that, with more opportunity for social experience or more prolonged periods of social contact, less variability would be observed. Genetic female rhesus monkeys, treated prenatally with testosterone propionate, display a developmental pattern for mounting behavior which resembles that of the genetic male and differs from that of the genetic female (Tables III and IV).

The changes induced in female rhesus monkeys by prenatal testosterone have subtle features and include characteristics of the individual that cannot be tabulated as frequency data. In this species, the display of the mature double-foot-clasp mount requires the complete cooperation of the partner. The full manifestation of the behavior could be easily prevented at any time if the partner withdrew or sat down after the initial contact. Just how this cooperation is elicited in the partner is a subtlety that we have not been able to analyze. It does not appear to be a simple matter of social dominance, insofar as our criteria for social dominance are concerned. Some other set of factors, which, in the case of heterosexual mounting, may include sexual attractiveness, appears to be involved. Whatever characteristics are essential for

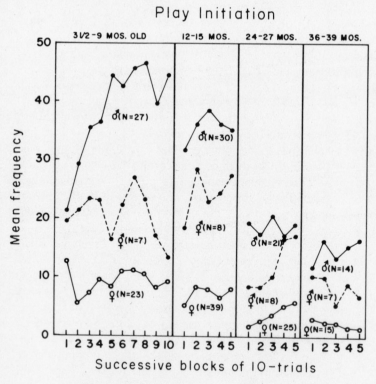

FIGURE 2 Average frequency of performance of play-initiation in standardized tests for social behavior by male (♂), female (♀), and prenatally testosteronized females (♀̄) throughout the first 39 months of postnatal life.

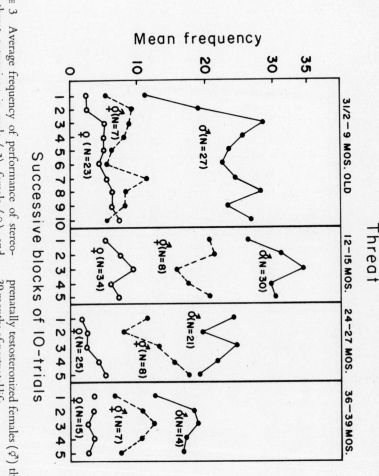

FIGURE 3 Average frequency of performance of stereotyped threat expressions in male (♂), female (♀), and

prenatally testosteronized females (♂̷) throughout the first
39 months of postnatal life.

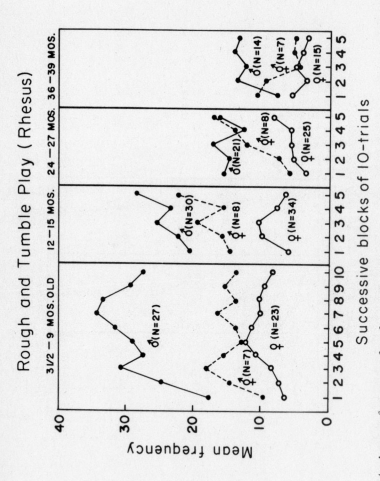

FIGURE 4 Average frequency of performance of rough-and-tumble play in male (♂), female (♀), and prenatally testosteronized females (♀) throughout the first 39 months of postnatal life.

Robert W. Goy

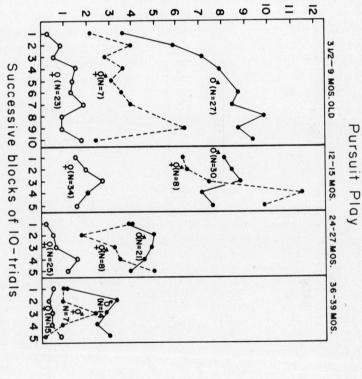

FIGURE 5 Average frequency of performance of pursuit play (chasing behavior) in male (♂), female (♀), and prenatally testosteronized females (♀♂) throughout the first 39 months of postnatal life.

463

the elicitation of cooperation in a partner by a mounter, females treated prenatally with testosterone seemed to possess these characteristics to a much greater extent than did normal females.

The experiments on rhesus monkeys demonstrate that the presence of testosterone during an embryonic or fetal stage contributes to the development of masculine patterns of social and mounting behavior, which are displayed only at later stages of life. Moreover, the changes induced in the behavior of treated individuals are not limited to behaviors controlled by later hormones, and the effects cannot in this case be interpreted solely as a permanent alteration in sensitivity of neural tissues to hormonal activation. Instead, it seems necessary to conclude that exogenous prenatal androgen alone is sufficient to cause the development in the genetic female of a variety of behaviors normally characteristic of the young developing male. Correspondingly, prenatal androgen alone (but from endogenous rather than exogenous sources) is sufficient to cause the development of these social behaviors in the genotypic male.

TABLE II

Average frequency of performance of four kinds of social behavior by normal males and females and by male and female rhesus gonadectomized at birth

		N	Threat	Play Initiation	Rough-and-Tumble Play	Pursuit Play
				Average Frequency per Animal per Block of 10 Trials		
Spayed	♀	3	7.0	4.0	3.6	.2
Intact	♀	23	5.6	9.2	9.0	1.1
Castrated	♂	2	35.0	49.2	39.3	5.3
Intact	♂	27	23.5	38.6	29.1	7.8

TABLE III

Changes with age in the frequency of performance of immature mounting postures by male, female, and prenatally testosteronized female rhesus

	3½-9 mos old		12-15 mos old		24-27 mos old		36-39 mos old	
	N	Av. Freq. of Mts per Animal per Block of 10 Trials	N	Av. Freq. of Mts per Animal per Block of 10 Trials	N	Av. Freq. of Mts per Animal per Block of 10 Trials	N	Av. Freq. of Mts per Animal per Block of 10 Trials
♂	27	2.8	30	2.1	21	1.5	14	0.9
♀	23	0.0	34	0.0	25	0.1	15	0.0
♀♂	7	1.0	8	0.5	8	0.4	7	0.3

TABLE IV

Changes with age in the frequency of performance of mature mounting posture by male, female, and prenatally testosteronized female rhesus

| | 3½–9 mos old | | 12–15 mos old | | 24–27 mos old | | 36–39 mos old | |
	N	Av. Freq. of Mts per Animal per Block of 10 Trials	N	Av. Freq. of Mts per Animal per Block of 10 Trials	N	Av. Freq. of Mts per Animal per Block of 10 Trials	N	Av. Freq. of Mts per Animal per Block of 10 Trials
♂	27	0.2	30	1.2	21	3.7	14	2.7
♀	23	0.0	34	0.0	25	0.0	15	0.0
⚥	7	0.1	8	1.0	8	1.1	7	0.9

Robert W. Goy

CONCLUDING REMARKS

A number of theoretical and experimental papers have adequately criticized the textbook view that sex is determined at the moment of fertilization (Chang and Witschi, 1956; Yamamoto et al., 1968; Turner, 1969). Such a point of view, although it may be adequate to describe the assemblage of genetic material at that moment in time, fails to provide insight into a wide variety of sexual phenomena known to biologists. For example, the occurrence of true functional hermaphroditism among many invertebrate forms clearly contradicts the concept that particular reproductive functions or capabilities are limited to a specific genetic endowment. Similarly, transformation from functional male to functional female with maturation not infrequently occurs among certain crustaceans (Charniaux-Cotton, 1962) and marine annelids. Among annelids of the genus *Ophryotrocha,* adult functional females can reconvert to males either when starved or when cut to pieces and allowed to regenerate. The genetic constitution very likely has not been altered during the sexual transformation in such individuals, any more than it has in a variety of decapod crustaceans, which live the first part of their lives as males and the later part as females.

Spontaneous sex reversal is more rare in vertebrate forms than among invertebrates. It is among vertebrates that the gonadal hormones as we know them (the estrogens and androgens) take on special importance in controlling the character of sexual development and, in some instances, are capable of completely overriding the differences in genetic constitution. That is to say, among vertebrates as among invertebrates, a single genetic constitution is compatible with either sexual phenotype. Parallels to complete spontaneous sex reversals have been produced experimentally in two classes of vertebrates (fishes and amphibians) by hormonal treatment, thus demonstrating that even among these higher forms the sexual genotype is not solely determinative. Among birds and mammals, the genetic endowment appears to limit the hormonal modification of morphological sexual characters more strongly, but complete reversals of the behavioral phenotype are possible.

It is surprising that among mammals, which show relatively greater complexity of neural development than do fishes and amphibians, behavioral characteristics should be influenced by the fetal and larval hormones to a nearly comparable degree. Nevertheless, the behavioral studies we have reviewed permit us to regard the genetic constitution of mammals as a plastic,

467

pluripotential matrix, highly susceptible to shaping and selection by environmental influences such as the hormones. For those mammalian species (guinea pig [Valenstein et al., 1955; Goy and Young, 1957]; rat [Hard and Larsson, 1968]; rhesus monkey [Mason, 1961; Harlow, 1965]; and human being [Money, 1963]) in which social experience also contributes to the development of sexual and sex-related behaviors, I propose the hypothesis that early hormonal influences predispose the individual to the acquisition of specific patterns of behavior.

The physiological basis for this predisposition to acquire sexually specific patterns of behavior may well be a unique organization of neural systems involved in the mediation of drive and reward. The experiments with rhesus monkeys can be interpreted broadly as suggesting that neural structures that have no dependence on the activational properties of hormones appear to be involved in the acquisition and maintenance of masculine social behavior. Speculatively, the hypothesis may be advanced that some of these neural structures are motivational in character and functionally related to the reinforcing events associated with, or derived from, the performance of such masculine activities as rough-and-tumble play, threatening, chasing, and prepubertal mounting. All these behaviors are displayed by infant and juvenile female, as well as male, monkeys. The distinction between the sexes is purely quantitative, and the reinforcing events involved in regulating the quantitative aspects of behavior are sexually specific.

REFERENCES

Allison, J. E., 1965. Testicular feminization. *Okla. Med. Ass.* 58: 378-380.

Allison, J. E., A. J. Stanley, and L. G. Gumbreck, 1965. Sex chromatin and idiograms from rats exhibiting anomalies of the reproductive organs. *Anat. Rec.* 153:85-91.

Barraclough, C. A., and R. A. *Gorski,* 1962. Studies on mating behaviour in the androgen-sterilized female rat in relation to the hypothalamic regulation of sexual behaviour. *J. Endor cinol.* 25: 175-182.

Beach, F. A., 1945. Hormonal induction of mating responses in a rat with congenital absence of gondal tissue. *Anat. Rec.* 92: 289-292.

Beach, F. A., and A. M. Holz, 1946. Mating behavior in male rats castrated at various ages and injected with androgen. *J. Exp. Zool.* 101:91-142.

Beach, F. A., R. G. Noble, and R. K. Orndoff, 1969. Effects of perinatal androgen treatment on responses of male rats to gonadal hormones in adulthood. *J. Comp. Physiol. Psychol.* 68:490-497.

Beach, F. A., and P. Rasquin, 1942. Masculine copulatory behavior in intact and castrated female rats. *Endocrinology* 31:393-409.

Beeman, E. A., 1947. The effect of male hormones on aggressive behavior in mice. *Physiol. Zool.* 20:373-405.

Bronson, F. H., and C. Desjardins, 1968. Aggression in adult mice: Modification by neonatal injections of gonadal hormone. *Science (Washington)* 161:705-706.

Chang, C.-Y., and E. Witschi, 1956. Genic control and hormonal reversal of sex differentiation in Xenopus. *Proc.* Soc. *Exp. Biol. Med.* 93:140-144.

Charniaux-Cotton, H., 1962. Androgenic gland of crustaceans. *Gen. Comp. Endocrinol. (Suppl.)* 1:241-247.

Crossley, D. A., and H. H. Swanson, 1968. Modification of sexual behaviour of hamsters by neonatal administration of testosterone propionate. *J. Endor cinol* 41:xiii-xiv (abstract).

Diamond, M., and C. L. Wong, 1969. Neonatal progesterone: Effect on reproductive functions in the female rat. *Anat. Rec.* 163:178 (abstract).

Eaton, G. G., 1969. Perinatal androgen's role in the ontogenesis of coital behavior in the male hamster (*Mesocricetus auratus*). University of California, Berkeley, doctoral thesis.

Feder, H. H., and R. E. Whalen, 1965. Feminine behavior in neonatally castrated and estrogen-treated male rats. *Science (Washington)* 147:306-307.

Gerall, A. A., and I. L. Ward, 1966. Effects of prenatal exogenous androgen on the sexual behavior of the female albino rat. *J. Comp. Physiol. Psychol.* 62:370-375.

Goldfoot, D. A., H. H. Feder, and R. W. Goy, 1969. Development of bisexuality in the male rat treated neonatally with androstenedione. *J. Comp. Physiol. Psychol.* 67:41-45.

Goy, R. W., 1968. Organizing effects of androgen on the behaviour of rhesus monkeys. *In* Endocrinology and Human Behaviour (R. P. Michael, editor). Oxford University Press, London, pp. 12-31.

Goy, R. W., W. E. Bridson, and W. C. Young, 1964. Period of maximal susceptibility of the prenatal female guinea pig to masculinizing actions of testosterone propionate. *J. Comp. Physiol. Psychol.* 57:166-174.

Goy, R. W., C. H. Phoenix, and R. Meidinger, 1967. Postnatal development of sensitivity to estrogen and androgen in male, female and pseudohermaphroditic guinea pigs. *Anat. Rec.* 157:87-96.

Goy, R. W., C. H. Phoenix, and W. C. Young, 1962. A critical period for the suppression of behavioral receptivity in adult female rats by early treatment with androgens. *Anat. Rec.* 142:307 (abstract).

Goy, R. W., and W. C. Young, 1957. Somatic basis of sexual behavior patterns in guinea pigs. *Psychosom. Med.* 19:144-151.

Goy, R. W., and W. C. Young, 1958. Responses of androgen-treated spayed female guinea pigs to estrogen and progesterone. *Anat. Rec.* 131:560 (abstract).

Grady, K. L., C. H. Phoenix, and W. C. Young, 1965. Role of the developing rat testis in differentiation of the neural tissues mediating mating behavior. *J. Comp. Physiol. Psychol.* 59:176-182.

Hard, E., and K. Larson, 1968. Dependence of adult mating behavior in male rats on the presence of littermates in infancy. *Brain, Behav. Evolut.* 1:405-419.

Harlow, H. F., 1961. The development of affectional patterns in infant monkeys. *In* Determinants of Infant Behaviour (B. M. Foss, editor). John Wiley and Sons, New York, pp. 75-97.

Harlow, H. F., 1965. Sexual behavior in the rhesus monkey. *In* Sex and Behavior (F.A. Beach, editor). John Wiley and Sons, New York, pp. 234-265.

Harris, G. W., 1964. Sex hormones, brain development and brain function. *Endocrinology* 75:627-648.

Harris, G. W., and S. Levine, 1962. Sexual differentiation of the brain and its experimental control. *J. Physiol.* (*London*) 163: 42P-43P.

Harris, G. W., and S. Levine, 1965. Sexual differentiation of the brain and its experimental control. *J. Physiol.* (*London*) 181:379-400.

Levine, S., and R. F. Mullins, Jr., 1966. Hormonal influences on brain organization in infant rats. *Science* (*Washington*) 152:1585-1592.

Mason, W. A., 1961. The effects of social restriction on the behavior of rhesus monkeys: II. Tests of gregariousness. *J. Comp. Physiol. Psychol.* 54:287-290.

Money, J., 1963. Psychosexual development in man. *In* Encyclopedia of Mental Health, Franklin Watts, Inc., New York, pp. 1678-1709.

Nadler, R. D., 1969. Differentiation of the capacity for male sexual behavior in the rat. *Hormones and Behav.* 1:53-63.

Noumura, T., J. Weisz, and C. W. Lloyd, 1966. *In vitro* conversion of 7-^{3}H

^{3}H progesterone to androgen by the rat testis during the second half of fetal life. *Endocrinology* 78:245-253.

Phoenix, C. H., R. W. Goy, A. A. Gerall, and W. C. Young, 1959. Organizing action of prenatally administered testosterone propionate on the tissues mediating mating behavior in the female guinea pig. *Endocrinology* 65:369-382.

Resko, J. A., 1967. Plasma androgen levels of the rhesus monkey: Effects of age and season. *Endocrinology* 81:1203-1212.

Resko, J. A., H. H. Feder, and R. W. Goy, 1968. Androgen concentrations in plasma and testis of developing rats. *J. Endocrinol.* 40:485-491.

Rosenblum, L. A., 1961. The development of social behavior in the rhesus monkey. University of Wisconsin, Madison, Wisconsin, doctoral thesis.

Stanley, A. J., and L. G. Gumbreck, 1964. Male pseudoherlinked recessive character. Program, 46th Meeting, The Endoctrine Society, Abstract no. 36.

Stanley, A. J., L. G. Gumbreck, and R. B. Easley, 1966. FSH content of male pseudohermaphrodite rat pituitary glands together with the effects of androgen administration and castration on gland and organ weights. Program, 48th Meeting, The Endocrine Society, Abstract no. 235.

Stern, J. J., 1969. Neonatal castration, androstenedione, and the mating behavior of the male rat. *J. Comp. Physiol. Psychol.* 69: 608-612.

Swanson, H. H., 1967. Alteration of sex-typical behaviour of hamsters in open field and emergence tests of neo-natal administration of androgen or estrogen. *Anim. Behav.* 15:209-216.

Tollman, J., and J. A. King, 1956. The effects of testosterone propionate on aggression in male and female C57BL/10 mice. *Brit. J. Anim. Behav.* 4:147-149.

Turner, C. D., 1969. Experimental reversal of germ cells. *Embryologia* 10:206-230.

Valenstein, E. S., W. Riss, and W. C. Young, 1955. Experiential and genetic factors in the organization of sexual behavior in male guinea pigs. *J. Comp. Physiol. Psychol.* 48:397-403.

Ward, I. L., 1969. Differential effect of pre- and postnatal androgen on the sexual behavior of intact and spayed female rats. *Hormones and Behav.* 1:25-36.

Whalen, R. E., 1964. Hormone-induced changes in the organization of sexual behavior in the male rat. *J. Comp. Physiol. Psychol.* 57:175-182.

Whalen, R. E., D. A. Edwards, W. G. Luttge, and R. T. Robertson, 1969. Early androgen treatment and male sexual behavior in female rats. *Physiol. Behav.* 4:33-39.

Wilson, J. G., and H. C. Wilson, 1943. Reproductive capacity in adult male rats treated prepuberally with androgenic hormone. *Endocrinology* 33:353-360.

Wilson, J. G., and W. C. Young, 1941. Sensitivity to estrogen studied by means of experimentally induced mating responses in the female guinea pig and rat. *Endocrinology* 29:779-783.

Yamamoto, T., K. Takeuchi, and M. Takai, 1968. Male-inducing action of androstenedione and testosterone propionate upon XX zygotes in the medaka, *Oryzias latipes. Embryologia* 10:116-125.

Young W. C., 1961. The hormones and mating behavior. *In* Sex and Internal Secretions, Vol. 2 (W. C. Young, editor). Williams and Wilkins, Baltimore, Maryland, pp. 1173-1239.

29

John Money is one of the pioneers in the study of human psychosexual disturbances. Since 1955 he has published an enormous number of papers and books in this area. Until recently he has concentrated on clinical material—studies of individuals who show some ambiguity of sexual gender. He has concentrated on environmental contributions to psychosexual gender including both pre- and postnatal hormonal influences. His theoretical position is largely based upon studies of hermaphrodites. He states that the sex of clinical assignment and rearing, if it is without ambiguity, is a better predictor of psychosexual orientation that any morphological or genetic properties of the individual. He argues for a great deal of postnatal plasticity in human sexual development.

The paper included in this volume represents a succinct and clear resume of his recent position. He points out that the nature-nurture dichotomy is an oversimplification and presents evidence that hormonal environment can completely alter the genetically determined phenotype. Part of the difference between Money and exponents of more physiologically determinist positions may be semantic; e.g., are pre- and postnatal hormonal influences to be considered environmental or constitutional in nature?

Money's current theory on the development of psychosexual identity is that it is the end product of a sexually dimorphic developmental sequence. The sequence normally begins with the dimorphism of the genetic code [XX or XY], thence to differentiation of gonadal structures [testes or ovaries], and finally to external genitalia and possibly neural differentiation involving the hypothalamus as well as other parts of the brain. At the beginning of each stage of the sequence, the organism is bipotential for the next phase of differentiation. Despite whatever central nervous system differentiation has occurred prenatally, Money feels that the human organism at birth is still largely bi-potential for gender-role differentiation.

Money differs from many of his associates in his stress on environmental contributions to psychosexual development, although such an emphasis is common among psychoanalysts. One of the key questions here is just what is *considered part of the environment. Many biologists and psychologists prefer to discuss behaviors that are subject to the nature-nurture controversy in terms of an interaction of innate and environmental factors. Organisms create their own environments, which in turn affect the working out of genetic determinants. The relative contribution of various components often varies from species to species. Therefore, it is difficult to determine how much generalization across species is possible as well as generalization from abnormal [hermaphroditic] to normal psychosexual development.*

Sexual Dimorphic Behavior, Normal and Abnormal*

John Money

MODIFICATION OF BEHAVIOR BY ENVIRONMENTAL ALTERATION OF THE GENOTYPE

In an earlier and more naive era of determinism in behavioral theory, if a particular feature of behavior was ascribed to heredity, it was thereby invested with an aura of being more genuine, durable, unmodifiable, and valid than behavior ascribed to environmental influence. To use the alliterative shibboleth of the nineteenth century, nature was assigned a higher scientific status than nurture in behavior theory. Today's experimental evidence requires a revision of such a naive point of view: it is actually possible environmentally to manipulate heredity so as to change the program of the genotype as expressed in the phenotype. The morphology of the organism can be changed, and its behavior as well. Sexually, the extent of the change may constitute a complete reversal of sexual dimorphism of morphology and of behavior.

This type of sexual reversal is well illustrated in the experiments of Yamamoto (1962) on the killifish, *orizeas latipes.* Yamamoto's

*From *Environmental Influences on Genetic Expression: Biological and Behavioral Aspects of Sexual Differentiation.* Fogarty International Center Proceedings no. 2, ed. N. Kretschmer and D. N. Walcher, Washington, D.C.: U.S. Government Printing Office, 1971.

experiments go one stage further, however, and demonstrate how environmental manipulation may change the very genotype itself and, with it, the genetic program for behavior.

Yamamoto exposed XY larvae of *orizeas latipes* (it is a viviparous salt and/or freshwater fish) to female sex hormone. Untreated, they would have differentiated as males. Treated, they differentiated as females. These XY females were, like normal XX females, able to breed with normal XY males and produce young: 25% of the second generation larvae were then chromosomally XX (female), 50% XY (male), and 25% YY, which, if left untreated, would differentiate as males. If, however, the YY were exposed to estrogen, they would differentiate as YY females. These YY females would, in adulthood, be fertile, like normal XX females, but their ova would contain only a Y instead of an X chromosome. In the succeeding generation it was, therefore, possible to breed YY females with YY males: 100% of the resultant progeny differentiated as YY males (unless they were experimentally exposed to estrogen). In the reverse of this experiment, Yamamoto was able to produce XX males by treating XX larvae with male sex hormone.

What of the behavior of YY males? Hamilton and his colleagues (1969) at the Downstate Medical Center, New York, tested YY and XY males, in 14 matched pairs, in competitive mating for single XX females; the YY males were clearly dominant. They induced 137 of 155 spawnings. They gained higher scores for number of contacts with females; quivers, including those at spawning; moving in quick circles around the females; and number of seconds spent alone with females. YY males spent more time chasing the XY males than vice versa, and made more quick circling movements around the XY males. When one male chased another male, he would bite the pursued if he caught up with him. Biting was done almost exclusively by the YY males. Several XY males had their fins lacerated as a result. XY males tended to avoid YY males by remaining at one corner of the tank, near the bottom. One may presume, as Hamilton did, that the presence of an extra Y chromosome, rather than the loss of an X, was responsible for the YYs' increased mating dominance. Be that as it may, the chief significance of increased dominance, in the present context, is that it was produced by environmental alteration of the genotype itself.

MODIFICATION OF BEHAVIOR BY ENVIRONMENTAL
ALTERATION OF THE PHENOTYPE

In the Yamamoto experiment, the first stage in altering the genotype was to alter the phenotype: the developmental male program of the XY genotype was suppressed by the addition of estrogen to the tanks in which the larvae had been spawned. A female program was thereby instituted instead, and the phenotype differentiated as female. At maturity, the breeding behavior was that of a female despite an atypical Y chromosome in 50% of the eggs.

Yamamoto's experiment is not the first in which the term cells have been reversed from ova to sperms, or vice versa, while still retaining their reproductive fertility. Many years ago, Witschi demonstrated that overripe toad eggs all developed as morphologic males. Not only the genetic males, but also the genetic females had the appearance of males and produced sperms, but without the male sex chromosome present in any of them (Witschi, 1956, 1965). Witschi and his co-workers (Chang and Witschi, 1955, 1956; Mikamo and Witschi, 1963) also succeeded in producing a similar reversal of genetic sex in toads by implanting sex hormones into the developing larvae. In 1964, Turner and Asakawa made a first step toward achieving the same result in a mammal by transplanting the gonads of fetal mice into a host animal, so that the fetal testis turned the fetal ovary into an ovotestis in which spermatogenesis progressed to the point of secondary spermatocytes. Burns (1961) had in 1956 used estradiol in the fetal oppossum to convert a would-be testis into an ovo-testis producing ovocytes.

It has not yet been reported experimentally possible to reverse the sex of differentiation completely from that of the genetic sex of the fertilized egg in mammals. Nonetheless the fish and amphibian experiments demonstrate how profound can be the reversal of everything pertaining to genetic sex: morphology, behavior, and fertility. These experiments require that one keep an open mind with regard to possible partial reversals of the expression of genetic sex in human beings, perhaps of direct relevance to sexual psychopathology, from causes as yet unknown.

The fish and amphibian experiments also point out a profoundly important principle in the theory of heredity versus environment (perhaps more appropriately designated as genetics versus environmentics). It is a principle that transcends the old dichotomy between nature and nurture by introducing the concept of the critical period. There is only a limited period during which a fertilized egg may be tampered with and forced to reverse the program for which it is genetically coded. After this limited or critical period, the die is cast and the program cannot be changed, or, having been changed, cannot revert.

MODIFICATION OF BEHAVIOR BY PARTIAL MODIFICATION OF THE PHENOTYPE: ANTIANDROGENIZATION

In mammals, though it has not proved experimentally possible to effect a complete sex reversal of the phenotype, it has proved relatively easy to reverse the phenotype of the external organs of sex. The principle involved may be simply stated as the principle of the masculine additive: add androgen at the critical fetal period when the external sex organs differentiate, and they will differentiate as male even in an XX fetus. Delete or suppress androgens at this critical period, and the external organs will differentiate as female, even in an XY fetus.

Experimental feminization of the male may be achieved surgically, by castrating the fetus *in utero,* and so depriving it of its own fetal testicular hormones. The alternative is pharmacologic feminization, which is achieved by injecting the pregnant mother with an antiandrogenic steroid that prevents the fetus from utilizing its own fetal androgen. The most successful antiandrogen so far discovered for this type of experiment is cyproterone. Neumann and his colleagues (1955, 1966) in West Berlin have produced XY rats that have completely female external organs. The gonads are testicles, undescended. The uterus and its fallopian tubes are not present as in a normal female, since the testes had been able in fetal life to secrete their Mullerian-inhibiting substance that prevented development of a uterus. Cyproterone does not interfere with this aspect of fetal development, only with the production of androgen.

Cyproterone administered to the fetus does not permanently impair the testes. They will secrete androgen at puberty. To permit the development of full feminine mating behavior at puberty, the testes are, therefore, removed and the animal is maintained on cyclic female hormones, estrogen and progesterone. Under these conditions, the mating behavior of these anti-androgenized males

477

is exclusively feminine. The stud males of the colony recognize them only as females.

There is no ethical reason to antiandrogenize the human fetus. Thus, there are no experimental or iatrogenic examples of this condition in the human species.[1] An exact analogue does occur, however, in the syndrome of testicular feminization or androgen insensitivity. This condition of insensitivity of all of the body's cells to androgen is genetically transmitted, probably as an X-linked recessive or a male-limited autosomal dominant, in the female line. The biochemistry of the defect in cellular response to androgen has not worked out. This defect remains continuous throughout life. The affected individual is, therefore, not only born with a female morphology, but develops with an exclusively female puberty, except for absence of the menses due to absence of the uterus. It is self-evident that a baby with female external genitals will be assigned and reared as a girl. Genetics notwithstanding, she differentiates a psycho-sexual identity as a girl (Money, Ehrhardt, and Masica, 1968). Typically, in fact, she fits the feminine stereotype rather closely, with a negligible tendency toward tomboyism. In childhood play her maternal interests are strong and in adulthood, when she marries and adopts children, she is a good mother. In teen-age, her dating and romantic interests are inseparable from those of her age-mates, except that she has the emotional hurdle of coping with the knowledge of her sterility.

Since the differentiation of a gender identity in girls with the androgen-insensitivity syndrome is feminine, it is obvious that the Y chromosome in their genetic constitution is unable to express itself. Its expression is defeated first by the feminizing hormonal events of fetal life and, subsequently, by the events and experiences of being reared as a girl.

MODIFICATION OF BEHAVIOR BY PARTIAL MODIFICATION OF THE PHENOTYPE: ANDROGENIZATION

The counterpart of antiandrogenization of the XY genotype is androgenization of the XX genotype. Experimental androgenization is relatively easy to accomplish in animals, namely,

---

1. One possibility, however, made evident in the animal experimental work of Gorski (1968) is that barbiturates taken by the pregnant mother may antagonize the influence of androgen in the fetus, which is rather frightening in its implications with respect to the human male.

by injecting the pregnant mother with androgen. A very considerable body of experimental literature has now accumulated on this topic, involving several species, including the rhesus monkey. When the dosage of androgen is sufficient, the external genitals of the female fetus are completely masculinized and the baby is born with a penis, foreskin, and fused scrotum (empty) instead of a clitoris, clitoral hood plus labia minora, and unfused labia majora.

There are two experimental traditions of androgenizing female animals. One relates directly to an interest in the behavior of masculinized females, the other to an interest in the pituitary control of estrous cycles. In briefest synopsis, the upshot of these two lines of work has been to show that partial fetal androgenization of estrous species, properly timed for the critical period, permanently unfeminizes the hypothalamic centers that govern feminine cycling of the pituitary and, at the same time, bizarrely disrupts the normal patterns of hypothalamically governed mating behavior appropriate to the phasing of the estrous cycle. In addition, fetal androgenization, especially when complete enough to result in the transformation of the clitoris into a penis, induces changes in the sexually dimorphic balance or frequency of behavior. Females with a penis gain scores on various frequency tests of behavior (behavior that may be in the repertory of both sexes) that deviate from the norms of their female controls in the direction of the male controls. These masculinized scores have been widely assumed to reflect a masculinization of the central nervous system.

From the human point of view, the most instructive androgenized females are the rhesus monkeys being raised at the Oregon Regional Primate Center (Young, Goy, and Phoenix, 1965; Phoenix, 1966). These penis-bearing females are, in brief, tomboys in their childhood behavior. They gained behavior scores for initiating play, engaging in rough-and-tumble play, making threatening gestures, and adopting the mounting position in sexual play that were closer to the scores of normal control males than normal control females. The oldest of these animals have reached adolescence. They have normal menstrual cycles. With maturity, they appear to lose the masculine trend of their behavioral scores, but the evidence is still incomplete.

In human beings, the closest parallel to experimental masculinization in animals is the iatrogenic condition of progestin-induced hermaphroditism in genetic females. This rare condition first appeared about fifteen years ago when synthetic progestins were first introduced on the market and prescribed for the purpose of preventing threatened miscarriage. Certain of these synthetic products (all of which are closely related to biologically active

479

androgens in chemical structure) proved to have a masculinizing influence on an occasional female fetus. In consequence, a baby is born with a greatly enlarged clitoris and partial fusion of the labia. The genital appearance in such an instance is the same as in an incompletely fused penis and scrotum in a genetic male. In general, the correct diagnosis is made at birth, and the baby is assigned and surgically corrected as a female. Hormonal puberty is normal, as for a female, and no endocrine treatment is necessary.

A study of the behavior of ten girls, in middle to late childhood and early adolescence, with the partial masculinization of progestin-induced hermaphroditism (Erhardt and Money, 1967; Ehrhardt, 1969) showed them, like their monkey counterparts, to manifest a strong degree of tomboyism as compared with experimental controls. Such a girl judges herself to be a tomboy, as do also her family and friends, and is rather proud of it. Her tomboyism is defined, perhaps above all else, by vigorous expenditure of muscular energy and an intense interest in athletic sports and outdoor activities in competition with boys. It is not especially associated with aggression and fighting, though the tomboy will take up for herself when challenged. She rather scorns feminine frills and elegant hairdos in favor of utilitarian styles. In childhood, maternalistic doll play is perfunctory, as is the attitude toward anticipated mothering of newborn infants in adulthood. Career ambitions come first; they are commensurate with high academic achievement and high IQ, which seem to be a correlate of the syndrome. Career does not, however, exclude the anticipation of eventual romance, marriage, and pregnancy, to be combined with career. There is no tendency toward lesbianism; this kind of tomboy girl does not express the feeling that she ought to have been a boy or the belief that she would be better off if she could change her sex.

The tomboyism of progestin-induced hermaphroditism is fairly closely paralleled in another hermaphroditic condition, the early-treated female adrenogenital syndrome (Ehrhardt, Epstein, and Money, 1968). In this syndrome, fetal masculinization is the product of excessive androgen secretion by abnormal adrenocortical function. Treatment is with cortisone from birth. In an earlier generation, prior to the discovery of cortisone as the agent that would prevent excessive and premature pubertal virilization, teen-agers and women with the virilizing stigmata of the adrenogenital syndrome had lesbian fantasies and/or desires significantly more often than do affected individuals of the current generation who have been successfully treated from birth. In the older patients one presumes that, whatever the masculinizing effect of fetal androgens on subsequent behavior, it was augmented by the continuing rapid masculinization of the body and its appearance after birth. The remarkable finding among these older, heavily masculinized patients, however, is that only a relatively small proportion did develop lesbian desires and behavior.

MODIFICATION OF BEHAVIOR BY SEX ASSIGNMENT AND REARING

The foregoing hermaphroditic findings all pertain to modification of the morphologic and behavioral phenotype of sex by events in the prenatal environment that interfere with genotypic expression. Hermaphroditism is of further scientific value in showing that the postnatal environment also may exert so strong an influence as to counteract the normal expression of the genotype in the differentiation of gender identity and gender role. The key evidence derives from matched pairs of hermaphrodites, each with the same ambiguity of external genital appearance and each with the same diagnosis, but one assigned and reared as a boy, the other as a girl. That such disparities can and do occasionally occur is not by design, but by reason of imprecise diagnosis, or of different traditions of deciding the sex of assignment in cases of maximum ambiguity.

Notwithstanding variations in such traits as maternalism, tomboyism, dominance, and responsiveness with genital arousal to visual and narrative erotic images (a masculine trait) versus haptic sensations (on which the female is dependent for genital arousal), the typical finding in matched pairs of hermaphrodites is that the gender identity and gender role differentiate in conformity with the sex of assignment and rearing. This conformity is of such strength that it may withstand even the ambiguous or contradictory appearance of the defective sex organs and the bodily effects of a contradictory hormonal puberty, namely, ugly virilization in a girl and partial androgen insensitivity with breast development, absence of the beard, and erectile inadequacy in a male. Ideally, of course, it is infinitely preferable that these contradictions do not exist, and that the growing boy or girl has no paradoxical information from the body as to his or her gender.

Even though contradictions of the body can be effectively circumvented in the establishment of a gender identity they constitute a severe hazard, not only because of their visible meaning to the child, but also because of their meaning to all others who have

481

dealings with him (or her). Ambiguity and uncertainty in the minds and actions of other people (children as well as adults) are probably the single most important factor in preventing a child from developing a consistent and unitary gender identity. Continuously made aware that something is wrong sexually, a child does not easily tolerate the cognitive dissonance of his ambiguity.

It is rare for a hermaphrodite to differentiate a hermaphroditic and ambiguous gender identity. Instead, a resolution of ambiguity is achieved by way of the principle of opposites. There are only two acceptable alternatives in sex: male and female. If one's assigned status as either appears unsatisfactory or obviously erroneous, then the simple solution is to consider a change to the other. Whatever the pros and cons, the alternative at least has the virtue of not yet having been proved wrong and unsatisfactory. All told, there are not very many hermaphrodites who develop a conviction that they should have their sex reassigned. Among those who do, there is no consistent relationship beeween the genetic sex, the assigned sex, and the reassignment desired. For example, a genetic female hermaphrodite assigned as a girl may feel compelled to live as a boy, whereas another of the same diagnosis and assigned as a boy may have the opposite conviction.

Cases of hermaphroditic sex reassignment thus may show the same contradiction between sex-chromosomal status and gender identity as is manifested in some unreassigned hermaphrodites. In both instances, the evidence indicates that experiences of sex assignment and rearing can interrupt and reverse the orderly progression of events that ensure for the majority of the human race a perfect positive correlation between sex-chromosomal status and gender identity. The correlation between sex chromosomes and sexually dimorphic behavior then becomes perfectly negative.

GENETICS AND GENDER IDENTITY

For generations mankind has lived with a popular and scientific folklore that something so intensely and personally unnegatable as one's own sense of gender identity must, in some way, be preordained in the genes. By the same token, anomalies of gender identity, as in hermaphrodites who seek sex reassignment, in anatomically normal transexuals who do the same, and in homosexuals of the more mundane varieties than transexualism, also would need, theoretically, to be preordained in the genes. All the experimental evidence, however, from sex-reversed fish to human hermaphrodites shows that such a simple-minded theory is untenable.

The theory needed in its place is one that sees gender identity as the end product of a sexually dimorphic development sequence. The sequence begins with the dimorphism of the genetic code as manifested in the XX and XY chromosomal dimorphism. From the genetic code, sexual dimorphism is translated into the dimorphism of embryonic differentiation of the gonads, which, through their hormonal secretion, in turn differentially regulate the dimorphism of first the internal reproductive structures and then the external genitalia. At the same time in embryonic life, gonadal secretion dimorphically regulates the differentiation of structures in the brain, specifically the hypothalamus, that in turn will regulate the sex-related functioning of the pituitary. In all probability gonadal secretion at this same time also dimorphically regulates other structures of the brain that will eventually be involved in the regulation of certain aspects of sexually dimorphic behavior, namely, those aspects that are phyletically widely distributed (like motherly attentiveness to the newborn or coital postures and movements).

At the commencement of each stage in the sequence, the organism is, in effect, bipotential for the next phase of differentiation. In the normal course of events, this bipotentiality will never show itself. Therefore, it must be inferred from the known clinical examples of anomalies in dimorphic differentiation and from cleverly conceived experiments designed to demonstrate it.

Despite whatever sexual dimorphism may already have differentiated in the central nervous system, the human organism at birth is still largely bipotential for dimorphism of gender-identity differentiation. More simply said, the individual's gender identity and role (identity is the subjective experience of role, and role is the enactment of identity) will differentiate in response to and in interaction with stimuli encountered after birth.

This state of affairs is analogous to the development and differentiation of bilingualism in a child with two native languages. At birth, the child has, like other members of the human race, differentiated a brain programmed to use language, subject to the proviso that it encounters language postnatally. When this brain encounters the vocal signals and auditory oscillations of two languages, it must accomplish the incredible feat of coding the two separately, which, incidentally, is easier if the contextual cues are different, as when the two languages are used by different people exclusively. Eventually the child is able to use each of the two languages, each as a completely self-contained and autonomous system. It is possible to use the one correctly only by excluding the other. The differentiation of a gender-identity role resembles bilingualism in that it requires a brain to code two systems, the male and the female. Whereas there are only certain cases of bilingualism in which one of the languages is censored or avoided, in the differentiation of gender identity one of the systems must routinely be negatively coded and suppressed. The other is positively coded and actively in operation. Thus one may say that a boy knows how to be a boy because he knows also how not to be a girl. The establishment of gender identity and role is an active process of differentiation (with total success not necessarily guaranteed). The analogy is with the painter and his canvas, not with the photographic image absorbed on a blank paper. The latter, unhappily, is the one tacitly assumed in almost all social-learning theories of sex-role formation through identification with role models.

Because the absorbent-sheet model does not apply, it is not so important that a child have a perfect model for gender identity and role as that, in the sum-total of his experiences, the masculine and the feminine are understood and experienced as different and not as equivocal or the same. What is masculine and what feminine is less important, in any given household and community, than the fact that they can be distinguished, even though extensive overlap is acceptable. This is the principle of dimorphic signals.

Gender identity and role are in an active phase of differentiation during the period of late infancy and early childhood. The differentiation process would appear to be a rather delicate one, rather easily subject to disruption, perhaps more so in boys than in girls. The disruption need not be self-evidently associated with sex. I suspect it may be, among other things, a sequel to insufficient infantile tactile stimulation (Harlow's 1965 monkey experiments are a prime paradigm here); to too much personal closeness or overcrowding; to life-threatening illness or death of a close family member; to family feuding with the child as pawn; to atypical early exposure to sexual activity or play of excessive dramatic impact, perhaps with insufficient prior opportunity for routine sexual play in childhood; and to equivocation or ambiguity in the parents' expectancies of masculinity or femininity for their sons or daughters. A brain lesion may disrupt gender-identity differentiation, but this effect is more generally seen in adulthood, as a deterioration, than in the formative years.

These various environmental events—and others yet to be identified—that may disrupt gender-identity differentiation may also leave permanent sequelae in the form of aberrations of sexual behavior. One cannot say, however, in this instance that environmental events modified genetic expression. The genetic code does not exhaustively program gender identity and role as male or female in the human species. The program in the genetic code spells out only a readiness to differentiate a gender identity and role (or in certain cases, like the XXY and XYY syndromes, perhaps impairs readiness). The details are, as in the case of language, programmed in the social code of interaction and learning. Herein lies ample opportunity for error of differentiation — for all the aberrations of psychosexual function, in fact. This is a manifestation of the range of the versatility and flexibility of response in our species, as compared with the stereotype in other species. It is a feature of man's phyletic heritage that environmental influences of the genetics of our behavior are vast in scope — more vast than in any other species.

REFERENCES

Burns, R. K. (1961). In *Sex and Internal Secretions,* W. C. Young, editor. Baltimore, Williams and Wilkins.

Chang, C. Y., and Witschi, E. (1955). *Proc. Soc. Exp. Biol. Med.,* 89, 150-152.

Chang, C. Y., and Witschi, E. (1956). *Proc. Soc. Exp. Biol. Med.,* 93, 140-144.

Ehrhardt, A. A., and Money, J. (1967). *J. Sex. Res.,* 3, 83-100.

Ehrhardt, A. A., Epstein, R., and Money, J. (1968). *Johns Hopkins Med. J.,* 122, 160-167.

Ehrhardt, A. A. (1969). Zur Wirkung Foetaler Hormone auf Intelligenz und geschlechtsspezifisches Verhalten. Ph.D. dissertation, Univ. of Duesseldorf, West Germany.

Hamilton, J. B., Walter, R. O., Daniel, R. M., and Mestler, G. E. Supermales (YY sex chromosomes) and ordinary males (XY): Competition for mating with females. *Animal Behavior. In* [*in press*].

Harlow, H. F., and Harlow, M. K. (1965). *Sex Research, New Developments,* John Money, editor. Holt, Rinehart and Winston.

Mikamo, K., and Witschi, E. (1963). *Genetics,* 48, 1411-1421.

Money, J., Ehrhardt, A. A., and Masica, D. N. (1968). *Johns Hopkins Med. J.,* 123, 105-114.

Neumann, F., and Elger, W. (1965). *Excerpta Medica,* International Congress Series No. 101, 169-185. Androgens in normal and pathological conditions.

Neumann, F., and Elger, W. (1966). *Endokrinologie,* 50, 209-225.

Phoenix, C. (1966). Psychosexual organization in nonhuman primates. Paper delivered at the Conference on Endocrine and Neural Control of Sex and Related Behavior. Dorado Beach, Puerto Rico.

Turner, C. D., and Asakawa, H. (1964). *Science,* 143, 1344-1345.

Witschi, E. (1956). In *Gestation,* Transactions of the Third Conference, C. A. Villee, editor. Princeton.

Witschi, E. (1965). *Archives d'Anatomie Microscopique et de Morphologie Experimentale,* 54, 601-611.

Yamamoto, T. (1962). *Gen. Comp. Endocrinology,* Supp. 1, 311-345.

Young, W. C., Goy, R. W., and Phoenix, C. H. (1965). *Sex Research, New Developments,* John Money, editor. New York, Holt, Rinehart and Winston.

30

At first glance Mitchell's paper does not appear to belong in the section of this volume concerned with the development of psychosexual differences. Unlike the other papers in this section, it is concerned only with empirical research. Mitchell's research involves careful analysis of mother-infant interactions in monkeys. A standardized scoring system was used in which mother-infant behaviors are measured in terms of the occurrence of a particular behavior during successive fifteen-second intervals of fifteen-minute test sessions. He found that maternal behavior was dependent upon the sex of the infant. In the first three months of the infant's life, mothers of females exhibited more affectional contacts with their infants than mothers of males. During the second three months, they groomed female infants more than males. Mothers of males presented more to their infants than mothers of females. They also played with and aggressed against male infants more than females.

Mitchell's work suggests that the mothers play an active role in promoting differential amounts of independence in the two sexes. Female infants both received and reciprocated more positive physical contact than did the males. Mothers of males restrained them less often than females and withdrew from them more.

These findings suggest a number of interesting possibilities that may be related to human psychosexual development. First, differences in the treatment of differently sexed young may be a characteristic of primate behavior rather than a product of human culture. Such behavior would still represent an environmental contribution to gender differentiation, but investigation of its origin would lie within the province of biology rather than sociology or anthropology. Second, the stimuli controlling differential maternal behavior in primates are still unknown, but Mitchell suggests in other studies that male infants are more active and bite their mothers more often than females. Thus *behavioral differences between the sexes at a very young age may trigger differences in their treatment, which in turn amplify the initial differences. Only a relatively small amount of physiological priming would be required to explain large differences in psychosexual gender. One would like to see behavioral analyses similar to those performed by Mitchell on adult-young relationships in primates who have been subject to hormonal manipulation.*

The mother's relation with the male infant was compared with the mother's relation with the female infant in 32 mother-infant pairs of rhesus monkeys. Mothers had more physical contact with female infants and restrained females more frequently than males. Mothers of males withdrew from, played with, and presented to their infants more often than did mothers of females. Males bit their mothers more often than did females. The frequency and form of mother-infant contacts depend on the behavior of the mother and on the age and sex of the infant.

Attachment Differences in Male and Female Infant Monkeys*

Gary D. Mitchell

Normal mother-infant relations in the subhuman primates have been studied extensively, both in the field (DeVore, 1963; Jay, 1963) and in the laboratory (Hansen, 1966). It has been generally recognized that male rhesus monkey infants are more active and more playful than female monkey infants (Hansen, 1966); yet no published laboratory studies have quantified the mother's relations with rhesus infants of different sex. It has been assumed that a normal rhesus monkey mother provides equivalent amounts of protection and punishment to a male and a female infant. Since Jensen, Bobbitt, and Gordon (1966, 1967) have reported sex differences in the mother-infant social interactions of pig-tailed monkeys, it is quite probable that similar differences exist in a closely related macaque, the rhesus monkey.

The present study incorporates data from three laboratory mother-infant experiments on the rhesus monkey. Since the mother's protection and punishment during the second 3 months

*From *Child Development,* 1968, *39* (2), 611-20.

of the infant's life is acknowledged to be quite different from the relations during the first 3 months (Hansen, 1966), the present study has two specific purposes: (1) to compare the first and second 90 days of the mother-infant relation and (2) to compare the mother's relation with the male infant to the mother's relation with the female infant.

METHOD

Subjects

An examination was made of the behavioral histories of mother-infant relations for 16 male infant and 16 female infant rhesus monkeys which had been reared at the University of Wisconsin Primate Laboratory. Twenty-eight of the mothers were jungle reared, and four were laboratory reared.

The maternal and infant behaviors discussed here are based on the first 6 months of data accumulated in studies conducted by Alexander (1966), Arling (1966), and Griffin (1966). The modified Hansen (1966) scoring system was used in all three studies. This is a standard Wisconsin system in which mother-infant behaviors are measured in terms of the occurrence of a particular behavior during successive 15-second intervals of 15-minute test sessions. A behavior is scored for one and only one 15-second period, even though it may occur several times during that interval. Although the original rearing conditions given to these mother-infant pairs differed in the three basic experiments, all 32 infants lived with their mothers 24 hours a day throughout the first 6 months.

Apparatus

The 32 mother-infant pairs lived in a standard Wisconsin playpen apparatus described by Hansen (1966).

Procedure

Two observers worked simultaneously, each observing a different mother-infant pair for 15 minutes, twice daily. The order of testing particular mother-infant pairs was balanced.

Symbols, corresponding to specific behavioral categories, were recorded in each scoring interval. Every 15 seconds a buzzer signaled the start of a new time period, and symbols were then entered in a subsequent row. Each row was subdivided into an upper section for maternal behaviors and a lower section for infant behaviors. The unit of the scoring system was the occurrence of a given motor pattern of behavior within a 15-second interval. The mother and infant behaviors which were recorded are defined below, and interobserver reliability coefficients for each of these behaviors, most of which are above .85, appear in Alexander (1966), Arling (1966), and Griffin (1966).

A. *Maternal Behaviors*

1. *Approach.* — Movement toward the infant of at least one body length.
2. *Withdraw.* — Movement away from the infant of at least one body length.
3. *Visual orient.* — Looking at the infant.
4. *Oral exploration.* — Oral examination of the infant, such as sniffing or mouthing.
5. *Manual exploration.* — Manual examination of the infant.
6. *Nonspecific contact.* — Diffuse body contacts with the infant, such as brushing against, falling upon, or bumping into the infant.
7. *Retrieval.* — Maternal restoration of ventral-ventral contact with the infant.
8. *Embrace.* — Providing active support for the infant, using the limbs.
9. *Clasp.* — Gripping the fur of the infant.
10. *Restrain.* — Active interference with the infant's attempts to leave the mother.
11. *Reject.* Pushing the infant away.
12. *Groom.* — Spreading and picking through the fur of the infant.
13. *Clasp-pull-bite.* — Mouthing, cuffing, slapping, or clasp-pulling the fur of the infant.
14. *Retrieval grimace.* — An expression consisting of retraction of the corners of the mouth alternated with lip smacking.
15. *Threat.* — (a) Flattening the ears, opening the mouth, and bobbing the head toward the infant; or (b) expression similar to the human frown, involving a wrinkling of the brow and a facial scowl.
16. *Present.* — Assumption of the female sexual position, involving a rigid posture and exposure of the genitalia to the infant.
17. *Play.* — (a) Mouthing, tumbling, and wrestling with the infant; or (b) infant-oriented approach or withdrawal movements accompanied by at least two bounces, caroms, or rebounds.
18. *Aggression.* — Biting or tearing the fur or flesh of the infant.
19. *Fear grimace.* — A retraction of the corners of the mouth, which exposes the teeth.
20. *Convulsive jerk.* — Violent shaking or shuddering of the body.

B. Infant Behaviors

1. *Embrace.* — One or both arms wrapped around the mother.
2. *Coo.* — A soft drawn-out "whoo" vocalization.
3. *Approach.* — Same definition as for maternal behavior.
4. *Withdraw.* — Same as for maternal behavior.
5. *Visual orient.* — Same as for maternal behavior.
6. *Oral exploration.* — Same as for maternal behavior.
7. *Manual exploration.* — Same as for maternal behavior.
8. *Nonspecific contact.* — Same as for maternal behavior.
9. *Gross contact.* — Full-body contact with the mother but not on her ventral surface.
10. *Ventral contact.* — The ventral surface of the infant contacts the ventral surface of the mother.
11. *Nipple contact.* — Oral contact with the mother's nipple.
12. *Clasp.* — Same as for maternal behavior.
13. *Submit.* — Assumption of a rigid posture in response to the contact activities of the mother.
14. *Clasp-pull-bite.* — Same as for maternal behavior.

Statistical Analysis

The Hansen system (1966) placed an upper limit on the obtained scores (60 per session); hence these scores do not represent the absolute frequencies of specific behaviors for the time periods sampled. The modified frequencies were subjected to a two-tailed Wilcoxon matched-groups, signed-ranks test, with the two sexes being matched for experimenter and early rearing condition. The same test was used to compare the first 3 months with the second 3 months for males and females separately. The significance level for all comparisons was .05. One-tailed probabilities were also presented when a difference which had been predicted from other studies (Jensen et al., 1966, 1967) reached the .05 level for a one-tailed Wilcoxin test.

RESULTS

Maternal Behavior

Table 1 presents the median frequencies for maternal behaviors with male and female infants during the two 90-day blocks. There were two obvious differences between the behaviors directed toward male infants and behaviors directed toward female infants. The mothers of female infants restrained their infants more frequently in the first 3 months. In the second 3 months, the mothers of males presented significantly more often than did mothers of females.

The one-tailed test, allowed by predictions from previously published studies (Jensen et al., 1966, 1967), revealed five more differences in maternal behavior which depended on the sex of the infant. In the first 3 months, mothers of female infants exhibited more nonspecific contact, more embraces, more clasps, and fewer withdrawals than did mothers of male infants. In the second 3

TABLE 1

MEDIAN FREGUENCIES OF MATERNAL BEHAVIORS TOWARD MALE AND FEMALE INFANTS AND PROBABILITY LEVELS OF WILCOXON TESTS

MATERNAL BEHAVIOR	0-3 MONTHS		SEX DIFF.	3-6 MONTHS		SEX DIFF.	AGE DIFF. P	
	M	F	(P)	M	F	(P)	M	F
1. Approach...	50.5	58.0	...	11.0	13.0	...	.01	.01
2. Withdraw..	50.0	17.5	*	33.0	23.5	...	...	...
3. Visual orient......	860.5	887.5	...	632.5	768.0	...	...	...
4. Oral explore.	26.5	39.0	...	13.5	9.5	...	.01	.01
5. Manual explore.....	31.5	40.0	...	3.5	5.0	...	.01	.01
6. Nonspecific contact.....	70.0	90.0	*	35.5	38.5	...	.01	.01
7. Retrieve....	48.5	70.5	...	1.5	3.5	...	.01	.01
8. Embrace....	1,210.0	1,432.5	*	353.5	323.5	...	.01	.01
9. Clasp......	32.5	44.0	*	23.5	28.5	...	.05	...
10. Restrain....	24.5	63.5	.05	0.0	1.0	...	.01	.01
11. Reject......	23.5	16.5	...	44.5	27.0	...	.05	...
12. Groom.....	164.0	189.5	...	32.5	75.5	*	.01	.02
13. Clasp-pull- bite........	25.0	17.0	...	33.0	28.0	...	...	...
14. Retrieval grimace....	12.5	11.5	...	0.0	0.5	...	.02	.05
15. Threat.....	23.0	54.5	...	85.5	79.0	...	.01	...
16. Present.....	6.5	4.0	...	9.0	5.0	.01	...	...

* Significant at the .05 level by a one-tailed Wilcoxon test.

months, moreover, female infants were groomed more often than were males.

There were two other infrequently occurring maternal behaviors which differed according to the sex of the infant: play and aggression. Nine out of 16 mothers of males played with their infants (a total of 90 times), while only one mother of a female infant played (a total of one time). Two mothers aggressed their infants, and both of these infants were males.

The mothers of both males and females initiated more behavior in the first 90 days than in the second 90 days. In the second 90-day block, the following behaviors decreased significantly for mothers of both males and females: approach, oral exploration, manual exploration, nonspecific contact, retrieval grimace, embrace, restrain, groom, and retrieval. Two behaviors which occurred infrequently also decreased significantly in the second 3 months: fear grimaces and convulsive jerks by the mother. Fear grimaces toward the infant occurred 55 times in the first 3 months and only 15 times thereafter. Some mothers jerked convulsively (102 times) during the first 90 days, but none jerked during the second 90. There were no sex differences associated with these two behaviors. Clasping also decreased significantly in the second 90 days, but for mothers of male infants only. Mothers of males showed a significant increase in rejection and threat in the second 90-day block.

Infant Behaviors

Male and female infants differed significantly in only one mother-directed behavior: clasp-pull-bite (see Table 2). Male infants exhibited this behavior significantly more often than did females.

Reliable decreases with age occurred for both male and female infants in the following categories: embrace, ventral contact, and nipple contact. Significant increases for both sexes were observed

TABLE 2

MEDIAN FREQUENCIES OF INFANT BEHAVIORS TOWARD MOTHER AND PROBABILITY LEVELS OF WILCOXON TESTS

INFANT BEHAVIOR	0–3 MONTHS		SEX DIFF. (P)	3–6 MONTHS		SEX DIFF. (P)	AGE DIFF. P	
	M	F		M	F		M	F
1. Embrace....	1,331.0	1,371.5	...	326.0	492.0	...	.01	.01
2. Coo........	25.0	29.5	...	72.5	67.5	...	...	.05
3. Approach...	341.0	330.0	...	658.0	469.5	...	.03	.01
4. Withdraw..	4.0	5.0	...	40.0	38.5	...	.01	.01
5. Visual orient....	433.5	428.5	...	668.5	706.0	...	...	.01
6. Oral explore.	119.5	126.5	...	40.0	51.5	...	...	.01
7. Manual explore...	51.0	64.5	...	32.5	36.0	...	...	.01
8. Nonspecific contact...	463.0	516.5	...	947.5	712.5	...	.01	.05
9. Gross contact...	117.0	166.5	...	167.5	96.5	...	...	.05
10. Ventral contact...	1,957.5	1,843.5	...	537.5	868.5	...	.01	.01
11. Nipple contact...	1,801.0	1,693.5	...	553.0	739.5	...	.01	.01
12. Clasp......	269.5	338.5	...	191.5	158.5	...	...	.01
13. Submit.....	5.5	6.0	...	4.5	4.0	...	...	...
14. Clasp-pull-bite......	1.5	3.5	...	6.5	3.5	.01	.01	...

in approach, withdraw, and nonspecific contact. Females showed stable increases in coo, visual orient, oral explore, and manual explore, and significant decreases in gross body contact and clasping, while males exhibited a significant increase in clasp-pull-biting.

Nonpunitive Physical Contact

Two general categories involving the total frequency of non-punitive physical contact were devised combining several behaviors: (*a*) *infant-initiated nonpunitive physical contact* included embraces, oral explores, manual explores, nonspecific contacts, gross body contacts, ventral contacts, nipple contacts, and clasp; and (*b*) *mother-initiated nonpunitive physical contact* included embraces, oral explores, manual explores, nonspecific contacts, retrievals, clasps, restrains, and grooms. Female infants received more nonpunitive physical contact from their mothers during the first 3 months than did male infants (see Table 3), and female infants seemed to reciprocate with a higher frequency of nonpunitive physical contact than did the male infants, although the latter difference was not significant.

DISCUSSION

If protection can be defined as close nonpunitive physical contact, the mothers protected the female infants more than the males. The frequencies of maternal restraint observed also supported this notion. The female infants both received and reciprocated more positive physical contact than did the males. The mothers of males did not differ significantly from the mothers of females in the amount of punishment administered to the infants, but they promoted independence in their male offspring by

TABLE 3

MEDIAN FREQUENCIES OF NONPUNITIVE PHYSICAL CONTACT
AND PROBABILITY LEVELS OF WILCOXON TESTS

	0–3 Months		Sex Diff. (P)	3–6 Months		Sex Diff. (P)	Age Diff. (P)	
	Male Infant	Female Infant		Male Infant	Female Infant		Male Infant	Female Infant
Mother initiated..	1,764.5	1,985.5	.05	461.5	634.5	...	.01	.01
Infant initiated..	6,126.5	6,543.5	...	3,205.0	3,409.5	...	.01	.01

not restraining them and by withdrawing from them. Higher activity in the male infants might have accounted for at least part of the depressed positive maternal contact. Male infants in the field have been reported to leave their mothers sooner than female infants (Itani, 1959), but Jensen et al. (1967) reported that the *mothers* of males as well as the male infants themselves withdrew from contact more frequently than mothers of females during the first 15 weeks of life. This finding was partially corroborated in the present report. The mothers apparently play an active role in promoting differential amounts of independence in the two sexes. The females remain closely attached to the mothers; the males interact more frequently with other members at the periphery of the troop. Field studies have described the behavioral repertoire of the female infants as being centered in the mature females and particularly in their own mothers (DeVore, 1963; Jay, 1963). The males, on the other hand, became the recipients of more social exploration and grooming from other members of the troop than did the female infants (Boelkins, personal communication, 1967). Differential activity levels again may account for some of this difference, but most of the grooming and exploration directed toward male infants by other members of the troop has been reported to occur when the infants were in physical contact with the mother (R.C. Boelkins, personal communication). There were apparently three behaviors which promoted independence in the male: (a) the mother's early withdrawal from contact with the male infant, (b) the high interest of the other troop members in the male infant, and (c) the male infant's own striving for independence from the mother.

Despite the relatively low level of positive physical contact between male infants and their mothers, the physical interaction that did occur was quite intense. Mothers of males were more frequently involved in bouts of social play with their infants, and this play involved vigorous bouncing and wrestling. Although these interactions were not observed frequently, even between males and their mothers, they were almost never seen between females and their mothers. In addition, mothers of males sexually presented more often to their infants than did mothers of females, and the only two infants aggressed by their mothers were males.

This high intensity of maternal interaction with the male infant can apparently be exaggerated when the mother has been socially deprived early in life. In the jungle-reared mothers of the present study, significant infant sex differences were not found in the frequencies of punishment. However, Arling (personal communication) observed that maternal punishment increased to the point of brutality in rhesus monkeys that had been socially deprived. In eight out of nine of Arling's brutal animals, the maternal brutality was directed toward a male infant.

In the present study, most infant-directed behaviors decreased from the first 90-day block to the second. However, there were some exceptions, such as punishing, rejections, and threats, which have been described as good indicants of the mother's transition into a second maternal stage (Hansen, 1966). Both the frequency and the form of maternal punishment changed with the age of the infant. Gentle mouthing by the mother occurred frequently in the first 90 days but changed in quality to biting in the second 90-day block, while rejection gradually increased over time. Hansen (1966) reported similar changes. The maternal convulsive jerk, a response which usually occurred when the infant bit the nipple, disappeared completely in the second 90-day block of the present study, and the pattern of mouthing and jerking slowly gave way to rejecting or pushing the infant away in the second 90 days. The increased frequency of male infant punishment administered by the mothers of the present study in the second 90 days was undoubtedly related to the increasing frequency of male infant clasp-pull-bites directed toward the mothers.

Mother-directed behaviors involving prolonged contact (e.g., embrace, ventral contact, nipple contact) decreased sharply in the second 90 days of life, while noncontact or brief-contact behaviors increased. There was a transition for both mother and infant away from an attachment restricted to physical contact to one including sensory and motor communicative skills. Coo vocalizations and visual orients increased with age in the infant, while threats and presents increased in the mothers. Coo vocalizations generally occurred more frequently in juvenile females than in juvenile males (Mitchell, in press), but this sex difference was not yet evident at 6 months of age.

In humans, it has been generally believed that sex differences are to a large extent experientially determined by a process called "sex-typing" (see Mussen, Conger, & Kagan, 1963, p. 286). The present data suggest that experiential variables may also influence the sex role of the monkey. A previous experiment at Wisconsin (Chamove, Harlow, & Mitchell, 1967) reported differential maternal-like infant-directed behaviors in sexually immature male and female monkeys. The females typically exhibited maternal-like affiliative patterns toward infants, whereas the males exhibited patterns of indifference or hostility. Such differences were observed in monkeys over a wide range of social rearing conditions but have been conspicuously absent in monkeys reared in social isolation (Mitchell, in press). These apparently biological sex differences become most marked in monkeys who have experienced real monkey mothering.

Generally speaking, in the rhesus monkeys, and probably in all primates, the mother's relations with the male and the female infant are very much alike. However, the differences that do exist may be crucial to the long-term development of the primate. For example, one would predict from the above data that over-protective mothering would lead to more social retardation in the male than in the female. A recent project at the Wisconsin Primate Laboratory found that overprotective primiparous mothering did in fact retard male infants more than female infants. Primiparous mothered males played very little and cooed very frequently (Mitchell, Ruppenthal, Raymond, & Harlow, 1966). These two behavioral patterns are characteristically female. Differences in mother-infant interaction apparently en*gender* differential long-term effects along a male-female continuum of behavior.

REFERENCES

Alexander, B. K. The effects of early peer deprivation on juvenile behavior of rhesus monkeys. Unpublished doctoral dissertation, University of Wisconsin, 1966.

Arling, G. L. Effects of social deprivation on maternal behavior of rhesus monkeys. Unpublished Master's thesis, University of Wisconsin, 1966.

Chamove, A. C., Harlow, H. F., & Mitchell, G. D. Sex differences in the infant-directed behavior of preadolescent rhesus monkeys. *Child Development,* 1967, *38,* 329-335.

DeVore, I. T. Mother-infant relations in baboons. In H. Rheingold (Ed.), *Maternal behavior in mammals.* New York: Wiley, 1963, Pp. 305-335.

Griffin, G. A. The effects of multiple mothering on the infant-mother and infant-infant affectional systems. Unpublished doctoral dissertation, University of Wisconsin, 1966.

Hansen, E. W. The development of maternal and infant behavior in the rhesus monkey. *Behaviour,* 1966, *27,* 107-149.

Itani, J. Paternal care in the wild Japanese monkey, *Macaca fuscata fuscata. Primates,* 1959, *2,* 61-93.

Jay, P. Mother-infant relations in langurs. In H. Rheingold (Ed.), *Maternal behavior in mammals.* New York: Wiley, 1963, Pp. 287-304.

Jensen, G. D., Bobbitt, R. A., & Gordon, B. N. Sex differences in social interaction between infant monkeys and their mothers. In J. Wortis (Ed.), *Recent advances in biological psychiatry.* Vol. 9. New York: Plenum, 1966. Pp. 283-293.

Jensen, G. D., Bobbitt, R. A., & Gordon, B. N. The development of maternal independence in mother-infant pigtailed monkeys, *Macaca nemestrina.* In S. A. Altmann (Ed.), *Social communication among primates.* Chicago: University of Chicago Press, 1967. Pp. 43-53.

Mitchell, G. D. Persistent behavior pathology in rhesus monkeys following early social isolation. *Folia primatologica,* in press.

Mitchell, G. D., Ruppenthal, G. C., Raymond, E. J., & Harlow, H. F. Long-term effects of multiparous and primiparous monkey mother rearing. *Child Development,* 1966, *37,* 781-791.

Mussen, P. H., Conger, J. J., & Kagan, J. *Child development and personality.* New York: Harper & Row, 1963.

SUGGESTED PAPERS AND PROJECTS

Papers:

1. Is aggression a biologically "masculine" characteristic?
2. Discuss the origins of psychosexual disorders in humans.
3. What is the hormonal basis for sexual differentiation?
4. What is the biological basis of biological determinism?

Projects:

1. Visit the zoo. What are similarities and differences in play patterns between primates and humans?
2. Differentiate between the terms "homosexual," "transexual," and "transvestite."
3. Note differences in the external gentalia of developing fetuses of both sexes. (This is much more effective if actual fetuses can be observed).
4. What effect would it have on you if you were told you had a chromosomal abnormality which changed your sexual classification?

ADDITIONAL REFERENCES

Beach, F. A. (Ed.) *Sex and behavior.* New York: Wiley, 1965.

Beckwith, L. Relationships between infants' vocalizations and their mothers' behaviors. *Merrill-Palmer Quarterly,* 1971, *17,* 211-26.

Clark, G., and Birch, H. G. Hormonal modification of social behavior. *Psychosomatic Medicine,* 1945, *7,* 321-29.

———. and ———. Hormonal modification of social behavior. *Psychosomatic Medicine,* 1946, 8, 320-31.

Garron, D. C., and Vander Stoep, L. R. Personality and intelligence in Turner's syndrome. *Archives of General Psychiatry,* 1969, *21,* 229-46.

Gross, C. G. Biology and pop-biology: Sex and sexism. Symposium presented at the meeting of the American Orthopsychiatric Association, Detroit, April, 1972.

Parke, R. D., O'Leary, S. E., and West, S. Mother-father newborn interaction: Effects of maternal medication, labor, and sex of infant. *Proceedings of the 80th Annual Convention of the American Psychological Association,* 1972, 85-86.

Stotler, R. *Sex and gender: On the development of masculinity and femininity.* New York: Science House, 1968.

Tobach, E. Some evolutionary aspects of human gender. *American Journal of Orthopsychiatry,* 1971, *41,* 710-15.

Section VI

The Unique Female Condition: Menstruation and Pregnancy

31 Introduction

An understanding of the hormonal events accompanying the menstrual cycle and pregnancy is essential in order to understand the issues generated by the study of the psychological phenomena accompanying these conditions.[1] The statement that the psychological state of the human female is affected by the rhythmic physiological changes of the menstrual cycle is questioned by few. The term "premenstrual syndrome" is commonly used in the medical and psychological literature to refer to the symptoms of cramps, head- and backaches, irritability, mood swings, tension, and/or depression which are present in 30 to 50 percent of normal young married women during the three or four days before the onset of menses (Moos, 1968). Impairment of cognitive function may also be present (Dalton, 1960a; Kopell et al., 1969). Sutherland and Steward (1965) found that only 17 percent of the women they investigated were completely free of some aspect of this syndrome. In fact, they propose the use of the term "cyclical phenomenon" to emphasize that such changes are typical and physiological rather than pathological in nature. Unfortunately most studies of the menstrual cycle and pregnancy are of small clinical or otherwise selected populations.

The most interesting studies of the psychological events attending the menstrual cycle are those that do not limit themselves to a simple listing of symptoms. A number of studies have indicated that affective swings in women during the premenstrual and menstrual periods may be correlated with an increase in number of suicide attempts (Mandell and Mandell, 1967), hospital admissions for accidents (Dalton, 1960b), hospital admissions for acute psychiatric illness (Dalton, 1959), and even visits to a clinic for minor illnesses of their children (Dalton, 1966). The latter phenomenon is of particular interest since clinic visits are attributed to the child's behavior and/or physical condition. Presumably the mother is unaware of the relationship of the menstrual cycle to her judgment of her child, and such behavior is therefore unlikely to be part of the culturally conditioned symptomology of menstruation.

---

1. A summary of the physiological changes associated with the menstrual cycle and pregnancy is included elsewhere in the book.

WOMAN: DEPENDENT OR INDEPENDENT VARIABLE?

Basic research into the behavior associated with the menstrual cycle is confused by the problem of how much of such behavior is culturally conditioned and how much is determined by the hormones present during various stages of the cycle. It is clear that most cultures, including our own, have menstrual taboos of varying degrees of severity (Stephens, 1961). Ivey and Bardwick (1968) investigated normal subjects over two complete cycles with a sensitive instrument measuring levels of anxiety, guilt, shame, and concern with death, mutilation, and separation. They found consistent and significant variations in anxiety level between ovulation and premenstrual samples for each subject. Estrogen is known to be a nervous system excitant while progesterone acts as a depressant on the central nervous system. Ivey and Bardwick conclude that endocrine changes greatly affect behavior so that in spite of personality differences, even in normal women behavior becomes predictable on the basis of cycle phase.

Ivey and Bardwick's study is somewhat better controlled than other studies of menstrual cycle behavior. A clinical population was not utilized and subjects served as their own controls. Nevertheless, there were some methodological problems in the study which limit the generalizability of its findings. For example, subjects knew they were participating in a study on menstruation. They apparently knew each other and the experimenter. Moreover, postexperimental interviews revealed that the subjects were aware that the study was about moods. As in Dalton's (1966) study, only a correlational relationship between menstrual phase and behavior was obtained. Nevertheless, these studies represent rather extreme positions on chemical causality.

A recent study by Paige (1971) represents the first attempt to analyze experimentally the etiology of the behavioral changes associated with the menstrual cycle. It is possible that menstrual symptoms are socially mediated emotional responses to a condition of the female body and the associated biological events represent a spurious correlation. Paige utilized the same method of analyzing the verbal content of speech as Ivey and Bardwick, but under conditions that disguised the purpose of the study. She asserts that her results were not determined either by self-selection or prior expectations of the subjects.

Paige's experimental design is a rather complex one that involves the comparison of individuals with natural menstrual cycles to those using two different types of oral contraceptives: combination types (an estrogen- and progesterone-like substance combined) and sequential type (an estrogen-like substance for most of the cycle and, in addition, a progesterone-like substance for the last four or five days of the cycle). She also compared those with a good deal of physical discomfort, especially bleeding under any condition with those who had little discomfort or bleeding). She found the usual cyclic affective changes for women not using oral contraceptives and none for users of a combination pill. Users of sequential pills, however, showed cyclic fluctuations, although to a much lesser extent than non-pill users.

Biochemically, the two pill-using groups were more similar to each other than to the non-pill group. Nevertheless, they showed striking differences from each other in the pattern of fluctuation of two components of affective state—anxiety and hostility. Although the sequential group showed less overall negative affect than the combination group, they showed a sharp rise in premenstrual anxiety similar to that of a natural cycle. Sequential pills reduce menstrual flow less than combination pills and heavy bleeders showed a greater rise of anxiety than light bleeders. Therefore, Paige attributes premenstrual anxiety as a response to a culturally conditioned negative self-image associated with bleeding. On the other hand, combination users had a greater overall amount of hostility than sequential users. Amount of hostility was correlated with the amount of progesterone in the pill used. Progesterone apparently increases the amount of monoamine oxidase (MAO) in the bloodstream. This substance is associated with mental illnesses involving mood fluctuations. Premenstrual hostility may be attributable to chemical factors. Thus Paige's study reveals a multideterminist causality pattern. Cultural factors may account for the premenstrual rise in anxiety while biological factors may account for the rise in hostility.

Paige's study avoids some of the methodological problems common to a number of studies involving oral contraceptives. These other studies have stressed the effect of a potent drug on behavior. They have also tended to concentrate on small clinical populations and to rely on self-report and retrospective recall methods of data collection. They would possibly tend to overemphasize the role of social expectations. Nevertheless, such studies (Moos, 1968; Silbergeld et al., 1971) have seemed to confirm the finding of mood flattening throughout the menstrual cycle when oral contraceptives are used.

These same methodological considerations limit the generalizability of studies of psychological behavior following child-bearing. It is estimated that 20-40 percent of all postpartum women experience some depression and/or cognitive impairment (Treadway et al., 1969). Studies of postpartum behavior, like those of menstrual behavior, tend to fall into two camps: those that emphasize biochemical factors and those that emphasize cultural or environmental factors. The Treadway et al. (1969) study is representative of studies that concentrate upon the effect of hormones upon the central nervous system. They simultaneously studied a large number of psychological and biochemical factors in hospitalized pregnant and nonpregnant women. Their study was particularly valuable since it did not select only subjects with a considerable degree of postpartum depression. They found a significant correlation between decreased norepinephrine in the bloodstream and increased depressive self-reports of pregnant and postpartum women compared to their nonpregnant controls. Norepinephrine is also reduced in certain kinds of clinical depressions. Treadway and his associates hypothesize that estrogen and progesterone levels affect norepinephrine and produce an increased biologic susceptibility to affective disorders in the period following childbirth.

It is important to understand why some women are resistant to the presumed biochemical stresses of menstruation and childbirth while others are not. Some students of the subject emphasize psychological factors as major determinants of premenstrual and postpartum syndromes. Coppen and Kessel (1963) find a high correlation between premenstrual syndromes and neuroticism. They found that women who complained of premenstrual irritability were also more irritable at other times.

Melges (1968) takes an extreme environmental position with regard to the nature of the factors predisposing severe postpartum reactions. He analyzed one hundred postpartum patients with a syndrome comprised of shame, helplessness, and confusion. He found no differences from controls in simple cognitive function. He claims that conflict over assuming the mothering role is the central precipitating stress. Women manifesting this syndrome tend to have had absent or inadequate mothers of their own. Far more than the expected percentage of affected mothers were younger children. There was a very high recurrence rate. Melges stresses the presense of a typical postpartum syndrome in three women following adoption of an infant as important evidence that the syndrome is nonphysiological in origin.

The major issue in the study of the psychological concomitants of menstruation and pregnancy is not whether such changes occur, but to what factors such changes are attributable. The nature-nurture argument, which has disappeared from most biological and psychological texts, continues here. The seemingly implacable correlation between physiological and behavioral events tends to seduce one into believing that such correlations must be causative.

There may be an implicit bias in this area because of the fact that, until recently, most researchers have been male. There is a tendency to ignore the 40 percent of women who do not show menstrual symptomology or the larger percentage who do not show significant postpartum depression. Moreover, despite rises in suicides, accidents, crimes, etc. during the premenstrual and menstrual period, women still have far lower rates in these activities than men (Dr. Estelle Ramey, personal communication). Researchers do not report negative results, so that only studies showing symptomology appear in the literature.

Controversy in this area can probably be resolved by an interactional approach. The factors underlying behavioral changes during the menstrual cycle and following childbirth are probably multidimensional. Chemical factors probably have a predispositional effect, but culture and personality probably also play a role. Good cross-cultural studies involving biochemical and behavioral measures are necessary to clarify the issues in this area.

REFERENCES

Coppen, A. and Kessel, N. Menstruation and personality. *British Journal of Psychiatry*, 1963, *109*, 711-21.

Dalton, K. Menstruation and acute psychiatric illness. *British Medical Journal*, 1959, 148-49.

———. *Effect of menstruation on schoolgirls' weekly work.* British Medical Journal, 1960, 326-28. (a)

———. Menstruation and accidents. *British Medical Journal*, 1960, 1425-26. (b)

———. *The influence of mother's menstruation on her child.* Proceedings of the Royal Society of Medicine, 1966, *59*, 1014-16.

Garcia, M. Hormonal interactions, menstruation and the oral contraceptives. Written especially for this volume.

Ivey, M., and Bardwick, J. Patterns of affective fluctuations in the menstrual cycle. *Psychosomatic Medicine*, 1968, *30*, 336-45.

Kopell, B. S.; Lunde, D.; Clayton, R. B.; and Moos, R. H. Variations in some measures of arousal during the menstrual cycle. *Journal of Nervous and Mental Diseases*, 1969, *148*, 180-87.

Mandell, A., and Mandell, M. Suicide and the menstrual cycle. *Journal of the American Medical Association*, 1967, *200*, 792.

Melges, F. T. Postpartum psychiatric syndromes. *Psychosomatic Medicine*, 1968, *30*, 95-108.

Moos, R. Psychological aspects of oral contraceptives. *Archives of General Psychiatry,* 1968, *19,* 87-94.

— — —. The development of a menstrual distress questionnaire. *Psychosomatic Medicine,* 1968, *30,* 853-67.

Paige, K. E. Effects of oral contraceptives on affective fluctuations associated with the menstrual cycle. *Psychosomatic Medicine,* 1971, *33,* 515-37.

Silbergeld, S.; Brast, N.; and Noble, E. P. The menstrual cycle: A double-blind study of symptoms, mood and behavior, and biochemical variables using Enovid and Placebo. *Psychosomatic Medicine,* 1971, *33,* 411-28.

Stephens, W. A cross-cultural study of menstrual taboos. *Genetic Psychology Monographs,* 1961, *64,* 385-416.

Sutherland, H., & Stewart, I. A critical analysis of the premenstrual syndrome. *Lancet,* 1965, *1,* 1180-83.

Treadway, C. R.; Kane, F. J.: Jarrahi-Zadeh, A.; & Lipton, M. A. A psycho-endocrine study of pregnancy and puerperium. *American Journal of Psychiatry,* 1969, *125,* 1380-86.

32

There is little doubt that the psychological state of the human female is affected by the rhythmic physiological changes known as the menstrual cycle. The menstrual cycle is an evolutionary invention of the primates and is not found in other species. The cycle affects both the ovaries and the uterus and is under the control of several pituitary hormones known collectively as gonadotropins.

No one knows what stimulus at puberty sets the female reproductive system cycling, but Dr. Garcia discusses the complex series of physiological events that recur with great regularity until either pregnancy or menopause ensues. A cycle begins with the secretion of follicle-stimulating hormone [FSH] by the pituitary in response to a signal from the hypothalamus. During this follicular stage of the cycle FSH alone stimulates the growth of the egg follicle in the ovary. An additional pituitary hormone, luteinizing hormone [LH], is also present. LH is mainly responsible for stimulating estrogen secretion by the ovary. Estrogen stimulates further follicular growth and is also responsible for the proliferation of the endometrial lining of the uterus.

Toward the end of the follicular stage some progesterone is secreted by the ovary. The increasing amount of estrogen and progesterone circulating in the bloodstream somehow stimulate a sudden release of LH at the middle of the menstrual cycle. This "ovulatory surge" appears to cause the release of the egg from its follicle. Estrogen reaches its peak level at this time. There may be two areas in the hypothalamus regulating LH release; one maintains a basal level of ovarian activity and the other regulates the "ovulatory surge." Both areas respond by decreasing LH secretion when large amounts of estrogen and progesterone are circulating in the bloodstream [the so-called negative feedback mechanism]. Oral contraceptives apparently work by depressing the center that regulates the surge. Thus women on "the pill" have apparently normal but anovulatory cycles.

After ovulation, the empty egg follicle is transformed into the corpus luteum, which acts as a gland secreting both estrogen and progesterone. During this luteal phase of the cycle there is an unexplained rise in basal body temperature, which persists until the next menstrual period. The rise in temperature is often used as a method for family planning.

The luteal phase persists about two weeks in women and during this period the corpus luteum secretes a gradually increasing level of progesterone. If implantation does not occur, the corpus luteum fails for some unexplained reason and estrogen and progesterone levels drop abruptly. With the fall of these hormones the lining of the uterus ceases being maintained. It sloughs off, bleeding occurs, and a new cycle begins with a new signal from the hypothalamus.

If implantation occurs, the corpus luteum is maintained and continues to secrete increasing amounts of progesterone until the placenta takes over as the chief source of this hormone. Progesterone level at the termination of pregnancy is more than nine times that of the peak level during the luteal phase of the menstrual cycle. Estrogen level is also much higher than its peak level at the time of ovulation. The level of both hormones in the bloodstream drops precipitously after birth.

Hormonal Interaction, Menstruation, and the Oral Contraceptives

Margarita Garcia

Hormones are chemical messengers manufactured by several classes of specialized tissue throughout the body. The hormone-manufacturing tissue can secrete its product into the bloodstream (endocrine glands) or to the exterior of the body (exocrine glands). However, the term "pheromone" has been reserved to refer to these external secretory products, leaving the term "hormone" to denote the chemical messengers that are secreted internally and carried by the bloodstream.

Chemically, hormones are molecules of varying structural complexity that can be classified as belonging to one of three general classes: peptides (e.g., insulin), catecholamines (e.g., adrenalin), and steroids (e.g., androgens and estrogens). These molecules are synthesized by the endocrine glands in the course of the normal metabolic degradation of foodstuffs. It is often found, especially among steroid hormones, that the manufacture of one type of molecule is nothing but a simple transformation in the structure of another, biologically active hormone. That is to say,

FIGURE 1

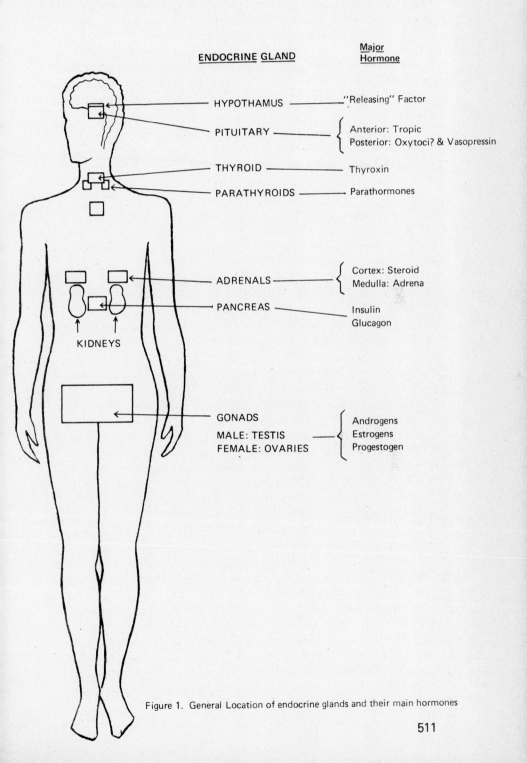

Figure 1. General Location of endocrine glands and their main hormones

there is a high degree of interdependence among several hormones such that one may serve as a substrate, or appear as an intermediary, in the spontaneous synthesis of another.

The endocrine system is a complex network of glands of relatively small size located throughout the body. As can be seen in Figure 1, this system includes the thyroid, parathyroids, adrenals, pancreas, and the pituitary gland, this latter of particular significance because of its role in regulating the action of the other glands.

MODE OF ACTION

Hormones act by influencing the activity of rather specific "target" cells located in organs at some distance away from the endocrine glands. This influence is regulatory in nature and can take the form of increasing or decreasing the normal activities of the target cells, promoting growth, aiding in the regeneration of lost tissue, etc.

One of the intriguing aspects of endocrine physiology is the precise orchestration of the release of hormones that occurs in the normal organism: they are secreted in the right amounts at precisely the right time. Finding what the "right time" is—i.e., finding the conditions that switch on or off a particular gland—has been the task of endocrinological research for many years.

We now know, for example, that the antidiuretic hormone (ADH) is secreted from the posterior lobe of the pituitary whenever the body has suffered some loss of water (ADH acts on the kidney to prevent excessive urination). We also know, as another example, that insulin is secreted by cells in the pancreas whenever a carbohydrate-rich meal has been ingested (insulin stimulates glucose utilization in all cells). But perhaps the best example of the sensitive sequential activity of glands is found in the cyclical release of the several hormones involved in sex and reproduction. The explanation of this fine control of patterns of hormonal release lies in the intricate relationship that exists among the diverse glands and can be best understood by referring to the *negative-feedback* model, as illustrated in Figure 2.

The model postulates the existence of a "master switch" (depicted in the figure as Organ A), which secretes its Hormone 1. The target organ of Hormone 1 is another gland (Organ B), which upon reception of the chemical agent starts secreting hormone. Hormone 2 will now exert its influence on its specific target organs, making them grow and so on. Since upon activation of Organ B

FIGURE 2

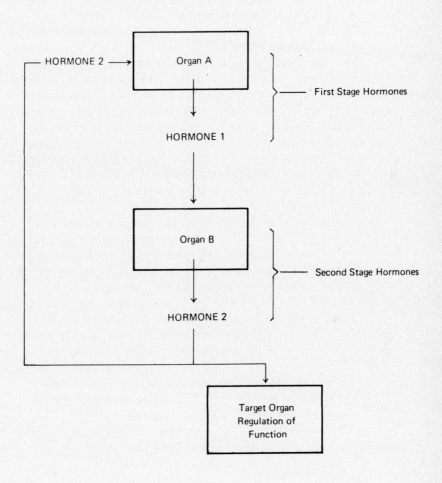

Figure 2. A two-stage negative feedback model

the level of Hormone 2 has been increased in the bloodstream, the heightened concentration of this hormone can be felt wherever there are suitable receptors for its detection. The negative-feedback model postulates that Organ A is also a target organ for the second stage hormone, but that its mode of action upon this master switch is one of inhibition. That is to say, Hormone 2 regulates Organ A by making it diminish its output of Hormone 1. Thus, as soon as this happens, Organ B is not stimulated any more, causing a decrease in blood levels of Hormone 2 and a subsequent removal of the inhibition being exerted upon Organ A. At a suitably low level, Organ A then restarts its production of the first-stage hormone and the cycle continues.

This two-stage negative-feedback model has been found useful in the understanding of the controlling mechanism of glandular secretion, but a situation that most closely approximates the endocrine system in higher mammals is represented by a three-stage negative-feedback model, as represented in Figure 3. The three-stage model differs from the previous one in the postulation of one additional step (Organ C, secreting Hormone 3) in the chain of events. Otherwise the rationale is the same: hormones are able to inhibit the release of other hormones and thus a self-regulating system ensues.

The precise mechanism of inhibition of release is not well understood, but there is no question that the experimental administration of, say, a high level of Hormone 3 results in a subsequent decrease in the blood levels of the first- and/or the second-stage hormones. It was precisely this understanding of the negative-feedback mechanism that permitted the development of the oral contraceptives, to be discussed below.

It must be emphasized at this point that the activity of endocrine glands is by no means as uniquely regulated as the foregoing explanation might have implied. A wide variety of internal as well as external stimuli can interfere at any stage of the negative-feedback loop and a much more complex modulation of endocrine function is, in fact, provided.

HIERARCHICAL CONTROL OF ENDOCRINE FUNCTION

When the anatomical connections of the different glands are examined, it is found that in only two cases (the posterior lobe of the pituitary and the adrenal medulla) is there any direct innervation from higher brain centers. Yet a wide variety of environmental stimuli are known to influence endocrine function. One perfect example of hormonal release triggered by an en-

FIGURE 3

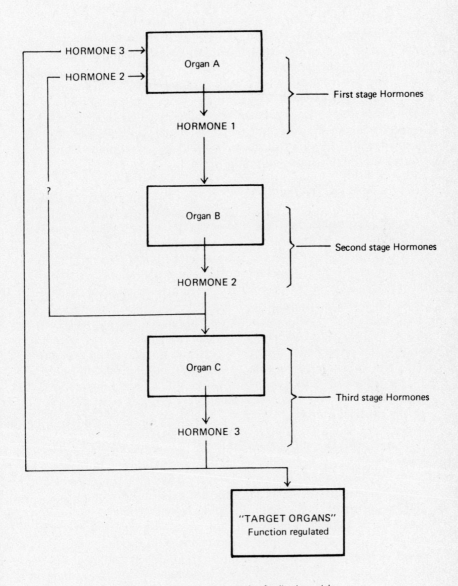

Figure 3. A three-stage negative-feedback model

vironmental situation is provided by the female rabbit: In this animal ovulation does not occur until *after* coitus. Other instances are provided in the cases of the adrenal cortex and the hormones involved in the regulation of the menstrual cycle. The adrenal cortex increases markedly its secretion of steroid hormones just after the organism has been subjected to some type of environmental stress such as a sudden temperature change, an intense light, or bodily restraint. Out-of-cycle menstrual bleeding can occur after a severe emotional upset such as being in a near-accident in an automobile.

Up to a few years ago there was no better explanation for this environmental-endocrine interaction than to say that the activity of glands was somehow "mediated" by higher brain centers. Recent research has shed some light on the hierarchical control of endocrine function by the brain, and we are beginning to understand the nature of this modulating mechanism.

The Hormones of theHypothalamus

The brain center that is in more direct control of endocrine function is the *hypothalamus,* an area about one-half inch in diameter located on the lower surface of the brain. Experimental destruction and/or stimulation of selected portions of the hypothalamus in lower animals has shown this structure to be essential in the regulation of such basic behaviors as the seeking and ingesting of food, sexual responsiveness, rage and attack reactions, "pleasure" experiencing, etc. In addition, it has been known for some time that certain hypothalamic cells have a secretory capacity, being able to manufacture and release hormones just like any other endocrine gland. According to the model presented in Figure 3, the hypothalamus corresponds most closely to the box depicted as "Organ A."

Two of the hypothalamic hormones are *vasopressin* (also known as the antidiuretic hormone, or ADH), and *oxytocin*. Both are stored on the *posterior* lobe of the pituitary gland after synthesis by the hypothalamic cells until called upon to exert their functions on their target organs in the body. Vasopressin has a blood-pressure-elevating function in addition to its direct role in water conservation: oxytocin promotes contraction of the uterus, which helps in expelling the fetus in parturition (in fact, injected oxytocin is used clinically to induce labor). Some workers also postulate that oxytocin release might occur during intromission so that the uterine contractions it promotes facilitate the ascent of spermatozoa in the female tract. Another important function of oxytocin is to stimulate milk ejection by the mammary glands in lactating mothers.

The rest of the hypothalamic hormones, secreted in minute amounts, are just beginning to yield to innumerable attempts at their identification. They are known collectively as the hypothalamic *releasing factors,* and are the ones that most closely resemble the activity of the Hormone 1 depicted in Figure 3. The releasing factors are secreted into a small network of capillaries at the base of the brain known as pituitary portal blood system. Upon reaching the *anterior* lobe of the pituitary gland, they induce this organ to secrete its own hormones.

By 1971, two of the hypothalamic releasing factors were finally purified and their chemical structure elucidated: the thyroid-releasing factor, or TRF, in charge of inducing the anterior pituitary to release its thyroid-stimulating hormone; and the lutein-releasing factor, or LRF, in charge of inducing the anterior lobe of the pituitary to release its luteinizing hormone, and also perhaps its follicle-stimulating hormone. A corticotropin releasing factor, or CRF, in charge of inducing the anterior pituitary to release its hormone, which stimulates the cortex of the adrenal glands, although biologically active, has resisted all attempts at its total purification so far.

The Hormones of the Anterior Pituitary

If the hypothalamus is the first structure in the hierarchical control of endocrine function and the hypothalamic releasing factors constitute the first-stage hormones, the second stage is provided by the anterior lobe of the pituitary gland and its group of hormones, known collectively as the *tropic* hormones.

The pituitary gland is a double organ located directly below the hypothalamus in a concavity of the sphenoid bone. Its posterior lobe is the storage place for the hypothalamic hormones oxytocin and vasopressin and it is functionally and anatomically quite different from its anterior lobe. It is to the anterior lobe of the pituitary that the term "master gland" of the body is most properly applied, and it is the anterior lobe that corresponds to the cell depicted as "Organ B" in Figure 3.

The series of tropic hormones of the anterior pituitary exert their stimulating function on other glands. Thus the thyroid-stimulating hormone (TSH) acts on the thyroid, and thyroxin is in turn secreted; the adrenocorticotropic hormone (ACTH) acts on the cortex of the adrenal glands, and the adrenal steroid hormones are in turn secreted; and the two gonadotropins (the follicle-stimulating hormone or FSH, and the luteinizing hormone, or LH) act on the gonads (i.e., the ovaries and the testes), and the estrogens, progestogens and androgens are in turn secreted. In addition to the tropic hormones, the anterior pituitary secretes three other hormones: growth hormone, prolactin, and the melanophore-stimulating hormone.

It is interesting to note that exactly the same gonadotropins are present in the anterior pituitary of both females and males. Hence their eventual end effect (of, for example, promoting the developing of secondary female or male sexual characteristics) is going to depend on what type of tissue acts as target organ for the gonadotropins.

In the female, the main action of the gonadotropin FSH is to stimulate the growth of the egg follicles in the ovaries. In the male, FSH stimulates the proliferation of spermatozoa. Similarly, the gonadotropin LH, acting in conjunction with FSH, stimulates the secretion of estrogen by the ovarian follicles and causes ovulation in the female; in the male, LH activates the Leydig cells of the testes with the consequent production of androgens.

The Hormones of the Gonads and the Adrenal Cortex

Although thyroxin (produced by the thyroid gland) represents an instance of a third-stage hormone as depicted in Figure 3, this discussion will focus on the *steroid* hormones instead. It should be pointed out in passing, however, that the main function of thyroxin is to stimulate the metabolic rate and thus thyroxin has a widespread action throughout the body.

Both the *gonads* and the *adrenal cortex* correspond to the cell depicted as "Organ C" in Figure 3, and the third-stage hormones that they produce belong to a family of closely related chemical compounds known collectively as the steroid hormones. Steroids include such compounds as cortisone, cortisol, androgens, estrogens, and progestogens.

The adrenal cortex. The cortex of the adrenals (a pair of glands located more or less atop the kidneys), in response to the action of pituitary ACTH, is known to produce a variety of steroid hormones that affect the metabolism of carbohydrates and minerals in just about every organ of the body. Animals die within a few days upon experimental removal of the adrenal glands. In humans, the condition of adrenal insufficiency known as Addison's disease leads to a severe clinical picture including failure of the kidney, low blood sugar level, reduced blood pressure and muscular weakness. These individuals have an extremely low tolerance for stresses of any kind, and death ensues unless a replacement therapy of adrenal steroids is established.

In normal circumstances, adrenal steroids (prompted by ACTH) are secreted in great amounts in response to physical stresses such as sudden changes in temperature, overcrowding, or restraint. In addition, it has been demonstrated that the adrenal steroids are also secreted in the monkey in a situation that is best described as inducing psychological rather than physical stress. When monkeys are placed in a situation in which electric shocks are automatically delivered every few minutes, they soon learn to press a lever that prevents the occurrence of the next shock. After the task is learned, this lever-pressing behavior can be maintained for a considerable period of time without the monkeys' receiving any actual shock at all, and without too many outward signs of emotional upset. If the level of adrenal steroid hormones is assessed, however, it is found to have increased by a significant amount during exposure to the psychologically stressful situation of having to respond in order to prevent the occurrence of a noxious stimulus.

The adrenal cortex also secretes androgens, progestogens, and estrogens in both males and females. Thus exactly the same hormones that are the specialty of the male and female gonads have an additional place of manufacture in the body. In fact, in patients with tumors of the adrenal glands there might appear large quantities of androgens or estrogens in the bloodstream with a consequent masculinizing or feminizing of such secondary sex characteristics as quality of voice, amount of hair in the body, etc.

The other third-stage hormones of interest to this discussion are those produced by the gonads: the ovaries and testes.

The ovaries. The ovaries are small, oval-shaped organs in charge of proliferating the female germ cells as well as of secreting the hormones that are going to guarantee the well-being of those germ cells. Under the microscope, the ovary reveals the existence of two main types of internal structures (*follicles* and *corpora lutea*) at various stages of growth and destruction. The individual development of a follicle or corpus luteum is correlated with the time elapsed since the last menstruation, and is directly stimulated by the action of pituitary FSH and/or LH.

The female germ cells (the eggs) are deposited in the passageway between ovaries and uterus by the rupture of a grown, mature follicle at the time of ovulation. From the wall of the ruptured follicle a corpus luteum differentiates and remains visible for about ten days before it too atrophies. Both the mature ovarian follicle and the corpus luteum elaborate estrogens and progestogens. In addition, the follicles also produce androgens (the characteristic hormone of the male testis) and a nonsteroid hormone called relaxin.

The estrogens of the human body are *estradiol-17-beta* and *estrone,* but a great variety of synthetic products having the same biological effects as naturally occurring estrogens have been commercially produced. Estrogens act on the uterus to promote growth of the endometrium; on the vagina to promote growth of the epithelium; on the cervix to augment the secretion of mucus; on the mammary glands to prime these organs for milk secretion. In addition to these specific effects on organs related to sex and reproduction, it must be noted that there is scarcely any tissue in the body that is not in one way or another a target organ for estrogens: they have been proved to have profound effects on the metabolism of calcium and phosphorous, on the metabolism of fats and proteins, and on the rate of secretion of the sebaceous glands of the skin. If one term must be applied as a general description of the action of estrogens throughout the body, it would be "promotion of tissue growth." Thus it comes as no surprise that excessive amounts of estrogens might be potentially harmful precisely because of its stimulating of cell divisions. Estrogens are, in fact, suspected of encouraging the formation of cancer in certain individuals.

Finally, fulfilling their role as third-stage hormones, estrogens complete the negative-feedback loop depicted in Figure 3, and by acting either on the hypothalamus itself or on the anterior pituitary (the exact mechanism has not been elucidated yet), they inhibit secretion of the pituitary gonadotropins.

The *progestogens* are a group of compounds capable of inducing "progestational" changes in the uterus, i.e., preparing the uterus for implantation of the fertilized egg, maintaining pregnancy, etc. The best known of the progestogens is *progesterone,* but there are at least two other naturally occurring progestogens and a wide variety of artificially produced progestogens.

Progestogens are secreted by the corpus luteum of the ovaries during the latter half of the menstrual cycle after ovulation has occurred. However, there are additional sources of progestogens in the body: the placenta in pregnancy and the adrenal glands in nonpregnant women and in males.

The *androgens* are the main hormones secreted by the Leydig cells of the testes, but again, they are also produced by the ovaries and the adrenal glands. Some examples of naturally occurring androgens are *androsterone* and *testosterone.*

Androgens are involved in the regulation of the pattern and amount of hair covering the body, voice changes, and skeletal configuration; they influence sperm production and act directly in

FIGURE 4

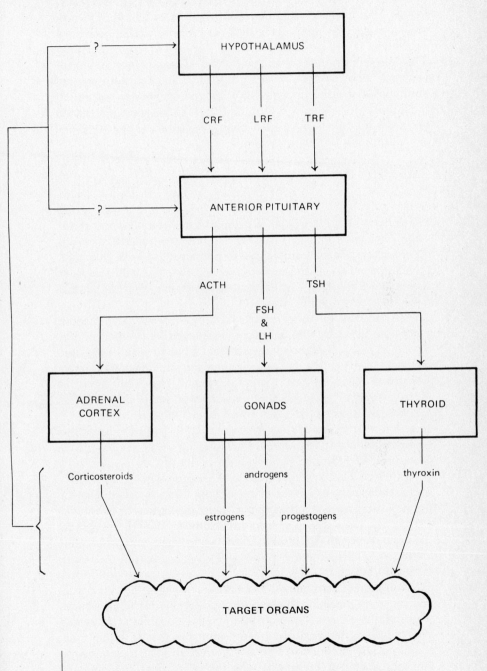

Figure 4. The negative feed back system of the hypothalamic-pituitary axis

521

maintaining the size and activity of the male accessory sex organs. Secretion of testicular androgens, like the other gonadal hormones, is regulated by the pituitary gonadotropins, which in turn are ultimately regulated by the total amount of gonadal hormones circulating in the bloodstream.

Figure 4 illustrates schematically the stages of the negative-feedback loop for hypothalamic, pituitary, adrenal, and gonadal hormones discussed above. The different stages correspond to those presented in Figure 3, but the names of the individual glands and their hormones have now been inserted.

THE MENSTRUAL CYCLE

The rhythmic patterns of release of first-, second-, and third-stage hormones of the hypothalamic-pituitary-gonadal axis are observable in the menstrual cycle of primates. Figure 5 illustrates an approximation of the individual events in the cycle, without claims to being an accurate representation of the actual magnitudes of hormone release.

Just because the onset of bleeding is an easily determinable event, the day that this happens is taken as "day one" of the menstrual cycle. Menstruation lasts from three to seven days, but the figure uses four days as an average representation of the first or *menstrual phase* of the cycle. It is not clear whether the hypothalamus produces its LRF or a different factor at this point, but with the onset of menses there is a gradual increase in the secretion of the pituitary gonadotropin FSH. This stimulates the young ovarian follicles to grow, thus marking the beginning of the next (proliferative or *follicular*) phase of the cycle.

As the follicles are growing under FSH prompting, they in turn secrete increasing amounts of estrogens. The increased level of this gonadal hormone starts then to exert the variety of peripheral effects explained above. Thus, for example, during this phase there is a demonstrable growth of the lining (endometrium) of the uterus.

Toward the end of the follicular phase, there is enough blood concentration of estrogens to activate the negative-feedback loop and cause an inhibition in the pituitary secretion of FSH. Maybe this is also the point at which the hypothalamus starts secreting LRF; maybe at this point the hypothalamus increases (rather than starts) its LRF production (the exact mechanism is not known). The fact is that at the end of the follicular phase the pituitary gonadotropin LH starts a sudden outpour coinciding with FSH

Margarita Garcia

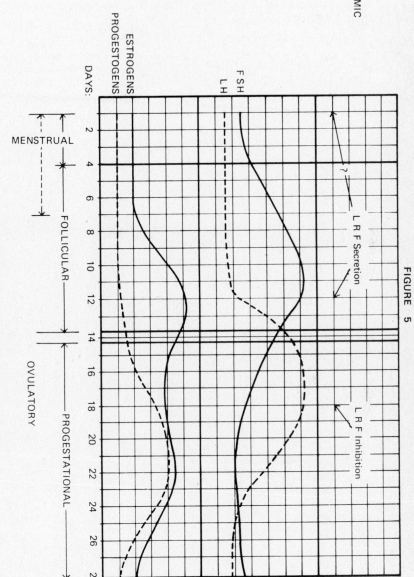

Figure 5. Patterns of release of hormones during the menstrual cycle

523

inhibition. When the balance between FSH and LH tilts in favor of the latter, the next or *ovulatory phase* of the cycle occurs.

Ovulation is the rupturing of the mature, fully grown follicle and the deposition of the female germ cells in the passageway between ovaries and uterus. This is the area where fertilization occurs if spermatozoa have entered the female tract. Ovulation occurs in mid-cycle, about two weeks after onset of menses.

After ovulation, the corpus luteum of the ovary begins to form out of the walls of the ruptured follicle, prompted by LH. The luteal or *progestational phase* of the cycle that has started will last for the last two weeks of the cycle. During this time, the newly formed corpus luteum, under the influence of the gonadotropin LH, secretes increasing levels of progestogens, while maintaining some production of estrogens at the same time. The uterine endometrium continues to grow, getting ready to accept the arrival of a fertilized egg.

If fertilization has not occurred, a functional degeneration of the corpus luteum starts by about day twenty-four of the cycle. This degeneration is preceded by decreased levels of the gonadotropin LH.

What causes pituitary inhibition of LH? This mechanism remains unknown. Consistent with the negative-feedback model presented above, it might be the case that the heightened levels of progestogens in the bloodstream are detected by the hypothalamus, causing inhibition of the LRF. However, some additional controlling mechanism has to exist because if the egg happens to get fertilized, the pituitary continues its release of LH. In pregnancy the corpus luteum does not degenerate but increases in size and secretes even larger quantities of progestogens. Later in pregnancy, the placenta takes over as the chief source of progestogen production, with the overall level of this hormone being maintained many times above the level of nonpregnant women until childbirth.

Nevertheless, the degeneration of the corpus luteum in the absence of fertilization has the immediate consequence of decreasing the supply of gonadal hormones. The endometrial lining of the uterus ceases to be properly maintained. At the point when progestogens fall to baseline levels, the bleeding occurs and the same events are repeated in the next cycle. The menstrual flow consists of the sloughed-off endometrium, rich in blood capillaries.

524

BRAND NAME	Manufacturer	ESTROGENIC AGENT		PROGESTATIONAL AGENT		
		Compound	Dosage (mg.)	Compound	Dosage (mg.)	Administration
ENOVID – E	Searle & Co. Chicago, Ill.	Mestranol	0.1	Norethynodrel	2.5	One tablet/day from day 5 to day 24 of cycle
ENOVID – 5 mg.	Searle & Co. Chicago, Ill.	Mestranol	0.075	Norethynodrel	5	Same
NORINYL – 1	Syntex Labs. Palo Alto, Calif.	Mestranol	0.05	Norethindrone	1	Same
NORINYL – 2	Syntex Labs. Palo Alto, Calif.	Mestranol	0.1	Norethindrone	2	Same
NORLESTRIN – 1	Parke-Davis Detroit, Mich.	Ethinyl estradial	0.05	Norethindrone Acetate	1	Same
NORLESTRIN – 25	Parke-Davis Detroit, Mich.	Ethinyl estradial	0.05	Norethindrone Acetate	2.5	Same
ORTHO · NOVUM – 1	Ortho Pharmaceuticals Raritan, N.J.	Mestranol	0.05	Norethindrone	1	Same
ORTHO · NOVUM – 2	Ortho Pharmaceuticals Raritan, N.J.	Mestranol	0.10	Norethindrone	2	Same
OVULEN	Searle & Co. Chicago, Ill.	Mestranol	0.10	Ethynodial Diacetate	1	Same
OVULEN – 21	Searle & Co. Chicago, Ill.	Mestranol	0.10	Ethynodial Diacetate	1	3 weeks on; 1 week off
PROVEST	Upjohn Co. Kalamazoo, Mich.	Ethinyl estradial	0.05	Medroxyprogesterone Acetate	10	One tablet/day from day 5 to day 24 of cycle

Table 1. Some commercially available oral contraceptives Combination Type

BRAND NAME	Manufacturer	Estrogenic Agent		Progestational Agent		Administration
		Compound	Dosage (mg.)	Compound	Dosage (mg.)	
C – QUEENS	Lilly & Co. Indianapolis, Ind.	Mestranol	0.08	Chlormadinone Acetate	2	Estrogen only from day 5 to day 18 estrogen-progestogen from day 20 to day 24
NOEQUEN	Syntex Labs Palo Alto, Calif.	Mestranol	0.08	Norethindrone	2	Estrogen only from day 5 to day 18 Estrogen-Progestogen from day 19 to day 24
ORACON	Mead Johnson Evansville, Ind.	Ethinylestradial	0.10	Dimethisterone	25	Estrogen only from day 5 to day 20; estrogen-progestogen from day 21 to day 25
ORTHO-NOVUM SQ	Ortho Pharmaceuticals Raritan, N.J.	Mestranol	0.08	Norethindrone	2	Estrogen only from day 5 to day 18; estrogen-progestogen from day 19 to day 24

Table 2. Some commercially available oral contraceptives Sequential Type

THE ORAL CONTRACEPTIVES

The oral contraceptives available today are synthetic estrogen-progestogen combinations of various concentrations. They have been developed to mimic the normal pattern of hormonal secretion in such a way that the ovulatory phase of the menstrual cycle is prevented from occurring.

There are two types of pills on the market: the combination and the sequential type. A list of some of the commercially available contraceptives is presented by brand name in Tables 1 and 2. In the *combination* type, each pill contains the given concentrations of both the endrogenic and the progestational agent. Administration starts on day five of the cycle and in most cases is continued daily for twenty consecutive days. The *sequential* type displays pills of two different colors, with the estrogenic agent alone being administered first (starting on day five and continuing for fourteen to sixteen days, depending on the brand), followed by the combination dosage of both estrogen and progestogen during the last four to six days. Based on the normal waxing and waning of hormones explained above, the sequential type approximates more closely the natural pattern of hormone release than the combination type.

A woman who starts taking the pill on day five of her menstrual cycle is going to receive an influx of external estrogen. As in the natural cycle, the endometrial lining of the uterus begins to grow, the vaginal epithelium also grows, there is an increase in secretion of cervical mucus, etc. Since the blood levels of estrogen have been artificially increased, the negative-feedback loop prevents the pituitary gland from secreting its FSH, which is what normally should be happening during this follicular stage of the cycle. As a consequence of this inhibition of gonadotropin release, there is a failure of follicle development. Since viable egg cells can be deposited only in the oviduct by the rupture of a mature follicle, FSH inhibition is one way of preventing ovulation.

In addition to the estrogenic agents, the progestational components of the contraceptive pills have independently demonstrated their capacity to inhibit gonadotropin secretion. Thus, not only is FSH suppressed, but the sudden increase in LH, characteristic of the pre-ovulatory point, is inhibited as well and the corpus luteum does not develop. However, the uterine endometrium never gets to know that these alterations have taken place. It had started to proliferate as a result of the action of the synthetic estrogens and now continues to do so when stimulated

527

by the synthetic progestational agent.

After twenty consecutive days on the pill of either type, when the woman stops medication, there is a sudden decrease in the blood levels of both hormones. In the presence of drastically reduced progestogen level, the uterine endometrium sloughs off and menstrual or "progestogen-withdrawal" bleeding occurs.

Based as they are on synthetic estrogen-progestogen combinations, the oral contraceptives have been shown to have innumerable side effects ranging from mild to severe reactions. After all, the gonadal hormones have widespread effects on the entire organism and any pre-existing condition can be exacerbated by the growth-promotion qualities of these hormones.

As a consequence, research is being aimed at the development of an alternative means of pituitary gonadotropin suppression. The recent elucidation of the structure of the hypothalamic LRF (the first-stage hormone in the negative-feedback mechanism) has provided a new avenue of attack. If, for example, a chemical antagonist to LRF could be developed, it could be administered to inhibit the release of pituitary gonadotropins. This intervention at an earlier stage of the negative-feedback loop could perhaps obviate the unwanted side effects of the estrogen-progestogen combinations.

33

Dr. Dalton is an English M. D. with a great deal of interest in the effect of menstruation on behavior. She has published a number of studies on the relationship between menstrual cycle phase and reports of illness, acute psychiatric admissions and frequency of accidents, and has written a book entitled *The Premenstrual Syndrome*. Her work is particularly interesting because it is concerned with behavior that does not appear to be linked to the menstrual cycle. In addition to the more serious behaviors already discussed, she has also studied the relationship between the menstrual cycle and schoolgirls' misbehavior and test-taking performance.

The study included in this volume appears to be the first one correlating women's paramenstrual period [the four premenstrual days and the four days of menstruation] with their behavior toward another individual; in this case, perception of their child's state of health. Dalton finds that there is a much higher than chance frequency that a mother will bring her child to a clinic for minor illnesses during her paramenstrual period than during other periods of the month. She suggests that this effect is due to impaired judgment and mental dullness, which decrease the mother's ability to differentiate between insignificant and real symptoms.

It should be emphasized that all of Dr. Dalton's interesting data are correlational in nature. To date, there have been no good experimental studies on the effect of menstruation on judgmental ability. Dalton has made no attempt to determine the origin of these effects. Her study lays the groundwork for a number of additional studies. What effect does the paramenstrual period have on clinic visits for serious illness? Is there any correlation between the severity of the mother's menstrual symptoms and her perception of her child's illness? Are these effects present in working as well as nonworking mothers?

The Influence of Mother's Menstruation on Her Child

Dr. K. Dalton

A London evening newspaper of October 1964 told of a young mother who had beaten up her 3-year-old daughter. In evidence the mother stated: "I suffer from my nerves, at certain times of the month it is worse than others." The husband said: "She seems to be quite uncontrollable. I have restrained my wife physically." This young woman was not one of my patients, but it reminded me of a similar instance in which one of my kind and motherly patients, in a fit of temper, had struck her child, fracturing her fibula. In her case these violent outbursts always occurred just before menstruation, and treatment for her premenstrual tension resulted in a happy and even-tempered mother.

Serious cases of premenstrual tension result in temporary loss of self-control and may result in acts of violence. What happens in the less serious cases? Does the child show any adverse manifestations to his mother's premenstrual irritability, depression and lethargy? The possibility that minor coughs and colds in children might be related to mother's menstruation was suggested by the following case:

CASE 1 BOY, AGE 3

This child was brought in November 1964 by his elder brother with the ultimatum "something must be done." He had been suffering from a "cold" since an attack of mumps in January 1964. During tea that day he had again sniffed loudly, when in his brother's words: "Mother really lost her temper and made me bring him here." He was healthy enough and unconcerned by the thick nasal catarrh coming from his nose. This was his first visit since mumps. Next day, his father confirmed that he had an undue share of recurrent colds, which had not been continuous, but each time one had cleared up there was a recurrence within a couple of weeks. The father agreed to bring the child regularly each week until the present cold cleared, to report immediately the development of a new cold and to record the onset and duration of all colds.

Dr. K. Dalton

The boys's mother, aged 35, was healthy, with normal menstruation, but admitted to being tired and irritable during the

Fig 1 **Case 1** *Chart showing relationship between the dates of the child's colds (X) and his mother's menstruation (P), 1964-5*

premenstruum. When the dates of the boy's colds were entered on the same chart as his mother's menstruation, it became evident that his colds were occurring during the mother's premenstruum (Fig. 1).

Following this positive correlation of the child's colds with his mother's menstruation it was decided to investigate this possibility further with mothers whose children were frequent attenders at the surgery. The mothers were asked to record on a periodicity chart the dates of their child's ailments. Most of the mothers were already keeping records of their own menstruation on the menstrual charts which are given routinely to patients in this practice. It was fascinating to observe the marked correlation in many cases of mother's menstruation to the child's minor, but recurrent symptoms.

SURVEY OF MINOR AILMENTS

When it became apparent that the mother's menstruation could influence the child's health adversely, it was decided to investigate all children attending for treatment of minor coughs and colds. The survey was limited to children, who fulfilled the following five

531

conditions: (1) Appeared well at the time of attendance. (2) No physical signs were elicited at examination, apart from nasal catarrh or cervical glands. (3) They were apyrexial at the time of the visit. (4) They attended surgery and were accompanied by their mother. (5) They were not in the prodromal stage of an infectious disease. Those occasions where the surgery attendance was primarily for some other member of the family and where, as an afterthought, at the end of the primary consultation the mother sought advice about her child's cough and cold, were excluded from the survey. In such cases it was not the timing of the child's ailment which had determined the time of the surgery attendance.

The period covered by the surgery was March 1965 to October 1965, thus excluding the winter months when infectious coughs and colds, in all members of the family and at all ages, are common. The survey was carried out in a single-handed general practice and all the children were seen by one observer. A proforma was prepared on which was noted the child's age, sex, position in family, duration of symptoms and the presence of nasal catarrh, cough, sore throat or vomiting. The mother was asked her age, parity, date of her last menstruation and whether she suffered from depression, irritability, tiredness, "bloatedness" or breast pains at the time of her menstruation.

DEFINITIONS

Paramenstruum is used in this study for the four days immediately before menstruation and the first four days of menstruation. In a normal cycle of twenty-eight days this would include Days 1-4 and Days 25-28.

Intermenstruum is used in this study for all days of the menstrual cycle except the four premenstrual days and the first four days of menstruation. In a cycle of twenty-eight days the intermenstruum would cover Days 5-24, and would be two and a half times the duration of the paramenstruum, but the intermenstruum can vary in length in short and long menstrual cycles. In the calculations of probability in this study the length of the intermenstruum is taken as twenty days.

RESULTS

During the eight months of the survey, 91 episodes of apyrexial coughs and colds were recorded among the children of 65 mothers. Forty-nine of these attendances (54%) occurred during the paramenstruum, and this percentage is much higher than the expected 28.5% in four groups, as shown in Table 1. The significance of this preponderance in these four groups is shown by the X^2 test on one degree of freedom and for each of these four groups the probabilities are very low. These results are therefore highly significant. Mothers attending during their paramenstruum claimed a slightly higher incidence of each of the premenstrual symptoms of depression, irritability, lethargy, bloatedness and mastitis.

In view of the significant findings of the effect of the mother's

Table 1

Distribution of children's attendances during mothers' paramenstruum

	Attendances during paramenstruum	Total attendances in group	χ^2 on 1 d.f.	Probability
All children	49 (54%)	91	28·4	0·001
Children aged under 2 years	15 (71%)	21	18·9	0·001
Only children	16 (67%)	24	16·8	0·001
Symptoms less than twenty-four hours	21 (66%)	32	21·8	0·001
Mothers aged under 30 years	12 (63%)	19	11·3	0·01

paramenstruum on the surgery attendance of her child, a survey has now been commenced to study the time of acute hospital admissions of children in relation to the time of their mother's menstrual cycle.

DISCUSSION

This study reveals that over half of all children attending surgery with minor coughs and colds attend during the eight days of the mother's paramenstruum. The children studied appeared normal at the time of examination, were unconcerned by their symptoms, responded to simple mixtures and did not require any further attention. Several of these children were brought within three hours of the onset of symptoms; sometimes a child had merely coughed (or possibly choked) during breakfast and the child attended the 9 o'clock surgery.

During the paramenstruum the mother is unable to assess the severity of her child's symptoms and fears these may be the early stages of a serious illness. Lowered judgment during the paramenstruum was blamed by Dalton (1960b) for the high

533

proportion of accidents during the paramenstruum, and she also showed that schoolgirl's work deteriorated at this time (1960a). Wickham (1958) demonstrated that intelligence test scores in women Army personnel were lowered during menstruation. These same factors of impaired judgment and mental dullness of the paramenstruum appear to be operating in the mother's assessment of her child's symptoms.

It is commonly recognized that the young mother with an only child is invariably overanxious about her child's illnesses and her inability to differentiate between insignificant and real symptoms sends her hurrying to the surgery or the telephone at the first sniff or cough. In this study all these factors are borne out with the additional finding that during the mother's paramenstruum they were increased.

Dalton (1964) has shown that premenstrual tension increases with age and parity, which would appear to be contrary to the findings of this study. A possible explanation may be that with greater experience the older mother with a large family has the effects of her premenstrual tension buffered by other members of the household.

There have been many surveys to show the adverse effects of the paramenstruum on various facets of a woman's life and, as has been pointed out, the menstrual influence of these surveys varies with a narrow margin (Dalton 1964). Thus, during the eight days of the paramenstruum 45% of schoolgirls' punishments were inflicted, 45% of industrial employees reported sick, there were 46% of acute psychiatric admissions and 49% of acute medical and surgical admissions, 49% of prisoners committed their crimes, 52% of emergency accident admissions were noted and 52% of acute pyrexias presented for diagnosis in general practice. This study would appear to be the first correlation of the effect of a woman's paramenstruum on other people's lives, in this case the children, and it is of interest that the menstrual influence of 54% corresponds closely to the narrow limits of 45-52% in the surveys quoted. It has often been suggested that a woman's premenstruum must have a significant effect on other people, as in marital quarrels where the husband suffers from his wife's irritability, in schools where the children suffer from a teacher's paramenstruum, in industry where factory workers are at the mercy of a forewoman in her paramenstruum, and even wrongdoers at the hands of a woman magistrate.

This study emphasizes the close and sympathetic relationship which develops between the young mother and her child. When the mother's well-being is affected during the paramenstruum, the child responds by a similar feeling of ill health, as manifested by nasal catarrh, cough or sore throat. Many general practitioners will recall occasions when they have treated the mother, even though it was the child for whom the advice was sought. The findings of this paper stress the paramenstruum as one of the many possible causes of recurrent minor ills in children and justifies treatment of the mother in these cases.

REFERENCES

Dalton K
1960a) *Brit. med. J.* i, 326.
(1960b) *Brit. med. J.* ii, 1425.
(1964) The Premenstrual Syndrome. London
Wickham M. (1958) *Brit. J. Psychol. 49*, 34.

34

One of the major problems in the study of the behavioral effects of the menstrual cycle is that most of the studies use self-reports of symptomology and mood as dependent variables. Presumably, women in such studies are aware of what their symptoms and emotional state "should be." The study by Ivey and Bardwick utilizes a measure of mood which should not have been able to relate directly to the menstrual cycle. They used Gottschalk's Verbal Anxiety Scale [VAS], which consists of five minutes of relatively free association on a "memorable life experience." An additional methodological advantage of their study over most others in the area is the use of subjects as their own controls. Four separate samples were taken from each subject, one during the premenstrual period and one at mid-cycle, for two complete menstrual cycles.

Ivey and Bardwick found that the premenstrual anxiety level was significantly higher than the anxiety level at ovulation for all subjects. They also found considerable hostility, depression, and non-coping themes during the premenstrual phase. Although their data are correlational in nature, they assert that there is a considerable relationship between affective fluctuation and endocrine changes or if endocrine level produces mood.

The chief methodological flaw in this study is that subjects knew that they were participating in a study on menstruation and postexperimental interviews indicated that the subjects knew the study was about moods. The subjects also knew each other and the experimenter. Nevertheless, the study is of great value. It indicates that the menstrual-cycle can affect the psychological behavior of normal women. Mood becomes predictable by menstrual phase in spite of individual differences in personality.

Patterns of Affective Fluctuation in the Menstrual Cycle*

Melville E. Ivey and Judith M. Bardwick

Twenty-six female college students aged 19-22 were tested for differences in anxiety level during the menstrual cycle. Ss were asked to talk for 5 min. on "any memorable life experience." These verbal samples were recorded at ovulation and 2-3 days preceeding the onset of menses during 2 complete menstrual cycles for each S. The samples were scored according to Gottschalk's (1961) Verbal Anxiety Scale (VAS) for Death, Mutilation, Separation, Guilt, Shame, and Diffuse Anxiety. The verbal samples were also examined for thematic variations.

The sensitivity of the VAS was confirmed, as it revealed consistent and significant variations in anxiety level between ovulation and premenstrual samples for each S. The premenstrual anxiety level was found to be significantly higher (p 0.0005) than that at ovulation over all Ss. Additional findings showed consistent themes of hostility and depression as well as themes of noncoping during the premenstrual phase of the menstrual cycle. In spite of individual differences between Ss, these findings indicate significant and predictable affective fluctuations during the menstrual cycle which correlate with endocrine changes. Qualitative data on "premenstrual syndrome" and psychosomatic aspects of premenstrual symptoms were also presented.

Because its periodic functioning is central to the female physically as well as psychologically, the reproductive system offers an ideal system for the physical expression of attitudes and emotions. There have been many studies on the psychodynamic characteristics of women who suffer such reproductive dysfunctions as infertility,[9,13] habitual abortion, [8,10,15] pseudocyesis,[7] and severe difficulties during pregnancy.[16] These studies were concentrated on psychological affects and their influence on psychology.

* From *Psychosomatic Medicine,* 1968, 30 (3), 336-44.

In 1942 Benedek and Rubenstein[4] did pioneer work in examining affects from another perspective, that of physiological influences on psychology. In studying the effects of endocrine changes upon psychological affects, they found that female psychiatric patients demonstrated striking and consistent psychodynamic manifestations related to particular hormonal phases of the menstrual cycle. They found passive-receptive tendencies to be correlated with progesterone production, and active heterosexual strivings with estrogen production. Benedek, in a later paper,[3] further characterized the premenstrual phase of the menstrual cycle as being high in feelings of fear about mutilation and death, sexual fantasies, anxiety, and depression. At ovulation she found almost no evidence of anxiety-related themes.

Shainess[11] found the low estrogen and progesterone phase just preceding menstruation to be generally associated with a yearning for love, feeling of helplessness, anxiety, and defensive hostility. Sutherland and Stewart[14] noted that premenstrual depression and irritability were associated with a wide range of unpleasant physical symptoms. These studies tend to confirm the hypothesis of psychosomatic interaction as a basis for affective changes evidenced in the menstrual cycle.

Psychosomatic studies of emotion need an easily administered psychological test that provides comprehensive and immediate measurement of the affect associated with a given physiological state. After Gottschalk et al.[5] conducted extensive studies of validity and reliability, Gottschalk's Verbal Anxiety Scale (VAS) seemed to offer a valuable method for handling this problem. Based on a content analysis of free-association verbal samples, this scale serves as a measure of preconscious and conscious anxiety manifested by the subject at the time of testing. The scale reliably differentiates between different populations on the basis of the anxiety being measured.[5]

Gottschalk et al.[6] used the VAS to measure affective changes in 5 subjects during the menstrual cycle. They reported that their results were not statistically significant across Ss, and attributed this result to the small size of the sample. Their data did suggest, however, a tendency for transient decreases in levels of anxiety and hostility during ovulation.

A purpose of the present study was to replicate the work of Gottschalk et al.[6] with normal subjects, using a larger sample, in an effort to obtain statistically significant results. Whereas in other previous research, selected neurotic and psychotic Ss were frequently used, the use of a normal population might show more universal applicability of findings indicating affective change during the menstrual cycle. With experimental controls and a larger sample of normal girls, we hope to find significant results that demonstrate the overwhelming and normal impact of physiological change upon emotions.

On the basis of the preceeding considerations, the following hypotheses were evolved. The difference in anxiety level between ovulation and premenstruation ought to be consistent for each individual S. Since it was hypothesized that the change in anxiety level would be a function of endocrine changes, the changes in anxiety level were expected to be consistent for all Ss. It was also predicted that the anxiety level for all Ss during premenstruation would be singificantly higher than at ovulation.

METHOD

Subjects

The Ss were 26 female college students 19-22 years of age. Twenty-two were members of 1 living unit, and 4 were members of another. All members of the first house volunteered, but 9 had to be dropped because of irregular cycles, absence during the testing period due to spring vacation, use of oral contraceptives, or other purely pragmatic problems. There seemed to be no reason to suspect a bias in this volunteer population.

Procedure

MENSTRUAL DATA. The Ss were asked to volunteer for participation in a "study of the menstrual cycle" and were given no indication as to any expected affective fluctuations. They were told that participation would involve four 10-min. interviews, 1 at ovulation and 1 premenstrually for 2 complete menstrual cycles. The interviews were to be arranged at their convenience. A cooperative group effort was encouraged, and because E was a member of the house from which the majority of Ss came, participation was encouraged and supported. Volunteers were asked to write down the date of onset of their most recent menstrual period and the approximate length of the cycle. Since many were uncertain, their participation began at the onset of their next period.

Because of the number of subjects and the voluntary nature of their participation, basal body temperature (low point preceding a rise in temperature indicating ovulation) was recorded for only 3 or 4 days preceding the scheduled ovulation of each girl as determined by the available menstrual history. This measure, coupled with verbal descriptions of ovulation symptoms and the observed onset of menses, was felt to give a fairly reliable estimate of the time of ovulation. Each girl was interviewed 4 times, twice premenstrually and twice at ovulation. Ovulation, when estrogen levels are highest, was determined by basal body temperature and menstrual history; for the majority of cases, this was 14-16 days following the onset of menses. The premenstrual interviews were conducted 2-3 days before scheduled menstruation, when both progesterone and estrogen levels are low.

INTERVIEW. At each session, the S was interviewed privately, at her convenience. She was asked to speak for 5 min. into a tape recorder about "any memorable life experience." After the 5-min. session, a general questionnaire, asking about any current problems or worries and about her physical health at that time, was administered. This was done to detect any sources of external stress that might contaminate the results. Following the 5-min. verbal sample at the first premenstrual interview, a detailed questionnaire on menstrual history was administered (for content see Table 3).

SCORING. The verbal samples were transcribed verbatim from the tapes. Two judges independently scored the typescripts using Gottschalk's analysis technique for the VAS.[10] Judges scored the samples clause by clause for indications of: (1) Death Anxiety, (2) Mutilation Anxiety, (3) Separation Anxiety, (4) Guilt Anxiety, (5) Shame Anxiety, and (6) Diffuse Anxiety. Under each of these categories, reference to the self (except as agent) received a score of 3; to animate others, 2; and to inanimate others, 1 (except in Categories 4, 5, and 6); denial was scored as 1. The total anxiety score for each sample is obtained by summing all items. To control for differences in verbal output in the 5-min. periods, the total score is divided by the number of words in the sample and then multiplied by 100. The square root of this final raw total anxiety score is used for all statistical comparisons.

While E was one judge, the other examiner trained in this technique had no knowledge of the Ss or of the particular menstrual phase corresponding to each sample. The tests were scored at random and the particular menstrual phase was not recorded on the typed sample. The use of code numbers prevented any knowledge of the particular S giving the sample. The interjudge correlation was .81, showing good scoring reliability. In addition, Dr. Gottschalk was kind enough to check one-third of our score samples and reported good consistency with his scoring.

Although hostility and depression are not included in Gottschalk's VAS, we also made a simple tabulation of the number of

TABLE 1. MEAN COMBINED ANXIETY SCORES FOR 26 FEMALE Ss AT OVULATION AND PREMENSTRUATION OVER 2 COMPLETE MENSTRUAL CYCLES

S (No.)	Mean combined ovulation scores	Mean combined premenstrual scores	Premenstrual minus ovulation score	Rank
1	1.10	1.90	+0.80	18
2	0.77	1.85	+1.08	22
3	1.30	1.35	+0.05	1
4	1.15	1.75	+0.60	12
5	1.29	2.75	+1.46	25
6	1.20	2.20	+1.00	19.5
7	1.70	2.40	+0.70	15.5
8	1.90	1.30	-0.60	12
9	1.60	1.50	-0.10	2
10	1.40	0.83	-0.57	10
11	0.90	1.45	+0.55	9
12	1.45	2.80	+1.35	24
13	1.05	1.50	+0.45	6
14	0.84	2.45	+1.61	26
15	1.70	2.70	+1.00	19.5
16	1.29	0.97	-0.32	5
17	1.65	1.13	-0.52	8
18	3.10	3.30	+0.20	3
19	1.75	2.40	+0.65	14
20	2.70	2.95	+0.25	4
21	0.90	1.65	+0.75	17
22	1.43	2.55	+1.12	23
23	2.90	3.60	+0.70	15.5
24	0.85	1.90	+1.05	21
25	1.60	2.20	+0.60	12
26	1.30	1.80	+0.50	7

Gottschalk's Verbal Anxiety Scale was used, and scores were taken from 5-min. free-association verbal samples.

TABLE 2. ANXIETY SCORES FOR 26 FEMALES Ss ARRANGED IN ORDER OF SAMPLING

Ss (No.)	Sample 1	Sample 2	Sample 3	Sample 4
1	O_1 1.8	PM_1 3.3	O_2 0.42	PM_2 0.52
2	O_1 0.24	PM_1 2.7	O_2 1.3	PM_2 1.0
3	O_1 1.5	PM_1 1.0	O_2 1.1	PM_2 1.7
4	O_1 1.2	PM_1 1.7	O_2 1.1	PM_2 1.8
5	O_1 2.3	PM_1 2.4	O_2 0.28	PM_2 3.1
6	O_1 1.1	PM_1 2.2	O_2 1.3	PM_2 2.1
7	PM_1 2.2	O_1 2.1	PM_2 2.6	O_2 1.4
8	PM_1 2.0	O_1 1.4	PM_2 1.8	O_2 1.2
9	O_1 1.5	PM_1 1.5	O_2 1.7	PM_2 1.5
10	PM_1 0.26	O_1 1.8	PM_2 1.4	O_2 1.7
11	O_1 1.5	PM_1 1.2	O_2 0.3	PM_2 1.7
12	O_1 1.6	PM_1 2.2	O_2 1.3	PM_2 1.4
13	PM_1 1.4	O_1 1.1	PM_2 1.6	O_2 1.0
14	PM_1 2.1	O_1 1.6	PM_2 2.8	O_2 0.08
15	PM_1 2.3	O_1 1.9	PM_2 3.0	O_2 1.5
16	O_1 2.3	PM_1 1.7	O_2 0.28	PM_2 0.24
17	O_1 1.3	PM_1 1.3	O_2 1.0	PM_2 0.95
18	O_1 3.4	PM_1 3.9	O_2 2.8	PM_2 2.7
19	PM_1 1.9	O_1 1.7	PM_2 2.7	O_2 1.8
20	O_1 3.3	PM_1 3.0	O_2 2.1	PM_2 2.9
21	O_1 0.9	PM_1 1.2	O_2 0.9	PM_2 2.1
22	O_1 1.9	PM_1 1.7	O_2 0.95	PM_2 3.4
23	O_1 3.6	PM_1 2.8	O_2 2.2	PM_2 4.2
24	PM_1 1.6	O_1 0.8	PM_2 2.2	O_2 0.9
25	O_1 1.6	PM_1 1.6	O_2 1.6	PM_2 2.8
26	O_1 1.2	PM_1 1.8	O_2 1.5	PM_2 1.7

O indicates ovulation; PM, premenstruation.

543

TABLE 3. ANXIETY CATEGORIES AT OVULATION AND PREMENSTRUATION

Ss (No.)	Death Anxiety d	rank	Mutilation Anxiety d	rank	Separation Anxiety d	rank	Guilt Anxiety d	rank	Shame Anxiety d	rank	Diffuse Anxiety d	rank
1	+2	+5	+22	+17	-11	-20	+5	+19.5	-1	-3.5	-1	-3.5
2	0		+13	+16	+3	+10.5	+1	+4.5	-1	-3.5	+6	+19.5
3	0		-2	-8.5	+1	+2	-5	-19.5	+3	+10.5	+1	+3.5
4	-1	-2.5	0		-2	-5.5	-3	-14.5	+9	+22	+5	+18
5	+8	+11	+1	+4	+10	+19	+3	+14.5	0		+1	+3.5
6	0		0		0		-1	-4.5	+4	+14	+4	+17
7	+4	+8	+1	+4	0		+3	+14.5	0		+3	+14
8	0		+1	+4	0		0		-6	-20	-11	-23
9	0		0		+3	+10.5	-1	-4.5	-1	-3.5	+3	+14
10	0		-1	-4	-3	-10.5	-1	-4.5	+2	+8	-2	-9
11	+2	+2.5	+1	+4	+3	+10.5	-2	-10	0		+2	+9
12	+3	+6.5	+1	+4	0		-1	-4.5	-1	-3.5	+2	+9
13	0		0		+4	+14.5	-1	-4.5	-1	-3.5	+3	+14
14	+5	+9	0		-1	-2	0		+4	+14	+3	+9
15	+6	+10	+1	+11.5	+2	+5.5	-3	-14.5	+8	+21	+6	+19.5
16	0		+1	+4	-8	-18	-1	-4.5	+5	-18	-1	-3.5
17	0		-4	-11.5	+3	+10.5	+1	+4.5	-2	-8	+2	+9
18	+11	+12.5	+2	+8.5	-4	-14.5	+7	+22	-3	-10.5	-3	-14
19	-3	-6.5	-7	-15	+24	+21	-3	-19.5	+4	+14	+3	+9
20	0		-3	-10	+2	+5.5	-2	-10	-4	-14	+7	+21
21	+11	+12.5	0		+5	+16	+3	+14.5	+2	+8	+8	+3.5
22	0		+1	+4	+1	+2	+2	+10	-5	-18	+8	+22
23			0		+6	+17	0		+15	+23		
24	-1	-2.5	+6	+14	+3	+10.5	0		+4	+14	+3	+14
25	+1	+2.5	+5	+13	+2	+5.5	+5	+19.5	+1	+3.5	0	
26							-3	-14.5	+5	+18	-1	-3.5
	T = 11.5		T = 45		T = 70.5		T = 104.5		T = 88		T = 49.5	
	N = 13		N = 17		N = 21		N = 22		N = 23		N = 24	
	z = 2.36		z = 1.49		z = 1.56		z = 0.715		z = 1.52		z = 2.87	
	p < 0.02		p = 0.14		p = 0.12		p = 0.50		p = 0.13		p < 0.01	

d Indicates the number of statements at premenstruation minus number of statements at ovulation; N, the number of Ss contributing in this anxiety category.

statements of hostility and depression in each 5-min. sample because these seemed to be recurrent affects. In addition, a general analysis of each sample was made to determine the most salient themes. Information from the menstrual history questionnaire was qualitatively evaluated.

RESULTS

The Wilcoxen test for 2 matched samples was used to compare the mean premenstrual anxiety scores with the mean anxiety scores for all subjects at ovulation. The premenstrual anxiety scores were found to be significantly higher at the .0005 level than those at ovulation (Table 1). The same test revealed no significant differences between the anxiety levels of the same cycle phase during the 2 different cycles.

When the sample scores were arranged in the order in which they were taken there was no evidence for a serial effect. We found no systematic increase or decrease in the anxiety scores from the first to the fourth sample (Table 2).

Because we were pressed for time, we were unable to prolong the experiment for the additional month which would have permitted a balanced design in which half of the Ss began participation at ovulation and half at premenstruation. Seven Ss began at premenstruation; they were Ss 7, 10, 13, 14, 15, 19 and 24. There is no systematic difference between these scores and those of the remaining Ss.

Using the Wilcoxen test (2-tailed approximation for small samples where N<25) for those Ss contributing to each category,[12] highly significant differences were noted in the categories of death and diffuse anxiety.

The ovulation and premenstrual anxiety scores were tabulated over all Ss, and the frequency of each type of anxiety at the 2 cycle phases was compared. The premenstrual Death Anxiety score was significantly higher than that at ovulation, ($p < 0.02$) as was the Diffuse Anxiety score ($p < 0.01$). Separation Anxiety, Mutilation Anxiety and Shame Anxiety were higher premenstrually—at the .14, .12, and .13 levels respectively—while Guilt Anxiety remained fairly constant over the 2 phases of the menstrual cycle (Table 3).

DISCUSSION

The statistical analysis lends strong support to the hypotheses. Every S was consistent when her mean anxiety levels, premenstrually and at ovulation, were compared. This was true for the 21 Ss whose anxiety level was higher at premenstruation as well as for the 5 Ss whose anxiety level was higher at ovulation. There was considerable variability in a S's response, largely due to the sensitivity of the measure to changes in situational anxiety.[5] Nevertheless, when the mean anxiety levels for all Ss were combined, the comparison between the premenstrual and ovulation anxiety levels showed the anxiety level at premenstruation to be significantly higher at the .0005 level.

Five of the 26 Ss showed a higher level of anxiety at ovulation. One of these Ss had a mean difference of only .10 between her mean ovulation and premenstruation scores. For 3 of the other 4 Ss, an examination of their ovulation questionnaires on "current situation" revealed that they all expressed more than the usual anxiety over some environmental factor at the time of the ovulation test sessions. Their concerns at that time ranged from the attempted suicide of a friend to the prospect of facing a great deal of make-up school work due to illness.

The presence of a lower level of anxiety at ovulation compared with that at premenstruation in 21 of these subjects confirmed Gottschalk's findings,[6] which had indicated a transient decrease in anxiety at ovulation. The fact that a higher level of premenstrual anxiety (significant at the .01 level) was present in this sample was consistent with other research.[3,6,11]

When the specific types of anxiety were examined, higher premenstrual incidence of Death, Mutilation, and Separation Anxiety in this normal population confirmed earlier findings of Benedek[4] with psychiatric patients. In the present study, as in Benedek's, the premenstrual phase was characterized by fear of mutilation and body damage. Also confirmed was Shainess' observation[11] of an increase at premenstruation in yearning for love, anxiety about being separated from love, and a feeling of helplessness in dealing with the situation.

A tabulation of the instances of hostility outward and the few instances of hostility inward (depression) suggested a trend towards higher premenstrual hostility as noted by Gottschalk[6] Shainess,[11] and Benedek,[3] as well as some tendency towards premenstrual depression (Sutherland and Stewart[14]). The inclusion of hostility and depression themes with those from the anxiety scale would increase the already significant differences between the affects expressed premenstrually and those seen at ovulation.

When the verbal samples were examined, consistently recurring themes unique to the hormonal phases were found. A constantly recurring theme at ovulation was a self-satisfaction over success or the ability to cope with a situation:

> . . . so I was elected chairman./ I had to establish with them the fact/ that I knew/ what I was doing./ I remember one particularly problematic meeting,/ and afterwards, L. came up to me and said/ "you really handled the meeting well."/ In the end it came out the sort of thing/ that really bolstered my confidence in myself./

Contrast this with a sample from the same girl premenstrually during the same cycle:

> They had to teach me how to water ski./ I was so clumsy/ it was really embarrassing/ 'cause it was kind of like saying to yourself/ you can't do it/ and the people were about to lose patience with me./

This type of thematic adequacy-inadequacy dichotomy appeared repeatedly in different forms, and while inadequacy could be scored in terms of separation and shame anxiety, the coping theme might have remained unrecognized without a clinical evaluation. Concern with coping was, however, a consistent theme and may be similar to Benedek's description of active striving at ovulation versus passive reception at premenstruation.[3]

Another theme which was not scorable on the anxiety scale, but which occurred often, was hostility. The incidence of hostility was much greater premenstrually than at ovulation:

> . . . talk about my brother and his wife./ I hated her./ I just couldn't stand her./ I couldn't stand her mother./ I used to do terrible things to separate them./

This hostile, sexually anxious, and incestuous verbal sample is in striking contrast to the sample from the ovulatory phase of the same cycle for the same girl:

> . . . talk about my trip to Europe./ It was just the greatest summer of my life./ We met all kinds of terrific people/ everywhere we went/ and just the most terrific things

happened./

Thematic consistencies were also evident in the samples scorable by the anxiety scale. For example, in the following sample from another girl, a theme of Death Anxiety was evident at premenstruation:

> I'll tell you about the death of my poor dog M./ . . . oh, another memorable event, my grandparents died in a plane crash./ This was my first contact with death/ and it was very traumatic for me/ . . . Then my grandfather died/ and I was very close to him./

In contrast, the sample at ovulation for the same girl:

> Well, we just went to Jamaica/ and it was fantastic/ the island is so lush and green and the a . . . water is so blue/ the place is so fertile/ and the natives are just so friendly./

Finally, the following was a clear example of premenstrual Mutilation Anxiety which provided a strong contrast with a very peaceful, contented ovulation narrative for still another girl during 1 menstrual cycle:

> . . . came around the curve and did a double flip and landed upside down./I remember the car coming down on my hand and slicing it right open/and all this blood was all over the place./Later they thought/ it was broken/ cause every time I touched the finger it felt/ like a nail was going through my hand./

At ovulation:

> We took our skis and packed them on top of the car/ and then we took off for up North./ We used to go for long walks in the snow/ and it was just really great, really quiet and peaceful./

These examples illustrate the pronounced and consistent variation between premenstrual and ovulatory anxiety levels in our normal subjects, both as measured by the anxiety scale and by independent thematic analysis.

In spite of the neutral explanation to Ss that this experiment aimed at investigating the menstrual cycle, it was felt that any possible contaminating knowledge or intuition by some Ss as to

TABLE 4. PREMENSTRUAL SYNDROME

Symptoms	(%)*
Diarrhea	12
Constipation	12
Headaches	15
Breast swelling	73
Backaches	41
Nausea	26
Change in sleeping habits	34
	(12 less, 22 more)
Stomach swelling	65
Change in eating habits	46
	(20 less, 26 more)
Irritability	65
Physical sensitivity	40
Spotting	7
Weight gain	40
Dream about sex	12
Feel sexy with boyfriend	31
Cramps	42
Skin eruptions	40
Depression	12

N = 26
* Percentage of population reporting a given symptom.

the expected mood swings should be ascertained. At the conclusion of the experiment, Ss were asked to write what they felt the aim of the experiment has been. Most Ss assumed we were studying moods, but in their evaluations did not mention specific affects such as anxiety, depression, or hostility, or expected mood changes. This result was encouraging, though future use of the scale might be better disguised if verbal samples were taken in conjunction with a cognitive task, seeming to place the experimental emphasis on the latter.

There was one unexpected experimental control. One S was interviewed on Day 14 of her menstrual cycle for an ovulatory sample. The sample was highly anxious, yielding a score of 2.8, significantly higher than her previous score of 1.4 at ovulation. Thematically there were references to death, mutilation, and separation. The next day, she began to menstruate, 2 weeks early.

The qualitative evaluation of the menstrual history questionnaire revealed several additional findings of interest. When asked if they experienced any symptoms before their periods by which they could tell they were about to menstruate, all girls reported at least 1 symptom. The average number of symptoms reported was 6.

The percentage of girls reporting particular symptoms (Table 4;
provided an interesting portrait of the "premenstrual syndrome"
for girls of this age (compare Sutherland and Stewart,[14] 1965).

It was suspected that those girls who had received childhood
gratification from the sick role (i.e., maternal attention, special
privilege) might exhibit a greater number of premenstrual symptoms. As expected, those girls who experienced fewer than the
average 6 symptoms reported little gratification from the sick role
as a child. Those girls reporting more than 8 symptoms, however,
indicated either extreme gratification from the sick role or, at the
other extreme, expressed bitterness at being neglected during
childhood illnesses. Thus, we see the use of the reproductive
system as an arena for the physical acting out of psychological
conflicts.[1,2] The girls who received extreme gratification from
childhood illness in the form of extra love and attention continued
to seek this source of gratification with premenstrual symptoms.
Those who were neglected when ill as children seemed to be
reacting to this neglect by demanding that attention be paid to
their premenstrual physical difficulties. This seems to be an
example of the classic psychosomatic etiology—the defensive
function of the physical (conversion) symptom in preserving
psychological balance in a socially acceptable way.

Although one might expect strong individual differences in
reaction, the Anxiety Scale and thematic analysis revealed consistent and significant mood swings unique to a particular menstrual phase. A conclusion which seems warranted is that these
physical, especially endocrine, changes so influence psychological
behavior that, in spite of personality differences, even in normal
subjects, psychological behavior becomes predictable on the basis
of menstrual cycle phase. Our results, coupled with those of
Gottschalk, Benedek, and Shainess have obvious, but nonetheless
exceedingly important pragmatic implications. The menstrual cycle
exercises gross influences on female behavior. That females may
cope or not cope, test anxious, hostile, or depressive, appear
healthy or neurotic on psychological tests, is due as much to
menstrual cycle phase as to core psychological characteristics.

SUMMARY

Twenty-six female college students, ages 19-22, being tested for
differences in anxiety level during the menstrual cycle, were asked
to talk for 5 min. on "any memorable life experience." These verbal
samples, which were recorded at ovulation and 2-3 days preceding

Melville E. Ivey and Judith M. Bardwick

the onset of menses during 2 complete menstrual cycles for each S, were scored according to Gottschalk's Verbal Anxiety Scale (VAS) for Death, Mutilation, Separation, Guilt, Shame, and Diffuse Anxiety. The verbal samples were also examined for thematic variations.

The sensitivity of the VAS was confirmed, as it revealed consistent and significant variations in anxiety level between ovulation and premenstrual samples for each S. The premenstrual anxiety level was found to be significantly higher (p 0.0005) than that at ovulation over all Ss. Additional findings showed consistent themes of hostility and depression as well as themes of noncoping during the premenstrual phase of the menstrual cycle. In spite of individual differences between Ss, these findings indicate significant and predictable affective fluctuations during the menstrual cycle which correlate with endocrine changes. Qualitative data on "premenstrual syndrome" and psychosomatic aspects of premenstrual symptoms were also presented.

REFERENCES

1. Bardwick, J. M. The need for individual assessment of Ss in psychosomatic research. *Psychol. Rep. 21,*81, 1967.
2. Bardwick, J. M. Psychosomatic Relations in Women. Unpublished data, 1967.
3. Benedek, T. "Sexual Function in Women and Their Disturbance." In *American Handbook of Psychiatry* (Vol. I), by Arieti, S., Ed. Basic Books, New York, 1959.
4. Benedek, T., and Rubenstein, B. *The Sexual Cycle in Women: The Relation Between Ovarian Function and Psychodynamic Processes.* Washington, D.C., National Research Council, 1942.
5. Gottschalk, L. A., Springer, K. J., and Gleser, G. C. "Experiments with a Method of Assessing the Variations in Intensity of Certain Psychological States Occurring During Two Psychotherapeutic Interviews." In *Comparative Psycholinguistic Analysis of Two Psychotherapeutic Interviews,* by Gottschalk, L. A., Ed. Internat. Univ. Press, New York, 1961.
6. Gottschalk, L. A., Kaplan, S., Gleser, G. C., and Winget, C. M. Variations in magnitude of emotion: A method applied to anxiety and hostility during phases of the menstrual cycle. *Psychosom Med 23,* 300, 1962.

7. Greaves, D. C., Green, P. E., and West, L. J. Psychodynamic and psychophysiological aspects of pseudocyesis. *Psychosom. Med. 22,*24, 1960.
8. Grimm, E. Psychological investigation of habitual abortion. *Psychosom. Med. 24,*369, 1962.
9. Peberdy, G. R. "The Psychiatry of Infertility." In *Studies of Infertility.*Blackwell Scientific Publishers. Oxford: Medical Press, 1958, 239, 703.
10. Seward, G. H. The question of psychophysiologic infertility: Some negative answers. *Psychosom. Med. 22,*24, 1960.
11. Shainess, N. A re-evaluation of some aspects of femininity through a study of menstruation: A preliminary report. *Compr. Psychiat. 2,*20, 1961.
12. Siegel, S. *Nonparametric Statistics.* McGraw-Hill, New York, 1956, p. 75.
13. Stone, A., Sandler, B., and Ward, M. E. Factors responsible for pregnancy in 500 infertility cases. *Fertil Steril 7,*1, 1956.
14. Sutherland, H., and Stewart, I. A critical analysis of the premenstrual syndrome. *Lancet 1,*1180, 1965.
15. Weil, E. J., and Tupper, G. Personality, life situation, and communication: A study of habitual abortion. *Psychosom. Med. 22*:448, 1960.
16. Zuckerman, M., Nurnberger, J., Gardner, S., Vandiver, J., Barrett, B., and den Breeijen, A. Psychological correlates of somatic complaints in pregnancy and difficulty in childbirth. *J. Consult. Psychol.* 27:4, 324, 1963.

35

Paige was a doctoral student of Bardwick and her study is an extension of that of Ivey and Bardwick, using the same dependent variable, the Verbal Anxiety Scale. Since hormonal concentration cannot ethically be manipulated in normal women, she cleverly chose her population in terms of hormonal levels resulting from their own manipulation; e.g., various varions of "the pill." She studied verbal output at various stages of natural menstrual cycles and for the same periods in individuals using several different kinds of oral contraceptive. Combination and sequential oral contraceptives release differential amounts of estrogen and progesterone at various stages of the anovulatory cycles they produce. Various contraceptives also differ in the dosage of estrogen and progesterone they contain. Thus Paige was able to examine subjects who differed only in their hormonal levels at the time of study.

Her hypotheses are rather complicated and are based upon a good deal of chemical knowledge and conjecture about the physiological effects of estrogen and progesterone. Her study has tended to differentiate behavior correlated with the paramenstrual phase which has a physiological basis from that which is a socially mediated response to a culturally abhorrent condition to the female body. Her study seems to indicate that premenstrual anxiety is a culturally conditioned response while premenstrual hostility may have a physiological basis.

She found that there were no cyclic fluctuations of anxiety in users of a combination contraceptive that maintains a high level of estrogen and progesterone throughout the cycle. Users of a sequential contraceptive [fifteen days of estrogen alone and then five days of estrogen and progesterone] showed a rise in premenstrual anxiety which was much less than that in women with natural cycles. Unfortunately, the type of contraceptive used is confounded with the degree of menstrual bleeding. However, by studying heavy and light bleeders [whether or not they used an oral contraceptive], she found that anxiety was more highly correlated with the severity of menstrual bleeding than with the hormonal level of the individual.

Hostility on the other hand, may be related to the

monoamine oxidase [MAO] level of the individual. MAO is a chemical found in many parts of the body which has been implicated in affective disorders. Estrogen appears to inhibit the MAO level while progesterone increases it. Users of combination contraceptives, which have larger amounts of progesterone than sequential contraceptives, have higher MAO levels than those using sequential pills and show more hostility throughout the cycle. Unfortunately, Paige did not measure the amount of MAO in the endometrium of her subjects, but inferred levels from other studies.

The study represents an interesting attempt to understand the etiology of mood fluctuation during the menstrual cycle, although it is still correlational in nature. We know that mood and hormonal level are related, but we do not know what causes what. The study is a clear improvement over other studies involving oral contraceptives since it does not concentrate upon the effects of a potent drug upon behavior. It is also unusual in that it makes use of a non-clinical population and does not rely upon retrospective measures of affect. Paige has suggested a method that relies upon differences already existing within a population to study phenomena that are not readily accessible to experimental manipulation.

Effects of Oral Contraceptives on Affective Fluctuations Associated with the Menstrual Cycle*

Karen E. Paige

Cyclic changes in the magnitude of negative affect were measured among a sample of 102 women who differed only in their use of oral contraceptives. Negative affect was measured by content-analyzing verbal speech collected at four different phases of the menstrual cycle under conditions that disguised the real purpose of the study. While women with natural menstrual cycles produced a U-shaped pattern of negative affect, women using combination oral contraceptives showed no cyclic affective changes. These results were not determined by self-selection, prior

---

*From *Psychosomatic Medicine*, 1971, *33* (6): 515-37.

expectations or reduction of physical discomfort among users of drug combinations. Further analysis suggested that the absence of affective fluctuations among users of drug combinations may be due, in part, to the effects of the drug on the intensity of menstrual flow, and in part, to its effects on MAO activity.

Periodic fluctuations in women's emotions during the menstrual cycle have been a topic of continuing discussion and research. Numerous clinical reports (1-10) and empirical studies (11-21) show that almost all women experience at least some increase in negative affect during the premenstrual and menstrual phases of the cycle, and a substantial proportion report these shifts as debilitating. Normal emotional behavior usually is resumed after menstrual bleeding stops, and continues until the next premenstrual phase.

The prevailing view among medical researchers is that these cyclic fluctuations in emotion are caused by fluctuations in the activity of female sex hormones (3, 12, 22-24). The emotional stability observed during intramenstrual phases is thought to be maintained by high hormone activity. The onset of depression, irritability and anxiety just before menstruation, and the days of emotional distress that follow are seen as a response to decreased estrogen and progesterone activity. During the cycle, a number of other biochemical changes occur that are frequently cited as intermediary links between fluctuations in female sex hormones and women's emotional shifts. For example, when estrogen and progesterone are decreasing premenstrually, a substantial increase in monoamine oxidase (MAO) activity is observed in various body tissues (25). Southgate et al (cited by Grant and Pryse-Davies [25]) has noted a tenfold increase in endometrial MAO activity which is believed to reflect similar increases in sensitive brain centers—e.g., the hypothalamus. The cyclic pattern of MAO activity is of particular interest since changes in MAO activity are often cited as a direct cause of emotional disorders similar to those experienced by menstruating women (22,24). Cyclic changes in adrenocorticoid levels (11,12,23,26), nerve excitability (27), and water and electrolyte metabolism (28,29) have also been observed in women. These changes are often believed to be influenced by fluctuations in estrogen and progesterone and, in turn, they determine cyclic emotional changes.

Although medical researchers acknowledge the importance of considering the effects of social and psychologic factors on women's mood cycles, it is commonly argued that the most fruitful direction of future research in this area is further specification of their biochemical origins (12,23,24). However, to date there is no empirical evidence to justify the assumption that the specific affective changes experienced during the menstrual cycle occur in direct response to specific biochemical changes. In fact, the whole question of physiologic distinctions among the various human emotional experiences must still be considered an open question. Correlational data, after all, do not demonstrate causality.

It must also be recognized that menstruation is a social, as well as physiologic, event. The menstrual process, and particularly menstrual bleeding, is surrounded by superstitution and taboo, and plays a central role in women's psychosexual development. Menstrual blood is universally abhorred, and its monthly flow has a significant impact on women's social and personal life. In nearly all societies, taboos exist to restrict the activities of menstruating women. These taboos range in severity from the banishment of women to menstrual huts to informal prohibitions against sex relations (30-35). In our own society, the menstrual sex taboo is commonly observed (36,37), and women always take great care to avoid any sign of menstrual blood. Menstruation is only discussed in private, if at all, and is viewed as unsanitary, inconvenient and embarrassing. The profound anxiety which menstrual bleeding causes in both men and women is well documented in folklore literature and numerous psychoanalytic protocols. Deutsch (6) and Benedek (3) argue that menstrual blood may offer reassurance of woman's reproductive capacity and femininity, but it also symbolizes sin, baseness, uncleanliness and woman's inferior social status.

It is equally plausible to suggest, then, that the cyclic shift in negative affect which coincides with the onset of menstrual bleeding may be determined by external factors. Menstruation-related depression, anger, irritability and anxiety could be socially mediated emotional responses to a woman's own bodily functions rather than a direct consequence of physiologic changes. If this were the case, then the biochemical events associated with periodic emotional distress would represent a spurious correlation between the time of menstruation and the affective response to menstrual blood.

Currently, an excellent opportunity exists to study systematically the possible causes of affective fluctuations in the menstrual cycle. Millions of women are using oral contraceptives for the purpose of preventing ovulation. One of the major consequences of using the drug is the elimination of many of those biochemical fluctuations usually cited as determinants of women's shifts in mood. During the use of oral contraceptives, fixed quantities of synthetic estrogen and progestin are administered daily for 20 or 21 days thus inhibiting secretion of natural estrogen and progesterone by the ovaries. The *combination* oral contraceptive brands artifically maintain high circulating levels of both hormones by including both progestin and estrogen in each tablet. During the use of the *sequential* brands, estrogen is taken alone for the first 15 or 16 days of the tablet cycle. A progestin is combined with estrogen only during the last 5 tablet days. There is some speculation that administration of these oral contraceptives alters the cyclic pattern of adrenocorticoid secretion and normal brain wave patterns (38), although the evidence is not yet conclusive.

There is good evidence, however, that the use of oral contraceptives eliminates the normal premenstrual increase in endometrial MAO activity (25). Grant and Pryse-Davies performed endometrial biopsies on women who were using either the combination or sequential brands and found that MAO activity remained relatively stable during the cycle. These researchers believe that this pattern reflects a similar pattern of MAO activity in the brain, and is the result of administering large doses of progestin. They also found significant differences in the overall magnitude of endometrial MAO activity between combination and sequential brand users. Throughout the cycle, endometrial MAO activity was greater among combination users than among sequential users. Moreover, the incidence of negative affect reported by their sample was directly related to group differences in cyclicity and magnitude of endometrial MAO activity; women using *both* types of oral contraceptive reported an absence of menstruation-related negative affect. However, women using combination brands reported a greater incidence of general negative affect during the cycle than women using sequential brands.

Another important consequence of using oral contraceptives is a substantial reduction in menstrual flow. The likelihood that menstrual flow will be reduced, however, depends largely on the type of oral contraceptive used. There is substantial evidence to suggest that only combination brands have a significant effect on menstrual flow. Most women using sequential brands report no change in the volume of flow, and some even report an increase (39-43). In contrast, the majority of women using combination brands report a substantial reduction in flow (40, 41,44). Often, menstrual bleeding constitutes 1 or 2 days of spotting, which requires little hygienic attention. Drill's review (40) shows that, among combination users, flow reduction is significantly more likely to occur among women using brands containing low (1 mg.) quantities of progestin than among women using brands containing higher (2 mg. or more) doses of progestin. For example,

Andrews and Andrews (45) found that 83% of women using 1-mg. brands experienced reduction in flow, while Drill's survey shows that only 8-52% of various samples using the 2-2.5 mg. brands report flow reduction (40). These data suggest that the volume of menstrual flow is most likely to be reduced among (a) women using 1-mg. combination brands, followed by (b) women using 2-2.5 mg. combination brands, and (c) those using sequential brands, in that order.

Each of the physiologic changes described could influence the typical pattern of fluctuations in negative affect during the menstrual cycle, and each is related somewhat differently to social versus biochemical determinants of these affective shifts. The differential effects of oral contraceptives on cyclic variability in the levels of female sex hormones, cyclic pattern of endometrial MAO activity, and volume of menstrual flow lead to a number of testable hypotheses about the origins of menstruation-related negative affect.

In the present study, the pattern of negative affect during the menstrual cycle was measured among women with natural cycles and among those using various oral contraceptives. Negative affect patterns were then compared between (a) combination brand users and women with natural cycles, (b) women experiencing different intensities of menstrual flow, and (c) women using different brands of oral contraceptives which are expected to have different effects on MAO activity. The following hypotheses were proposed about each of these comparisons:

EFFECTS OF COMBINATION BRANDS
ON CYCLIC NEGATIVE AFFECT

As noted, the use of combination oral contraceptive brands eliminates normal fluctuations in circulating levels of female sex hormones during the cycle. Normally, progesterone does not begin to circulate until the last half of the cycle. Estrogen levels, however, begin to increase after menstruation and remain high throughout most of the cycle. A few days before the next menstruation, both estrogen and progesterone levels decrease rapidly and only minimal circulating levels are observed during menstruation. During the use of combination oral contraceptives, however, high levels of *both* progestin and estrogen are continually circulating during the cycle, with only a temporary reduction to

558

Karen E. Paige

permit withdrawal bleeding.

The first hypothesis concerns the relationship between the pattern of estrogen-progestin activity and that of negative affect during the combination oral contraceptive cycle. If there is any relationship between the variability in female sex hormone activity during the menstrual cycle and the variability in negative affect, then the following prediction should be supported:

> 1. The artificial maintenance of constantly high levels of estrogen and progestin during the use of combination brands should eliminate the typical U-shaped pattern of negative affect fluctuations during the menstrual cycle. In geometric terms, the pattern of negative affect among combination users should be described by a straight line with zero slope.

The critical statistical test of this hypothesis is comparison of the amount of variability in negative affect accounted for by the cycle phase between women using combination oral contraceptives and those with natural cycles. The effects of cycle phase on negative affect variability should be 0 for combination users, but substantially greater than 0 for nonusers.

The following two hypotheses test alternate explanations of possible mechanisms by which the pattern of sex hormone variability may determine affective changes.

MENSTRUAL FLOW AND THE MAGNITUDE OF MENSTRUAL NEGATIVE AFFECT

It is possible that fluctuations in female sex hormones during the cycle only indirectly influence the cyclic shift in negative affect by determining the amount of endometrial tissue sloughed off as menstrual blood. Instead, menstruation-related negative affect could be a direct emotional response to menstrual flow.

Normally, menstrual bleeding may continue for a period of 5-7 days. During this time, women are constantly reminded of the negative social attitudes about menstruation. They are expected to abstain from sex relations and to avoid public cognizance of menstrual bleeding by attending to various hygienic tasks (e.g., changing menstrual pads). If menstruation-related emotional distress occurs in response to menstrual flow rather than to underlying biochemical changes, then any condition in which the flow is substantially reduced should also reduce the magnitude of negative affect.

The differential effects of oral contraceptive brands on the intensity of menstrual flow provide an opportunity to test this hypothesis. The difference in magnitude of negative affect during menstruation was compared among the following subgroups of oral contraceptive users: (a) sequential users versus combination users, (b) women using combination brands containing 1 mg. progestin versus those using combination brands containing 2-2.5 mg. progestin, (c) combination users with normally heavy flow versus those with reduced flow estimated from self-report data. In each of the comparisons, only women most likely to experience normally heavy flow were expected to produce the typical increase in menstrual negative affect. Women likely to experience reduced flow were expected to produce a substantially lower magnitude of negative affect at menstruation. The following results were predicted:

2(a). During menstruation, sequential brand users should produce the typical increase in negative affect; combination brand users should not experience an increase in negative affect.

2(b). During menstruation, women using 2-2.5 mg. combination brands should produce a greater magnitude of negative affect than women using 1 mg. combination brands.

2(c). During menstruation, combination users reporting normally heavy flow should produce a greater magnitude of negative affect than women reporting a reduction in flow.

It is also possible to test the relationship between women's adherence to social expectations about the behavior of menstruating women and the intensity of menstrual flow. The menstrual sex taboo is an excellent example of the cultural abhorrence of menstrual blood. Menstruating women are generally expected to abstain from sex for as many as 5-7 days. However, if menstrual bleeding is scanty and subsides within 1 or 2 days, as is common among oral contraceptive users, it is possible that the taboo will be ignored.

If there is a relationship between adherence to the menstrual sex taboo and the intensity of menstrual bleeding, then the following prediction should be supported:

2(d). Women who experience a reduction in flow during the use of oral contraceptives should be less likely to observe the menstrual sex taboo than women with normally heavy flow (whether or not they use oral contraceptives).

An empirical relationship between the magnitude of menstrual negative affect, menstrual flow intensity and adherence to the menstrual sex taboo, regardless of hormones levels, would suggest a causal link between negative social attitudes about menstruation and the experience of menstrual distress.

MAO ACTIVITY AND THE PATTERN OF NEGATIVE AFFECT

Variability in the activity of female sex hormones during the cycle is also believed to influence endometrial MAO activity, and possibly brain MAO activity. Estrogen is thought to inhibit MAO activity and thus maintain normal emotional behavior in women. However, the normal increase in progesterone premenstrually is thought to stimulate MAO activity and consequently increase negative affect. Grant and Pryse-Davies suggest that administration of high quantities of progestin in oral contraceptives causes the observed absence of premenstrual increase in endometrial MAO activity. This absence, in turn, brings relief from menstruation-related negative affect among women who are using both sequential and combination oral contraceptive brands.

If menstruation-related negative affect is directly related to increased MAO activity, and if use of oral contraceptives eliminates the cyclic shift in MAO activity, then the following hypothesis should be supported:

3(a). The magnitude of negative affect should remain constant throughout the cycle for *both* women using sequential brands and those using combination brands.

Grant and Pryse-Davies also found that the general level of endometrial MAO activity was lower among sequential users throughout the cycle than among combination users. They suggest that the lower MAO activity among sequential users is due to MAO-inhibiting qualities of the highly estrogenic sequential

561

tablets. Self-report data on these women showed also that sequential users reported a lower incidence of depression, anger and irritability during the cycle than did women who used combination brands. Grant and Pryse-Davies conclude that the absolute magnitude of endometrial MAO activity is directly related to the magnitude of negative affect experienced during the cycle. This finding should be supported by the present study.

If the general level of endometrial MAO activity during the cycle is related to the general magnitude of negative affect, and if sequential oral contraceptives inhibit MAO activity to a greater extent than combination brands, then,

3(b). The magnitude of negative affect for women who use sequential brands should be consistently lower than that for women using combination brands.

A replication of the Grant and Pryse-Davies results regarding group differences in negative affect patterns during the cycle would suggest a biochemical interpretation of menstrual negative affect fluctuations.

There have been numerous previous studies on the emotional changes experienced by women using oral contraceptives (25, 36, 40-44, 46-62). However, most have focused on the possible psychologic consequences of using a highly potent drug, rather than examining oral contraceptives as a means of studying the etiology of mood fluctuations in the menstrual cycle. Although the findings of some of these studies have implications for effects of the drug on mood changes, methodologic problems inherent in many of the studies make it difficult to generalize beyond the populations studied. Many are clinical in nature, use patient populations, and report contradictory findings concerning women's emotional reactions to oral contraceptives. Large-scale clinical tests of various oral contraceptives often report the incidence of menstruation-related symptoms, but rarely present comparative data on the incidence of these symptoms among a control population. Well designed empirical studies, such as that by Moos (58), have compared the relative incidence of negative affect among oral contraceptive users and nonusers during the cycle. However, they have relied on self-report and retrospective recall data which, for our purposes, make it difficult to assess whether differences in cyclic mood patterns are due to underlying biochemical changes or to social expectations about which emotions are appropriate to each phase of the cycle. In the present study, the method by which women were selected and tested minimized the effects of social bias. Women were not told the purpose of the study during testing, and negative affect was measured by an instrument that is not distorted by retrospective or prior expectations about menstruation.

METHOD

Sample selection. The general strategy of this field experiment was to measure cyclic changes in the magnitude of negative affect among a sample of women who differed only in their use of oral contraceptives. Initially, 470 wives of university graduate students were asked to volunteer for a study of sex differences in linguistic and personality styles. Seventy-six percent indicated willingness to participate. Pretest interviews were conducted to select a homogeneous sample of women and to determine which women use oral contraceptives and which had natural menstrual cycles. On the basis of the interview, women were eliminated who were pregnant or postpartum, foreign-born, regular users of drugs that could affect emotional states, mentally or physically disabled, or lived too far outside the university area for interviewing.

Groups. The final sample included 102 women who, for the purpose of data analysis, comprised the following groups: (a) The *Normal* group consisted of 38 women who had either never used oral contracep /es (N = 32) or had discontinued their use at least 6 months prior to testing (N = 6). Cycle lengths were determined at least 1 months prior to testing, so that testing would occur during the same hormone phase for all women. Cycle lengths were estimated according to the procedure suggested by Potter et al (63), and in many cases, by using a woman's own record of basal temperature and weight changes. Women were told that such information was one of the many necessary controls for a scientific study on sex differences. Also, information on cycle lengths was gathered along with extraneous questions regarding the cover story. (b) The *Combination* group consisted of 52 women who had been taking the same brand of oral contraceptives for at least 6 months prior to testing. Twenty-six women were using a 1-mg brand (Ortho-Novum-2 or Ovulen-1), 18 were using a 2-mg brand (Ortho-Novum-2 or Norlestrin), and 8 were using a 2.5-mg. brand (Enovid-E). All brands contain 0.10 mg of an estrogen compound, mestranol, in addition to the 1-2.5 mg progestin. Each brand, except Ovulen, consists of 20 tablets; Ovulen consists of 21 tablets. Using the 28-day menstrual cycle as the reference cycle, all women being menstrual bleeding on Day 1. The first table is taken on Day 5 and the last on Day 24 (or Day 25 for Ovulen). The withdrawal period between tablet cycles lasted between 6 and 8 days, with menstrual bleeding beginning about 2-4 days after taking the last tablet. The cycle days on which women were tested were determined simply by knowing how many tablets were taken at the time of the pretest interview, the number of tablets in the series, the duration of menstrual flow, and the length of the withdrawal period. (c) The *Sequential* group consisted of 12 women,* of which 10 were using C-Quens (15 tablets of 0.08 mg mestranol followed by 5 tablets of 0.08 mg mestranol and 2 mg progestin), and 2 were using Oracon (16 tablets of 0.10 mg mestranol followed by 5 tablets of 0.10 mg mestranol and 2.5 mg progestin). For all women, the withdrawal period lasted between 7 and 8 days. Menstrual bleeding occurred between 2 and 4 days after the last tablet was taken. The cycle days on which women were tested were determined in the same way as described for the Combination group.

Test days. The actual day on which testing took place varied with each woman, since cycle lengths vary. For the sake of clarity, however, the test cycle days are referred to as the fourth, 10th, 16th and 26th days of the average 28-day cycle. The cycle days on which all women were tested may be described as follows: (a) Day 4: All women are experiencing menstrual bleeding. For the Normal group, estrogen and progesterone levels are substantially lower than at other cycle phases. Since women in the Combination and Sequential groups are between tablet cycles, circulating levels of estrogen and progestin are reduced. (b) Day 10: For the Normal group, this is the estrogen phase during which estrogen levels are increasing rapidly, but ovarian progesterone is minimal and perhaps absent. Women in the Combination group have been taking estrogen-progestin tablets for 6 days, and those in the Sequential group have been taking only estrogen tablets for 6 days. (c) Day 16: For the Normal group, Day 16 refers to the midcycle, or ovulation, phase. Estrogen levels are high, and progesterone is beginning to increase. Women in the Combination group have been taking estrogen-progestin tablets for 12 days, and those in the Sequential group have been taking only estrogen for 12 days. (d) Day 26: For the Normal group, both estrogen and progesterone levels are decreasing rapidly, and endometrial MAO activity is presumably increasing substantially. Since women in

---

* The *Sequential* group originally included 26 women. However, due to faulty data collection procedures by one interviewer, data on 14 of these women are invalid and could not be included in the analysis.

both Combination and Sequential groups have just stopped taking estrogen-progestin tablets, high levels of both hormones are still circulating. However, there is no increase in endometrial MAO activity for either oral contraceptive group. Menstrual bleeding has not yet begun for any woman in the sample.

Testing procedures. Negative affects were measured by a content analysis technic of speech samples collected and scored according to procedures described by Gottschalk et al (64). Women were tested at home on each of the 4 test days. Each woman was asked to speak for 5 minutes about any memorable experience in her life. The verbal samples were recorded on tape under the supervision of an experienced female interviewer who usually left the room during testing. The sequence in which women were tested was varied in order to control for a series effect that may occur when affective states are measured over time. The starting points for the interview series were randomly distributed over the 4 test days within each group. Testing followed the same format each day, and each woman was tested by the same interviewer throughout the series. Additional tests were administered at each interview (word-matching and drawing completion) to maintain the cover story about the purpose of the study. At the last test session, additional background data were collected, and the real purpose of the study revealed.

Scoring. As specified by Gottschalk et al (64), the content of each verbal sample was assessed for the magnitude of nine kinds of negative affect: (a) Death Anxiety, (b) Shame Anxiety, (c) Separation Anxiety, (d) Mutilation Anxiety, (e) Guilt Anxiety, (f) Diffuse Anxiety, (g) Inward Hostility, (h) Outward Hostility, and (i) Ambivalently Directed Hostility. The numerical scores for the first six categories were summed together to form an *Anxiety Scale,* and the scores for the last three categories were summed together to form a *Hostility Scale.* All nine categories were then summed together to form a *Total Negative Affect Scale.* The formula used to derive each of the three affect scores is

$$\sqrt{\frac{100f_1w_1 + f_2w_2 + \ldots + f_nw_n + .5}{N}}$$

where f_n is the frequency per unit of time of any relevant verbal sample, w_n is the weight applied to such verbal references, and N is the number of words in the sample. Four advanced graduate students in psychology scored the verbal samples without knowledge of either the group or cycle day to which the sample belonged. Interscorer correlations ranged from 0.86 to 0.91.

Validity. Previous studies have shown the Gottschalk scales to be valid measures of the U-shaped pattern of negative affect fluctuations that are known to occur during the menstrual cycle (15, 16). For our purposes, the usefulness of the scales depended on their sensitivity to the decrease in negative affect between menstruation (Day 4) and midcycle (Day 16), and between mid-cycle and premenstruation (Day 26) among those in the Normal group in this study. Table 1 shows the mean negative affect scores produced by the Normal group. These results show that each of the three scales are, indeed, valid measures of these shifts in negative affect. The decrease in mean scores between Days 4 and 16 and the increase in mean scores between Days 16 and 26 are statistically significant when measured by the Total Negative Affect and Hostility scales. The affective fluctuations measured by the Anxiety scale show the same U-shaped pattern, although only the shift between Days 4 and 16 is statistically significant.

RESULTS

Hypothesis I: Differences in Negative Affect Patterns Between Normal and Combination Groups

The first hypothesis predicted that the typical U-shaped pattern of negative affect should not occur for the Combination group. Instead the magnitude of negative affect produced by the Combination group should be constant throughout the cycle.

The group differences in mean negative affect scores are presented graphically in Fig 1-3. Observation of the differences between the affect curves of the Normal and Combination groups shows clearly that this hypothesis is confirmed. Whether measured by the Total Negative Affect scale, or its two components, Anxiety and Hostility, the curvilinear fluctuations in mean negative affect scores produced by the Normal group obviously do not occur for the Combination group.

Two statistical tests were performed to analyze these group differences in negative affect patterns as measured by each of the three scales. First, two-way analyses of variance were performed for repeated measures and unequal Ns, including tests of the simple main effect of cycle day on the magnitude of negative affect for each group individually (65). Second, the strength of association between cycle day and negative affect was estimated according to the method described by Hays (66). Table 2 presents the results of the analyses of variance of negative affect scores by group and cycle day for each of the three scales.

Total negative affect. The results show that group alone (main effect A) has no effect on the magnitude of Total Negative Affect, irrespective of cycle day. This indicates that the magnitude of negative affect which women experience during the cycle averages out to the same, regardless of whether they use oral contraceptives. Tests of the simple main effect of cycle day on negative affect for each group individually show that cycle day for the Normal group (b at a_1) has a significant effect ($P<0.01$) on the magnitude of Total Negative Affect scores. Cycle day for the Combination group only (b at a_2), however, has no effect whatsoever on the magnitude of Total Negative Affect scores ($P<0.95$).

For the Combination group, the estimated amount of variability (w^2) in Total Negative Affect accounted by the day of the menstrual cycle is 0, as compared to 7.6% for the Normal group. This means that 100% of the estimated variability in negative affect accounted for by the cycle day is eliminated for the Combination group.

Anxiety. The analysis of variance of Anxiety scores by group and cycle day shows again that there is no systematic effect of group alone (A) on the average magnitude of Anxiety. Tests of the simple main effect of cycle day for Normal and Combination groups separately (b at a_1, and b at a_2, respectively) show that cycle day significantly affects the magnitude of Anxiety scores for the Normal group ($p<0.05$) but does not significantly affect the magnitude of Anxiety for the Combination group ($0.25<P<0.10$).

The estimated amount of variability in Anxiety scores accounted for by the cycle day alone is 0.94% for the Combination group, as compared to 5.2% for the Normal group. The variability in Anxiety for the Combination group, then, is reduced by about a factor of 5.

Hostility. The results of the analysis of Hostility scores show the same results. Group alone (A) had no systematic effect on the magnitude of Hostility experienced during the menstrual cycle. Although cycle day (B) had a signficant effect on Hostility scores, the tests of the simple main effect of cycle day on Hostility for each group individually indicates that all of this effect is attributable to the Normal group (b at a_1) ($P<0.001$). Cycle day has no effect whatsoever on the magnitude of Hostility for the Combination group (b at a_2) ($P<0.99$). The estimated amount of variability in Hostility scores accounted for by the cycle day alone is 0 for the

Table 1. Normal Group: Differences in Mean Negative Affect Scores Between Menses (Day 4) and Midcycle (Day 16), and Between Midcycle (Day 16) and Premenses (Day 26)

Scale	Menses-Midcycle Shift			Midcycle-Premenses Shift		
	Mean comparisons	t^*	P	Mean comparisons	t	P
Total Negative Affect	2.519 vs 2.115	3.873	<0.001	2.115 vs 2.561	2.972	<0.005
Anxiety	1.932 vs 1.614	3.142	<0.005	1.614 vs 1.768	1.549	<0.10
Hostility	1.402 vs 1.227	1.836	<0.05	1.227 vs 1.756	3.886	<0.001

* t Values are for paired comparisons described by Hays (66).

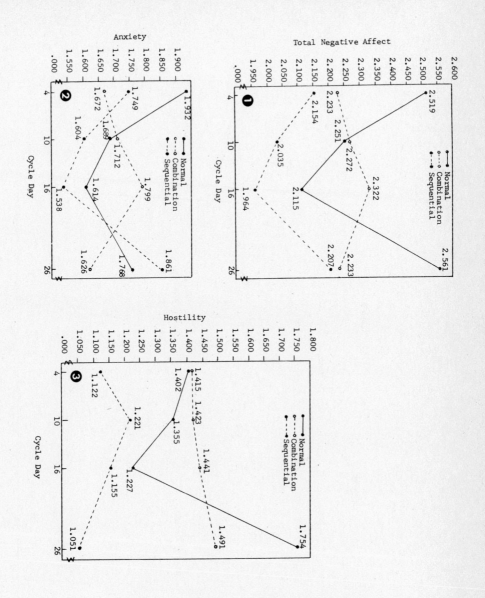

Fig 1. Differences in cyclic patterns of Total **Negative** Affect mean scores between Normal, Combination **and** Sequential groups. **Fig 2.** Differences in cyclic **patterns** of Anxiety mean scores between Normal, Combination and Sequential groups. **Fig 3.** Differences in cyclic patterns of Hostility mean scores between Normal, Combination and Sequential groups.

Table 2. Analyses of Variance of Negative Affect Scores by Group and Cycle Day for Each Scale

Source	SS	df	MS	F	P
TOTAL NEGATIVE AFFECT SCALE					
Group (A)	0.768	1	0.763	2.909	NS
Error a	23.215	88	0.264		
Day of cycle (B)	1.178	3	0.393	0.854	NS
A × B	4.381	3	1.460	3.147	< 0.05
Error b	120.018	264	0.418		
b at a_1	5.233	3	1.744	4.172	< 0.01
b at a_2	0.334	3	0.111	0.265	> 0.95
ANXIETY SCALE					
Group (A)	0.3641	1	0.3641	0.5299	NS
Error a	60.4610	88	0.6870		
Cycle day (B)	0.7673	3	0.2557	0.1081	NS
A × B	2.7259	3	0.9086	3.8418	< 0.01
Error b	62.4428	264	0.2365		
b at a_1	2.1232	3	0.7077	2.9923	< 0.05
b at a_2	1.3699	3	0.4566	1.9306	$0.25 < p < 0.10$
HOSTILITY SCALE					
Group (A)	0.000	1	0.000	0.000	NS
Error a	54.735	88	0.615		
Cycle day (B)	3.021	3	1.007	2.970	< 0.05
A × B	2.224	3	0.741	2.185	< 0.10
Error b	89.600	264	0.339		
b at a_1	5.784	3	1.928	5.678	< 0.001
b at a_2	0.075	3	0.025	0.074	> 0.99

Normal group, and 13.8% for the Combination group.

Effects of Self-Selection, Expectations and Symptom Reduction on Group Differences in Negative Affect Patterns

Although statistical analyses show clearly that cyclic negative affective fluctuation are eliminated for the Combination group, there is the possibility that these results are confounded by some third variable correlated with both affect and use of oral contraceptives.

Self-selection. Since this was a field study rather than a laboratory experiment, women could not be randomly assigned to control and experimental conditions. Therefore, factors were investigated that may have determined the self-selection of women into the 2 groups, and consequently account for the differences in negative affect patterns. The initial selection of women insured some degree of sample homogeneity, since only white, native-born, married, middle-class women were asked to participate. Additional analysis showed that women were not self-selected into the 2 groups on the basis of age, parity, education or father's education (index of social class origin). Psychologic factors often mentioned as important determinants of menstrual attitudes and symptomology were also examined as possible determinants of oral contraceptive use as well. The factors examined, age at menarche, reaction to menarche, mother's attitudes about menstruation, amount of preparation for menarche, and degree of menstrual discomfort recalled during teens did not differentiate between the 2 groups. Table 3 presents the proportional representation of women in the 2 groups according to each of these factors. Since these factors do not distinguish between the composition of the Combination group and that of the Normal group, it is unlikely that they account for observed group differences in negative affect patterns. As a final check, however, within-group differences in negative affect curves according to each factor were examined. Regardless of each factor, women in the Normal group always produced the typical U-shaped pattern of negative affect fluctuations observed for the group as a whole. This pattern was never observed for within-Combination group comparisons.

Reduction of physical discomfort among combination users. A number of previous studies have reported a decrease in the incidence of common menstruation-related physical symptoms among oral contraceptive users (40, 41, 50, 52, 58). In this study as

Table 3.   Proportional Representation of Women in Normal and Combination Groups According to Demographic and Psychologic Factors Thought to Determine Self-Selection

Data	Normal group	Combination group	Total (%)*	χ^2	P
Parity					
Parous	47 (22)	53 (25)	100 (47)		
Nonparous	37 (14)	63 (24)	100 (38)	0.257	< 0.75
Educational attainment					
High School diploma	46 (11)	54 (13)	100 (24)		
College or more	41 (26)	59 (38)	100 (64)	0.038	< 0.90
Age (yr)					
21–24	36 (15)	64 (27)	100 (42)		
25–29	46 (16)	54 (19)	100 (35)		
30–33	63 (5)	37 (3)	100 (8)	2.256	< 0.50
Religion					
Catholic	56 (10)	44 (8)	100 (18)		
Jew	46 (6)	54 (7)	100 (13)		
Protestant	37 (21)	63 (36)	100 (57)	2.026	< 0.50
Father's Education					
Noncollege	52 (27)	48 (25)	100 (52)		
College	27 (10)	73 (26)	100 (36)	2.902	< 0.10
Age at menarche (yr)					
10–11	39 (7)	61 (11)	100 (18)		
12–13	48 (25)	52 (26)	100 (51)		
14–15	26 (5)	74 (14)	100 (19)	2.168	< 0.50
Amount of prior information					
a great deal	61 (12)	39 (19)	100 (31)		
some	45 (18)	55 (22)	100 (40)		
little or none	31 (6)	69 (10)	100 (16)	0.824	< 0.75
Initial reaction to menarche					
Negative	42 (15)	58 (21)	100 (36)		
Positive	39 (13)	61 (20)	100 (33)		
Neutral	44 (8)	56 (10)	100 (18)	0.127	< 0.95
Mother's attitude about menses					
Negative	37 (10)	63 (17)	100 (27)		
Positive	39 (13)	61 (20)	100 (33)		
Neutral	43 (12)	57 (16)	100 (28)	0.363	< 0.90
Number of symptoms during teens					
Few (0–3)	35 (15)	65 (29)	100 (44)		
Many (4–7)	50 (19)	50 (19)	100 (38)	1.484	< 0.25

* Some data missing; thus total sample not represented.

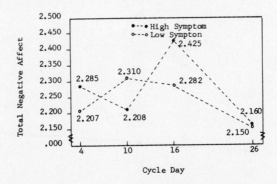

Fig 4. Differences in Total Negative Affect patterns between high- and low-symptom complainers—Combination group.

well, self-report data on the incidence of menstrual and premenstrual physical symptoms showed that women in the Combination group reported fewer symptoms than those in the Normal group. All women were asked to indicate whether they experienced any of the following symptoms associated with menstruation: cramps, bloating, constipation, backaches, headaches, breast tenderness and weight gain. The mean number of symptoms reported by the Normal group was 4, as compared to 2.3 for the Combination group. This raised the possibility that reduction in menstrual discomfort among women in the Combination group may account for the absence of negative affective fluctuations. Within the Combination group, the relationship between degree of menstrual discomfort and negative affect pattern was examined by comparing the negative affect curves of women with high and low symptoms. Women with high symptoms—ie, the average or above-average number of symptoms reported by the Normal group. Women with low symptoms were those reporting fewer symptoms (0-3) than the average for the Normal group. If negative affective fluctuations were related to physical discomfort, then the high-symptom group should produce the same U-shaped pattern observed for the Normal group. Only women with low symptoms should show no affective shifts.

As shown in Fig. 4, reduction of menstrual discomfort associated with oral contraceptive use does *not* account for the absence of U-shaped affective fluctuations among the Com-

573

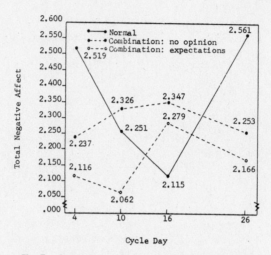

Fig 5. Comparison of Total Negative Affect patterns between Normal group and subgroups of Combination group—women **with** expectations about emotional effects of oral contraceptives and women **without** expectations (eg, no opinion).

bination group. Both high-and low-symptom groups continue to show the same absence of menstrual cycle fluctuations observed for the group as a whole.

Prior expectations about oral contraceptives. It has also been suggested that the extent to which oral contraceptive users experience emotional changes during the menstrual cycle depends on their prior expectations about the beneficial effects of the drug (44, 51). The women in the Combination group may experience no affective fluctuations because they expect the drug to bring relief to menstrual emotional distress. To test this possibility, women in the Combination group were asked whether or not they believed oral contraceptives were supposed to eliminate either (a) premenstrual tension, (b) depression or (c) irritability. The results showed that 11 women believed the drug was supposed to eliminate one or more of these symptoms of menstrual distress, and the remaining 40 had no opinion.

The negative affect curve of the 11 women who did believe that oral contraceptives reduced menstrual distress was compared to that of the 40 women with no opinion. Inspection of Fig 5 clearly reveals that women's beliefs about the effects of oral contraceptives on menstrual emotional symptoms do not explain the

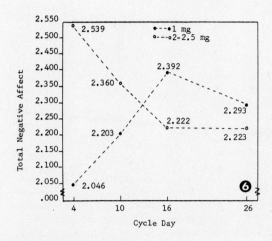

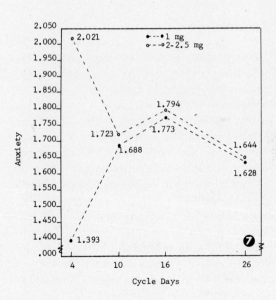

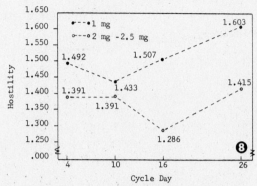

Fig 6. Differences in cyclic patterns of Total Negative Affect mean scores between women in Combination group using 1-mg brands and those using 2–2.5 mg brands. **Fig 7.** Differences in cyclic patterns of Anxiety mean scores between women in Combination group using 1-mg brands and those using 2–2.5 mg brands. **Fig 8.** Differences in cyclic patterns of Hostility mean scores between women in Combination group using 1-mg progestin brands and 2–2.5 mg brands.

absence of affective fluctuations for the Combination group. Instead of producing a U-shaped affect pattern, women *without* expectations produce the same pattern of negative affect during the cycle as women *with* expectations.

These results show that Normal versus Combination group differences in negative affect patterns during the menstrual cycle cannot be explained in terms of self-selection, reduction of physical discomfort during oral contraceptive use, or expectations about the effects of the drug on menstruation-related discomfort.

Hypothesis II: Menstrual Flow and Menstrual Negative Affect

The second hypothesis proposed that the high magnitude of negative affect normally experienced during the menstrual phase may be an emotional response to visible evidence of menstrual bleeding, and only incidentally associated with reduction in estrogen and progesterone levels. If this was the case, then a reduction in menstrual flow would also reduce the magnitude of menstrual negative affect.

To test this hypothesis, mean negative affect scores at Day 4 (menses) were compared between subgroups of women most likely to experience a reduction in menstrual flow, and subgroups of women most likely to experience normally heavy flow.

Sequential versus Combination comparison. It was predicted that the Sequential group would produce the same increase in Day 4 negative affect observed for the Normal group, despite the fact that they are more similar to the Combination group in terms of drug-induced biochemical changes (eg., endometrial MAO activity).

Comparisons of negative affect curves as measured by Total Negative Affect, Anxiety and Hostility may be observed in Fig 1, 2 and 3, respectively. Inspection of these curves reveals that the Sequential group pattern of Total Negative Affect (Fig 1) is most similar to that of the Normal group. This U-shaped pattern, however, is entirely due to the Anxiety component (Fig. 2). The Anxiety curve in the Sequential group is strikingly similar to that of the Normal group, with very little difference in the magnitude of anxiety expressed at each cycle day tested. However, inspection of the Hostility curves (Fig 3) reveals a different trend. Instead of producing a U-shaped pattern of Hostility during the cycle, the Sequential group produces a pattern of Hostility scores most similar to that of the Combination group.

While the Sequential group, like the Normal group, shows substantial increase in Total Negative Affect at Day 4, the *absolute* level is still lower than that of the Combination group. For the Anxiety measure alone, however, the absolute level for the Sequential group is *higher* than that of the Combination group. Although the difference in Anxiety means is not statistically significant, the difference is in the expected direction. Therefore, the 2 groups most likely to experience normally heavy menstrual flow experience a greater magnitude of Anxiety at menstruation than the group most likely to experience a reduction in flow.

Combination group dosage comparison. If the magnitude of negative affect at Day 4 is related to menstrual flow intensity, then women using the brands containing 1 mg progestin should produce a lower Day-4 negative affect score than those using higher dosages. As shown in Fig 6-8, this prediction is supported for Total Negative Affect and Anxiety, but not for Hostility. The curves presented in Fig 6 show that only at Day 4 is there a difference in mean Total Negative Affect between the 2 dosage groups. During the remainder of the cycle, the means are essentially the same for each group. As predicted, only at menstruation is the mean magnitude of Total Negative Affect for the 1-mg group significantly lower than that for the 2-2.5 mg group

577

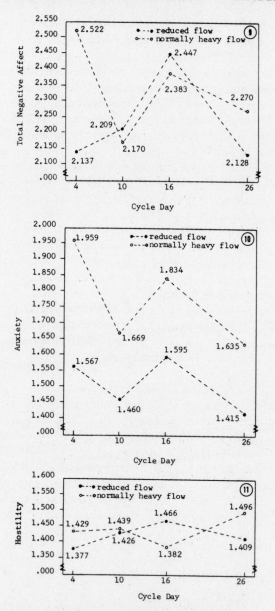

Fig 9. Differences in cyclic patterns of Total Negative Affect mean scores between women in Combination group reporting reduced and normally heavy flow. **Fig 10.** Differences in cyclic patterns of Anxiety mean scores between women in Combination group reporting reduced flow and normally heavy flow. **Fig 11.** Differences in cyclic patterns of Hostility mean scores between women in Combination group reporting reduced flow and normally heavy flow.

578

Karen E. Paige

($t = 2.952$, $P < 0.005$). Inspection of Fig 7 indicates that the difference in the means of Total Negative Affect at Day 4 is entirely due to the Anxiety component. The 1-mg group produces a significantly lower magnitude of Anxiety at Day 4 than the 2-2.5 mg group ($t = 3.451$, $P < 0.001$), although there is no difference in Anxiety scores at the other 3 cycle days. Figure 8 shows that the magnitude of Hostility at Day 4 is not related to dosage level. The Hostility means at Day 4 are not significantly different between dosage groups. In fact, throughout the cycle, the patterns of Hostility produced by each dosage group are the same as the pattern produced by the Combination group as a whole.

Combination group self-reported flow. It was also predicted that, regardless of dosage level, women reporting a reduction in menstrual flow while using oral contraceptives would experience a lower magnitude of negative affect at Day 4 than women reporting no change in flow.

Although women were not asked about the intensity of menstrual flow during regular interviews, 67% ($N = 34$) of the Combination group was questioned during later telephone interviews. Of these, 23 reported a substantial decrease in flow since the use of oral contraceptives. Eleven women reported that the drug had not affected the intensity of menstrual flow. None reported an increase in flow.

The curves presented in Fig 9-11 indicate that the hypothesis is confirmed again for Total Negative Affect and Anxiety. Figure 9 shows that only at Day 4 is there a significant difference in Total Negative Affect scores between women with normal and reduced flow ($t = 1.681$, $P < 0.06$). The group differences in Anxiety patterns (Fig 10) show that women with reduced flow produce a significantly lower magnitude of Anxiety at Day 4 than those with normal flow ($t = 1.866$, $P < 0.05$). The group with reduced flow experiences less Anxiety during each of the remaining 3 cycle days as well. However, group differences in Anxiety means at each of these cycle days are not statistically significant.

Hostility curves (Fig 11) clearly show that the magnitude of hostility at Day 4 is not related to self-reported flow intensity. Women reporting normal flow produce only a slightly higher level of Hostility during menstruation than those with reduced flow. However, the Hostility means for the 2 groups show the same pattern throughout the cycle observed for the group as a whole.

In sum, the results of each of the three comparisons strongly suggest a relationship between menstrual *Anxiety* and the intensity of menstrual flow. In none of the comparisons, however, was the magnitude of menstrual Hostility related to estimated flow intensity.

Table 4. Differences in Proportion of Women Who Refrain From Sex Relations During Menstruation Depending on Intensity of Flow

Refrain from sex at menses	Normally heavy flow	Reduced flow	χ^2	P
Yes	62 (29)	35 (8)		
No	38 (18)	65 (15)		
Total	100 (47)	100 (23)	3.482	<0.05

Menstrual flow and adherence to the menstrual sex taboo. The final prediction concerned the relationship between the intensity of menstrual flow and conformity to social expectations regarding the behavior of menstruating women. It was expected that women experiencing a reduced menstrual flow would be less likely to adhere to the universal menstrual sex taboo.

In the present sample, 55% of the women indicated that they abstain from sex relations during menstruation. The possibility that sexual abstinence was related to flow intensity was examined by comparing the proportion of women who abstain with normally heavy flow with those experiencing a reduction in flow. Women with normally heavy flow are all those in the Normal group and those in the Combination group who reported no change in flow while using the drug. Women with reduced flow are those in the Combination group reporting a substantial reduction in flow while using the drug. As Table 4 shows, sexual abstinence during menstruation is significantly related to the intensity of menstrual flow ($\chi^2 = 3.482$, $P<0.06$). Women with reduced flow are significantly less likely to abstain than women with normal flow.

Reduced menstrual flow, then, is associated with *both* lower Anxiety during menstruation and less likelinood of adhering to the menstrual sex taboo, which lends support to the social explanation of menstrual distress.

Hypothesis III: MAO Activity and Negative Affect Patterns

A biochemical explanation of cyclic fluctuations in negative affect was tested by attempting to replicate the findings of Grant and Pryse-Davies who attribute premenstrual onset of depression and irritability to the sudden increase in MAO activity. They found that (a) neither premenstrual irritability and depression nor premenstrual increases in endometrial MAO activity occurred among oral contraceptive users, but that (b) among oral contraceptive users, both the incidence of depression, anger and irritability *and* the level of endometrial MAO activity throughout the cycle were greater among combination brand users than among users of the sequential brands. These results suggest a direct relationship between the level of MAO activity and the magnitude of negative affect during the cycle.

In this study, the affective states described as depression and irritability are measured by the Hostility scale. Inspection of Fig. 3, which compares the Hostility curves for the Normal, Combination and Sequential groups, clearly indicates that group differences in Hostility patterns during the cycle replicate the self-report findings of Grant and Pryse-Davies. First, the most substantial shift in Hostility for the Normal group occurs during the premenstrual phase (Day 26), which is the cycle phase during which endometrial MAO activity increases rapidly. The premenstrual shift in Hostility does not occur for either oral contraceptive group. For the Sequential as well as the Combination group, the magnitude of Hostility remains relatively constant during the cycle. Second, the Sequential group maintains a consistently lower magnitude of Hostility than the Combination group, as predicted. The grand Hostility mean for the Sequential group is 1.137 as compared to 1.443 for the Combination group, a difference which is significant at the 0.01 level ($t = 2.593$). Therefore, the two predictions about negative affect patterns, expected to occur in response to MAO activity, are supported for Hostility.

DISCUSSION

The results of this study indicate that fluctuations in negative affect commonly experienced during the menstrual cycle do not occur among women using combination oral contraceptives. Self-selection factors, the effects of oral contraceptives on menstrual discomfort, and women's expectations about the effects of the drug on menstrual distress did not account for this finding.

Further analysis demonstrated, however, that the absence of anxiety (but not hostility) fluctuations among those in the Combination group can be attributed largely to the effects of the drug on menstrual flow. When women most likely to experience reduced flow were compared to those most likely to experience normally heavy flow, *only* those with reduced flow show no increase in menstrual phase anxiety. Women using oral contraceptives who most likely experience normally heavy flow show the same increase in menstrual anxiety observed in women with natural menstrual cycles.

One might argue that physiologic changes coinciding with menstrual bleeding explain the results, rather than flow intensity. First, the low dosage of progestin used by women most likely to have reduced flow may have caused the lower anxiety levels. Second, women with reduced flow may experience less physical discomfort while bleeding, and consequently express less anxiety.

With respect to the dosage argument, although reduced flow is associated with the use of low progestin brands, there is no reason whatsoever to believe that progestin activity should affect anxiety level at only one phase of the cycle. Progestin activity, after all, is continuously active throughout the tablet cycle. If the use of progestin has some yet unspecified direct influence on the magnitude of anxiety, then one should reasonably expect the effect to be observed throughout the cycle rather than just at menstruation. The differences in anxiety patterns by dosage level clearly indicate that this is not the case. Only at menstruation is there a significant difference in anxiety means by dosage group. At each of the remaining 3 cycle days, there are no differences in mean anxiety scores between the 2 dosage groups. When flow intensity was estimated on the basis of self-report data, women with reduced flow showed lower anxiety not only at menstruation but throughout the cycle. However, a large proportion of these women were using the higher dosage brands as well as the 1-mg brands. Dosage level alone, then, cannot account for this result.

The second argument that may be raised suggests that women with reduced flow may experience less physical discomfort during the menses, and consequently experience less anxiety. Analysis of the relationship between complaints of physical symptoms and flow intensity, however, show that symptom complaints were not significantly less frequent among women with reduced flow than among women with normal flow.

The empirical relationship between the intensity of menstrual flow and the magnitude of menstrual anxiety thus raises the possibility that emotional disturbances most often associated with menstruation are a socially mediated response to a woman's own bodily functions. The woman perceives the bleeding, must take sanitary precautions, and becomes anxious in social situations because of possible embarrassment. This is, of course, a hypothesis which is contrary to most medical opinion on the causes of menstrual distress. Nevertheless, the results of this study suggest that it may in fact be true, particularly for menstrual anxiety.

Further analysis provided a number of reasons to suggest that menstrual distress is related to the intensity of menstrual flow. First, sexual abstinence during menstruation was shown to be significantly related to flow intensity. Women experiencing normally heavy flow, whether or not they used oral contraceptives, were almost twice as likely to abstain than women experiencing a reduced flow. Further examination also showed that sexual abstinence could not be accounted for by the degree of physical discomfort at menstruation: Women who did *not* abstain were just as likely to report menstrual physical discomfort as did those who abstained. Reduced menstrual flow, then, is associated with lower anxiety *and* ignoring the menstrual sex taboo. As noted earlier, menstruating women are specifically forbidden to engage in sexual relations in nearly all societies. Stephens (33) and Young and Bacdayan (35) have shown that cultural variation in the severity of menstrual restriction is related to specific aspects of the social structure and socialization process, such as indices of male sexual anxiety and castration fears, social rigidity and male solidarity. In our own society, the menstrual sex taboo is still commonly observed, despite the fact that medical evidence shows that it is neither physically harmful nor unsanitary.

It should also be mentioned that the data showed an association between women's emotional reaction to menarche and adherence to the menstrual sex taboo. In this sample, 70% of the women with negative reactions to menarche adhere to the sex taboo as compared with only 40% of the women with positive reactions, and 54% of those with no emotional reaction. Since reactions to menarche were based on recall data, these findings cannot be taken as evidence of actual menarche experience. Instead, they may be another index of women's subjective feelings about how one should react to the menstrual process.

While the social explanation seems reasonable for menstrual anxiety, replication of the Grant and Pryse-Davies results regarding group differences in hostility (depression, anger and irritability) suggests that one aspect of the menstrual cycle mood fluctuations may be biochemically determined. As discussed earlier, Grant and Pryse-Davies found that the magnitude of depression, anger and irritability during the cycle was directly related to the magnitude of MAO activity in endometrial tissue. These researchers believe that endometrial MAO activity reflects similar changes in MAO in sensitive brain centers, and that such biochemical changes determine emotional behavior. At present, of course, one can only state that the activity of MAO as well as that of other biochemical agents (e.g., adrenocorticoids) is *correlated* with observed emotional changes. The direction of causality is still unclear. Indeed, there is abundant evidence to suggest that biochemical changes occur in *response* to socially mediated emotional changes as shown by the work on biochemical reactions to stress and other psychologic states (24, 67). Nevertheless, the kinds of affects measured by the Hostility scale are those which Grant and Pryse-Davies found to be associated with changes in endometrial MAO activity. In this study, premenstrual increase in Hostility produced by the Normal group was not observed for either the Combination or Sequential group. Also, the general level of Hostility was significantly lower for the Sequential than for the Combination group, as predicted.

SUMMARY

This study attempted to determine possible causes of menstruation-related affective fluctuations by comparing the patterns of negative affect in women with natural cycles and in those who use oral contraceptives. Negative affect was measured at four different phases of the menstrual cycle by an instrument that is not distorted by self-report or social expectations about menstruation. All hypotheses tested in the study made predictions about the relationship between the magnitude of negative affect (anxiety and hostility) among oral contraceptive users and menstrual cycle phase. Women with natural cycles were used as a control group, since cyclic mood patterns during the natural cycle have already been established.

The first hypothesis, which predicted that cyclic affective changes should be eliminated for combination oral contraceptive users, was supported. One hundred percent of the variability in Total Negative Affect scores accounted for by the cycle day was eliminated for the Combination group. Individual analysis of Hostility and Anxiety scores revealed that (a) the estimated strength of association between Hostility and the cycle day was 0, and (b) the estimated strength of association between Anxiety and the cycle day was 0.94 for the Combination group.

The question of spuriousness was considered by examining factors that may determine the results other than oral contraceptive use. It was shown that group differences in negative affect patterns could not be determined by self-selection, prior expectations or differences in physical discomfort.

Two additional hypotheses were tested in order to examine possible mechanisms by which oral contraceptives eliminate mood fluctuations. One hypothesis proposed that oral contraceptives reduced menstruation-related negative affect by reducing the intensity of menstrual flow. This hypothesis was supported for Anxiety, which suggests that menstrual anxiety is a socially mediated response to menstrual bleeding.

A third hypothesis proposed that oral contraceptive use eliminated mood fluctuations by eliminating cyclic shifts in endometrial MAO activity, as argued by previous researchers. Examination of group differences in Hostility patterns replicated the findings of Grant and Pryse-Davies about the relationship between endometrial MAO activity and negative affect in women.

REFERENCES

1. Abraham K: Manifestations of the female castration complex, Selected Papers on Psychoanalysis. Edited by K. Abraham, London, Hogarth, 1948, pp. 338-369.
2. Balint M: A contribution to the psychology of menstruation. Psychoanal Quart 6:346, 352, 1937.
3. Benedek T: Sexual function in women and their disturbance, American Handbook of Psychiatry. Vol. I. Edited by S. Arieti. New York, Basic Books, 1959.
4. Benedek, T, Rubenstein B: The sexual cycle in women: the relation between ovarian function and psychodynamic processes. Psychosom Med 1:246-270, 1939.
5. Chadwick M: The psychological effects of menstruation. Nervous and Mental Diseases Monograph Series 56:1952.
6. Deutsch H: Psychology of Women. Vol. I. New York, Grune & Stratton, 1944.
7. McCance,R.A., Luff M, Widdowson, E: Physical and emotional periodicity in women. J Hyg 37:571-611, 1957.
8. Rose RA: Menstrual pain and personal adjustment. J Personality, 17:287-307, 1949.
9. Shainess, N: A re-evaluation of some aspects of feminity through a study of menstruation: a preliminary report. Comp Psychiat 2:20-26, 1961.
10. Silbermann I: A contribution to the psychology of menstruation. Int J Psychoanal 6:346-352, 1937.
11. Coppen A, Kessel N: Menstruation and personality. Brit J Psychiat 109:711-721, 1963.
12. Dalton, K: The Premenstrual Syndrome. Springfield, Iil, Charles C Thomas, 1964.
13. Fluhmann, CF: Management of Menstrual Disorders. Philadelphia, WB Saunders, 1956.
14. Garron D, Shekelle R: Mood, personality, and the menstrual cycle. Unpublished data, 1969.
15. Gottschalk L, Kaplan S, Gleser G, et al: Variations in magnitude of emotion: a method applied to anxiety and hostility during phases of the menstrual cycle. Psychosom Med 24:300-311, 1962.
16. Ivey M, Bardwick, J: Patterns of affective fluctuations in the menstrual cycle. Psychosom Med 30:336-345, 1968.
17. Levitt E, Lubin B: Some personality factors associated with menstrual complaints and menstrual attitudes. J Psychosom Res 11:267-270, 1967.
13. Moos R: The development of a menstrual distress questionnaire. Psychosom Med 30: 853-867, 1968.

Karen E. Paige

19. Moos R, Kopell B, Melges F, et al: Fluctuations on symptoms and moods during the menstrual cycle. J Psychosom Med 13:37-44, 1969.
20. Paulson MJ: Psychological Concomitants of Premenstrual Tension. Unpublished dissertation, University of Kansas, 1956.
21. Sutherland H, Stewart I: A critical analysis of the premenstrual syndrome. Lancet 1: 1180-1183, 1965.
22. Coppen A: The biochemistry of affective disorders. Brit J Psychiat 113:1237-1264, 1967.
23. Janowsky D, Gorney R, Kelly B: 'The curse': vicissitudes and variation of the female fertility cycle; Part I: psychiatric aspects. Psychosomatics 7:242-246, 1966.
24. US Department of Health, Education, and Welfare, National Institute of Mental Health, Mental Health Reports-3. Public Health Service Publication No. 1876, Washington, DC, Government Printing Office, 1969.
25. Grant C, Pryse-Davies J: Effects of oral contraceptives on depressive mood changes and on endometrial monoamine oxidase and phosphates. Brit Med J 28:777-780, 1968.
26. Rees L: The premenstrual tension syndrome and its treatment. Brit Med J 1:1014-1016, 1953.
27. DeCara E: EEG studies of the bioelectrical activity of the brain during the menstrual cycle. Acta Neurol 13:617-637, 1958.
28. Eichner E, Watner C: Pre-menstrual tension. Med Times 83:771-778, 1955.
29. Ferguson J, Vermillion M: Premenstrual tension. Amer J Obstet Gynec 9:615-619, 1957.
30. Bettelheim B: Symbolic Wounds. Glencoe, Free Press, 1954.
31. Ford C, Beach F: Patterns of Sexual Behavior. New York, Harper & Row, Ace Books, 1951.
32. Hays H: The Dangerous Sex. New York, G.P. Putnam's Sons, 1964.
33. Stephens W: A cross-cultural study of menstrual taboos. Genetic Psychology Monographs 64:385-416, 1961.
34. Webster H: Taboo—A Sociological Study. Stanford, Stanford University Press, 1942.
35. Young F, Bacdayan A: Menstrual taboos and social rigidity. Ethnography 4:225-240, 1965.
36. Paige K: Unpublished data.
37. Tietze C: Forward. Int J Fertil Steril 12: 65, 1967.
38. Scott J: Personal communication.
39. Balin H, Wan L: Chlormadinone, a potent synthetic oral progestin: evaluation of 1002 cycles. Int J Fertil 10:127-131, 1965.
40. Drill VA: Oral Contraceptives. New York, McGraw-Hill,

1966.

41. Goldzicher J, Rice-Wray E: Oral Contraceptives. Springfield, Ill, Charles C Thomas, 1966.

42. Mears E: Clinical experience in the use of oral contraceptives. Proc Roy Soc Med 57: 204-207, 1964.

43. Palma E, Onetto E: Our experience with a combination of estrogen-progestin in birth control. Dec Congr Chileno Obstet Gynocol 2:615-617, 1963.

44. Pincus G, et al: Effectiveness of an oral contraceptive. Science 130:81-85, 1959.

45. Andrews WC, Andrews MC: Reduction of side-effects from ovulation suppression by the use of new progestin combinations. Fertil Steril 15:75, 1964.

46. Bakker CB, Dightman C: Side-effects of oral contraceptives. Obstet Gynec 28:373-379, 1966.

47. Chernick B: Side effects of cyclic therapy with norethindrone and mestranol. Fertil Steril 16:445-454, 1965.

48. Daly R, Kane F, Ewing J: Psychosis associated with the use of a sequential oral contraceptive. Lancet 2:2444-2445, 1967.

49. Dickenson J, Smith G: A new and practical oral contraceptive agent: norethindrone with mestranol. Canad Med Ass J 89:242-245, 1963.

50. Advisory Committee on Obstetrics and Gynecology, Food and Drug Administration: Report on the Oral Contraceptives. Washington, DC, US Govt. Printing Office, August 1969.

51. Garcia C. Wallach E: Biochemical changes and implications following long-term use of oral contraceptives. Fertility and Family Planning. Edited by SJ Behrman, et al. Ann Arbor, University of Michigan Press, 1969.

52. Glick ID: Mood and behavioral changes associated with the use of oral contraceptives: a review of the literature. Psychopharmacologia 10:363-374, 1967.

53. Kane FJ: Mood and behavioral changes with progestational agents. Brit J Psychiat 113:265-268, 1967.

54. Kane FJ, Ewing J, Keeler H, et al: Mood and behavioral changes with the use of progestational steroids. Presented at the Annual Meeting of the American Psychiatric Association, New York City, May 3-7, 1965.

55. Kane FJ, Keeler MH: use of Enovid in postpartum mental disorders. Southern Med J 58:1089-1092, 1965.

56. Kroger WS, Peacock JF: Psychophysiological effects with an ovulation inhibitor. Psychosomatics 9:67-70, 1968.

57. Lewis A, Hoghughi M: An evaluation of depression as a side effect of oral contraceptives. Brit J Psychiat 115:697-701, 1969.

58. Moos R: Psychological aspects of oral contraceptives. Arch Gen Psychiat 19:87-94. 1968.
59. Murawski B, Sapir P, Shulman N, et al: An investigation of mood states in women taking oral contraceptives. Fertil Steril 19: 50-63, 1966.
60. Simpson G: Enovid in treatment of psychic disturbances associated with menstruation. J Dis Nerv System 23:589-590, 1962.
61. Swanson D, Barron A, Floren A, et al: The use of norethynodrel in psychotic females. Amer J Psychiat 120:1101-1103, 1964.
62. Zell J, Crisp W: A psychiatric evaluation of the use of oral contraceptives. Obstet Gynec 23:657-661, 1966.
63. Potter R, Burch T, Matsumoto S: Long cycles, late ovulation, and calendar rhythm. Int J Fertil 12:127-140, 1967.
64. Gottschalk L, Winget C. Gleser G: Manual of Instructions for Using the Gottschalk-Gleser Content Analysis Scales. Berkeley, University of California Press, 1969.
65. Winer BJ: Statistical Principles in Experimental Design. New York, McGraw-Hill, 1962, p 311.
66. Hays W: Statistics for Psychologists. New York, Holt, Rinehart, Winston, 1963.
67. Mason J: Organization of Psychoendocrine Mechanisms. Psychosomatic Medicine. Vol. 30. No. 5, Part II, 1968.

36

Recently a colleague requested some information on the effect of childbirth on the mother. To our surprise, there have been very few nonclinical studies on the effect of pregnancy or the early postpartum period on behavior. This study by Treadway and his associates is one of the better studies in the area. It is somewhat unusual in that both biochemical and psychological measures were taken from the same individuals. It is also unusual in that the individuals studied were chosen prior to childbirth and therefore did not represent extreme examples of postpartum reactions. Nevertheless, the small sample size in the study [twenty-one pregnant women] is typical of the area.

Despite the fact that none of the women showed severe postpartum reactions, the authors found some cognitive impairment, increased social introversion, and increased neuroticism. They also found a significant decrease in norepinephrine during pregnancy and following delivery. There was a significant correlation between norepinephrine depletion and depressive ratings in pregnant women, but not in their hospitalized non-pregnant controls. They suggest that norepinephrine depletion during pregnancy and the puerperium may be interpreted as an increased biologic susceptibility to affective disorders during these periods. Environmental stresses associated with maternal responsibility will tend to exaggerate the effect upon an organism already lacking an ability to rebound due to physiological factors.

Unfortunately, the study tends to stress biochemical and medical jargon to such a degree that intelligibility is affected. However, little work has been done by psychologists on the psychological changes related to pregnancy and childbirth. The fact that the present study represents one of the better controlled ones indicates the great need for more investigations in this important area.

This study suggests, as does the preceding one by Paige, that the relationship between hormonal level and emotional behavior in the menstrual cycle and pregnancy is the result of a combination of physiological and psychological factors.

These studies raise a number of questions that might be answered experimentally. What is the relationship between norepinephrine depletion and affect in mammals? What are the statistics on depressive disorders during the puerperium in various cultures? What is the relationship between norepinephrine level and depression within each individual studied? And, lastly, why are so few nonclinical studies available in these interesting areas?

A Psychoendocrine Study of Pregnancy and Puerperium*

C. Richard Treadway, Francis J. Kane, Jr., Ali Jarrahi-Zadeh, and Morris A. Lipton

To investigate the relationship between hormonal changes associated with pregnancy and the increased incidence of psychiatric disturbances during the postpartum period, the authors conducted a controlled psychological and biochemical assessment of 21 women during pregnancy and the puerperium. On the basis of the findings reported here, they speculate that the increased incidence of clinically significant disorders among women in the postpartum period may be due to the increased environmental stresses of maternal responsibilities in association with lack of rebound from the biochemical changes of pregnancy.

Depressive and other psychoses have long been known to occur in a small number of women in the puerperium (20). Previously, clinicians viewed these psychoses as no different from psychoses occurring at other times of life (4, 45), but recent studies have shown that there is a disproportionate increase in the incidence of psychoses in the first month after parturition (32, 37, 47). Other studies (23, 24, 25) have demonstrated that 20 to 40 percent of postpartum women experience some degree of dysphoria and/or cognitive dysfunction, although primarily of non-psychotic proportions.

---

* From *American Journal of Psychiatry*, 1969, 125 (10, 1380-86.

It has not been determined whether these psychotic and nonpsychotic disorders are the sequelae of the psychological stress of childbearing and maternal responsibilities, of biochemical changes in the puerperium, or of some combination of these factors. Current biochemical findings in other types of affective disorders at least suggest that similar biochemical changes might be a factor in postpartum depressive disturbances.

The successful use of therapeutic agents which alter catecholamine metabolism and the associated findings of catecholamine changes in depression (5, 11, 26, 39) have led to the development of a hypothesis of affective disorders which, as stated by Schildkraut (42), proposes that "some, if not all, depressions may be associated with a relative deficiency of norepinephrine at receptor sites in the brain while elations may be associated with an excess of this amine." Comprehensive reviews of the evidence for this hypothesis have been published by Schildkraut (42), Bunney (5), Kety (26), and Prange (36). Steroid changes associated with depression and mania have also been reported by a number of authors (6, 11, 16, 17, 27), who found that 17-hydroxycorticosteroids (17-OHCS) generally tend to be decreased in mania and elevated in many patients with depression. Bunney and associates (7) have found that 17-OHCS elevations in depressed patients tend to be correlated with degrees of "psychic distress."

Other evidence to suggest that hormonal changes in the puerperium might be related to postpartum psychiatric disturbance is found in catecholamine studies of female animals and humans. In animals a linkage between gonadal hormones and catecholamines has been demonstrated. Studies of uterine binding of epinephrine (E) in animals have shown that there is a marked decline in uterine E in postpartum rats (49) and that the capacity of the uterus to bind circulating E is endocrine-sensitive, rising fourfold between diestrous and estrous (8, 12, 51).

Also, uterine binding of E in animals is known to be high with increased estrogen levels and lowered by progesterone, reserpine, or guanethidine (8, 40, 50). Pregnant rabbits show norepinephrine (NE) concentrations at placental sites reduced to three percent of nonpregnant values (8). Plasma studies have shown that the concentration of NE in plasma from estrous and pregnant animals is significantly lower than from diestrous animals (19). Meyerson, in a series of animal experiments, has demonstrated alterations in sexual behavior secondary to alterations in biogenic amines by reserpine, tetrabenazine, and MAO inhibitors (30). Anton-Tay and Wurtman have produced evidence indicating increased turnover of NE in brain in response to gonadectomy (1).

593

Although plasma E and NE in humans have been found normal during the third trimester of pregnancy, labor, and the post-partum period (22, 44), studies of urinary excretion of catecholamines have demonstrated a significant rise in NE on the day following delivery (52). Simionescu and associates (43) measured E and NE in the urine of pregnant and postpartum women. Normal E and NE values were found in the ninth month, although total urinary catecholamines increased in the immediate ante-partum period. This increase was more marked for NE than for E. During labor, the total catecholamines increased, and E increased more than NE. In the immediate postpartum period NE was maintained at a high level whereas E diminished. Later in the puerperium the total catecholamines diminished even below the control levels.

Plasma 17-OHCS have been reported to rise slowly during human pregnancy, to increase sharply but briefly after delivery, and then to fall rapidly during the early puerperium (2, 3, 9, 14, 15). No significant change in urinary excretion of 17-OHCS has been observed (9). Corticosteroids and catecholamines have not previously been obtained simultaneously during pregnancy and puerperium.

In summary, quantitative changes in catecholamine and steroid levels have been demonstrated in association with depression; changes in catecholamines have been shown to occur as a result of changes in gonadal hormones in animals; and changes in urinary catecholamines in the puerperium have been demonstrated in humans. These findings suggested to the authors of this project the importance of a combined psychological and biochemical assessment of women during pregnancy and the postpartum period.

METHOD

Twenty-one pregnant subjects and nine nonpregnant control subjects matched for age were admitted to a clinical research unit for two three-day periods of study separated by six-week intervals. All subjects had a minimum of a high school education. No subjects with significant medical or psychiatric illnesses were used. Pregnant subjects were limited to first or second pregnancies.

The pregnant women were studied approximately six weeks prior to delivery and were transferred to the clinical research unit on the first or second day after delivery. Meals while on the unit were limited to a VMA-free diet, and physical activity was limited to walking on the ward. No drugs were used.

After an initial day of adjustment to the ward on each admission to the unit, two 24-hour urine collections were made. All urines were collected in bottles which contained 15 ml. of 6N hydrochloric acid and which were refrigerated from the start of collection. Biochemical determinations on all urines of each subject (after both admissions) were performed in a single day and in duplicate in order to avoid variations in assay. Urines were measured for volume and creatinine and were analyzed for epinephrine (E), norepinephrine (NE), metanephrine (MN), normetanephrine (NMN), 3-methoxy-4-hydroxymandelic acid (VMA), and 17-hydroxycorticosteroids (17-OHCS). E and NE were determined by a modification of the Crout method (10), MN and NMN by the technique of Taniguchi (46), VMA by the Pisano method (33), and 17-OHCS by the Porter-Silber reaction (34). All biochemical values were expressed in amounts per gram of creatinine per 24 hours. All biochemical determinations were performed without knowledge of psychological state.

Psychological assessments were made on the second and third days of each admission. Measures used included the Minnesota Multiphasic Personality Inventory (MMPI) (21): the Nowlis Mood Adjective Check List (MACL) (31), the Neuroticism Scale Questionnaire (NSQ) of Cattell (41), and the Porteus Maze (35) and Trail Making (38) tests. MMPI subscores were obtained for hypochondriasis (Hs), depression (D), hysteria (Hy), psychopathic deviance (Pd), masculine-feminine orientation (Mf), paranoia (Pa), psychasthenia (Pt), schizophrenia (Sc), hypomania (Ma), social introversion (Si), repression (R), and anxiety (A).

MACL tests were evaluated for total scores and for aggression, concentration, deactivation, social affection, anxiety, depression, egotism, pleasantness, activation, nonchalance, skepticism, startle, cognitive, and labile subscores. NSQ tests were evaluated for total scores and for sensitive, depressive, submissive, and anxious subscores. The time in seconds required to complete the Porteus Maze and Trail Making tests was recorded as the score for each subject.

RESULTS

Complete psychological and biochemical data were collected on all of the pregnant and nonpregnant subjects. The data from two pregnant women who had cesarean sections were not used. Statistical analysis of the data was done by t-test comparisons of the data from the pregnant women with those obtained on the first admission of the nonpregnant control subjects and comparisons of the data from the postpartum women with those obtained on the second admission of the nonpregnant control subjects.

Clinical evaluation of the pregnant and postpartum women demonstrated no serious depressions, although there were brief episodes of tearfulness and increased lability of mood in many of the postpartum women. There was also dramatic clinical evidence of cognitive impairment in several women in the postpartum group. One college graduate was completely unable to perform serial 7 subtractions and sent out her birth announcements listing her infant's weight as 13 pounds 6 ounces instead of the correct weight of 6 pounds 13 ounces. Another patient forgot an entire day and could not remember the visit of her parents on the previous day.

On the MMPI, pregnant subjects had significantly higher scores on hypochondriasis, an indication of their increased concern with health and bodily functions. They also had significantly decreased scores on feminine orientation. Both pregnant and post-partum women had significantly increased social introversion scores, an indication of decreased interest in social contacts and activities and increased interest in self.

On the MACL, pregnant women scored significantly lower in startle responses than did their controls. This means that they gave themselves lower ratings for being startled or shocked than did their controls. Postpartum women showed increased scores of deactivation, social affection, and pleasantness. This means that they described themselves as a group as being in a pleasantly sluggish drowsy state.

On the NSQ, depressive ratings were significantly increased in both pregnant and postpartum women. This means that they more frequently checked items found empirically to discriminate between neurotically depressed and nonneurotic persons (41). Postpartum women, in comparison with their controls, also had increased total neuroticism scores.

No changes in Porteus Maze times were observed in pregnant or postpartum women, but postpartum women did show significant increased in time required to complete the Trail Making Test.

Analysis of the biochemical data indicated that postpartum women showed increases in 17-OHCS and E that were not quite statistically significant. NE was significantly lower in both pregnant and postpartum women. NMN was increased in both pregnant and postpartum women, but only the increased values in pregnancy attained statistical significance. No significant changes in MN or VMA were observed.

A statistically significant correlation (.76) was found between reduced NE levels and increased NSQ depressive scores in pregnant but not in postpartum or control subjects. No other significant correlations were found between psychological and biochemical variables. A summary of psychological and biochemical findings is presented in figure 1.

FIGURE 1
Summary of Statistically Significant Psychological and Biochemical Findings

PREGNANT SUBJECTS   POSTPARTUM SUBJECTS

MMPI   ↑ Concern with health and bodily functions   ———

      ↓ Feelings of femininity

      ↓ Interest in social contacts and activities   ↓ Interest in social contacts and activities

MACL   ———   ↑ Feelings of deactivation

      ———   ↑ Feelings of social affection

      ———   ↑ Feelings of pleasantness

      ↓ Startle responses   ———

NSQ   ———   ↑ Total neuroticism

      ↑ Depression   ↑ Depression

Trail making   ———   ↑ Time

Urine   ↓ NE   ↓ NE

      ↑ NMN   ———

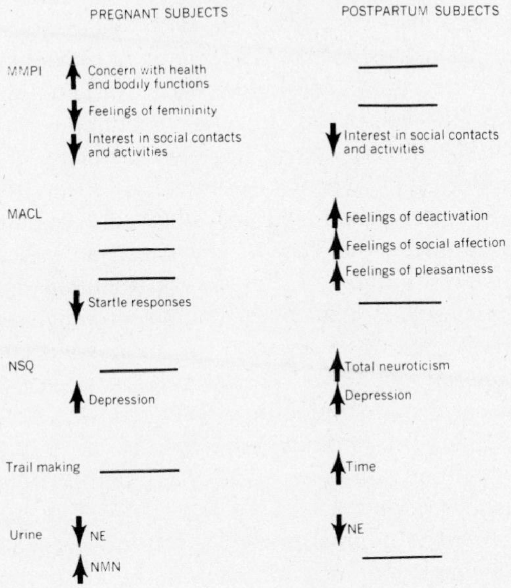

DISCUSSION

To our knowledge this study represents the first attempt to study simultaneously psychological and biochemical factors in pregnant and postpartum women in an effort to obtain correlations between these two parameters of functioning. Although one-to-one concordance between psychological functioning and the excretion of urinary metabolites can hardly be expected, this design is in the time-honored tradition of psychosomatic research in which such correlations are initially sought.

In designing the study, consideration was given to the findings of Mason (28) and Tolson (48) that the stress of hospitalization itself causes elevations in the urinary excretion of corticosteroids and catecholamines. Hospitalized pregnant and post-partum women were therefore compared with hospitalized control subjects, and all subjects were given an initial night of adjustment to the ward on each admission before beginning the collection of urines and psychological data. Also, all psychological tests were given in the same sequence in order to avoid differences in scores which might occur with the reduction of the stress of hospitalization over time.

The psychological findings can be divided into three categories, depending upon whether they occur in the antepartum, postpartum, or in both periods. Pregnant women compared to their controls show an increased concern with health and bodily functions (MMPI Hs scale), decreased feelings of femininity (MMPI Mf scale), and a decreased tendency to be startled (MACL). Postpartum women compared to their controls had increased neuroticism (NSQ), described themselves as being in a pleasantly sluggish drowsy state (MACL deactivation, social affection, and pleasantness scales), and showed significant increases in time required to complete the Trail Making Test, an indication of impaired cognitive function. As previously mentioned, there were also several dramatic clinical evidences of impaired cognitive function. These findings lend support to those authors who have described altered cognitive function in the postpartum period, especially in association with puerperal psychoses (20, 23, 24).

The psychological findings common to both pregnant and postpartum women compared to their controls were a decreased interest in social contacts and activities (MMPI Si scale) and increased feelings of depression (NSQ depressive scale).

The biochemical findings can be attributed primarily to two causes, the gonadal hormone changes associated with pregnancy and the termination of pregnancy. The increased levels of E and 17-OHCS in the postpartum period (not statistically significant) are probably due to the stress of delivery or to other factors associated with the termination of pregnancy such as unbinding from plasma proteins.

The decreased NE and increased NMN in pregnancy and puerperium (increased NMN was not statistically significant in puerperium) are probably attributable to gonadal hormone changes associated with pregnancy. The decreased NE in the puerperium is especially impressive in view of the increase in E in this period. One possible explanation of the decreased NE and increased NMN is an increased utilization of available NE due to a reduction in receptor sensitivity by gonadal hormone changes.

Of particular interest is the significant correlation between reduced NE levels and increased NSQ depressive ratings of pregnant women compared to their controls. It is tempting to postulate from the data that a reduction in NE linked to gonadal hormone changes of pregnancy might be responsible for the increased depression. Such a hypothesis would correlate well with the current catecholamine hypothesis of affective disturbance but would have to include two assumptions.

The first is that the decreased urinary excretion of NE results from both brain and peripheral NE decreases. This assumption can now be made only tentatively since the urinary excretion of NE and its metabolites cannot be separated into central and peripheral components. The second assumption is that the depression observed in pregnant and postpartum women on psychological testing is similar except in degree to clinically observed depressions in these periods.

If one accepts these tentative assumptions, the reduced NE in the pregnant and postpartum periods may be interpreted as an increased biologic susceptibility to affective disorders in these periods. The fact that the increased incidence of clinically significant disorders occurs primarily in the postpartum period may be attributable to the increased environmental stresses associated with maternal responsibilities in this period and to lack of rebound from the biochemical changes of pregnancy. The fact that not all women with reduced NE in pregnancy and puerperium become seriously depressed does not seem crucial, since studies with reserpine and alpha-methyldopa indicate that not all persons with reduced brain NE secondary to these drugs become depressed (42).

The question of which gonadal hormone change is responsible for the decreased NE cannot presently be answered with any certainty. However, progesterone would seem to be a likely hormone for consideration. It has been previously shown to have central nervous system depressant effects (18, 29) and has also been shown to alter adrenergic function in animals (13). One may indeed speculate that the depression seen during pregnancy in this study is due to the effect of a depressant hormonal substance, progesterone, and that the continued depression in the postpartum period when progesterone levels are greatly reduced is due to a lingering depletion of brain NE caused by the sustained elevation of progesterone during pregnancy.

SUMMARY

A combined psychological and biochemical study of pregnancy and puerperium has been described. Pregnant subjects showed an increased concern with health and bodily functions, decreased feelings of femininity, and a decreased tendency to be startled. Postpartum women showed increased neuroticism, described themselves as being in a pleasantly sluggish drowsy state, and showed evidence of impaired cognitive function. Both pregnant and postpartum women had a decreased interest in social contacts and activities and increased feelings of depression.

Increased levels of E and 17-OHCS in the postpartum period (not statistically significant) were probably due to the stress of delivery or to other factors associated with the termination of pregnancy (such as unbinding from plasma proteins). Decreased urinary NE and increased NMN in pregnancy and puerperium (increased NMN not statistically significant in puerperium) were thought to reflect an increased utilization of available NE due to a reduction in receptor sensitivity by gonadal hormone changes associated with pregnancy.

A significant correlation was observed between the decreased urinary NE and increased depression. A tentative hypothesis is presented that a reduction in NE linked to gonadal hormone changes produces an increased biologic susceptibility to affective disorders in pregnancy and puerperium.

REFERENCES

1. Anton-Tay, F., and Wurtman, R.J.: Norepinephrine Turnover in Rat Brains After Gonadectomy, Science 159:1245, 1968.
2. Appleby, J.I., and Norymberski, J.K.: The Urinary Excretion of 17-Hydroxycorticosteroids in Human Pregnancy, J. Endocrinol. 15:310-319, 1957.
3. Birke, G., Gemzell, C.A., Plantin, L.O., and Robbe, H.: Plasma Levels of 17-Hydroxycorticosteroids and Urinary Excretion Pattern of Ketosteroids in Normal Pregnancy, Acta Endocrinol. 27:389-402, 1958.
4. Boyd, D.A.: Mental Disorders Associated with Childbearing, Amer. J. Obstet. Gynecol. 43:148-163 and 43:335-349, 1942.
5. Bunney, W.E., and Davis, J.M.: Norepinephrine in Depressive Reactions, Arch. Gen. Psychiat. 13:483-494, 1965.
6. Bunney, W.E., and Fawcett, J.A.: Possibility of a Biochemical Test for Suicidal Potential, Arch. Gen. Psychiat. 13:232-239, 1965.
7. Bunney, W.E., Mason, J.W., and Hamburg, D.A.: Correlation Between Behavioral Variables and Urinary 17-Hydroxycorticosteroids in Depressed Patients, Psychosom. Med. 27: 299-308, 1965.
8. Cha, K.S., Woo-Choo, L., Rudzik, A., and Miller, J.W.: A Comparison of the Catecholamine Concentrations of Uteri from Several Species and the Alterations Which Occur During Pregnancy, J. Pharmacol. Exp. Ther. 148:9-13, 1965.
9. Cohen, M., Stiefel, M., Reddy, W.J., and Laidlaw, J.C.: The Secretion and Disposition of Cortisol During Pregnancy, J. Clin. Endocrinol. 18:1076-1092, 1958.
10. Crout, R.J.: "Catecholamines in Urine," in Seligson, D., ed.: Standard Methods in Clinical Chemistry, vol. 3. New York: Academic Press, 1961, p. 62.
11. Curtis, G.C., Cleghorn, R.A., and Sourkes, T.L.: The Relationship Between Affect and the Excretion of Adrenaline, Noradrenaline and 17-Hydroxycorticosteroids, J. Psychosom. Res. 4:176-184, 1960.
12. Fischer, J.E., Kopin, I.J., and Wurtman, R.J.: Effects of Lumbar Sympathectomy on the Uterine Uptake of Catecholamines, Nature 203:938-939, 1964.
13. Fullerton, A., and Morrison, J.F.B.: A Comparison of Certain Responses of the Vascular System of Rats After the Administration of Progesterone and Oestrogen, J. Endrocrinol. 33:75-81, 1965.

14. Gemzell, C.A.: Blood Levels of 17-Hydroxycorticosteroids in Normal Pregnancy, J. Clin. Endocrinol. 13:898-902, 1953.
15. Gemzell, C.A.: Variations in Plasma Levels of 17-Hydroxycorticosteroids in Mother and Infant Following Parturition, Acta Endocrinol. 17:100-105, 1954.
16. Gibbons, J.L.: Cortisol Secretion Rate in Depressive Illness, Arch. Gen. Psychiat. 10:572-575, 1964.
17. Gibbons, J.L., and McHugh, P.R.: Plasma Cortisol in Depressive Illness, J. Psychiat. Res. 1:162-171, 1962.
18. Gibbs, F.A., and Reid, D.E.: The Electroencephalogram in Pregnancy, Amer. J. Obstet. Gynecol. 44:672-675, 1942.
19. Green, R.D., and Miller, J.W.: Catecholamine Concentrations: Changes in Plasma of Rats During Estrous Cycle and Pregnancy, Science 151:825-826, 1966.
20. Hamilton, J.A.: Postpartum Psychiatric Problems. St. Louis: C.V. Mosby Co., 1962, p. 18.
21. Hathaway, S.R., and McKinley, J.C.: Booklet for the Minnesota Multiphasic Personality Inventory. New York: Psychological Corporation, 1943.
22. Israel, S.L., Stroup, P.E., Seligson, H.T., and Seligson, D.: Epinephrine and Norepinephrine in Pregnancy and Labor, Obstet. Gynecol. 14:68-71, 1959.
23. Jarrahi-Zadeh, A., Kane, F.J., Van de Castle, R., and Ewing, J.A.: Emotional and Cognitive Disturbances Associated with the Childbearing Period, read at the 123rd annual meeting of the American Psychiatric Association, Detroit, Mich., May 8-12, 1967.
24. Kane, F.J., Jarman, W.H., Keeler, M.H., and Ewing, J.A.: A Clinical Psychiatric Survey of Postpartum Patients, read at the Fourth World Congress of Psychiatry, Madrid, Spain, September 1966.
25. Kear-Colwell, J.J.: Neuroticism in the Early Puerperium, Brit. J. Psychiat. 111:1189-1192, 1965.
26. Kety, S.: Catecholamines in Neuropsychiatric States, Pharmacol. Rev. 18:787-798, 1966.
27. Kurland, H.D.: Steroid Excretion in Depressive Disorders, Arch. Gen. Psychiat. 10: 554-571, 1964.
28. Mason, J.W., Sachar, E.J., Fishman, J.R., Hamburg, D.A., and Handlon, J.H.: Corticoid Responses to Hospital Admission, Arch. Gen. Psychiat. 13:1-8, 1965.
29. Merryman, W.: Progesterone "Anesthesia" in Human Subjects, J. Clin. Endocrinol. Metab. 14:1567-1569, 1954.
30. Meyerson, B.J.: Estrus Behavior in Spayed Rats After Estrogen or Progesterone Treatment in Combination with Reserpine or Tetrabenazine, Psychopharmacologia 6:210-218, 1964.

31. Nowlis, V.: "Research with the Mood Adjective Check List," in Tomkins, S.S., and Izand, C.E., eds.: Affect, Cognition and Personality. New York: Springer, 1965, pp. 353-389.
32. Paffenbarger, R.S.: The Picture Puzzle of the Postpartum Psychosis, J. Chron. Dis. 13:161-173, 1961.
33. Pisano, J.J., Crout, R.J., and Abraham, D.: Determination of 3-Methoxy-4-Hydroxymandelic Acid in Urine, Clin. Chim. Acta 7:285-291, 1962.
34. Porter, C.C., and Silber, R.H.: A Quantitative Color Reaction for Cortisone and Related 17, 21-Dihydroxy-20-Ketosteroids, J. Biol. Chem. 85:201-207, 1950.
35. Porteus, S.D.: The Porteus Maze Test and Intelligence. New York: Psychological Corporation, 1950.
36. Prange, A.J., Jr.: The Pharmacology and Biochemistry of Depression, Dis. Nerv. Syst. 25:217-221, 1964.
37. Pugh, T.F., Jerath, B.K., Schmidt, W.M., and Reed, R.B.: Rates of Mental Diseases Related to Childbearing, New Eng. J. Med. 268:1224-1228, 1963.
38. Reitan, R.: The Relation of the Trail Making Test to Organic Brain Damage, Consult. Psychol. 19:393-394, 1955.
39. Rosenblatt, S., and Chanley, J.D.: Differences in the Metabolism of Norepinephrine in Depressions, Arch. Gen. Psychiat. 13:495-502, 1965.
40. Rudzik, A.D., and Miller, J.W.: The Effect of Altering the Catecholamine Content of the Uterus on the Rate of Contractions and the Sensitivity of the Myometrium to Relaxin, J. Pharmacol. Exp. Ther. 138:88-95, 1962.
41. Scheier, I.H., and Cattell, R.B.: Handbook for the Neuroticism Scale Questionnaire. Champaign, Ill.: Institute for Personality and Ability Testing, 1961.
42. Schildkraut, J.J.: The Catecholamine Hypothesis of Affective Disorders: A Review of Supporting Evidence, Amer. J. Psychiat. 122: 509-522, 1965.
43. Simionescu, S., and Carapancea, M.: Study of the Reactivity of the Neuroadrenergic System in Pregnant Women, During Labor, in the Postpartum Period and in the Puerperium, Stud. Cercet. Fiziol. 9:375-383, 1964.
44. Stone, S.L., and Piliero, S.J.: Epinephrine and Norepinephrine in Pregnancy, Obstet. Gynecol. 16:674-678, 1960.
45. Streker, E.A., and Ebaugh, F.C.: Psychosis Occuring During the Puerperium, Arch. Neurol. Psychiat. 15:239-252, 1926.
46. Taniguchi, K., Kakimoto, Y., and Armstrong, M.D.: Quantitative Determination of Metanephrine and Normetanephrine in Urine, J. Lab. Clin. Med. 64:469-484, 1964.

WOMAN: DEPENDENT OR INDEPENDENT VARIABLE?

47. Tetlow, C.: Psychosis of Childbearing, J. Ment. Sci. 101:629-639, 1955.
48. Tolson, W.W., Mason, J.W., Sachar, E.J., Hamburg, D.A., Handlon, J.H., and Fishman, J.R.: Urinary Catecholamine Responses Associated with Hospital Admission in Normal Human Subjects, J. Psychosom. Res. 8:365-372, 1965.
49. Wurtman, R.J., Axelrod, J., and Kopin, I.J.: Uterine Epinephrine and Blood Flow in Pregnant and Post-parturient Rats, Endocrinology 73:501-503, 1963.
50. Wurtman, R.J., Axelrod, J., and Potter, L.T.: The Disposition of Catecholamines in the Rat Uterus and the Effect of Drugs and Hormones, J. Pharmacol. Exp. Ther. 144: 150-155, 1964.
51. Wurtman, R.J., Chu, E.W., and Axelrod, J.: Relation Between the Oestrous Cycle and the Binding of Catecholamines in the Rat Uterus, Nature 198:547-548, 1963.
52. Zuspan, F.P., Nelson, G.H., and Ahlquist, R.P.: Alterations of Urinary Epinephrine and Norepinephrine: The Antepartum, Intrapartum and Postpartum Periods, Amer. J. Obstet. Gynecol. 99:709-721, 1967.

37

Melges' study is included because it represents an extreme environmental approach to postpartum syndromes. He investigated one hundred postpartum patients with a syndrome comprised of shame, helplessness, and confusion. He found no differences from controls in simple cognitive function or in EEGs. He suggests that conflict over assuming the mothering role is the central precipitating stress. Most of the women showing the syndrome had absent or inadequate mother figures. Melges' psychoanalytically oriented position stresses that these mothers have lost their ability to distinguish between themselves and their children. As evidence of the environmental causality of the syndrome, he cites the cases of three women who manifested an identical syndrome following adoption of an infant.

Feminist leanings would tend to make one seek for environmental etiologies, but it must be recognized that Melges' study contains a number of serious flaws. First, all of his subjects were selected because they showed severe postpartum reactions. We have no information on the frequency of deficient maternal models in women who do not show severe reactions. Second, in citing similar syndromes in adoptive mothers, Melges is confusing effect with cause. Both a rare recessive gene and thalidomide produce phocomelia [limb reduction], but lack of limbs in any few newborns would not tell one the agent responsible. Third, many of the mothers in this study showed the syndrome before leaving the hospital when maternal cares are presumably at their lowest ebb. One would also like to know the effect of psychiatric treatment upon behavior with such a high recurrence rate [44 percent]. Nevertheless, Melges' data on the sibling position of the patients [mostly from the youngest two thirds of the family] indicate that environment probably does play a role in this syndrome.

Postpartum Psychiatric Syndromes*

Frederick T. Melges

Study of 100 postpartum patients pointed to a syndrome comprised of feelings of shame, helplessness, and confusion. Lack of difference between these patients and control subjects in performance on serial-7 subtractions and digit span as well as in frequency analysis of the EEG militates against the existence of a toxic delirious state. Conflict over assuming the mothering role was a central precipitating stress. For the most part, this conflict stemmed from the rejection of the patient's own mother as an adequate model and distorted communications about care of the infant. Problems in maternal identification may be accentuated in the puerperium by the neonate's incapacity to specify guidelines for his care. Since the ambiguities of infant care are greater in the early puerperium, this factor may, in part, account for the high recurrence rate of postpartum distress in these women as well as the onset of illness largely within the first 10 days postpartum.

When an infant is born into a family, it is usually a time of rejoicing and happiness. Why is it, then, that some women become bewildered and even psychotic at this time? Why is it, as Pugh *et al.*[1] have shown, that there is a four- to fivefold increase in risk of mental illness (especially psychosis) for women during the first 3 months after delivery?

Our of a host of possible variables, our research focused on two key questions which might explain the increased vulnerability: (1) Do postpartum psychiatric syndromes represent a delirium? In the many studies reviewed by Hamilton,[2] a delirium frequently has been assumed on the basis of mental confusion, without supporting evidence from electroencephalographic and cognitive changes. (2) Is there a conflict over mothering in these women and, if so, what are its determinants? Rejection of the infant has been noted in some studies,[3-5] but it has been most often considered as a consequence of other stresses and not as a central facet of puerperal illness. The term "mothering" is here restricted

---

* From *Psychosomatic Medicine*, 1968, 30 (1), 95-108.

to refer to those activities and attitudes necessary for the care of an infant of 3 months or younger.

METHODS

One-hundred patients were included in the sample, being selected according to two criteria: (1) the onset of psychiatric illness took place within 1 month prepartum to 3 months postpartum and (2) the psychiatrist in charge of the patient deemed childbearing to be a significant factor in the onset or exacerbation of mental illness.

The median age was 28.0 years (range: 17-46). Ninety-one patients received inpatient care; 9 had out-patient care. Sixty-two patients were division status (unable to afford private psychiatric care); 38 were private patients. The modal education was that of a high school graduate) 21% were college graduates. The sex of the infant from the delivery under consideration was as follows: male 46; female 53. (One was a macerated stillborn whose sex could not be determined.) The median gravidity was 3.0, with a range of 1-11. The median parity was 3.0, with a range of 1-9. Two patients had twins. Three patients were included in the study because of the onset of psychiatric illness in relation to the adoption of an infant. As there were 3 unwed mothers in the sample, 3 babies were given up for adoption.

Since the study was essentially exploratory, the data are based primarily on psychiatric workups, including some EEG, PBI, and psychological tests. For the span of 3 years, the writer interviewed 74 patients; of these, he was the responsible psychiatrist for 13 and was involved in the diagnostic workup and management of 27 other patients. Information on 26 patients who had been admitted prior to 1962 was gleaned solely from the hospital chart. These case histories, along with a review of the literature, [2-8] served as a guideline for the construction of a data sheet centering on items related to delirium and precipitating stress. Problems of mothering were paramount, as has also been observed by Romano. The data sheet was then used for the analysis of the charts and conduct of the interviews, which began in an open-ended fashion and progressed toward greater structure until all categories had been covered. For those patients not treated or managed by the writer, time taken for interviews averaged 3 hr. (range: 1-7). Serial observations were made on all in-patients. The interview data were then collated with information in the hospital chart, from family interviews, from teaching conferences, and from talks with the attending psychiatrists, medical students, and nurses. Insofar as was possible, inferential material was avoided; the patient's verbalizations were taken at face value with regard to her puerperal experience, her past and present object relations, and what she deemed to be her major conflicts. Since the data therefore represent conscious reports and behavioral observations, the more elusive unconscious factors are not dealt with.

Although the literature,[2, 10] has repeatedly assumed that deliria stemming from postpartum endocrine and fluid-balance changes account for the prominent mental confusion in such syndromes, there have been no specific tests directed to this hypothesis. Slowing of the alpha rhythm of the EEG and impairment of cognitive tests of concentration and attention are specific deficits found in delirium.[11] Thus, the following procedures were directed to this question of delirium. (1) The serial substraction of 7 from 100 and the digit span were the tests used for judging attention and concentration. Since the most rapid endocrine and metabolic changes take place within the first 2 weeks postpartum,[12] it was decided to compare those patients who were admitted within 2 weeks postpartum (N = 18) with those admitted beyond 2 weeks, then comparing both of these groups to another general psychiatric population of 50 patients (33 women; 17 men). The latter sample had no instances of organic brain disease. (2) Fifteen EEGs were obtained for those patients in whom delirium was being considered from a clinical standpoint. (3) Since hypothyroidism has been implicated as the cause of the confusion,[2] 14 PBI tests were obtained. (4) In light of the high recurrence rate of postpartum distress, 6 patients with a history of previous postpartum psychiatric reaction (5 schizophrenic and 1 depressive reactions) were tested within 1 month before delivery and at 3 days postpartum for a subsequent pregnancy, using EEG, serial-7, and digit-span tests. Nine multiparous women without such a history served as a control sample for pre-to postpartum changes, again having each subject also serve as her own control. During delivery and the first 2 days postpartum, all patients received the same drugs, including anesthetic preparations. Drugs were eliminated for at least 24 hr. prior to each testing period. The alpha rhythm of the EEGs was determined by Engel's method.[13] When serial EEG changes are reported as nog significant, there was less than a 0.5-eps change in alpha frequency.

For all other comparisons, the student t test was the statistical method used. When a result is reported as not significant, it did not reach the .05 level. Since the descriptive data were incomplete or indefinite in some instances, the results are reported in terms of percentages. The latter pertains only when N is over 50; below that, actual numbers are given.

RESULTS

Before dealing specifically with the issue of delirium and the nature of the precipitating stress, the characteristics and background features will be outlined.

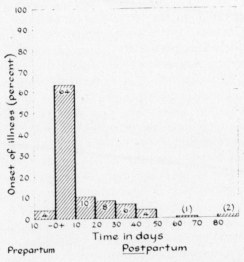

FIG. 1. Graph indicates time relationship of delivery to onset of illness.

Characteristics of the Syndromes

As shown in Fig. 1, 64% of the poastpartum psychiatric syndromes (PPS) experienced the onset of illness within the first 10 postpartum days. The median onset was 4 days postpartum (range: 10 days before delivery to 89 days postpartum). Of the 4 patients whose illness began before delivery, the symptoms did not become incapacitating until after delivery. Sixteen patients had the onset of distress on the *first* day postpartum. This finding militates against the so-called "latency period" of 3 days[14] as a supposed physiological protective period prior to the decrement of various hormones.

The diagnostic breakdown, which reflects the discharge diagnosis of the responsible psychiatrist, is given below.

609

Schizophrenic reaction	51
Neurotic depressive reaction	25
Personality disorder	11
Psychoneurotic reaction	4
Manic depressive reaction	4
Psychotic depressive reaction	2
Other	3

No patient was diagnosed as having an acute brain syndrome or a delirium. Although there was a predominance of schizophrenic reactions, this label was often found wanting: (1) many psychiatrists preferred the terms "schizo-affective" or "atypical psychotic reaction," and (2) even though the official psychiatric nomenclature in the United States contains no term for PPS, such as "post-partum depression" or "postpartum psychosis," the description "postpartum" was nevertheless appended to the discharge diagnosis in 66 of the cases.

The following symptoms, centering around delirioid phenomena, were tabulated. Confusion, often marked by uncertainty and indecision, was present in 91.7% of the patients. Disorientation to time (more than 2 days off) was present in 19.1% but only 2.2% were disoriented to place. Depersonalization, "dreamy" states, *deja vu,* misidentification, and distractability were common in those patients disoriented to time. Changes in time sense were prevalent in 89.7%. Both the perception of the passage of time and the orientation in time according to past, present, and future were often distorted, as has been noted.[15] As one patient stated, "I am going so far into the past that I cannot hold onto the present." Of the patients, 81% had insomnia; 63.4% were excited and restless. Irritability occurred in 94.6%, especially when the mothers were frustrated by their infants. Rapid changes in mood, fluctuating from tears to gaiety in a matter of minutes, took place in 79.7%. Inexplicable crying occurred in 94.5%. Feelings of shame, helplessness, and depression were the most pervasive affects, often resulting from a feeling of inadequacy.

Thus, the essential characteristics consist of an early puerperal onset of a schizophreniform or depressive illness—marked by labile mood, shame, changes in time sense, and confusion (without disorientation) in the majority of cases.

Predisposing and Background Factors

In considering predisposition, the most important finding was that of a high recurrence rate of postpartum distress. (1) Soon after their *first* delivery, 34 patients required psychiatric care; 30 experienced severe "postpartum blues" (lasting more than 2 weeks); 11, slight to moderate "postpartum blues" (lasting less than 2 weeks); 11, no reaction; and no data on 14 for the first puerperium. This degree of distress is in contrast to the Yalom et al.[16] study of 39 normal postpartum women in whom crying spells, though occurring in 67% of the women, were largely limited to less than 1-2 hr.; also, depression usually remitted within 24 hr. (2) The median duration of the previous "postpartum blues" (defined as distress precluding normal every-day activity) for the present sample was 30 days (range: 1-86), indicating quite a prolonged duration compared to the often-noted transitory reactions, which rarely last over 1-2 days.[16-18] (3) This tendency toward recurrent postpartum distress can best be seen in the high percentage of pregnancies resulting in either "postpartum blues" or PPS. Here, for each multigravidous woman, the percentage of pregnancies complicated by such reactions was calculated. Of a total of 313 pregnancies for 81 multigravidous women, the mean percentage of postpartum emotional disturbances ("postpartum blues" plus PPS) per individual was 76.1% (S.D. 29.9). The mean percentage of "postpartum blues," considered separately, was 31.8% (S.D. 25.6). The mean percentage of PPS per individual was 43.5% (S.D. 25.6), indicating roughly half of the pregnancies necessitated postpartum psychiatric care.

Other background features will be briefly mentioned: 51% of the women knew of severe emotional postpartum reactions among their relatives (23.3% for their mothers; 16.3% for their sisters). Further, 50% gave a history of severe premenstrual tension, i.e., anxiety, irritability, and depression that disrupted their every-day activities; 31% had moderate premenstrual tension. The position of the patient within the sibling order of her family paralleled Jansson's findings[10] of fewer eldest children: 41% came from the youngest third; 35% from the middle third; and 24% from the eldest third.

The Question of Delirium

In view of the prevalent but untested motion that PPS represent acute organic brain syndromes[2, 10] secondary to puerperal metabolic abnormalities, the following negative results militate against this assumption. (1) Despite confusion and disorientation ($p < .01$) in the 18 patients admitted within 2 weeks after delivery (the period of rapid endocrine changes), there was no significant difference between the performance of these patients and the later admissions on the serial-7 and digit-span tests. Moreover, the performance of each group of PPS on these cognitive tests did not differ from 50 other psychiatric patients. (2) Of the 15 patients who had EEGs to rule out clinically suspected deliria, the mean frequency of alpha rhythm was 9.00 (S.D. 2.83). There was no instance of EEG slowing indicative of a delirium.[11] (3) For the 14 PBI determinations, the mean value was 5.5ug. (S.D. 1.24), which is clearly within normal limits. (4) Finally, over the course of a subsequent partus, the 6 patients with a history of a previous PPS showed no significant pre- to postpartum differences on cognitive and EEG tests when compared to results in the 9 control subjects. Three of the 6 patients went on to require postpartum psychiatric treatment, but their EEGs, serial-7, and digit-span on the third day postpartum were not different from the prepartum-testing results. One patient developed an acute schizophrenic reaction on the fourth day postpartum — 1 day after the second battery of tests, which showed no change from the prepartum exams. Three weeks postpartum, when the patient was still psychotic, she was given another EEG, which did not differ from her previous two.

Thus, there was no evidence for a classical delirium. It is still possible, however, that puerperal endocrine changes in these women may produce a syndrome similar to a "steroid psychosis," in which cognitive impairment and EEG slowing may not take place.[19] Future research should be directed to those hormones such as progesterone and prolactin which are known to influence maternal behavior in animals.[20] Along this line, there was evidence for symptomatologic changes in connection with the first puerperal menstrual period and with the ingestion of progestational agents for contraceptive purposes. Also, the median onset of illness at four days postpartum coincides with lactational changes.

Nature of the Precipitating Stress

Table 1 delineates some of the most frequent psychological difficulties reported by the patients in this study. The percentages represent the totals within the categories of the data sheet. Each category was broken down into major, moderate, slight, and none in order to give a rough quantification of the degree of distress experienced. The classification is therefore primarily a convenient descriptive scheme which was found to be highly relevant to the patients' paramount concerns. The sub-categories overlap, but the "major" difficulties of the main headings are mutually exclusive: thus, 68% of the women had a major conflict with mothering, 10% with an object loss, 15.3% with "entrapment," and 6.6% with miscellaneous factors. These various categories will be illustrated

TABLE 1. CLASSIFICATION OF POSTPARTUM PRECIPITATING STRESS

	Major (%)	Moderate (%)	Slight (%)	None (%)
Conflict over mothering	68.0	26.0	1.0	2.0
Problems with identification				
Ambivalent identification with patient's own mother	49.0	39.0	4.0	8.0
Overidentification with baby	8.0	39.1	12.1	40.5
Difficulty with masculine-feminine identification	7.6	51.2	24.3	16.6
Distorted communication networks				
Conflicting messages	25.0	59.2	2.6	13.1
Lack of feedback from baby	6.8	50.0	1.7	41.3
Lack of rewards from husband	12.1	21.2	19.8	46.5
Difficulty in coping with task of mothering	30.0	58.0	3.0	9.0
Denial of mothering role	12.3	33.7	14.6	39.3
Hostility toward infant				
Primary*	2.4	14.6	13.4	69.5
Secondary	14.1	61.1	7.0	17.6
Object loss	10.0	24.0	22.0	43.0
Loss of baby	5.0	9.0	2.0	84.0
Loss of own mother or motherfigure	2.0	16.0	3.0	79.0
Loss of pregnant state	8.6	10.7	4.3	76.3
Other loss (includes change of plans)	13.0	16.0	3.0	68.0
Accentuation of "entrapment" feelings	15.3	48.3	10.9	27.4
Miscellaneous	6.6	43.3	33.3	46.6

* Hostility central in precipitating or maintaining illness.

WOMAN: DEPENDENT OR INDEPENDENT VARIABLE?

by citing case histories and adding other supporting evidence.

Conflict Over Mothering

Conflict over mothering was the area of greatest difficulty for the majority of women. Some of the most prominent features are exemplified by the following case history.

A 17-year old primiparous woman was admitted on the twelfth day postpartum in a confused, semicatatonic state. Pregnancy and delivery had been normal, except for some hyperemesis during the first trimester. Two days postpartum, the patient became irritable and was given to mood swings. Three days postpartum, when she was to leave the hospital with her baby, she had a 4-hr. crying spell, feeling that she wanted to be "taken care of" and "didn't want to be a mother" because she felt "incapable." When home, her husband noted that she became nervous when the infant cried and would not feed it. She claimed that she herself could "feel" when the infant was hungry. Six days postpartum, the patient stated that the baby was dead and asserted that she and her own mother were the same person. Later, she felt that her mother was "coming to strangle" her, though she had not seen her mother since age 6, when her mother was committed to a state hospital. The patient talked of wanting to go back to her childhood and, in the emergency department, was observed in the fetal position, asking if she could go "pee-pee" and "poo-poo." She kept calling for her mother and repeatedly misidentified the nurse as "Mommy." History revealed that, after the commitment of her own mother, the patient had two step-mothers, both of whom rejected her. Her confusion of her own identity in relationship to these various maternal figures was a pervasive and recurrent theme.

This case portrays many of the sub-categories under the main heading of "conflict over mothering" in Table 1, which will be discussed separately.

Ambivalent identification with the patient's own mother. The re-activation of problems of maternal identification in the above case history is typical, and 88% of the women experienced major to moderate difficulties in this sphere. The evidence for this "ambivalent identification" was derived essentially from the following findings. (1) the patients' vociferous repudiation of their own mothers (or mother-substitutes) as adequate models, (2) their recognition of an increased tendency to behave similarly to their own mothers since their delivery, and (3) their dread of becoming like their own mothers. Since this category turned out to be the most important, it will be dealt with at some length.

The accentuation of identification during the puerperium was often portrayed by the patients taking on symptoms which their mothers had. For example, one patient felt she was a "dead mother" and that her nose, cheeks, and skin were being "eaten away"; her own mother had died of lupus erythematosus when the patient was 8 years old. Another patient developed "spells" and "jerks," even though her neurological and EEG exams were normal; her own mother had been incapacitated with epileptic attacks. The following case history exemplifies the re-enactment of a symbiotic, hostile tie between mother and child during the puerperium.

A 20-year old primiparous woman was admitted on the seventh day postpartum after a serious suicidal attempt. Chief complaint: "I was afraid I would hurt the child." On the second day postpartum, the patient developed incapacitating anxiety about her ability to care for the infant, fear that her mother would usurp her role, and guilt over hostility toward the child. She openly denounced her own mother and refused all contact with her. She was confused and felt that her "mind had stopped — it was as if time did not exist."

History revealed that the patient had an interlocking relationship with a schizophrenic mother who was plagued with obsessions about being a "bad mother." The patient was an only child and, at that, an "accident." Ever since the patient was 6 years old, she had assumed the role of caring for her own mother. During the patient's pregnancy, the mother prophesied that her daughter's child would turn out to be a contorted animal, reflecting the mother's obsession with sodomy. After delivery, the daughter felt her mother's "thoughts had gotten to her." She, too, felt like a "bad mother," resembling not only her own mother, but also her controlling, rigid maternal grandmother. About 1 month after the patient came into the hospital, the patient's mother had to be admitted because of obsessional guilt for having "caused" her daughter's illness.

This type of matriarchal line of a controlling, rejecting mother (going back to the grandmother) was a definite finding in 7 other patients and suggestive in many others.

Using Schaefer's circumplex model for classifying maternal behavior, [21] 58.3% of the patients' mothers were described as concomitantly controlling and rejecting; 80.2% were rejecting; 70.0% were controlling. The breakdown, based on the patients' descriptions plus actual observations of many of the patients' mothers, is as follows: permissive-rejecting, 12; permissive-accepting, 3; controlling-rejecting, 56; controlling-accepting, 9;

permissive, 1; controlling, 2; rejecting, 9; accepting, 4; insufficient data, 4.

Further data on the patients' mothers suggest that these women were inadequate models for mothering: 13% had been judged psychotic at one time; 30.4% received psychiatric care; 23.6% suffered a severe postpartum emotional disturbance; and 23% were either separated or divorced. Twenty-seven of the mothers had used symptoms of illness to control their families. Fourteen were dead at the time of their daughter's puerperal mental illness; 7 died before their daughters reached the age of 12.

Although control data are needed, developmental clues suggest that some patients may have repudiated the mothering role early in childhood. For example, 35% had played with dolls only slightly or not at all. One patient's favorite pastime was to stick pins in dolls and imagine them suffering. Another had a fetish for wax dolls, which she would melt on the radiator. Of the patients, 39% had served as baby;sitter only slightly or not at all. On the other hand, 8 patients had been forced to assume the role of "child mother" because of their own mothers' absence, death, or chronic illness.

Finally, 3 patients had a "postpartum equivalent reaction" secondary to the adoption of an infant. Each of these patients, within a few days after the arrival of the baby, became confused and conflicted about her capacity to mother, showing great lability of affect. Each had a controlling mother who had inhibited them from making decisions of their own. Curiously, all 3 patients were highly disorganized and perplexed, despite the fact that no puerperal physiological changes were taking place, suggesting that such confusion can have a nonorganic basis. The following case captures the essential features of these "postpartum equivalent reactions," which were remarkably similar to the other patients with an ambivalent identification with a controlling-rejecting mother.

A 41-year-old social worker, who had been childless for her 5 years of marriage, became giddy and confused upon the arrival of her adopted male infant — an event she had been anticipating for 18 months. Within 2 days, she was insomniac, garrulous, and felt inadequate as a mother, fearing that she might harm the child. She thought her mother-in-law was trying to usurp her role as mother. On admission, she was unable to do serial-7 or digit-span tests and manifested flight of ideas, labile affect, and auditory hallucinations. Background history revealed that the patient had a domineering, cold mother who inhibited the patient from making any decisions of her own. The mother was described as a "large, dominant woman, a licensed real estate broker, the undisputed head of the household" who apparently dictated how the patient should look after her two younger sisters — a role that the patient resented. The patient's psychiatrist volunteered that the precipitating stress was the assumption of the mothering-feminine role which carried with it the identification with her own rejecting mother.

Overidentification with the baby was a major problem for 8% of the patients and a moderate problem for another 39.1%. This difficulty largely revolved around changing from the role of being cared for to assuming the caretaking role. As one patient stated, "I would like to be a child again and start all over, but I'm not the baby . . . I'm the mother." Another patient mumbled that she was "way back in the past" and her behavior mimicked that of a baby: she could not hold her head up; she cried in a high-pitched breathless whine; she gurgled and patted herself on the chest while leaning forward to induce burping.

Difficulty with masculine-feminine identification. About 8% of the patients openly asserted that they would rather have been men, and another 51.2% stated that they were more like their fathers than their mothers. A severe tomboy phase, often extending into high school, was reported by 70.6%.

Turning now from identification problems to distorted communication networks, the pervasive theme was the lack of positive reinforcement in mothering the infant.

Conflicting messages was a severe problem for 25% and a moderate difficulty for another 59.2% of the patients. Here, conflicting and ambiguous communications came not only from the infant, but also from other significant objects, such as the patient's mother, sisters, mother-in-law, and husband, who often gave insistent but discrepant advice as to how to care for the infant. Moreover, the new mother was often reluctant to take any advice or to give any hint of her inadequacy, for she felt that her conduct as a mother was a test of her worth and femininity.

Many mothers were perplexed also by the infant's crying, as portrayed by the following patient's statement: "When they cry, you don't know what they're crying for. . . . You do everything under the sun you can think of to do, and they still cry. . . . I get upset after a few minutes. . . . I feel that I am not being a good mother when I don't know what to do for him. I feel stupid, and it makes me mad to take care of him because I don't seem to be meeting his needs. I don't know what he wants half of the time, and I feel stupid when I hear other people tell me what it is."

Crying was often interpreted as angry rejection of the mother coupled with a desperate demand for help; this sometimes bordered on a classical "double-bind" situation in that the mother felt she had to respond despite the frequent possibility of failure to appease the infant.

Lack of feedback from the baby. Not only was interaction with the infant perplexing, but also it consisted of a rather global form of communication, punctuated by either gross distress and crying versus quiescence, with little positive reinforcement for the mother during the early puerperium. The infant's incapacity to give specific needs was a major difficulty for 6.8% of the patients and a moderate difficulty for another 50%. Some mothers felt as if they were "talking to a dummy" or dealing with a "vegetable." There was not the "give-and-take" of adult interaction; rather the axis of reinforcing activity was from mother to infant, especially during the first month postpartum when the babies evinced little smiling and cooing.

Since the infants gave them little feed-back on their mothering activities, the new mothers had to turn either to themselves or to others for guidance and rewards. Because many of the patients found little reward for mothering through identifying with their own mothers, they frequently became extremely dependent on the approval of other persons, especially the husband. If the latter remained detached or overly critical, the patient was left to herself again, puzzled by her lack of warmth and affection for her baby.

Lack of rewards from husband: Some of the husbands remained surprisingly uninvolved in their wives' struggle with mothering. It was rare for 12.1% of the husbands to give reinforcement for their wives' mothering duties, and another 21.2% were moderately disengaged. Five husbands increased their outside activities, such as taking on extra jobs, writing a book, etc., in order to get away from the home. This detachment is typified by one husband who nonchalantly left his wife off at the hospital before she delivered each of her 3 children, while he returned to work.

Difficulty in coping with the task of mothering was a major problem for 30% and a moderate problem for 58% of the patients. Many patients felt overwhelmed by the demands placed upon them after the birth of the baby: not only did they have to care for the infant, but also they had to attend to their houses, meals, laundry, husbands, and interested guests and relatives. Moreover, if they had other children, the arrival of the infant often prompted regression and sibling rivalry in the older children, who then made even greater demands on the mother. A vicious circle frequently ensued, in which the mother's distress augmented the children's distress, and vice versa. Some patients felt unduly stressed by having too many young children to care for at one time.

Also included in this category are women who felt shamed because breast feeding was not adequate, guilty because of illness of the infant, hostile because they were not getting the help they expected from the husband, mother, etc. Of course, any fatigue or confusion — whether induced by physiological or psychological factors — aggravated this difficulty in coping.

Denial of mothering role. This was severe in 12.3% and moderate in another 33.7% of the patients. One patient was repulsed by the task of kissing her children good-night; her major concern was to "get away from the kids." Eleven patients attempted to get jobs outside the home within the first 2 months postpartum. When denial was prominent, these mothers responded to their infants mechanically, shunning emotional involvement and, consequently, getting little satisfaction from mothering. Since it was practically impossible to carry out this denial of mothering in the postpartum period, the use of this defense precipitated even more difficulty.

Hostility toward the infant. Only 2.4% of the patients had severe "primary" hostility toward their infants, i.e., overt fears of actively inflicting harm on them, which were central in precipitating or maintaining illness. Another 14.6% had fleeting thoughts of harming their infants. Such thoughts, especially that of infanticide, transfixed the patients with guilt; they frequently ruminated, "How could a mother have such thoughts? Why would a mother harm her helpless child?" Another 14.1% of the patients had major and 61.1% moderate "secondary" hostility toward their infants, i.e., anger stemming from a host of other conflicts and manifested as wishes and actions to leave the infant rather than actively to harm him. Along these lines, most of our postpartum patients had difficulty in tolerating and expressing their own aggressive ideas — for fear of rejection or disapproval of others. And for many, any anger toward the infant was unthinkable and shameful.

In summary, the conflict over mothering stemmed largely from an ambivalent identification with a controlling-rejecting mother which led to the repudiation of the mothering role, especially if the reinforcements from the concurrent environment were sparse and ambiguous.

Object Loss

The actual or threatened loss of a significant object constituted a major precipitating stress for 10% of the patients. Patients were included in this general category of precipitating stress if they had either an overwhelming object loss, or an incapacitating admixture of some of the below-listed types of object losses seen in the puerperium.

Loss of baby was a major precipitating stress for 5% of the patients. Two infants died; 3 were given up for adoption. In another 9%, there was a threatened loss of the baby, through either infantile illness or intervention by a relative.

Loss of own mother or mother-figure constituted a major stress for 2% of the patients; another 16% experienced moderate difficulty because their mothers were no longer available, or because the birth of the infant reawakened memories of loss of their mothers.

Loss of pregnant state. About 9% of the patients experienced this as a major stress. These patients stated that they wanted to be pregnant again, and that they missed the felicitous attention they received when they were pregnant. Included within this category are 5 patients who were upset by the change in "body image" upon delivery.

Other loss. This residual category turned out to be quite important for 13% of the patients and moderately significant for another 16%. A frequent finding was the necessity of giving up some cherished and carefully laid out plans for the future after the arrival of the baby. For example, the care of the infant interfered with the pursuit of a career more than some mothers had anticipated. Or, a 43-year-old woman was preparing for travels and rest with her retired husband when another pregnancy appeared unexpectedly. Other factors consisted of the loss of freedom, loss of youth, and the necessity of moving from a familiar home to a new setting which would accommodate the infant.

There were no instances of the loss of the husband, either through death, separation, or divorce during the puerperium. But, as noted above, the husbands were frequently detached.

Accentuation of "Entrapment" Feelings

The feelings of "entrapment" was a major precipitating stress in 15.5% of the women and a moderate stress for another 48.3%. The arrival of the baby ensnared the mother in a marriage or other social situation from which she wanted to be free. In such instances there was often a more overt battle between husband and patient, as opposed to the above-mentioned aloofness and disengagement of the husband.

Miscellaneous

About 7% of the patients had major and 43.3% moderate difficulties which resided in conflicts other than those mentioned. Examples of this category are fearful states associated with physical illness of the patient (such as postpartum hemorrhage), competition with sisters and friends, financial difficulties, etc.

COMMENT

An adequate explanation of the postpartum psychiatric syndromes must account for the following essential features, found in this study and many others: the onset of illness soon after delivery, the high postpartum recurrence rate of mental illness in these women, and the marked confusion, shame, and labile affect. A metabolic derangement—recurring during rapid endocrine changes each pueperium and resulting in a delirium—could explain these findings.[2] But cognitive and EEG tests produced no evidence for a delirium.[11] Moreover, since 3 patients developed a similar syndrome in connection with the adoption of an infant, it is doubtful that organic factors alone explain the syndrome. Victoroff[5] reports 3 and Tetlow[4] describes 6 other postadoption psychoses, claiming that they were similar to those of their puerperal psychotic patients. While it is still possible that hormonal changes may make these women more vulnerable during the puerperium, it may prove fruitful to entertain a more *psychological* hypothesis. Briefly, the postulate is this: A conflict in assuming the mothering role, activated by caring for a helpless, relatively noncommunicative infant, led to *identity diffusion*[22] in these postpartum women. This factor may have accounted for the prominent confusion. The mothering of a noncommunicative infant hindered self-definition, for there was a relative lack of interpersonal feed-back and less distinction between "self" and "other" in the early mother-child relationship. Moreover, identity as a mother was impaired because these women either lacked adequate maternal models or repudiated their own mothers as models.

Let us examine the postulate in terms of the basic findings. (1) The onset of illness took place within the first month postpartum for 82% of the PPS. This is the period when the infant is most noncommunicative. The median onset of 4 days postpartum coincides with the time most women were discharged from postnatal hospital care to assume major responsibility for their infants. Thus, the onset of illness may not wholly relate to puerperal metabolic changes, but rather may stem from the conflicting messages and ambiguities surrounding the care of the infant. Over 75% of the patients stated that these factors were a major to moderate stress. In particular, they found infant crying perplexing in that it was interpreted as raging rejection as well as desperate need of the mother.

(2) The high recurrence rate may also relate to the ambiguities of communication and identification which reoccur postpartum in connection with mothering a neonate. For the sample of multiparous women as a whole, 43.5% of the pregnancies of each woman (expressed as an average) resulted in postpartum psychiatric care. This contrasts markedly with the low incidence of

PPS in the general population, which is roughly 1 per 1000 deliveries. [2]

(3) The prominent confusion, shame, and labile affect could also be explained on the basis of a conflict over mothering, resulting in identity diffusion. Confusion was found in 91.7%, but in contrast to the usual findings of an acute brain syndrome, disorientation to time was present in 19.1% and only 2.2% were disoriented to place. Carlson[23] has described an acute nonorganic confusional state in relatively healthy college students, usually arising at the time of psychosocial shifts and new commitments. Most of the students had previously formed a compliant, dependent relationship, largely through guilt and fear, with their unstable, rejecting, and controlling parents. When faced with an adult commitment, they found they had inadequate repertoires and personal identity to meet the task — resulting in feelings of failure, irritability, and confusion. Similar feelings of inadequacy, confusion, and dependency on domineering yet rejecting mothers were also noted in this and other postpartum samples,[4-6, 24] but the possible interrelation of these factors have not been spelled out. Since 68% of the postpartum women gave evidence for a major conflict over mothering, it is possible that the ambivalent and vacillating commitment to mothering led to the acute confusional state. But why?

Essentially, by disavowing their own mothers, these women were bereft of a plan of action in a situation which demanded action, leading to untoward emotion and confusion. [25] Their sense of identity and feelings of competence became fragmented in that they were mothers without knowing how to act. The following postulates tie together the most prominent stresses found in this study (Table 1) into a process which may explain the onset of identity diffusion in these women. (1) Giving birth to a neonate who has extensive needs committed these women to mothering. (2) Since the young infant was incapable of specifying guidelines for his care, yielding little positive reinforcement, the new mothers became more dependent on the images and plans of action provided by significant maternal figures of her past and present. Her own mother was an important reference point. (3) This tendency to seek guidelines from maternal figures was further accentuated if: her own mother had been controlling, as 70% of them were, thereby inhibiting the patient from developing self-direction and repertoires of her own; when the concurrent environment offered little on-going reinforcement for her mothering activities, as evidenced by the lack of rewards from the husband and the discrepant advice from many others; and when current stresses, resulting in object loss, frustration, and feelings of "entrapment," prompted the woman to recapture earlier periods of equilibrium, i.e., to regress—in this way, their own mothers' maternal behavior increasingly became a reference or model for their own program of action. (4) However, since their own mothers had often repudiated the mothering role, or were judged as inadequate maternal models, the increased identification entailed conflict—it was an ambivalent identification. Moreover, since 80% of their own mothers had rejected the patients, the identification often led to the new mothers' rejection of their own infants, despite conscious wishes to be unlike their own mothers. As Victoroff states, ". . . they . . . reject their children as they themselves were rejected."[5] The identity of the new mothers in this situation therefore vacillated: they felt helpless without the images of their mothers, yet ashamed when like their own mothers. Indecision, perplexity, and a loss of a sense of personal efficacy mounted. Uncertain in their role as mother and yet without a positive maternal model, these women felt lost and confused.

In essence, then, it is postulated that identity diffusion, stemming from identification and modeling problems in assuming the care of a relatively noncommunicative infant, may account for the early puerperal onset, the high recurrence rate, and the syndrome of labile affect, as well as feelings of shame and confusion in these postpartum women.

CONCLUSION: A NOTE OF TREATMENT

Ideally, the patient should not be separated from her child, for this often confirms her suspicion that she is an inadequate mother. Useful tacks are getting family members to assist the patient with mothering, or, with hospitalized patients, allowing for frequent visits with the children and even admitting the infant with the mother. A number of institutions[26, 27] have found the latter procedure to be of value and, of 16 joint mother-infant admissions to our hospital, it was found beneficial in 10 instances in that continual reinforcement and encouragement of mothering activities helped these patients find themselves as mothers. The staff's concern for the infant, rather than for the mother, occurred with 2 joint admissions and varied with 4 others, thereby aggravating the mother's shame and feeling of incompetence. Thus, careful attention should be directed to bringing the baby in at the proper time: when the mother, staff, and other patients are prepared to reinstate the patient as mother.

SUMMARY

The study of 100 women, whose onset of psychiatric illness

began from 1 month prepartum to 3 months postpartum, delineated the following features of "postpartum" psychiatric disorders. 1. The peak onset was close to the time of delivery (median onset, 4 days postpartum), indicating the psychiatric illness is not incidental to the puerperium. 2. The high recurrence rate of postpartum distress suggests that these women were vulnerable during most of their puerperal periods. 3. For the most part, the rapidly fluctuating affective and confusional symptoms were not adequately described by the usual nosological categories.[2][10] 4. Lack of difference between these patients and control subjects in performance on serial-7 subtractions and digit-span tests as well as in frequency analysis of the EEG militates against the existence of a toxic delirious state. 5. It is postulated that the high incidence of confusion most likely stems from identity diffusion, certering around a conflict in assuming the mothering role. 6. In the majority of patients, this conflict appeared to result from the patients' repudiation of their own mothers as adequate models. 7. Even though the patients' maternal identification was ambivalent, the puerperium intensified the need for maternal models as the infant was incapable of communicating guidelines for his care. 8. Hormonal changes may make some women more vulnerable, but since 3 patients became bewildered shortly after the adoption of an infant, it appears that the psychological conflict over mothering can precipitate a confusional syndrome in the absence of postpartum physiological changes.

REFERENCES

1. Pugh, T.F., Jerath, B.K., Schmidt, W.M., and Reed, R.B. Rates of mental disease related to childbearing. *New Eng J Med 268:*1224, 1963.
2. Hamilton, J.A. *Postpartum Psychiatric Problems.* Mosby, St. Louis, 1962.
3. Brew, M.F., and Seidenberg, R. Psychotic reactions associated with pregnancy and childbirth. *J. Nerv Ment Dis* 111:*408,* 1950.
4. Tetlow, C. Psychoses of childbearing. *J. Ment Sci 101:*629, 1955.
5. Victoroff, V.M. Dynamics and management of para partum neurophathic reactions. *Dis Nerv Syst 13:*291, 1952.
6. Benedek, T. *Psychosexual Functions in Women.* Ronald, New York, 1952.
7. Bibring, G.L., Dwyer, T.F., Huntington, D.S., and Valenstein, A.F. "A Study of the Psychological Processes in Pregnancy and of the Earliest Mother-Child Relationship." In *The Psychoanalytic Study of the Child.* International Universities Press, New York, 1961, vol. 16, p. 9.
8. Deutsch, H. "Motherhood." In *Psychology of Women.* Grune, New York, 1945, vol. 2.
9. Romano, J. Psychosocial aspects of obstetrical-gynecological practice: Implications for education and research. *Bull Sloane Hosp Wom 10:*267, 1964.
10. Jansson, B. Psychic insufficiences associated with childbearing. *Acta Psychiat Scand (Suppl) 172:*1, 1964.
11. Engel, G.L., and Romano, J. Delirium, a syndrome of cerebral insufficiency. *J Chronic Dis 9:*260, 1959.
12. Benson, R.B. Endocrinology of the puerperium. *Clin Obstet Gynec 5:*639, 1963.
13. Engel, G.L., Romano, J., Ferris, E.B., Webb, J.P., and Stevens, C.D. A simple method of determining frequency spectrums in the electroencephalogram. *Arch Neurol Psychiat 51:*134, 1944.
14. Karnosh, L.J., and Hope, J.M. Puerperal psychoses and their sequelae. *Amer J Psychiat 94:*537, 1937.
15. Melges, F.T., and Fougerousse, C.E., Jr. Time sense, emotions, and acute mental illness. *J Psychiat Res 4:* 127, 1966.
16. Yalom, I.D., Moos, R.H., Lunde, D.T., and Hamburg, D.A. The "post-partum blues" syndrome: description and related variables. Unpublished data.
17. Pleshette, S., Asch, S.S., and Chase, J. A study of

anxieties during pregnancy, labor, the early and late puerperium. *Bull NY Acad Med 32:*436, 1956.

18. Robin, A.A. The psychological changes of normal parturition. *Psychiat Quart 36:*129, 1962.

19. Glaser, G. H. EEG activity and adrenal cortical dysfunction. *Electroenceph Clin Neurophysiol* 10:366, 1958.

20. Riddle, O. Prolactin or progresterone as key to parental behavior: A review. *Anim Behav 11:*419, 1963.

21. Schaefer, E.S. A circumplex model for maternal behavior. *J Abnorm Psychol 9:*226, 1959.

22. Erikson, E.H. "Identity and the Life Cycle." In *Psychology Issues,* International Universities Press, New York, 1959, vol. 1.

23. Carlson, H.B. Characteristics of an acute confusional state in college students. *Amer J Psychiat 114:*900, 1958.

24. Ostwald, P.F., and Regan, P.F. Psychiatric disorders associated with childbirth. *J Nerv Ment Dis 125:*153, 1957.

25. Pribram, K.H., and Melges, F.T. "Emotion: The Search for Control." In *Handbook of Clinical Neurology,* Vinken, P.J., and Bruyn, G.W., Eds. North-Holland Publishing Co., Amsterdam. (In press.)

26. Grunebaum, H.U., and Weiss, J.L. Psychotic mothers and their children: Joint admission to an adult psychiatric hospital. *Amer J Psychiat 119:*927, 1963.

27. Baker, A.A., Morison, M., Game, J.A., and Thorpe, J.G. Admitting schizophrenic mothers with their babies. *Lancet 29:*237, 1961.

38 The Case for Human Cycles

Rhoda Kesler Unger

The argument that women are "slaves of their chemistry" has been used against women for some time. It is wielded by the husband who wishes to explain his wife's sudden outbursts of rage in purely physical terms, as well as by the politicians who wouldn't consider letting women run for high office because for several days each month they are not "in complete control of themselves." Underlying this conception is the assumption that was made by most endocrinologists until the late 1940s: the male body is basically stable and its normal state is one of constancy. During the 1950s and 1960s, however, Halberg and his associates (Halberg, 1969) made it clear that healthy men on a regular sleep schedule showed a regular rise and fall of adrenal hormone levels in blood and urine, a cycle that occurred every twenty four hours. Free-running cycles in various chemical and behavioral measures have been found in virtually every species studied. They are called circadian from the Latin *circa dies*, or around a day. An exposition on the origins of this basic rhythm are beyond the scope of this book; however, current thought has it that these oscillations are a direct result of our inherited structure being acted upon by a world that changes on a twenty-four-hour cycle. An organism that is physiologically tuned to the twenty-four-hour vibration of the planet would have a greater survival value than one that isn't (Pittendrigh, 1960).

One of the most dependable indicators of circadian functioning is body temperature. It remains at a plateau during the day and drops a degree or two during the night. This represents a significant drop in metabolic activity, and people awake at this point in their cycles function poorly (Klein et al., 1968). Pulse rates, respiration rates, and urine flow rates follow similar rhythms (Halberg and Hamburger, 1964; Haus and Halberg, 1966). Scheving and Pauly (1967) observed cyclic changes in the blood composition of rats. Clotting time was shortest at the beginning of their rest period and was 50 percent longer at the middle of their activity period. The levels of gamma globulin, the blood protein that contains a large number of immune antibodies, also varied according to a circadian rhythm.

The liver, via storage and release of glycogen, plays a crucial role in maintaining blood sugar levels. It has been shown (Sollberger, 1964) that human glycogen levels begin to decline in the late afternoon. By early morning, the liver has used up most of its glycogen. Increased irritability may be related to the resultant mild hypoglycemia.

Sleep itself is the essence of periodicity. Not only does it occur regularly every twenty-four hours, but the ninety-minute Stage 1 to 2 to 3 to 4 to REM cycle has been well established. There is some evidence suggesting that the ninety-minute undulations of brain waves carry on into the waking day in the form of a "basic rest and activity cycle" (Kleitman, 1963). This would help explain the waxing and waning of attention span, sudden onsets of drowsiness or daydreaming, and similar mood changes of which we are usually unaware, but which are quite marked in young children.

Cyclic variations in the release of adrenal hormones appear to be most directly implicated with mood change. Curtis et al. (1966) compared healthy and depressed patients for the levels of 17-hydroxy-corticosteroid (an adrenal hormone) at different hours. Distressed males showed higher amplitude of change in daily adrenal rhythms than either normal men or women. Normal women showed a flatter curve than men, while distressed women showed even less circadian change than normal women. Depressed groups appear to have greater variability in their adrenal rhythms than normal individuals. In addition, there may be phase differences. In one such study (Halberg et al., 1968), healthy people showed their peak excretion of urinary 17-ketosteroids around midday, while the depressed patients showed their peak excretion around late afternoon.

The monthly cycle of women may have less conspicuous counterparts in men. Unfortunately, there has been virtually no research done in this particular area. The basic source of most information appears to be a nontechnical article on the subject written by Dr. Estelle Ramey for Ms. magazine (Ramey, 1972). The article has been cited in a number of professional publications. An additional source of information are two volumes by Luce (1970, 1971). She notes that Sanctorius, a seventeenth-century doctor, weighed healthy men over long periods of time and discovered a monthly weight change of one to two pounds. Halberg and Hamburger (1964) described a sixteen-year study of daily urines in one man and found a near-monthly cycle of adrenal hormones in addition to the aforementioned daily one. Hersey (1931) conducted a year-long study on twenty-five industrial workers who were average in intelligence and overtly "normal." He found long-term trends that were typical for each individual. The men rated themselves each day on an emotional scale and showed mood variations typically ranging from four to nine weeks in periodicity. One twenty-two-year-old man showed a 4-5-week cycle with a variance no greater than that of the menstrual cycle. During low periods he was indifferent, apathetic at work and at home, and temporarily abandoned his artwork. Recently Japanese scientists have attempted to study such long-term cycles in men in an effort to avert industrial accidents. Their results, however, have not yet been translated.

These results emphasize that the relationship between biochemistry and behavior is not limited to females. To date, no one has elucidated their possible chemical bases. However, one recent study has found a relationship between chemistry and affect in a noncyclic phenomenon. Persky, Smith, and Basu (1971) found a significant correlation between the amount of testosterone in the bloodstream and hostility in healthy young men. The amount of testosterone present is also related to rank in the dominance hierarchy in many primates (Johnson, 1972).

These data are not intended to deny the reality of the menstrual cycle or the various symptoms and changes in behavior associated with it. However, they may serve to place it in its proper perspective along with the many other biological cycles that rule the lives of all of us, male or female.

REFERENCES

Curtis, G.C.; Fogel, M. L.; McEvoy, D.; and Zarate, C. The effect of sustained effect on the diurnal rhythms of adrenal cortical activity. *Psychosomatic Medicine, 1966, 28, 696-713.*

Halbert, F. Chronobiology. *Annual Review of Physiology,* 1969 *31.* 675-725.

Halberg and Hamburger, C. 17-ketosteroid and volume of human urine weekly and other changes with low frequency. *Medicine,* 1964, *47,* 916-25.

Halberg, Vestergaard, P. and Sakai, M. Rhythmometry on urinary 17-ketosteroid excretion by healthy men and women and patients with chronic schizophrenia; possible Chronobiology. in depressive illness. Cited in G. G. Luce, *Biological Rhythms in psychiatry and medicine.* Chevy Chase, Md.: U.S. Department of Health, Education and Welfare, 1970.

Haws, E., and Halbert, F. Circadian phase diagrams of oral temperature and urinary functions in a healthy man studied longitudinally. *Acta Endocrinologica,* 1966, *51,* 215-23.

Hersey, P. Emotional cycles of man. *Journal of Mental Science,* 1931, *77,* 151-69.

Johnson, R. *Aggression in man and animals.* Philadelphia: Saunders, 1972.

Kleitman, N. *Sleep and wakefulness.* Chicago: University of Chicago Press, 1963.

Luce, G. G. *Biological rhythms in psychiatry and medicine.* Chevy Chase, Md.: U. S. Department of Health, Education and Welfare, 1970.

———— *Body time.* New York: Pantheon, 1971.

Persky, H.: Smith, K. D., and Basu, G. K. Relation of psychologic measures of aggression and hostility to testosterone production in man. *Psychosomatic Medicine,* 1971, *33,* 515-37.

Pittendrigh, C. S. Circadian rhythms and the circadian organization of living systems. *Symposia on Quantitative Biology,* 1960, *25,* 159-82.

Ramey, E. Men's cycles. *Ms.,* January, 1972.

Scheiring, L. E. and Pauly, J. E. Daily rhythmic variation in blood coagulation time in rats. *Anatomical Record,* 1967, *157,* 657-65.

Sollerberger, A. The control of circadian glycogen rhythms. *Annals of the New York Academy of Sciences,* 1964, *117,* 519-53.

SUGGESTED PAPERS AND PROJECTS

Papers:

1. Discuss the relationship between the menstrual cycle and behavior as considered in psychology.
2. Discuss the effects of pregnancy upon the psychology of the mother.
3. Discuss postpartum psychosis: environmental vs. physiological factors.
4. Discuss postpartum and menopausal depressions. What physical and environmental factors do these periods have in common?

Projects:

1. Keep daily records of your moods for two months, noting any fluctuations. Females should note on which days they are menstruating.
2. Ask the following questions of several people (include males and females in your sample): If scientists developed a foolproof method—free of any physical or psychological side effects—to eliminate menstruation while preserving your ability to become pregnant if and when you wanted to, would you want to eliminate menstruation? (If you are a male, would you want your wife or girl friend to do so?) Please briefly give the reasons for your answer.
3. Discuss the question of whether abortion or giving birth is more likely to result in psychological disturbance.
4. Interview three women at their time of ovulation and menstruation. Are there any reported or observable differences in moods between these segments?

ADDITIONAL REFERENCES

Bardwick, J. *Readings in the psychology of women* pt. 6. New York: Harper & Row, 1972.

Herzberg, B. N. Body composition and premenstrual tension. *Journal of Psychosomatic Research,* 1971, *15,* 251-57.

— — —, and Coppen, A. Changes in psychological symptoms in women taking oral contraceptives. *British Journal of Psychiatric Medicine,* 1970, *116,* 161-64.

Luce, G. G. *Biological rhythms in psychiatry and medicine.* Bethesda, Md.: Public Health Service publication no. 2088, 1970.

Moos, R. H.; Kopell, B. S.; Meltes, I. D.; Yalom, D.T.; Lunde, R. B.; and Hamburg, D. A. Fluctuations in symptoms and moods during the menstrual cycle. *Journal of Psychosomatic Research,* 1969, *13,* 37-44.

Reynolds, E. Variations of mood and recall in the menstrual cycle. *Journal of Psychosomatic Research,* 1969, *13,* 163-66.

Section VII

Female Achievement:
Internal vs. External Barriers

39 Introduction

"Achievement behavior refers to the evaluation of performance against some standard of excellence. Many of the studies concerned with achievement behavior have stressed the development of achievement in children as well as the characteristics of achievement-oriented children, adolescents, and adults (e.g., Crandall, Katovsky, and Preston, 1960; Crandall, Dewey, Katovsky, and Preston, 1964).

Rather than examining achievement behavior, a number of other investigators, such as McClelland (1953), have focused on the study of achievement motivation or the need for achievement (nAch). Many of these studies have been concerned with male achievement motivation and have used males as subjects. McClelland used male-oriented TAT (Thematic Apperception Test) type pictures as the basis for scoring need for achievement. When sex was treated as a variable it often appeared as a by-product of the statistical analysis. However, as research based on McClelland's scoring system[1] continued, interest grew in the female Ss, who were found to score much lower in need for achievement than the males, and much higher in need for affiliation.

In a study by Veroff et al. (1953), the achievement motive was examined in high school and college-age women. Whereas male Ss increased their mean need for achievement scores on the TAT following the experimental procedure, the females did not. In addition, both males and females gave more achievement-related responses to pictures with men in them. Thus, both sexes saw achievement and success as male traits.

Crandall (1969), using a number of studies covering many age ranges and involving different types of problems, also reported that males consistently gave higher estimates of expectancy of success. This was true even in instances where prior female performance had been better than that of males. Females were less confident than males when approaching new intellectual tasks. When both negative and positive success-related cues were presented, females focused on the negative ones in contrast to

---

1. Despite its usage, this measure has low reliability for nAch scores. There has also been difficulty in replicating studies that use the TAT test as a measure of nAch.

males, who focused on the positive cues. It is puzzling that despite the positive reinforcement girls receive for obtaining high grades in the elementary school years from teachers, parents, and other socializing agents, they underestimate their ability even in these early grades.

Turner (1964) attempted a sociological analysis of the complex problem of women's ambition. He collected questinnaire data from 1441 high school students, male and female. Analysis of the data showed that females were less ambitious than males on educational and material levels. Turner reports that males placed more emphasis on prestige, women on esteem.

Perhaps females generally are underachievers, as the above studies would indicate. This immediately raises the questions of whether other studies continue to support these findings, and if so, what factors operate on the female to make her an underachiever in contrast to males. Other studies, regardless of method employed, do report low achievement motivation for females. However, before examining some of the internal or personal barriers to achievement, it must be noted that not all women are underachievers.

Many studies have looked at the differences among women in achievement motivation. Lesser, Krawitz, and Packard (1963) point out that female achievers had higher achievement scores for female pictures than for male pictures, but the underachievers attributed higher achievement scores to the male pictures. The achiever sees other females as achievers too. She has not resigned herself to the culturally defined role of woman as someone who can experience success only vicariously through her husband or some other male figure. A study by French and Lesser (1964), in which women Ss at all-women colleges had higher nAch scores than did women attending coed colleges, supports this contention. The woman in the coed situation is forced into competition with men and she faces the conflict between achievement and rejection of woman's role. Those women who valued intellectual attainment had to reject the traditional woman's role. In the all-women school, the female is competing only with other females and does not have as great a conflict between her role as a woman and intellectual achievement.

The finding that some women score higher in nAch than others was also supported by Baruch (1967) in a cross-sectional study of Radcliffe alumnae. She employed the sex pictures previously used by Veroff (1953) and found that Radcliffe alumnae had much higher achievement imagery than did a nationwide sample of women. Baruch also reported a temporal cycle in women's nAch and return to paid employment. Women out of college five years had a disproportionate number with high nAch scores, but for those ten years out of school there was a steady decline in the scores. Married woman with high nAch, who are out of college twenty years or more, are likely to be pursuing careers, but this is not true of those with low nAch. But for those out of college fifteen years, even with a rise in nAch, there were no significant correlation between nAch and career if there were young children at home. The college-educated women in the nationwide sample resembled the Radcliffe alumnae in the temporal pattern. However, for those with less than twelve years of school there was a steady decline of nAch with age. For women with a high school education, those between twenty-one and twenty-four years of age scored high on nAch, but this declined for those between thirty and thirty-nine years, with some rise for subsequent years. It isn't really surprising that Radcliffe graduates should have higher nAch than women in a national sample. By gaining admission to this prestigious college as well as by competing for degree requirements, they have accepted achievement striving as compatible with their feminine identity. In contrast many women with a limited education feel that any hope of a career has passed along with the years. They have stifled the personal achievement strivings they may have had earlier.

Another study involving differences among females in achievement motivation was conducted at Radcliffe with a group of wives of graduate students (Blumen-Lipman, 1972). All had previously attended college. They ranged in age from eighteen to fifty-four years. Respondents were grouped into two categories: those who held a traditional view of woman's role—i.e., that woman's place is in the home and the male is the only one responsible for financial support of the family—and those who held a contemporary view, that the relationship between the sexes should be egalitarian. Twenty-six percent of the respondents adhered to the traditional view and 73 percent to the contemporary view.

In many ways these two groups were similar, but many more of the women with a contemporary view of woman's role had a higher aspiration level than did those women with a traditional view. Women with the contemporary view tended to come from homes where neither parent or just the mother was dominant. Women with a contemporary view are reported to have a critical mother, those with traditional views a critical father.

Importance of the parents' influence on achievement motivation was also suggested by Crandall, Katkovsky, and Preston (1962). In their study, boys' achievement motivations were positively associated with their achievement efforts. For the girls, expectations and effort were either negatively or nonsignificantly related. The authors feel this may be due to parents' reinforcing or approving boys who have high aspirations while reprimanding the girls for unfeminine boasting.

This conflict that women have between achievement vs. maintaining their femininity was explored by Horner (1969). The woman who succeeds is concerned about rejection by males because she is too assertive or competitive. Horner found striking differences in responses given to questions of success, depending on whether the central figure in the story was male or female. The female Ss verbalized their inner conflict, showing the ambiguity with which they viewed success. Male Ss did not exhibit this conflict.

In her more recent paper (1972) Horner extends this theme through extension of her original research and through examination of other studies. Horner believes that most women have a motive to avoid success because they expect negative consequences such as social rejection and/or feelings of being unfeminine as a result of succeeding. This motive to avoid success is more characteristic of high achievement-oriented, high ability women than of low achievement-oriented, low ability women and is more likely to appear in competitive achievement situations. Sixty-five percent of Horner's women Ss gave responses that were filled with negative consequences associated with achievement. They associated excellence in women with loss of feminity, social rejection, personal or societal distrust, or some combination of these. In contrast, 90 percent of the men in the study showed strong positive feelings, indicating increased striving, confidence in the future, and a belief that this success would be instrumental in providing other goals, such as a secure and happy home.

Horner reports some surprising findings in her more recent data. There has been an increase in the fear of success imagery or negative consequences of success in the male Ss. Successful male figures are viewed as lacking a social consciousness and having selfish personalities. Horner states that the recent data also indicate something of a backlash phenomenon. The negative attitudes toward successful women have increased since that time and have intensified to a disporportionately greater extent than have the positive ones. This has been observed for female as well as male Ss.

Horner also points out that contrary to previous research, the motive to avoid success showed no relationship with the affiliative motive, which was also measured. Horner also notes that attitudes of parents were not significant in arousing the motive to avoid success. The families of the females who scored high on this motive in her initial study placed a high premium on competence and independence, which has been shown to be conducive to the development of high achievement motivation. The attitudes of male peers toward the appropriate role of women appears to be the most significant factor in arousing the motive to avoid success.

Horner's own work and the other related work she reviewed indicate that the problem of achievement motivation in women is more complex than simply calling it a function of the traditional sex-role orientation held by those women having a high motive to avoid success. There seems to be a complex relationship between the internal personality factors or motives and certain situational factors that determine both the expectancy a female has about the consequences of her actions and the value of these consequences to her in that situation.

Alper (1971) and Hoffman (1972b) disagree with some of Horner's conclusions. Alper's study represents an interesting attempt to extend Horner's work. She finds a similar percentage of Ss who showed the motive to avoid success. Alper reports that it is not success in general that women fear, but success in a culturally sex-inappropriate field. Alper's findings also suggest that parents *are* important antecedents to this motive in that "lows" experienced an egalitarian upbringing, including a nurturant father, while "highs" apparently were exposed to an authoritarian child-rearing pattern and a punitive, devaluing father.

In contrast to Horner, Hoffman (1972) notes that one of the factors that prevents a woman from reaching the peak of her intellectual potential is her high need for affiliation. A women is often more concerned with the establishing and maintaining rapport than in besting an opponent in an intellectual argument. Hoffman cites evidence from several studies which shows that even in preschool and early elementary grades little girls' achievement behavior is motivated by a desire for love rather than mastery. The author believes that these achievement patterns can be traced to early childhood learning experiences. While little boys are learning strategies for coping with their environment as well as developing feelings of self-confidence and independence, little girls are learning to be effective and safe through affiliative relationships. Little girls are more fearful of their environment and lack self-confidence in their ability to master it, and Hoffman believes that this is due to inadequate parental encouragement of little girls' early independence strivings. Another reason why little girls feel that their safety and effectiveness lie in their affiliative relationships is because the separation of the little girl's "self" from her mother is delayed or inadequate since she is the same sex as the mother and shares the same sex-role expectations. On the other hand, the little boy's awareness that the mother is a different person from himself and that her wishes are different from his increases the child's striving for independence and autonomy. Hoffman believes that the parent is likely to react with unambivalent pleasure to boys' first motoric endeavors, while these same attempts by the girl toddler are likely to produce anxiety feelings in the mother which are conveyed to the little girl and produce in her a sense of incompetence. Hoffman concludes that many girls experience too much protection and rapport with their mother, which results in an unwillingness or an inability to deal with stress as adults as well as a lack of motivation for autonomous achievement. While boys learn to be effective through mastery, girls learn to be effective by eliciting the help and protection of others. Finally, Hoffman suggests that women's affiliative needs may be due to feelings of incompetence and may therefore have a neurotic quality.

Regardless of whether a woman is motivated to fail or to succeed, and if the former, regardless of the source of the conflict that produced this internal motivational barrier, women also face external barriers that block achievement.

Women are discriminated against in admission to college and graduate school, in obtaining jobs, particularly high status ones, and in job advancement. Unfortunately, women as well as men are perpetrators of this discrimination. This discrimination, sometimes overt but usually covert, can only reinforce an existing motive to fail with its resultant lack of achievement. A vicious cycle begins. "Women don't achieve so let's not hire them or admit them unless they're exceptional." A woman who has difficulty being admitted or hired loves her aspiration. She wants approval and hesitates to effect entry into a field where she's not wanted. She too incorporates the sex-role stereotype that a woman belongs at home or should only work in female sex-typed occupations. Perhaps only the high achievement-motivated woman is able to overcome the external barriers.

Little research has been conducted specifically on job discrimination against black women, but Turner and Turner (1971) attempted to relate ethnic background of respondant to subjective perceptions of the occupational opportunity structure in American society. Black females perceived significantly more occupational discrimination against women than did white females. The authors attribute this finding to the fact that an occupational career is a realistic prospect for the black female, but not for the white female who has been socialized to expect her primary involvement to be her home and family. Thus, since the white female does not go through the "reality testing" with regard to employment that the black women does, she is less likely to make a realistic assessment of this situation.

Another study indicates that both women and blacks are discriminated against in admissions to college. Walster, Cleary, and Clifford (1971) sent applications for admission to a random sample of 240 colleges and universities in all parts of the United States. The applications were identical except for race and sex; there were three levels of ability among applicants: low, medium, and high. At the low ability level, there was a significant sex by ability interaction effect; males were preferred over females (both black and white). This effect disappeared at the higher levels. When all levels of ability were taken into account, the sex difference approached significance at the .05 level (p < 06). Since most students in the high school population were at the lowest ability level, this trend is not surprising. Only when a woman is exceptional is she judged objectively.

Contrary to the author's hypothesis, and despite the increase in college enrollment of blacks, the latter were not accepted more frequently than whites regardless of ability level. Black women were treated the same as white women.

In contrast to Walster et al.'s empirical study, Ekstrom (1972) presents a review paper that examines some of the problems women face in pursuing postsecondary education. One of these is the practice of refusing admittance to women in programs in "inappropriate" fields as well as the practice of setting a ceiling on the number of qualified women admitted while accepting men with lower qualifications. She points out that one argument that is used for limiting the number of women into Ph.D. programs is that they will marry, raise families, and never use their training, but Ekstrom refers to a study by Astin which showed that 9l percent of women Ph.D.s were employed. Another obstacle encountered is age restrictions on admittance to graduate schools. This affects women more than men because women usually drop their education to marry and raise a family. When the youngest child is in school, usually when the mother is about thirty-five years old, she may attempt to pursue her studies again but is refused admittance to graduate programs because she is considered too old. Sex biases also exist in the granting of scholarships, grants, etc. The only area where women receive more money than men is in loans. Women are often told that women students are not serious enough to receive loans or that they must be more qualified than men in order to receive financial aid. By requiring full-time attendence in college to be eligible for financial aid, married women again lose out because they are more likely than men to be part-time students since they are the ones responsible for taking care of the children and household tasks. Without financial aid many women find that the cost of tuition, books, and a sitter while they are in classes or in the library is prohibitive, and either postpone their education until they are older or give it up entirely.

Another barrier women encounter is that many schools require continuous enrollment and may not allow students to have a leave of absence for maternity or family emergencies. Women are also prejudiced against in the granting of teaching assistant-ships and hiring practices. Ekstrom quotes from the Berkeley study, which found that women are often told by department heads that they would be unable to get jobs in major universities. Ekstrom states that this often becomes a self-fulfilling prophecy when these same chairmen also refuse to hire women as members of the faculty. The attitudes of faculty and staff are further ob-stacles to the women's pursuit of postsecondary education. Ekstrom cites one study that relates how attempts were made by members of an architecture department to get women ar-chitectural students to switch into interior decorating, and another case of a woman graduate student who won an award as the best graduate student but was told by her department chairmen that he would not recommend her for a fellowship because of her sex. The lack of women faculty and administrators creates a shortage of role models for women considering academic careers, which results in another obstacle to women in their attempt to pursue higher education. In addition, many college counselors, both male and female, hold sex-role biases and make statements that reflect negative attitudes toward women entering male occupations. Family and society pressures often deter a women in her pursuit of postsecondary education. Ekstrom reports on a study by Mitchell which showed that only 7.3 percent of the women Ph.D.s in her study were actively encouraged in their educational goals by their husbands; the remaining husbands were either nonsupportive or neutral.

Another problem encountered by married women is the frequent moving around necessitated by their husbands' careers. Since many colleges make it very difficult if not impossible to receive credit for courses taken at another institution, many women find this an insurmountable obstacle and drop out of school altogether. The attitudes of family and friends who disapprove of a woman going on for graduate studies because it is not considered traditional behavior for a woman, as well as the demands of society that a women should be engaged in volunteer or other work beneficial to the community, create psychological barriers to a women in postsecondary education. The author points out that the woman wishing to pursue higher education often finds herself required to fill a greater number of roles than her male counterpart does. She quotes one female Ph.D. who said that the emotional strain caused by trying to excel in the role of student, mother, wife, and community worker is almost unbelieveable, a task that only the exceptional survive. The woman's own attitudes, motivation, and personality variables are often factors that prevent her from pursuing higher education. Ekstrom notes that in high school women students are rewarded for being passive, dependent, and avoiding conflict while in college aggressiveness, competitiveness, and independence are rewarded. Thus, she says, a woman is constantly battling between the old behaviors and the new. Ekstrom notes that the socialization process women receive encourage them to develop personalities that are at odds with those characteristics needed for obtaining a higher education. In addition, women are taught that they are intellectually inferior to men.

When females attempt to become part of the "man's world of work," their sex also presents an obstacle.

Epstein (1969) points out that women have difficulty entering various professional fields, particularly those sex-typed as male. She cites census figures that indicate that despite the great increase of women in the work force, the percentage of women in many fields has remained approximately the same. In medicine for example, women constituted 6.8 percent of all physicians in 1960. This was not very different from the 6.0 percent of 1910. In some fields the percentage of women has even decreased. Thus, the percentage of women college faculty members has shown a steady decline from 32% in 1930 to 19 percent in 1960—right back to the 1910 level.

Even when women do enter male-dominated fields, they still run into barriers that exclude them from the highest levels. They are not accepted as protégées and are excluded from the colleague system. This exclusion from entry into top-level positions affects woman's salary, her activity, and her autonomy. Women in turn confirm this image of a lack of female ability by limiting their contributions and interactions with others on the job. They are afraid of encountering rebuffs. Women go still further in incorporating the standards of their professions by favoring exclusion of other women.

Many of these same points were noted by White (1970), who limited her discussion to the external barriers faced by women in the sciences.

Fidell (1971) carried out an empirical study that supported the reports of Epstein and White. Fidell found that women are discriminated against on the basis of their sex when applying for positions within the field of academic psychology. Identical resumes with either a male or female name attached were sent to

643

numerous chairmen of psychology departments. Each chairman received ten resumes and were asked to indicate the desirability of each candidate as well as the likely rank at which each would be hired. Obtensibly they were helping San Fernando Valley State College (Fidell's school) in a long-range study of the careers of recent Ph.D.s. Either a male or female name was inserted in a particular resume among those given to each chairmen.

The response rate was high. Despite psychologists' contention that they look at data objectively, the male applicants were consistently rated higher and placed at higher academic ranks than were identically described females. Fidell presents evidence for covert discrimination in academic hiring.

Many people claim that external barriers are justified. They state that it is more important for a man to have the high-level job since he will not leave the work force for marriage or pregnancy. They also feel that a woman's working will have negative effects on her children.

A woman may leave the work force temporarily upon the birth of a child, but pregnancy leaves built into the job situation help ensure her return. Absentee rates are low for married women.

Lois Hoffman explores the effects of the professional woman's work on her children (1972a). She states that there is considerable evidence to support the idea that maternal employment has positive effects, particularly on girls. The results of several studies indicate that the adolescent daughters of working mothers have been found to be active, autonomous girls who admire their mothers but are not unusually close to them. Hoffman says that for girls of all ages, maternal employment contributes to a concept of the female role which includes a wider range of activities, fewer restrictions, and a self-concept that incorporates these aspects of the female role. The optimum conditions for a highly achieving female includes the presence of an affirmative role model, independence training, and finally a good relationship with a father who encourages his daughter to be independent and highly achieving while accepting her as a female.

Hoffman asserts that these conditions are more likely to be found in the family that includes a professional mother. She supports her assertion by citing evidence from several studies. One study by Birnbaum shows that professional mothers expressed pleasure over their children's movement toward independence but the nonworking mother was disturbed over her child's independence strivings. The nonworking mother probably felt her own importance diminish along with the child's reduced need for her. The nonworking mother also seemed to be unduly concerned over her children's health and safety, which also suggests that she is overprotective.

There is data to support the contention that husbands of working women are likely to be more encouraging and supportive of their daughters. Evidence from many studies shows that husbands of working women are more actively involved in the care of children; results from other studies show that the father's active involvement in the care of his child has a positive effect on the child regardless of sex.

Hoffman cites evidence that shows that women who do well in college but do not pursue a career seek vicarious satisfaction through the achievement of their children. About fifteen years after graduation from college, these women experience a rise in their achievement need; they have low self-esteem and tend to be easily depressed; they are concerned about their competence, especially their competence as a mother.

Hoffman says that on the whole, existing data show that professional women have done quite well as mothers. But she suggests that this may be because they experienced guilt feelings about having a career, which led them to make compensatory responses that had a positive effect on their children's development. However, she also points out that many professional women have reduced their work load when their children are young, and that this might be one of the reasons why maternal employment does not have an adverse effect on the child's development.

Thus, if the mother overcomes internal and external barriers to achieve on the job, high achievement is also fostered in her daughters. Overcoming external barriers may lead to high need for achievement for females in the following generation.

It is fruitless to argue whether internal or external barriers produce the greatest havoc in terms of female achievement. They feed on each other and both must be surmounted.

REFERENCES

Alper, T. G. Achievement motivation in college women. Paper presented at the meeting of the Eastern Psychological Association, New York, April 1971.

Baruch, R. The achievement motive in women: Implications for career development. *Journal of Personality and Social Psychology,* 1967, *5,* 260-67.

Blumen-Lipman, J. How ideology shapes women's lives. *Scientific American,* 1972, *226,* 34-42.

Crandall, V. C. Sex differences in expectancy of intellectual and academic reinforcement. In C. P. Smith (Ed.), *Achievement-related motives.* New York: Russell Sage Foundation, 1969.

Crandall, V. J., Katkovsky, W., and Preston, A. A conceptual formulation of some research on children's achievement. *Child Development,* 1960, *31,* 784-97.

————, ————, and ————. Motivation and ability determinants of young children's intellectual achievement behaviors. *Child Development,* 1962, *33,* 643-61.

————, Dewey, R.; Katkovsky, W.; and Preston, A. Parents' attitudes and behaviors and grade-school children's academic achievement. *Journal of Genetic Psychology,* 1964, *104,* 53-66.

Ekstrom, R. B. Barriers to women's participation in post-secondary education: A review of the literature. In S. Ball and P. Cross, *Barriers to women's continuing education,* symposium presented at the meeting of the American Psychological Association, Honolulu, September 1972.

Epstein, C. F. Encountering the male establishment: Sex-status limits on women's careers in the professions. *American Journal of Sociology,* 1969, *75,* 1094-98.

Fidell, L. S. Empirical verification of sex discrimination in hiring practices in psychology. *American Psychologist,* 1971, *25,* 1094-98.

French, G., and Lesser, G. S. Some characteristics of the achievement motive in women. *Journal of Abnormal and Social Psychology,* 1964, *68,* 119-28.

Hoffman, L. W. The professional woman as mother. *Successful women in the sciences,* symposium presented at the New York Academy of Sciences, New York, May 1972 (a).

————. Early childhood experiences and women's achievement motives. *Journal of Social Issues,* 1972, *28,* 129-55 (b).

Horner, M. Fail: Bright women. *Psychology Today,* November 1969, *3,* (6), 36ff.

————. Toward an understanding of achievement related conflicts in women. *Journal of Social Issues.* 1972, *28,* 157-74.

Lesser, G. S.; Krawitz, R. N.; and Packard, R. Experimental arousal of achievement motivation in adolescent girls. *Journal of Abnormal and Social Psychology,* 1963 *66,* 59-66.

McClelland, D. C.; Atkinson, J. W.; Clark, R. A.; and Lowell, E. L. *The achievement motive.* New York: Appleton-Century-Crofts, 1953.

Turner, C. B., and Turner, B. F. Perception of the occupational opportunity structure, socialization to achievement, and career orientation as related to sex and race. *Proceedings of the American Psychological Association,* Washington, D.C., 1971, *6.*

Turner, R. H. Some aspects of women's ambition. *American Journal of Sociology,* 1964, *70,* 271-85.

Veroff, J., Wilcox, S., and Atkinson, J. W. The achievement motive in high school and college age women. *Journal of Abnormal and Social Psychology,* 1953, *43,* 108-119.

Walster, E., Cleary, T., and Clifford, M. M. The effect of race and sex on college admission. Paper presented at the meeting of the Eastern Psychological Association, New York, April 1971.

White, M. S. Psychological and social barriers to women in science. *Science,* 1970, *170,* 413-16.

40

Crandall's paper is an attempt to correlate students' expectancy of intellectual achievement with previous reinforcement. It includes a number of studies using various types of intellectual problems as well as a wide range of age groups. Although task and age group varied, the results were basically the same: the females did not approach new intellectual tasks with as much confidence as the males, even though their past intellectual performance had been better. For example, students at Antioch College indicated prior to each registration period the grades they expected to receive that semester. At the end of their academic careers, SS' expectancies were compared with their actual grades. Males' expectancies were significantly higher than the females'. The females continually estimated their future academic performance lower than their past grades would warrant, whereas the males continued to estimate higher than their previous grades.

Another study revealed that when both male and female Ss received some cues that told them that they were capable and others that told them that they were not, the females focused on the negative aspects and the males on the positive.

Some interesting questions are generated by this paper. Why should elementary school girls, who traditionally receive higher grades than boys and who presumably also receive positive reinforcement for intellectual achievement during that age period, underestimate their ability and lack the confidence of boys in approaching new intellectual tasks? Findings would suggest that men are either undefeatable optimists or else must feel terribly frustrated when they discover that they have less ability than they had assumed. Does this contribute to the higher levels of aggression found in males?

This is a well-written, provocative study; the results hang together. It is related to other research in this area concerned with internal barriers to achievement.

Sex Differences in Expectancy of Intellectual and Academic Reinforcement

Virginia C. Crandall

Much research in achievement motivation or achievement behavior is carried out under theoretical systems which are basically expectancy X value formulations. While various investigators have found a number of additional constructs helpful in increasing prediction, expectancy and value remain central in their theoretical models. Because of this, it is imperative that we delineate the relationships of each of the two fundamental constructs to antecedent and response variables, not only to validate the utility of these intervening variables, but also to understand better how they develop and how they affect behavior. The series of studies to be described here deals with one of the major variables, expectancy of reinforcement, and specifically with sex differences in expectancy estimates. Obviously, a status variable like sex does not in itself explain the dynamic processes that determine the formation of expectancies. Nevertheless, if we can establish that a difference in expectancy is consistently associated with the subject's sex, perhaps this phenomenon will suggest hypotheses about differences in the processes which determine expectancies that might come about because of the individual's history as a member of that sex. Our aims, then, in the studies to follow, are first, to demonstrate the consistency of differences in expectancy estimates between males and females, and second, to describe some beginning probes into the possible determinants of this difference.

THE DEFINITION OF EXPECTANCY

There are many disparate experimental paradigms and measures which have been used for the study of expectancy, and from these dissimilar operations it is apparent that the concept of expectancy has been defined in a variety of ways. In addition, several symbols and terms have been used to label what seem to be the same kind of expectancy. In order that the reader will better understand that form of expectancy with which we are concerned in the studies to follow, I will distinguish among three uses of the construct.

1. *Expectancy: the nature of the reinforcement available in a given situation.* This form of expectancy is synonymous with the individual's perception of the *kind* of reinforcement which he sees as likely to ensue from his behavior in a particular situation. For example, when one individual sits down at a bridge table, he may perceive that this situation provides an opportunity to demonstrate his card-playing *skill*; that is, the situation, as he sees it, provides reinforcements for achievement. Another individual, on the other hand, may structure the situation as primarily an affiliative one; he may be smiled at, spoken to, laughed with, and can exchange news and gossip. When the individual has generalized such an expectancy *across* situations, carries it with him, and "reads into" a variety of circumstances the expectation that they contain reinforcements relevant to a given need, Veroff[1] has labeled this a "disposition expectancy." As he says, "Such an expectancy about achievement would be the expectancy to see achievement possibilities in any ambiguous situation. The stronger the expectancy, the more likely the person is to see achievement in *any* setting." This form of expectancy, then, deals with the degree to which the individual perceives that reinforcements for a given need are available in a given situation. The reward or punishment value of that reinforcement is not the issue here. To use the first bridge player again as an example, this form of expectancy does not deal with whether he expects to win or lose; it deals with the strength of his certainty that card-playing skill is the issue.

2. *Expectancy: the agent responsible for the occurrence of an outcome event.* This is the individual's expectation that his own behavior is or is not responsible for an outcome event. For example, in most probability learning studies, where the subject predicts whether a particular light will occur on the next trial or whether a card of a particular suit will turn up, expectancy estimates are being given for an event that he does not produce and whose occurrence he cannot control. This is in contradistinction to expectancy measures taken in situations where the outcome event is *contingent* upon the subject's instrumental behavior. This latter is the kind of event that the subject is predicting in most achievement tasks, for such tasks are usually presented in such a way that the outcome is perceived by the subject as dependent on his own skill. When the laboratory or life situation

1. J. Veroff, "Assessment of Motives Through Fantasy" (Paper given at Midwestern Psychological Association, 1961); and "Theoretical Background for Studying the Origins of Human Motivational Dispositions," *Merrill-Palmer Quarterly,* 11 (1965), 3-18

is somewhat ambiguous, however, then individuals may vary in the degree to which they feel that their own behavior causes the

3. *Expectancy: the ability to obtain a specific reinforcement or class of reinforcements.* This form of expectancy is relative to the subject's perception of his own skill. It is the height of the probability held by the individual that his instrumental behavior will be adequate to obtain a single, specified reinforcement, or alternatively, the level of reinforcement on a single continuum which he predicts his behavior is able to elicit. That is, we can ask a subject what the odds are, or how certain he is that he is able to get 100 per cent (or any other given score) on a task, or we can ask him what score from 1 to 100 he expects to get. This is the form of expectancy which Atkinson and others[2] refer to as "subjective probability of success" (P_s) and it is this kind of expectancy with which we are dealing in the studies to follow. It will be noted that this kind of expectancy already assumes some positive value of the preceding two forms of expectancy. For example, in work in achievement the task characteristics, the instructions presented, or some other cues in the situation have already made it clear to the subject that *he* must perform some instrumental act in order to obtain the reinforcement and that the reinforcements which are available to him are those for achievement, that is, they are being given for the competence of his performance. The question remaining is "How good will that instrumental act be? How skilled am I in the behavior necessary to acquire that kind of rein-forcement?" If I am unskilled, I will estimate that the odds are poor that I can get a score of 100 per cent, and/or I will predict that I can only get a particular score of $100-x$.

It is readily apparent that such expectations will depend on the kinds of skills involved. While it is possible to ask a subject "How good are you at doing *things*?" it is likely that he will find it hard to answer such a question, and will respond with something like, "Well, that all depends on what sort of 'things' you mean." In other words, he finds it difficult to generalize over varying skill areas. For example, one's expectancy of reinforcement might be high in activities requiring intellectual skill, but low in those dependent upon athletic prowess, or vice versa. And even within those areas, one might expect to do well in basketball but poorly at swimming, well at handling abstract ideas or logic but poorly in tasks requiring memory.

---

2. J. W. Atkinson, "Motivational Determinants of Risk-Taking Behavior." *Psychological Review, 64* (1957), 359-372; J. W. Atkinson *et al.,* "The Achievement Motive. Goal Setting, and Probability Prefe-rences," *Journal of Abnormal and Social Psychology, 60,*(1960), 27-36.

Virginia C. Crandall

THE PREDICTION OF BEHAVIOR FROM EXPECTANCY

Although most investigators of achievement behavior use multidimensional theories, it is sometimes useful to examine the predictive utility of each single component variable. Since the work to be described below is based on a theoretical model which is primarily (though with modifications and additions) an expectancy X value formulation, it is necessary to hold value relatively constant in order to examine the relationship of expectancy to behavior. In order to do this an achievement area has been chosen where it might be said, at least broadly, that most subjects hold some positive value for that sort of achievement reinforcement. In today's culture, which puts so much emphasis on academic and intellectual achievement, perhaps it is safe to assume that being bright and getting good grades have a positive valence for most children. Given, then, that these constitute desirable goals, we would predict that the child who holds a strong expectancy that his effort is capable of producing good grades in school, or a good score on an intellectual task or a game requiring intellectual skill — this child should spend more time and effort in studying and in related intellectual and academic activities than should the child who does not expect to be able to attain the rewards. On the other hand, for the child who holds a low expectancy of reinforcement, it may seem useless to persist in attempts to reach the goal even though he may value it, because he does not feel that it is possible for him to obtain those reinforcements. The approach behaviors of the low expectancy child, then, should be more limited than those of the child with high expectancy.

This hypothesis has been tested. Forty children (20 males and 20 females, ages 7, 8 and 9) were given an expectancy measure in the laboratory. [3] Each child was shown a sequence of eight mazes which became increasingly more complex. He was told that the maze at the one end was so easy that "Most children your age can easily do this one," and the last maze was described as so difficult that "Very few children your age are able to do this one." He was also told that he was about to be tested on this task and, starting from the easiest level, he was asked to indicate which mazes he would be able to do. A similar procedure was followed with a task that required that he remember and recall groups of toy objects after each group was uncovered for only three seconds. The

---

3. V. J. Crandall, W. Katkovsky, and A. Preston, "Motivational and Ability Determinants of Young Children's Intellectual Achievement Behaviors," *Child Development, 33* (1962), 643-661.

number of toy objects in each group increased over the eight levels of the task. For both procedures, the stimuli at each end of the range were exposed, but all remaining stimuli were covered. This was done in order that the subject could not rehearse the solutions or give a specific expectancy for a particular maze or group of objects to remember. Thus, he was made to generalize his estimate of his skill on mazes and memory-for-objects from past rein-forcements in tasks or situations that he perceived as requiring similar kinds of intellectual abilities. The highest level in the sequence at which the subject estimated he would be able to perform in each of the two tasks was averaged and considered an index of his generalized expectancy for intellectual reinforcement, for these tasks require intellectual skills, rather than artistic skill, or athletic skill, or some other.

The children were then put in an unstructured, free-play situation, and observers recorded the amount of time they chose to spend with intellectual puzzles, quiz games, reading materials, flash cards, checkers, chess, etc. They also observed and rated the intensity of concentration and effort the children displayed while they were engaging in those intellectual activities. The observers were specifically instructed to disregard the competence or quality of the child's products or performance so that the ratings would reflect only *goal-approach* behaviors. In accordance with the hypothesis, it was predicted that children who expected to be highly successful on those intellectual tasks should evidence more of these approach behaviors toward intellectual goals than should children who expected to be less successful.[4]

4. Skills and abilities, per se, do not seem relevant to such behavioral measures as persistence, choice of task, intensity of striving, effort expended, etc., for these behaviors would seem to be determined by motivational factors. That is, for example, it seems most logical that it is not skill itself, but the child's *perception* of his skill, that will dictate whether or not he will choose the task, persist in his attempts to obtain reward, and work diligently toward that end. His perception of his ability may or may not be congruent with that ability. It is our con-ception that skill or ability itself does not constitute a dynamic, ac-tivating variable, but lies dormant or latent until and unless the subject is motivated to approach the goal. Even though measures of ability may *statistically* relate to goal-approach behaviors, they do not explain the dynamic processes through which that approach is made to occur. Thus, actual abilities, even if it were possible to obtain pure measures of them, would not seem to be theoretically appropriate predictors. When, on the other hand, one is predicting *competence* of per-formance or excellence of product, then it would seem that both level of skill and motivational factors might be considered to attain finer prediction. For example, correct solution of a Chinese puzzle would depend upon spatial relations skills, in addition to the factors motivating the child to attempt to solve it. In a study of E. Battle ("Motivational Determinants of Academic Competence," *Journal of Personality and Social Psychology*, 4 [1966], 634-642) in which report-card grades were used as a "product" measure, it was found, as

The girls' expectancy estimates did not bear a significant relationship to the approach behaviors. For the boys, however, the expectancy estimates predicted both the intensity of their efforts in the intellectual activities as well as the amount of time they chose to spend in them $(r = 5.58$ and $.40, p < .01$ and $.05$ respectively).

In another study done in our laboratory, Battle[5] used 74 older children at the junior high school level, and found that *both* boys' and girls' expectations in mathematics predicted the amount of time they would persist in an attempt to solve a difficult math "magic square" problem. The correlation for boys was .52 and for girls .38 (both $p <01$). For both sexes this time, height of expectancy had predicted the amount of goal-approach behavior that occurred.

Feather,[6] too, found that college-age subjects in general, who had high initial expectations of success on a difficult perceptual reasoning problem, persisted significantly longer in an attempt to solve it than did those subjects who had low initial expectancies.

A second motivational function of expectancy may lie in its more immediate effects in a present performance situation. For example, Tyler[7] has demonstrated that randomly selected subjects who were *given* a high expectancy of success (through "encouraging" remarks from the examiner during pretest trials) more frequently reached the correct solution of a novel pattern-learning problem than did those subjects who were given a low expectancy (through "discouraging" remarks). In addition, it was found that significantly more subjects in the low expectancy group than in the high expectancy group attempted to give the proper series of responses by rote memorization, rather than attempting to conceptualize the logical steps involved in the solution of the problem.

would be expected, that children who were above the mean on both IQ and expectancy earned higher grades than those who were low on both measures. Nevertheless, those subjects who had low IQ but high expectancy had significantly higher grades than those who had high IQ but low expectancy. Thus, even with a competence measure, expectancy of reinforcement was a more powerful determinant of that performance than was ability when the two factors were in opposition.

5. E. Battle, "Motivational Determinants of Academic Task Persistence," *Journal of Personality and Social Psychology,* 2 (1965), 209-218.

6. N. T. Feather, "Persistence at a Difficult Task with Alternative Task of Intermediate Difficulty," *Journal of Abnormal and Social Psychology,* 66 (1963), 604-609.

7. B. B. Tyler, "Expectancy for Eventual Success as a Factor in Problem Solving Behavior," *Journal of Educational Psychology,* 49 (1958), 166-172.

Feather [8] also found that subjects in whom a high expectancy was induced with previous success trials were able to perform better on a subsequent anagrams task than those who were given a low expectancy with previous failure trials. It seems reasonable to assume that confidence in one's ability to perform well in the achievement task at hand may facilitate the maximum discrimination, abstraction, integration, recognition, and other cognitive processes that are necessary for correct problem solution, whether it is working on an experimental task, playing a competitive game, doing an assignment, writing a test, working a problem on the blackboard, reciting in class, or whatever. When, on the other hand, the child's expectancy is low, it may serve a debilitating function and prevent optimum cognitive performance, especially under test pressure or in situations where his intellectual product is open to public assessment. I am proposing, then, that low expectancy of reinforcement in a valued-goal area may underlie test anxiety, but this has yet to be established empirically.

Whether or not low expectancy actually calls forth the affective response of anxiety, however, we would expect it to function to depress performance. It may simply be that the low expectancy child decides, quite reasonably and without anxiety, that it is useless to try and he is wasting his time.

It then seemed reasonable to us that the greater approach behaviors of high expectancy children should result in the acquisition of more information and better problem-solving skills. These, in turn, should be reflected in higher grades and achievement test socres. Thus, expectancy measures should predict such measures of academic competence, but in a "derivative" fashion, that is, via the more extensive academic effort which is associated with a higher expectancy.

The expectancy is, in fact, related to final academic competence has been demonstrated by others as well as ourselves. The report on "Equality of Educational Opportunity" [9] is a good example. Embedded in a more extensive questionnaire were three questions asking the child how bright he thought he was in comparison with other students, whether he sometimes felt he was unable to learn, and whether the teachers presented the material too fast for him. While Coleman *et al.* apply the term "self-concept" to the responses from these three items, it is not difficult to infer also that

8. N. T. Feather, "Effects of Prior Success and Failure on Expectations of Success and Subsequent Performance," *Journal of Personality and Social Psychology*, 3 (1966), 287-298.

9. J. S. Coleman *et al.*, *Equality of Educational Opportunity* (Superintendent of Documents, Catalog No. FS 5: 238: 38001 [Washington, D.C.: Government Printing Office, 1966]).

this measure reflects the child's expectancy of reinforcement in intellectual-academic situations. In fact, these authors state, "If a child's self-concept is low, if he feels he cannot succeed, then this will affect the effort he puts into the task and thus, his chance of success."[10] Results from this nationwide study of aproximately a million children in 6th, 9th, and 12th grades indicate that this variable was more predictive of school achievement among white students than any of the thirty or so other attitudinal, demographic, and situational variables studied. Among non-white students it was the second most-predictive measure.

The prediction of academic competence from expectancy is demonstrated in Figures 1 and 2. These figures are based upon results from six different studies from our own project. Actually these several studies had been aimed primarily at the investigation of other issues. The original focus of each of the studies dictated the particular sample used and the exact nature of the task upon which the subjects made their expectancy estimates. Nevertheless, in each case, the subjects had given some sort of intellectual or academic expectancy and we obtained the students' academic

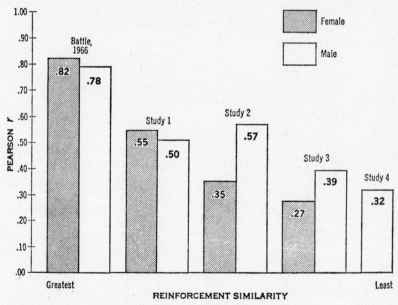

Figure 1. Prediction of report-card grades from expectancy estimates as a function of degree of similarity between reinforcements on which expectancy estimates were based and grades.

---

10. *Ibid.*, 281.

grades and current achievement test scores (where they were available). The sample sizes range from 70 to 256 in these studies and all of the correlations are significant with *p* values (two-tailed) of at least .01 or better.

Figure 1 presents the correlations of various kinds of intellectual or academic expectancy estimates with *report-card grades*. The bars representing the correlations have been arranged along a dimension representing the degree of similarity of the reinforcements on which the expectancy estimate was based, to the reinforcements represented in report-card grades. That is, it would be expected that prediction of a given grade should be strongest if the subject has been asked to give a specific expectancy based on past feedback in that particular course, next most strong if he is basing his estimate on past academic work in other courses, next if he is asked about his intellectual capability, least if he is giving his expectancy relative to another skill area. Another way of saying it might be that when the task characteristics or the instructions for the expectancy measure cause the subject to focus on less relevant past reinforcements, prediction should be reduced to the degree that those past reinforcements are decreasingly relevant. In such a case the measured expectancies require increasingly greater generalization to the reinforcements represented in final course

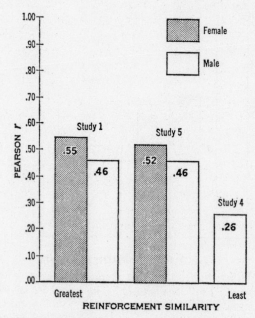

Figure 2. *Prediction of achievement test scores from expectancy estimates as a function of degree of similarity between reinforcements on which expectancy estimates were based and achievement test scores.*

grades and may be presumed to be less commensurate with the specific academic expectancy which determines the individual's approach behavior toward that academic goal. A brief description of the expectancy measures used in these studies follows:

In the *Battle study*[11] junior high students gave separate estimates in early spring of the grades in math and English they thought they would receive at the end of the year. The bars represent the average (computed from z to r transformations) of the correlation of English expectancy to final English grade and of math expectancy to final math grade.

In *Study 1,* 12th grade high school students were asked for their estimates of their "true or native ability" in math, English, social science, and physical science. In this case we might assume that the subjects were giving us an estimate of what might be called their aptitude for each discipline, probably based primarily on grades received in past courses in that discipline, but also on reinforcements in other situations requiring the skills of that subject-matter area. Each of these estimates was correlated with the grade the student received in the course he was currently taking in that discipline. Again the average of the correlations (using z to r transformations) is represented in the bars.

In *Study 2,* the expectancy statements were made by college students at the beginning of an Introductory Psychology course. They were asked to estimate the final grade they anticipated receiving in the course, and these estimates were correlated with the grade they actually did receive. Since this was their first course in a new field, expectancies at the beginning of the course would have to be generalized from broader referents, perhaps primarily previous reinforcements of a general academic nature.

In *Study 3,* the estimates were given for a novel digit-symbol substitution task. These subjects were 8th graders and the examiner gave them an intellectual set for the task by telling them this was a type of task found in many intelligence tests. Here, in order for prediction to have occurred, we have broadened even further the demand for generality to those reinforcements that the subject conceives of as any indexes of his "brightness." These estimates were related to the average of grades received on the next report card.

In *Study 4,* 8th grade male subjects gave estimates for a novel angle-matching task. (There were no female subjects in this study.) Of course, it would not be expected that a very strong relationship would be found here, since this angle-matching task, with no intellectual set given for it, probably did not appear to be a matter of academic or intellectual skill, but of perceptual skill. In fact, the

---

11. Motivational Determinants of "Competence."

subjects were told "This is a test to see how well you can match up figures." It has been added to Figure 1 simply to demonstrate that there is still *some* generality of expectancies even from this remote skill area in order for any prediction to grades to have occurred at all.

Figure 2 presents correlations of the same expectancy estimates with *standardized achievement test scores* in those schools where current test scores were available to us (Studies 1 and 4 above).

Study 5 does not appear in Figure 1 because we had only achievement test scores for this sample. These were 9th grade students who were asked to make estimates on the same angle-matching task used in Study 4 above, with the exception that these subjects were helped to attain an intellectual set by explaining to them that this sort of task is often found on intelligence tests. We substantiated this assertion by showing them briefly the spatial relations section (Section 7) of the California Test of Mental Maturity.

As the reader can see, these correlations with achievement test scores do not run quite as high as those with grades.

If the correlations for Study 4 are omitted because the angle-matching task with no intellectual set appeared to have little connection with academic-intellectual reinforcements, the correlations from the remaining studies average .53 with grades and .50 with achievement test scores (*z* to *r* transformations). As the figures demonstrate, correlations are sometimes a bit higher for one sex, sometimes for the other, but height of expectancy on novel intellectual tasks or for future grades before they are earned, does predict those future grades at approximately equal levels for both sexes.

STUDIES DEMONSTRATING SEX DIFFERENCES IN EXPECTANCY

In view of the fact that expectancy does seem to facilitate approach behaviors,[12] it is important to note that girls' expectancy estimates are consistently lower than boys'. The following studies demonstrate these sex differences and are a beginning attempt to elucidate some of the reasons for such differences.

Study A

A group of the elementary school-age children (aged 7 years 2

---

12. Battle, "Motivational Determinants of Persistence"; Crandall *et al.*,

months—12 years 2 months) in the Fels longitudinal sample, 17 boys and 24 girls, were given six different kinds of intellectual tasks from which expectancy estimates were obtained. It was thought that an average expectancy derived from six tasks should yield a reliable measure of the child's general intellectual expectancy. Stimuli for all tasks were especailly constructed in our laboratory. Each of the six tasks was presented to the subject in eight levels of graduated difficulty as in the procedure used by Crandall et al.[13] As before, the child was told he would be tested subsequently on the tasks. The most difficult level at which he predicted he would be able to perform constituted his expectancy estimate for that task. The tasks were:

1. *Estimating blocks.* Estimating the number of blocks in irregularly shaped constructions of greater and greater size and complexity, after each construction was uncovered for only ten seconds.

2. *Logical relations.* Solving easy to difficult "brain teasers."

3. *Spatial relations.* Constructing increasingly difficult jigsaw puzzles of *solid* colors.

4. *Numerical skill.* Solving easy to difficult addition problems without the aid of writing materials.

5. *Memory for objects.* Naming all toys in a group after seeing stimuli for ten seconds (from three objects, easiest, to twelve objects, hardest).

6. *Mazes.* Increasingly difficult.

Since all tasks were similarly presented in eight levels of difficulty, expectancy estimates were summed over all six tasks for each subject and the average of his six estimates was calculated. The mean of the males' average expectancies was 6.3 ($SD = 0.64$) and the females' mean was 5.6 ($SD = 0.76$). The t between these means is 3.04, $p < .01$, two-tailed. (In fact, girls' mean estimates were lower than boys' for each individual task.) The females, then, approached these new intellectual tasks with a significantly lower assessment of their intellectual skills than the males.

Was there any reason to believe that the males' estimates should realistically be higher? Perhaps the boys' past histories of intellectual reinforcement had been more positive in nature, resulting in a realistic expectancy that they would be able to perform very well on the new tasks presented to them here. Since these were *novel* intellectual tasks, it is obvious that the child could have had no reinforcement history on these particular tasks which he could

"Motivational and Ability Determinants"; Feather, "Effects of Prior Success"; Tyler, "Expectancy for Eventual Success."

13. Crandall et al., "Motivational and Ability Determinants."

use to form his current expectancy for his own performance. For this reason, it would have been necessary for him to use some generalization of the level of reinforcement he had received in other past intellectual situations.[14] Thus, intelligence test scores were used as an index of the adequacy of his performance in such past situations. If the child had received reinforcement at a level fairly commensurate with that adequacy, then it seemed logical that he would have derived an expectancy for success in current intellectual task situations approximately equivalent to his IQ level.

Because male subjects had higher expectancy estimates we would anticipate that their IQ scores would also be higher. Analysis of the IQ scores, however, proved otherwise. The subjects' most recent Stanford-Binet scores from the Fels files yielded a mean for the males of 107 ($SD = 11.7$) while the females' mean was 114 ($SD = 15.7$). The t between these means was *not* significant. Thus, even though the girls' IQ was slightly, though nonsignificantly, higher than the boys', their intellectual expectancies were significantly lower than the boys'. It seemed, then, that children of the two sexes had used their similar past feedback very differently in forming their expectancies.

To investigate this issue in a more precise manner, a single difference score was needed. Since expectancy scores and IQ scores could not be compared directly, it seemed most appropriate to make the comparison between the individual's relative position on the one dimension and his relative position on the other. Thus, the scores for all subjects were combined for each measure and transformed into standard z scores. The IQ z score was then subtracted from the expectancy z score to yield a discrepancy (D) score for each individual. If IQ level and level of expectancy had indeed been commensurate, then each subject's discrepancy score would have resulted in a value of zero. As can be seen in Figure 3, however, where males' and females' D scores are presented separately, most of the males have higher z scores on the expectancy distribution than on the IQ distribution ($+Ds$) while the reverse obtained for females (-Ds).

Of the 17 boys in the group, 13 had positive D scores, one had a D score of 0 and only 3 had negative D scores. The converse was true for the girls. Seventeen of the 24 girls had negative D scores

---

14. The expectancy tasks used here had been intentionally designed to be novel to the child, since a large proportion of the intellectual tasks and situations he ordinarily meets are, by virtue of his inexperience, new to him. When the individual is confronted with tasks that are unfamiliar to him he is compelled to use his previous successes and failures on tasks that he perceives as most nearly relevant to the particular task at hand in order to predict his probable success in the current task. It seemed important to attempt to investigate the origins of such current

and only 7 of them had positive *Ds*. The chi square for these data is significant (10.42, $p < .01$). Thus, the two sexes made estimates in opposite directions. The girls did not approach these new intellectual tasks with as confident expectancies of reinforcement as did the boys, even though their past intellectual performance had been similar. As indicated in Figure 3 the boys' mean discrepancy score was $+ .80$ ($SD = 1.05$); the girls' mean was $- .56$ ($SD = 1.44$). Because of their opposite directions, those means were significantly different *from one another* ($t = 3.24$, $p .005$). When the signs were removed from the *D* scores, however, the absolute amount of discrepancy from the zero value previously suggested was about equal for the two sexes ($t = 0.39$, *n.s.*).

As a beginning, the following three determinants were considered as possibilities which might account for these distortions in estimate:

1. Perhaps the child's *verbal report was a nonveridical statement* of his or her internally held expectancy. It might be that his verbal expectancy estimate had been distorted by some factor which, in this context, could be considered a response set since it influences the verbal estimates over and above the internally felt expectations that are assumed to determine approach behaviors.

(a) One such influence might be that the child was *responding to some sort of perceived cultural demand*. Perhaps the girls felt that the examiner would approve of them if they were modest about their intellectual skills, while the boys felt that they should appear confident and upward striving.

(b) Another influence upon estimates might be the *value the child holds for intellectual-academic reinforcements*. It may be that the more the child values intellectual reinforcements, that is, the more he *wants* to do well on intellectual and academic tasks, the more his verbal estimate might be wishfully pulled upward. Previous theory and empirical findings are contradictory on this issue. A negative relationship between value and expectancy has been proposed or found by some investigators[15] and a positive relationship by others.[16] Some theories propose that the two

---

task expectancies because it has been empirically demonstrated at several age levels that such expectancies are consistently predictive of current approach behaviors and competence of performance.

15. S. K. Escalona, "The Effect of Success and Failure upon the Level of Aspiration and Behavior in Manic-Depressive Psychoses," *University of Iowa Study of Child Welfare*, 16 (1940), 199-302; L. Worell, "The Effect of Goal Value upon Expectancy," *Journal of Abnormal and Social Psychology*, 53 (1956), 48-53.

16. F. W. Irwin, "Stated Expectations as Functions of Probability and Desirability of Outcomes," *Journal of Personality*, 21 (1953), 329-335;

variables are independent of one another,[17] while still other investigators have found the two variables related only under certain special circumstances.[18] ATkinson[19] proposes that expectancy and value are generally independent, but negatively related in achievement tasks. However, the studies testing these propositions have differed significantly from one another in design, the nature of the samples used, the form of expectancy measured, and/or the task characteristics. Thus, comparisons cannot be made and the present issue remains unresolved.

2. There is also the possibility that these expectations are not simply distorted verbal responses but that males and females actually form different internal expectations. It may be that these differences are the result of *different reinforcement histories* for the two sexes. While it does not seem likely, there is the possibility that males and females have actually received differential feedback from reinforcing agents even when their performances has been equivalent. Since Crandall,[20] Crandall, Good and Crandall,[21]

R. Jessor and J. Readio, "The Influence of the Value of an Event upon the Expectancy for Its Occurrence," *Journal of General Psychology,* 56 [1957], 219-228 K. MacCorquodale and P. Meehl, "Preliminary Suggestions as to a Formalization of Expectancy Theory," *Psychological Review,* 60 (1953),55-63;R.W.Marks, "The Effect of Probability, Desirability, and 'Privilege' on the Stated Expectations of Children," *Journal of Personality,* 19 (1951), 332-351.

17.J. B. Rotter, *Social Learning and Clinical Psychology* (New York: Prentice-Hall, 1954); E. C. Tolman, *Purposive Behavior in Animals ar.d Men* (Berkeley : University of California Press, 1949).

18. H. Burdick, "The Effect of Value of Success upon the Expectation of Success" (Technical Report #14, Contract Nonr 3591 01] Office of Naval Research, NR 171-803 [Lewisburg, Pa., Bucknell University, 1965]); Burdick and N. Stoddard, "The Relationship Between Incentive and Expectations of Success" (Technical Report #7, Contract Nonr 3591 [01] Office of Naval Research NR 171-803 [Lewisburg, Pa.: Bucknell University, 1964]); V. J. Crandall, D. Solomon, and R. Kellaway, "Expectancy Statements and Decision Times as Functions of Objective Probabilities and Reinforcement Values," *Journal of Personality,* 25 (1955), 192-203; Crandall, Solomon, and Kellaway, "The Value of Anticipated Events as a Determinant of Probability Learning and Extinction," *Journal of Genetic Psychology,* 58 (1958), 3-10; H. Hess and R. Jessor, "The Influence of Reinforcement Value on Rate of Learning and Asymptotic Level of Expectancies," *Journal of General Psychology,* 63 (1960), 89-102.

19. Atkinson, "Motivational Determinants of Behavior"; J. W. Atkinson, *An Introduction to Motivation* (Princeton:D Van Nostrand Co., 1964).

20. V. C. Crandall, "Reinforcement Effects of Adult Reactions and Non-Reactions on Children's Achievement Expectations," *Child Development,* 34 (1963), 335-354.

21. V. C. Crandall, S. Good and V. J. Crandall, "Reinforcement Effects of

Feather,[22] and others have shown that expectations are increased by positive reinforcement and decreased by negative reinforcement, it is possible that the reinforcement histories of males have been more positive and/or less negative than those of females. When responding to comparable intellectual performance, perhaps parents, teachers, and other socializing agents give male children more praise and less criticism than females, and females more criticism and less praise than males. Thus, their different expectancies may be warranted simply because they have been given more of the one than the other.

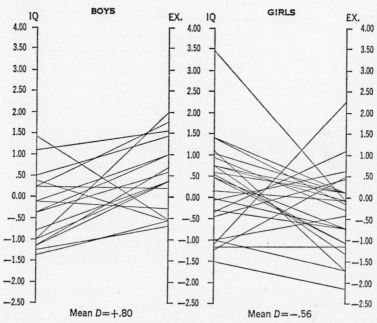

Figure 3. Discrepancies between Fels children's Stanford-Binet scores and their average expectancy estimates for six novel intellectual tasks.

3. Finally, internally held expectations may differ because the two sexes are *differentially sensitive to positive and negative reinforcements.* Even if boys and girls do actually receive objectively equal reinforcements, it may be that when those reinforcements are negative, the girls' expectancies are more sharply reduced by them than the boys'. And/or perhaps boys are more responsive to positive reinforcement and raise their expectancies more than do girls under such circumstances. If this were to turn

<hr>

Adult Reactions and Nonreactions on Children's Achievement Expectations: A Replication Study," *Child Development,* 35 (1964), 485-497.

22. "Effects of Prior Success."

out to be the case, the task would then be to find the antecedents of this differential assimilation of positive and negative feedback, but it would be necessary first to demonstrate whether sex differences in sensitivity to the reinforcements do, in fact, exist.

Or it may turn out to be some combination of differential reinforcement histories and sensitivity. While there has been much work done on cross-sex and same-sex examiner influence in social reinforcement and on the use of parent praise and criticism, there seems to be no empirical evidence bearing upon sex differences in reinforcement histories or reinforcement sensitivity in the intellectual area.

As mentioned in 1(a) above, it was thought that the discrepancy between a child's expectancy and his past performance might be a function of the child's attempt to state to the examiner an estimate which he thought he *should* hold, rather than that which he actually *did* hold. If this were true the greater the child's need for the examiner's approval, the more his estimate might be distorted. Perhaps such need might have produced the too-modest estimates of the girls and the inflated estimates of the boys.

To measure the desire to present a socially acceptable facade to the examiner, our sample of Fels children were given our Children's Social Desirability scale.[23] This forty-seven-item scale has previously been demonstrated to have some validity as a measure of the individual's concern with others' approval-disapproval.[24] The scale was administered individually and orally. For this sample the girls' mean on the social desirability scale was 26.4, $SD = 11.7$; the boys' mean was 23.6, $SD = 10.8$. The t between these means was not significant.

The IQ—expectancy D scores of the sample were arranged on a single dimension running from high positive, through consonant, down to high negative discrepancies. Correlations between the social desirability measure and the discrepancy scores, however, did not reveal any association for either of the sexes (boys' $r = .08$, girls' $r = .00$). Thus, the distortion represented in discrepancy scores could not be readily assigned to the desire to obtain social approval.

In 1(b) above, it was reasoned that the more the child valued intellectual reinforcements (i.e., the more he wanted to do well on

23. V. C. Crandall, V. J. Crandall, and W. Katkovsky, "A Children's Social Desirability Questionnaire," *Journal of Consulting Psychology*, 29 (1965), 27-36.

24. V. C. Crandall, "Personality Characteristics, and Social and Achievement Behaviors Associated with Children's Social Desirability Response Tendencies," *Journal of Personality and Social Psychology*, 4 (1966), 477-486.

these intellectual tasks), the more his verbal estimate might be wishfully driven upward. Therefore, we gave these children a measure of Intellectual-Academic Attainment Value, a measure of the importance they placed on doing well in intellectual and academic endeavors as opposed to getting reinforcements of other kinds. (See Appendix A.) This measure was especially constructed for the purposes of this study. It was made up of sixteen forced-choice items, each of which paired an intellectual or academic reinforcement with a reinforcement from the need areas of affiliation, dependency, dominance, physical comfort, and leadership. For example, "If you could have whatever you wanted, would you rather: (a) Be able to do well in your school work, or (b) Have lots of kids like you?"

This scale was also administered individually and orally. The girls' mean was 10.7, $SD = 2.6$; the boys' mean was 10.8, $SD = 3.5$.

Scores from this measure also did not correlate with the discrepancies of either sex (boys' $r = .18$, girls' $r = .13$). Thus, the value a child held for intellectual reinforcement did not cause his (or her) verbal estimate to be "pulled" upward. Again, distortions in estimate could not be assumed to be a function of a verbal response set.

Study B

The following findings bear upon the possibility that males and females may *assimilate* the same past reinforcements differently in forming their expectancies. That is, given past feedback *known* to be equivalent for the two sexes, will succeeding expectancy estimates still differ? The data to be presented were gathered from the entire class (except for foreign students) who enrolled at Antioch College in 1963 ($N = 380$). At entrance, and at each subsequent quarter's registration, expectancy estimates were obtained by asking the students to list the courses they were registering for and to circle on a 12-point scale the grade they expected to receive in each course at the end of the term. The scale was represented at each interval as follows: A,A−,B +,...D−,F. At the end of each quarter the grades the students actually had been given were obtained from the college registrar. It was considered that the grades the subject received for the preceding quarter were the most immediate referent available for him to use in estimating his grades for the coming quarter.

Table 1 contains the means and standard deviations of the grades received and the grades expected by each sex and the tests

TABLE 1   *Tests of Difference Between College Males' and Females' Grade Point Averages and Expectancy Estimates*

Grade Point Average	Males			Females			t	p
	N	Mean	SD	N	Mean	SD		
End 1st Quarter	170	7.54	1.97	210	7.82	1.95	1.39	n.s.
End 2nd Quarter	166	7.75	2.00	205	8.14	1.72	1.83	n.s.
End 3rd Quarter	145	8.06	1.93	187	8.31	1.91	1.21	n.s.
Expectancy								
Beginning 1st Quarter	164	9.34	1.34	207	8.90	1.24	3.37	.01
Beginning 2nd Quarter	158	9.40	1.21	195	8.73	1.19	5.21	.01
Beginning 3rd Quarter	128	9.42	1.11	160	8.97	1.10	3.41	.01
Beginning 4th Quarter	115	9.50	1.21	152	9.05	1.14	3.11	.01

of difference between sexes on each measure. If the reader will refer to the first expectancy estimates he will note that even at the beginning of the first quarter in college, before any college courses were taken, the boys' *initial* estimates of their probable grades in their first courses were significantly higher than those of the girls. Significant differences between the expectancies of the two sexes continued for each of the remaining quarters of this analysis, and the males consistently gave the higher estimates. This was true even though there were no significant differences in the grades received by the two sexes. The males did not receive higher grades to warrant their higher expectancies; in fact, inspection of the boys' and the girls' mean grades reveals that the girls' grades were slightly, though nonsignificantly, higher than the boys' for each quarter.

In order to examine the accuracy or reality of the estimates, the grades of each six for each preceding quarter can be compared with their estimates at the beginning of the next quarter. It will be noted that although these girls have lower mean expectancies than the boys, as was true of the younger Fels girls on their novel tasks, these college girls' estimates of their grades for each quarter were slightly higher than their own past grades. The males' estimates, however, like those of the young Fels boys, were again well above the past feedback they had received.

Table 2 presents between-sex comparisons of these discrepancies. Each of the three tests of difference demonstrates that the males overestimated significantly more than did the females each quarter. It will also be noted in the table that the absolute size of the discrepancy scores for each sex decreased as the subjects had more experience in college.

TABLE 2   *Discrepancies Between Last Grades Received and Estimate of Grades for Succeeding Quarter*

	Males			Females				
	N	Mean	SD	N	Mean	SD	t	p
Gr. 1st Qtr. to Ex. 2nd Qtr.	157	+1.86	1.92	194	+.87	1.93	4.78	<.001
Gr. 2nd Qtr. to Ex. 3rd Qtr.	124	+1.60	2.08	157	+.71	1.65	3.89	<.001
Gr. 3rd Qtr. to Ex. 4th Qtr.	112	+1.29	1.90	150	+.57	1.70	3.17	<.01

(Subsequent analyses of the discrepancy scores for the remainder of the five years of this study demonstrate that the sex differences in discrepancies noted in Table 2 continue, although these differences are slightly attenuated during the latter portion of the students' enrollment. An analysis of the difference between the overall average D scores for the full five-year period, however, was significant at the .001 level (males' $M = 1.00$, $SD = 1.07$; females' $M = 0.29$, $SD = 1.09$; $t = 4.34$). Although the females' mean D scores for the last several quarters were more often slightly positive than negative, the generally decreasing size of those scores led us to examine the *number* of students of each sex who had + and -D scores in their last academic year. Of the 129 students with sufficiently complete data to remain in the sample at that time, there were 57 females and 72 males. Thirty-three of the females had negative D scores, only 24 had positive ones; of the males, only 27 had negative D scores and 45 had positive ones. The chi square for these data is 5.32, $p < .05$. Thus, at the end of their academic careers more girls actually estimated lower than their past grades would warrant while more boys continued to estimate higher than their preceding grades. This is the same sex differentiated tendency initially noted in the younger Fels children with their novel task estimates.)

Study C

What would happen if a novel intellectual task were given to a sample of subjects of ages roughly comparable to those of the college students? If the reinforcements given the males and females *during* the task were exactly equal, would the two sexes assimilate this reinforcement differently? Would they change their estimates (pretest to posttest) in different amounts, even though they had been given the same feedback? As part of a larger longitudinal study of achievement, various achievement measures were given to the young adults (18-26 years old) in the Fels sample.

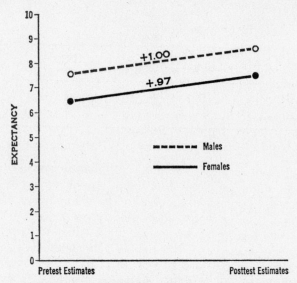

Figure 4. Mean changes in expectancy estimates after 80 per cent positive reinforcement on a novel intellectual task (Fels young adults).

At the time of this analysis 18 females and 23 males had been tested. One of the intellectual tasks required the storage, recall, and reproduction of different patterns of geometric figures which varied in color as well as form. The task was an adaptation of one developed by Glanzer, Huttenlocher, and Clark.[25] This modified form of the task involved twelve different storage loads and required that the subject recall a particular combination of ten of them on each trial. Six geometric forms (star, heart, square, triangle, diamond, and circle) in two colors (black and white) were used. Each stimulus consisted of some combination of five of the various black and white forms drawn on a rectangular card. The subject was given a complete set of cutouts of the six forms in black and a duplicate set in white. The stimulus card was shown the subject for ten seconds, then removed, and he was asked to reproduce the pattern of figures using his set of cutouts. After the task was explained to the subject, but before it was actually administered, his expectancy was obtained by asking him, "I am going to give you ten of these patterns now. How many do you think you will get right?" The task was sufficiently complex that the subjects were somewhat unsure of their responses until they were told "right" or "wrong" by the examiner. This allowed the

25. M. Glanzer, J. Huttenlocher, and W. H. Clark, "Systematic Operations in Solving Concept Problems," *Psychological Monographs,* 77 (1963), 1, Whole No. 564.

examiner to manipulate the reinforcements to adhere to a designated schedule. All subjects were failed on trials 4 and 6 and succeeded on the remaining eight trials of the ten-trial series. Exactly the same verbal reinforcing statements were used for all subjects and the examiners were of the same sex as the subjects. After the series of ten trials, a second expectancy estimate was obtained in a similar fashion. It was expected, of course, that most individuals would raise their expectancies after this 80 per cent positive reinforcement schedule, but the point at issue was to determine whether the females would raise their estimates as much as the males. Perhaps this was why girls came to intellectual situations with lower expectancies—the positive feedback they receive in daily life does not have as great a reinforcing value for them as for males.

The first expectancy estimates of the females in this task, as in the preceding studies, were again lower than those of the males. The mean of the women's first estimate was 6.53, $SD = 1.74$; the men's mean was 7.57, $SD = 1.90$. The resulting t was 2.08, $p < .05$. After the series of trials, the mean of the females' posttest estimate was 7.50, $SD = 1.50$, and the males' mean was 8.57, $SD = 1.03$. The t of 2.64 between these means was again significant, this time at the .02 level. Again, the women's estimates were significantly lower than those of the men. Change scores were computed for each subject, constants added, and the t computed, in order to determine whether there were differences in the degree to which subjects of the two sexes were affected by the same reinforcements from the examiners. The females' mean change score was .97 while the males' mean was exactly 1.00. This difference between the sexes ($t = 0.06$) was obviously nonsignificant. These mean changes in expectancy are illustrated in Figure 4. Thus, although females started and ended the task with estimates significantly lower than the males, they did not seem to be any more or less sensitive to the same reinforcements than were the males, since the two sexes changed their expectancies equivalent amounts.

After all Ss had received the reinforcement schedule of eight successes and two failures in the task, it is obvious that the most realistic posttest estimate would be eight. It should be noted that the mean of the females' second estimate was 7.50 while that of the males' was 8.57. The difference between the posttest estimates and a theoretically expected estimate of 8.00 was computed for subjects of each sex. The t between these D scores for males and females was 0.04, clearly nonsignificant. Each sex, then, reflected past feedback with about equal amounts of accuracy, but the males again were somewhat optimistic and the females somewhat pessimistic relative to the reinforcements they had received for their own performance.

Certainly, however, the social reinforcement on the laboratory task given these young adults is far from comparable to the IQ scores used as an index of past performance for the little Fels children. Although both samples of females estimated low, and both samples of males estimated high relative to these different indexes of past performance, it will be necessary in future studies to control for, or *systematically* vary, each index across age when examining developmentally the manner in which the two sexes reflect past feedback in making their estimates. So far, however, it appears that the opposite direction of distortion in these estimates on new intellectual tasks may be predicted from sex regardless of age.

Even though the Fels young women started from lower levels of expectancy than the men, it should be noted that they were able to raise their estimates *during* the task just as much as the young men did. If this were the case in their daily experience, what then had made them and the Antioch College women and the young Fels girls give lower expectancies to begin with?

Study D

It occurred to us that the reinforcement given the Fels young women in the laboratory might be quite unlike their natural rein-forcement histories in a very important respect. Perhaps the 80 per cent positive reinforcement schedule on a problem they had never tried before constituted such strong and clear-cut reinforcement that it created a "situational demand" to raise one's expectancy estimate for it. The laboratory reinforcement was more consistent and uniform than is normally the case in daily life. Depending on the idiosyncratic standards held by various reinforcing agents, the child's degree of competence on a particular task may exceed or fall short of that standard and he will receive praise, reproof, or fairly neutral feedback accordingly. It is well known that some teachers "grade hard," others are "easy graders." Mother may say that a score of 85 on a test is "great work," Dad may say it is "so-so," an older sibling may assess it as "pretty poor." When these sorts of inconsistent feedback occur, it may be that girls are more sensitive to the negative aspects of that inconsistency, while the positive ones are more strongly reinforcing for boys.

For the next study, then, feedback was controlled so that it contained different percentages of inconsistency or contradiction. The task was a novel digit-symbol substitution task and the 8th grade subjects were instructed that this was a test of intellectual competence. Expectancies were taken using a measure of social comparison. The task was explained to each subject and he was told that it was like part of an intelligence test. He was handed a legal-size sheet of paper with fifty small stick figures running down the length of the sheet. The top one was labeled "does the best on this test," the bottom was labeled "does the poorest on this test." He was asked to circle the child he would turn out to be when we finished testing everyone. Thus, expectancies could range from 1-50, and did. The subject was then assigned to a reinforcement condition so that 6 groups of boys and 6 groups of girls were matched across sex and across conditions on the basis of those initial expectations ($N=204$, 17 per cell). To obtain matched groups on initial expectancy, data from an additional 24 male and 28 female subjects were discarded.

After each trial the subject was given the feedback on his performance via a display panel of ten lights. He was told that each light represented one of ten schools in which the test had previously been given. The sample was divided among 6 reinforcement schedules: 80 per cent positive, 80 per cent negative, 60 per cent positive, 60 per cent negative, 50 per cent positive, and 50 per cent negative. In the positive conditions the subject was informed that each of the lights which came on after each trial meant that he had "beaten the kids at that school." The negative conditions were produced by telling the subject that when any light came on it meant that "the kids at that school had beaten" him. The total task consisted of ten trials.

This form of feedback was adopted to provide the inconsistency with which a particular piece of performance (here a single trial) might be reinforced in daily life. In other words, the subjects were given quite-consistent-and-mostly-positive reinforcement, quite-consistent-and-mostly-negative, on down to highly inconsistent feedback which was half positive or half negative. The change score between pre-and posttest expectancies was considered the index of the manner in which the reinforcements had been assimilated. This change score, then, constituted the dependent variable on which a 2x2x3 analysis of variance was computed. That is, there were the two sexes, by the two directions or signs of the reinforcement (positive and negative) by the percentage of reinforcement for each trial (80 per cent, 60 per cent, 50 per cent) — which indicated the amount of inconsistency. Because it was anticipated that girls might react more strongly to negative conditions but less strongly to positive conditions, while the converse might be true for boys, it was expected that there would be no main effect for sex. Collapsing across conditions of opposite sign for each sex would probably preclude a significant F ratio for sex. The portion of the analysis relevant to the sex differences under investigation, then, would be a sex x sign interaction, indicating that the girls reacted more to negative reinforcements, boys more to positive, and perhaps a sex x sign x per cent of reinforcement interaction indicating a greater difference between the sexes, each sex in its predicted direction, in the more inconsistent 50-50 conditions than in the more consistent 80-20 conditions.

The results are shown in Table 3. As predicted, there was no main effect for sex, but neither did the expected interactions occur. The main effect for per cent of reinforcement ($F = 18.01$) simply indicates that for all children (i.e., with sex and sign of reinforcement collapsed) the 80 per cent conditions caused more change than the 60 per cent conditions, which were more effective than the 50 per cent conditions. Secondly, the main effect for sign ($F = 32.84$) indicates that, for children of *both* sexes, the negative conditions as a group caused greater decreases in expectancy than the positive conditions caused increases, even though the positive and negative conditions were objectively equal mirror images of one another. Previous research,[26] however, had already demonstrated this latter phenomenon, and it did not contribute anything to the explanation of the sex differences in response to reinforcement for which the study had been designed. At least as it had been tested here, males and females did not respond differently from one another to either positive or negative reinforcement, nor to inconsistent mixtures of them.

The reader will remember that one of the hypotheses entertained earlier was that the children might be responding to cultural demands for different verbal behavior by the two sexes. These pressures may require that if a girl is to be *feminine* she must be modest in stating her intellectual capabilities; if a boy is to be *masculine* he should appear "upward striving" and confident. Perhaps, then, the more masculine a boy was, the more his expectancy estimate would exceed his past feedback, and the more feminine a girl, the more her estimate would fall below the level of her past reinforcement. To examine this possibility, the femininity subscale from the California Psychological Inventory[27] was given to the total sample of 256 children.

Again, the child's past grades were used as an index of the most specific and concrete feedback he had received about his in-

26. Crandall, "Reinforcement Effects"; Crandall, Good, and Crandall, "Reinforcement Effects: A Replication Study."

27. H. C. Gough, *The California Psychological Inventory* (Palo Alto: Consulting Psychologists Press, 1957).

Virginia C. Crandall

tellectual capability. Boys' and girls' grades and their initial estimates on the novel task were each transformed into z scores so that a discrepancy between these z scores could be computed. It should be remembered that all subjects might have retained their same relative positions on both grade and expectancy z distributions, resulting in zero D scores, or that changes in either direction in those relative positions might be randomly distributed among males and females. Of the 126 boys in the sample, however, 90 had *positive* discrepancy scores; of the 130 girls, 92 had *negative* discrepancies. That is, about 70 per cent of the boys estimated high relative to their past feedback, and about 70 per cent of the girls estimated low relative to theirs ($X2$ = 37.18, $p.<.001$). In addition, the mean *amount* of the boys discrepancy was exactly equal to the mean *amount* of discrepancy of the girls (boys = ⅓.52, girls = −.52), although the two sexes had again taken the opposite directions found in the previous studies.

TABLE 3 *Analysis of Variance of Expectancy Change Scores*

Source of Variation	df	Mean Square	F	p
Sex	1	7.84	.16	n.s.
Sign (Pos. vs. Neg.)	1	1603.84	32.84	p < .01
Per cent Reinforcement	2	879.57	18.01	p < .01
Sex × Sign	1	34.60	.71	n.s.
Sex × Per cent Reinforcement	2	28.23	.58	n.s.
Sign × Per cent Reinforcement	2	22.97	.47	n.s.
Sex × Sign × Per cent Reinforcement	2	11.22	.23	n.s.
Within Group	192	48.84		

We arranged the discrepancy scores into a single dimension running from high positive through consonant down to high negative discrepancies and found a correlation with femininity scores of −.34 ($p<.001$) for the total group of subjects. While the variance held in common was not large, it appeared that there was some tendency for the more feminine child to estimate relatively low compared to his past beedback, and the more masculine one to estimate relatively high.

However, masculinity and femininity are obviously associated with biological sex and it has already been shown that particular kinds of discrepancy scores were associated with sex. Thus, it seemed possible that the obtained correlation of −.34 between masculininity-femininity and discrepancy scores for the total group was caused by the common association of those variables with biological sex. Measures of relationship cannot in themselves ever

675

establish cause, of course, but if, *within* each sex, greater and less femininity were to be associated with negative and positive *D* scores respectively, it would be much more persuasive. The correlations for the sexes separately, however, were essentially nothing for either sex (boys = .03, girls = -.08). If the reader will refer to Figure 5, it will be seen that the generally negative relationship for the total group is spurious. It is clear that masculinity-femininity as measured by the California Psychological Inventory is strongly associated with biological sex; there is, in fact, practically no overlap for the boys' and the girls' distributions. Since the boys had more positive *D* scores and the girls more negative ones, it is these two facts which are accounting for the negative correlation with femininity for the total group. It will be seen that the distributions for each sex separately reveal no relationship at all between *D* scores and femininity for either sex. Thus, again, discrepancy between feedback and estimate could not be explained simply by cultural demands to make sex-appropriate verbal statements about one's ability, and it seemed necessary to continue to entertain the possibility that the internally held expectations of the two sexes were actually different.

In addition to the experimental data dealing with inconsistency and direction of reinforcement, and the femininity measure, there was still another source of data available to us for this subject sample which might provide some insight into the differential formation of expectancies. The particular school from which these subjects came used a rather extreme form of homogeneous grouping in that it had divided these 8th grade children into nine ability levels. One of the rationales sometimes given for homogeneous ability grouping is that the child of poor ability is better able to maintain his confidence in his capability if he is in daily contact with others like himself and does not have to compare himself constantly with very capable children, as would be the case in a system where children of all abilities are put together. For this to be true, however, the child would have to ignore the assessment of the external world around him which sees him as one of the members of a group of low ability. In order to do this he must be oblivious to the larger world of parents, teachers, school administration, and peers outside his own classroom, and be cognizant of only the smaller group in his own room. If that were the case, then the child's assessment of his intellectual ability should be determined primarily by his relative standing within his own daily classroom and it should be influenced very little by the height of his ability group in the whole school. It seemed to us, however, that ability group level would constitute reinforcement of loaded value for most children.

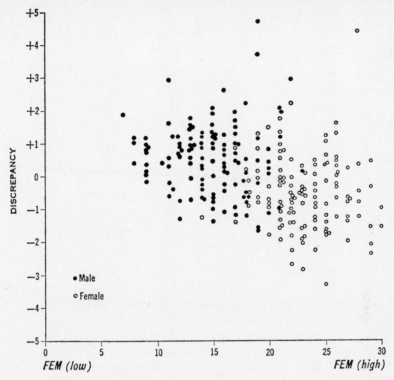

Figure 5. Discrepancies between past grades and novel digit-symbol esti-mates as a function of femininity.

For this reason analyses of variance for unequal *Ns* were computed for each of the sexes separately (126 boys, 130 girls) using ability group placement and standing within classroom as the independent variables and initial expectancy estimates on the novel digit-symbol task as the dependent variable. Subjects for this analysis were not used from the extreme groups 1 and 9.[28] The remaining seven groups were trichotomized into high (groups 2 and 3), medium (groups 4, 5, 6) and low (groups 7 and 8). The subjects from each of the several classrooms were also classified into thirds within their own rooms, using the range of grade point

---

28. Groups 1 and 9 were omitted partially to avoid possible ceiling effects on *D* scores and partially because these groups, by virtue of their special programs, were somewhat outside the main stream of the regular academic program of the school. Group 1 was an accelerated group with a very individualized, enriched program; group 9 was a slow learners' group made up of children of below 80 IQ. In addition, we felt that the latter children might be unable to give meaningful expectancy estimates.

averages in a child's own classroom as the criterion on which to divide them.

Table 4 gives the means for each sex using this double classification. For the boys it will be seen that, in general, the means of their expectancies drop with decreases in both ability group level and standing within class. It will be noted, however, that the differences between ability groups (row means) are a good deal greater than those produced by differences in standing within one's own classroom (column means). The analysis of variance reflected this fact and yielded an $F = 69.88$, $p < .01$, for height of ability group, while standing within class did not significantly affect the boys' expectancies ($F = 0.65$). The interaction term was also nonsignificant ($F = 0.67$). The boy's assessment of his intellectual capability, then, was significantly associated with the level of the ability group he had been put into, but was not associated with his standing among his peers in his own classroom.

TABLE 4

Means of Expectancy Estimates on a Novel Intellectual Task (Digit-Symbol with Intellectual Set) Classified by Standing within Classroom and Ability Group Level

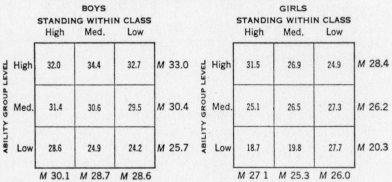

BOYS

ABILITY GROUP LEVEL	STANDING WITHIN CLASS: High	Med.	Low	
High	32.0	34.4	32.7	*M* 33.0
Med.	31.4	30.6	29.5	*M* 30.4
Low	28.6	24.9	24.2	*M* 25.7
	M 30.1	*M* 28.7	*M* 28.6	

GIRLS

ABILITY GROUP LEVEL	STANDING WITHIN CLASS: High	Med.	Low	
High	31.5	26.9	24.9	*M* 28.4
Med.	25.1	26.5	27.3	*M* 26.2
Low	18.7	19.8	27.7	*M* 20.3
	M 27.1	*M* 25.3	*M* 26.0	

For the girls, in general, the same thing is true. Ability group level was again significant ($F = 4.55$, $p < .025$) while standing within classroom was not ($F = 0.67$, *n.s.*). Inspection of individual cell means will reveal, however, that although the girls' expectancies in the top ability group (the top row) drop a little as standing within class goes down, those in the medium and low ability group levels actually *rise* as the standing within class decreases. This yielded a significant interaction term in the analysis of variance for the girls ($F = 2.84$, $p < .05$). Not only was ability grouping not maintaining the expectancy of intellectual success for the low ability group child *of either sex,* but girls who had lower classroom standing in the low and medium ability groups seemed to be resorting to some sort of inflated, unreal self-assessment.

To determine more definitely whether these girls' estimates were disproportionately high, the discrepancies between report-card grade and expectancy z scores were examined through this same double classification. These appear in Table 5. The reader will note that both boys and girls in the three cells around the upper left corners of each table give more conservative, cautious estimates than their past feedback might warrant. These are the children who are actually in pretty good positions as to both ability group level and standing within their own classrooms. Those in the lower right cells are in poorer positions on both counts and it can now be seen that boys, as well as girls, in those poorer positions give inflated estimates. Although this was already apparent for the girls in Table 4, it could not be observed for the boys in that table because the expectancy estimates reported there had not yet been "anchored" to the grades the children had been receiving.

The most revealing part of Table 5, however, in relation to the sex difference phenomenon is in the cells that lie along the lower left to upper right diagonals. These cells represent the groups of children who have inconsistent or contradictory feedback about their performance. That is, the children in the lower left cells are in a low ability group but high in their own classrooms, while the children in the upper right cells are in a high ability group but are poorest in their own rooms. In the very center cell feedback is so

TABLE 5

Means of Discrepancies Between Past Grades and Current Expectancy Estimates on a Novel Intellectual Task (Digit-Symbol with Intellectual Set) Classified by Standing Within Classroom and Ability Group Level

BOYS				GIRLS		
STANDING WITHIN CLASS				STANDING WITHIN CLASS		
ABILITY GROUP LEVEL	High	Med.	Low	High	Med.	Low
High	−.74	−.01	+.73	−.87	−.94	−.76
Med.	−.33	+.54	+1.34	−.93	−.06	+.92
Low	+.19	+.62	+1.05	−.83	+.02	+1.63

679

neutral on both counts as to provide little to go on. It should be noted that under these conditions the boys' expectations are elevated, the girls' are depressed. In other words, when feedback is neutral or inconsistent and contradictory, the two sexes resolve the conflict in the opposite ways—the ways that have previously been found to be most characteristic of each sex.

A further analysis of variance was then computed to determine whether the sex differences under conditions of contradictory feedback were in fact significant. Subjects of both sexes were reclassified as to direction and consistency of feedback. Those who were either high-high or high-medium as to ability group and standing within classroom (upper left cells in Tables 4 and 5) were considered as having received quite consistently positive feedback; those who were low-low or low-medium (lower right cells in Tables 4 and 5) were considered to have had fairly consistent negative feedback. Those who were high-low or low-high on the two dimensions or medium on both (the diagonal cells) were classified as the "contradictory and neutral" group. Means for these groups are given in Table 6. The main effect for sex yielded an F ratio of 23.45 ($p < .001$, that for type of reinforcement was 38.32 ($p<001$), and there was no significant interaction ($F=0.98$). Tests of dif-

TABLE 6

Means of Discrepancies Between Past Grades and Current
Expectancy Estimates on a Novel Intellectual Task
(Digit-Symbol with Intellectual Set) Classified by
Sex and Consistency and Direction of Reinforcement

	Consistency and Direction of Reinforcement				
Sex	Consistent Positive	Contradictory & Neutral	Consistent Negative		
Males	−.35	+.51	+.96	M	+.52
Females	−.91	−.52	+.62	M	−.52
	M −.75	M +.03	M +.86		

Virginia C. Crandall

ference between cell means demonstrated that even though males and females both estimated low in the consistent positive condition, the females, true to their sex, estimated significantly lower than did males ($t = 3.01$, $p < .01$). Differences between the sexes in the consistent negative condition were also in the expected direction with the boys estimating even more positively than the girls, but here the difference in response was not significant ($t = 0.92$). It has been observed elsewhere[29] that on some occasions the effect of negative reinforcement can be so strong as to "wipe out" the effect of individual differences, and that may be what has happened here. The opposite response of the two sexes to "contradictory and neutral" feedback is, of course, very significantly different ($t = 5.62$, $p < .001$).

If the two sexes assimilated *this* contradictory feedback differently in forming their expectancies, why didn't they show differences with the inconsistent reinforcements given them on the digit-symbol task? One possibility is that the method of communicating inconsistency, the use of lights displayed simultaneously for each trial to represent beating or losing to different schools, was not actually assimilated as inconsistency, and thus did not produce the conflict or dissonance which may be necessary to bring about the sex-differentiated distortion. It may be that the subjects simply interpreted the several lights as one single reinforcement of greater (80 per cent) or lesser (50 per cent) strength. To reexamine this hypothesis experimentally a different feedback procedure will have to be used.

The most probable reason for the significant results from the "real-life" school situation, however, is that the ability group and classroom factors are of much longer duration, involve many people's assessments of them, and touch upon a larger area of their lives, so to speak, than did our little laboratory task. The reinforcements that can be inferred from those school classifications probably have much greater value or impact.

SUMMARY OF STUDIES AND SUGGESTIONS FOR FUTURE RESEARCH

What conclusions can be drawn from these several studies? That girls give estimates of their own intellectual and academic

---

29. Crandall, "Reinforcement Effects"; Crandall, Good, and Crandall, "Reinforcement Effects: A Replication Study."

681

capabilities lower than do boys seems quite well established and consistent over the various ages studied. Relative to their own past academic performance, the boys are overoptimistic, while the girls are at first slightly hopeful but become more pessimistic as their college careers progress. As to their capability in new intellectual situations, the girls' estimates are relatively *lower* than their past performance would indicate; the boys' estimates are equivalently higher.

Much additional research needs to be done before the two latter phenomena can be established conclusively across age levels. The measures of past feedback used as base lines to estimate the appropriateness of expectancies on new intellectual tasks have varied across age levels and they are extremely incomplete samples of the child's reinforcement history. And the use of intelligence test scores from which to infer reinforcement histories is a particularly crude measure. Much more accurate and complete reinforcement histories, at least in the intellectual skill area, are necessary, and comparable measures must be used at all age levels. In addition, the past grades to current academic grade estimates must be reexamined at other developmental periods. This latter, as opposed to the former problem, can be examined fairly readily.

The sex differences found do not seem amenable to prediction through indexes of cultural demand for sex-appropriate verbal responses. Of course, it may be that so far the proper tools have simply not been used to test this possibility adequately. It will be remembered that the verbal response hypothesis was based on the premise that males were trying *to appear* masculine and females feminine in giving their estimates. Thus, it would seem advisable to try a masculinity-femininity subscale measure that did not disguise its purpose. Because the Femininity Subscale of the California sex as the criterion, many of the items do not have face validity as masculine or feminine. Thus, they do not allow the respondent to display an attempt *to appear* masculine or feminine. At any rate, since it is not yet possible to assign these sex differences to some sort of response set, it would seem advisable to continue to entertain the possibility that they are real.

The two sexes do not seem to assimilate laboratory task reinforcements differently, but there does seem to be a real difference in the way they derive their expectancies from contradictory life-school situations. When they have cues which tell them that on the one hand they are capable, on the other hand they are not, the girls seem to focus on the negative aspects of the situation, boys on the positive.

Do the sexes get different feedback from the culture? Girls, if anything, get more positive feedback, at least in the form of grades in the early school years. Nevertheless, from these grades as well as other behaviors, perhaps parents and other socializing agents give more praise to boys, more criticism to girls for their intellectual performance. Or perhaps they hold higher standards for girls, making it harder for a girl to produce a product that will meet their approval. These variables have been analyzed from some parent data in our files and no significant differences were found in the amount of praise or criticism for intellectual performance given by mothers or fathers to sons than to daughters. Nor do we find any differences in the standards held by parents of either sex for the intellectual performance of sons than of daughters. However, these parent data are mostly self-report data. It would seem advisable to obtain better measures through direct observation in the home and on structured tasks that are presented to the child in the parents' presence or on which parents and child work together — task situations similar to those used by Hess and Shipman,[30] Rosen and D'Andrade,[31] and Solomon and colleagues.[32]

IMPLICATIONS FOR PSYCHOLOGICAL ADJUSTMENT AND FUTURE ACHIEVEMENT

Probably more attention has been given here to the low estimation of girls than to the high estimation of boys. Perhaps such concern is unwarranted since girls' performance, at least at earlier ages, is as good as, or better than, boys'. In view of this fact, the motivational quality of expectancy may be called into question. However, the studies by Battle,[33] Crandall et al.,[34] Feather,[35] and Tyler[36] in which expectancy relates to clear mea-

30. R. Hess and V. Shipman, "Early Experience and the Socialization of Cognitive Modes in Children," *Child Development,* 36 (1965), 869-886; and "Cognitive Elements in Maternal Behavior," in J. P. Hill (ed.), *Minnesota Symposia on Child Psychology,* Vol. 1 (Minneapolis-St. Paul: University of Minnesota Press, 1967).

31. B. Rosen and R. D'Andrade, "The Psychosicial Origins of Achievement Motivation," *Sociometry,* 22 (1959), 185-218.

32. D. Solomon, T. V. Busse, and R. J. Parelius, "Parental Behavior and Achievement of Lower-Class Negro Children" (Paper read at APA, Washington, D.C., September, 1967).

33. "Motivational Determinants of Persistence."

34. "Motivational and Ability Determinants."

35. "Persistence at a Difficult Task" and "Effects of Prior Success."

36. "Expectancy for Eventual Success."

sures of approach, and the several studies cited earlier in which novel task estimates relate to current or future grades earned would seem to argue to a motivational interpretation of expectancy. In addition, since higher expectancy is positively related to performance for girls *within their own sex* it might be said that girls who *are* able to hang on to a confident expectancy are the ones among their own sex who are able to perform best. The overall difference in performance *between* the sexes may prove to be attributable to other motivational factors in which girls have the advantage, such as, for example, intellectual attainment value[37] and perceptions of internal control.[38]

Nevertheless, Sontag, Baker, and Nelson[39] found significantly fewer girls than boys whose intelligence test scores had risen over the elementary school years, and significantly more girls than boys whose mental test scores had declined. It may possibly be that it is these lower expectations of girls that eventually, though not immediately, result in this poorer intellectual performance.

If these lower expectancies are, in fact, actually subjectively held, it is unfortunate that females must work under such a disadvantage. It has been suggested elsewhere[40] that girls frequently use achievement as a means of obtaining love, affection, approval from others—what Atkinson would call "ex-

---

37. Crandall, Katkovsky, and Preston, "Motivational and Ability Determinants."

38. *Ibid.*; V. C. Crandall, W. Katkovsky, and V. J. Crandall, "Children's Beliefs in Their Own Control of Reinforcements in Intellectual-Academic Achievement Situations," *Child Development,* 36 (1965), 91-109; P. McGhee and V. C. Crandall, "Beliefs in Internal-External Control of Reinforcements and Academic Performance," *Child Development* 39 (1968), 91-102.

39. L. W. Sontag, C. T. Baker, and V. L. Nelson, "Mental Growth and Personality Development: A Longitudinal Study," *Monographs of the Society for Research in Child Development,* 23 (1958), Serial 68.

40. V. C. Crandall, "Achievement Behavior in Young Children," *Young Children,* 20 (1964), 77-90; V. J. Crandall, "Achievement," in H. W. Stevenson (ed.), *Child Psychology* (The 62nd Yearbook of the National Society for the Study of Education Part I [Chicago: University of Chicago Press, 1963], 416-459; V. J. Crandall *et al.*, "Parents' Attitudes and Behaviors and Grade School Children's Academic Achievements," *Journal of Genetic Psychology,* 104 (1964), 53-66; F. B. Tyler, J. Rafferty, and B. Tyler, "Relationships Among Motivations of Parents and Their Children," *Journal of Genetic Psychology,* 101 (1962), 69-81; P. S. Sears, "Correlates of Need Achievement and Need Affiliation and Classroom Management, Self-Concept, and Creativity" (Unpublished manuscript, Laboratory of Human Development, Sanford University, 1962).

trinsic" rewards, But in order to obtain these valued goals girls must perform on tasks and in situations in which they feel less capable. If, in addition, the female "hunts for" and is unduly sensitive to reproof whenever the situation provides inconsistent feedback, it seems as though she has little chance of raising her expectancy.

On the other hand, if these are nonveridical verbal responses and females state low expectancies because the culture demands that they make such self-deprecatory statements in order for their behavior to be considered sex-appropriate, while at the same time the culture generally places a high value on intellectual competence, it would seem that females are put in another kind of psychological bind. They are supposed to *perform* competently in academic and intellectual situations, but are not supposed to *say* that they *are* competent. Whether internally held or erroneously stated, these low expectancies would not seem to bode well for their psychological integrity, comfort, self-esteem, or freedom from anxiety.

Although most attention has been given to the girls throughout this discussion because of their lower estimates, perhaps the boys' continued overestimation warrants as much attention. If the males truly *feel* highly confident, that should help them to continue to approach intellectual goals, which in turn should result in increased skill and insure future gratification. But if achievement pressures have forced them to defend by overstating, because it is too threatening to think of oneself as less capable intellectually, then there is cause for concern for them, too. It may be that their relatively poorer performance in this greatly valued intellectual area has forced them to be defensive about it.

The research findings presented here are meant to constitute only a very preliminary progress report. While the sex differences are consistent and stable through several age levels and with a variety of methods of measurement, little success has been achieved in the search for their antecedents. Any of the three possibilities presented here (differential reinforcement histories, differential sensitivity to positive and negative reinforcements, and culturally determined sex-appropriate verbal statements) or some combination of these antecedents may be found to underlie the observed differences, for the suggested antecedents are certainly not mutually exclusive. Or the origins of these sex differences may be found to lie in antecedents not yet probed here at all.

41

This study was clear and straightforward and typical of many of the studies carried out in the 1950's and 1960's which were concerned with female achievement motivation and characteristics of the high and low achiever.

In previous experiments of this type pictures of males were found to produce higher achievement scores than pictures of females when both were shown to females. Results of this paper showed that only underachievers fitted this pattern. The female achievers in contrast had higher achievement scores to female pictures than to male pictures.

The authors feel that this is consistent with social role interpretations, and that social conditions have different impacts on different girls. One could conclude that "underachievers" had resigned themselves to the culturally defined role of women, i.e. passive, dependent, etc. and destined to experience success only vicariously through their husbands or other male figures. The "achiever" is assertive and competitive, thus she perceives other females also to be achievers which could account for the higher achievement scores she gives to pictures of women.

In order to reconcile these findings with other studies when females were not divided into high and low achievers but considered as a single group, one must conclude that females in general are "underachievers." [The Horner and Hoffman papers consider the cultural basis which produces this internalized lack of desire and resultant failure to achieve.] Questions are raised but not answered by this study as to what factors produce high achievement motivation in some females contrary to the general pattern.

Experimental Arousal of Achievement Motivation in Adolescent Girls*

Gerald S. Lesser, Rhoda N. Krawitz, and Rita Packard

2 groups of female high school students (40 achievers and 40 underachievers, matched for IQ) were exposed to 2 experimental conditions. (Neutral and Achievement Oriented) and 2 types of pictures (those depicting males and those depicting females). The overall effect of the experimental achievement arousal conditions for all girls was nonsignificant. However, a highly significant 2nd-order interaction effect was obtained: the achievement motivation scores of achievers increased significantly in response to Achievement Oriented conditions when they produced stories to pictures of females but did not increase in response to pictures of males; by contrast, the achievement motivation scores of underachievers increased significantly in response to Achievement Oriented conditions when they produced stories to pictures of males but did not increase in response to pictures of females.

An impressive body of theoretically consistent information has accumulated which describes the operation of achievement motivation in male subjects. Studies of achievement motivation in men have demonstrated increases in achievement motivation scores in response to experimental achievement arousal conditions which stress intelligence and leadership ability (e.g., Lowell, 1950; McClelland, Clark, Roby, & Atkinson, 1949; Veroff, Wilcox, & Atkinson, 1953), and have described significant relationships between achievement motivation and risk taking behavior (Atkinson, 1957; Atkinson, Bastian, Earl, & Litwin, 1960; Atkinson & Litwin, 1960), conformity (Davage, 1956; Samelson, 1958), work partner selection (French, 1956), problem solving effectiveness (French, 1958; French & Thomas, 1958), learning (e.g., Hurley, 1957; Johnston, 1955; Lowell, 1952), academic performance (Pierce & Bowman, 1960; Ricciuti & Sadacca, 1955), speech behavior (Wagner & Williams, 1961), etc. However, the few

*From *Journal of Abnormal and Social Psychology,* 1962, 66 (1), 59-66. Footnotes have been renumbered.

comparable studies of achievement motivation in female subjects have shown neither consistency with the findings for men nor internal consistency with each other. The general theory of achievement motivation which has evolved to date (Atkinson, 1957, 1958; McClelland, Atkinson, Clark, & Lowell, 1953) confines its empirical supports to research with men and is forced to ignore the dynamics of achievement motivation in women because of the scarcity, ambiguity, and inconclusiveness of the empirical findings. This, of course, has been a formidable restriction on comprehensive theory construction.

One area of confusion in the results on samples of women (e.g., Veroff et al., 1953) is the apparent failure of female subjects to show the expected increase in n Achievement scores when exposed to experimental achievement arousal conditions which stress "intelligence and leadership ability." Almost a decade ago, McClelland et al. (1953) stated:

Women do not show an increase in n Achievement scores as a result of achievement-involving instructions. . . . Why then don't women's scores increase under experimental arousal? This is the puzzler. Two possible explanations—invalidity of the scoring for women, scores too high to go higher—have been eliminated. Apparently the usual arousal instructions simply do not increase achievement striving in women . . . " (p. 178).

Substantially the same unresolved state of affairs remains today. In general, we know very little about the operation of achievement motivation in female subjects, and, specifically, the lack of response to experimental achievement arousal conditions has not been explained. Field (1951) supplied some clarification of the experimental arousal issue by demonstrating that, although manipulating achievement orientation by reference to intelligence and leadership does not increase achievement motivation scores in women, experimental conditions which arouse a concern about social acceptance produce increases in their n Achievement scores.

One research result has been reported in the literature on achievement motivation which suggests that, for certain female samples, the experimental instructions which appeal to intelligence and leadership ability can produce an increase in achievement motivation scores. Angelini (1955), employing a sample of Brazilian college women, found significant increases in n Achievement following experimental instructions which appeal to intelligence and leadership ability, and also found that this increase exceeded the increase produced by experimental conditions which arouse concern about social acceptance. Angelini explains the discrepancy between the results on Brazilian and American college women by indicating that in Brazil, where opportunities for higher education are greatly limited, only highly competitive girls who have placed great stress on intellectual accomplishment will succeed in enrolling in a university. It is reasonable to conclude that the achievement goals of Angelini's sample of Brazilian college women are more career or intellectually oriented than the more socially oriented objectives of the average American female subject.

Thus, it appears possible that the failure to demonstrate increases in achievement motivation in American women in response to experimental conditions stressing intelligence and leadership ability is related to the fact that the female subjects employed were insufficiently concerned with standards of intellectual excellence and with achieving through the development of intellectual skills. There are, of course, certain settings in which great emphasis is placed upon the intellectual accomplishments of girls. One such institution is the Hunter High School for intellectually gifted girls; this is a seventh through twelfth grade demonstration school associated with Hunter College of the City University of New York. Hunter High School sets extremely high expectations and demands for intellectual achievement, provides intense scholastic stimulation, and emphasizes competitive achievement goals which require long-range planning and persistence, including the pursuit of college training. The presence of a strong intellectual achievement orientation at Hunger High School is reflected in the following facts: (a) admission is highly competitive—only outstanding elementary school students are advised to apply and from this highly selected group of about 4000 candidates, approximately 150 are admitted; (b) more than 99% of Hunter High School girls proceed to college (and, of the remaining few, most choose other forms of advanced training, such as nursing); (c) no high school in New York State receives a higher percentage of State Regents Scholarships; ordinarily, about 75% of Hunter High School's graduating seniors receive this competitive award; (d) although no precise tabulations exist, a very large percentage of graduates win scholastic recognition in college and proceed to professional careers.

Girls attending Hunter High School might, thus, be expected to display a concern for competitive standards of excellence and achievement comparable to the concern of the Brazilian college women in Angelini's (1955) sample, and it was hypothesized that Hunter High School students would display the same increases in achievement motivation scores in response to experimental conditions emphasizing intelligence and leadership ability which were shown by previous samples of men and by Brazilian college women. While no specific direction of results was predicted, it was further expected that academic "achievers" and "underachievers" might respond differently to the experimental achievement arousal conditions and to pictures depicting male or female characters.

METHOD

Subjects

The subjects were 80 juniors and seniors (ranging in age from 15-8 to 18-3 years) at Hunter High School. These girls are primarily from middle-class families.

Because it appeared likely that there would be differences in response to experimental instructions stressing intelligence and leadership ability between girls who were successfully meeting the academic demands of the school and girls who were not, the 80 students were divided into two equal matched groups of 40 achievers and 40 underachievers. Achievers in the junior class had cumulative scholastic grade averages in the first quartile for the four preceding semesters and in the senior class had first quartile grades for five of six preceding semesters; underachievers in the junior class had cumulative scholastic grade averages in the fourth quartile for the four preceding semesters and in the senior class had fourth quartile grades for five of the six preceding semesters.

Achievers were individually matched with underachievers for IQ score — Terman-McNemar (1941) Test of Mental Ability. The mean IQ score for the 40 achievers was 132.36 ($SD = 6.40$) and for the 40 underachievers was 131.86 ($SD = 7.42$); thus, the groups did not differ significantly in IQ ($t = 0.71$, $p < .05$).

In order to accumulate a sufficient number of matched subjects, the experiment was spread over a 2-year period. In 1958, 20 achievers and 20 underachievers were drawn from the junior and senior classes, and, again in 1960, 40 matched subjects were drawn from the junior and senior grades. All experimental sessions were conducted by the same female experimenter (assisted by another female experimenter) in 1958 and in 1960 under identical classroom conditions.

Experimental Conditions

Each student was exposed to two group experimental sessions

separated by one week, the first under Neutral conditions and the second under Achievement Oriented conditions. The Neutral and Achievement Oriented conditions employed in this experiment were identical to those described originally by McClelland et al. (1953, pp. 101-104) and used widely thereafter (e.g., Atkinson & Reitman, 1956; Martire, 1956). In general, the neutral condition is one in which no experimental attempt is made either to arouse achievement motivation or to create an especially relaxed condition; the objective is to elicit the normal motivation level of the subject in an everyday school setting. The achievement oriented condition introduces strong achievement cues in the form of special instructions in order to arouse achievement related motives.

Measure of n Achievement

Content analysis of thematic stories provided the measure of achievement motivation. The group testing procedure which was followed for collecting the stories is described in detail elsewhere (Atkinson, 1958, p. 837; McClelland et al., 1953, pp. 97-99).

Each of the 80 subjects wrote 12 thematic stories, 6 under neutral experimental conditions (3 to pictures in which a male was the central figure and 3 in which a female was the central figure), and 6 different stories under achievement arousal conditions (3 to pictures of males and 3 to pictures of females).

The 12 pictures were selected from those used in previous research on achievement motivation. The 6 pictures depicting females as central figures were derived from the research of Veroff, Atkinson, Feld, and Gurin (1960, pp. 3-4), and the 6 pictures of males are described by McClelland et al. (1953, p. 375). These 12 pictures were divided into the following four sets of 3 pictures each:

Female Set A
Woman (mother) seated by a young girl reclining in chair.
Group of four women, one standing, the others seated facing each other.
Woman kneeling and applying a cover to a chair.

Female Set B
Two women preparing food in a kitchen.
Two women standing by a table in a laboratory; one woman is working with test tubes.
A woman in the foreground with a man standing behind and to the side.

TABLE 1

MEAN n ACHIEVEMENT SCORES OF ACHIEVING AND UNDERACHIEVING GIRLS UNDER NEUTRAL AND ACHIEVEMENT ORIENTED EXPERIMENTAL CONDITIONS TO PICTURES CONTAINING FEMALE AND MALE CHARACTERS

Group	N	Experimental conditions								Total for all experimental conditions and pictures	
		Neutral				Achievement oriented					
		Three female pictures		Three male pictures		Three female pictures		Three male pictures			
		M	SD	M	SD	M	SD	M	SD	M	SD
Achievers	40	4.80	2.39	5.43	2.61	6.03	2.82	4.78	2.17	5.26	2.56
Underachievers	40	2.93	2.40	4.18	2.82	2.25	2.22	6.20	2.47	3.89	2.91
Total for all subjects	80	3.86	2.58	4.80	2.56	4.14	2.91	5.49	2.44		

Male Set C

Two men ("inventors") in a shop working at a machine.

Boy in foreground with vague operation scene in background.

Father and son.

Male Set D

Two men, in colonial dress, printing in a shop.

"Lawyer's" office: two men talking in a well-furnished office.

"Cub reporter" scene—older man handing papers to a younger man.

The thematic stories were scored according to the method of content analysis (Scoring system C) also described in detail elsewhere (Atkinson, 1958, pp. 179-204, 685-735; McClelland et al., 1953, pp. 107-138, 335-374). Interjudge scoring reliability (Spearman rank-order correlation coefficient) was .93 for the six-story protocols of 30 subjects.

TABLE 2

ANALYSIS OF VARIANCE OF n ACHIEVEMENT SCORES OF
ACHIEVING AND UNDERACHIEVING GIRLS UNDER
NEUTRAL AND ACHIEVEMENT ORIENTED EX-
PERIMENTAL CONDITIONS TO PICTURES
CONTAINING FEMALE AND MALE
CHARACTERS

Source	SS	df	MS	F
Between subjects				
Groups (G)	149.88	1	149.88	16.60*
Error (b)	704.72	78	9.03	
Total between	854.60	79		
Within subjects				
Pictures (P)	104.66	1	104.66	15.06*
Experimental conditions (E)	18.53	1	18.53	2.53
P × E	3.40	1	3.40	1.45
P × G	169.65	1	169.65	24.41*
E × G	3.00	1	3.00	0.41
P × E × G	104.66	1	104.66	44.73*
Error$_1$ (w)	542.44	78	6.95	
Error$_2$ (w)	571.22	78	7.32	
Error$_3$ (w)	182.19	78	2.34	
Error$_T$ (w)	1295.85	234	5.54	
Total within	1699.75	240		
Total	2554.35	319		

* $p < .001$.

Design

Both groups of female subjects (achievers and underachievers) were exposed to both experimental conditions (Neutral and Achievement Oriented) and both types of pictures (those depicting males and those depicting females). For the variable of groups each achieving subject was matched for IQ with an underachieving control. For the variables of experimental conditions and pictures each subject was used as his own control, being exposed to both experimental sessions and to both male and female pictures. Thus, since there were one between-subjects variable (groups) and two within-subjects variables (experimental conditions and pictures), a 2x2x2 Type VI analysis of variance design described by Lindquist (1956) was employed.

A succession of studies (e.g., Birney, 1958; Haber & Alpert, 1958; Jacobs, 1958; Murstein, 1961) has shown the crucial influence upon the motivational content of stories of the cue strength of the thematic apperception pictures. No fully adequate technique for comparing and equating the relative cue strengths of thematic pictures has as yet been developed. In order to be able to unequivocally attribute any observed increases in achievement motivation scores to the experimental conditions rather than to the differential cue strength of the pictures used under Neutral and Achievement Oriented conditions, the sets of pictures were counterbalanced. Since the total experimental procedure was conducted first in 1958 and then repeated in 1960 with samples of equal size, the counterbalancing of sets of pictures was used; the data from the two administrations were then pooled in the Type VI analysis of variance design described. The effect of order of presentation for different combinations of sets of pictures could not be computed because all possible combinations of order of presentation were not represented; that is, the combinations A-B, C-D and B-A, D-C were used in counterbalancing, but A-B, D-C and B-A, C-D did not appear.

RESULTS

Table 1 presents the mean achievement motivation scores for the eight subgroups. Bartlett's test for homogeneity of variance indicated that analysis of variance was not inappropriate for these data.

Table 2 presents the Type VI (Lindquist, 1956) analysis of variance. This table indicates that the overall effect of the experimental conditions was nonsignificant; thus, the major expectation of this study, that experimental conditions stressing intelligence and leadership ability would produce an increase in achievement motivation scores for this sample of girls, was not confirmed. Also, the experimental conditions were apparently no more effective in producing an increase in the achievement motivation scores of the achievers than of the underachievers (i.e., the interaction between experimental conditions and groups was also nonsignificant). However, the second order interaction effect of Pictures x Experimental Conditions x Groups was highly significant ($F = 44.73$, $p < .001$). Thus, the achievement motivation scores of achievers increase significantly in response to Achievement Oriented conditions when they produce stories to pictures of females but do not increase in response to pictures of males; by contrast, the achievement motivation scores of underachievers increase significantly in response to Achievement Oriented conditions when they produce stories to pictures of males but do not increase in response to pictures of females.

The other significant results presented in Table 2 indicate that the achievers have higher n Achievement scores than underachievers for all experimental conditions and types of pictures combined ($F = 16.60$, $p < .001$), the pictures depicting males produce higher n Achievement scores than pictures depicting females for all groups and experimental conditions combined ($F = 15.06$, $p < .001$); However, this difference is attributable to the scores of underachievers and not of achievers, since for both experimental conditions combined, achievers produce higher n Achievement scores to female pictures than to male pictures while underachievers produce higher n Achievement scores to male pictures than to female pictures ($F = 24.41$, $p < .001$).

Numerous studies (e.g., Ricciuti & Sadacca, 1955; Veroff et al., 1960) have demonstrated the importance of controlling for individual differences in verbal fluency in computing scores derived from thematic content. However, the correlation coefficient obtained in the present study between n Achievement scores and number of words in the story protocols ranged from -.01 to -.10. These negligible coefficients may have resulted from the fact that word fluency showed little variability; all of the subjects in this experiment showed great verbal fluency and very few brief protocols were obtained. This finding is consistent with earlier reports (e.g., Atkinson, 1950) in which negligible correlation coefficients were found between n Achievement scores and length of protocol when the sample was homogeneous and structuring questions were used in the test administration. Since the correlation coefficients in the present study were so small (accounting for no more than 1% of the shared variance between n Achievement scores and length of protocol), no attempt was made to correct for individual differences in verbal fluency.

DISCUSSION

Contrary to expectation, the experimental introduction of Achievement Orientation conditions did not produce an overall increase in achievement motivation scores for this sample of girls. However, a highly significant second order interaction effect emerged: achieving girls did display the expected increase in achievement motivation scores under achievement orienting conditions, but only when responding to stimuli depicting females; underachieving girls also displayed the expected increase in achievement motivation scores under achievement orienting conditions, but only when responding to stimuli depicting males.

A suggested interpretation is that the achieving girls perceive intellectual achievement goals as a relevant part of their own female role; in contrast, the underachieving girls perceive intellectual achievement goals as more relevant to the male role than to their own female role. Since the achievers and underachievers have equivalent intellectual capabilities, the discrepancy between them in their perception of the strivings and behaviors relevant to female and male roles may also represent a reasonable explanation for their differential academic performance. These interpretations are consistent with growing evidence (e.g., Moss & Kagan, 1961) that the production of thematic material is strongly influenced by the subject's conception of what behaviors are appropriate to the hero's social roles.

The application of such a social role model to the finding that achieving girls respond to experimental arousal conditions with increased achievement imagery when reacting to female figures but not when reacting to male figures is relatively direct. The achievement strivings of these girls are aroused by the experimental instructions stressing intelligence and leadership, and this increase in achievement motivation is expressed imaginally in response to the female figures since these female characters and their activities are most directly related to the girls' own strivings.

The concept of achievement motivation as a generalized pattern of strivings must be added to the social role interpretation when it is applied to the finding that the underachieving girls respond to experimental arousal conditions with increased achievement imagery only to male figures. If achievement motivation in this sample of underachieving girls is composed of generalized strivings to excel, then these generalized achievement strivings, when aroused, will be expressed imaginally by assigning increased achievement directed activity to the male figures for whom achievement behaviors are considered more appropriate. Thus, this social role interpretation suggests that when the achievement imagery of underachieving subjects is engaged by experimental instructions stressing intelligence and leadership, the increased generalized achievement imagery is attached to the figures whom the underachievers perceive to be the usual and proper agents for action directed toward achievement.

Margaret Mead (1949) has obseved that the adolescent girl in our society begins to realize that her attempts to achieve place her in competition with men and elicit negative reactions from them; our society, thus, defines out of the female role ideas and strivings for intellectual achievement. The results of the present research suggest that these social conditions have different impacts upon different girls. It appears that the girl who retains a perception of the female role as including intellectual achievement goals succeeds intellectually under conditions of strong academic competition with other girls; by comparison, the girl who accepts the social prescription that intellectual achievement strivings are relevant to the male role and not the female role does not succeed as well in intellectual competition with other girls.

Other results of the present study are consistent with a social role interpretation and may help to explain previously reported findings on samples of women. Veroff et al. (1953) report that female high school students produce greater n Achievement scores to pictures of men than to pictures of women, while Angelini (1955) reports higher scores for Brazilian college women responding to pictures of females than for Brazilian college men responding to pictures of men. In the present study, the pictures of men elicited more achievement imagery than pictures of women only for the underachievers and not for the achievers. Table 1 shows that for the underachievers, the mean n Achievement score to pictures of men significantly exceeds the mean score to pictures of women under both Neutral and Achievement Orientation conditions. However, for the achievers, the mean n Achievement score to pictures of men was significantly lower than the mean score to pictures of women under Achievement Orientation conditions, and under Neutral conditions the mean scores to pictures of men and women were not significantly different.[1]

An alternative theoretical model, based upon the concepts of approach-avoidance conflict and conflict produced displacement,

---

1. In the absence of additional empirical evidence on the operation of achievement motivation in women, the social role explanation is not more fully developed here. However, this theoretical approach is being expanded in a study of the characteristics of achievement motivation in college women conducted currently by Elizabeth G. French and the senior author of this paper.

has previously proved fruitful in research on achievement needs (e.g., Atkinson, 1954, 1957), aggression (e.g., Lesser, 1958), and sexual needs (e.g., Clark, 1952; Clark & Sensibar, 1956). This conceptualization, introduced by Lewin (1931) and elaborated by Miller (1948, 1951), has become a conventional model for discussions of needs which are ordinarily accompanied by some degree of attendant anxiety. While this model may ultimately prove to be of great value in conceptualizing the results of studies on the characteristics of achievement motivation in women, it is not clear at this time that it would unequivocally predict the present results.

However, no matter what theoretical model is applied, it is apparent that attempts to clarify the impact of experimental achievement arousal conditions upon female subjects must consider the interaction among the nature of the experimental conditions, the characteristics of the stimuli used to elicit thematic material, and the relative accomplishment of the subjects in achievement performance.

One further comparison should be noted between the present results and the findings of earlier research. While a recent study by Pierce and Bowman (1960) on a sample of gifted high school girls reports the absence of a significant relationship between achievement motivation scores and academic performance (when only pictures of men were used in assessing achievement motivation of the female subjects), studies relating academic performance to achievement motivation in samples of men have reported either strong relationships (e.g., McClelland et al., 1953; Morgan, 1952; Pierce & Bowman, 1960; Rosen, 1955) or at least moderate relationships (e.g., Morgan, 1953; Ricciuti & Sadacca, 1955). The present study obtained a highly significant difference between achieving and underachieving girls in their achievement motivation scores, even with IQ controlled through the matching of subjects. The significant interaction of Pictures x Groups reported in Table 2 indicates that the difference in achievement motivation scores between achievers and underachievers occurred in response to pictures of females but did not occur in response to pictures of males. Thus, the discrepancy between the positive findings of this study and the negative results of Pierce and Bowman in relating achievement motivation to academic performance in girls may be explained by the absence in the latter study of stimuli which allow the relationship to be displayed. Despite the present evidence, Atkinson's (1958, p. 605) caution is still appropriate: that no simple explanation of the complex behaviors referred to by the variable of academic achievement can be expected through the consideration of the strength of any single motive alone.

REFERENCES

Angelini, A. L. Um novo método para avaliar a motivaçaõ humano. [A new method of evaluating human motivation] *Bol. Fac. Filos. Cienc. S. Paulo.*, 1955, No. 207.

Atkinson, J. W. Studies in projective measurements of achievement motivation. Unpublished doctoral dissertation, University of Michigan, 1950.

Atkinson, J. W. Explorations using imaginative thought to assess the strength of human motives. In M. R. Jones (Ed.), *Nebraska symposium on motivation: 1954.* Lincoln: Univer. Nebraska Press, 1954, Pp. 56-112.

Atkinson, J. W. Motivational determinants of risk-taking behavior. *Psychol. Rev.,* 1957, *64,* 359-372.

Atkinson, J. W. (Ed.) *Motives in fantasy, action, and society.* Princeton: Van Nostrand, 1958.

Atkinson, J. W., Bastian, J. R., Earl, R. W., and Litwin, G. H. The achievement motive, goal-setting and probability preferences. *J. abnorm. soc. Psychol.,* 1960, *60,* 27-36.

Atkinson, J. W., and Litwin, G. H. Achievement motive and test anxiety conceived as motive to approach success and motive to avoid failure. *J. abnorm. soc. Psychol.,* 1960, *60,* 52-63.

Atkinson, J. W., and Reitman, W. R. Performance as a function of motive strength and expectancy of goal attainment. *J. abnorm. soc. Psychol.,* 1956, *53,* 361-366.

Birney, R. C. Thematic content and the cue characteristics of pictures. In J. W. Atkinson (Ed.), *Motives in fantasy, action, and society.* Princeton: Van Nostrand, 1958. Pp. 630-643.

Clark, R. A. The projective measurement of experimentally induced levels of sexual motivation. *J. exp. Psychol.,* 1952, *44,* 391-399.

Clark, R. A., and Sensibar, Minda R. The relationships between symbolic and manifest projections of sexuality with some incidental correlates. *J. abnorm. soc. Psychol.,* 1956, *50,* 327-334.

Davage, R. H. Effect of achievement-affiliation motive patterns on yielding behavior in two-person groups. Unpublished doctoral dissertation, University of Michigan, 1956.

Field, W. F. The effects of thematic apperception upon certain experimentally aroused needs. Unpublished doctoral dissertation, University of Maryland, 1951.

French, Elizabeth G. Motivation as a variable in work partner selection. *J. abnorm. soc. Psychol.,* 1956, *53,* 96-99.

French, Elizabeth G. The interaction of achievement motivation and ability in problem solving success. *J. abnorm. soc. Psychol.,* 1958, *57,* 306-309.

French, Elizabeth G., and Thomas, F. H. The relation of achievement motivation to problem solving effectiveness. *J. abnorm. soc. Psychol.,* 1958, *56,* 45-48.

Haber, R. N., and Alpert, R. The role of situation and picture cues in projective measurements of the achievement motive. In J. W. Atkinson (Ed.), *Motives in fantasy, action, and society.* Princeton: Van Nostrand, 1958. Pp. 644-663.

Hurley, J. R. Achievement imagery and motivational instructions as determinants of verbal learning. *J. Pers.,* 1957, *25,* 274-282.

Jacobs, B. *A* method for investigating the cue characteristics of pictures. In J. W. Atkinson (Ed.), *Motives in fantasy, action, and society.* Princeton: Van Nostrand, 1958. Pp. 617-629.

Johnston, R. A. The effects of achievement imagery on maze-learning performance. *J. Pers., 1955, 24, 145-152.*

Lesser, G. S. Conflict analysis of fantasy aggression. *J. Pers.,* 1958, *26,* 29-41.

Lewin, K. Environmental forces in child behavior and development. In C. Murchison (Ed.), *A handbook of child psychology.* Worcester, Mass.: Clark Univer. Press, 1931. Pp. 94-127.

Lindquist, E. F. *Design and analysis of experiments in psychology and education.* Boston: Houghton Mifflin, 1956.

Lowell, E. L. A methodological study of projectively measured achievement motivation. Unpublished master's thesis, Wesleyan University, 1950.

Lowell, E. L. The effect of need for achievement on learning and speed of performance. *J. Psychol.,* 1952, *33,* 31-40.

McClelland, D. C., Atkinson, J. W., Clark, R. A., and Lowell, E. L. *The achievement motive.* New York: Appleton-Century-Crofts, 1953.

McClelland, D. C., Clark, R. A., Roby, T. B., and Atkinson, J. W. The projective expression of needs: IV. The effect of the need for achievement on thematic apperception. *J. exp. Psychol.,* 1949, *39,* 242-255.

Martire, J. G. Relationships between self-concept and differences in the strength and generality of achievement motivation. *J. Pers.,* 1956, *24,* 364-375.

Mead, Margaret. *Male and female.* New York: Morrow, 1949.

Miller, N. E. Theory and experiment relating psychoanalytic displacement to stimulus-response generalization. *J. abnorm. soc. Psychol.,* 1948, *43,* 155-178.

701

Miller, N. E. Comments on theoretical models illustrated by the development of a theory of conflict behavior. *J. Pers.,* 1951, 20, 82-100.

Morgan, H. H. A psychometric comparison of achieving and nonachieving college students of high ability. *J. consult. Psychol.,* 1952, *16,* 292-298.

Morgan, H. H. Measuring achievement motivation with picture interpretation. *J. consult. Psychol.,* 1953, *17,* 289-292.

Moss, H. A., and Kagan, J. Stability of achievement and recognition seeking behaviors from early childhood through adulthood. *J. abnorm. soc. Psychol.,* 1961, *62,* 504-513.

Murstein, B. I. The role of the stimulus in the manifestation of fantasy. In J. Kagan & G. S. Lesser (Eds.), *Contemporary issues in thematic apperceptive methods.* Springfield, Ill.: Charles C. Thomas, 1961. Pp. 229-273.

Pierce, J. V., and Bowman, P. H. Motivation patterns of superior high school students. *Coop. res. Mongr.,* 1960, No. 2, 33-66. (USDHEW Publ. No. OE-35016).

Ricciuti. H. N. and Sadacca, R. The prediction of academic grades with a projective test of achievement motivation: II. Cross validation at the high school level. Princeton: Educational Testing Service, 1955.

Rosen, B. C. The achievement syndrome: A psychocultural dimension of social stratification. *Amer. sociol. Rev.,* 1955, *21,* 203-211.

Samelson, F. The relation of achievement and affiliation motives to conforming behavior in two conditions of conflict with majority. In J. W. Atkinson (Ed.), *Motives in fantasy, action, and society.* Princeton: Van Nostrand, 1958. Pp. 421-433.

Terman, L. M., and McNemar, Q. *Tests of mental ability.* New York: World Book, 1941.

Veroff, J., Atkinson, J. W., Feld, Sheila C., and Gurin, G. The use of thematic apperception to assess motivation in a nationwide interview study. *Psychol. Monogr.,* 1960, *74,* (12, Whole No. 499).

Veroff, J., Wilcox, Sue, and Atkinson, J. W. The achievement motive in high school and college age women. *J. abnorm. soc. Psychol.,* 1953, *48,* 108-119.

Wagner, R. F., and Williams, J. E. An analysis of speech behavior in groups differing in achievement imagery and defensiveness. *J. Pers.,* 1961, *29,* 1-9.

42

Matina Horner, the president of Radcliffe College, became extremely well known for her research on women's fear of success. While exploring the basis for sex differences in achievement motivation, Horner found that women have a conflict between achievement or success on the one hand vs. maintaining their "femininity" or sex-role stereotype on the other. If the woman succeeds, she worries about being rejected by males because she is too competitive or too aggressive. Male Ss did not show similar conflicts. They were very positive and direct about achievement.

In this more recent, well-written and enjoyable paper, which reviews several research studies in this area, the same theme recurs. Highly competent, achievement-motivated young women have a conflict. They can choose to express their abilities or else maintain their feminine image. It is an "either-or" proposition, and the conflict is even more intense in a society that is achievement-oriented. The woman who leaves the mainstream of achievement will pay for it in emotional and interpersonal difficulties.

Horner mentions another somewhat ancillary problem. In the future the role of a mother and housewife, which is centered around having children and which is still the major source of self-esteem for women, will have to be restricted in the light of the ever growing population problem. Horner reports that the alternatives of acquiring self-esteem through achievement and success in activities outside the home seems both inevitable and necessary.

This paper discusses in more depth some of the points empirically reported by Crandall. Horner looks for causes and solutions.

Toward an Understanding of Achievement Related Conflicts in Women*

Matina S. Horner

The motive to avoid success is conceptualized within the framework of an expectancy-value theory of motivation. It is identified as an internal psychological representative of the dominant societal stereotype which views competence, independence, competition, and intellectual achievement as qualities basically inconsistent with femininity even though positively related to masculinity and mental health. The expectancy that success in achievement-related situations will be followed by negative consequences arouses fear of success in otherwise achievement-motivated women which then inhibits their performance and levels of aspiration. The incidence of fear of success is considered as a function of the age, sex, and educational and occupational level of subjects tested between 1964 and 1971. Impairment of the educational and interpersonal functioning of those high in fear of success is noted and consequences for both the individual and society are discussed.

The prevalent image of women found throughout history, amidst both scholarly and popular circles, has with few exceptions converged on the idea that femininity and individual achievements which reflect intellectual competence or leadership potential are desirable but mutually exclusive goals. The aggressive and, by implication, masculine qualities inherent in a capacity for mastering intellectual problems, attacking difficulties, and making final decisions are considered fundamentally antagonistic to or incompatible with femininity. Since the time of Freud's treatise on the "Psychology of Women," the essence of femininity has been equated with the absence or "the repression of (their) aggressiveness, which is imposed upon women by their constitutions and by society [Freud, 1933, p. 158]." For instance:

---

* From *Journal of Social Issues*, 1972, *28* (2), 157-75.

. . . it is highly probable that the undoubted superiority of the male sex in intellectual and creative achievement is related to their greater endowment of aggression. . . . The hypothesis that women, if only given the opportunity and encouragement, would equal or surpass the creative achievements of men is hardly defensible [Stoff, 1970, p. 68]. Each step forward as a successful American regardless of sex means a step back as a woman [Mead, 1949].

It has taken us a long time to become aware of the extent to which this image of woman has actually been internalized, thus acquiring the capacity to exert psychological pressures on our behavior of which we are frequently unaware.

It is clear in our data, just as in Broverman, Vogel, Broverman, Clarkson, and Rosenkrantz (1970), that the young men and women tested over the past seven years still tend to evaluate themselves and to behave in ways consistent with the dominant stereotype that says competition, independence, competence, intellectual achievement, and leadership reflect positively on mental health and masculinity but are basically inconsistent or in conflict with femininity.

Thus despite the fact that we have a culture and an educational system that ostensibly encourage and prepare men and women identically for careers, the data indicate that social and, even more importantly, internal psychological barriers rooted in this image really limit the opportunities to men.

A PSYCHOLOGICAL BARRIER
TO ACHIEVEMENT IN WOMEN

Maccoby (1963) has pointed out that a girl who maintains the qualities of independence and active striving which are necessary for intellectual mastery defies the conventions of sex appropriate behavior and must pay a price in anxiety. This idea is encompassed in the conceptualization (Horner, 1968) of the Motive to Avoid Success (M_{-s}) which was developed in an attempt to understand or explain the major unresolved sex differences detected in previous research on achievement motivation (Atkinson, 1958;

705

WOMAN: DEPENDENT OR INDEPENDENT VARIABLE?

McClelland, Atkinson, Clark, & Lowell, 1953). When it was first introduced as a psychological barrier to achievement in women, the Motive to Avoid Success was conceptualized within the framework of an expectancy-value theory of motivation as a latent, stable personality disposition acquired early in life in conjunction with standards of sex role identity. In expectancy-value theories of motivation, the most important factors in determining the arousal of these dispositions or motives and thereby the ultimate strength of motivation and direction of one's behavior are: (a) the expectations or beliefs the individual has about the nature and likelihood of the consequences of his/her actions, and (b) the value of these consequences to the individual in light of his/her particular motives. Anxiety is aroused, according to the theory, when one expects that the consequences of action will be negative. The anxiety then functions to inhibit the action expected to have the negative consequences; it does not, however, determine which action will then be undertaken. In other words, within this framework, avoidance motives inhibit actions expected to have unattractive consequences. They can tell us what someone will *not* do, but not what he *will* do. The latter is a function of which positive-approach motives and tendencies are characteristic of the individual (Atkinson & Feather, 1966; Horner, 1970a).

With this in mind, I argued that most women have a motive to avoid success, that is, a disposition to become anxious about achieving success because they expect negative consequences (such as social rejection and/or feelings of being unfeminine) as a result of succeeding. Note that this is not to say that most women "want to fail" or have a "motive to approach failure." The presence of a "will to fail" would, in accordance with the theory, imply that they actively seek out failure because they anticipate or expect positive consequences from failing. The presence of a motive to avoid success, on the other hand, implies that the expression of the achievement-directed tendencies of most otherwise positively motivated young women is inhibited by the arousal of a thwarting disposition to be anxious about the negative consequences they expect will follow the desired success.

A review of the results of the several studies carried out over the past few years, summarized in Table 1, substantiates the idea that despite the emphasis on a new freedom for women, particularly since the mid sixties, negative attitudes expressed toward and about successful women have remained high and perhaps even increased and intensified among both male and female subjects.

706

Matina S. Horner

INDIVIDUAL DIFFERENCES IN THE STRENGTH
OF THE MOTIVE TO AVOID SUCCESS: ITS
ASSESSMENT AND FUNCTIONAL SIGNIFICANCE

It was hypothesized (Horner, 1968) that the motive to avoid success would be significantly more characteristic of women than of men, and also more characteristic of high achievement oriented, high ability women who aspire to and/or are capable of achieving success than of low achievement oriented, low ability women who neither aspire to nor can achieve success. After all, if you neither want nor can achieve success, the expectancy of negative consequences because of success would be rather meaningless It was sssumed that individual differences in the strength of the motive to avoid success would not be manifested in behavior unless aroused by the expectancy that negative consequences would follow success. This is most likely to occur in competitive achievement situations in which performance reflecting intellectual and leadership ability is to be evaluated against a standard of excellence and *also* against a competitor's performance. Once aroused, the tendency or motivation to avoid success would inhibit the expression of all positive motivation or tendencies to do well and thus should have an adverse effect on performance in these situations. It was assumed, furthermore, that the negative incentive value or repulsive aspects of success should be greater for women in interpersonal competition than in noncompetitive achievement situations, especially against male competitors.

In order to test our hypotheses about the presence and impact of the motive to avoid success, it was necessary to develop a measure of individual differences in the motive. At the end of the Standard Thematic Apperceptive Test (TAT) for measuring the achievement motive, in which verbal leads rather than pictures were used, an additional verbal lead connoting a high level of accomplishment in a mixed-sex competitive achievement situation was included. The 90 females in the initial study responded to the lead "After first term finals, Anne finds herself at the top of her medical school class." For the 88 males in the sample, the lead was "After first term finals, John finds himself at the top of his medical school class." The subjects were predominantly freshmen and sophomore undergraduate students at a large midwestern university.

A very simple present-absent system was adopted for scoring fear of success imagery. The specific criteria used as an indication

TABLE 1

INCIDENCE OF FEAR OF SUCCESS IMAGERY IN SAMPLES TESTED, 1964–1970

Study	Year Data Gathered	Nature of the Sample	N	Subjects Showing the Response TAT Format (Standard Verbal Cue) N	%
Horner, 1968	1964	*College Freshmen & Sophomores*	178		
		Males	88	8	9.1
		Females	90	59	65.5
Horner & Rhoem, 1968	1967	*All Female*			
		Junior High (7th grade)	19	9	47.0
		Senior High (11th grade)	15	9	60.0
		College Undergraduates	27	22	81.0
		Secretaries	15	13	86.6
		Students at an Eastern University			
Schwenn, 1970	1969	Female Juniors[a]	16	12	75.0
Horner, 1970b	1969	Female Juniors/Seniors	45	38	84.4
		Same Subjects[a]	45	34	75.5
		Female Law School Students	15	13	86.6
Watson, 1970	1970	Female Summer School Students	37	24	65.0
Prescott, 1971	1970	Male Freshmen	36	17	47.2
		Female Freshmen	34	30	88.2
		Same Females 3 months later	34	29	85.3

[a] Questionnaire format employed.

of the motive to avoid success were developed in accordance with Scott's (1958) results. His data show what happens in a TAT when a person is confronted with a cue or situation that represents a threat rather than a goal, or simultaneously represents a goal and a threat. These can be found in Horner (1968, 1970b). Briefly, the Motive to Avoid Success is scored as present if the subjects, in response to a thematic lead about a successful figure *of their own sex,* made statements in their stories showing conflict about the success, the presence or anticipation of negative consequences because of the success, denial of effort or responsibility for attaining the success, denial of the cue itself, or some other bizarre or inappropriate response to the cue. In accordance with our hypothesis, fear of success imagery dominated the female responses and was relatively absent in the male responses.

In response to the successful male cue, more than 90% of the men in the study showed strong positive feelings, indicated increased striving, confidence in the future, and a belief that this success would be instrumental to fulfilling other goals—such as providing a secure and happy home for some girl. For example, there was the story in which John is thinking about his girl, Cheri, whom he will marry at the end of med school and to whom he can give all the things she desires after he becomes established. He decides he must not let up, but must work even harder than he did before so as to be able to go into research. Fewer than 10% of the men responded at all negatively and these focussed primarily on the young man's rather dull personality.

On the other hand, in response to the successful female cue 65% of the girls were disconcerted, troubled, or confused by the cue. Unusual excellence in women was clearly associated for them with the loss of femininity, social rejection, personal or societal destruction, or some combination of the above. Their responses were filled with negative consequences and affect, righteous indignation, withdrawal rather than enhanced striving, concern, or even an inability to accept the information presented in the cue. There was a typical story, for example, in which Anne deliberately lowers her academic standing the next term and does all she subtly can to help Carl, whose grades come up. She soon drops out of med-school, they marry, and Carl goes on in school while she raises their family.

Some girls stressed that Anne is unhappy, aggressive, unmarried, or that she is so ambitious that she uses her family, husband, and friends as tools in the advancement of her career. Others argued that Anne is a code name for a non-existent person created by a group of med students who take turns taking exams and writing papers for Anne. In other words, women showed significantly more evidence of the motive to avoid success than did the men, with 59 of the 90 women scoring high and only 8 of the 88 men doing so. (The chi square difference of 58.05 was significant at $p < .0005$).

The pattern of sex differences in the production of fear of success imagery found in the first study has been maintained in the subsequent samples of (white) men and women tested since that time (see Table 1). The major difference has been an increase, noted over the past two years, in the extent to which fear of success imagery or negative consequences are expressed by male subjects in response to cues about successful male figures, who have come increasingly to be viewed as lacking a social consciousness and having "Waspish" or selfish personalities; e.g., "John will finish med school with very high honors—marry the fattest woman in town and become an extremely rich and self-centered doctor."

The fact that college students of both sexes, but especially the men, are currently taking an increasingly negative view of success as it has been traditionally defined is reflected in another set of recent data collected in the winter of 1970 (Prescott, 1971). Forty-seven percent of the 36 male freshmen undergraduates in this sample responded with negative imagery to the cue. This was a significant increase with respect to previous male samples. Even in this sample, however, significant sex differences in the presence of fear of success imagery were maintained. Thirty, or 88%, of the 34 women tested scored high in fear of success compared with 17, or 47%, of the 36 men tested ($x^2 = 13.43$, $p < .01$). Furthermore, the content of the stories differed significantly between the sexes. Most of the men who responded with the expectation of negative consequences because of success were not concerned about their masculinity but were instead likely to have expressed existential concerns about finding a "non-materialistic happiness and satisfaction in life." These concerns, which reflect changing attitudes toward traditional kinds of success or achievement in our society, played little, if any, part in the female stories. Most of the women who were high in fear of success imagery continued to be concerned about the discrepancy between success in the situation described and feminine identity. In the past two years, the manifest content of this concern has been demonstrated in several new themes that were not evident in previous work. Take, for example, the story in which Anne feels out of place and has "*a fear of becoming a lesbian . . . maybe she shouldn't have cheated* on the exam, then the other men would have felt better about her being stupid"; or, that in which she wants to go on to a career in law and doesn't particularly want children: "Her husband wants to do as well as she is, but feels unable to. She will go on in law school. *He will substitute sugar for her pills so she gets knocked up.* She has the baby—in between lectures—and an hour later is back at the books. He hits his head against the wall."

One of the objectives of several studies done was simply to observe the incidence of Fear of Success imagery in female subjects at different ages and at different educational, occupational, and ability levels. The specific content of the verbal lead used in each sample was altered so as to make the situation described more consistent and meaningful with respect to the age, educational level, and occupation of the subjects being tested. For instance, in the junior high and high school levels the cue used was "Sue has just found out that she has been made valedictorian of her class." The results summarized in Table 1 show that the incidence of M-s in the samples we've tested has ranged from a low of 47% in a 7th grade junior high school sample to a high of 88% in a sample of high ability current undergraduate students at a high ranking eastern school (see Table 1). The incidence of fear of success found in a sample of administrative secretaries in a large corporation, all of whom were able high school graduates, was also high (86.6%). In each of the female *college* samples tested so far, fear of success imagery has ranged from 60%-88%.

THE IMPACT OF M____s ON LEVELS OF ASPIRATION AND PERFORMANCE IN ACHIEVEMENT-ORIENTED SITUATIONS

In light of the vast sex differences found in the presence of Fear of Success imagery it seemed very important to study the differential impact of individual differences in the motive to avoid success on performance and levels of aspiration in achievement-oriented situations, and, furthermore, to understand what personal and situational factors are most effective in arousing the motive or in keeping it in check.

In accordance with the theory, the motive to avoid success is believed to affect performance only in situations in which it is aroused. The assumption that fear of success is aroused in situations in which there is concern over or anxiety about competitiveness and its aggressive overtones was tested and received support in the first study (Horner, 1968). For 30 male and 30 female subjects it was possible to compare the level of their performance on a number of achievement tasks in a large mixed-sex competitive situation with their own subsequent performance in a strictly noncompetitive but achievement-oriented situation in which the only competition involved was with the task and one's internal standards of excellence. This was the best group on which to test the hypothesis because each subject acted as his own control for ability effects. Thirteen of the 17 girls in this group who had scored high in the M_{-s} performed at a significantly lower level in the mixed-sex competitive condition than they subsequently did in the noncompetitive condition. Twelve of the 13 girls in the group who had scored low in fear of success on the other hand did better under the competitive condition, as did most of the male (2/3) subjects in this group (Horner, 1968). In other words, in accordance with the hypothesis only 1 of the 13 girls low in fear of success showed the performance decrement under competition which was characteristic of the girls high in fear of success. (The chi square difference between the groups was 11.37, $p < .01$).

Anxiety about success was the only one of the four other psychological variables for which individual differences were assessed in the study that predicted female performance. It is important to note that the motive to avoid success showed no relationship with the strength of the affiliation motive nor did the latter predict to the performance of the female subjects. The results of this part of the study clearly indicated that young women, especially those high in the motive to avoid success, would be least likely to develop their interests and explore their intellectual potential when competing against others, especially against men.

These conclusions, drawn from the preceding *within* subject analysis, were supported by comparing the questionnaire responses of all 90 female subjects who had been randomly assigned *between* each of three experimental conditions, two competitive and one noncompetitive. Following her performance in one of the experimental achievement-oriented conditions, each subject was asked to indicate on a scale, "How important was it for you to do well in this situation?" In both competitive conditions the mean level of importance reported by subjects high in anxiety about success was significantly lower than for subjects low in anxiety about success ($p < .05$). In the noncompetitive condition the difference, although short of the conventionally accepted level of significance ($p < .10$), was in the same direction. For subjects high in motive to avoid success, differences in mean level of importance between the noncompetitive condition and each of the competitive conditions were significant ($p < .05$); but no significant differences were found between the conditions for the subjects low in motive to avoid success. A more complete discussion of these results can be found in Horner (1968).

Arousing or Minimizing M$_{-s}$

Schwenn's (1970) results in a small pilot study of 16 women at an outstanding eastern women's college began our exploration of the elements of both a personal and situational nature present during the college experience which arouse the motive to avoid success. Most of the students arrive at the highly select school dedicated to the idea of distinguishing themselves in a future career, even if they are not sure what it will be. According to Schwenn's data, by the time these women are juniors most have changed their plans and aspirations toward a less ambitious, more traditionally feminine direction. This is similar to Tangri's (1969) findings at a large midwestern university. Although Schwenn's sample was small, approximating a case study approach, the findings were useful in raising a number of important questions for further exploration.

Schwenn used a questionnaire and intensive interviews to explore the impact on behavior of the motive to avoid success. Particular attention was paid to how this motive influences the educational and career aspirations of these very bright and highly motivated young women especially at a time in our society when self-actualization and the equality of women are drawing much public attention. All the girls in the sample were doing well and had grade point averages of B or better. Nevertheless, 12 of the 16 girls showed evidence of fear of success on a modified questionnaire version of the TAT cue. In this version subjects are not asked to write a thematic story but are asked instead simply to describe the person represented in the cue. The same scoring criteria are used for both forms and evidence of fear of success from both is highly correlated (Horner, 1970b). Subjects whose descriptions indicated the possible presence of a motive to avoid success manifested their anxiety in several ways. To begin with, they prefer not to divulge the fact that they are doing well or have received an "A" to male peers, preferring instead to make their failures known. The more successful they were the less likely they were to want to say so. All 3 of the girls who had straight A averages would prefer to tell a boy that they have gotten a "C" than an "A." Most of the girls with B's preferred to report an "A." Whereas all 4 of the girls whose descriptions manifested low fear of success said they were more likely to report an "A" to a male friend (sometimes coupled with an explanation), only one-third of the 12 girls indicating high fear of success were likely to do so.

Even more important perhaps is the fact that only 2 of the 16 girls in the sample had in fact after three years of college changed their

713

plans toward a more ambitious or more traditionally masculine direction. The rest report changes in their majors and future career plans toward what *each of them considered to be for her a more traditional, appropriately feminine, and less ambitious one,* i.e., to work for a politician instead of being a politician, to teach instead of going to law school, to become a housewife instead of any number of things.

Individual differences in evidence of M-s were very effective in predicting these patterns of behavior. Eleven of the 12 girls in the study whose descriptions suggested the presence of high fear of success had actually changed their aspirations toward a more traditional direction. Only one of the four evidencing low fear of success did so. A Fisher test showed this difference to be significant at better than the .05 level.

Just how important it is to attend to an individual's subjective expectations and evaluation of certain careers was clearly emphasized by the subject who changed her career goals from medicine to law because "Law School is less ambitious, it doesn't take as long . . . is more flexible in terms of marriage and children. It is *less masculine* in that it is more accepted now for girls to go to law school." The others who changed their aspirations from law school to "teaching" or "housewife" apparently did not hold the same expectations about a law career.

Although several of the girls had started out majoring in the natural sciences with the intent of pursuing a medical career, all were now, as juniors, majoring in traditionally females areas like English, fine arts, French, and history. These findings reflect the idea that no one seriously objects to a higher education in a woman provided the objective is to make her a generally educated and thus a more interesting and enlightened companion, wife, and/or mother. The objections arise only when the individual's objectives become more personal and career-oriented, especially in nontraditional areas. These findings are, furthermore, consistent with a subsequent analysis of data gathered from the 90 female subjects in the initial study (Horner, 1968). This analysis showed that 88.9% of the 59 girls high in fear of success were majoring in the humanities and 56% of the 31 low in anxiety about success were concentrating in the less traditional natural sciences like math and chemistry.

Two factors explored by Schwenn in her study as the ones most likely to arouse the motive to avoid success and thus to negatively influence the achievement strivings of these girls were the parental attitudes and those of the male peers toward appropriate sex role behavior.

The 16 girls in this sample lend support to Komarovsky's (1959) argument that in the later college years girls experience a sudden reversal in what parents applaud for them; i.e., whereas they have previously been applauded for academic success these girls now find themselves being evaluated "in terms of some abstract standard of femininity with an emphasis on marriage as the appropriate goal for girls of this age."

This is again consistent with the results of a follow up analysis of data gathered in the initial study which showed that 78% of the 59 girls who scored high in fear of success came from predominantly upper middle and middle class homes, with fathers who were successful business or professional men. Their families placed a premium value on competence and independence, and this is just the kind of background that McClelland and others (see McClelland, 1961) have shown to be conducive to the development of high achievement motivation, the expression of which is subsequently viewed as inconsistent with a feminine sex-role stereotype. This provides the basis for the conflict manifested in the motive to avoid success. Only 33% of the 31 subjects who had scored low in fear of success, on the other hand, had backgrounds of this type; the rest of the low fear of success girls came from primarily lower middle class homes.

There was apparently no relationship in the Schwenn study between shifts in the attitudes of the parents and fear of success in the girls, nor did there appear to be any direct indication that parents had influenced anyone to turn away from a role-innovative type of career. If anything, the unintended effect appears to be in the opposite direction—as in the case of the girl who said, "There is a lot of pressure from my mother to get married and not have a career. This *is one reason I am going to have a career* and wait to get married."

Some girls even report being motivated for careers by the negative examples set by their mothers.

> My mother is now working as a secretary, but she didn't work until now. I don't want to end up like that.
> Another reason I am going to have a career and wait to get married is a reaction to my mother's empty life.

How much of this is a pattern really restricted to this sample or one that can be generalized is an important question which remains to be seen in later studies.

Attitudes of Male Peers

The attitude of male peers toward the appropriate role of

women, which they apparently do not hesitate to express, appears to be a most significant factor in arousing the motive to avoid success. In the Schwenn Study (1970), the girls who showed evidence of anxiety about success and social rejection and had altered their career aspirations toward a more traditional direction were either not dating at all (those with the all A averages) or were dating men who do not approve of "career women." When asked, for instance, how the boys in their lives feel about their aspirations, frequent responses were "they laugh," "think it's ridiculous for me to go to graduate school or law school," or "say I can be happy as a housewife and I just need to get a liberal arts education." Several indicated they were "turning more and more to the traditional role" because of the attitudes of male friends whose opinions were important: "I need someone [a man] to respect me and what I want to do, to lend importance to what I sense is important." This is consistent with the idea, frequently reported in the literature, that women are dependent on others for their self-esteem and have difficulty believing they can function well autonomously.

Those girls on the other hand who had scored low in fear of success or those who had scored high in fear of success but were continuing to strive for innovative careers were either engaged to or seriously dating men who were not against nor threatened by their success. In fact, they expected it of their girls and provided much encouragement for them: "I would have to explain myself if I got a C."

One of the factors distinguishing the couples in this second group from those in the first is a mutual understanding, either overt or covert, that the boy is the more intelligent of the two: "He's so much smarter . . . competition with him would be hopeless." This fact or belief seems to be sufficient to keep the motive from being aroused and affecting the behavior of the girls in this second group. Tension exists between the couples in the first group rooted in the fear that she is the more intelligent one.

The importance of male attitudes is being further tested in a current study which looks at how fear of success influences the expectations and performance of young (college) girls when competing against their own boyfriends, as compared to how well they have done in a previous noncompetitive setting. The attitudes of the boyfriends toward achievement in women are assessed prior to performance in this situation. It is hypothesized that negative attitudes on the part of the men will be significantly correlated with arousal of fear of success in their girl friends, which will be manifested in performance decrements by the girls when competing against their boyfriends.

As our work has progressed it has become increasingly clear that the problems of achievement motivation in women are more complex than simply the matter of whether or not women have internalized a more or less traditional view of the female role. A complex relationship or interaction appears to exist between the girl's internal personality dispositions or motives and certain situational factors which determine the nature of the expectancy a girl has about the consequences of her actions and the value of these consequences to her in that situation. It is these latter factors which determine whether or not internalized dispositions will be aroused and therefore influence behavior. Does, for instance, the girl care about the male competitor and possible rejection that may ensue if she does better than he does?

CONSEQUENCES OF THE MOTIVE TO AVOID SUCCESS

As indicated, our data argue that unfortunately femininity and competitive achievement continue in American society, even today, to be viewed as two desirable but mutually exclusive ends. As a result, the recent emphasis on the new freedom for women has not been effective in removing the psychological barrier in many otherwise achievement motivated and able young women that prevents them from actively seeking success or making obvious their abilities and potential. There is mounting evidence in our data suggesting that many achievement-oriented American women, especially those high in the motive to avoid success, when faced with the conflict between their feminine image and developing their abilities and interests, disguise their ability and abdicate from competition in the outside world—just like Sally in the Peanuts cartoon who at the tender age of five says: "I never said I wanted to *be* someone. All I want to do when I grow up is be a good wife and mother. So . . . why should I have to go to kindergarten?" When success is likely or possible, threatened by the negative consequences they expect to follow success, young women become anxious and their positive achievement strivings become thwarted. In this way, their abilities, interests, and intellectual potential remain inhibited and unfulfilled.

A subsequent analysis of the data in the initial study (Horner, 1968), together with that of our most recent studies, shows however that these processes do not occur without a price, a price paid in feelings of frustration, hostility, aggression, bitterness, and confusion which are plainly manifested in the fantasy productions of young women. This was made clear by a comparison of the thematic apperceptive imagery written in response to the cue

"Anne is sitting in a chair with a smile on her face" by women who had scored high in fear of success with that by those who had scored low. In response to the "smile cue," more than 90% of those low in fear of success imagery wrote positive, primarily affiliative stories centering on such things as dates, engagements, and forthcoming marriages, as well as a few on successful achievements. On the other hand, less than 20% of the 59 women who scored high in fear of success responded in this way. The rest of the responses, if not bizarre, were replete with negative imagery centering on hostility toward or manipulation of others.

Stories characteristic of the girls low in fear of success are exemplified by the following:

> Her boyfriend has just called her . . . Oh boy. I'm so excited what shall I wear . . . Will he like me? I am so excited. Ann is very happy. Ann will have a marvelous time.
>
> Anne is happy—she's happy with the world because it is so beautiful. It's snowing, and nice outside—she's happy to be alive and this gives her a good warm feeling. Well, Anne did well on one of her tests.

In comparison, the stories written by girls high in fear of success were dramtically different and distressing. Consider these examples:

> Anne is recollecting her conquest of the day. She has just stolen her ex-friend's boyfriend away, right before the High School Senior Prom because she wanted to get back at her friend.
>
> She is sitting in a chair smiling smugly because she has just achieved great satisfaction from the fact that she hurt somebody's feelings.
>
> Gun in hand she is waiting for her stepmother to return home.
>
> Anne is at her father's funeral. There are over 200 people there. She knows it is unseemly to smile but cannot help it . . . Her brother Ralph pokes her in fury but she is uncontrollable . . . Anne rises dramatically and leaves the room, stopping first to pluck a carnation from the blanket of flowers on the coffin.

At this point we can only speculate about how much of what was expressed in the fantasy productions of these girls was a true reflection of their actual behavior or intents, and secondly, if it was, what repercussions there might be. The psychodynamic causes and consequences of these differences are among a number of yet unanswered questions.

The results from data gathered by Watson (1970) as part of a larger study show a significant relationship between presence of the motive to avoid success and self-reported drug taking which is relevant to the psychodynamic issues raised. The drug taking measure involved a questionnaire estimate by the subjects of their frequency of use of drugs such as marijuana, LSD, and speed. Of the 37 college women in Watson's study, 24 (65%) scored high in fear of success. Of these, 13 described themselves as using drugs frequently, 6 moderately, and 5 never. Of the 13 girls low in fear of success, only 1 was a heavy drug user, 5 were moderate, and 7 never used them. The chi square difference between the groups was 8.12, with $df = 2$, $p < .05$. Whereas 54% of the high fear of success girls reported heavy drug usage, only 7.7% of the low fear of success girls did so.

The causal direction of this observed relationship can only be a matter of speculation at this point. Just what the functional significance of heavy drug use is for high fear of success women remains a question that must be considered along with the rest of the data showing that negative consequences for women ensue when the expression of their achievement needs or efficacious behavior is blocked by the presence of the motive to avoid success.

CONCLUSIONS

It is not unreasonable now to speculate that what we have observed in the laboratory does in fact extend into and influence the intellectual, professional, and personal lives of men and women in our society.

In light of the high and, if anything, increasing incidence of the motive to avoid success found among women in our studies (see Table 1), the predominant message seems to be that most highly competent and otherwise achievement motivated young women, when faced with a conflict between their feminine image and expressing their competencies or developing their abilities and interests, adjust their behaviors to their internalized sex-role stereotypes. We have seen that even within our basically achievement-oriented society the anticipation of success, especially in interpersonal competitive situations, can be regarded as a mixed blessing if not an outright threat. Among women, the anticipation of success especially against a male competitor poses a threat to the sense of femininity and self-esteem and serves as a potential basis for becoming socially rejected—in other words, the anticipation of success is anxiety provoking and as such inhibits otherwise positive achievement-directed motivation and behavior. In order to feel or appear more feminine, women, especially those high in fear of success, disguise their abilities and withdraw from the mainstream of thought, activism, and achievement in our society. This does not occur, however, without a high price, a price paid by the individual in negative emotional and interpersonal consequences and by the society in a loss of valuable human and economic resources.

The issues addressed here are particularly important in light of the population problems now facing society and the appeals being made to women to have fewer children. Inasmuch as having children is one of the major sources of self-esteem for women, it becomes necessary to have other options for enhancing self-esteem available to those who will respond to appeals to avoid overpopulation. Achievement in the outside world is one such possibility, but one which we have found is not at present a viable option because of the presence of psychological barriers like the motive to avoid success. It is clear that much remains to be done to respond fully to the issues raised and to understand the factors involved in the development and subsequent arousal of a motive to avoid success.

REFERENCES

Atkinson, J. W. (Ed.) *Motives in fantasy, action, and society.* Princeton, N.J.: Van Nostrand, 1958.

Atkinson, J. W., and Feather, N. T. *A theory of achievement motivation.* New York: Wiley, 1966.

Broverman, I. K., Vogel, S. R., Broverman, D. M., Clarkson, F. E., and Rosenkrantz, P. S. Sex role stereotypes and clinical judgments of mental health. *Journal of Consulting and Clinical Psychology,* 1970, *34,* (1), 1-7.

Freud, S. The psychology of women. In *New introductory lectures on psychoanalysis.* New York: Norton, 1933. (Republished: 1965).

Horner, M. Sex differences in achievement motivation and performance in competitive and non-competitive situations. Unpublished doctoral dissertation, University of Michigan, 1968.

Horner, M. Femininity and successful achievement: A basic inconsistency. In J. Bardwick, E. M. Douvan, M. S. Horner, and D. Gutmann (Eds.), *Feminine personality and conflict.* Belmont, Calif.: Brooks-Cole, 1970 (a).

Horner, M. The motive to avoid success and changing aspirations of college women. Unpublished manuscript, Harvard University, 1970 (b).

Horner, M., and Rhoem, W. The motive to avoid success as a function of age, occupation and progress at school. Unpublished manuscript, University of Michigan, 1968.

Komarovsky, M. Functional analysis of sex roles. *American Sociological Review,* 1959, *15,* 508-516.

Maccoby, E. Women's intellect. In S. M. Farber and R. H. L. Wilson (Eds.). *The potential of women,* New York: McGraw-Hill, 1963.

McClelland, D. C., Atkinson, J. W., Clark, R. A., and Lowell, E. L. *The achievement motive.* New York: Appleton-Century-Crofts, 1953.

McClelland, D. C. *The achieving society.* New York: Van Nostrand, 1961.

Mead, M. *Male and female.* New York: Morrow, 1949. (Republished: New York; Dell, 1968).

Prescott, D. Efficacy-related imagery, education and politics. Unpublished honors thesis, Harvard University, 1971.

Schwenn, M. Arousal of the motive to avoid success. Unpublished junior honors thesis, Harvard University, 1970.

Scott, W. A. The avoidance of threatening material in imaginative behavior. In Atkinson, J. W.(Ed.), *Motives in fantasy, action and society.* Princeton, N.J.: Van Nostrand, 1958.

Starr, A. *Human Aggression.* New York: Bantam, 1970.

Tangri, S. Role innovation in occupational choice. Unpublished doctoral dissertation, University of Michigan, 1969.

Watson, R. Female and male responses to the succeeding female cue. Unpublished manuscript, Harvard University, 1970.

43

This paper surveys the literature and discusses another type of conflict that interferes with women's achievement. The focus of this paper is the conflict between a woman's desire for success and her fear of a loss of femininity as well as a fear of being rejected socially. Hoffman maintains that studies point out that women have greater affiliative needs then men do; therefore this problem or conflict between need for affiliation and need for achievement is much more acute for women.

Hoffman theorizes that the female child is not given adequate encouragement in early independence strivings; and since she is the same sex as the mother, she has fewer confrontations with problems or challenges. Girls are rewarded for love, rather than mastery of a challenge or independence strivings, and this strengthens their affiliative needs. In contrast, Hoffman points out studies that conclude that boys are more motivated to conquer challenging tasks, which would strenghten their motive to achieve.

After these childhood experiences, in college years we see the young woman who is intellectually equal or superior to her male colleagues, but who suppresses her achievement motivation because she is more interested in "pleasing" her competition in order to "affiliate" rather than to succeed.

This well-written, thoughtful, and thought-provoking review article expands our critical thinking about the internal reasons underlying woman's failure to achieve and reach her potential.

Early Childhood Experiences and Women's Achievement Motive*

Lois Wladis Hoffman

Research findings in child development are reviewed to shed light on female achievement motives. It is suggested that females have high needs for affiliation which influence their achievement motives and behavior, sometimes enhancing and sometimes blocking them. Since girls as compared to boys have less encouragement for independence, more parental protectiveness, less pressure for establishing an identity separate from the other, and less mother-child conflict which highlights this separation, they engage in less independent exploration of their environments. As a result they develop neither adequate skills nor confidence but continue to be dependent upon others. Thus while boys learn effectance through mastery, the effectiveness of girls is contingent on eliciting the help of others. Affective relationships are paramount in females and much of their achievement behavior is motivated by a desire to please. If achievement threatens affiliation, performance may be sacrificed or anxiety may result.

The failure of women to fulfill their intellectual potential has been adequately documented. The explanations for this are so plentiful that one is almost tempted to ask why women achieve at all. Their social status is more contingent on whom they marry than what they achieve; their sense of femininity and others' perception of them as feminine is jeopardized by too much academic and professional success; their husband's masculinity, and hence their love relationship as well as their reciprocal sense of femininity, is threatened if they surpass him; discrimination against women in graduate school admittance and the professions puts a limit on what rewards their performance will receive; their roles as wives and mothers take time from their professional efforts and offer alternative sources of self-esteem. Perhaps most important, they have an alternative to professional success and can opt out when

---

* From *Journal of Social Issues,* 1972, 28 (2), 129-55.

the going gets rough. A full scale achievement effort involves painful periods of effort and many a man would drop out if that alternative were as readily available as it is to women. (Indeed, the Vietnam war and the new distrust of the old goals have provided young men with just such an opportunity and many have grabbed it.) But women's underachievement must have roots deeper even than these, for the precursors of the underachieving woman can be seen in the female child.

Even at preschool age girls have different orientations toward intellectual tasks than do boys. Little girls want to please; they work for love and approval; if bright, they underestimate their competence. Little boys show more task involvement, more confidence, and are more likely to show IQ increments. Girls have more anxiety than boys and the anxiety they have is more dysfunctional to their performance. There are also differences in the specific skills of each sex: Males excel in spatial perceptions, arithmetical reasoning, general information, and show less set-dependency; girls excel in quick-perception of details, verbal fluency, rote memory and clerical skills.

Boys and girls enter the world with different constitutional make-ups, and recent studies show that parents treat boys and girls differently even from birth. Social roles are first—and most impressively—communicated through parent-child relations and events in early childhood may have an impact that cannot later be duplicated in effectiveness.

As a result, interest in women's intellectual achievement has led a number of people to look to the child development data for insights. A few of the limitations of these data will be discussed first, for a number of extravagant generalizations are being drawn from them.

LIMITATIONS OF CHILD DEVELOPMENT DATA

Relativity

Child development data are often relative to a given group. Thus a statement about girls who are "high on aggression" usually means high relative to the other girls studied. If they are compared to boys who are "high on aggression" even in the same study, the actual aggressive behavior may be very different. Boys are considerably more aggressive than girls; a girl who is high on aggression may resemble a boy whose aggressive behavior is coded as average. She may also differ from the boys with respect

725

to the form of aggression and the personality syndrome of which it is a part. It should not be surprising then to discover that the antecedent conditions of high aggression are different in boys and girls. They might very well be different even if the dependent variables were identical, but the fact is that they are not. We are comparing oranges with apples and discovering to our surprise that they grow on different trees.

This problem not only applies to the dependent variables, but also to the independent variables studied, usually parent behavior or the parent-child relationship. To use an actual finding, Kagan and Moss (1962) found that maternal protectiveness during the first three years was negatively related to adult achievement behavior for girls. This was not true for boys and in fact the relationship was positive although not statistically significant. This is an important finding to which we will return, but here it should be pointed out that we cannot tell from these correlations whether or not the actual maternal behavior is different for high achieving boys and girls. Girls are subject to more overprotection than boys and the same amount of protective behavior may be relatively low for a girl but average or high for a boy.

Baumrind (1970) has pointed out that obtaining data on the differential treatment (or behavior) of boys and girls is difficult because, even in behavioral observations, when the observer knows the sex of the child, "an automatic adjustment is made which tends to standardize judgments about the two sexes."

Generalizability

The problem of generalizing results obtained with one population to another occurs throughout the social sciences. It is particularly acute when the variables involve relative terms. "High parental coerciveness" in a middle class sample may not be considered high in a lower class sample. Furthermore, most empirical generalizations hold only within certain contexts. Variations in social class, parent education, rural-urban residence, family structure, and ethnicity—as well as changes over time—may make the generalizations inapplicable.

As an interesting case in point, it is impossible to generalize white sex differences to blacks for the patterns of sex differences are very different in the two groups. Studies of blacks will be important in interpreting the etiology of sex differences in intellectual performance for in many ways the black male resembles the white female. For both, school performance has been largely irrelevant to adult goals and there are interesting similarities in the patterns of achievement scores that may reflect this (Tulkin, 1968;

Jensen, 1970). In a study of conformity and perceptual judgment by Iscoe, Williams, and Harvey (1964), black males and white females were more influenced by others than were black females and white males. Similarities between black males and white females argue against constitutional explanations, for these two groups share neither hormones nor race—but they do share environmental handicaps.

Maturation

Another difficulty in interpreting sex differences among children pertains to differences in the maturity of boys and girls. The newborn girl is one month to six weeks developmentally ahead of the boy. At school entrance she is about one year ahead, depending on the index of growth used. Growth does not proceed equally on all fronts and the intellectual growth rate is not related to the physical (Bayley, 1956). These different degrees of maturity complicate the comparison between the sexes.

Conceptualization

Ambiguous concepts are a problem in many fields. The so-called inconsistencies in the child development data often upon close examination turn out to be inconsistencies in the researcher's summaries and concluding statments rather than in the actual findings. If examined in terms of the operational definitions, contradictory studies sometimes turn out to be dealing with different phenomena that have been given the same label. Among the particularly troublesome concepts that are important in the sex-difference literature are identification and dependency (Bronfenbrenner, 1960; Maccoby & Masters, 1970).

FEMALE ACHIEVEMENT ORIENTATIONS

There are very few studies that have empirically connected socialization experiences to sex differences in achievement orientations. As a matter of fact, there are few studies of sex differences in child rearing practices in general, and existing data— most of which were originally collected for other purposes—are subject to the limitations mentioned above. Promising new approaches sensitive to identifying sex differences may be found in the studies of parent-child interaction with neonates (Moss, 1967; Moss & Robson, 1968; Moss, Robson, & Pedersen, 1969; Lewis,

1969; Goldberg & Lewis, 1969; Kagan, 1969; Kagan, Levine, & Fishman, 1967). These are mainly longitudinal studies which will make their most valuable contributions in the future, but some have already examined relationships between maternal behavior and cognitive orientations.

Probably the richest current area in the study of sex differences has to do with cognitive styles. Witkin, Dyk, Faterson, Goodenough, & Karp (1962) as well as other investigators have ben interested in differences in perceptions of and approaches to problems. For example, some people are more affected by background stimuli than others. In a task in which the subject is asked to line up a rod until it is perpendicular, the fact that the frame around the rod is tilted will affect the judgment of some respondents more than others. Those most affected by the tilting frame are said to be field dependent. This body of research has revealed a number of personality traits that are associated with performance on the task, and a number of cognitive skills such as mathematical ability that seem to be closely tied to field independence. These personality traits describe differences between the sexes; the corresponding cognitive abilities similarly differentiate.

For example, Maccoby (1963, 1966)[1] has pointed out that girls are more conforming, suggestible, and dependent upon the opinions of others. These traits in turn have been related to field dependency, inability to break the set of a task, and IQ's that tend to decrease rather than increase over the years. She suggests that these same traits in females might also account for their superior performance on spelling and vocabulary tests, and their inferior performance on tests involving analytic thinking, spatial ability, and arithmetic reasoning. Additional discussion on this issue can be found in Kagan (1964), Sherman (1967), Silverman (1970), and Kagan and Kogan (1970).

The actual linkage between these personality traits and the cognitive styles has not been established, nor has the etiology of sex differences in personality. Some of the infancy studies mentioned above are making inroads. Thus the finding that mothers spend more time in face-to-face verbalizations with infant girls (Kagan, 1969; Moss, 1967; Goldberg & Lewis, 1969) may be tied to the observation that female infants are more verbally

---

1. These reviews by Maccoby and reviews by Kagan (1964), Becker (1964), Glidewell, Kantor, Smith, and Stringer (1966), Oetzel (1966), Garai and Scheinfeld (1968), Silverman (1970), Kagan and Kogan (1970), and Bardwick (1971) will be referred to throughout the paper where a point is supported by several studies that are adequately reported in the review.

responsive and to the later superiority of females in verbal ability. Verbal responsiveness may also result from the fact that girls' hearing is superior to that of boys (Garai & Scheinfeld, 1968). Also relevant is a study with 10-year-olds in which observations of mother-daughter interaction in task solving showed that girls good in math or spatial relations were left to solve tasks by themselves while the mothers of girls higher on verbal skills (the more typical female pattern) were more intrusive with help, suggestions, and criticism (Bing, 1963).

The present paper will focus on an area that is even less explored: the question of motivation for top intellectual performance. There are data that the very brightest women more often than comparable men stop short of operating at their top intellectual level. Terman and Oden (1947) have shown that gifted girls did not as adults fulfill their potential as often as gifted boys. Rossi (1965a, 1965b) has summarized data indicating that even those few women who do go into science and the professions rarely achieve eminence.[2]

These data reflect in part the factors mentioned earlier— alternative choices in life that have been available to women but not to men, barriers to career opportunities that exist because of women's family roles, and discrimination in the professions which limits the rewards obtainable. The concern here is not with these factors, however, but with a deeper, more psychologically-based motivation that occurs in women. The most relevant data come from the work of Horner (1968, 1972) who has demonstrated with a projective story completion measure a "fear of success" among able college women. Furthermore, women who indicate fear of success show poorer performance in a competitive task than when the same task is performed alone. In interpreting her results, Horner suggests that this fear exists in women because their anticipation of success is accompanied by the anticipation of negative consequences in the form of social rejection or loss of femininity.

The idea that the affiliative motive can be dysfunctional to performance is supported by another of Horner's findings. Men who were motivated both to achieve and to affiliate showed a performance decrement when asked to compete with another man. Horner suggests this decrement may have resulted from a conflict of motives since "out-performing a competitor may be antagonistic to making him a friend."

---

2. Simon, Clark, and Galway (1970), on the other hand, have reported that the woman PhD who is employed full time publishes as much as her male colleagues.

AFFILIATIVE NEEDS AND ACHIEVEMENT

There is agreat deal of evidence that females have greater affiliative needs than males (Oetzel, 1966; Walberg, 1969) and therefore the conflict between affiliation and achievement probably will occur more often for women. It seems that, apart from direct concerns with whether or not their behavior is sufficiently "feminine," academic and professional women frequently allow their concern with affective relationships to interfere with the full use of their cognitive capacities. In group discussion and in intellectual argument, women often seem to sacrifice brilliance for rapport.

However, while the findings of the Horner studies (1972) and our observations of professional women focus attention on the dysfunctions of affiliative motivations for performance, there are data indicating that the desire for love and approval can also have a positive effect. In fact, the Crandalls (V. J. Crandall, 1963; V. C. Crandall, 1964) as well as others (Garai & Scheinfeld, 1968) have suggested that achievement behavior in girls is motivated not by mastery strivings as with boys, but by affiliative motives.

In two very different studies, nursery school and elementary school girls' achievement efforts were motivated by a desire for social approval to a greater extent than were boys'. In the nursery school study the attempt was also made to motivate the children by appeals to mastery strivings; this technique succeeded with boys but failed with girls (Lahtinen, 1964). In the study with elementary school children, achievement motives in boys were related positively to achievement test scores. Among the girls, affiliative motives, not achievement motives, were so related (Sears, 1962, 1963). Other studies with nursery school and elementary school children found affiliative behavior and achievement efforts positively related in girls, but boys showed no such relationship (Tyler, Rafferty, & Tyler, 1962; Crandall, Dewey, Katkovsky, & Preston, 1964). Similarly with adult women, the achievement arousal techniques that are effective with males have failed with females (Veroff, Wilcox, & Atkinson, 1953; Horner, 1968), but appeals to social acceptability have been successful (Field, 1951).

There are also several studies that indicate that throughout grade school boys are more motivated than girls to master challenging tasks when social aproval is not involved. When given the opportunity to perform an easy or more difficult task, to work on a puzzle they had already solved or one they had failed, to pursue further or escape a difficult problem, boys are more likely to choose the more difficult and challenging, girls to choose the task that promises easy success or to leave the scene (Crandall & Rabson, 1960; Moriarity, 1961; McManis, 1965; Veroff, 1969).

From these studies it appears that female achievement behavior even at preschool or early grade school ages is motivated by a desire for love rather than mastery. When achievement goals conflict with affiliative goals, as was the case in Horner's projective responses and in the competitive situation in which her fear-of-success girls showed less competent performance, achievement behavior will be diminished and/or anxiety result. This does not mean that academic performance is lower for females in general since it is often compatible with affiliative motives. In elementary schools, excellence is rewarded with love and approval by parents, teachers, and peers. Even in the lower socioeconomic class, sociometric studies show that academic excellence in girls is rewarded with popularity (Glidewell et al., 1966; Pope, 1953). In college, however, and in professional pursuits, love is less frequently the reward for top performance. Driving a point home, winning an argument, beating others in competition, and attending to the task at hand without being side-tracked by concern with rapport require the subordination of affiliative needs.

In short, the qualities needed for sustained top performance — especially as an adult — are not typically part of a girl's make-up. She wants approval and so she performs well in school. She works for good grades. And indeed throughout grammar school, high school, and college, she obtains higher grades than boys (Oetzel, 1966; Garai & Scheinfeld, 1968). If overachievement is thought of as grades exceeding IQ's, then girls as a group are more overachieving than boys. But girls are less likely to become involved in their task; they are less motivated by strivings for mastery. In McClelland's sense of *achievement* (McClelland, Atkinson, Clark, & Lowell, 1953) — competition with a standard of excellence — they fall short.[3]

This affiliative need may be particularly germane to achievement patterns because it may be rooted in early experiences when the child is learning patterns of effectance. When little boys are expanding their mastery strivings, learning instrumental independence, developing skills in coping with their environment and confidence in this ability, little girls are learning that effectiveness — and even safety — lie in their affectional relationships. The idea expressed by Kagan (1964) that boys try to "figure the

---

3. Women have obtained scores on McClelland's test of achievement motivation under neutral conditions that are as high or higher than those obtained by men under arousal conditions; however, researchers have questioned the validity of the measure for women (see McClelland et al., 1953; and Horner, 1968).

task" and girls try to "figure the teacher" seems rooted in early childrearing practices and reinforced by later experiences.

STATEMENT OF THEORY

It is the thesis here that the female child is given inadequate parental encouragement in early independence strivings. Furthermore, the separation of the self from the mother is more delayed or incomplete for the girl because she is the same sex with the same sex role expectations, and because girls have fewer conflicts with their parents. As a result, she does not develop confidence in her ability to cope independently with the environment. She retains her infantile fears of abandonment; safety and effectiveness lie in her affective ties. These points will now be elaborated and supportive data brought in where available.

The Development of Independence, Competence, and Self-Confidence

All infants are dependent; as the child matures his independence strivings increase. Observers have often been impressed with what White (1960) calls the *effectance motive*—the child's need to have an effect upon his environment. Thus the child grasps and releases, reaches and pulls, and in the course of doing this he learns about his environment and his ability to manipulate it. He develops cognitive abilities, and he develops a sense of effectiveness—a sense of competence through increasingly successful interaction with his environment.

As the infant matures, the feats he undertakes get scarier. Increasingly they involve separating the self from the mother and leaving the security of that unity. Early independence explorations seem to take place most successfully with the parent present; the child moves toward independence so long as the "safety man" is in sight. As he gains confidence, the parent's presence becomes less and less necessary.

Very likely this period—somewhere between a year and three or four years of age—is critical in the development of independence and competence (Erikson, 1959; Veroff, 1969; White, 1960; Stendler, 1963). By critical, we mean a period when independence and competence orientations are more efficiently learned than at other times. There is a rapid building up of notions about the self and about the world.

Although theories differ as to the exact timing and differential importance of the events occurring in this period, all would probably agree on the minimal requirements for the development of independence and competence. Thus if the infant is deprived of affection, rejected, or prematurely pushed toward independence, he will not have a secure base from which to build true independence. The dependency that results from a short shrift in early affective ties is probably of a distinct kind (Stendler, 1963). We do not think it is more characteristic of girls, nor that it is sufficiently common to the nonpathogenic middle class family to be useful in understanding prevalent female achievement orientations.

Even with an adequate affective base, independent behavior does not happen automatically. It requires not only opportunities for independent behavior but also actual parental encouragement. Evidence for this can be found in Baumrind's research (Baumrind & Black, 1967; Baumrind, 1971) which indicates that competence comes not from permissiveness but from guidance and encouragement. The first steps a child takes are exciting but also frightening, and cues from the mother can greatly influence the subsequent behavior. The mother's delight is part of her independence training; her apprehension constitutes training in dependence.

Further, if the child's early independence behaviors are to be followed by more, these ventures must be reasonably in accord with his abilities. Repeated success such as these will have the important effect of developing in the child a sense of competence. There may be a delicate timing mechanism—premature independence can backfire; but the parent who withholds independence opportunities too long and indeed does not encourage independent behavior will also fail to produce an independent child. (It is possible that the appropriate timing is different for boys than girls due to differences in abilities and maturation rates.)

The awareness that the mother is a separate person whose wishes are not the same as his serves to increase the child's striving for autonomy and independence. Both Erikson and White see the period between one and three as the battle for autonomy. At this age the child's motoric explorations often require parental interference. The span of consecutive action is such that interference can be frustrating for the child and completions gratifying. Toilet training usually occurs around this time. The child thus enters into conflict with his mother; out of this conflict, if it does not involve his humiliation and defeat, the child will emerge with "a lasting sense of autonomy and pride [Erikson, 1959]" and "a measure of confidence in his own strength [White, 1960]."

THE EMPIRICAL FINDINGS

Independence Training: Sex Differences

Early exploratory behaviors in which the child interacts effectively with his environment are seen here as crucial in building up a sense of competence. In this respect males have a number of advantages.

Infant studies. Studies of neonates suggest a higher activity level on the part of the male, while females demonstrate greater tactile sensitivity and a lower pain threshold (Garai & Scheinfeld, 1968). From these predispositions alone we could expect more exploratory behavior on the part of male infants, but to compound the matter observations of mothers with neonates show that even controlling for the differences in activity levels, mothers handle and stimulate males more than females (Moss, 1967, undated). And a study by Rubenstein (1967) suggests that such maternal attentiveness facilitates exploratory behavior.

Kagan and Lewis and their associates have also reported differences in maternal behavior toward male and female infants (Kagan, Levine, & Fishman, 1967; Goldberg & Lewis, 1969). Whether the maternal behavior is primarily a response to infant predispositions or a cause of the differences is not definitely established, but there is some evidence that both influences occur. That maternal behavior is not entirely a response to the infant is indicated by relationships found between the mother's infant care and her orientations prior to the child's birth. For example, Moss (1967) reports that mothers were interviewed two years before they gave birth and rated on their attitudes toward babies. A positive attitude toward babies was found to relate significantly to the amount of responsiveness later shown to her 3-week-old infant. This same investigator also found mutual visual regard—one of the earliest forms of mother-infant communication—to be related to maternal attitudes expressed before the birth (Moss & Robson, 1968). On the other hand, that maternal behavior is not the sole determinant of the infant's behavior is indicated by the fact that the sex differences in tactile stimulation and pain thresholds mentioned above have been established for infants less than four days old and still in the hospital nursery (Garai & Scheinfeld, 1968; Silverman, 1970). An interaction hypothesis seems most tenable in the light of the present data.

One of Moss's mother-infant interaction findings is particularly pertinent to the theory presented in this paper (1967, undated). He reports data on the mother's responsiveness to the infant's cries and notes that this sequence—baby cries and mother responds with the needed care—is important in shaping the infant's response to the mother as a supplier of comfort. The more closely the mother's caretaking behavior is related to the infant's cries, the more effectively will the child "regard the mother as having reinforcing properties and respond to her accordingly [Moss, undated, p. 10]." The correlation obtained between maternal contact and infant irritability was statistically significant for females but not for males. The mothers did not attend to the female infants more than the male (less, in fact) but their attention was more closely linked to the infant's state of need as expressed by crying. This finding if borne out by further research could be very important for several reasons. First, it could signify the beginning of a pattern of interaction between mothers and daughters in which the daughters quickly learn that the mother is a source of comfort; and the mother's behavior is reinforced by the cessation of crying. The sheer presence of the mother would soon signal the satisfaction of the infant's needs. Second, there is agreement among most investigators that there are critical periods in infancy when learning takes place so efficiently that long range behaviors are effected by simple but pertinently timed events; this might be such a critical period. Third, even if this is not a critical period, the finding may reflect an orientation of mothers toward daughters that is often repeated beyond the infancy period.

In any case, one thing appears certain from this body of research on early mother-infant interaction: There are sex differences in both maternal and infant behavior during the first year of life. That sex role learning is begun so early should not be surprising. Sex is a primary status—the first one announced at birth. The mother is very much aware of it. Her early behaviors toward the infant are not deliberate efforts to teach the child his proper sex role, but she has internalized society's view and acts accordingly. She acts toward her son as though he were sturdy and active and she is more likely to show pleasure when his behavior fits this image. Her daughter is her doll—sweet and delicate and pink. The mother's behavior reflects this perception, and if the child exhibits behavior consistent with the female stereotype, such as dependency, she is not as likely to discourage it as she would with a son.

Independence training in childhood. Moving from early infancy, we find studies that link independence training and the parent's achievement orientations to the child's competence (Baumrind & Black, 1967) and achievement orientations (Winterbottom, 1958; Rosen & D'Andrade, 1959), but few examining sex differences in the independence and achievement training children receive. It is our view that because of parental attitudes toward male and female

735

children which reflect their culturally assigned roles, males receive more effective independence training and encouragement.

An adaptation of the Winterbottom measure for use with parents of younger children was developed by Torgoff (1958). Using this measure, Collard (1964) asked mothers of 4-year-olds to indicate the ages they thought parents should expect or permit certain child behaviors. For example, the parents were asked at what age they believed parents should: (a) begin to allow their child to use sharp scissors with *no* adult supervision, (b) begin to allow their child to play away from home for long periods of time during the day without first telling his parents where he will be. The answers to these questions yielded two measures—*independence granting* and *achievement induction.* Mothers of girls responded with later ages than mothers of boys. This difference was significant for the independence-granting items and it was particularly strong in the middle class. The achievement induction scores were not significantly different for the two sexes, but close inspection of the data revealed that, for the middle class, mothers of girls indicated an earlier age for only two of the 18 items making up the scale. One of the two exceptions was "sharing toys" which may have more to do with inter-personal relationships than with achievement.

Parental anxiety and protectiveness. Still another difference in the independence training received by boys and girls may stem from parental ambivalence: Parents may show more unambivalent pleasure in sons' achievements than in daughters'. The young child's first motoric adventures can produce anxiety in the mother as well as the child, just as they produce pleasure for both. It seems likely that for the parent of a boy there is a particular pride in the achievement and less of a feeling of the child's fragility; as a result there is a clearer communication of pleasure in the achievement per se. A beaming mother when the child takes his first steps may have a very different effect than the mother who looks anxious while holding out loving arms. In the former case, the task itself becomes the source of pleasure (in reinforcement terms the reward is closer to the act). In the latter case, the mother is saying in effect, "You may break your neck en route, but I will give you love when you get here." The mother's indications of anxiety as the child moves toward independence make the child doubt his own competence, for mothers are still omniscient to the young child.

There is some indirect evidence for this view. Despite the greater maturity and sturdiness of the female infant (Garai & Scheinfeld, 1968), parents think of them as more fragile. Furthermore, behavioral observations of infants have shown that male infants are handled more vigorously (Moss, 1967). The setting of later ages for granting autonomy to girls, as indicated in the Collard (1964) study mentioned earlier, suggests that parents are more protective, if not more anxious, toward girls. For example, parents report allowing boys to cross busy streets by themselves earlier, though they are not motorically more advanced than girls and their greater motoric impulsivity would seem to make this more dangerous. And we do know that infants pick up the subtle attitudes of their caretakers. This was demonstrated in the well known study by Escalona (1945) in which the infant's preference for orange or tomato juice depended heavily on the preference of the nurse who regularly fed him. The infant had no way of knowing his nurse's preference except through sensing her attitude as she fed him.

Another kind of parent behavior that is detrimental to the development of independence might be called *over-help.* Mastery requires the ability to tolerate frustration. If the parent responds too quickly with aid, the child will not develop such tolerance. This shortcoming—the tendency to withdraw from a difficult task rather than to tackle the problem and tolerate the temporary frustration— seems to characterize females more than males. This has been demonstrated in the test situations mentioned earlier, and Crandall and Rabson (1960) have also found that, in free play, grade school girls are more likely than boys to withdraw from threatening situations and more frequently to seek help from adults and peers. The dysfunctions of this response for the development of skills and a sense of competence are clear. There are no data to indicate that over-help behavior is more characteristic of parents of girls, but such a difference seems likely in view of the greater emphasis placed on the independence training of boys.

Clearly more research is needed to identify differences in the independence and achievement training—and in any over-protection and over-help—that parents provide boys and girls. Even if the differences we have described are definitely established, it will still need to be shown that this pattern of parental protectiveness and insufficient independence training is a major contributor to an inadequate sense of personal competence in girls. It should be pointed out, however, that this inference is consistent with the findings that girls are more anxious than boys, more likely to underestimate their abilities, and more apt to lack confidence in their own judgment when it is contrary to that of others (Sarason, 1963; Sarason & Harmatz, 1965; Sears, 1964; Crandall, Katkovsky, & Preston, 1962; Hamm & Hoving, 1969). There is also evidence that the above pattern is reinforced by the later socialization experiences of girls. Several investigators report that while dependency in boys is discouraged by parents, teachers, peers, and the mass media, it is more acceptable in girls (Kagan &

Moss, 1962; Kagan, 1964; Sears, Rau, & Alpert, 1965). Data from the Fels study (Kagan & Moss, 1962) are particularly interesting in this respect, reporting that childhood dependency predicted to adult dependency for females but not males, the converse being true for aggression. Their interpretation is that pressure is exerted on the child to inhibit behaviors that are not congruent with sex role standards (Kagan, 1964).

Establishing a Separate Self: Sex Differences

Same sex parent as primary caretaker. Separation of the self is facilitated when the child is the opposite sex of the primary caretaker. Parsons (1949, 1965) and Lynn (1962, 1969), as well as others, have pointed out that both males and females form their first attachment to the mother. The girl's modeling of the mother and maintaining an identity with her is consistent with her own sex role, but the boy must be trained to identify with his father or to learn some abstract concept of the male role. As a result, the boy's separation from the mother is encouraged; it begins earlier and is more complete. The girl, on the other hand, is encouraged to maintain her identification with the mother; therefore she is not as likely to establish an early and independent sense of self. If the early experiences of coping with the environment independently are crucial in the development of competence and self-confidence, as suggested previously, the delayed and possibly incomplete emergence of the self should mitigate against this development.

There are no studies that directly test this hypothesis. As indirect evidence, however, there are several studies showing that the more identified with her mother and the more feminine the girl is, the less likely she is to be a high achiever and to excel in mathematics, analytic skills, creativity, and game strategies. For example, Plank and Plank (1954) found that outstanding women mathematicians were more attached to and identified with their fathers than their mothers. Bieri (1960) found that females high on analytical ability also tended to identify with their fathers. Higher masculinity scores for girls are related positively to various achievement measures (Oetzel, 1961; Milton, 1957; Kagan & Kogan, 1970), as are specific masculine traits such as aggressiveness (Sutton-Smith, Crandall, & Roberts 1964; Kagan & Moss, 1962). The relation between cross-sex identification and cognitive style for both boys and girls is discussed also by Maccoby (1966).

For several reasons the above studies provide only limited support for our view. First, there is some evidence, though less consistent, that "overly masculine" males, like "overly feminine" females, are lower on various achievement-related measures (Maccoby, 1966; Kagan & Kogan, 1970). Second, the definitions and measures of femininity may have a built-in anti-achievement bias. Third, the question of the mother's actual characteristics has been ignored; thus the significant factor may not be closeness to the mother and insufficient sense of self, as here proposed. The significant factor may be identifying with a mother who is herself passive and dependent. If the mother were a mathematician, would the daughter's close identification be dysfunctional to top achievement?

Clearly the available data are inadequate and further research is needed to assess the importance of having the same sex as the primary caretaker for personality and cognitive development.

Parent-Child conflict. Establishing the self as separate from the mother is also easier for boys because they have more conflict with the mother than do girls. Studies of neonates suggest, as mentioned above, that males are more motorically active; this has also been observed with older children (Garai & Scheinfeld, 1968; Moss, 1967; Goldberg & Lewis, 1969). Furthermore, sex differences in aggressive behavior are solidly established (Oetzel, 1966; Kagan, 1964), and there is some evidence that this is constitutionally based (Bardwick, 1971). Because of these differences, the boy's behavior is more likely to bring him into conflict with parental authority. Boys are disciplined more often than girls, and this discipline is more likely to be of a power assertive kind (Becker, 1964; Sears, Maccoby, & Levin, 1957; Heinstein, 1965). These encounters facilitate a separation of the self from the parent. (While extremely severe discipline might have a very different effect, this is not common in the middle class.)

One implication of this is that girls need a little maternal rejection if they are to become independently competent and self-confident. And indeed a generalization that occurs in most recent reviews is that high achieving females had hostile mothers while high achieving males had warm ones (Bardwick, 1971; Garai & Scheinfeld, 1968; Maccoby, 1966; Silverman, 1970). This generalization is based primarily on the findings of the Fels longitudinal study (Kagan & Moss, 1962). In this study "maternal hostility" toward the child during his first three years was related positively to the adult achievement behavior of girls and negatively to the adult achievement behavior of boys. Maternal protection, on the other hand, as mentioned earlier, related negatively to girl's achievement and positively to boy's.

In discussions of these findings "maternal hostility" is often equated with rejection. There is reason to believe, however, that it may simply be the absence of "smother love." First, the sample of cooperating families in the Fels study is not likely to include extremely rejecting parents. These were primarily middle class parents who cooperated with a child development study for 25 years. They were enrolled in the study when the mother was pregnant, and over the years they tolerated frequent home visits, each lasting from 3 to 4 hours, as well as behavioral observations of their children in nursery school and camp. Second, we have already pointed out that what is "high hostility" toward girls, might not be so labeled if the same behavior were expressed toward boys. It is interesting to note in this connection that "high hostility" toward girls during these early years is related positively to "acceleration" (i.e., the tendency to push the child's cognitive and motoric development) and negatively to maternal protectiveness. Neither of these relationships is significant for the boys (Kagan & Moss, 1962, p. 207). Further, the mothers who were "hostile" to their daughters were better educated than the "nonhostile." In addition to being achievers, the daughters were "less likely to withdraw from stressful situations" as adults. The authors themselves suggest that the latter "may reflect the mother's early pressure for independence and autonomy [p. 213]."

Our interpretation of these findings then is that many girls experience too much maternal rapport and protection during their early years. Because of this they find themselves as adults unwilling (or unable) to face stress and with inadequate motivation for autonomous achievement. It is significant that the relationships described are strongest when the early years are compared to the adult behavior. Possibly the eagerness to please adults sometimes passes as achievement or maturity during the childhood years.

While excessive rapport between mother and son occurs, it is less common and usually of a different nature. The achievement of boys may be in greater danger from too much conflict with parents—there being little likelihood of too little.

The danger for girls of too much maternal nurturance has been pointed out by Bronfenbrenner (1961a, 1961b) and is consistent with data reported by Crandall, Dewey, Katkovsky and Preston (1964). The finding that girls who are more impulsive than average have more analytic thinking styles while the reverse pattern holds for boys also fits this interpretation (Sigel, 1965; Kagan, Rosman, Day, Phillips, & Phillips, 1964). That is, impulsive girls may be brought into more conflict with their mothers, as in the typical pattern for boys. Maccoby (1966) has suggested that the actual relationship between impulsivity and analytic thinking is curvilinear: The extreme impulsivity that characterizes the very impulsive boys is dysfunctional, but the high impulsivity of the girls falls within the optimal range. In our view, the optimal range is enough to insure some conflict in the mother-child relationship but not so much as to interfere with the child's effective performance.

Inadequate Self-Confidence and Dependence on Others

Since the little girl has (a) less encouragement for independence, (b) more parental protectiveness, (c) less cognitive and social pressure for establishing an identity separate from the mother, and (d) less mother-child conflict whichhighlights this separation, she engages in less independent exploration of her environment. As a result she does not develop skills in coping with her environment nor confidence in her ability to do so. She continues to be dependent upon adults for solving her problems and because of this she needs her affective ties with adults. Her mother is not an unvarying supply of love but is sometimes angry, disapproving, or unavailable. If the child's own resources are insufficient, being on her own is frustrating and frightening. Fears of abandonment are very common in infants and young children even when the danger is remote. Involvement in mastery explorations and the increasing competence and confidence that results can help alleviate these fears, but for girls they may continue even into adulthood. The anticipation of being alone and unloved then may have a particularly desperate quality in women. The hypothesis we propose is that the all-pervasive affiliative need in women results from this syndrome.

Thus boys learn effectance through mastery, but girls are effective through eliciting the help and protection of others. The situations that evoke anxiety in each sex should be different and their motives should be different.

The theoretical view presented in this paper is speculative but it appears to be consistent with the data. In the preceding sections we have reviewed the research on sex differences in early socialization experiences. The theory would also lead us to expect that owing to these differences females would show less self-confidence and more instrumental dependency than males.

The data on dependency are somewhat unclear largely because the concept has been defined differently in different studies. These findings have been summarized by Kagan (1964), Oetzel (1966), Garai and Scheinfeld (1968), and the concept of dependency has been discussed by Maccoby and Masters (1970). The balance of the evidence is that females are more dependent, at least as we are using the concept here, and this difference appears early and continues into maturity. Goldberg and Lewis (1969) report sex differences in dependency among one-year-olds, but Crandall and his associates (Crandall, Preston, & Rabson, 1960; Crandall & Rabson, 1960) found such differences only among elementary school children and not among preschoolers. It should be noted, however, that even differences that do not show up until later can have their roots in early experiences. For example, independence training at a later age may require a sense of competence based on early successes if it is to be effective.

The findings on self-confidence show that girls, and particularly the bright ones, underestimate their own ability. When asked to anticipate their performance on new tasks or on repetition tasks, they give lower estimates than boys and lower estimates than their performance indicates (Brandt, 1958; Sears, 1964; Crandall, Katkovsky, & Preston, 1962; Crandall, 1968). The studies that show the girls' greater suggestibility and tendency to switch perceptual judgments when faced with discrepant opinions are also consistent with their having less self-confidence (Iscoe, Williams, & Harvey, 1963; Allen & Crutchfield, 1963; Nakamura, 1958; Hamm & Hoving, 1969; Stein & Smithells , 1969)[4] Boys set higher standards for themselves (Walter & Marzolf, 1951) As mentioned earlier, difficult tasks are seen as challenging to males, whereas females seek to avoid them (Veroff, 1969; Crandall & Rabson, 1960; Moriarty, 1961; McManis, 1965). Thus the research suggests that girls lack confidence in their own abilities and seek effectance through others (Crandall & Rabson, 1960). Affective relationships under these conditions would indeed be paramount.

The findings indicating that this is the case—that affective relationships are paramount in females—were summarized earlier in this paper. The data suggest that they have higher affiliative needs and that achievement behavior is motivated by a desire to please. If their achievement behavior comes into conflict with affiliation, achievement is likely to be sacrificed or anxiety may result.

IMPLICATIONS

If further research provides support for the present developmental speculations, many questions will still need answering before childrearing patterns used with girls can be totally condemned. Even from the standpoint of achievement behavior, I would caution that this paper has only dealt with the upper end of

4. Girls do not conform more to peer standards which conflict with adult norms (Douvan & Adelson, 1966), even though they conform more when group pressure is in opposition to their own perceptual judgments.

the achievement curve. Indices of female performance, like the female IQ scores, cluster closer to the mean and do not show the extremes in either direction that the male indices show. The same qualities that may interfere with top performance at the highest achievement levels seem to have the effect of making the girls conscientious students in the lower grades. Is it possible for the educational system to use the positive motivations of girls to help them more fully develop their intellectual capacities rather than to train them in obedient learning? The educational system that rewards conformity and discourages divergent thinking might be examined for its role in the pattern we have described.

Although childrearing patterns that fail to produce a competent and self-confident child are obviously undesirable, it may be that boys are often prematurely pushed into independence. Because this paper has focused on achievement orientations, it may seem that I have set up the male pattern as ideal. This is not at all intended. The ability to suppress other aspects of the situation in striving for mastery is not necessarily a prerequisite for mental health or a healthy society. The more diffuse achievement needs of women may make for greater flexibility in responding to the various possibilities that life offers at different stages in the life cycle. A richer life may be available to women because they do not single-mindedly pursue academic or professional goals. And from a social standpoint, a preoccupation with achievement goals can blot out consideration of the effect of one's work on the welfare of others and its meaning in the larger social scheme.

A loss in intellectual excellence due to excessive affiliative needs, then, might seem a small price to pay if the alternative is a single-minded striving for mastery. But the present hypothesis suggests that women's affiliative needs are, at least in part, based on an insufficient sense of competence and as such they may have a compelling neurotic quality. While I have not made the very high achievement needs more characteristic of males the focus of this paper, they too may have an unhealthy base. By unraveling the childhood events that lead to these divergent orientations we may gain insights that will help both sexes develop their capacities for love and achievement.

REFERENCES

Allen, V. L., and Crutchfield, R. S. Generalization of experimentally reinforced conformity. *Journal of Abnormal and Social Psychology,* 1963, *67,* 326-333.

Bardwick, J. M. *The psychology of women: A Study of biosocial conflict.* New York: Harper and Row, 1971.

Baumrind, D. Socialization and instrumental competence in young children. *Young Children,* 1970, December, 9-12.

Baumrind, D. Current patterns of parental authority. *Developmental Psychology Monograph,* 1971, *4,* (1, Pt. 2).

Baumrind, D., and Black, A. E. Socialization practices associated with dimensions of competence in preschool boys and girls. *Child Development, 1967, 38, 291-327.*

Bayley, N. Growth curves of height and weight by age for boys and girls, scaled according to physical maturity. *Journal of Pediatrics,* 1956, *48,* 187-194.

Bayley, N. Developmental problems of the mentally retarded child. In I. Phillips (Ed.), *Prevention and treatment of mental retardation.* New York: Basic Books, 1966.

Becker, W. Consequences of different kinds of parental discipline. In M. L. Hoffman and L. W. Hoffman (Eds.), Review of child development research. Vol. 1. New York: Russell Sage, 1964.

Bieri, J. Parental identification, acceptance of authority and within-sex differences in cognitive behavior. *Journal of Abnormal and Social Psychology,* 1960, *60,* 76-79.

Bing, E. Effect of childrearing practices on development of differential cognitive abilities. *Child Development,* 1963, *34,* 631-648.

Brandt, R. M. The accuracy of self-estimate: A measure of self concept. *Genetic Psychology Monographs,* 1958, *58,* 55-99.

Bronfenbrenner, U. Freudian theories of identification and their derivatives. *Child Development,* 1960, 31, 15-40.

Bronfenbrenner, U. Some familial antecedents of responsibility and leadership in adolescents. In L. Petrullo and B. M. Bass (Eds.), *Leadership and interpersonal behavior.* New York: Holt, Rinehart, & Winston, 1961 (a).

Bronfenbrenner, U. Toward a theoretical model for the analysis of parent-child relationships in a social context. In J. Glidewell (Ed.), *Parent attitudes and child behavior.* Springfield, Illinois: Thomas, 1961 (b).

Coleman, J. S. *The adolescent society.* Glencoe, Illinois: Free Press, 1961.

Collard, E. D. Achievement motive in the four-year-old child and its relationship to achievement expectancies of the mother. Unpublished doctoral dissertation, University of Michigan, 1964.

Crandall, V. C. Achievement behavior in young children. *Young Children,* 1964, *20,* 77-90.

Crandall, V. C. Sex differences in expectancy of intellectual and academic reinforcement. In C. P. Smith (Ed.), *Achievement-related motives in children.* New York: Russell Sage, 1968.

Crandall, V. J. Achievement. In H. W. Stevenson (Ed.), *Child Psychology: The 62nd Yearbook of the National Society for the Study of Education.* Part I. Chicago: University of Chicago Press, 1963.

Crandall, V. J., Dewey, R., Katkovsky, W., and Preston, A. Parents' attitudes and behaviors and grade school children's academic achievements. *Journal of Genetic Psychology,* 1964, *104,* 53-66.

Crandall, V. J., Katkovsky, W., and Preston, A. Motivational and ability determinants of young children's intellectual achievement behaviors. *Child Development,* 1962, *33,* 643-661.

Crandall, V. J., Preston, A., and Rabson, A. Maternal reactions and the development of independence and achievement behavior in young children. *Child Development,* 1960, *31,* 243-251.

Crandall, V. J., and Rabson, A. Children's repetition choices in an intellectual achievement situation following success and failure. *Journal of Genetic Psychology,* 1960, *97,* 161-168.

Douvan, E. M., and Adelson, J. *The adolescent experience.* New York: Wiley, 1966.

Erikson, E. H. Identity and the life cycle. *Psychological Issues,* 1959, *1,* 1-171.

Escalona, S. K. Feeding disturbances in very young children. *American Journal of Orthospychiatry,* 1945, *15,* 76-80.

Field, W. F. The effects of thematic apperception upon certain experimentally aroused needs. Unpublished doctoral dissertation, University of Maryland, 1951.

Garai, J. E. and Scheinfeld, A. Sex differences in mental and behavioral traits. *Genetic Psychology Monographs,* 1968, *77,* 169-299.

Glidewell, J. C., Kantor, M. B., Smith, L. M., and Stringer, L. A. Socialization and social structure in the classroom. In L. W. Hoffman and M. L. Hoffman (Eds.), *Review of child development research.* Vol. 2. New York: Russell Sage, 1966.

Goldberg, S., and Lewis, M. Play behavior in the year old infant: Early sex differences. *Child Development,* 1969, *40,* 21-31.

Hamm, N. K., and Hoving, K. L. Conformity of children in an ambiguous perceptual situation. *Child Development,* 1969, *40,* 773-784.

Heinstein, M. *Child rearing in California.* Bureau of Maternal and Child Health, State of California, Department of Public Health, 1965.

Horner, M. S. Sex differences in achievement motivation and performance in competitive and non-competitive situations. Unpublished doctoral dissertation, University of Michigan, 1968.

Horner, M. S. Toward an understanding of achievement related conflicts in women. *Journal of Social Issues,* 1972, *28,* (2).

Iscoe, I., Williams, M., and Harvey, J. Modifications of children's judgements by a simulated group technique: A normative developmental study. *Child Development,* 1963, *34,* 963-978.

Iscoe, I., Williams, M., and Harvey, J. Age, intelligence and sex as variables in the conformity behavior of Negro and White children. *Child Development,* 1964, *35,* 451-460.

Jensen, A. R. The race X sex X ability interaction. Unpublished manuscript. University of California, Berkeley, 1970.

Kagan, J. Acquisition and significance of sex-typing and sex-role identity. In M. L. Hoffman and L. W. Hoffman (Eds.), *Review of child development research.* Vol. 1. New York: Russell Sage, 1964.

Kagan, J. On the meaning of behavior: Illustrations from the infant. *Child Development,* 1969, *40,* 1121-1134.

Kagan, J., and Kogan, N. Individuality and cognitive performance. In P. H. Mussen (Ed.), *Carmichael's manual of child psychology.* Vol. 1. New York: Wiley, 1970.

Kagan, J., Levine, J., and Fishman, C. Sex of child and social class as determinants of maternal behavior. Paper presented at the meeting of the Society for Research in Child Development, March 1967.

Kagan, J., and Moss, H. A. *Birth to maturity.* New York: Wiley, 1962.

Kagan, J., Rosman, B. L., Day, D., Phillips, A. J., and Phillips, W. Information processing in the child: Significance of analytic and reflective attitudes. *Psychological Monographs,* 1964, *78,* 1.

Lahtinen, P. The effect of failure and rejection on dependency. Unpublished doctoral dissertation, University of Michigan, 1964.

Lewis, M. Infants' responses to facial stimuli during the first year of life. *Developmental Psychology,* 1969, *1,* 75-86.

Lynn, D. B. Sex role and parental identification. *Child Development,* 1962, *33,* 555-564

Lynn, D. B. *Parental identification and sex role.* Berkeley: McCutchan, 1969.

Maccoby, E. E. Sex differences in intellectual functioning. In E. E. Maccoby (Ed.), *The development of sex differences.* Stanford, California: Stanford University Press, 1966.

Maccoby, E. E. Woman's intellect. In S. M. Farber and R. H. L. Wilson (Ed.), *The potential of woman.* New York: McGraw-Hill, 1963.

Maccoby, E. E., and Masters, J. C. Attachment and dependency. In P. H. Mussen (Ed.), *Carmichael's manual of child psychology.* Vol. 2. New York: Wiley, 1970.

McClelland, D. C., Atkinson, J. W., Clark, R. A., and Lowell, E. L. *The achievement motive.* New York: Appleton-Century-Crofts, 1953.

McManis, D. L. Pursuit-rotor performance of normal and retarded children in four verbal-incentive conditions. *Child Development,* 1965, *36,* 667-683.

Milton, G. A. The effects of sex-role identification upon problem solving skill. *Journal of Abnormal and Social Psychology,* 1957, *55,* 208-212.

Moriarty, A. Coping patterns of preschool children in response to intelligence test demands. *Genetic Psychology Monographs,* 1961, *64,* 3-127.

Moss, H. A. Laboratory and field studies of mother-infant interaction. Unpublished manuscript, NIMH, undated.

Moss, H. A. Sex, age, and state as determinants of mother-infant interaction. *Merrill-Palmer Quarterly,* 1967, *13,* 19-36.

Moss, H. A., and Robson, K. S. Maternal influences in early social visual behavior. *Child Development,* 1968, *39,* 401-408.

Moss, H. A., Robson, K. S., and Pedersen, F. Determinants of maternal stimulation of infants and consequences of treatment for later reactions to strangers. *Developmental Psychology,* 1969, *1,* 239-247.

Nakamura, C. Y. Conformity and problem solving. *Journal of Abnormal and Social Psychology,* 1958, *56,* 315-320.

Oetzel, R. M. The relationship between sex role acceptance and cognitive abilities. Unpublished masters thesis, Stanford University, 1961.

Oetzel, R. M. Annotated bibliography and classified summary of research in sex differences. In E. E. Maccoby (Ed.), *The development of sex differences.* Stanford, California: Stanford University Press, 1966.

Parsons, T. *Essays in sociological theory pure and applied.* Glencoe, Illinois: Free Press, 1949.

Parsons, T. Family structure and the socialization of the child. In T. Parsons and R. F. Bales (Eds.), *Family socialization and interaction process.* Glencoe, Illinois: Free Press, 1965.

Plank, E. H., and Plank, R. Emotional components in arithmetic learning as seen through autobiographies. In R. S. Eissler et al. (Eds.), *The psychoanalytic study of the child.* Vol. 9. New York: *Inter. Univ. Press, 1954.*

Pope, B. Socio-economic contrasts in children's peer culture prestige values. *Genetic Psychology Monographs,* 1953, *48,* 157-220.

Rosen, B. C., and D'Andrade, R. The psychosocial origins of achievement motivations. *Sociometry,* 1959, *22,* 185-218.

Rossi, A. S. Barriers to the career choice of engineering, medicine, or science among American women. In J. A. Mattfeld and G. G. Van Aken (Eds.), *Women and the scientific professions: Papers presented at the M.I.T. symposium on American Women in Science and Engineering, 1964.* Cambridge, Massachusetts: M.I.T. Press, 1965 (a).

Rossi, A. S. Women in *science:* Why so few? *Science,* 1965, *148,* 1196-1202 (b).

Rubenstein, J. Maternal attentiveness and subsequent exploratory behavior in the infant. *Child Development,* 1967, *38,* 1089-1100.

Sarason, I. G. Test anxiety and intellectual performance. *Journal of Abnormal and Social Psychology,* 1963, *66,* 73-75.

perimental conditions. *Journal of Personality and Social Psychology,* 1965, *1,* 499-505.

Sears, P. S. Correlates of need achievement and need affiliation and classroom management, self concept, and creativity. *Unpublished manuscript. Stanford University,* 1962.

Sears, P. S. The effect of classroom conditions on the strength of achievement motive and work output of elementary school children. Final report, cooperative research project No. *OE-873,* U.S. Dept. of Health, Education, and Welfare, Office of Education, Washington, D.C., 1963.

Sears, P. S. Self-concept in the service of educational goals. *California Journal of Instructional Improvement,* 1964, *7,* 3-17.

Sears, R. R., Maccoby, E. E., and Levin, H. *Patterns of child rearing.* Evanston, Illinois: Row, Peterson, 1957.

Sears, R. R., Rau, L., and Alpert, R. *Identification and child rearing.* Stanford: Stanford University Press, 1965.

Sherman, J. A. Problems of sex differences in space perception and aspects of intellectual functioning. *Psychological Review,* 1967, *74,* 290-299.

Sigel, I. E. Rationale for separate analyses of male and female samples on cognitive tasks. *Psychological Record,* 1965, *15,* 369-376.

Silverman, J. Attentional styles and the study of sex differences. In D. L. Mostofsky (Ed.), *Attention: Contemporary theory and analysis.* New York: Appleton-Century-Crofts, 1970.

Simon, R. J., Clark, S. M., and Galway, K. The woman Ph.-D.: A recent profile. Paper prepared for a workshop of the New York Academy of Sciences, New York, February 1970.

Stein, A. H., and Smithells, J. Age and sex differences in children's sex role standards about achievement. *Developmental Psychology,* 1969, *1,* 252-259.

Stendler, C. B. Critical periods in socialization. In R. G. Kuhlen and G. G. Thompson (Eds.), *Psychological studies of human development.* New York: Appleton-Century-Crofts, 1963.

Sutton-Smith, B., Crandall, V. J., and Roberts, J. M. Achievement and strategic competence. Paper presented at the meeting of the Eastern Psychological Association, April 1964.

Terman, L. M., and Oden, M. H. *The gifted child grows up.* Stanford, California: Stanford University Press, 1947.

Torgoff, I. Parental development timetable. Paper presented at the meeting of the American Psychological Association, Washington, D. C., August 1958.

Tulkin, S. R. Race, class, family, and school achievement. *Journal of Personality and Social Psychology,* 1968, *9,* 31-37.

Tyler, F. B., Rafferty, J. E., and Tyler, B. B. Relationships among motivations of parents and their children. *Journal of Genetic Psychology,* 1962, *101,* 69-81.

Veroff, J. Social comparison and the development of achievement motivation. In C. P. Smith (Ed.), *Achievement-related motives in children.* New York: Russell Sage, 1969.

Veroff, J., Wilcox, S., and Atkinson, J. W. The achievement motive in high school and college age women. *Journal of Abnormal and Social Psychology,* 1953, *48,* 108-119.

Walberg, H. J. Physics, femininity, and creativity. *Development Psychology,* 1969, *1,* 47-54.

Walter, L. M., and Marzolf, S. S. The relation of sex, age, and school achievement to levels of aspiration. *Journal of Educational Psychology.* 1951, *42,* 258-292.

White, R. W. Competence and the psychosexual stages of development. In M. Jones (Ed.), *Nebraska Symposium on Motivation.* Lincoln, Nebraska: University of Nebraska Press, 1960.

Winterbottom, M. R. The relation of need for achievement to learning experiences in independency and mastery. In J. W. Atkinson (Ed.), *Motives in fantasy, action, and society,* Princeton: Van Nostrand, 1958.

Witkin, H. A., Dyk, R. B., Faterson, H. F., Goodenough, D. R., and Karp, S. A. *Psychological differentiation.* New York: Wiley, 1962.

44

Epstein, a sociologist at Queens College, notes many of the external barriers women face in determining their status in occupations "sex-typed" as male, i.e., in fields where it is expected that the large majority will be men. Despite women's entry, during the past fifty years, into occupations from which they were once excluded, women are still frequently excluded from favored positions and from the colleague system, both of which determine access to the highest level of various professions. Men, who predominate at the highest levels, have mixed feelings about identifying women as suitable to membership in these inner circles, since women are not readily accepted by other male colleagues already in the inner circle. They might even prefer her to a male as an assistant, but not as a successor.

Not being accepted in the upper echelons will in turn affect such things as the woman's contributions in her particular field, her visibility, her income, her autonomy, and her activity in professional organizations.

Women help to perpetuate their own exclusion. Afraid of rebuffs, they limit their professional interactions, helping to confirm the image of their own lack of ability. What is even worse is that women favor exclusion of other women. This behavior is also seen as appropriate.

Epstein also notes the factors that were important to those few women who proved to be successful professionals, such as performance in fields that can be rated by measurable standards, acceptable of their roles as women as well as professionals, age and length of career, and being part of a high ranking institution.

Epstein feels that more radical changes are needed in American society to eliminate the problems of women as occupational deviants.

Encountering the Male Establishment: Sex-Status Limits on Women's Careers in the Professions*

Cynthia F. Epstein

Despite impressive extensions in the scope of women's social and political rights, there have been few extensions of sex-linked boundaries in the prestigious, male-dominated professions. This paper identifies the processes and structure of the professions in the United States which act to limit women's participation and achievement within them. Because their sex status is defined within the culture of professions as inappropriate, women find that the institutionalized channels of recruitment and advancement, such as the protégé system, are not available to them. Various modes of behavior on the part of women and their colleagues are described which are consequences of women's minority position and which reinforce it. Social changes affecting the traditional structures and opening careers in the professional hierarchy are discussed.

During the past half-century women have entered many upper-level occupations and positions from which they were once excluded, and their general level of involvement in the labor force has risen. But their participation in the occupations of highest rank — among them the professions of law, medicine, teaching in higher education, and the sciences — has not kept pace with these developments nor has their access to the elite levels of the professions been greatly improved. Further, despite pressures to implement the equalitarian values in American culture and extensions of women's social and political rights, there have been no accompanying extensions of the sex-linked boundaries existing in the occupations of high prestige in this society.

The processes which undermine women's motivations for professional careers and work against their completion of the necessary education, their entry into practice after training, and their aiming at the highest levels of performance in professional

---

*From: *American Journal of Sociology,* 1970, *75*(6) 965-82.
Footnotes have been renumbered.

practice have been described in various works. (Rossi 1965; Bernard 1964; Friedan 1963; Komarovsky 1953; Epstein 1970). Here I wish to focus on one set of these processes; those anchored in the structures of the professions and having the consequence of causing women's sex status to become salient[1] in the professional role, equal to or above the occupational status. We will also draw attention to the consequences of "sex-typing"[2] and of "status-set typing"[3] in the professions which have made the professions almost exclusively male. The important processes which underlie these questions are: (1) the colleague system of the professions, especially at the upper levels; (2) the sponsor-protégé relationship, which determines access to the highest levels of most levels of most professions; (3) the demands of the specific professions' "inner" structure and its attendant patterns of social interaction which are, under most circumstances, incompatible with the sex-role expectation repertory of even those women engaged in professional careers; and (4) the sex-typing of occupations, which reinforces these processes in linking occupational roles and sex roles.

This analysis applies not alone to women, but to others who possess statuses (such as age or race) which are culturally defined as "inappropriate" when held in conjunction with certain occupational statuses. That is, those persons whose status-sets do not conform to the expected and preferred configuration cause discordant impressions on members of the occupational network and the society at large: the black physician, the Jewish Wall Street lawyer, and the football-hero philosophy professor all generate such discordance.

---

1. Part of the analysis which follows draws on Robert K. Merton's conceptualization of the dynamics of status-sets, presented in lectures at Columbia University over the past years, but as yet unpublished. According to Merton, the "salient" status is the one that is focused upon—made salient—in the interaction under analysis. The salient status may be the one that is most germane to the interaction but it may be one that is inappropriate to the situation. The black teacher who is invited to join a faculty because he is black, not because his professional status merits the offer, has had his racial status made salient.

2. According to Merton, "occupations can be described as 'sex-typed' when a very large majority of those in them are of one sex and when there is an associated normative expectation that this is as it should be."

3. Thus I have labeled it "status-set typing" when a class of persons who share a key status (e.g., lawyer) also share other matching statuses (e.g., white, Protestant) and when it is considered appropriate that this be so.

WOMAN: DEPENDENT OR INDEPENDENT VARIABLE?

SEX-TYPING OF OCCUPATIONS

One element of "status-set typing" is the sex-typing of occupations. The typing of certain occupations as male or female has consequences for entry to them and performance within them by persons who possess the "wrong sex." Those occupations defined as male provide a social context uncomfortable for women. Those who seek entry to them are regarded as deviants and are subjected to social sanctions. As a result, few women attempt to enter such fields, and those who do often are blocked from the opportunity structure.[4]

As Table 1 shows, women lawyers have increased from 1 percent of the profession in 1910 to 3.5 percent in 1950, but there has been no change in this percentage for the past ten years. Women now form 6.8 percent of the medical profession, an all-

TABLE 1

WOMEN AS PERCENTAGE OF ALL WORKERS IN SELECTED PROFESSIONAL OCCUPATIONS (USA, 1900–1960)

Occupation	1960	1950	1940	1930	1920	1910	1900
College professors, president, instruction....	19.0	23.0	27.0	32.0	30.0	19.0	...
Doctors..............	6.8	6.1	4.6	4.0	5.0	6.0	...
Lawyers[a]............	3.5	3.5	2.4	2.1	1.4	1.0	...
Engineers............	0.8	1.2	0.3	...	...	...	...
Dentists.............	2.1	2.7	1.5	1.8	3.2	3.1	...
Scientists............	9.9	11.4	...	...	...	...	...
Biologists............	28.0	27.0	...	...	...	...	...
Chemists.............	8.6	10.0	...	...	...	...	...
Mathematicians.......	26.4	38.0	...	...	...	...	...
Physicists............	4.2	6.5	...	...	...	...	...
Nurses...............	97.0	98.0	98.0	98.0	96.0	93.0	94.0
Social workers........	57.0	66.0	67.0	68.0	62.0	52.0	...
Librarians...........	85.0	89.0	89.0	91.0	88.0	79.0	...
Clergy..............	5.8	8.5	2.2	4.3	2.6	1.0	4.4

SOURCE.—U.S. Bureau of the Census of 1963, vol. 1, table 202, pp. 528–33. 1900–50 statistics from U.S. Department of Labor 1954, p. 57.
[a] The lack of change in the percentage of women lawyers is even more striking if one uses the adjusted figures of Hankin and Krohnke (1965):

1963	1960	1957	1954	1951	1948
2.7	2.6	2.7	2.3	2.5	1.8

4. In fields which are not sex-typed or have not yet become sex-typed, or where there are few expectations concerning what would constitute an appropriate status-set to complement the occupational status, opportunities for women are great. As far as I know, computer programming is an occupation which has not become typed and many bright women and minority group members have been drawn to the field.

754

time high, but not a striking increase over the 6.1 percent of ten years before or since 1910, when women constituted 6 percent of the profession. The percentage of women college teachers has gone down steadily since 1930 from 32 percent to 19 percent today. Although the U.S. census figures are now almost ten years old, and there are certain indicators of increasing participation by women in some fields such as law,[5] it is doubtful that a really new trend is emerging.

Some occupations which have remained predominantly male in the United States are, in other countries (most notably the Communistic-block nations), regarded as female occupations. In the Soviet Union, women constitute 75 percent of the medical profession, 30-40 percent of the judges, and 28 percent of the engineers; in Denmark, they make up 70 percent of the dental profession.

Yet even in these countries women's share of the leading positions in the professions is meager. While social definitions regarding the "proper" sex of a practitioner are important in determining the sex-composition of an occupation, the sex-ranking of occupations provides an added inhibitor of women's advancement. High-ranking occupations in all societies are typically male (Goode 1964, p. 70). Medicine does not rank low in the Soviet Union, but it does not rank nearly as high as in the United States. For all occupations in all societies, as one approaches the top, the proportion of men increases and the proportion of women decreases. In the Soviet Union, for example, only the tiniest proportion of professions of surgery within the great teaching universities and research institutes are women (Dodge 1966); in the United States, although women constitute close to 20 percent of the academic ranks of higher education, few women attain the rank of full professor in the institutions of highest prestige.

It is evident that the dynamics of recruitment and involvement at the higher echelons of professions are different than they are at the lower levels and that they militate against the participation of women. Further, these processes are integral to the "culture" of the professions as we know them and may not be intentionally exclusionary. Of course, cultural attitudes tied to women's roles and women's biologically linked characteristics interweave with these processes in making the woman professional's sex-status salient in the course of her career.

---

5. The enrollment of women in some law schools has increased in recent years. The University of Notre Dame Law School admitted women for the first time in the fall of 1969. The 20 women comprised 12 percent of the entering class, an unusually high proportion for law school classes (*New York Times,* September 14, 1969).

CHARACTERISTICS OF PROFESSIONS

Professions share many characteristics of communities (Goode 1957; Merton, Reader, and Kendall 1957). They tend toward homogeneity and are characterized by shared norms and attitudes. The work of the professions depends greatly on mutual understanding between practitioners and common standards of behavior which permit them control of their share without much intervention from the state or lay public.

Interaction in professions, especially in their top echelons, is characterized by a high degree of informality, much of it within an exclusive, club-like context. As Hughes (1962) describes these qualities, professionalism "indicates a strong solidarity of those in an occupation. . . . The very word 'profession' implies a certain social and moral solidarity, a strong dependence of one colleague upon the opinions and judgments of others" (Hughes 1962, pp. 124-125).

Thus, it is difficult for someone not equipped with a status-set of appropriate statuses to enter the exclusive society, to participate in its informal interactions, to understand the unstated norms,[6] and to be included in the casual exchanges.

The Protégé System

Entry to the upper echelons of many professions is commonly gained through the protégé system. This system, linked to the colleague system, operates both to train personnel for certain specialties (special areas of surgery or corporate law, for example), and to assure continuity of leadership. These fields are marked by the interplay between the formal and informal relationships of the practitioners. At certain levels one must be "in" to learn the job. Becker and Strauss (1956) point out that "until a newcomer is accepted [in these fields] he will not be taught crucial trade secrets," much less advance in the field.[7]

The sponsor-protégé (or master-apprentice) relationship may inhibit feminine advancement. The sponsor is apt to be a man and will tend to have mixed feelings about accepting a woman as protégé. Although the professional man might not object to a female assistant — and might even prefer her — he cannot easily

6. Goffman (1963, p. 129) points out that "more is involved than norms regarding somewhat statis status attributes . . . that failure to sustain the many minor norms important in the etiquette of face-to-face communication can have a very pervasive effect upon the defaulter's acceptability in social situations."

7. The work of Hall (1948) illustrates this for medicine. See also Smigel (1964, pp. 100-102).

identify her (as he might a male assistant) as someone who will eventually be his successor. He may therefore prefer a male candidate to a female in the belief that she has less commitment to the profession. When the woman is accepted as a protégé, her other role-partners—husband, father, child, etc.—may be jealous and suspicious of her loyalty to the sponsor and her dependence on him. The sponsor's wife may also resent the intimacy of the relationship between the sponsor and his female protégé and object to it.[8]

If the sponsor wants to minimize his risks in adopting recruits, the collegial group will not favor an unsuitable member likely to weaken its intimacy and solidarity and it may exert pressure on the sponsor to pick the protégé with whom it will be comfortable (see Etzioni 1961, p. 260).

For a sponsor, a protégé (1) eases the transition to reitrement (Hall 1948; Hughes 1945); (2) gives him a sense of continuity of his work, and (3) gives some assurance that his intellectual offspring will build on his work. It is considered unwise to depend on a woman for these.

Even if she serves an apprenticeship, the female professional may not get the sponsor's support in gaining entry to the inner circles of the profession—support which a male neophyte would expect as a matter of course. The sponsor may exert less effort in promoting a female student for career-line jobs. First, he may believe that she is financially less dependent on a career position than a man might be.[9] Second, because of her presumably highly contingent commitment and drive (she might forego all for marriage, after all), he might only reluctantly introduce her or recommend her to colleagues.

However, it is often true that a protégé relationship may be more important to the women than a man, and that a male sponsor may make an extra effort to promote a female protégé because he is aware of the difficulties she faces. In fact, she may only be able to

---

8. A number of placement officers in law schools report that it is difficult to place female graduates with solo practitioners. The reason offered, evidently considered as legitimate, is that the men complain that their wives would object.

9. A dramatic example of this is the Ruth Benedict-Franz Boas elationship in the Columbia University Anthropology Department. Boas regarded Ruth Benedict, as the wife of Stanley Benedict, "amply supported and with the obligation of a wife, someone for whose talents he must find work and a little money, someone on whom he could not make extreme demands and for whom he need not be responsible" (Mead 1959 p. 342-43). Later, when Ruth Benedict separated from her husband and pressed for professional standing, Boas got her an assistant professorship. (The illustration is cited in Bernard [1964, pp. 105-6].)

TABLE 2

PERCENTAGE OF PROFESSIONAL
WORKERS IN SELECTED OCCU-
PATIONS IN GOVERNMENT SER-
VICE BY SEX (1960)

Occupation	Male	Female
Dentists.......	0.03	10.0
Lawyers.......	14.0	27.0
Doctors.......	14.0	30.0
Engineers......	17.0	32.0

SOURCE.—U.S. Bureau of the Census 1963,
p. 277.

rise or gain notice in a field because she is a protégé, although this form of entry is not as important for others. I have suggested elsewhere (Epstein, in press) that women in professional life seem to find jobs and feel most comfortable in situations which are highly particularistic and are considered a unique exception to the general rule excluding women (e.g., because a particular woman is brilliant, or is in partnership with her husband), or in highly bureaucratized situations, such as government service, where strictly universalistic criteria, such as standing on competitive examinations, are applied. In fact, as Table 2 shows, women professionals go into government service in far greater proportions to their number than do men. In this respect, they are much like other minority groups, such as Negroes.[10]

This pattern tends to be self-perpetuating. Women tend to select these two kinds of work situations because they know they will meet least opposition. Placement offices in professional schools often fit women students to government work and counsel them to avoid high-prestige firms or research centers. This means that many women never even enter environments where contacts are made for protégé relationships essential to entering the elite corps of their professions. Even within these environments, it is often true that women are guided into peripheral or low-ranking

---

10. A larger proportion of nonwhites than whites are employed by the government in practically every occupational category in the professional and technical group in the census. For example, 20.1 percent of Negro lawyers and judges go into government work as contrasted with 14 percent of whites; 24.7 percent of Negro physicians contrasted with 14.8 percent of whites (U.S. Bureau of the Census 1963, p. 284).

specialties where their work is not likely to draw the elite's attention.[11]

Later progress in a woman's career may be inhibited by similarly limited access to fellow practitioners and peers and their clubs and associations—the circle in which job opportunities are made known and informal recommendations are made. Hall (1948) illustrates the interdependence of career advancement and sponsorship by specifying the channels through which younger doctors of proper class and acceptable ethnic origins are absorbed into the inner fraternity of the medical profession. He notes that perpetuation of this fraternity depends on a steady flow of suitable recruits.

Performance Criteria

The collegial relationship is also important in the assessment of the performance of professionals. Although adequacy of performance may be simple to judge at lower levels of a profession, the fine distinctions between good and superior performance require subtle judgments. Members of professions affirm that only peers can adequately judge performance at these levels (as opposed to the lay public or outside agencies); they know the standards, they know the men, and they can maintain control. And the professionals typically close ranks to maintain control when their autonomy is threatened. At higher levels, high stakes are often involved: legal decisions can affect people's lives or huge sums of money; medical decisions can assure a patient's life or death. Although there are gross guidelines for the behavior of professionals at these levels, formal scrutiny is minimal and the social controls exercised by peers act most effectively to prevent deviance. The professions depend on intense socialization of their members, much of it by immersion in the norms of professional culture even before entry; and later by the professional's sensitivity to his peers. These controls depend on a strong network cemented by bonds of common background, continual association, and affinity of interests.

Not only do contacts with professional colleagues act as a control system, they also provide the wherewithal by which the professional may become equipped to meet the highest standards of professional behavior. As we know, the learning of a profession

11. A disproportionate number of women lawyers specialize in the low-ranking speciality of matrimonial law and a disproportionate percentage of women doctors practice psychiatry, a relatively low-ranking medical specialty. For a further analysis see Epstein (1970, chap. 4).

is not completed with graduation from the professional school. Techniques and experience must still be acquired in interaction with established practitioners. This is true also for acquiring new knowledge.[12]

Evidence suggests that women professionals are not involved in the collegial networks to the extent that men are.[13] Thus they are excluded from the situations in which they can learn and are also excluded from the social control system which lets them know how well they perform (Epstein 1969).

The judgment of whether a professional is "top" rank is contingent on a number of elements linked to the collegial system:

Contributions. — Definitions of "contributions" vary from field to field but each profession has norms regarding quality and quantity of contributions deemed adequate for consideration as high-level performance. Women probably do make proportionately fewer contributions to their professions than do men (in male-dominated professions) although there is some evidence to the contrary (Simon, Clark, and Galway 1967). Few women have achieved fame for discoveries in science, designing great architectural structures, devising new surgical techniques, or the triumphant argument of cases before the Supreme Court. If publication in the academic professions is used as a criterion, it is probably true that women are responsible for proportionately fewer books and articles considered important to their fields. Even if one does not use standards of "greatness," it is not commonly believed that women do very much publishing at all.[14] The colleague and network systems are probably important in assessing these "facts." These are some of the dynamics involved:

a) Contributions must be visible to be noted; work from the larger and more prestigious institutions probably has a greater chance of being noticed than work performed at lesser-known

---

12. Sir Alfred Egerton has noted, in fast-moving sciences, "of the total information extant, only part is in the literature. Much of it is stored in the many brains of scientists and technologists. We are as dependent on biological storage as on mechanical or library storage." It is to this source of unpublished information that access may be more limited for women than for men (cited by Bernard 1964, p. 303).

13. Bernard's (1964, p. 152) study of women zoologists showed that women faculty members at colleges had less contact with fellow scientists than did the men there. They were less likely than other scientists to attend meetings of professional societies. They were also less likely than male scientists to be on regular mailing lists for reprints of researchers. Women on the staffs of universities seemed to do better in becoming part of the communications network.

14. For a review of some surveys on women's productivity see Epstein (1970, p. 171).

institutions.[15] Women are less likely to be affiliated with large and prestigious institutions.[16]

b) Contributions are also made visible by the activity of senior men in the field to promote them or by joint publications with those in eminent positions.[17] I tentatively suppose that women's contributions are not promoted as much as men's and that they less often collaborate with those in eminent positions.

On the other hand, women professionals in male-dominated professions have greater visibility than men simply because they are a small minority. At professional meetings they are physically more visible (as are Negroes), and their written work identifies their sex by name. When their work is good, it may get even greater notice than that of men who perform at the same level of competence.

Performance. —Not only are written or material works assessed in considering a person for a place at the top, but also the quality of his general performance. Colleagues "get to know" a man by their exposure to his work in the courtroom, at the operating table, in the laboratory. Performances bearing the labels of well-known institutions are more apt to attract public notice; further, the great men who will make the judgments are at the great institutions and are likely to be in a better position to judge the potential of the young who are already in their midst.

The relative invisibility of the woman professional's performance stems directly from women's disadvantageous position in the structure of the professions. They are not only routed into less visible positions, such as library research, but the specialties in which they predominate are typically regarded as the less important and less demanding ones, and their skills in them count for less.

---

15. This is an example of the "halo" effect of the institution on the author of a piece of work where his identity is not commonly known. Cole and Cole (1968) have found that the visibility of physicists, for example, is highly correlated with the rank of department in which they work.

16. In 1963, 82 percent of women faculty members, contrasted with 74 percent of the men, worked in colleges and technical institutions with a faculty numbering under 200; 18 percent of the women as contrasted with 26 percent of the men teaching in colleges were in institutions with more than 200 faculty.
    Women faculty members were also affiliated with smaller universities to a greater extent than were men (Dunham, Wright, and Chandler 1966, pp. 64-65).

17. Zuckerman (1967, p. 393) finds, for example, that Nobel laureates who themselves had laureate "masters" received the prize, on the average, nine years earlier than scientists who had not studied with a prize winner.

Incomes are lower in the professional specialties in which women predominate. Women lawyers in a relatively unlucrative field, such as matrimonial law, are less apt to gain distinction and advance in a firm because they are unable to contribute substantially to the firm's total profits. Women are also seldom given the accounts of important clients; their comparatively unimportant clients cannot effectively press for their promotion.[18]

Women also tend less than men to be in positions where they can exercise the greatest autonomy. Figure 1 indicates that women who work in the male-dominated professions are self-employed to a far lesser degree than are men. They are also less likely to be in high-ranking, decision-making positions if they are on the staffs of institutions, or in professional or business firms.

Associations. — Membership and participation in professional associations characterizes the active professional and reinforces his ties to colleagues and work. At professional meetings information is traded about new techniques and theories, and informal judgments are exchanged about the profession's rising "stars." Professional friendships develop into personal relationships at the cocktail hours, and at committee and dinner meetings. The appointment of members to special committees may publicize their achievements to their colleagues.

Women are less active in professional organizations than are men, particularly at the decision-making levels. It is generally believed, but not generally proven, that proportionately fewer women than men join professional organizations (see Fava 1960, pp. 171-72; Bernard 1964, p. 152; Simon et al. 1967, p. 234; Epstein 1970, p. 185 ff.). Certainly, however, women's past participation and performance in professional organizations has been limited.

Women's reticence to participate in these associations is due in part to past discrimination against women in some cases in the recent past, although no professional organization today excludes women from membership. In cases where there were no legal barriers based on sex (or where they were removed), women were nevertheless made to feel unwelcome. Women have been barred particularly from full participation at decision-making levels. They are seldom elected to prestigious committees or to executive posts. In the field of sociology, out of a total of 57 presidents, only one woman has been elected to serve as president of the American Sociological Association. In the American Psychological Association too, they have been continuously underrepresented in

---

18. See Smigel's evaluation of client sponsorship as a path to partnership in a large firm (1964, pp. 100-102).

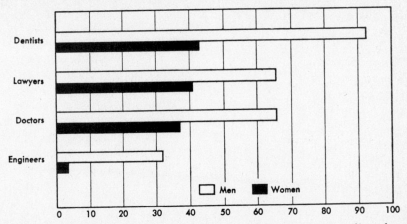

F<small>IG</small>. 1.—Proportion of males and females in selected professions who are self-employed.
Source: U.S. Bureau of the Census 1963, table 21, p. 277.

posts of distinction.[19] In law, they tend to serve disproportionately on bar association committees concerned with family law[20] (reflecting their high representation in the specialties of matrimonial law, custody, adoption, etc.) and not on the committees of high rank.

To some extent the establishment of women's professional organizations has served to deflect women's participation in the general professional groups. Some women's organizations were formed because the general organizations had formal or informal bans on female membership.[21] Following the removal of these

19. Mitchell (1951, p. 200) reported that women had not become fellows, officers, committee chairmen, committee members, editors, representatives to other organizations, members of the Council of Representatives, members-at-large, on the Executive Committee, or division presidents of the American Psychological Association in proportion to their numbers and qualifications. Only as secretaries have they served in proportion to their numbers. In 1968 no women held major offices.

20. For example, in a listing of the principal committees and members of the New York County Lawyers' Association for 1967-68, women served on fourteen of thirty-seven committees, and some appeared on more than one (*New York Times,* August 6, 1967, p. 37). Of a total of 1,103 members of the State Bar of California serving on committees, only eighteen are women (letter from Karl E. Zellman, Assistant Secretary, State Bar of California, March 21, 1967).

21. For example, the National Council of Women Psychologists was established in 1942, after it became clear that the Emergency Committee in Psychology of the National Research Council was continuing to omit women from its plans for the wartime use of psychologists (Mitchell 1951, p. 193). The National Association of Women Lawyers

barriers, they have generally managed to keep their inner sanctums free of women.[22] Male clubs which recruit members cross-occupationally and which are also centers of informal contacts between those at the top, by their very definition exclude women. Prestigious clubs, such as the Harvard and Princeton Clubs, permit women entry only on ludicrously limited bases, and their resistance to full integration is dramatized to the women by certain symbolic devices; among them are separate women's entrances and restaurants limited to male patronage during lunch hours. Of course, there is no shortage of places for male and female colleagues to lunch together but many men seem to favor the club setting, and when women go along, they must use "the back entrance" (the Harvard Club), if they are admitted at all.

Dedication to the profession. — The ideal professional is one whose work dominates the other parts of his life. As his professional associations blend into personal friendships, so his working and leisure hours may merge. Although styles of work differ, the professional's involvement with his craft is generally expressed by the long hours he puts in. Because women professionals do not or cannot work the same number of hours as their male colleagues (Table 3), their commitment is suspect and they are not deemed colleagues in the full sense of the word.

Exclusivity of the elite. — The collegial system has the further consequence of creating an image of exclusivity which reinforces professional boundaries. Even if inner circles do not act to explicitly exclude "inappropriate" members, outsiders are loath to place themselves in a situation which they anticipate would be embarrassing or uncomfortable. Women, as members of an inappropriate category often practice self-exclusion and limit their professional interactions. Although they might or might not be rebuffed if they initiated contact, the situation is often never put to

---

and other women's bar associations were also formed in response to exclusion by the men. There are also separate professional associations for women in the fields of medicine (founded 1915), dentistry (founded 1921), engineering (founded 1950), geography (founded 1925), and certified public accounting (founded 1933). It is interesting to note that in professions typed as female, there are no separate men's organizations, nor have men been legally excluded from membership at any time.

22. New York attorney Doris Sassower, former president of the New York Women's Bar Association, tells of the experience of Florence Allen, Chief Judge of the U.S. Court of Appeals, Sixth Circuit, who, when appointed as a federal judge, found the resistance of fellow judges so great that they refused to look at her or speak to her, except when forced to by the business at hand (speech delivered at the Waldorf Astoria Hotel, May 13, 1967, on the occasion of the first Florence E. Allen Award).

the test.[23] The woman's self-imposed limits on professional interaction often complete the self-fulfilling prophecy of her ineptitude. To a large extent, this behavior results in her acceptance of the prevailing image of professions as societies of men.

Women often not only exclude themselves, but favor exclusion of other women. They accept the image and definitions of this behavior as appropriate. The more informal the professional context, the more willing women seem to concede the "rightness" of their exclusion.[24]

TABLE 3

WEEKLY HOURS WORKED BY EMPLOYED ENGINEERS, SCIENTISTS, AND TECHNICIANS, BY SEX, 1960

OCCUPATION	MEAN No. HOURS		No. HOURS WORKED (%)					
			Men			Women		
	Men	Women	1–34	35–40	41+	1–34	35–40	41+
Engineers	42.8	38.6	1	67	32	9	82	9
Scientists	42.1	38.6	5	68	27	11	75	14
Biologists	43.0	39.1	6	58	36	12	66	21
Chemists	41.6	38.8	4	72	24	9	80	11
Mathematicians	41.4	38.6	3	74	23	6	87	7
Physicists	41.6	*	5	72	23	18	59	23
Professors-instructors:								
Biological sciences	43.6	33.8	17	28	54	37	28	35
Chemistry	40.8	*	25	25	50	41	26	33
Engineering	42.5	*	15	32	53	60	20	20
Mathematics	36.4	35.4	34	30	36	37	31	32
Physics	40.5	*	26	26	48	54	...	46
Technicians:								
Medical and dental	42.2	38.5	10	51	39	15	61	24
Electrical and electronic	42.2	39.8	3	70	27	5	81	14
Other engineering and physical science technicians	41.5	38.7	4	71	25	8	80	12
Lawyers and judges	46.7	38.9	6	33	59	22	47	28

SOURCE.—U.S. Bureau of the Census 1963, table 13. Statistics (except for lawyers) cited in Rossi (1965).
* Mean not shown when the case base is less than 1,000.

---

23. Some of the women lawyers I interviewed, for example, avoided joining colleagues at lunch. One commented, "Sometimes when the natural thing to do would be to join an associate and a client at lunch if you were a man, you feel, well, maybe I'd better not. It might be awkward for them. They might want to talk about something and might feel constrained."
24. A lawyer described her feelings in this way: "There was a camaraderie in the County (Law) Association—a terrific spirit. In other associations the members are very staid . . . but there everybody knows one another and they joke. They were prejudiced against admitting women but I think they were justified. It's not the same with a woman around. They aren't free to express themselves, to tell off-color stories—they should have that."

THE INTERACTIONAL SETTING

Because women don't "fit" well in the professional structure just described, their appearance in the collegial networks as legitimate coprofessionals often causes a considerable amount of role-confusion. Male colleagues typically are unable to engage in the normal collegial relationship with them and instead fall back on the traditional norms governing male-female interaction.

Performance of the professional task may be seriously inhibited, when not only colleagues but clients focus on the sex-status instead of the occupational status of women. This occurs, for example, when a patient responds to a woman physician first as a woman and only second as a doctor, instead of as a doctor primarily and perhaps exclusively—the appropriate response in a professional relationship. This kind of social response colors both the attitude and behavior of the woman practitioner and forces her to work out ways to counter violations of the norms of professional relationships by her role partners. The following consequences may occur:

1. Women in professional life feel self-conscious [25] about being women, with the result that they are unsure of how they will be received. [26] They may overreact to conceal or inhibit "womanly attributes," and overconform or overproduce in an attempt to make up for their situationally downgraded status. [27] Women lawyers may, as noted earlier, try to be unobtrusive and not create

25. There is considerable congruence here between women professionals and other individuals who have some highly visible objectionable characteristic, trait, or status. Like them, during contacts with "normals" the woman may feel that she is "on," having to be self-conscious and calculating about the impressions she is making, to a degree and in areas of conduct which she assumes others are not (Goffman 1963, pp. 13-14, 33).

26. This problem is identified by Barker (1948, p. 34) in pointing to the uncertainty of status for the disabled person over a wide range of social interactions, including employment. "The blind, the ill, the deaf, the cripples, can never be sure what the attitude of a new acquaintance will be, whether it will be rejective or accepting, until the contact has been made. This is exactly the position of the adolescent, the light-skinned Negro, the second generation immigrant, the socially mobile person and the woman who has entered a predominantly masculine occupation."

27. These two types of behavior are, of course, examples of "compulsive" behavior or overconformity (identified by Merton 1957, pp. 131-60), whereby adherence to norm prescriptions in spite of the situational context may weaken role relationships and in addition impede the accomplishment of the goal.

"trouble" or attract attention by holding back in conversation or by accepting work which keeps them in "invisible" positions where they do not have individual clients.[28] They thereby accept and reinforce the common definitions about the inappropriateness of their presence in the field in which they have chosen to work.

2. Similarly the role partner—colleague, supervisor, client—may try to compensate[29] by being overly solicitous, congenial, courtly, underdemanding,[30] or overdemanding in the professional interaction.

3. Status discrepancies make continuous role definition necessary during interactions which should be routine. Thus, all group members are sensitized to problems of ambiguity and are forced to form new ground rules (i.e., establish norms) for the situation. When the inappropriate status of the person's status set is activated in the professional context, refocusing of the interaction to the appropriate status must occur so that the professional task may be accomplished.

SITUATIONS WHERE FOCUSING ON SEX-STATUS WILL BE MINIMIZED

In view of the difficulties which are apt to be encountered by the woman professional in the course of her working life, I interviewed successful women professionals at length about the factors that had helped them in their careers. They described situations and patterns of professional life which helped to avoid or minimize the problems commonly faced by professional women. These were of the following types:

---

28. White's data showed that women see fewer clients than do men (1967, p. 1093).

29. Compensation may be a consequence of the discomfort persons feel in interaction with a stigmatized person, or, in our case, the person with a deviant status. Since he doesn't know how to act, because he feels sorry for the person with the stigma, or because he resents him for causing an awkwardness, the role partner tries to assuage his guilt by being extra-nice (Goffman 1963).

30. As with the cripple, the woman professional's accomplishments are often judged by a different set of standards than the man's. Thus minor accomplishments may be assessed as signs of remarkable and noteworthy capacities "in the circumstances." This may well be interpreted as a "put down" on the part of whoever is judging the accomplishment.

Formality in the professional context. —Where the working environment was formal and the tasks well defined, role partners were not unsure about the norms of governing the interactions. For example, where authority patterns and the division of labor were clearly laid out, men would not feel disturbed by a woman giving instructions.

Defined standards of performance. —If there was no indecision about how to rate performance because the outcome could be measured and lead to a specific result, relationships with role partners were easier. For example, although it is difficult to evaluate the enduring quality of philosophical ideas, it is less difficult to evaluate the efficiency of a newly designed motor for a given piece of equipment. In cases where ability had been clearly demonstrated, other criteria for inclusion in the team become less important. Women in professional life counsel neophytes to make an effort to become experts in some specialty, because their special talents will then be sought out regardless of attitudes concerning women "in general."

Correlatively, where role partners in the professional encounter have a high stake in the task at hand and are dependent on each other for performance and information, women experience little difficulty. For example, an industrial engineer will show respect for the female patent lawyer who is charging him $60 an hour for consultation services, and she, in turn, is motivated to keep the relationship professional if she wishes to keep him as a client.

Flexibility of role-playing. —Where the woman wins acceptance of her sex status as natural and unobtrusive, she has fewer professional difficulties. Collegial relationships demand that role partners shift easily from formal roles to informal ones, from professional colleague to "one of the boys." Women must perform the functional equivalent of this flexibility in role-switching, but not imitate it. Women who act "professional" but not especially formal or aggressive, who try to be gracious as women and not to be one of the boys, are said to be able to make the best impression on men and gain their acceptance. Often sex status intrudes less when it is permitted expression in normal sex-role behavior. For example, women who work in top law firms or hospitals report that male colleagues are used to treating women in a courtly manner and can work best with women who respond graciously. Women who tell off-color jokes or demand always to be treated just like the men cause their colleagues discomfort. Attempts to suppress sex-role behavior in such contexts only succeed in making it obtrusive.

Supervision of the professional interaction. —It was easier for professional women where third parties supported the professional interaction. The professor of medicine instructing a male and a female medical student in a laboratory, for example, ensures that the relationship is task directed (see Goode 1960).

Length of career and length of professional relationships. —In time, men and women in professional relationships usually establish ground rules to govern behavior and eliminate awkwardness which flows from being unsure of whether to focus on the norms governing interaction between men and women or those which govern the relationship between colleagues. For example, women lawyers who had worked in a firm for a number of years and who had early set a precedent of paying their own way, were not reticent in inviting colleagues to lunch. Of course, age itself gives the woman a certain amount of authority and if she has gained eminence, problems are further reduced. Not only do many of the feminine role components attached to the female sex status become less intrusive in professional interactions as the woman grows older (it is probably safe to say that in most cases as the woman ages, her sexual appeal becomes less an object of focus), but her position is bolstered by the rank derived from her experience and her age.

High rank of institution. —When the firm or organization is of high rank and good reputation, it is probably more likely that a woman can expect fair and open treatment than if she were at an institution of lower rank. One encounters more adherence to norms at the top and, once a member of an elite group, the woman professional may count on being treated by the universalistic criteria appropriate to the situation. In low-ranking institutions, practitioners tend to be relatively insecure about their own abilities and financial security, and the woman may become a scapegoat. Perhaps this is simply a case where once the woman is "in," she is truly "in."

Women, like others with statuses which do not conform to cultural preferences, must learn the dynamics of handling inappropriate responses to them as well as the skills of their trade. Some are protected by social structure more than others; some have greater personal skill in handling people and ambiguities. The more a woman can depend on the environment filtering out responses to her sex status which intrude on accomplishing the professional task, and the more she has perfected techniques for handling responses, the more likely she is to continue at her work and proceed along a "normal" career sequence. American women may leave professional careers at almost any point, no matter how high the investment in it or the amount of talent shown for it, with a high degree of cultural approval (Epstein 1969). We suspect that those who enter professional life and who remain within it are from environments in which obstacles are minimal, or they have, for idiosyncratic reasons, been able to define the obstacles as minimal.

CHANGES IN THE STRUCTURE OF PROFESSIONS

I have examined some of the causes of the woman professional's failure to fulfill her career potential. I have also noted some of the factors which can, depending on the case, mitigate this failure. It would be well to close by drawing attention to some of the changes in American society and in the professions, which may have consequence for women's career patterns.

At this time, the most important change seems to be the loss of prestige of traditional elite centers to new foci of professional interest, notably those in the spheres of public welfare and service. Whether or not it proves to be temporary, many of today's gifted young professionals are no longer eager to enter the traditional inner corps of the professions, and are instead being drawn to the new fields of professional opportunity. This seems to be particularly so in law and medicine, where there are signs of a breakdown in the collegial structure and an increasing challenge to the traditional insistence on recruits of particular types.

This disruption of traditional processes, coupled with the recently renewed movement toward women's occupational equality, should bring some important changes in the direction of women's greater participation in the professions. But probably far more radical changes than these, both in the institutions of the economy and the family, will be necessary to eliminate the peculiar problems of professional women, along with the cultural and occupational views of them as deviants.

REFERENCES

Barker, Roger. 1948. "The Social *Psychology* of Physical Disability." *Journal of Social Issues 4:22-54.*

Becker, Howard, and Anselm Strauss. 1956. "Careers, Personality and Adult Socialization." American Journal of Sociology 62:253-63.

Bernard, Jessie. 1964. *Academic Women.* University Park: Pennsylvania State University Press.

Cole, Jonathan, and Stephen Cole. 1968. "The Visibility and the Structural Bases of Awareness of Scientific Research." *American Sociological Review* 33:397-413.

Dodge, Norton T. 1966. *Women in the Soviet Economy.* Baltimore: Johns Hopkins Press.

Dunham, Ralph E., Patricia Wright, and Marjorie O. Chandler. 1966. *Teaching Faculty in Universities and Four-Year Colleges.* Washington, D.C.: Office of Education.

Epstein, Cynthia Fuchs. 1969. "Women Lawyers and Their Profession: Inconsistency of Social Controls and Their Consequences for Professional Performance." Paper presented at 64th Annual Meeting of American Sociological Association, September 4, San Francisco, Calif. Mimeographed.

― ― ―. In press. *The Woman Lawyer.* Chicago: University of Chicago Press.

Etzioni, Amitai. 1961. A *Comparative Analysis of Complex Organizations.* New York: Free Press.

Fava, Sylvia Fleis. 1960. "Women in Professional Sociology." *American Sociological Review* 25:271-72.

Friedan, Betty. 1963. *The Feminine Mystique.* New York: Norton.

Goffman, Erving. 1963. *Stigma: Notes on the Management of Spoiled Identity.* Englewood Cliffs, N.J.: Prentice-Hall.

Goode, William J. 1957. "Community within a Community: The Professions." *American Sociological Review* 22:194-200.

― ― ―. 1960. "Norm Commitment and Conformity to Role-Status Obligations." *American Journal of Sociology* 66:246-58.

― ― ―. 1963. *World Revolution and Family Patterns.* New York: Free Press.

― ― ―. 1964. *The Family.* Englewood Cliffs, N.J.: Prentice-Hall.

Hall, Oswald. 1948. "The Stages of a Medical Career." *American Journal of Sociology* 53:327-36.

Hankin, F., and D. Krohnke. 1965. *The American Lawyer.* 1964. Statistical Report 29. Chicago: American Bar Association.

Hughes, Everett. 1945. "Dilemmas and Contradictions of Status." *American Journal of Sociology* 50:353-59.

— — —. 1962. "What Other." In *Human Behavior and Social Processes,* edited by Arnold Rose. Boston: Houghton Miffin.

Komarovsky, Mirra. 1953. *Women in the Modern World: Their Education and Their Dilemmas.* Boston: Houghton Mifflin.

Mead, Margaret, and Frances Kaplan, eds. 1965. *American Women.* New York: Scribner's.

Merton, Robert K. 1957. *Social Theory and Social STructure.* Glencoe, Ill.: Free Press.

Merton, Robert K., George Reader, and Patricia L. Kendall, eds. 1957. *The Student-Physician.* Cambridge, Mass.: Harvard University Press.

Mitchell, Mildred B. 1951. "Status of Women in the American Psychological Association." *American Psychologist* 6:193-201.

New York Times. 1969. "20 Women to Study Law at Notre Dame." September 14.

Rossi, Alice S. 1965. "Barriers to the Career Choice of Engineering, Medicine or Science among American Women." In *Women and the Scientific Professions,* edited by Jacquelyn A. Mattfeld and Carol G. Van Aken. Cambridge, Mass.: M.I.T. Press.

Simon, Rita James, Shirley Merritt Clark, and Kathleen Galway. 1967. "The Woman Ph.D.: A Recent Profile." *Social Problems* 15:221-36.

Smigel, Erwin O. 1964. *The Wall Street Lawyer.* New York: Free Press.

U.S. Bureau of the Census. 1963. *1960 Subject Reports. Occupational Characteristics.* Final Report PC (2)-7A. Washington, D.C.: Government Printing Office.

U.S. Department of Labor. 1954. *Changes in Women's Occupations, 1940-1950.* Women's Bureau Bulletin No. 253. Washington, D.C.: Government Printing Office.

White, James J. 1967. "Women in the Law." *Michigan Law Review* 65:1051-1122.

Zuckerman, Harriet A. 1967. "Nobel Laureates in Science: Patterns of Productivity, Collaboration and Authorship." *American Sociological Review* 32:391-403.

45

Psychologists state that it is very important for them as scientists to look at data objectively. Yet this study shows that when it comes to appraising job prospects of male and female psychologists with similar academic qualifications, they reveal a decided lack of objectivity.

Fidell enlisted the aid of her chairman at San Fernando Valley State College and sent out descriptions of prospective academic job applicants to numerous chairmen in psychology departments across the country. Identical resumes of fictional male and female psychologists were sent to these various chairmen, who were asked to indicate the desirability of these individuals as faculty members and at what ranks they would be hired. This was obstensibly part of a long-range study of the careers of ten recent Ph.D.s. Each chairman received a resume with either a male or a female name inserted. A high percentage cooperated in this survey.

Not too surprisingly, male applicants were favored by these predominantly male chairmen. Thus male applicants were consistently placed at higher ranks than similar females. They were also rated as more desirable as colleagues, but not significantly so.

Many psychologists would have doubted that such results could occur among themselves. Others would claim they as individuals could never be guilty of such biased judgment. Yet Fidell has presented evidence for the type of discrimination that does exist in present hiring practices.

Empirical Verification of Sex Discrimination in Hiring Practices in Psychology

L. S. Fidell

The proportion of women in academic positions has declined from about 28% in the 1930s to 20% in the 1960s. As pressure to hire members of racial minority groups increases and federal funds are cut back, there may be a further decline in the proportion of women in academic positions.

Furthermore, the jobs that women hold in academic institutions are different from the jobs that men hold (Bernard, 1964). A thorough study of the positions of women in academic sociology departments (Rossi, 1970) revealed that women are more likely than men to teach undergraduate courses and to hold part-time positions. Women are also less likely than men to hold positions at advanced levels or at prestigious institutions.

The dearth of women in highly prestigious institutions is frequently attributed to two factors: an assumed tendency for women to leave academics in favor of family and a lower productivity of women. Rossi (1970) has collected data which speak to the first point:

> After twenty years of an academic career, 90 per cent of the men had reached a full professorship, something achieved by only 53 per cent of the single women and 43 per cent of the married women. From these data it seems clear that it is sex and not the special situation of married women that makes the greatest difference to career advancement [p. 9].

To the second point, although it may be that women do not produce as many publications as men (Bernard, 1964), preliminary results suggest that differences in publication rates may be exclusively at the full professor level. Female lecturers and assistant professors and women in nonacademic positions may, in fact, publish more than their male counterparts.[1]

Some women have recently begun to attribute their lack of

---

1. L. S. Fidell & Co. Porro. Publication Rates of Men and Women in Psychology. Study in progress, 1970.

academic advancement to tacit discrimination on the basis of sex. Freeman (1969) has documented numerous examples of discrimination against women in the social sciences faculties at the University of Chicago from 1852 to the present. At the 1969 APA Convention, all of the women who participated in the Women's Caucus reported experiencing sex discrimination at least once during their professional careers.[2] However, firm empirical corroboration of such claims has never been reported. Accordingly, it was the purpose of the current study to determine empirically whether or not discrimination against women exists in hiring for academic positions in psychology.

METHOD

One of two forms, A and B, was sent to the chairmen of each of the 228 colleges and universities in the United States offering graduate degrees in psychology. Each form contained 10 paragraphs describing the professional behavior of hypothetical psychologists. The chairman (or the person most closely associated with departmental hiring practices) was asked to "judge your *current* impression about the chances of his getting an offer for a full-time position." The respondent was asked to indicate the desirability of the candidate described in each paragraph on a scale from 1 (totally unacceptable) to 7 (highly desirable) and to indicate at what level the candidate should be offered a position (professor, associate professor, assistant professor, research associate, lecturer, other). At the end of the survey, the respondent was asked to rank order the 10 people using 1 as the least and 10 as the most desirable rank.

The letter that accompanied each form stated that the survey was the first stage in a long-range study of the careers of 10 young PhDs. The goal of the survey was claimed to be estimation of the objective desirability of the 10 people chosen for long-range study, so that their future job offers and choices could be evaluated systematically.[3] The people were all said to have held academic positions since obtaining their doctorates five years ago. The letter was sent out under the names of the Chairman of the Department of Psychology, San Fernando Valley State College, and the author.

Each of the 10 paragraphs describing a hypothetical candidate varied dichotically along nine dimensions. The dimensions were experimental versus clinical interests, compatibility with

2. E. Kaplan, personal communication, 1970.

3. The author sincerely regrets the use of deception in the cover letter but feels it was essential to the goals of the study.

colleagues, publication rate, prestige of degree-granting institution, intelligence, seriousness of purpose, emphasis on
teaching or research, significance of publications, and marital
status. Dichotic levels of each dimension were assigned randomly
to each paragraph with the constraint that five candidates were
attributed one level of each dimension and five the other level.
Marital status was an exception; six paragraphs described married
and four described unmarried candidates. Low intelligence was
indicated by exclusion from mention of this variable in the appropriate paragraphs. The paragraphs employed in the survey are
reproduced in the appendix.

The difference between Forms A and B was that on Form A the
paragraphs describing Ross, Baxter, LaSalle, and Norton had
feminine first names and proper pronouns, while on Form B the
paragraphs describing Wilson, Guyer, Pinney, and Clavel had
feminine first names and pronouns. The wording of all paragraphs
on both forms was otherwise identical.

The paragraphs describing Wiley and Pointer had male first
names and pronouns on both forms to control for potential effects
due to different forms and to constrain the percentage of
paragraphs describing women to 40% on each form. Forms A and
B were sent to equal numbers of the 228 schools by random
assignment.

RESULTS

A total of 155 (68%) of the forms were returned. Eight of the
respondents declined to answer the questions but described the
criteria used by their departments to select faculty. Of the 147
respondents who completed the forms, 75 filled out Form A and 72
filled out Form B.

Clear sex differences were obtained in response to the question,
"At what level should this candidate be offered a position?" The
proportion of responses at each academic level for men and
women appears in Table 1. As may be seen from Table 1, women
received greater numbers of offers at the assistant professor level
or lower than men. Across all paragraphs, the modal level of offer
for women was assistant professor, while for men it was associate
professor. There were no responses of full professor when the
paragraphs described women, although several such responses
were made to the Norton paragraphs when it described a man. The
Komolgorov-Smirnov test of the similarity of two distributions was
applied to the proportions at each academic level, collapsed across

TABLE 1

PROPORTION OF RESPONSES AT EACH ACADEMIC LEVEL FOR MEN AND FOR WOMEN

Paragraph	"Other"	Lecturer	Research associate	Assistant professor	Associate professor	Full professor
Ross						
James	.01	.00	.01	.47	.50	.00
Janet	.07	.03	.01	.51	.38	.00
Baxter						
Albert	.33	.07	.03	.49	.08	.00
Alice	.33	.08	.05	.43	.11	.00
Wilson						
Eugene	.26	.05	.00	.55	.14	.00
Edith	.31	.14	.03	.44	.08	.00
LaSalle						
Thornton	.00	.00	.07	.19	.74	.00
Thelma	.03	.00	.12	.28	.57	.00
Guyer						
Donald	.05	.01	.03	.52	.39	.00
Donna	.03	.01	.04	.64	.28	.00
Pinney						
Thomas	.10	.01	.03	.36	.49	.00
Theresa	.05	.08	.03	.39	.44	.00
Norton						
Jonathan	.00	.00	.01	.15	.75	.08
Joan	.03	.01	.04	.24	.68	.00
Clavel						
Patrick	.03	.03	.00	.34	.59	.01
Patricia	.03	.03	.00	.50	.44	.00
Men	.10	.02	.02	.39	.46	.01
Women	.11	.05	.04	.43	.37	.00
Wiley						
Form A	.12	.05	.01	.53	.28	.00
Form B	.13	.03	.01	.62	.19	.01
Pointer						
Form A	.08	.01	.01	.32	.57	.00
Form B	.01	.05	.00	.43	.50	.00

TABLE 2

MEANS AND STANDARD DEVIATIONS OF DESIRABILITY
RATINGS FOR MEN AND WOMEN

Paragraph	M	SD	M_{diff} Men − Women
Ross			
James	3.29	1.26	+.32
Janet	2.97	1.17	
Baxter			
Albert	1.69	.78	−.19
Alice	1.88	.93	
Wilson			
Eugene	2.20	1.16	+.27
Edith	1.93	1.08	
LaSalle			
Thornton	4.88	1.37	+.25
Thelma	4.63	1.28	
Guyer			
Donald	3.95	1.42	−.17
Donna	4.12	1.39	
Pinney			
Thomas	3.39	1.44	+.17
Theresa	3.22	1.47	
Norton			
Jonathan	5.89	1.07	+.16
Joan	5.73	.99	
Clavel			
Patrick	4.96	1.50	+.47
Patricia	4.49	1.48	
Wiley			
Form A	3.19	1.37	
Form B	3.18	1.42	
Pointer			
Form A	4.31	1.50	
Form B	4.28	1.39	

all eight paragraphs, for men and for women. The probability that the two distributions are the same is less than .01 ($x^2 = 11.74$, $df = 2$).

The means and standard deviations of the desireability ratings of the 10 paragraphs are provided in Table 2. For six of the eight paragraphs, less desirable mean ratings were made when the paragraphs described women rather than men. This difference, while in the direction predicted by the sexual discrimination hypothesis, is not significant by either a sign-rank test or a T test of the average difference in means across all paragraphs.

The mean desirability ratings for the control paragraphs (Wiley and Pointer) were very similar on the two forms. However, there was a difference between Forms A and B with respect to level of employment for the two control paragraphs. Form A produced slightly higher employment responses for both paragraphs than did Form B. Due to the counterbalancing of paragraphs, this factor should have produced differences in favor of the sexual discrimination hypothesis for paragraphs Ross, Baxter, LaSalle, and Norton, and differences against the hypothesis for the other four experimental paragraphs. Nonetheless, higher levels of employment were indicated for males on all of the experimental paragraphs except the one describing Baxter.

The rank ordering of paragraphs was completed by 70 of the 75 respondents to Form A, and by 68 of the 72 respondents to Form B. Five of the eight paragraphs (Clavel, LaSalle, Guyer, Ross, and Pinney) generated a higher mean rank order when they described men than when they described women (recall that 1 was the least, and 10 the most favored rank). The average rank order for the paragraphs when they described men was 8.88 and when they described women it was 8.12.

DISCUSSION

The hypothesis that academic departments of psychology discriminate in hiring on the basis of sex has received consierable support. The level at which a PhD would be offered a position apparently depends not only on the person's academic credentials, but also on the person's sex. The distributions of level of appointment were higher for men than for women. Further, men received more "on line" (academic positions leading to tenure) responses than women. Only men were offered full professorships.

Several anomalies were observed in the data. The Baxter paragraph, when it described a woman, was both rated more desirable and offered a slightly higher average level of appointment. However, little encouragement can be derived from this reversal because the Baxter paragraph was the least desirable of the paragraphs, and 33% of the responses to it were "Do not hire at any level." The paragraph describing Guyer is particularly interesting in that the person was rated slightly more desirable when female, but was offered a higher academic position when male.

A measure of encouragement may be taken from the desirability data. That the paragraphs were not ranked significantly less desirable when they described women may indicate that sexual equality in hiring is achievable. A less optimistic viewpoint is that written policy is more egalitarian than daily practice. A more powerful survey instrument than the current one might reveal further evidence of sex discrimination.

REFERENCES

Bernard, J. *Academic women.* University Park: Pennsylvania State University Press, 1964.

Freeman, J. Women on the social science faculties since 1892. Speech presented at the Minority Groups Workshop of the Political Science Association Conference, and the University Panel on the Status of Women, Chicago, winter 1969.

Rossi, A. S. Status of women in graduate departments of sociology: 1968-1969. *American Sociologist,* 1970, *5*, 1-12.

APPENDIX

The following are the paragraphs used in the survey [Form B had the words in parentheses inserted for the words immediately preceding them]:

Dr. Janet [James] Ross is a very bright and devoted experimental psychologist who received her [his] degree from Standord. Since graduation she [he] has published 11 articles, all competent but none of major importance. Her [His] emphasis would appear to be on teaching rather than research. Her [His] interactions with her [his] colleagues are few and sometimes abrasive. Dr. Ross is married.

Dr. Alice [Albert] Baxter received her [his] degree in clinical psychology from the University of Washington. She [He] gets along well with her husband [his wife] but is not overly popular with her [his] colleagues. Although she [he] appears serious about her [his] career as a researcher she [he] has published only two articles in the last five years, neither in prestigious journals.

Dr. Eugene [Edith] Wilson, a man [woman] of powerful intellect, received his [her] degree in clinical psychology from the U. C. Berkeley. Although his [her] primary professional interest is in teaching, he and his wife [she and her husband] spend considerable time and effort in recreational sailing and fishing. He [She] has published two papers since he [she] completed his [her] dissertation, neither of which received much acclaim. He [She] does not expend much effort in maintaining affable relations with his [her] colleagues.

Dr. Thelma [Thornton] LaSalle is a highly intelligent, deadly serious experimental psychologist from the University of New Mexico. Although she [he] collaborates well with both colleagues and graduate students, she [he] seems to prefer research to teaching. Dr. LaSalle published 10 articles since receiving her [his] degree, most of them in the Journal of Experimental Psychology. Dr. LaSalle has remained single.

Dr. Donald [Donna] Guyer is an experimental psychologist who received his [her] degree from the University of Michigan. To the extent that he [she] emphasizes anything professionally, he [she] emphasizes research over teaching. His [Her] three publications since graduation were read with considerable interest. He [She] is well liked by his [her] colleagues. Dr. Guyer is single.

781

Dr. Lucas Wiley is a clinical psychologist whose primary interest is in research. He graduated from the University of Connecticut five years ago and has published two important papers since then. He is well liked by his colleagues but, because of his numerous non-psychological interests, not considered entirely dedicated to his profession. He is single.

Dr. Michael Pointer received his Ph.D. in experimental psychology from Harvard. He has published an average of two papers a year since graduation but not on topics of current interest. His primary interest is in teaching rather than research and he gets along better with his own students than his colleagues. Dr. Pointer is unmarried.

Dr. Thomas [Theresa] Pinney is considered highly intelligent by his [her] colleagues but does not get along well with many of them. He [She] is not respected as a serious professional although he [she] graduated from the University of Wisconsin and publishes two or three competent, if not definitive, papers a year. His [Her] primary interest is thought to be in teaching. His wife [Her husband] is also a teacher.

Dr. Joan [Jonathan] Norton is an experimental psychologist dedicated to her [his] research and to her [his] career. She [He] has published twelve papers, some of major significance, since her [his] graduation from the University of Arizona. She and her husband [He and his wife] are quite friendly and get along well with her [his] colleagues.

Dr. Patrick [Patricia] Clavel received his [her] doctorate in clinical psychology from Western Reserve University. He [She] is considered both highly intelligent and very serious about his [her] academic goals. His [Her] students feel that he [she] is more interested in them than in his [her] research. He [She] works well with his [her] colleagues on committees, but has added only three articles to his [her] vita since graduation. These articles have, however, been well received professionally. Dr. Clavel is married.

SUGGESTED PAPERS AND PROJECTS

Papers:

1. Only the name has been changed. Discuss the evaluation of identical male and female achievements.
2. What factors underlie situations in which women are discriminated against vs. those in which they are not?
3. Discuss the concept of the *competent* woman as a social deviant.
4. Review the work on "fear of success" in both males and females.

Projects:

1. Review the obituary columns of a newspaper every day for a specified period and note the number of females and the number of males listed and what their accomplishment or status was which warranted an obituary.
2. Interview five women who have been successful in one field: music, athletics, business, the arts. What are the factors in their personal histories which explain their high achievement motivation?
3. Compare the occupational goals parents desire for their boy and girl children. Are there any sex differences on the basis of religion, ethnic group, or socioeconomic status?
4. Obtain demographic information about students in this class (age, sex, marital status, sex of siblings, employment, status of mother, GPA). Are they distinguishable from students in a course in either child psychology or experimental psychology?

ADDITIONAL REFERENCES

Bachtold, L. M., and Werner, E. G. Personality profiles of women psychologists. *Developmental Psychology,* 1971, *5,* 273-78.

Berens, A. E. Socialization of need for achievement in boys and girls. *Proceedings of the 80th Annual Convention of the American Psychological Association,* 1972, *7,* 273-74.

Gross, A. E. Sex and helping: Intrinsic glow and extrinsic show. Paper presented at the 80th Annual Convention of the American Psychological Association, Honolulu, September 1972.

Horner, M. S. *Sex differences in achievement motive and performance in competitive and non-competitive situations.* Doctoral dissertation, University of Michigan. Ann Arbor, Mich., 1968.

Lipman-Blume, J. The development and impact of female role ideology. Paper presented at the Radcliffe Institute Conference, Cambridge, Mass., April 1972.

O'Leary, V. E., and Braun, J. S. Antecedents and personality correlates of the academic careerism in women. *Proceedings of the 80th Annual Convention of the American Psychological Association,* 1972, *7,* 277-78.

Oberlander, M. I., Frauenfelder, K. J., and Heath, H. The relationship of ordinal position and sex to interest patterns. *Journal of Genetic Psychology,* 1971, *119,* 29-36.

Rose, H. A., and Elton, C. F. Sex and occupational choice. *Journal of Consulting Psychology,* 1971, *18,* 456-61.

Ryckman, R. M., and Sherman, M. F. Interactive effects of locus of control and sex of subject on confidence ratings and performance in achievement-related situations. Paper presented at the 80th Annual Convention of the American Psychological Association, Honolulu, September 1972.

Smith, C. P., and Smith, C. H. Why don't women succeed? *New Society,* October 1972, *22,* 577-79.

Stein, A., and Bailey, M. The socialization of achievement motivation in females. Paper presented at the 140th meeting of the American Association for the Advancement of Science, Washington, D.C., December 1972.

Tangri, S. S. Determinants of occupational role innovation among college women. *Journal of Social Issues,* 1972, *28,* 177-99.

Turner, B. F. Socialization and career orientation among black and white college women. Paper presented at the 80th Annual Convention of the American Psychological Association, Honolulu, September 1972.

Turner, R. H. Some aspects of women's ambition. *American Journal of Sociology,* 1964, *70*, 271-85.

Veroff, J. Social comparison and the development of achievement motivation. *Achievement-related motives in children,* ed. C. P. Smith. New York: Russell Sage Foundation, 1969.

Some Aspects of Female Sexual Behavior: an Overview

Florence L. Denmark

There are many facets of the human female sexual response, in terms of both arousal and appetite, which have recently become subject to investigation. Beginning with the work of Kinsey (1949, 1953), and continuing on through the extension of Kinsey's work to the laboratory studies of Masters and Johnson (1966), this topic has become one of considerable interest as well as impact on our sexual values.

In the nineteenth century, according to the sex manuals, sex was almost strictly for men. A modest woman submitted to her husband and did not want any sexual gratification for herself.

A double standard is still perpetuated in more recent manuals. In *Love Without Fear,* Chesser (1947) points out how important it is for each sex to retain its own sex characteristics. He notes that sexual freedom is foreign to feminine nature. Other manuals, e.g., Hall (1965) state that women don't enjoy sex without love, although men can. Even "J" in *The Sensuous Woman* (1971) perpetuates this double standard by pointing out how women can use sex to land a man—not vice versa.

Despite the available and continuing work on female sexuality, even very current sex manuals are filled with misinformation. Thus Barbara Seaman (1972) points out the errors made by David Reuben in his popular book, *Everything You Always Wanted to Know About Sex but Were Afraid to Ask* (1969).

Before trying to sell many copies of a "hot" book, sex popularizers would do well to review the extant research that has tried to answer some of the following questions: What information is known about the vaginal vs. clitoral orgasm? How does the ease of sexual arousal of females compare to that of males? What kind of stimulation does the arousing? How does the duration and intensity of sexual activity in the female compare with that of the male? If differences exist in sexual activity, are they biologically or culturally determined? We will not attempt to answer all of these questions, but even raising them indicates that glib answers will not be fruitful compared to laboratory investigations.

Kinsey's work (1948, 1953) opened up the field of sex research as an acceptable scientific discipline. Kinsey has been criticized for problems of sampling, especially the overrepresentation of some groups and the underrepresentation of others in his samples. The volunteer nature of his sample has been particularly singled out for attack. Despite these methodological criticisms, many expected findings emerged which were generally supported in later, laboratory research.

Contrary to physicians' warning, Kinsey (1953) found that wives who experienced orgasm prior to marriage had a far better rate of orgasm during marital intercourse. This was true regardless of whether the premarital orgasm occurred through masturbation, petting, intercourse, homosexual play, or fantasy.

Kinsey also concluded that the anatomic structures that are most essential to orgasm are practically identical in the male and female, e.g., mouth, penis and clitoris, and organs of touch. He downgrades the importance of the vagina in contributing to the arousal of the female, a point we will return to later on.

Kinsey notes that orgasm is essentially the same in both male and female. They are alike in physiological changes (e.g., blood pressure, pulse rate, respiration) associated with sexual response. Of particular interest is the point Kinsey makes that females can respond to orgasm as quickly as males. There is no evidence to support the statement that women are slower in their capacity to reach orgasm.

Kinsey does conclude that males respond more to psychological stimuli than do females. Thus he found that men, but rarely women, became aroused by viewing pornography. Levi (1969) found evidence in line with Kinsey's view. However, he also found that some women are highly aroused by visual stimuli, even more so than men, but the average female is less aroused than the male. According to Masters and Johnson (1966), female disinterest in the nude male figure may soon disappear. Women will react to sexual anatomy as men do if society permits them to.

Kinsey points out that while *levels* of sexual response may be modified by increasing available supplies of androgen, there is no reason to believe that hormonal therapy will modify *patterns* of sexual behavior. Money (1961) has shown that androgen is the hormone of eroticism for both men and women; i.e., it serves to maintain erotic imagery, sensations, and actions for both sexes.

For women, androgen is of adrenal origin. Money also notes that sex hormones have no direct effect on the direction or content of erotic inclination in humans. The latter is determined by experience.

Photographic and instrumental observations were carried out during coitus and other sexual activity by Masters and Johnson (1966). Their research findings were later described in easily understood, explicit language by Brecher and Brecher (1966). Masters and Johnson graphed the physiology of the four phases of the female sexual response: excitement, plateau, orgasmic, and resolution. They also observed multiple orgasm as contrasted with repeated orgasm, and disproved the myth that a woman is limited to one climactic orgasm. These multiple orgasms do not differ physiologically from single orgasms except that they are multiple. They are not "minor" experiences. Given suitable conditions and effective stimulation, most women are capable of experiencing intense multiple orgasms. Sherfey (1966, 1972) confirmed this finding.

Masters and Johnson also report that there is not a vaginal orgasm as distinct from a clitoral orgasm. Physiologically there is only a sexual orgasm.

Freud had asserted that women can have two types of orgasm, either a clitoral or a vaginal one. A mature woman transfers her sexual response from the clitoris to the vagina. If a woman is unable to make this transfer, she remains immature and frigid. This distinction in type of orgasm has permeated much of the psychoanalytic and sexual literature, and it has been a source of concern to many women. Masters and Johnson's research should quiet these worries, since they show vaginal and clitoral orgasms are the same. The clitoris participates fully even when no effort is made to stimulate it directly.

Gillespie (1969) briefly summarizes the work of both Masters and Johnson (1966) and Sherfey (1966), and offers evidence that supports the idea that the clitoris is the center of female sexuality. Gillespie goes into detail about how the clitoris can be stimulated indirectly during copulation. He feels that the term "vaginal orgasm" should be used to denote thrusting movements in the vagina in contrast to local stimulation of the clitoris. Gillespie believes that the vaginal orgasm is one more bogey that must be put to rest before we can proceed to establish a valid, viable, "psychoanalytic" view of women.

Koedt, a founder of the radical feminist movement, goes one step further (1970). The theme of her paper is that the "vaginal orgasm" does not exist; that all orgasms occur through stimulation of the small penis-like organ called the clitoris (either directly or indirectly as during coitus) or else psychologically. Taking this into account, Koedt suggests that we may have to redefine our concept of "sexuality," and, in fact, perhaps re-establish a new "normal" or "standard" sexual position, as the old one is not mutually enjoyable for both sexes. It favors the male.

Koedt goes on to say that Freud is the "father" of the vaginal orgasm; she attacks him for basing his theory on the assumption that "women were inferior appendages" rather than basing it on female anatomy. She then cites anatomical evidence that supports her own theory, which describes the clitoris as the "organ of pleasure." Koedt further asserts that women who believe the myth of the vaginal orgasm are either confused or lying. Moreover, Koedt asserts that men wish to maintain the myth of the vaginal orgasm for a number of reasons that can be summed up under the headings of fear, selfishness, and the desire to maintain control over women.

Masters and Johnson did not discount the vagina. They reported that *all* orgasms, regardless of clitoral stimulation, include vaginal contractions. However, to reiterate, they reported only one type of physiological response, including indirect clitoral stimulation, for every orgasm.

Readers are referred to the article by Sherfey (1966, reprinted in book form 1972) for a comprehensive summary of Masters and Johnson's work as well as a complete presentation of female sexual physiology as compared to the male's.

Sherfey deals with the clitoral vs. vaginal orgasm and concludes that vaginal orgasms cannot occur without at least indirect clitoral stimulation. She goes on to discuss the process utilized by women to reach orgasm. Sherfey feels that the female has an insatiable sexual drive, which had to be suppressed in order for modern civilization to appear. Basically the more orgasms achieved, the more that can be achieved.

Sherfey, an analytic feminist herself, feels her findings will strengthen psychoanalytic theory. Whether or not one has a psychoanalytic bias, Sherfey's article can be appreciated as a review of physiology and of research in female sexuality. However, when reading Sherfey one should also be aware of the valid factual and theoretical criticisms made by Money and Athanasiou (1973) and by Tobach (1973).

One of the criticisms leveled at the research in female sexuality is that responses are based on observations of largely middle-class Americans, who have volunteered for these projects. Although they will not be covered in any depth, some mention should be made of the studies of sexual behavior being carried out in other cultures. One example would be the work of anthropologist

William Davenport (1966), who carried out sex-research field studies in Melanesia. Davenport presents a full picture of sex life on a district of one island in the group. Sexual propriety, heterosexual as well as homosexual contact, marriage and divorce are all detailed. Sexual intercourse between husband and wife is assumed to be natural and pleasurable. Deprivation is believed to be harmful.

Rainwater (1971) tells us that lower-class males in the United States, Mexico, Puerto Rico, and elsewhere are concerned with achieving their own sexual pleasure without regard to the woman's needs. In contrast, the Mangaians, peoples of Polynesia, aim to have their partners achieve orgasm several times to their one (Marshall, 1971). No woman is frigid there. When women are expected to enjoy sex, they do.

Studies such as these are necessary to round out our knowledge of female sexuality in order to distinguish variable and culturally determined human responses from those which have a biological basis.

Another type of criticism aimed at sex research focuses on the entire approach taken by sexologists today. An example of this would be the attack on the work of Masters and Johnson by Leslie Farber (1966). Farber is a practicing psychoanalyst who feels that the new approach to the study of sex is dehumanizing and mechanical. Moreover, he feels that too much emphasis is put on the importance of the female orgasm. Farber notes that even though the female does not experience orgasm with regularity (except during masturbation), she is nevertheless happy and contented. Woman is satisfied with her difference from man and wouldn't want it otherwise, claims Farber.

Farber is very cynical about the use of new techniques and concepts concerning sex; he believes that mutually enjoyable sex—i.e., mutual orgasm—is not possible.

Gelfman (1969) also touches on the possibility that the dehumanizing emphasis on adequate sexual function and gratification may prevent a couple from establishing a genuine loving relationship.

Questions have also been raised about the motives of the volunteers—e.g., were they coerced or perhaps exhibitionists?—as well as the general immorality of conducting research in sexual behavior. However, there was no evidence of coercion; volunteers wanted to contribute to scientific progress, and in some cases to enhance their own enjoyment of sex. This laboratory research on humans does not supercede other approaches; it supplements them.

The last decade or so has opened up new vistas in exploring and

791

understanding sexuality. The diversity and challenges of the research in this area can be seen in Zubin and Money's (1973) collection. The recent reawakening of women, asking and answering questions about their own sexuality, has fostered this interest. In addition, science and technology have developed an open study of sexuality as another aspect of human reality. More research on sexuality is essential, since before deciding what is correct or appropriate one first needs knowledge of what is.

REFERENCES

Brecher, R., and Brecher, E. *An analysis of human sexual response.* New York: Signet, 1966.

Chesser, E. *Love without fear.* New York: Roy Publishers, 1947.

Davenport, W. Sexual patterns and their regulation in a society of the southwest. In F. A. Beach (Ed.), *Sex and behavior.* New York: Wiley, 1965.

Farber, L. I'm sorry dear. In Brecher, R., and Brecher, E. (Eds.), *Analysis of human sexual response.* New York: Signet, 1966.

Gelfman, M. A post-Freudian comment on sexuality. *American Journal of Psychiatry,* 1969, *126,* 651-57.

Gillespie, W. H. Concepts of vaginal orgasm. *International Journal of Psychoanalysis,* 1969, *50,* 495-97.

Hall, R. *Sex and marriage.* New York: Planned Parenthood, 1965.

"J." *The sensous woman.* New York: Lyle Stuart, 1971.

Kinsey, A. C., Pomeroy, W. B., and Martin, E. *Sexual behavior in the human male.* Philadelphia: Saunders, 1948.

— — —, — — —, Martin, E., and Gebhard, P. H. *Sexual behavior in the human female.* Philadelphia: Saunders, 1953.

Koedt, A. *The myth of the vaginal orgasm.* Pittsburgh: Know, Inc., 1970.

Levi, L. Sympatho-adrenomedullary activity, diuresis, and emotional reactions during visual sexual stimulation of human females and males. *Psychosomatic Medicine,* 1969, *31,* 251-68.

Marshall, D. Sexual behavior on Mangaia. In D. S. Marshall and R. C. Suggs (Eds.), *Human sexual behavior.* New York: Basic Books, 1971.

Masters, W. H., and Johnson, V.E. *Human sexual response.* Boston: Little, Brown, 1966.

Money, J. Sex hormones and other variables in human eroticism. In W. C. Young (Ed.), *Sex and internal secretion.* Baltimore: Williams and Wilkins, 1961.

— — — and Athanasiou, R. Review of M. J. Sherfey, *The nature and evolution of female sexuality. Contemporary Psychology,* 1973, *18,* 593-94.

Rainwater, L. Marital sexuality in four "cultures of poverty." In D. S. Marshall and R. C. Suggs (Eds.), *Human sexual behavior.* New York: Basic Books, Inc., 1971.

Reuben, D. *Everything you always wanted to know about sex but were afraid to ask.* New York: McKay, 1961.

Seaman, B. *Free and female.* New York: Coward, McCann & Geoghegan, 1972.

Sherfey, M. J. The evolution and nature of female sexuality in relation to psychoanalytic theory. *Journal of the American Psychoanalytic Association,* 1966, *14*, 28-128.

———. *The nature and evolution of female sexuality.* New York: Random House, 1972.

Tobach, E. Review of M. J. Sherfey, *The nature and evolution of female sexuality. Contemporary Psychology,* 1973, *18*, 594-95.

Zubin, J., and Money, J. (Eds.) *Contemporary sexual behavior: Critical issues in the 1970's.* Baltimore: Johns Hopkins University Press, 1973.

SUGGESTED PAPERS AND PROJECTS

Papers:

1. Discuss the relationship of courses in the psychology of women to courses in human sexuality.
2. Discuss new views and reconsider old ones on female sexuality.
3. Discuss various methods of contraception and their effects on sexual responsiveness.
4. Discuss the effectiveness and the ethical implication of sex clinics.

Projects:

1. Ask five males and five females if they ever had sexual intercourse. Is there a sex difference in response?
2. Ask five males and five females about their sexual fantasies. Is there a sex difference in response?
3. Discuss the social implications of the view that homosexuality is as acceptable as heterosexuality.
4. Define the term "rape." Interview several policemen on the subject. Do they believe rape is possible?

Bell, R. R., and Gordon, M. *The social dimension of human sexuality.* Boston: Little, Brown, 1972.

De Martino, M. F. *The new female sexuality.* New York: Julian Press, 1969.

Diamond, M. A critical evaluation of the ontogeny of human sexual behavior. *Quarterly Review of Biology,* 1965, 40, 147-75.

Ford, C., and Beach, F. *Patterns of sexual behavior.* New York: Harper, 1951.

Giese, H. (Ed.) *Sexuality of women.* New York: Stein & Day, 1970.

Gittelson, N. *The erotic life of the American wife.* New York: Doubleday, 1972.

Hampson, J. L., and Hampson, J. G. The ontogenesis of sexual behavior in man. In W. C. Young (Ed.), *Sex and internal secretions,* vol 2. Baltimore: Williams & Wilkins, 1961.

Hariton, E. B. The sexual fantasies of women. *Psychology Today,* 1973, *6,* 39-44.

Kaplan, H. S. *The new sex therapy.* New York: Brunner/Mazel, 1974.

Petras, J. W. *Sexuality in society.* Boston: Allyn and Bacon 1973.

Seaman, B. *The sex life of the contemporary woman.* New York: C. P. Putnam, 1969.

ADDITIONAL REFERENCES

Bardwick, J. *Psychology of women.* New York: Doubleday, 1970.

———. *Readings on the psychology of women.* New York: Harper & Row, 1972.

Beauvoir, S. de. *The second sex.* New York: Bantam, 1961.

Bebel, A. *Woman under socialism.* New York: Schocken Books, 1971.

Bernard, J. *Women and the public interest.* Chicago: Aldine, 1971.

———. *The future of marriage.* Cleveland: World, 1972.

Bird, C. *Born female.* New York: McKay, 1968.

Cade, T. (Ed.) *The black woman: An anthology.* New York: New American Library, 1970.

Carter, H., and Glick, P. G. *Marriage and divorce.* Cambridge: Harvard University Press, 1970.

Chesler, P. *Wonder woman.* New York: Holt, Rinehart & Winston, 1972.

DeWit, G. O. *Symbolism of masculinity and femininity.* New York: Springer, 1963.

Ellman, M. *Thinking about women.* New York: Harcourt Brace, 1968.

Epstein, C. F. *Woman's place: Options and limits in professional careers.* Berkeley: University of California Press, 1970.

——— and Goode, W. *The other half: roads to women's equality.* Englewood Cliffs, N. J.: Prentice-Hall, 1971.

Farber, S., and Wilson, R. H. L. *The potential of women.* New York: McGraw-Hill, 1963.

Fogarty, M., Rapoport, R., and Rapoport, R. *Sex, career, and family.* Beverly Hills, Cal.: Sage, 1971.

Flexner, E. *Century of struggle: The women's rights movement in the United States.* Cambridge, Mass.: Belknap Press, 1966.

Friedan, B. *The feminine mystique.* New York: Norton, 1963.

Garskorf, H. H. (Ed.) *The psychology of women's liberation: Readings.* Belmont, Cal.: Brooks Cole, 1971.

Ginzberg, E. *Life styles of educated women.* New York: Columbia University Press, 1966.

Gordon, M. *The nuclear family in crisis.* New York: Harper & Row, 1972.

Gornick, V., and Morgan, B. K. *Women in sexist society.* New York: Basic Books, 1971.

Greer, G. *The female eunuch.* New York: McGraw-Hill, 1971.

Grey, A., (Ed.) *Man, woman, and marriage.* New York: Atherton, 1970.

Hays, H. R. *The dangerous sex: The myth of feminine evil.* New York: Putnam, 1969.

Herschberger, R. *Adam's rib: A defense of modern women.* New York: Harper & Row, 1970.

Hole, J., and Levine, E. *Rebirth of feminism.* Chicago: Quadrangle Books, 1972.

Kanowitz, L. *Women and the law: The unfinished revolution.* Albuquerque: University of New Mexico, 1969.

Kontopoulos, K. Women's liberation as a social movement. In C. Safilios-Rothschild (Ed.), *Toward a sociology of women.* Lexington, Mass.: Xerox College Publications, 1972.

Kraditor, A. *Up from the pedestal: Landmark writings in the American woman's struggle for equality.* Chicago: Quadrangle Books, 1968.

Laing, R. D., and Esterson, A. *Sanity, madness, and the family.* Baltimore: Penguin, 1970.

Lederer, W. *The fear of women.* New York: Grune & Stratton, 1968.

Lifton, R. J., (Ed.) *The woman in America.* Boston: Beacon Press, 1971.

Masters, R. E. L., and Lea, E. *The anti sex: The belief in the natural inferiority of women: Studies in male frustration and sexual conflict.* New York: Julian Press, 1964.

Mead, M. *Sex and temperament in three primitive societies.* New York: Morrow, 1935.

— — —. *Male and female.* New York: Dell, 1968.

Mill, J. S. *On the subjection of women* (1869). New York: Fawcett, 1971.

Miller, B. F., Rosenberg, E. B., and Stackowski, B. L. *Masculinity and femininity.* Boston: Houghton Mifflin, 1971.

Millet, K. *Sexual politics.* New York: Doubleday, 1970.

Mitchell, J. *Woman's estate.* New York: Random House, 1972.

Money, J., and Ehrhardt, A. A. *Man and woman, boy and girl: Differentiation and dimorphism of gender identity.* Baltimore: Johns Hopkins University Press, 1972.

Montague, A. *The natural superiority of women.* New York: Macmillan, 1953.

Morgan, R., Ed. *Sisterhood is powerful: An anthology of writings from the women's liberation movement.* New York: Vintage, 1970.

Myrdal, G. *An American dilemma,* vol. 2. New York: Harper, 1944, 1962. (See the extensive appendix devoted entirely to the analogy between blacks and women.)

Rainwater, L. *And the poor get children.* Chicago: Quadrangle Books, 1960.

Reeves, N. *Womankind.* Chicago: Aldine, 1971.

Roszak, B., & Roszak, T. (Eds.) *Masculine/feminine.* New York: Harper & Row, 1969.

Safilios-Rothschild, C. (Ed.) *Toward a sociology of women.* Lexington, Mass.: Xerox College Publications, 1972.

Schneier, M. *The essential historical writings.* Westminster, Md.: Vintage Books, 1972.

Sherman, J. A. *On the psychology of women.* Springfield, Ill.: Charles C. Thomas, 1971.

Sinclair, A. *The emancipation of the American woman.* New York: Harper & Row, 1965.

Skolnick, A. S., and Skolnick, J. H. *Family in transition: Rethinking marriage, sexuality, child rearing, and family organization.* Boston: Little, Brown, 1971.

Smuts, R. W. *Woman and work in America.* New York: Schocken Books, 1971.

Wollstonecraft, M. *A vindication of the rights of women.* New York: Van Nostrand Reinhold, 1970.

Special Issues of Journals

Women in the professions: What's all the fuss about: *American Behavioral Scientist,* 1971, *15* (2).

The women's movement. *American Journal of Orthopsychiatry,* 1971, *41* (5).

Changing women in a changing society. *American Journal of Sociology,* 1973, *78* (4).

Sexism in family studies. *Journal of Marriage and the Family,* 1971, *33* (3).

New perspectives on women. *Journal of Social Issues,* 1972, *28* (2).

Women and education. *School Review,* 1972, *80* (2).

Who discriminates against women? *International Journal of Group Tensions,* 1974, *4* (1).

Glossary

Glossary

Achievement induction
> The symbolic or ceremonial bringing into a state of success or mastery.
>
> Initial mastery or success experience.

Achievement imagery
> Fantasy products related to goal mastery and success. The symbolic activities of task completion and fulfillment.

Achievement
> A motive toward goal mastery and success.

Acculturation
> A process marked by the transmission of traits and characteristics between diverse groups, resulting in new patterns.
>
> The process of socialization.

Achievement motivation
> Desire to gain mastery or skill in given tasks, in order to satisfy an internal or a cultural criterion of excellence.

Adrenal glands
> A pair of endocrine glands above the kidneys. Each gland consists of two parts, the adrenal cortex, which produces life-essential steroids, and the adrenal medulla, which produces the stimulants adrenalin and noradrenalin.

Adrenergic
> Term applied to nerve fibers that when stimulated release epinephrine at their endings.

Affectional relationships
> Emotion-based or emotion-oriented connections with other persons.

Affective behavior
> Emotional, feeling-based responses or activities.

Affiliation
> The state of being in close interpersonal relations with other persons.

Analysis of variance
> A statistical method of ascertaining if fluctuations in one or more dependent variables differ from chance expectancy when handled as a function of stated experimental variables.

Analytic Tasks or functions
> Procedures based on the belief that a complex process can best be understood by separating it into its component parts, and that improvement of the component parts will result in improvement of the more complex whole.

Ancillary
Subordinate, subsidiary, or auxiliary.

Androgen
Any of the male sex hormones, the agents that stimulate male development in the embryo and the activity of the male sex organs at puberty. Produced mainly by the testis, but also by the adrenal cortex and the ovary. Several related steroid hormones, varying in biological strength and effectiveness, qualify as androgens.

Anovulatory cycle
The ovary does not produce a ripe follicle and endometrial changes are minimal.

Antecedents
Influential or significant events, activities, or conditions of an individual's earlier life. Also, ancestors or forefathers.

Anthropomorphism
The tendency to view that which is not personal or human in terms of personal or human qualities or characteristics.

Antinepotism
Being opposed to the gaining of benefit solely from one's relationship to a member of the family; often used to rationalize discrimination against women.

Anxiety
Apprehension of danger. A psychoneurosis characterized by morbid fear. Uneasiness or fear of what might happen.

Auto-erotic stimulation
Masturbation; sexual gratification obtained without the participation of any individual except oneself.

Autonomic nervous system
A system of nerve cells consisting of medulla and spinal cord, nerve fibers and ganglia outside the central nervous system whose activities are beyond voluntary control.

Bimodal
Characterized by possessing two statistical modes.

Bisexuality
Possessing sexual desire for members of both sexes. Also, the condition of possessing traits (physiological or psychological) typical of both sexes.

Breast envy
Desire in the male for possession of female breasts and female status. Accompanied by feelings of anger and jealousy. May lead to feelings of inferiority.

Castration
Emasculation. The removal of the testicles or ovaries. Destruction or inactivation of the gonad.

Castration complex

Fear in a male of mutilation or removal of his penis. In psychoanalytic theory, the complex originates in the son's incestuous craving for the mother and his fear of the anger of a dominant father.

Catecholamine

One of a group of similar compounds having a sympathetic action. Such compounds include dopamine, norepinephrine and epinephrine.

Cathected

Invested with libidinal energy.

Cervix

The neck or cylindrical lower part of the uterus, which projects down into the vagina.

Chi square

A statistic used to show the extent to which observed frequencies depart from those expected according to chance or some other probability of occurrence.

Chi square analysis

A statistical test of goodness of fit, performed to determine if an observed frequency distribution differs significantly from a frequency distribution expected according to chance.

Cholinergic

Term applied to nerve endings that liberate acetylocholine.

Chromosome

A microscopic body that contains the genes or hereditary determiners. The number of chromosomes is constant for each species; it is 46 in man.

Circadian Rhythm

Noting or pertaining to rhythmic biological cycles recurring at approximately twenty-four-hour intervals.

Clitoral orgasm

Orgasm or sexual climax occurring as the result of stimulation of the clitoris.

Clitoridectomy

Excision or amputation of the clitoris; female circumcision.

Clitoris

The small, hooded organ at the top of the female vulva, comparable to the penis in the male.

Cognitive restructuring

Reorganizing the way an individual sees the physical and social worlds, including all his facts, concepts, beliefs and expectations and the patterns of their interactions.

Cognitive strategy

The mental process used to determine procedure that is adopted in an effort to achieve some goal, like the solution of a problem. May also be used for dissonance reduction.

Coitus

Sexual intercourse; characterized by insertion of the penis in the vaginal orifice.

Collapsing categories

Process of simplification whereby many categories of data are condensed into fewer categories for some logical or theoretical reason. Usually performed to aid statistical interpretation.

Compensatory responses

Reactions which are defenses against feelings of inferiority and inadequacy. Usually marked by an attempt to substitute for the defect in some manner, or to draw attention away from it.

Concept of self

A person's perception of his own feelings, behavior, and desires. His attitudes toward the person that he is.

Congenital

Present at birth.

Content analysis

A detailed, systematic categorization of the manifest and latent content of the various kinds of verbal materials. Obtained by the classification, tabulation, and evaluation of their key symbols and themes, in order to determine their meaning and probable effect.

Continuum

Something in which a fundamental character is discernible amid a series of variations.

Copulation

The act of joining; sexual union, coitus.

Corpus luteum

A small yellow body that develops within a ruptured ovarian follicle. It is an endocrine structure secreting progesterone and estrogens.

Correlation

A mutual or reciprocal relation between two variables.

Covert process

Responses that cannot be directly observed, such as thoughts, glandular reactions, etc.

Critical period

Period in maturation when the organism is physiologically "ready" to learn a certain response; thus, the period of greatest potential for certain behaviors. May also refer to a period of greatest stress or danger.

Cue strength

Strength of the drive that operates to stimulate an organism to make a certain response.

Cyclicity

The quality or state of being recurrent at definite periods or cycles.

Cyclic pattern or activity

A course or series of events that recur regularly and usually lead back to the starting point.

Cyclothyme

A person possessing a temperament characterized by alternation of lively and depressed moods. One who experiences sudden mood swings.

Delusion

A false belief; that is, one not based on reality.

Demographic

Referring to the dynamic balance of a population, especially in terms of its density and capacity for expansion or decline.

Dependency

Something that is determined or conditioned by someone else or something else relying on another for support.

Dependent variable

Response measures of behavior linked up to an independent variable.

Desexigate

To deemphasize or minimize appeals to sexual interest in.

Detumescence

Reduction or subsidence of a swelling. In this book we refer to vaginal detumescence.

Dichotic

Separated into two; composed of a pair or pairs.

Differentiation

A process of becoming different from the original condition, that is, more variegated, definite, and complex.

Also, being able to see a whole as composed of different parts, to be evaluated differently.

Dimorphic behavior

Behavior or responses occurring in two different forms or conditions, as male and female sex-role behavior.

Dimorphism

Two different forms or conditions occurring between two individuals or kinds of individuals that might be expected to be similar or identical.

Displacement

The transfer of behavior directed toward one person or object to a substitute person or object. Operating as an ego defense mechanism, it may serve to redirect emotional charges toward less dangerous objects.

Dysfunctional
> Pertaining to impaired, disturbed, abnormal, or nonadaptive functioning. Failing to serve a useful purpose.

Ectoderm
> The outermost of the three primary layers of an embryo; it becomes the skin and nervous system.

Edema
> An observable accumulation of excessive clear watery fluid in tissues, which may result in swelling. In sexual edema of the female, the accumulated fluid in the pelvic tissues passes through the vaginal wall to form the vaginal lubrication.

Effectance, effectance motive
> Drive or need to be purposeful or satisfied, or to accomplish something, in two areas at the same time, e.g., at home and at work.

Ego
> That part of the personality most in contact with the real world; the conscious, logical part of the mind which mediates between needs and reality.

Ego instincts
> According to Freud, those instincts that relate to the person's struggle for survival, especially the instincts for self-preservation, aggression, and hate.

EEG
> Abreviation for electroencephalogram: the record of alternating currents of brains waves in the cortex.

Embedded figures task
> Test of spacial discrimination where the subject is asked to isolate simple figures camouflaged by more complex figures.

Embryo
> Embryo
> The developing human individual from the time of implantation to the end of the eighth week after conception. Also, that which is as yet undeveloped, lacking final form and differentiation.

Embryogenesis
> The formation and development of the embryo.

Empirical
> Originating in or based on factual information, observation, or direct sense experience; able to be confirmed, verified, or disproved by observation or experiment.

Empirical verification
> The confirmation of truth or accuracy by empirical means, that is, in a manner directly observed or experienced.

Enculturation
  The process through which an individual learns the traditional content of a culture and assimilates its customs and norms.
Endoderm; entoderm
  The innermost of the three primary cell layers of the early embryo; it develops into the epithelium of the digestive tract and its derivatives.
Endometrium
  The mucous membrane lining of the inner surface of the uterus.
Erotic imagery
  Fantasy products and symbolic activities pertaining to sexual stimulation and gratification.
Estrogen
  The hormone responsible for the development and maintenance of female secondary sexual characteristics and preparation of the uterus for pregnancy. Several different but related steroid hormones qualify as estrogens.
Estrus
  "Heat." The part of the sexual cycle of female animals when they are receptive to the male, and when conception can occur.
Etiology
  Causation; all the factors that contribute to a disease or an abnormal condition. The study of disease-causing factors.
Expectancy
  Response readiness; sometimes a general term for cognitive determinants of a response.
Ex post facto
  After the fact. Formulated after the fact on the basis of current conditions or knowledge.
External barriers to achievement
  Problems or conditions in the outside world which interfere with achievement, such as discrimination or poverty.
Extrovert
  A person whose personality is characterized by interests directed toward the external environment of things and people rather than toward inner experiences and solitude. One who is sociable and outgoing.
Face validity
  Type of test validity in which the items *look* as if they measure what the test is supposed to measure. Face validity is determined by superficial examination of the test, and considers only obvious relevance.
Fallopian tubes
  Oviducts; the tubes leading down from each ovary to the

uppermost part of the uterine cavity. They carry the egg released from the ovary to the uterus for implanting.

Fear of success

A condition, particularly likely in females, derived from negative societal sanction for female aggressiveness. Success in achievement istuations may imply aggressiveness, and therefore threaten a loss of femininity to some females.

Fellatio

Insertion of the penis into the mouth, by a partner of either sex, for purposes of sexual stimulation and gratification.

Femina sapiens

Womankind; sentient, conscious, thinking woman.

Feminist therapist

A therapist who is aware of sex-role stereotypes, but attempts not to succumb to them personally, or to impose them on women clients. A therapist who helps a woman to see "psychosexual confusion" as the result of sex-role stereotypes, and helps her see how these stereotypes are culturally taught. Helps a woman expand her perception of her options, including those that men supposedly see as "unattractive"; e.g., aggressiveness, assertiveness. A therapist who believes a woman can make it on her own.

Fetus

The developing organism during the latter part of prenatal development, usually after the eighth week following conception.

Follicle stimulating hormone (FSH)

Hormone secreted by the anterior pituitary gland under the influence of which the follicles of the ovary begin to develop. Stimulates the secretion of estrogen by the ovaries.

Follicular phase

The time period prior to ovulation when the follicle increases in size preparatory to discharge of the ovum into the fallopian tube.

Fugue

A dissociative reaction in which the individual flees one life and establishes a different life elsewhere. He is amnesic for his past life, but his abilities remain unimpaired and he maintains the semblance of normality.

Fugue state

A state or condition of being amnesic for one's past life, while having established a new life in the present.

Genitalia

External sexual organs of men and women. The reproductive organs.

Gestalt theorist
 One who advocates the theoretical approach to psychology which emphasizes patterns or principles of organization rather than elements, taking the view that the whole is more than the sum of its parts.

Glans
 The conical vascular body forming the tip of the penis or clitoris.

Gonad
 A generic term referring to both female and male sex glands. Also the embryonic sex gland before differentiation into definitive testes or ovaries.

Gonadotropin glandotropic
 Generic term for hormones that stimulate production of sex hormones. A gonad-stimulating hormone.

Hallucination
 An imaginary sense perception for which there is no appropriate external stimulus.

Hera
 Greek name for Juno, the wife of Jupiter. She became queen of the gods and mistress of heaven and earth. She presided over marriage and was patron of female virtue.

Hermaphrodite
 A person with a congenital condition of sexual ambiguity, such that both male and female generative organs exist in the same person, whose sex therefore is not clearly defined as exclusively male or exclusively female.

Heterosexual
 One whose sexual interest or activity is toward a member of the opposite sex. Also, of or pertaining to different sexes.

Homologue
 An organ or part of one animal which corresponds in some way (position, structure, but not function) to an organ or part of another animal. A corresponding part.

Homosexual
 A person whose sexual interest or activity is with members of his (or her) own sex. Also, of or pertaining to the same sex.

Homosexuality
 A condition in which an individual is sexually attracted to a member or members of his own sex.

Homosociality
 The state of associating or interacting with persons of one's own sex.

Hormic
 Purposely directed toward a goal. Goal-oriented.

Hormones

Particular organic products of living cells, which produce a specific effect on the activity of cells in other parts of the body, where they are transported by body fluids.

Hypothalamus

A portion of the upper brain stem lying beneath the thalamus. Usually considered to include vital autonomic regulatory centers.

Hysterectomy

Surgical removal of the uterus.

Identification

An ego mechanism in which a person responds as if he and another are one. Also, a process in which a child tries to imitate the behavior of certain of his elders, in order to participate vicariously in their strengths and triumphs.

Idiosyncratic

Peculiar to the individual; eccentric.

Illusion

A perception that is an inaccurate or false interpretation of the actual stimuli.

Independence granting

Conducive to or encouraging of an individual's tendency to make his own thoughts and decisions, apart from any undue influence by others.

Independent variable

The stimulus, response, or organismic variable which is manipulated by an experimenter.

Innate drive

A drive or motive that is the result of hereditary causes rather than of specific experiences.

Inner directed

Pertaining to a person who, within limits set by tradition, makes his own decisions and formulates his own values.

Instrumental behavior

Actions or behaviors that help to bring a person closer to or into contact with a sought goal.

Interaction

The combined effect of two or more independent variables on a dependent variable.

Internal barriers to achievement

Barriers or obstacles to achievement arising from within the person, rather than from the real world. For example, lack of self-confidence, extreme shyness or fear of people, fear of responsibility or challenge.

Internalization

The making of the standards or values of another person or

group a part of one's own value system and beliefs.

Introvert

A person characterized by a tendency to prefer his own thoughts and company to those of other people. One who tends to avoid social contacts.

In vivo

In the living body of a plant or animal.

Klinefelter's syndrome

Symptoms include hypogonadism with testicular atrophy, underdevelopment of secondary sex characteristics, absence of sperm, and frequently eunuchoidal physique. Cause is a chromosomal anomaly—XYY.

Komologorev-Smiriokev test of 2 distributions

A two-sample statistical test used to determine whether two populations are distributed in the same fashion.

Labia (sing. labium)

Lips. The folds at the margin of the vulva. The labia majora are the outer folds, covered with public hair. The labia minora are the inner folds, covered with mucous membranes, wrinkled and hairless.

Laboratory

An environment that provides opportunity for systematic observation, experimentation, or practice.

Level of aspiration

The performance or standard for which a person is striving, and in terms of which he may judge his own behavior.

Lexicon

The volcabulary of a language, an individual speaker, a subject, or a group. Also, an account, record, or compendium.

Libidinal cathexis

The investment of libidinal energy in a person, object, idea, or activity.

Libidinal development

Stages or directions libidinal energy takes at various points in maturation. The first, till age five, is oriented toward acquiring survival skills. The second is sexually oriented and continues till middle age, when the third, spiritual, philosophical stage begins.

Libidinal instinct

Emotional or psychic energy, often expressed in terms of desire for sexual outlet or gratification.

Libido

In psychoanalytic theory, a basic instinctual force in the person, embracing, among other instinctual drives, the drive for sexual gratification.

Logogram

A graphic sign or conventionalized picture that represents a word or an object.

Lordosis

Abnormal anterior convexity of the spine. Arching of the back. Normal response of many female animals during "heat" or period of receptivity to male.

Luteal phase

Correlates with the development of a corpus luteum, and is time during which the endometrium is prepared for reception of a fertilized egg.

Luteinizing hormone (LH)

A gonadotropic hormone in the pituitary gland which induces release of the egg from the graafian follicle, and formation of this follicle into a corpus luteum.

Manifest Anxiety Scale (MAS)

Scale designed and validated by Taylor, and used to assess anxiety level as indicated by specific external factors.

Marginal woman

A female experiencing conflict between her former cultural norms and sex stereotypes, and a new set of norms.

Masturbation

Erotic stimulation involving the genitals, commonly resulting in orgasm, achieved by manual or other manipulation exclusive of sexual intercourse or coitus.

Menopause

That period which marks the permanent cessation of menstrual activity. Usually occurs between thirty-five and fifty-eight years old.

Menstrual cycle

The complete cycle of physiologic changes in the female, from the beginning of one menstrual period to the beginning of the next.

Monoamine oxidase (MAO)

A group of enzymes that act as catalysts in the oxidative decomposition of the biogenic amines, tyramine, tryptamine, serotonin, noradrenalin, etc. The breakdown of these substances can be inhibited by MAO inhibitors.

Mons

A body part raised above or delineated from surrounding structures. The mons pubis is the raised area of eminence at the front of the body.

Morphogenesis

The formation and differentiation of cells, tissues, and organs, which results in the form and structure of various body parts.

Also may refer to the regeneration of a body part that has been damaged or cut off.

Morphology

The structure or form of something; its makeup.

Also, a branch of biology that studies the forms, relationships, and development apart from their function.

Motive to avoid success

A (primarily female) need to avoid success or achievement because of the existence of penalties for success, especially social disapprobation and loss of feelings of femininity.

Multipara

A female who has delivered two or more live children.

Narcissism

Overevaluation of oneself and one's achievements. Excessive self-love, possibly to the point of sexual desire for or love of one's own body.

Also, the developmental stage when an infant is oriented primarily toward his own needs and sensations.

Narcissistic cathexis

The investment of libidinal energy in oneself.

"Nature vs. nurture"

The problem of the relative influence of heredity and of environment in the development of organisms.

Negative feedback

A high level of estrogen signals the pituitary to decrease production of PSH and to release luteinizing hormone which induces ovulation. FSH and LH act together to produce a surge of estrogen, which further inhibits production of FSH.

Neonate

A new born child. An infant less than one month old.

Neophyte

A young or inexperienced practicioner; a beginner.

Also, a new convert.

Neurosis

A mild functional personality disorder or aberration characterized by conflicts and anxieties which interfere with the management of everyday problems. A variety of symptoms may appear, but reality contact remains good.

Nonveridical

That which does not conform to objective reality.

Norepinephrine synthetic noradrenaline

A hormone of the adrenal medulla and one of the catecholamines. It is a biogenic amine that acts as a transmitter substance in the autonomic nervous system and the central nervous system.

Norms

Standards of behavior applied to members of a group or culture. Norms specify expectations about rights and privileges in role relationships, and are enforced by sanctions.

Nurturance

Nourishment or support during stages of growth.

Obfuscate, denigrate

Obfuscate: To confuse, becloud, or make obscure or unnecessarily complex.

Denigrate: To blacken or make dark. To cast aspersion on the character of, or to belittle.

Oedipal conflict

Conflict engendered in the young male in the Oedipal stage. The strength of the boy's sexual impulses and his pleasure in masturbation conflict with his castration anxiety, the result of fear of parental anger and retribution against sexual impulse and pleasure.

Oedipus complex

In psychoanalytic theory, the sexual attraction of the male child to his mother. More generally, a stage during early development when the child has a sexual attraction to the parent of the opposite sex.

Onanism

Masturbation, self-gratification.

Also, coitus interruptus.

Ontogenetic

Pertaining to the development of the individual organism, as opposed to phylogenetic.

Ontogeny

The biological development of the individual organism.

Oral character

A trait pattern originating in early socialization centering on eating. Manifested by an extreme interest in food and activities of the mouth, need for approval, optimism, and similar traits.

Oral contraceptive

Conception preventative taken orally, usually in pill form.

Orgasm

The climax of sexual excitement typically occurring near the end of coitus. Accompanied by ejaculation in the male, and a complex series of pleasurable muscular spasms in both male and female.

Outer-directed

Pertaining to a person whose values and behaviors are almost totally dictated or determined by his contemporaries, by others.

Ovariectomy

The excision of an ovary or portion of an ovary.

Ovary

One of the two almond-shaped glands in the female which produce reproductive cells called ova and two hormones: estrogen and progesterone.

Ovulation

The periodic ripening and rupture of the mature graafian follicle and the discharge of the ovum. It occurs approximately fourteen days before the next menstrual flow.

Paramenstrual period

Pertaining to the time period just before and during menstruation.

Parasympathetic nervous system

Part of the autonomic nervous system which operates when the organism is at rest.

Parity

The state of a female in terms of having borne live children. For example, nulliparity is the state of having borne no children; primiparity, the state of having had one child.

Particularistic

Based upon a particular situation or relationship rather than upon general principles.

Patriarchy

Male supremacy in the social organization, manifested by the superior position of the father in the family or clan, legal dependence of wives and children, and the reckoning of descent and inheritance through the male line.

Peer

One who is of the same or equal standing with another; an equal.

Penis

The cylindrical copulatory organ of the male. Also serves as the channel by which urine leaves the body.

Perceptual motor tasks

Learning to make an overt motor response that is not primarily verbal, when a concrete nonverbal stimulus situation is presented.

Phylogeny

The racial history or evolutionary development of a specific kind of organism or genetically related group of organisms, such as a family or species.

Phylogenetically

Having to do with the evolutionary development of a species, race, or other related group. Based on natural evolutionary relationships.

815

Phylogenetic scale

The evolutionary development and growth of a genetically related group or race.

Pituitary

Also called the hypophysis. A small gray, rounded body attached to the base of the brain. It is an endocrine gland secreting a number of hormones which may regulate many bodily processes.

Polarization

A division, as of groups or forces, into two opposites.

Also, the concentration around opposing extremes of usually conflicting groups or interests formerly aligned along a continuum.

Polyandry

A kind of polygamy in which one woman has two or more husbands at the same time.

Polygyny

A form of polygamy in which one man has two or more wives at the same time.

Polymorphous pervert

One who obtains sexual gratification in many ways.

Postpartum

The period following childbirth.

Postpartum depression or reaction following childbirth

A sense of despair or despondency after childbirth.

Potentiation

The synergistic action of two substances, e.g., hormones, in which the total effects are greater than the sum of the two substances.

Pre- and post-test

A research design in which comparisons are made of measurements taken before and after intervention.

Premenstrual period

The period of time preceding menstruation.

Prepartum

The period before delivery, that is, any time during pregnancy.

Prepuce

The foreskin or fold of skin covering the head of both the penis and the clitoris.

Primal fantasies

Images in the mind (imagination) having to do with the beginnings of people, individually and/or collectively.

Probability level

The probability that an event (object or person) will occur. It is equivalent to the relative frequency of occurrence of that event (object or person) in the population under consideration.

Progesterone

A hormone secreted by the corpus luteum after ovulation. Responsible for secretory changes in the endometrium that are characteristic of the luteal phase of the cycle.

Progestins

The collective term for all the related chemicals that have progesterone-like effects. Includes those released by the corpus luteum and placenta as well as those produced synthetically.

Projective technique

Any diagnostic psychological technique or procedure that utilizes ambiguous, unstructured stimuli to reveal a person's basic attitudes, conflicts, and so on.

Psychobiology

A broad, eclectic view of human behavior which stresses the pluralistic nature of behavior and the need for maintaining a holistic approach.

Psychopathology

Disordered, dysfunctional psychological and behavioral functioning, as in mental illness.

Also, the study of such disordered functioning.

Psychosexual

Pertaining to the mental, emotional, and behavioral aspects of the biological process of sexual differentiation. Also pertaining to mental and emotional attitudes about sexuality, and to the physiological psychology of sex.

Psychosexual Neutrality

Not belonging to, or associated with, either sex, psychologically or physiologically. Possessing characteristics belonging to neither of the two sexes.

Psychosis

A severely disordered mental condition, accompanied by peculiar and inappropriate reactions to the environment (loss of contact with reality), personality breakdown, and inability to handle everyday problems.

Psychosomatic symptoms

Physiological symptoms or complaints that are the result of a neurosis or a prolonged stress situation.

Puberty

Period in life of rapid change during which persons of both sexes become functionally capable of reproduction.

Pubescent

Having reached or arrived at puberty, the period of being capable of reproducing sexually. Manifested by maturation of the genitals and secondary sexual areas, and by the onset of menstruation in females.

Reaction formation
A defense mechanism in which dangerous feelings or impulses are blocked from cnsciousness or from overt behavior by the adoption of opposite types of behavior and attitudes.

Reality testing
Behavior directed toward testing or exploring the nature of the person's social and physical environment. May refer to testing social limits of permissiveness.

Reinforcement
The strengthening of an association between a stimulus and a response.

Rod and frame task
Test of spatial discrimination. The subject in a darkened room faces a luminous rod and frame. He must move the rod until it is in a true vertical position.

Sanguinic
Cheerfully optimistic; eagerly hopeful or confident.

SAT
Scholastic Aptitude Test. Academic aptitude test given to high school seniors, as one of the college entrance criteria. A test of potential for higher education.

Schizophrenia
A functional psychosis marked by emotional blunting and distortion, disturbed thought processes, and withdrawal from reality.

Schizothyme
A person who manifests withdrawn behavior, resembling that of schizophrenia, but who remains within the bounds of normality.

Seizure
A sudden attack, as of a disease or sickness.

Self-actualization
The life-line process of becoming a more complete person. Based on theory that people are innately virtuous and that normal, healthy development permits each person to actualize his own true nature and fulfill his potentialities.

Self-fulfilling prophecy
A fixed, often pessimistic, expectation about one's abilities or accomplishments, which predisposes the person to behave in such a way that the expectation is met. That is, the self-held "prophecy" or expectation is fulfilled or realized by oneself.

Sex reversal
Condition attained through surgery in hermaphrotides, such

that sex is changed from male to female or vice versa.

Also, in experimental embryology, and experimental procedure in which the established sex is reversed during embryological development.

Sex role

Pattern of behavior and social position defined in a cultural or subcultural group as being appropriate to a person because of his or her sex. Both rights and duties are associated with the role.

Sex-role stereotype

Displaying or adopting all or most of the behaviors traditionally associated with one's sex role, as delineated by one's culture.

Sexual differentiation

Behavior or physiological development which becomes more variegated, definite, and complex in separate ways for each sex.

Significance (statistical)

In statistical analysis, the degree to which an observed valud can be explained as a chance occurrence. Significant data have a very low probability of having occurred by chance.

Social desirability

A tendency to respond, especially on personality tests, in a manner preceived as being generally approved of, even if the response does not apply to, or is not characteristic of, the person involved.

Socialization

The processes through which a person acquires the thought and behavior patterns of his culture.

Sign rank test

A statistical test of significance which utilizes not only the sign of an observation but also its rank in order of absolute magnitude.

Space form blindness

Impairment of visual functioning such that one is unable to perceive figures accurately from ground.

Spearman-Brown correction

A formula for the estimation of the reliability coefficient of a psychological or educational test. It is in times as long as a basic test for which the reliabilities are known.

Split-half reliability

A statistical method for checking reliability, in which a single administration of the instrument (test) is made, the test split into two halves, which are scored separately, and the correlation coefficient between the two scores is obtained.

S.D. (Standard deviation)

A statistical device used for describing the variability of

measurements. Obtained by summing the squared differences of the mean, dividing by the number of cases, and extracting the square root.

Stereotype
A belief or attitude that is widespread in society and oversimplified in content. Generally resistant to change.

Sublimated creativity
A creative drive, such as for painting or writing, which is a substitute for something else, such as a frustrated or socially unacceptable sexual drive.

Superego
In psychoanalytic theory, that part of the personality established by the resolution of the Oedipus complex, representing moral and ideal standards. More generally the person's internalized moral standards, based on a sense of guiilt and personal responsibility.

Sympathetic nervous system
Part of the autonomic nervous system. It mobilizes the resources of the body for use in work and special emergencies.

Teleologic
Pertaining to or having the quality of design, purpose, final intention, or cause.

Temporal pattern
The unified impression produced by a succession of stimuli, as in rhythm.

Testicular feminization syndrome, also called androgen insensitivity syndrome.
Congenital. Girls or boys who appear normal manifest a swelling or lump in the groin or absence of pubic hair after puberty. There may be no female internal development, a blind vagina with no menstruation or fertility.

Testosterone
The male hormone obtained from the tissues of the testicles. Affects secondary sexual characteristics.

TAT (Thematic Apperception Test)
A projective test of personality and motivation in which the subject responds to pictorial stimuli by telling stories about them.

Thematic stories
Statements or accounts (as in TAT) in which an idea, ideal, or orienting principle is dominant or recurrent.

Transsexualism
The act of living and passing in the role of the opposite sex, before or after having attained hormonal, surgical, and legal sex reassignment.

Transudation
    The complete passage of a fluid through a membrane. Results from a difference in hydrostatic pressure.

T test
    A test of significance in which the ratio of a value to its standard error is obtained.

Turner's syndrome
    Characterized by dwarfism, webbed neck, and sexual infantilism. Almost confined to females. There is an absence of primordial follicles from the ovary. Cause is one absent sex chromosome, XO.

Unconscious
    Not present in consciousness; the aspect of behavior hidden from direct awareness. In psychoanalytic theory, the part of the personality where forgotten or repressed memories and desires are stored.

Underachievement
    Performance or behavior that is beneath the expected or potential level of the performer.

Vagina
    The canal that leads from the uterus of a female to the external opening of the genital canal.

Vaginal orgasm
    Sexual climax occurring primarily as the result of coital stimulation of the vagina.

Validity
    The degree to which a measuring instrument (such as a test) actually measures what it was designed to measure. Obtained by correlating test scores with a criterion of the variable involved.

Vascularity
    Provided with arteries and veins or ducts.

Vas deferens
    The tube that conveys sperm and semen away from the testes; the spermatic cord.

Verbal Anxiety Scale (VAS)
    Test designed by Gottschalk, 1961, to measure levels of anxiety. It is very sensitive to changes in current, real anxieties.

Viscera (sing. viscus)
    Organs of the body enclosed in the four large body spaces: the head, chest, abdomen, and pelvis. Most commonly refers to the organs in the abdominal cavity.

Viviparity
    Condition of producing living young instead of eggs.

Vulva
    The external parts of the female genital organs.

821

Vulvectomy

The surgical procedure in which all the external female genitalia are removed, plus all possible blood vessels and lymphatics. Performed only in the case of cancer of the area.

WAIS

Adult Intelligence Scale devised by Wechsler. Consists of six verbal subtests and five performance subtests.

WISC

Children's Intelligence Scale devised by Wechsler, 1949. Yields I.Q. score which utilizes mental age and performance on a series of verbal and performance subtests.

Withdrawal

A reaction of intellectual, physical, or emotional retreat. A person may try to relieve feelings of frustration by withdrawing from the attempt to attain his goals.

Z score

A standard score converted to a scale with a standard deviation of one and a mean of zero.

INDEX

Abolitionists, and women's suffrage movements, 95

Acceptance, social, and achievement, 690, 698

Achievement behavior, 635-645; and affiliation needs, 723-743; expectancy, and sex roles, 649-685; motivation, and sex roles, 687-702; and sex-role stereotype conflicts, 703-720, 740. *See also* Success, fear of

Adoption, sex-role, defined, 220, 233

Adrenal cortex, hormones, 518-519

Advertising, sex-role stereotypes in, 13, 26

Affect, and menstrual cycle behavior, 537-551, 553-585

Affiliation, need for, and achievement, 419, 430, 635, 723-743

Age, discrimination, and postsecondary education, 641

Aggression: and androgen, 458; and anxiety, 711; relative sex differences, 725-726; sex-typing and reinforcement of, 250, 257

Androgen: and behavior modification, 477-481; and cognitive abilities, 362-363; fetal excess, and psychosexual identity, 440, 458-466; and sex reversal, 477-478; and sexual response, 788

Androgenization, 478-481

Anger. *See* Rage

Anna O., case of, 156-157

Anterior pituitary, hormones, 517-518

Antiandrogenization, 477-478

Anxiety: and achievement expectancy, 705-720; and cognition testing, 301, 311-312, 656-657; menstrual cycle levels of, 505, 537-551, 553, 556, 566-567; parental, and independence training, 736-737; sex-role conflicts and, 12, 705, 741

Assimilation, of men and women, 107

Behavior: clinical judgments of, stereotypes and, 163-175; female superiority in, attributes, 318-320; male superiority in, attributes, 320; maternal, 506, 614-624; modification of, 474-485; mother-infant, in primates, 488-497; paramenstrual, perception of child's health, 529-535; parental role, sex differences, 247-260; psychosexual development, genetic and endocrine aspects, 447-468; sex differences in, factors; 219-228; sexual, disorders, 205-207; sexual dimorphic, 474-485; sexual response, 787-792; social, disorders, 207-208; survival *vs.* sexuality, as basis for, 177-191; and testosterone levels, 629. *See also aspects of behavior (e.g.,* Affect; Aggression; Hostility; Independence; Rage); Achievement; Mental health and illness; Psychotherapy

Biology, sexuality and, 177-191, 226-228

Breast envy, 177, 190-191

California Psychological Inventory, 674-676, 682

Castration: fetal, and sex reversal, 477-478; and sexual behavior, 451-454

Castration complex, 119, 127-136

Childbirth. *See* Pregnancy; Puerperium

Children: and achievement expectancy, 653-685, 694-695, 696, 697; behavior, during mother's menstrual cycle, 530-532; and psychiatric symptomatology, 145-146; sex-role perceptions of, 14-15, 101; as source of self-esteem, 720

Circadian rhythms, 627-629

Clitoris: in Freud's system, 119-120, 133; as unique organ, 123-124

Cognition: sex differences in, 299-434; and achievement expectancy, 655; and childbirth, 505, 595, 596, 598, 600; environmental factors, 367-376, 409-415; perceptual strategies, 395-406; physiological factors, 311-342, 355-364; social factors, and problem solving, 417-431; space perception, 379-390

Communication: and marriage, 94; and psychiatric symptomatology, 145-146

Competence, sex differences in rating, 32-40

Contraceptives, oral, 527-528; and delirium, 612; and menstrual cycle behavior, 553-585

Creativity, and competence evaluations, 36, 39

Culture: and achievement motivation, 689-691, 698; and menstruation, 197; and penis envy, 188; and pregnancy, 203; and sex roles, 16, 24-26, 112, 225-228, 275-291; and sexuality, 790-791

Dante, and Beatrice, 94

Darwinism, 178-179

Day care centers, 110

Delirium, postpartum syndromes and, 611-612, 621, 624

Dependency, as sex-typed behavior, 250, 741-742. *See also* Affiliation; Independence, development of

Depression: and menstrual cycle symptomatology, 537-550; during pregnancy and puerperium, 595-596, 599-600, 610; and rage, 209-210

Discrimination, sexual: and academic hiring practices, 773-779; and achievement motivation, 640; and college admissions, 641. *See also* Minority group, women's status as

Disorders; genetic and hormonal, 437, 439-440, 450; learning, male frequency, 306; physical, and rage, 200-205; sexual behavior, and rage, 205-207; social, and rage, 207-208. *See also* Behavior; Identity; *names of disorders*

Dominance, parental, and sex-role preferences, 263-274

Dora, case of (Freud), 154-155

Drugs: postpartum antidepressants, 593; and success fears, 719

Effectiveness and safety, sex differences, 731, 732

Emancipation, capitalism and, 22, 23, 189

Endocrine physiology, 509-528. *See also* Hormones; Menstrual cycle

Entrapment, feeling of, and postpartum syndromes, 620

Estrogen: cognitive abilities and, 311-342; menstrual cycle function, 509-528

Expectancy, achievement and, 649-685

Examiners, experimenters, or researchers, sex of, as data variable, 266, 369, 409-415, 417-431, 506-507. *See also* Therapists

Family planning, menstrual cycle method of, 509

Fellatio, 131

Femininity. *See* Stereotypes, sex-role

Feminism, 23-24, 93, 104-112, 278; and mental illness interpretation, 137-160

Fiction. *See* Literature; Myths and Legends

Freud, Sigmund, 11, 56, 119-120, 122, 127-136, 150, 152, 179, 705, 789

Friedan, Betty, 104, 106

Genetics, and gender identity, 482-485

Gide, Andre, 23

Gonads, hormones, 518-524

Gottschalk: Figure tests, 315, 316; Verbal Anxiety Scale (VAS), 537-551

Hermaphroditism: progestin-induced, and gender identity, 480-483; true, 467

Hiring practices, academic, and sex discrimination, 773-779

Homosexuality: and culture, 790; economic aspects, 183; and psychiatric symptomatology, 145; and therapist choice, 144. *See also* Lesbianism

Hormones: behavior modification and manipulation, 219, 447-468; 474-485; chemistry and classification of, 510-512; circadian rhythms and, 527-529; control of endocrine function, 514-522; menstrual cycle and, 498-500; mode of action, 512-514; negative affect and, 555-585; and

postpartum disturbances, 592-600. *See also specific names;* Contraceptives; Menstrual cycle
Hostility: during menstrual cycle, 504-505, 538-550, 553-585; success fears and, 717-718
Hypothalamus, hormones, 516-517

"Ideal women": femal perception, 73, 76-77, 78-81, 82, 83; inventory of values, 74-75, 78, 79, 80; male perception, 73, 77-81, 82-83
Identification: gender, and genetics, 482-485; with infant, postpartum, 616-617; masculine-feminine, difficulty with, 617-627; maternal, at childbirth, 614-617; sex-role, defined, 220, 232-234. *See also* Sex-roles, identification
Independence, development of, 723, 732-738. *See also* Dependency
Inferiority complex, and penis envy, 132
Intelligence: and achievement, 689-702; and success fears, 703-722
Inventory of Feminine Values, 74-75
IQ (Intelligence quotient): and achievement expectancy, 662, 666, 682, 684; children's and parents', 302; and sex-role learning, 225
ITSC (sex-role preference test), 267, 268-269, 271-272

Jealousy, penis envy and, 133, 134
Journals, women's. *See* Literature

Labor, sexual division of, 109-111; development, biological and societal, 278-287; and role sharing, 111-112
Language, sex-role stereotypes and, 13
Learning disorders, male frequency, 306
Legal institutions, women's status and, 287-291
Lesbianism, 710, 788; sex-role conflicts and, 206-207. *See also* Tomboyism
Literature (magazine fiction; journals; periodicals; textbooks), sex-role stereotypes in, 26; children's stories and elementary readers, 14, 55-68;

questionnaires in, 22; thematic content analysis, women's magazines, 13-14, 42-53. *See also* Myths and Legends

Magazines. *See* Literature
Males: biological rhythm in, 627-629; breast envy, 122, 190-191; mental health of, 121
MAO (monoamine oxidase), 322; and affect during menstrual cycle, 505, 553-585
Marginal woman concept, 100-102
Marriage: non-monogamous, 183, 287; and psychotherapy, compared as institutions, 137-149. *See also* Labor, sexual division of
Masculinity. *See* Stereotypes, sex-role
Masturbation: in Freudian system, 133-134; and orgasm expectations, 788
Maturation, sex differences in, 727
Menstrual cycle, 501-629; and affective behavior, 504-505, 537-551, 553-585; male equivalent, 627-629; and oral contraceptives, 505, 527-528, 553-585; physiology, 504, 509-528; symptomatology, culturally-conditioned, 503-504, 529-535; taboos and mythology, 197-198, 504. *See also* Pregnancy; Puerperium
Mental health and illness: feminist interpretation, 138-160; incidence, sex differences, 121-122, 147-149; postpartum syndromes, 605-624; survival *vs.* sexuality and, 177-191; sex-role stereotyped clinical assessments, 163-175. *See also* Behavior; Psychotherapy; Therapists
Minority group, women's status as, 16, 86-113, 758, 761; caste-class conflict, 95-98; definitions, 86-88; discriminations, 91-92, 612; feminism and, 104-112; majority attitude acceptance, 13; marginal woman concept, 100-102; mental health standards and, 173; and problem of generalizability, 726-727; psychological characteristics, 88-89;

race relations cycle, 98-100; social distance and, 92-95; subculture aspects, 90

More, Hannah, 89

Mothering, conflict over, 506, 614-624. *See also* Puerperium

Mother-whore complex, 187-188

Morisot, Berthe, 27

Motivation. *See* Achievement

Myths and legends, women in, 119; Eve and Mary, 196-199; Hebrew, 182; mother-whore, 12, 21, 187-188; Upanishad, 181; vaginal orgasm superiority, 123. *See also* Literature; Stereotypes sex-role

Nash, Ogden, 60, 63

National Women's Party, 88

National Organization for Women (NOW), 104; bibliography of non-sexist children's literature, 68

Negroes. *See* Minority group, women's status as

Neurophysiology, and cognitive functioning, 355-357, 360-364

Neutrality, psychosexual, 437, 440-441. *See also* Psychosexual development

Norepinephrine levels, and childbirth, 506, 591, 592, 593-600

Nurturance: and cognitive abilities, 419, 430; and sex-role stereotyping, 278-283, 740

Occupations. *See* Professions; Working women

Oedipus complex, 119, 127-136

Onanism. *See* Masturbation

Orgasm: clitoral, 787-790; multiple, 789, 791; vaginal, 123, 151, 789-790

Ovaries, 454, 519-520, 521

Pacifism, and sex-role stereotyping, 27, 29

Parasympathetic nervous system, and cognitive functioning, 323-324, 327-328, 362-364

Parents: and achievement motivation, 637-638, 723-724, 726; conflict with child,

739-741; permissiveness, and sex differences,223, 247-249, 255, 256-258; power, and sex-role identification, 263-274

Passivity, and sex-role stereotyping, 27-29, 186, 195-196, 200

Paternity, 287-288

Penis envy, 119, 121, 122, 127, 131-136, 177, 221. *See also* Breast envy

Phylogenetics, and power, 182-184

Physical disorders, and sex-role conflict, 200-205

Popularity, and academic achievement, 731

Pornography, 788

Postpartum period. *See* Puerperium

Power: parental, and sex-role identification, 263-274; *vs.* sexuality, as main drive, 177-191

Pregnancy, psychological and biochemical aspects, 591-600

Professions: discrimination in hiring, 773-779; sextyping of, 754-755; and women, 751-770. *See also* Achievement; Success, fear of; Working women

Progesterone, 504, 509-510, 520

Proust, Marcel, 100

Psychology, discriminatory practices within, 773-779

Psychosexual development: bipotentiality, 440-441; 449-461; and hormones, 437-439, 447-472; parental reinforcement, 442-444, 487-500

Psychotherapy: Freudian, 119-120, 122, 123, 127-136, 143-158, 177-191; male bias within, 121-122, 138-139, 142-144, 149-150, 159-160, 163-174; as middle-class institution, 121, 137, 139, 142, 158-159; symptomatology of women, 122-123, 124, 139-141, 145-147, 195-213. *See also* Therapists.

Puerperium: biochemical aspects, 591-595, 596-600; environmental aspects, 605-627; postpartum syndrome, 505-507, 596, 609-627. *See also* Menstrual

Race relations cycle, compared with sex relations, 98-100

Rage: as expression of role conflict, 122-123, 195-200; manifestations of, 200-210; and therapy, 210-213

Rape, and sex-role conflict, 205-206

Rearing, and gender identity, 481-482. *See also* Nurturance

Reinforcement: and expected behavior, 651, 652; sex differentiation of, 247-260

Researchers. *See* Examiners

Rod and Frame Test, 315-316, 359

Self-actualization: rejection of, 16; sex differences, 738-740

Self-concept, 16, 22. *See also* Feminism

Self-confidence, and independence training, 741-742

Self-fulfilling prophecy effect: and achievement expectancy, 305; and postsecondary education, 642

Sendak, Maurice, 63

Seuss, Dr., 63

Sex differences: in achievement, 649-685, 687-699, 703-720, 723-743; in cognition, 299-307, 311-342, 355-364, 367-376, 379-390, 395-406, 409-415, 417-431; development of, 231-243, 247-260, 263-274; in occupation and professions, 751-770, 773-779

Sex reversal: hormone-induced, 467, 474-485; spontaneous, 467

Sex roles: and achievement, 410-411, 649-685, 705-706, 713-715; acquisition of, components, 231-243; adoption of, 220, 233; biological and cultural factors, 209-228; cultural differences in, 275-291; equivalency, trend toward, 275-276; identification with, 220-225, 231, 233-243, 410, 411; parental influence on, 247-260, 263-274, 715; preference for, 233, 236-237. *See also aspects of sex roles;* Behavior; Stereotypes, sex-role

Sex typing: mother-infant behavior, 488-497; occupations, 751-770

Sexual differentiation and behavior; hormonal influences, 447-468; modification of, 474-485. *See also* Behavior

Slave, women as, 146, 147

Stereotypes, sex-role: abolition of, and minority groups, 84-112; achievement and career effect, 31-40; in children's literature, 55-68; and clinical judgments of mental health, 163-174; femininity, 19-30; in magazine fiction, 41-53; male-female perceptions of, 71-83; and success, 703-720

Success, fear of, 703-720; and affiliation needs, 639-640; male peer attitude and, 638, 715-717; motives for, 707-719; parental influence, 638; psychological aspects, 705-706

Suffrage movement, 95, 99, 104, 105

Survival drive, *vs.* sexuality, 177-191

Sympathetic nervous system, cognitive functioning and, 320-323, 360-362

Taboos, and menstruation, 556, 559, 560, 580, 582, 583

TAT (Thematic Apperception Test), 635, 707, 709-710

Temperature, body, and metabolic functioning, 627

Testes, hormones of, 520

Therapists, gender of, 141, 142-144, 149-160, 167, 172, 174

Thurber, James, 63, 64

Tomboyism, 478, 479, 480, 481

Turner's Syndrome, 449-450

Twain, Mark, 64

Underachievement, 636-645; and affiliation needs, 723-743; and anxiety, 724-725. *See also* Success, fear of

Values, Inventory of Feminine, 74-75

Verbal Anxiety Scale, 537-551

WAIS (Wechsler Adult Intelligence Scale), 299, 300

WISC (Wechsler Intelligence Scale for Children), 300, 409, 411-412, 413, 415

Women, and other women: competition among, 106, 109; in examinations, 305; identification with the aggressor, 13, 40, 200; prejudicial evaluations, 12, 31-40, 108; within professions, 13, 32, 37, 108, 109, 735; self-denigration, 12-13, 98, 149. *See also* Feminism;

Minority group, women's status as

Woolf, Virginia, 63

Working women: children of, attitudes, 14, 15, 644, 645; competition with men, 99; family life of, 110-112, 644-645; in literature, 14, 41, 66; and menstruation, 534. *See also* Professions